THE CIVIL WAR PAPERS OF
GEORGE B. MCCLELLAN

Books by Stephen W. Sears

THE CENTURY COLLECTION OF CIVIL WAR ART

HOMETOWN U.S.A.

THE AUTOMOBILE IN AMERICA

LANDSCAPE TURNED RED
THE BATTLE OF ANTIETAM

GEORGE B. MCCLELLAN
THE YOUNG NAPOLEON

THE CIVIL WAR PAPERS OF GEORGE B. MCCLELLAN
SELECTED CORRESPONDENCE, 1860–1865

MAJOR GENERAL GEORGE B. McCLELLAN,
photographed by Mathew Brady

HARVARD COLLEGE LIBRARY

THE CIVIL WAR PAPERS OF GEORGE B. McCLELLAN

SELECTED CORRESPONDENCE, 1860–1865

EDITED BY
STEPHEN W. SEARS

DA CAPO PRESS

First Da Capo Press edition 1992

This Da Capo Press paperback edition of *The Civil War Papers of George B. McClellan* is an unabridged republication of the edition published in New York in 1989. It is reprinted by arrangement with Ticknor & Fields.

3 4 5 6 7 8 9 10 02010099

Published by Da Capo Press, Inc.
A Member of the Perseus Books Group

Manufactured in the United States of America

Library of Congress Cataloging in Publication Data

McClellan, George Brinton, 1826-1885. Correspondence. Selections
The civil war papers of George B. McClellan: selected correspondence, 1860-1865 / edited by Stephen W. Sears.
p. cm.
Originally published: New York: Ticknor & Fields, 1989.
Includes index.
ISBN 0-306-80471-9
1. McClellan, George Brinton, 1826–1885–Correspondence. 2. Generals–United States–Correspondence. 3. United States–History–Civil War, 1861-1865. I. Sears, Stephen W. II. Title.
[E467.1.M2A4 1992] 91-29681
973.7 41 092–dc20 CIP

CONTENTS

INTRODUCTION

THIS COLLECTION of General George B. McClellan's Civil War correspondence presents him in a wide variety of wartime roles — army commander, theater commander, general-in-chief, grand strategist, battlefield tactician, military executive, political partisan, presidential candidate. Among Union commanders, only Grant and Halleck matched McClellan's range of military positions; overall, his combination of roles made him unique in the war years.

General McClellan served on active duty for something over eighteen months, from late April 1861 to early November 1862. He was in the upper echelons of command from the very beginning. When he was appointed major general of volunteers on April 23, 1861, and then major general in the regular army on May 14, it ranked him second only to Winfield Scott, the general-in-chief. After directing operations in the western theater as head of the Department of the Ohio and campaigning in western Virginia, he was summoned to Washington following the Bull Run debacle to organize and train the Army of the Potomac — the task he always regarded as his greatest wartime accomplishment. During the same period, in the winter of 1861–1862, he served for four months as general-in-chief of all the Union armies. His Peninsula campaign in the spring and summer of 1862 was one of the major operations of the war. In the Second Bull Run campaign his role was peripheral but highly controversial. His operations in Maryland that fall witnessed, at Antietam, what is still the bloodiest single day of battle in the nation's history. When he was relieved of command seven weeks after Antietam, he was the army's senior general.

Until the emergence of Grant and Sherman, McClellan was unqestionably the best-known military figure in the North, and he stands alongside those two generals in the importance of his impact on the war. No one came close to matching him as a center of controversy. In the election of 1864 some 1.8 million of his fellow citizens voted for him as the Democratic nominee for president, and if on Election Day he lost to Lincoln by a full ten percentage points, his vote count nonetheless represented a sizable constituency. By any measure, George McClellan was a figure to be reckoned with in the Civil War years.

This first collection of his wartime papers includes a surprising number of previously unpublished military letters and dispatches, many of them of considerable historical importance. Very little of his personal correspondence has been published, or published as he wrote it, until now. Of the 813 pieces of correspondence selected for this volume, 260, nearly a third, have not been in print before, and another 192 — his letters to his wife — appear here uncensored for the first time.

Although McClellan military correspondence may be found in greater or lesser amounts scattered through some twenty volumes of the *Official Records* of the Civil War armies — and in volumes of the *Official Records* of the navies as well — the compilers of these war records had by no means the entire body of McClellan's military documents from which to choose. Hundreds of his dispatches remained unseen in his personal papers.

When he took final leave of the Army of the Potomac at Warrenton Junction, Virginia, on November 11, 1862, McClellan carried away with him virtually all the army's headquarters papers. The new commander, Ambrose Burnside, can have inherited little more than current paperwork. That winter and into the spring of 1863 McClellan and his staff, stationed in New York City, worked through this mass of records in the course of preparing the final report of his tenure as commander of the Potomac army. This book-length work, when it was published in 1864, contained page after page of the general's letters and telegrams selected to document — and to rationalize — his actions. As delivered to the War Department, the manuscript of McClellan's *Report on the Organization of the Army of the Potomac, and of Its Campaigns in Virginia and Maryland* was accompanied by numerous maps and 263 reports by subordinates, but nothing more of the army's records was returned to the government.

McClellan regarded what remained in his hands — copies of his dispatches and dispatches received from others, unofficial and informal communications to and from him, drafts and memorandums and planning papers, intra-army battlefield messages and communications of every kind and in great number — as his property; only the contents of his *Report* and what related directly to it (such as the reports of his subordinates) were by his description public documents belonging to the government. On one occasion, at the request of the War Records Office, he supplied copies of a few papers bearing on his western Virginia campaign, but on the whole he contributed almost nothing to the *Official Records* project in the postwar years. In 1896, eleven years after McClellan's death, his son, New York congressman George B. McClellan, Jr., loaned a few of his father's dispatch books to the War Records compilers, and the considerable number of dispatches they utilized from them in the supplementary volumes of the *Official Records* suggests how much more complete the official historical record of the war for the years 1861 and 1862 might have been had the McClellan Papers in their entirety been made available from the first.

In selecting the contents of this volume, only McClellan's letters, telegrams, memorandums, and certain documents such as proclamations and addresses to his army have been considered, and only what is signed or unmistakably written by him. Correspondence signed by others "by command of General McClellan" is not included unless found in manuscript in his hand. Due to their length, his official campaign reports have also been excluded; they are few in number in any event, and readily available in the *Official Records* or, in the case of his *Report,* in separate book form as well. Other types of material excluded are matters of everyday military routine, orders and endorsements of little significance, multiple drafts, and, in private correspondence, perfunctory acknowledgments. To avoid repetition, when McClellan wrote several accounts of an event, the most complete and intrinsically valuable has been selected. When all else was equal, the unpublished was given precedence over the published.

All of McClellan's strategic papers and campaign plans are included here, as well as everything of significance bearing on his tactical decisions. In matters of military administration, as many representative examples of his actions as possible have been chosen. Virtually everything he wrote, officially and privately, bearing on the issues, policies, and politics of the war, and his roles in it, has been included. The purpose is to present, as nearly as the material allows, a comprehensive narration of events as General McClellan wrote it at the time.

By the nature of his elevated rank and service, the bulk of his official correspondence was with top officials of the government and the high command of the army — President Lincoln; Secretary of War Simon Cameron and his successor, Edwin M. Stanton; and the general-in-chief, first Winfield Scott and later Henry W. Halleck. McClellan wrote his first letter to Lincoln hardly a month after taking up his command in Ohio; the final dispatches he wrote as head of the Army of the Potomac were to the president. As a consequence, most military topics of significance in the years 1861 and 1862 are touched on here, often at the highest levels of decision-making.

McClellan wrote a remarkably large share of his military correspondence himself, and almost everything that relates to matters he regarded as important can be found in his handwriting. Seventy percent of this collection is in his autograph. While the military letters he sent were often in his hand, he not infrequently drafted letters to be copied for sending by an aide or clerk, keeping the draft for his files, and these autograph drafts, rather than the addressees' copies, are utilized here. Much the same is true of his military telegrams. It was McClellan's usual habit to write out dispatches for his telegrapher, who then copied and enciphered them for sending, a process repeated in reverse by the receiving operator. When found, these originals have been used instead of any later copies made during the telegraphic process. He less often retained copies of his personal correspondence, however, and many letters survive solely in the recipient's papers. For correspondence surviving only in the form of copies, the earliest version has been used.

A few excerpts from his private correspondence appeared in William Starr Myers's 1934 biography, *General George Brinton McClellan: A Study in Personality*, but among his personal writings certainly the best known are the excerpts from the wartime letters to his wife that appeared in his posthumous memoirs, *McClellan's Own Story*, published in 1887. McClellan had married Mary Ellen Marcy (called Ellen, or Nell or Nelly in these letters) in May 1860, eleven months before he took command of Ohio's volunteer troops. During their separations he tried to write her every day, and whenever possible he sent her a daily telegram as well. She followed a similar regimen in her replies. In his letters he told her everything of his emotions and opinions and motives; she was, he assured her, his alter ego, "you, who share all my thoughts...." Nothing else he wrote was so revealing of himself. Periodically during his life McClellan had kept a diary, and these letters to his wife, in their frequency and content, have very much the flavor of a daily diary. They give a special quality of immediacy to his accounting of events, and from the historian's perspective there is regret that on occasion their separations ended. This is particularly true for most of the period when McClellan was general-in-chief, in the winter of 1861–1862, and Mrs. McClellan joined him in Washington.

In his biography of Lincoln, the historian J. G. Randall termed these home letters "a kind of unstudied release, not to be taken too seriously," but this judgment was based on only slight familiarity with the larger body of the general's correspondence, especially his personal correspondence. In fact McClellan's actions frequently followed the patterns he spelled out to his wife. While in these letters he did indeed vent his feelings in outspoken opinions about Lincoln and his administration and its policies and the people in it, there was nothing unstudied (or even necessarily private) about this. He repeated the same views, sometimes in even more forceful terms, to prominent leaders of the Democratic opposition, and he assuredly intended them to be taken seriously.

In the mid-1870s, while assembling material for his memoirs, McClellan had copied portions of a large number of these letters in a notebook under the heading, "Extracts from letters written to my wife during the war of the Rebellion." From the content and uninhibited frankness of these extracts it is clear enough that he had no thought of their publication but simply intended them as reminders to himself, while writing his memoirs, of his wartime attitudes toward events. On the evidence of what he included, it seems equally clear that what he left out of these copies — which he indicated by ellipsis marks — was nothing more than personal matter. The several surviving original letters written to his wife in 1863 and 1864 that are printed in their entirety here suggest the often personal content, such as professions of his love, that he would logically have deleted in making the copies.

Following the general's death in 1885 his literary executor, William C. Prime, found the notebook among his papers and made the decision to print these extracts as part of *McClellan's Own Story,* which he was then assembling for publication. Feeling that his friend's personal qualities were not fully enough represented in these extracts, Prime persuaded the McClellans' daughter, May, to comb the original letters for more personal and private matter. Her copies, made in 1886, mark the last time these original letters McClellan wrote while on active service can be accounted for. (Similarly, only a handful of his wife's letters to him, and a few of her telegrams, are known to have survived.) Editor Prime combined the two sets of copies, had them transcribed (with less than scrupulous concern for accuracy), put them in what he took to be chronological order, severely censored them through cutting and alteration, and let them serve as eleven of the book's forty chapters.

In preparing the letters for publication in this volume, the editorial license practiced by Prime has been revoked. The copies by McClellan and his daughter have been retranscribed in their entirety and dates corrected or supplied. Where May McClellan copied more of a particular letter than her father had included, the letter has been reassembled based on content and on McClellan's usual pattern of writing. The daily telegrams to his wife that are of interest are included, but not the many simply stating the condition of his health and that of her father, Chief of Staff Randolph B. Marcy.

While on campaign he addressed by far the largest share of his private correspondence to his wife — his sole relaxation, he once told her, was "reading your letters & writing to you" — but occasionally he found time to write to other members of his family and to those he regarded as his supporters on the home front. Next to his wife the personal correspondent he wrote to most frequently in the years 1860–1865 was Samuel L. M. Barlow, an old friend and prominent New York Democrat who in 1864 became his unofficial political manager. These letters to Barlow, thirty-seven of which are included here, present perhaps the clearest picture of McClellan's views on major political issues and on his place in Civil War politics.

EDITORIAL PROCEDURES

General McClellan wrote rapidly in a distinctive and well-formed hand, with an innate concern for spelling and syntax, and his correspondence has required no editorial alterations to be easily readable. His abbreviations and sometimes minimal punctuation create no ambiguity. The letters and dispatches appear here exactly as he wrote them, except that the positioning of headings, salutations, and signatures is made uniform. Any necessary correction or clarification, most often in matters of date and place of writing, is placed within brackets or in the annotations. The ellipses McClellan indicated in his copies of letters to his wife are retained.

The arrangement is in chapters conforming to the major phases of his wartime career and intermixes military and personal documents in chronological order. The context and circumstances of their writing is noted in the chapter introductions. A fuller account of events and McClellan's role in them will be found in Stephen W. Sears, *George B. McClellan: The Young Napoleon* (New York: Ticknor & Fields, 1988). McClellan sometimes added to a private letter through the course of a day or even over two days, and in such cases it is placed according to the earliest date or time mentioned. Where the chronology is not explicit or obvious, placement is based on McClellan's writing habits. He did office work in the morning, for example, and often ended his day with a letter to his wife.

Routine, minor editing or correcting done by McClellan has been incorporated here without notice, as has any necessary decoding from cipher messages. However, where there is crossed-out material of substance or interest, it has been indicated and restored within brackets. For example, the original content of his telegram written to General Halleck during the Battle of Antietam, which he altered before sending, reveals something of his true feeling in the midst of that great battle. A long passage that on second thought he decided to cut from a letter of December 5, 1862, to General Charles P. Stone gives (for another example) new details on that officer's arrest for alleged disloyalty.

Following each document is its description by manuscript type and its source. Citation to the McClellan Papers in the Manuscript Division of the Library of Congress includes the collection volume number followed by the microfilm reel number. Citation to the Civil War records in the National Archives is by the record group (RG) and number, followed by the microfilm series and reel number, or by the entry number. Citation is also made to previous printing in *The War of the Rebellion: A Compilation of the Official Records of the Union and Confederate Armies* or the *Official Records of the Union and Confederate Navies in the War of the Rebellion,* using the abbreviations *OR* and *NOR,* respectively. Addressees and other persons mentioned are identified the first time they appear but not subsequently unless there is a significant change in status or position; the index serves as a guide to these identifications. Where relevant, the communication to which McClellan was responding, and the answer he received, are summarized in the annotations.

The following manuscript abbreviations are used:

AD	Autograph Document
ADS	Autograph Document Signed
ADf	Autograph Draft
ADfS	Autograph Draft Signed
AL	Autograph Letter or Telegram
AL copy	Autograph Letter or Telegram copy by McClellan
AL copy; copy	In reference to McClellan's letters to his wife, a copy in part by McClellan and in part by his daughter
ALS	Autograph Letter or Telegram Signed
Copy	Copy not made by McClellan
D	Document
Df	Draft
DP	Document Printed
DS	Document Signed
LS	Letter or Telegram Signed

THE CIVIL WAR PAPERS OF
GEORGE B. MCCLELLAN

ONE

COMMAND IN THE WESTERN THEATER

DECEMBER 27, 1860–JULY 22, 1861

AT THE OUTBREAK of war in April 1861, George McClellan was living in Cincinnati and serving as president of the eastern division of the Ohio and Mississippi Railroad. He had resigned from the army in 1857 to enter the railroad business, first with the Illinois Central and then, in August 1860, with the Ohio and Mississippi. As the first letters here suggest, he had followed the course of the secession crisis closely and hoped that compromise might settle the sectional conflict, but he was not optimistic. The decision for war did not surprise him.

At the time of his resignation, Captain McClellan had been considered one of the most promising young officers in the service. Graduating from West Point second in class in 1846, he was commissioned in the Corps of Engineers and served capably in the Mexican War. A wide range of increasingly important peacetime assignments followed. He was best known for his year-long service as an observer in the Crimean War and an analyst of the organization of European armies. When President Lincoln called for troops to put down the rebellion, the North's three most populous states all sought the thirty-four-year-old McClellan to command their forces.

The offers from Ohio and Pennsylvania may be traced here; New York's bid, not mentioned in McClellan's correspondence, reached him (like Pennsylvania's) after he had taken the position of major general of Ohio's volunteer troops. It is clear that his first preference had been for a high command with the Pennsylvania forces, and that it was more by chance — a misdirected telegram — than by any other cause that he went to war in the western theater. There is every likelihood that had he headed the Pennsylvania Reserves in the eastern army rather than the Department of the Ohio the course of his Civil War career — or at least the early phases of it — would have been very different.

McClellan's letter of April 27 to Winfield Scott, composed just four days after he took up his military duties, is noteworthy for being the first strategic plan by a Union general for carrying on the war on a large scale. It was a seriously flawed plan, as General Scott pointed out, but it inspired Scott in his reply to formulate a strategy of his own, the Anaconda Plan, which featured a blockade of Southern ports and an advance on the line of the Mississippi River. The correspondence here with and about Scott, some of it previously unpublished, reveals the roots of McClellan's conflict with the general-in-chief, which would grow and worsen in the coming months.

When McClellan was named to head the Department of the Ohio on May 3, his command initially consisted of the states of Ohio, Indiana, and Illinois; subsequently it included western Pennsylvania and western Virginia and (on June 6) the state of Missouri. He would play only a minor role in operations in the Mississippi Valley before a new Western Department was formed on July 3. He made his headquarters in Cincinnati and for the most part focused his attention as department commander on the Ohio River line, and specifically on Kentucky and western Virginia.

In dealing with Kentucky's proclaimed neutrality and with the threat of a Confederate occupation of strategically important western Virginia, McClellan first displayed the combining of military and political objectives that would mark the entire course of his wartime service. In his proclamation to the people of western Virginia (May 26) and in his letter to General Scott on Union policy toward Kentucky (June 5), for example, he made clear his belief that slavery must not become an issue in the war. He emphasized as well a benevolent attitude toward Southern civilians in the war zone. "All private property whether of secessionists or others must be strictly respected," he ordered (July 14), "and no one is to be molested merely because of political opinions."

From June 21 onward, General McClellan was in the field in a month-long campaign in western Virginia that involved him in a single action, at Rich Mountain on July 12. This first experience of field command is described in revealing detail in his dispatches to his subordinates and to Washington, and in his letters to his wife. In operations marked more by maneuver than by pitched battle, the Union forces in the region were everywhere victorious. "Our success is complete & secession is killed in this country," McClellan telegraphed Washington on July 14.

It was the first important Northern success of the war, and McClellan's role in it, as both military administrator and field commander, took on added significance when the Federal army in the eastern theater was defeated a week later at Bull Run. On July 22, 1861, General McClellan was ordered to Washington to take command of what he was to christen the Army of the Potomac.

To Samuel L. M. Barlow

Private

My dear S L M Cincinnati Dec 27 [1860]

We arrived here two or three days ago & found our house desolate — my wife's mother & sister having been suddenly called off to St Jo by the serious illness of Maj Marcy[1] — to day we hear that he is out of danger, so we are merry again after our sad Christmas.

I find very little *excitement* here, but a great deal of quiet determination. In a conversation with a very intelligent Republican, from Indiana, this morning I put to him the direct question whether he & his friends are willing to run the Missouri Compromise line to the Pacific & to repeal the Personal Liberty Bills — he replied that they would gladly do the first & more than the second — that they were perfectly willing that when a fugitive slave was rescued, or impediments thrown in the way of his arrest & return, that the *county* should pay his full value. I am sure that this is the feeling of the Republican party in the West. More than this — the feeling of *all* people here is that the North West will do justice to the South if they will give us time — but that if they go off half cocked & listen to nothing but the Republican politicians at Washington (who, from the nature of the case, cannot represent the *present* feeling of the North) we will meet the consequences unitedly, let it be war or peace — but the general opinion is that it will be *war*.

Most men here acknowledge that the South has much to ask that the North ought to & would grant — at the same time we think that in many things the South is in the wrong. Great Scott! I did not intend to preach politics — of which you must be sick enough — so I will ask pardon & change the subject. Some little affairs have turned up here which make it important that I should know *confidentially* what Bacon's[2] movements will probably be. Does he intend leaving the road, &, if so, when? I have been told here that he was about to engage in some business which would take him away from St Louis. Please let the question & answer be between ourselves.

My wife desires her kindest remembrances to Mrs B & yourself, not forgetting Miss Carrie — we were very sorry not to see Mrs B again — on the whole I don't know that I regret it, for I really began to be jealous of her — my better half was so much fascinated by her.

It is becoming so dark that I must close.

Your sincere friend
Geo B McClellan

S L M B Esq

ALS, Barlow Papers, Huntington Library. Barlow was a New York lawyer, railroad executive, and Democratic party leader.

1. Maj. Randolph B. Marcy, GBM's father-in-law. 2. Henry D. Bacon, an executive with the Ohio and Mississippi Railroad.

To Thomas C. English

My dear Thomas Cincinnati Feb. 7 1861

You will probably be surprised to hear from me, & in truth I have not a great deal to say — but it struck me that I would write before the mails are entirely stopped. I presume that you are in the midst of a great deal of excitement — there is little or none here in the cold blood of the North. I have yet strong hopes that the existing difficulties will be satisfactorily arranged. The feeling among the *people* in this vicinity is strongly in favor of doing justice to the South & leaving out the ultra men in certain limited districts, I think that feeling is prevalent in the North. I do believe that the border states will be satisfied, & that being accomplished, I think the further steps of satisfying all the other slave states save South Carolina will not be difficult.

I was very, very sorry to miss you in Phila. — had I had the slightest idea that you were coming on so soon I would have strained a point & waited for you. Nelly was very anxious to see you, & she begs me to say that when you next come north you *must* pass through Cincinnati if it is a possible thing for you to do it. We have taken a house here for three years. I hope the disturbances in the country may not make it necessary for me to change my plans as to living here. I suppose you will make no change in regard to the children — no state of affairs between the sections can make it unpleasant for them to be in Phila. while going to school — tho there may be considerations at home which would affect it.

Nelly sends her love.

Yours affectionately
Geo B McClellan

Mr. T. C. English

Copy, McClellan Papers (A-11:5), Library of Congress. English, GBM's brother-in-law, lived in Mt. Pleasant, Ala.

To Fitz John Porter

Ohio & Mississippi Railroad Company,
Eastern Division President's Office
Cincinnati, April 18, 1861

My dear old Fitz

Your welcome note has just reached me.[1]

I have already received an intimation that I have been proposed as the Comdr of the Penna Reserves, & asked if I would accept — replied yes! If Genl Scott would say a word to Gov Curtin in my behalf I think the matter could be easily arranged.[2]

Say to the Genl that I am ready as ever to serve under his command; I trust I need not assure him that he can count on my loyalty to him & the dear old flag he has so long upheld.

I throw to one side now all questions as to the past — political parties etc — the Govt is in danger, our flag insulted & we must stand by it. Tho' I am told I can have a position with the Ohio troops I much prefer the Penna service — I hope to hear something definite from them today & will let you know at once. Help me as far as you can.

Ever yours
McC

My wife is on a trip to Fort Randolph with her father & mother. Very pressing business here requires my presence for a few days.

ALS, Nicholson Collection, Huntington Library. Maj. Porter was stationed in the Adjutant General's Office in Washington.

1. Porter wrote GBM on Apr. 15 urging him to take a high command in the Pennsylvania or Ohio volunteers. McClellan Papers (A-11:5), Library of Congress. 2. General-in-Chief Winfield Scott; Andrew G. Curtin, governor of Pennsylvania.

To Robert Patterson

Ohio & Mississippi Railroad Company,
Eastern Division President's Office
Cincinnati, April 18 1861

Maj Genl Patterson
General

Your telegram of today is received. I at once replied "what rank & when do you want me." I have some very important business on hand here that will necessarily detain me a few days — it is not private business, but that of my employers, so that I feel bound to attend to it. One cannot in a day break off from such a business as that entrusted to me.

On every account — yours, mine, & the good of the service — I think the rank of Chf Engineer ought to be that of a Brig Genl — I could be of much more use to you in that than in a lower grade. I hope to hear from you by letter tomorrow, when I can at once determine.

I expect two of the principal owners of the Road here tonight — & feel that it is only proper to inform them before taking so decided a step.

Trusting that you will understand the nature of my delay, & that I shall have the pleasure of serving once more under your orders[1]

I am, General, your sincere friend
Geo B McClellan

The reason for my enquiring about the rank is that before receiving your telegram I have received intimations that a high command would be tendered me.

ALS, Miscellaneous Collections, Huntington Library. Maj. Gen. Patterson commanded Pennsylvania's three-month volunteers.

1. GBM had served under Patterson during the Mexican War.

To William Dennison

Private

His Excellency W Dennison

My dear Sir Cincinnati April 18/61

Your telegram of yesterday is received. In mine to Gen Bates[1] I had reference to the policy of retaining in Cincinnati, for its defence, a large portion of the organized Volunteer Companies belonging here.

It is clear that Cincinnati is the most important strategical point in the valley of the Ohio, both from its position & the resources it will furnish to the party holding it.

Should the Confederate States operate west of the Alleghenies, Cincinnati will doubtless be their objective point.

If it is left defenceless it would afford too great a temptation to lawless men, who by a sudden incursion might do a great deal of mischief.

I suggest that immediate steps should be taken to guard effectually against the latter evil & that means should secretly be proposed to pave the way for meeting the more formidable attempt first alluded to.

It appears to me that no time should be lost in arming & rendering efficient several regiments of Volunteers in this city for home service — I would send no men away from here until a sufficient well armed & organized force is raised to protect the city fully from insult. I would offer inducements & all facilities for gaining this end.

I think the "Home Guard" movement now in progress here is an ill advised one, tho' prompted by good motives; they will prove to be inefficient from the fact that they have no common head. It would be far better to organize regiments under the Militia Law, with the distinct understanding, if necessary, that they are not liable to be drafted for foreign service. The entire armed forces of all kinds in Cinc. should be in every respect under the orders of the militia officer comdg the District.

I understand that there is not a single powder magazine on this side of the River! Of arms there are next to none, especially of heavy guns. Both of these fatal defects should be remedied at once with regard to the first mentioned contingency. I think that the ground around Cincinnati should be carefully studied (especially on the south bank of the river), so that a plan of defence could be drawn up, all ready to be acted upon when the necessity for it arises. The most important thing to be done, in this connection, is to select the points on the Covington side to be occupied by field works, should it become necessary to do so, in order to cover the city on that side; the plans of the works should be carefully studied & arranged, the necessary form fixed upon, intrenching tools, & artillery provided so that no time would be lost when the emergency arises. It may well be that the necessity for all this will not occur, but there is only one safe rule in war — i.e. to decide what is the very worst thing that can happen to you, & prepare to meet it.

By proper precautions I think that this city can be rendered secure, & the available power of the state left free to act in other quarters.

Should my views strike you as correct I will gladly communicate with you more in detail if you care about my doing so. I hope that you will regard this letter as strictly confidential.

AL retained copy, McClellan Papers (A-11:5), Library of Congress. Dennison was governor of Ohio.

1. Brig. Gen. Joshua H. Bates, Ohio militia.

To Winfield Scott

Lt Genl Winfield Scott
Comdg U.S. Army
General:

Head Quarters Ohio Volunteers
Columbus Ohio April 23 1861

I have the honor to inform you that I have been appointed by the Governor of Ohio as the Major General Commanding all the Ohio troops called into the service of the Genl Govt, & to report for duty accordingly.

I wish to lay before you as full a statement as is now in my power of the condition of my command & its necessities.

There are four full Regts at Cincinnati, ready to be mustered into the service, some 3500 men encamped near this city, and about 600 at Cleveland; large numbers are now en route here, more than enough to complete the requisition — this state will supply 50,000 if desired.[1]

I have seen the men at Cincinnati & this city — I have never seen so fine a body of men collected together — the material is superb, but has no organization or discipline.

Capt Granger has probably mustered into service the Cleveland detachment today; Gov Dennison has telegraphed him to proceed at once to Cincinnati to muster in four Regts tomorrow; Major Burbank will commence mustering in the troops at this place tomorrow.[2]

Of the troops at Cincinnati two Regts have been encamped for four days, a third Regt goes into camp tomorrow. The Legislature will tomorrow authorize the Gov. to accept the services of eight Regts in addition to the 13 already called for.

None of these troops have any camp equipage, except some 100 state tents here, & about 20 at Cincinnati; we will probably be able to hut them.

I may say that we have no arms nor ammunition — for there are only some 480 muskets at Cincinnati & some 1400 here, many of the latter being rifles (without bayonets) & altered flint locks; we have in the state about 900 Rifled Muskets. I propose using these, & such of the Rifles as I can provide with bayonets in forming picked Battalions of Riflemen.

The Gov. received information today that 10,000 percussion muskets had been ordered here from Watervliet, & that the accouterments will be sent from Pittsburg as soon as manufactured, also that 200,000 cartridges would be forwarded. We have 19 6 pdr guns at Cincinnati, a battery of 6 guns (with fairly drilled cannoneers) at Marietta, & 6 indifferent guns here.

I cannot urge too strongly the absolute necessity of our receiving at once at least 10,000 stand of arms in addition to those now ordered here, & that as many as possible of these be of the new pattern Rifled-Musket; — cannot the St Louis, or the Dearborn Arsenal supply us? We will need the corresponding accouterments, & should have at least 5,000,000 cartridges, as I am anxious to perfect the men in target practice.

The state has thus far been very unsuccessful in its efforts to purchase arms in the East. Of camp equipage we need a full supply for 20,000 men; we require knapsacks, clothing, some means of transportation etc.

I find myself, General, in the position of a Comdg Officer with nothing but men — no arms or supplies.

I would respectfully request that Maj Fitz John Porter may be assigned to the position of Adjt Genl of the Ohio troops, to report to me at Cincinnati; Capt Jno H Dickerson as Qtr Mr Genl; Maj R B Marcy as Paymaster;[3] a Comsy of Subsistance. I also think it very necessary that I should have at least one officer of Engrs, of Topographical Engrs, & if possible two of Ordnance. The state is willing to undertake the manufacture of some iron field guns & guns of position for the defence of the Ohio River frontier; to carry out the project it is necessary that we should have an experienced officer of the Ordnance Corps, while another will be required to superintend the issue, care, & repairs of arms & ammunition. Whenever the necessities of defence at Washington etc will justify it I would be glad to have McCook's & Wilson's Regts (1st & 2nd Ohio, now at Lancaster or Harrisburg) ordered back here, if you intend that my command shall operate on the Ohio line.[4]

I propose, until receiving orders from you, to establish my command in a Camp of Instruction at some point near Cincinnati, where I will get them into shape as soon as possible. Until I hear from you I will consider it my duty to take all possible measures for the protection of Cincinnati & the line of the Ohio, from the Great Miami to Wheeling; I will obtain all the information possible in regard to ground opposite Cincinnati on the Ky side, & without attracting attention take all the steps necessary to occupy the heights when the moment arrives.[5] I will take steps by the use of secret service money to obtain early information as to any hostile movements from the south.

A few heavy guns & howitzers would be very desirable at Cincinnati in case it should become necessary to occupy heights on the Ky side, or to return the fire of hostile batteries.[6] We ought to have *at least* one light battery, & I will do what I can to organize one or more while awaiting your further orders.

A force of cavalry will also be very necessary for patrol duty. I make these suggestions in the supposition that it will be, for the present at least, my duty to provide for the defence of the frontier.

It would be well that I should have some understanding with the Comdt of the Indiana troops, by which a movement on Louisville could be made, should it become necessary in order to relieve a pressure upon Cincinnati.

If I am correct in supposing that for the present my command is to be kept together & charged with the defence of the Ohio, or a movement in advance should political events require it, I would recommend that it be formed into a Corps d'Armee & furnished with suitable batteries, & a cavalry force — a battalion of regulars would be of great assistance. I would urge the immediate dispatch of the staff officers I have asked for — you can imagine the condition in which I am, without a single instructed officer to assist me.[7]

I will take steps to secure the safety of the Railways in Ohio, & will make such arrangements with the Railway Managers as to enable me to control their entire resources.

I am Genl very respectfully yr obdt svt
Geo B McClellan
Maj Genl O.V.M.

12 24 pdrs
6 8″ howitzers
6 12 pdrs
2 8″ mortars
2 10″ "
2 8″ Columbiads

ALS retained copy, McClellan Papers (A-11:5), Library of Congress. *OR*, Ser. 1, LI, Part 1, pp. 333–34. This transcription combines two drafts written by GBM. The copy sent to Washington included the variations noted below.

1. Ohio's share of the president's call for 75,000 militia was thirteen regiments, or about 10,000 men. 2. Mustering officers Capt. Gordon Granger, Mounted Rifles, and Maj. Sidney Burbank, 1st U.S. Infantry. 3. Maj. Porter, Capt. John H. Dickerson, and Maj. Marcy were staff officers in the Adjutant General's Office, Quartermaster's Office, and Paymaster General's Office, respectively. 4. These three-month regiments had been ordered to Washington. 5. The copy sent to Washington included at this point the sentence: "I will be careful to do nothing that can compromise the Government in any way with the inhabitants of Kentucky." 6. The list of requested ordnance in the postscript (except the last item)

appeared here in the letter as sent. 7. Gen. Scott's adjutant, Lt. Col. E. D. Townsend, replied on Apr. 30: "The general very much regrets it will not be possible to place at your disposal the officers for whom you ask, except Major Marcy.... The very large number of resignations just in an emergency,... sufficiently explains the necessity for asking you to do as well as you can with the talent and zeal you can find in your command." *OR*, Ser. 1, LI, Part 1, pp. 342–43.

To Joseph W. Alsop

The State of Ohio, Executive Department
Columbus, April 24, 1861

My dear Mr Alsop

They have passed the law allowing the Govr to appoint the Maj Genl Comdg — I receive my commission this morning, & am to have the command of all the Ohio troops called into the service of the Genl. Govt., together with the defence of the State.[1] I am already overwhelmed with business — up till late in the morning. Sent off last night long dispatch to Genl Scott reporting in full.[2]

Hope to return to Cincinnati to night. Feel in my own element.

Truly yours
Geo B. McClellan

My regards to Mr Bartlett[3]

ALS, Alsop Family Papers, Yale University Library. Alsop was president of the Ohio and Mississippi Railroad.

1. On Apr. 23 the Ohio legislature passed a special bill for GBM's benefit, permitting the governor to apppoint any Ohio resident a major general rather than only a member of the state militia. 2. GBM to Scott, Apr. 23, *supra*. 3. Edwin Bartlett, an officer of the Ohio and Mississippi Railroad.

To Andrew G. Curtin [TELEGRAM]

[Columbus] Apl 24 [1861]

Your telegram to Chicago never reached me.[1] Before I heard from you that you wanted me in any position I had accepted the command of the Ohio forces. They need my services & I am bound in honor to stand by them. I regret that I cannot command the Penna troops, and thank you for the offer.

G. B. McClellan

Gov Curtin
Harrisburg

ALS (telegram sent), McClellan Papers, Illinois State Historical Library.

1. Gov. Curtin's misdirected telegram offered GBM command of the Pennsylvania Reserves.

To Allan Pinkerton

Allan Pinkerton, Esq.
Dear Sir:— Columbus, Ohio, April 24, 1861.

I wish to see you with the least possible delay, to make arrangements with you of an important nature. I will be either here or in Cincinnati for the next few days — here to-morrow — Cincinnati next day. In this city you will find me at the Capitol, at Cincinnati at my residence.

If you telegraph me, better use your first name alone. Let no one know that you come to see me, and keep as quiet as possible.

Very truly yours,
Geo. B. McClellan
Maj. Gen'l Comd'g Ohio Vols.

Allan Pinkerton, *The Spy of the Rebellion* (New York, 1883), pp. 140–41. Pinkerton, a Chicago private detective, became head of GBM's intelligence-gathering operations.

To Ohio Volunteer Militia

General Order, Head Quarters, Ohio Volunteer Militia,
No. 1. [Columbus] April 25th, 1861

By the direction of the Governor of Ohio, the undersigned hereby assumes command of the Ohio Volunteer Militia mustered into the service of the United States.

In doing so, he desires to call the attention of the officers and men to the fact, that discipline and instruction are of as much importance in war as mere courage. He asks for and expects the cheerful co-operation of the entire command in his efforts to establish discipline and efficiency, the surest guarantees of success.

Until the organization is perfected, many inconveniences must be endured, for the sudden exigency, which has made it necessary to call so largely upon your patriotism, has rendered it impossible for the authorities to make, in an instant, the requisite preparation.

We do not enter upon this war as a pastime, but with the stern determination to repel the insults offered to our flag, and uphold the honor and integrity of our Union.

In the coming struggle, we have not only battles to fight, but hardships and privations to endure, fatigue to encounter.

The General Commanding does not doubt, that the spirit which has prompted you to leave your homes and those most dear to you, will support you firmly in the future.

He asks your willing obedience and full confidence — having obtained that, he feels sure that he can conduct you to glory, and to victories that will ensure safety to your homes and lasting repose to the country.

Geo. B. McClellan,
Major General O.V.M.

DP, McClellan Papers (A-11:5), Library of Congress.

To Winfield Scott

Lieut Genl Winfield Scott
Comdg U.S. Army
General:

Head Quarters O.V.M.
Columbus Ohio April 27 1861

Communications with Washington being so difficult, I beg to lay before you some views relative to this region of country, & to propose for your consideration a plan of operations intended to relieve the pressure upon Washington, & tending to bring the war to a speedy close.

The region North of the Ohio, and between the Mississippi and the Alleghenies, forms one grand strategic field in which all operations must be under the control of one head, whether acting offensively or on the defensive.

I assume it as the final result that hostilities will break out on the line of the Ohio.

For two reasons it is necessary to delay this result, by all political means, for a certain period of time.

1st To enable the North West to make the requisite preparations now very incomplete.

2nd That a strong diversion may be made in aid of the defense of Washington, & the Eastern line of operations.

First urging that the General Govt. should leave no means untried to arm & equip the Western States, I submit the following views.

Cairo should be occupied by a small force, say 2 Battalions, strongly entrenched, & provided with heavy guns, & a gun boat to control the river.

A force of some 8 battalions to be in observation at Sandoval (the junction of the Ohio & Miss, & the Illinois Central Railways) to observe St Louis, sustain the garrison of Cairo, & if necessary to reinforce Cincinnati.

A few Companies should observe the Wabash below Vincennes.

A Division of about 4000 men at Seymour, to observe Louisville, & be ready to support Cincinnati or Cairo.

A Division of 5000 men at or near Cincinnati.

Two Battalions at or near Chillicothe.

Could we be provided with arms, the North West has ample resources to furnish 80,000 men for active operations, after providing somewhat more than the troops mentioned above for the protection of the frontier.

With the active army of operations it is proposed to cross the Ohio at, or in the vicinity of Gallipolis, & move up the valley of the Great Kanawha on Richmond; in combination with this Cumberland [Md.] should be seized, and a few thousand men left, at Ironton or Gallipolis, to cover the rear & right flank of the main column — the presence of this detachment & a prompt movement on Louisville, or the heights opposite Cincinnati would effectually prevent any interference on the part of Kentucky. The movement on Richmond should be conducted with the utmost promptness, & could not fail to relieve Washington, as well as to secure the destruction of the Southern Army if aided by a decided advance on the Eastern line.

I know that there could be difficulties in crossing the mountains, but would go prepared to meet them.

Another plan could be, in the event of Kentucky assuming a hostile position, to cross the Ohio at Cincinnati or Louisville with 80,000 men, march straight on Nashville, & thence act according to circumstances.

Were a battle gained before reaching Nashville, so that the strength of Kentucky & Tennessee were effectually broken, a movement on Montgomery, aided by a vigorous [offensive] on the Eastern line, towards Charleston & Augusta, should not be delayed. The ulterior movements of the combined armies might be on Pensacola, Mobile & New Orleans.

It seems clear that the forces of the North West should not remain quietly on the defensive, & that under present circumstances, if the supply of arms is such as to render it absolutely impossible to bring into the field the numbers indicated above their offensive movements would be most effective on the line first indicated; but if so liberal supply can be obtained as to enable us to dispose of 80,000 troops for the active army, then the 2nd line of operations could be the most decisive.

To enable us to carry out either of these plans, it is absolutely necessary that the Genl Govt should strain every nerve to supply the West with arms, ammunition & equipments.

Even to maintain the defensive we must be largely assisted.

I beg to urge upon you that we are very badly supplied at present, & that a vast population, eager to fight, are rendered powerless by the want of arms — the nation being thus deprived of their aid.[1]

I have the honor to be, General, very respectfully yours
Geo B McClellan
Maj. Genl. Comdg O.V.

ALS, Records of the Adjutant General's Office, RG 94 (M-619:41), National Archives. *OR,* Ser. 1, LI, Part 1, pp. 338–39.

1. Gen. Scott's May 2 endorsement on this letter reads in part: "As at the date of this letter Genl. Mc. knew nothing of the intended call for two years' volunteers, he must have had the idea of composing his enormous columns of three months' men . . . , that is, of men whose term of service would expire by the time he had collected & organized them. . . . 2. A march upon Richmond from the Ohio would probably insure the revolt of Western Virginia. . . . 3. The general eschews water transportation by the Ohio & Mississippi, in favor of long, tedious & *break-down* (of men, horses & wagons) marches. 4. His plan is to subdue the seceded states, by piecemeal, instead of enveloping them all (nearly) at once,

by a cordon of posts on the Mississippi to its mouth, . . . & by blockading ships of war on the sea-board. . . .''

To Lorenzo Thomas

Col L. Thomas
Adjt General U.S.A. Head Quarters OVM
Colonel: Columbus Ohio April 27 1861

I have the honor to request that Capt G. Granger, Regt Mounted Rifles, may be assigned to duty as Division Inspector of my Division. The Captain is now engaged in mustering in troops at Cincinnati & will be available for duty in a few days.

I have also to request that Lt O M Poe, Topl Engrs, now stationed at Detroit may be assigned to duty on my staff.

I hope that my request to have Major Fitz John Porter, & Capt Dickerson assigned to duty with my Division may be at once complied with. You will see that in organizing a force of 30,000 men it is very necessary that I should have such officers.

I found Lt McCleary, 6th Infty, on leave of absence & have taken him temporarily on my staff. I hope he may be allowed to remain there, as I shall probably in a few days ask to have him as one of my Aides-de-Camp.[1] I shall commence tomorrow moving the men into a camp of instruction on the Little Miami Railroad 17 miles from Cincinnati, a fine turnpike 12m in length also leads from it to Cincinnati.

From this position I can move the command rapidly to any point where it may be required.

In three days I shall have 7 Regts at Camp Dennison (the permanent camp), & 4 Regts at Camp Harrison 6 miles from Cincinnati.

By the end of the week the Cleveland & Columbus camps will be abandoned, & there will be some 17 Regts at Camp Dennison.

By the end of two weeks there will be 24 Regts in that camp, unless I find it necessary in the mean time to detach some Regts toward Marietta. My desire is to concentrate the whole command in this camp, & to thoroughly organize, discipline & drill them. By the end of six weeks I hope they will be in condition to act efficiently in any direction where they may be required.

I hope that my wish can be carried out, & that I may not be required to take my men under fire until they are reduced to some order & discipline.

Should they be required to act together I would desire to organize some batteries & cavalry.

Some squadrons of regular cavalry & regular batteries would be desirable.

We are very deficient in small arms, guns, ammunition & equipment — I have been doing all in my power to overcome these deficiencies, & most earnestly urge upon the consideration of the General in Chief the necessity of furnishing me with these supplies at once. Give me these & I will provide the men.

Money & a Subsistence officer should be sent at once — we have no U.S. money, & I am working with money furnished by the State.

The state will call 30 Regts (in all) into service, all of which they place under my command; 13 are now called out. 75 can be furnished by this state alone if you can arm us.

In hopes that you will find it in your power to comply at once with my requests

I am, Colonel, very respectfully your obedient servant
Geo B McClellan
Major Genl

In a few days I will probably move my Head Quarters to Cincinnati or Camp Dennison; there is a good deal of excitement in Cincinnati.

ALS, Records of the Adjutant General's Office, RG 94 (M-619 :37), National Archives. *OR*, Ser. 1, LI, Part 1, pp. 339–40. Col. (later Brig. Gen.) Thomas was the army's adjutant general.

1. Of the officers mentioned — Capt. Granger, Lt. Orlando M. Poe, Maj. Porter, Capt. Dickerson, and Lt. John McCleary — only Poe and Dickerson were assigned to GBM's command.

To Robert Patterson

Maj Genl Robt Patterson
Comdg Dept
General

Head Quarters OVM
Cincinnati, April 29 1861

Your dispatch is received. I have not a single Regiment in condition to take the field or perform efficient service.

There has been great delay in mustering in the troops & no supplies arms or money have been received from Washington — not even orders.

I have urged the Head Quarters for supplies, & am obliged to use the money of the State & act altogether on my own responsibility.

I am moving the troops into a Camp of Instruction where I propose organizing, equipping, & arming them — & will get them ready for service in the shortest possible time.

We have no arms yet & none of my Regts ought to be sent away from here in their present condition.

I have written to the Genl in Chief proposing a plan of operations which would keep the Ohio, Indiana & Illinois contingents west of the Alleghenies.

I am, General, very truly yours
Geo B McClellan
Maj Genl

ALS retained copy, McClellan Papers (A-11:5), Library of Congress.

To Winfield Scott

Lt. Genl Winfield Scott
Comdg the Army
General

Head Quarters OVM
Cincinnati May 7 1861

I have the honor to acknowledge the receipt of your confidential letter of the 3rd.[1] From certain remarks in an order transmitted to me by Col Townsend I learn that it has been decided to place me in command of a new Dept.[2]

I beg to thank you, General, for this mark of your confidence, & to assure you that you may rest satisfied that I will leave nothing undone to assist in carrying out your plans.

When I have time to think over the matter carefully I hope you will permit me to make such suggestions as to details as my intimate knowledge of the country may cause to occur to me.

I will do all I can, General, to reconcile public feeling here to the necessary delay. You are entirely correct in supposing this to be the greatest difficulty we have to encounter.

I fully appreciate the wisdom of your intentions & recognize the propriety of all your military dispositions, & will quietly urge the necessity of preparation.

Even if I did not agree with you I have that implicit confidence in the General under whom I first learned the art of war that would free me thereby to carry out his views.

I am respectfully very truly yours
Geo B McClellan

ALS retained copy, McClellan Papers (C-3:62), Library of Congress.

1. Gen. Scott's letter of May 3 outlined his so-called Anaconda Plan, the main features of which were a blockade of the Southern coasts and an advance down the Mississippi River to New Orleans. ***OR***, Ser. 1, LI, Part 1, pp. 369–70. 2. On May 3 GBM was named to the command of the Department of the Ohio.

To Winfield Scott

Personal

Lieut General Winfield Scott
Commanding U.S. Army
General.

Head Quarters O.V.M.
Cincinnati Ohio May 9th 1861

I feel assured that you not only will not misunderstand me, but that you will patiently bear with me while I make an appeal to you that involves the entire interests of my command and of the West.

I assumed control of an unorganized mass of men, with neither arms, clothing, equipments, supplies, discipline, instruction, nor money. I had no staff, not one single instructed Officer to assist me, no orders, no authority to do anything.

I knew that it must be your intention that the troops should be rendered efficient in the shortest possible time, and that economy should be introduced. I felt that from the very many instances of official and personal kindness I have received from you, I could implicitly rely upon your support in any reasonable measures, that might be taken by me. Please remember too, that for several days we were entirely cut off from all communication with Washington[1] and that it was but fair to suppose that it might at any moment prove necessary for me to move to the assistance of the General under whom I learned my first lessons in War, and whom I have been and ever shall be ready to support to the bitter end.

Under these circumstances I, for many days, performed in person the duties of all the Staff Depts, imperfectly it is true, but perhaps as fully as one man could. Knowing that Capt. Dickerson was unemployed I wrote to Gen Harney begging him to lend me the Captain, in his absence Major McKinstry[2] was kind enough to send the Capt to me, and I at once put him at work. Capt Burns[3] providentially made his appearance with no duty on his hands — I took the opportunity and kept him until I could obtain your approval. These Officers have done themselves infinite credit; they have introduced system and economy — every thing is going on in the regular order, and they have saved many thousands of dollars for the General Government.

I learn that the corresponding departments in Illinois and Indiana are totally disorganized, and I counted upon these Officers to introduce among the Volunteers from those States a system as good as that now existing in Ohio. I cannot supply their places — there are no men in these states competent to perform the duty.

If you will give me these two Officers, General, I will undertake that they shall perform the whole duty of their Dept's in the district to the command of which I may be assigned — without them I feel that there is no possibility of organizing the service. I would also urge that I may be allowed to retain Captain Granger, whose Regt. is in New Mexico. He knows now most of the Volunteers from this State, and is really indispensable to assist me in my efforts to instruct the Officers & introduce discipline.

Next to maintaining the honor of my country, General, the first aim of my life is to justify the good opinion you have expressed concerning me, and to prove that the great soldier of our country can not only command armies himself but teach others to do so. I do not expect your mantle to fall on my shoulders, for no man is worthy to wear it, but I hope that it may be said hereafter that I was no unworthy disciple of your school. I cannot make an army to carry out your views, unless I have the assistance of instructed soldiers. There are multitudes of brave men in the West, but no soldiers. I frankly and most earnestly call upon you to supply the want. I need, not only the Officers I have named, but a first rate Adjutant General and two good Aides de Camps. Major Porter is my preference as Adjt. General — if I cannot have him, I would be glad to have Capt. Williams.[4] Webb of the 5th Infantry and young Kingsbury just graduating would suit me well as Aides.[5]

The condition of things out here really makes an Ordnance Officer necessary — Capt Reno[6] would be glad to serve with me and I would be very glad to have him.

I have written frankly to you, General, for I am sure you will understand me and will not misinterpret my motives, the good of the service is what I seek. I cannot work without tools — I cannot be every where and do every thing myself. Give me the means and I will answer for it that I will take care of the rest.[7]

I have urgent demand for heavy guns, none are yet within my reach, notwithstanding your orders. It is absolutely necessary that a competent Officer should at once go to Cairo, and give directions, as to its defence — I have none at my disposal, and have not the authority to go myself.

Not one dollar have I yet received from the Genl. Gov. not any expression of opinion as to the steps I have taken. Excuse General, the length of this, the matter is urgent and I cannot well place it in a smaller compass. I ask your personal attention to it, and whatever the decision may be I will cheerfully acquiesce, and take my measures accordingly.

I am very respectfully your obt svt
Geo B McClellan
Maj Genl

LS, McClellan Papers, New-York Historical Society. *OR,* Ser. 1, LI, Part 1, pp. 373–74.

1. Maryland secessionists had cut Washington's rail and telegraph lines. 2. Brig. Gen. William S. Harney, commander of the Department of the West, at St. Louis; Maj. Justus McKinstry, of his staff. 3. Capt. William W. Burns, Commissary General's Office. 4. Capt. Seth Williams, Adjutant General's Office. 5. 1st Lt. William A. Webb, 5th U.S. Infantry; 2nd Lt. Henry W. Kingsbury, West Point 1861. 6. Capt. Jesse L. Reno, Ordnance Office. 7. Of the officers mentioned, Dickerson, Burns, and Williams were assigned to GBM's staff.

To William Dennison

Gov Wm Dennison
Columbus
Governor

Head Quarters Dept of the Ohio
Cincinnati May 13 1861

My reasons for advising that there should be no haste in sending the State Troops to the frontier, unless political reasons demanded it, are that I am in daily expectation of hearing from Washington the policy of the Govt, & that most of the information I obtain from the frontier indicates that the moral effect of troops directly on the frontier would not be very good, at least until Western Virginia has decided for herself what she will do. You no doubt are better posted than I am, & if it is clear that the Union men will be strengthened by the movement of course it will be made.

For military reasons I would prefer awaiting Lt Poe's return before selecting the points to be occupied — he should be here in a day or two, & we can then act understandingly.[1] I am pressed by Gov Morton[2] for troops & heavy guns along his frontier. Yates[3] wants all the troops at East St Louis & a battery of heavy guns there. Guns are also wanted at Cairo. With no means of supplying these demands it is sometimes a little difficult to satisfy them.

The apathy in Washington is very singular & very discouraging. The order placing me in command of the Dept was issued on May 3 — I have not yet received it! I can get no answers except now & then a decided refusal of some request or other — perhaps that is a little exaggerated, but the upshot of it is that they are entirely too slow for such an emergency, & I almost regret having entered upon my present duty.

No money has yet arrived.

I drew today on the Treasury of the State for $1250 on account, of next session — some $4000 or $5000 more should be placed to my credit in the Commercial Bank before the close of the week — the beginning of the session will be the most expensive.

I fear I shall have to go to Cairo in the morning — dare not leave here now until I hear from Harney & see Benham & Bell[4] — will go to you at the earliest moment.

Very truly yours
Geo B McClellan
Maj Genl

ALS retained copy, McClellan Papers (C-3 :62), Library of Congress.

1. Lt. Poe of GBM's staff had been sent into Kentucky and western Virginia to gather intelligence. 2. Oliver P. Morton, governor of Indiana. 3. Richard Yates, governor of Illinois. 4. Capt. Henry W. Benham, Corps of Engineers; Maj. William H. Bell, Ordnance Office.

To E. D. Townsend

To Col E D Townsend
A.A.G. — Head Quarters Dept of the Ohio
Colonel — Cincinnati May 17 1861

The intelligence I have from Western Virginia is not encouraging. The Union men there lack courage, I fear. From a long conversation with a well informed & reliable person this morning I have gathered some facts that may serve to corroborate information in your possession. The gist of the information was about as follows — viz: Harper's Ferry held by not over 2500 men, including those at Point of Rocks & the outposts; their arms, discipline etc. bad; no entrenchments erected on either side of the river; no guard at Shepherd's Town, where there is a good ford, & roads leading to Charlestown & Keys Ford. I would suggest a movement in that direction as the readiest method of driving the rebels from Harper's Ferry.

You are aware that the structures of the B & O RR most liable to injury are west of Cumberland. I beg to call to the attention of the Genl in Chief the importance of occupying Cumberland without delay — I learn that the population there, at Piedmont, Grafton etc are loyal — the importance of occupying Cumberland cannot be overestimated. In connection with that movement I propose moving one Regt of State troops to a point near Bellaire, another to a point in the vicinity of Marietta, another to Athens, another to Jackson on the Portsmouth RR. I wish to keep these away from the frontier, but near enough to produce a certain moral effect.

If Cumberland & Hancockstown can be occupied by the Maryland Troops now called out, it would probably be the best arrangement; if this cannot be done troops might be moved down from Pittsburg, if there are any there disposable.

Is it true as stated in the papers that Western Penna & Western Virginia have been added to my Dept? I have received no notification to that effect.[1]

The Union men of Kentucky express a firm determination to fight it out — yesterday Garret Davis[2] told me "we will remain in the Union by voting if we can, by fighting if we must, & if we cannot hold our own we will call on the General Govt to aid us." He asked me what I would do if they called on me for assistance & convinced me that the majority were in danger of being overpowered by a better armed minority.

I replied that if there were time enough I would refer to General Scott for orders — if there was not time, that I would cross the Ohio with 20,000 men, if that were not enough with 30,000, & if necessary with 40,000, but that I would not stand by & see the loyal Union men of Kentucky crushed. I have strong hopes that Kentucky will remain in the Union, & the most favorable feature of the whole matter is that the Union men are now ready to abandon the position of "armed neutrality," & to enter heart & soul into this contest on our side. I hope yet to pay a visit to the Hon Jefferson Davis at Montgomery.

I expect the three Randall Companies[3] tomorrow — will place them at Camp Dennison for the present. I hope to receive permission to mount more than one battery — I do not like the idea of being without regular batteries.

to nine regiments, but be brought up to twenty.[2] I have as yet received neither instructions nor authority. My hands tied until I have one or the other. Every day of importance.[3]

G B McClellan
Maj Genl

Hon Simon Cameron
Secy of War Washington D C

ALS (telegram sent), McClellan Papers (C-3 :62), Library of Congress. *OR,* Ser. 1, II, p. 642. Cameron was secretary of war.

1. A referendum on Virginia's ordinance of secession was scheduled for May 23. 2. Ohio was called on for nine regiments of three-year volunteers to supplant the thirteen regiments of three-month men. 3. Winfield Scott replied on May 21 that he was "surprised at your complaint to the Secretary of War against me that you are without instructions or authority and with your hands tied." He reviewed his communications to GBM on the subject, and added: "It is not conceived what other instructions could have been needed by you." *OR,* Ser. 1, LI, Part 1, pp. 386–87.

To E. D. Townsend

Col E D Townsend AAG
Colonel

Head Quarters Dept of the Ohio
Cincinnati May 21 1861

Gov Dennison has sent to me copies of his telegraphic communication of yesterday to the Lieut Genl comdg, with the Genl's reply.[1] A movement into Western Virginia may become necessary any day — so, also, it may at any moment become imperative to move into Kentucky, in order to save the loyal men of that state. With my present force it would be very dangerous to make these movements, particularly in view of the condition of the troops & the administrative branches. If we are to carry on this war in earnest, & in a manner to insure success, there should be at least 40,000 troops available for active operations in this Department, & the means of transportation should be provided, as well as clothing & equipment. Not less than 20, & if possible 30, Regts should be called for from this state.

I was extremely sorry a few moments since to receive a dispatch from the Adjt General stating that no recruits can be allowed for companies from Randall — there are between 400 & 500 recruits at Newport Barracks,[2] & plenty can be had by opening rendezvous on this side of the river.

I am very respectfully yr obdt svt
Geo B McClellan
Maj Genl USA

ALS retained copy, McClellan Papers (C-3 :62), Library of Congress. *OR,* Ser. 1, LI, Part 1, p. 383.

1. Gov. Dennison's telegram of May 20 reported intelligence that Confederate troops were advancing on Grafton and Clarksburg in western Virginia. Scott replied that the matter was "within the competency of Gen McClellan to whom please refer." McClellan Papers (B-7:46). 2. Newport Barracks was a recruiting depot at Newport, Ky.

To Lorenzo Thomas

Genl L Thomas
Adjt Genl U.S.A. Head Qtrs Dept of the Ohio
General Cincinnati May 21 1861

I have the honor to acknowledge the receipt of your communication of the 14th inst, enclosing my appointment as a Major General in the U.S. Army.

I accept the appointment & herewith return my oath of allegiance to the U.S. duly executed.

I beg, General, that you will convey to the Presdt, the Secretary of War, and the Lieut General Commanding, my most sincere & heartfelt thanks for this distinguished honor.

I confess it is with great diffidence that I enter upon the discharge of the momentous duties pertaining to my office, and with a grave sense of their magnitude & responsibility. I hope, however, that by bringing to the task a firm determination to devote my best abilities to the service of my country, I may succeed in justifying the exalted opinion of those to whom I am indebted for the post.

I am, General, very respectfully yours
Geo B McClellan
Maj Genl U.S. Army

ALS, Records of the Adjutant General's Office, RG 94 (M-619:37), National Archives.

To Winfield Scott [TELEGRAM]

To Gen. Winfield Scott Morris Ind [May 24, 1861]

Will do what you want. Make it clean sweep if you say so. Answer Cincinnati.[1]

G. B. McClellan

Received copy, Records of the Office of the Secretary of War, RG 107 (M-504:9), National Archives.

1. Sent by GBM when he was attending a military conference in Indiana, this telegram was in reply to Scott's of the same date, calling on him to counteract the Confederate advance on Grafton in western Virginia. *OR,* Ser. 1, II, p. 648.

To William Dennison [TELEGRAM]

To/Gov Wm Dennison
Columbus Ohio [Cincinnati] May 25/61

Genl. Scott is as you are aware eminently sensitive, and does not at all times take suggestions kindly from military subordinates especially when they conflict with his own preconceived notions.

In view of this, and of the importance of his hearty cooperation in future military operations in this Department, I beg to suggest that you request Gov. Yates by telegraph in carrying out the objects of his mission at Washington not to use my name in such a way as to disturb the sensitive complexion of the General's mind.[1]

Retained copy, McClellan Papers (A-12:5), Library of Congress.

1. Gov. Yates of Illinois was to deliver a "memorial" on military policy in the western theater to Gen. Scott. *OR*, Ser. 1, LII, Part 1, pp. 146–47.

To the Troops of the Department of the Ohio

Hd Qtrs Dept of the Ohio
Soldiers Cincinnati May 26 1861

You are ordered to cross the frontier & enter upon the soil of Virginia.

Your mission is to restore peace & confidence, to protect the majesty of the law, & to rescue our brethren from the grasp of armed traitors. You are to act in concert with Virginia troops,[1] & to support their advance.

I place under the safeguard of your honor the persons & property of the Virginians — I know that you will respect their feelings & all their rights.

Preserve the strictest discipline — remember that each one of you holds in his keeping the honor of Ohio & of the Union.

If you are called upon to overcome armed opposition, I know that your courage is equal to the task — but remember that your only foes are the armed traitors — & show mercy even to them when they are in your power, for many of them are misguided.

When under your protection the loyal men of Western Virginia have been enabled to organize & arm they can protect themselves, & you can then return to your homes with the proud satisfaction of having preserved a gallant people from destruction.

G B McClellan

ADS, McClellan Papers (A-12:5), Library of Congress. *OR*, Ser. 1, II, p. 49.

1. The 1st Virginia (Union).

To the Union Men of Western Virginia

Virginians! [Cincinnati, May 26, 1861]

The General Govt has long enough endured the machinations of a few factious rebels in your midst. Armed traitors have in vain endeavored to deter you from expressing your loyalty at the polls;[1] having failed in this infamous attempt to deprive you of the exercise of your dearest rights, they now seek to inaugurate a reign of terror & thus force you to yield to their schemes & submit to the yoke of the traitorous conspiracy dignified by the name of the Southern Confederacy. They are destroying the property of the citizens of your state, & ruining your magnificent railways. The Genl Govt has heretofore carefully abstained from sending troops across the Ohio, or even from posting them along its banks, although frequently urged by many of your prominent citizens to do so. It determined to await the result of the late election, desirous that no one might be able to say that the slightest effort had been made from this side to influence the free expression of your opinion, although the many agencies brought to bear upon you by the rebels were well known. You have now shown, under the most adverse circumstances, that the great mass of the people of Western Virginia are true & loyal to that beneficent Govt under which we & our fathers have lived so long. As soon as the result of the election was known the traitors commenced their work of destruction.

The Genl Govt cannot close its ears to the demand you have made for assistance. I have ordered troops to cross the river. They come as your friends & brothers — as enemies only to the armed rebels who are preying upon you.

Your homes, your families & your property are safe under our protection. All your rights shall be religiously respected. Notwithstanding all that has been said by the traitors to induce you to believe that our advent among you will be signalized by interference with your slaves, understand one thing clearly — not only will we abstain from all such interference but we will on the contrary with an iron hand, crush any attempt at insurrection on their part.

Now that we are in your midst I call upon you to fly to arms & support the Genl Govt.

Sever the connection that binds you to traitors — proclaim to the world that the faith & loyalty so long boasted by the Old Dominion are still preserved in Western Virginia, & that you remain true to the Stars & Stripes.

AD, McClellan Papers (A-12:5), Library of Congress. *OR*, Ser. 1, II, pp. 48–49.

1. The far western counties had opposed the Virginia ordinance of secession in the May 23 referendum.

To E. D. Townsend

Lt Col E D Townsend A.A.G. | Head Qtrs Dept of the Ohio
Colonel | Cincinnati May 30 1861

I have the honor to report the successful occupation of Grafton without the loss of a single life. My previous dispatches have informed you of the circumstances under which the movement was undertaken & the orders given for carrying it into effect.[1]

The movement was greatly delayed by the necessity of repairing the burned bridges — I constantly advised Col Kelly[2] to use great caution & I am happy to say that he has been able to combine it with unusual energy.

He promptly arrived at the burned bridge; at once set a working party at preparing timber for repairs, moved an advanced guard forward to the very important bridge over the Monongahela at Fairmont, & seized all the secessionists he could find.

At 11 o'clock this a.m. he moved forward & reached Grafton at 2.30 p.m.

The secessionists had evacuated the place before his arrival.

The Colonel will pursue them on the Beverly Road in the morning, & endeavor to capture at least some arms that they sent away before they started. I cannot commend too highly the prudence & energy displayed by Col Kelly in this movement — he has in every instance carried out his instructions, & has displayed very high military qualities — I beg to recommend to the Genl that he may be made a Brig Genl of the Va Volunteers.[3]

It is a source of very great satisfaction to me that we have occupied Grafton without the sacrifice of a single life. Col Stedman's[4] advance from Parkersburg has not been so prompt as that of Col Kelly — he has met with many difficulties on his route. I am happy to say that the movement has caused a very great increase of the Union feeling. I am now organizing a movement on the valley of the Great Kanawha — will go there in person & endeavor to capture the occupants of the secession camp at Buffalo, & return in time to direct such movements in Ky or Tenna as may become necessary.

I will make a more detailed report when I receive Col Kelly's full report.

I am very respectfully yr obd svt
Geo B McC
Maj Genl USA

ALS retained copy, McClellan Papers (A-12:5), Library of Congress. *OR,* Ser. 1, II, pp. 49–50.

1. These dispatches and instructions are in *OR,* Ser. 1, II, pp. 44–48. 2. Col. Benjamin F. Kelley, 1st Virginia. 3. Kelley was so commissioned, to date from May 17. 4. Col. James B. Steedman, 14th Ohio.

To Abraham Lincoln

Unofficial

His Excellency Abraham Lincoln
Presdt of the US
Sir

Head Quarters Dept of the Ohio
Cincinnati May 30 1861

I avail myself of the return of Lieut Nelson[1] to inform you briefly of what has been said to me by some of the leading Union men of Kentucky in regard to the recent distribution of arms among them. They uniformly represent that the effect has been extremely beneficial, not only in giving strength to the Union party & discouraging the secessionists, but that it has proved to the minds of all reasonable men that the Genl Govt has confidence in their loyalty & entertains no intention of subjugating them. I am confidently assured that very considerable numbers of volunteers can be raised in Western Virginia as well as in Ky, & I would most respectfully urge that an ample supply of arms be placed at my disposal to arm such regiments — we shall need in addition equipment, money, & clothing. The issue of the arms to Kentuckians is regarded by the staunch men as a masterpiece of policy on your part, & has — if I may be permitted to say so — very much strengthened your position among them.

A very delicate question is arising as to Western Ky — that portion west of the Tenna River; Lieut Nelson will explain to you that a convention is now being held at Mayfield which may declare the "Jackson Purchase"[2] separate from Ky, its annexation to Tenna, & that this will be followed by an advance of Tenna troops upon Columbus & Paducah. The Union men say that immediately upon this being done they will call upon Gov Magoffin[3] to drive out the invaders, & that, should he fail to do so, they will at once call upon me to aid them. I will respond to this call without delay — & should they delay in making it, will endeavor to find means to cause Genl Pillow to repeat his Cerro Gordo movement without violating the soil of Ky.[4] I am informed that my proclamation to the Western Virginians[5] has produced the happiest effect in Kentucky — it not being possible for me to refer the matter to Washington, I prepared it in great haste & on such a basis as my knowledge of your Excellency's previous course & opinions assured me would express your views — I am confident that I have not erred in this very important matter — if I have, a terrible mistake has been made, for the proclamation is regarded as expressing the views of the Presdt, & I have not intimated that it was prepared without authority.

I received the information that two bridges on the B & O RR had been burned, at a late hour on Sunday P.M. [May 26] & at once made all my arrangements by telegraph — in the hurry I could only endeavor to express your views & shall be very much gratified to learn that you approve of what I have done.

I am preparing to seize the valley of the Great Kanawha, there are some 1200 secessionists encamped there — I shall go there in person with from three to four rgts & endeavor to capture them — then to occupy the Gauley Bridge, & return here in time for any necessary movement on Ky. By occupying Grafton & Gauley Bridge we hold the passes thro' the mountains between Eastern & Western Va. It is also possible that I may occupy Guyandotte — a small hot bed of secession. By that means I hope to secure Western Virginia to the Union.

Rest assured that I will exert all my energies to carry out what I suppose to be your policy, & that I will be glad to be informed if I have misconstrued your views.

Should it not be in the power of the Govt to send Lt Nelson back to distribute arms, I would be glad to have him attached to my staff, on account of his intimate relations with the Union men of Ky.

I am very respectfully your obd svt & friend
Geo B McClellan
Maj Genl USA

ALS, Lincoln Papers, Library of Congress.

1. Lt. William Nelson, USN. 2. So named for Andrew Jackson, who played a leading role in its purchase from the Chickasaw Indians in 1818. 3. Beriah Magoffin, governor of Kentucky. 4. Maj. Gen. Gideon Pillow, Tennessee militia. GBM served under him in Mexico at the Battle of Cerro Gordo, which was an American victory despite Pillow's blundering. 5. GBM to the Union Men of Western Virginia, May 26, *supra.*

To Abraham Lincoln

His Excellency Abram Lincoln
Presdt of the U.S. — Head Qtrs Dept of the Ohio
Sir — Cincinnati June 1 1861

I take the liberty of asking your favorable consideration of a request that involves not only the efficiency of my command, but to a certain extent my personal feelings.

I wish to ask of you the appointment of Inspector General (in the place of Col Mansfield,[1] promoted) for Maj R B Marcy of the Pay Department, with the earnest request that he may be assigned to my command as the Chief of my staff.[2]

I need not advert to the eminent services rendered to the Govt by this admirable soldier — they are known to all who have kept themselves informed of the operations of our active army in the West — his numerous explorations, his trying & successful march over the mountains, in the dead of winter, from Camp Bridger to New Mexico, are familiar to all.[3] I may be permitted to add that my intimate personal & official relations with him show him to be possessed of precisely those qualities that I need in my advisor & chief of staff.

You will double my efficiency if you can find it possible to place Major Marcy in the position I refer to.

I have a large & unorganized command — requiring only instruction, discipline, & organization to make it the best Army in the world — to effect this I must have the necessary staff, & my first wish is to have Major Marcy in the place I have referred to.

I feel very deeply that the honor of the West is to a great extent in my keeping — I know that your excellency will share my wish to raise the reputation of the Western troops to the highest point — & I feel sure that you will grant my urgent request. If Maj M cannot be made Inspector Genl I hope that he may command a Brigade of Regulars under me.[4] I am, sir, very respectfully

your obedient servant
Geo B McClellan
Maj Genl USA

ALS, Records of the Office of the Secretary of War, RG 107 (M-492:10), National Archives.

1. Brig. Gen. Joseph K. F. Mansfield, promoted to command of the Department of Washington. 2. Maj. Marcy, GBM's father-in-law, was then serving as inspector general in the Department of the Ohio. 3. This march was made in the winter of 1857–58, during the Mormon War. 4. Secretary of War Cameron replied on June 8 that the post had been filled. RG 107 (M-492:10), National Archives. Marcy was appointed inspector general in the regular army on Aug. 9, 1861, and served as GBM's chief of staff with the rank of brigadier general.

To Winfield Scott

Lt Genl Winfield Scott
Head Quarters Army
Washington D.C.

Head Quarters Dept of the Ohio
Cincinnati June 5 [1861]

General

Your telegram in relation to Mr Rousseau was received.[1] I am informed that Mr. R. is a perfectly reliable Union man but that he is too impolitic for the present moment. I have watched the Kentucky movement with far more than ordinary care &, I think, understand it. It is my firm belief that the Union party is gaining strength every day, & that with care & great tact the State may be saved to the Union.

You are aware that there are two elections yet to take place in that state — one on June 20th for members of Congress. Another Aug. 4th for the State Legislature. The Union men are sure that they can carry both of these, if no undue elements of excitement are introduced into the canvass. You are also aware that the present legislature elected long since, is nearly secession & does not truly represent the feeling of the people.

Bearing in mind that the Kentuckians desire to remain in the Union *without a revolution, under all the forms of law & by their own action,* you will see, General, how important it is that they should be treated with the utmost delicacy until the elections are over.

To carry out this policy I urge that no troops be sent into Kentucky (except in an emergency, to which I will presently refer), that no comdr be appointed to the Dept of Kentucky, at least until he has some troops to command, & above all things that the comdg genl be either a Kentuckian or a man particularly acceptable to the Kentuckians.

If Tenna troops invade the state of Ky then we should act promptly and send reinforcements to drive them out — but let the first invasion take place from the South; not from here. It is my opinion that arms, equipment and funds should at once be placed at my disposal to arm my troops. I expect before I send this letter to see gentlemen from the other side on this subject, & am informed that we can have a thousand real Kentuckians in Covington & its vicinity, and at least ten thousand in Louisville, who will march anywhere and fight anybody. But it would be vain to muster these men before we can provide for them, & I think that instant action should be taken.

I send to-night a thoroughly reliable gentleman, a Kentuckian by birth, & a man of standing and intellect, to confer with leading Kentuckians; I ask as a great favor that all action may be deferred until I can report the result of his visit. I trust, General, that my action in the Grafton matter will show you that I am not given to procrastination but I feel so keenly the vital importance of keeping Kentucky in the Union that I must urge delay until we know exactly what we are doing.

I am convinced that it would be disastrous in the extreme to send either Col. Guthrie or his command to Ky. Were they real Kentuckians, as I at first believed, the case might be very different.[2]

I do not think that too much importance can be attached to the necessity of allowing the elections to proceed quietly, & I hope that no one will be detailed to command the Dept of Kentucky until Col. Anderson's health will permit him to enter upon the duty.

I think the advantage to be gained by delay, will far more than counterbalance the disadvantage arising from the shipment of provisions from Louisville for a short time.

I am very respectfully yr obdt svt
Geo B McClellan
Maj Genl USA

LS retained copy, McClellan Papers (C-3:62), Library of Congress.

1. Gen. Scott's telegram of June 4 proposed Lovell H. Rousseau of Louisville as commander of the newly established Department of Kentucky in place of the ailing Col. Robert Anderson. *OR,* Ser. 1, LII, Part 1, p. 157. 2. Col. James B. Guthrie, an earlier candidate for the Department of Kentucky post, was opposed by GBM on the grounds that he was not a native Kentuckian, and that his regiment contained more Ohioans and Indianians than Kentuckians. *OR,* Ser. 1, LII, Part 1, pp. 156–57.

To Thomas A. Morris [TELEGRAM]

[Cincinnati, June 20, 1861][1]

I will move from Parkersburg on the flank & rear of your opponents. My force will be sufficient to fight a battle. I leave to you the care of Cheat River, which you will strongly reinforce & hold at all hazards.

Concentrate on Grafton if you cannot certainly hold Phillipi. I trust to you entirely the defence of Phillipi, Grafton & Fairmont. I will recall towards Parkersburg when I move, the troops on that road, leave a sufficient garrison there & advance prepared to fight whatever I meet. Be prudent but do not give one inch that you can avoid. Have urged Genl Scott to send a strong column by Cumberland on Romney to cut off retreat of the rebels.[2] Be cool & firm & we will gain the first brilliant success.

G B McClellan
Maj Genl USA

Genl T A Morris

ALS (telegram sent), McClellan Papers (B-41 :61), Library of Congress. Brig. Gen. Morris commanded the force that on June 3 had routed the Confederates at Philippi, Va.

1. Date supplied from a draft of this telegram. McClellan Papers (B-13 :6). 2. GBM's June 19 telegram called for this column to be furnished by Maj. Gen. Patterson, commanding the Department of Pennsylvania. *OR,* Ser. 1, II, p. 706.

To Mary Ellen McClellan

Marietta June 21/61

I must snatch a few moments to write you. We got off about 11 1/2 yesterday morning & had a continual ovation all along the road.[1] At every station where we stopped, crowds had assembled to see the "Young General." Gray-headed old men & women; mothers holding up their children to take my hand, girls, boys, all sorts, cheering and crying, God bless you! I never went thro' such a scene in my life & never expect to go thro' such another one. You would have been surprised at the excitement. At Chillicothe the ladies had prepared a dinner & I had to be trotted through. They gave me about 20 beautiful bouquets, & almost killed me with kindness. The trouble will be to fill their expectations, they seem to be so high. I could hear them say, "He is our own general"; "Look at him, how young he is"; "*He* will thrash them"; "He'll do," &c, &c ad infinitum.

We reached here about 3 in the morning, & at once went on board the boat, where I got about 3 hours sleep until we reached Parkersburg. I have been hard at work all day for I found everything in great confusion. Came up here in the boat alone an hour ago & shall go back to Parkersburg in 2 or 3 hours. . . .

We start from Parkersburg at 6 in the morning. With me go McCook's rgt (9th Ohio), Mack's Company (4th US Artillery), the Sturgess Rifle Co., a battery of 6 guns (Loomis) & 1 company of Cavalry (Barker's Illinois).[2]

Two Indiana rgts leave in the morning just after us. I shall have 5 additional rgts at Grafton tomorrow afternoon. I shall have some 18 rgts, 2 batteries, 2 co's of cavalry at my disposal — enough to thrash anything I find. I think the danger has been greatly exaggerated & anticipate little or no chance of winning laurels. . . .

A terrible storm is passing over us now — thunder & lightning terrible in the extreme. . . .

AL copy; copy, McClellan Papers (C-7:63/D-10:72), Library of Congress. Mrs. McClellan would remain in Cincinnati until December 1861, when she joined GBM in Washington.

1. GBM left Cincinnati by train on June 20 to take command of the campaign in western Virginia. 2. These were units of the headquarters escort.

To E. D. Townsend

Col E D Townsend
A.A.G. — Head Qtrs Dept of the Ohio
Colonel — Parkersburg June 22 1861

I reached here yesterday morning, hoping to move forward during the day, but was delayed by want of wagons & the disorganization to be expected on the part of new troops moving for the first time into the field. In a few minutes (now 7 am) I shall move with the advance to Clarksburg — taking one regiment Infty, 2 detached co's (1 of regulars), 1 battery, & a company of cavalry. 2 Indiana regts will follow during the morning, two Ohio regts tomorrow. Two other Ohio regts will reach Grafton via Bellair today. Reports from the front are somewhat contradictory, but agree in representing the enemy in strong force near Piedmont & Beverly. Notwithstanding that Genl Morris & others seem sure that we have a large force to contend with, I now am inclined to doubt it. I will without delay beat them up in their quarters & endeavor to put an end to their attempts in this direction.

I have, I think, force enough to fight them wherever I find them.

Genl McCall[1] telegraphs that Cumberland will be reinforced on Monday [June 24] — if that is accomplished we should be able to cut off the force near Piedmont.

As I cannot learn yet the quality of their troops (there are reports that there are some regiments of the regular Confederate troops), I shall be cautious in my movements.

I feel very much the absolute necessity of more Commsy & Qtr Mr officers — also of cavalry. I hope the Lt Genl will find it in his power to let me have the companies of 1st Cavalry now at Leavenworth.

I received on the *18th* inst. the order adding Missouri to my Dept[2] — my arrangements for coming here to take command were so far advanced that it was not possible for me to go to Missouri. I shall go there immediately on my return from this state.

I move hence on Clarksburg & will act thence according to the information I receive — either move in force on the rear of the enemy at Beverly, or go on to Piedmont.

Excuse, Colonel, the hurried nature of this.

Very respectfully your obdt svt
Geo B McClellan
Maj Genl USA

ALS, Richards Collection, Boston University Library. *OR,* Ser. 1, II, p. 194.

1. Brig. Gen. George A. McCall, Pennsylvania Rerserves. 2. This order was dated June 6.

To Mary Ellen McClellan

Grafton Sunday June 23/61

... We did not reach here until about 2 in the morning & I was tired out....

Today I have been so busy that I did not know until 10 mins. ago that it is Sunday & cannot yet realize the fact. Everything here needs the hand of the master & is getting it fast. I shall hardly be able to move from here for a couple of days — so difficult is it to get these Mohawks[1] in working trim....

The weather is delightful here — we are well up in the hills & have the mountain air....

AL copy, McClellan Papers (C-7:63), Library of Congress.

1. A pejorative term for volunteers in the Mexican War.

To the Inhabitants of Western Virginia

To the Inhabitants of Western Virginia:

Head-Quarters, Department of the Ohio.
Grafton, Va., June 23d, 1861.

The army of this Department, headed by Virginia troops, is rapidly occupying all Western Virginia. This is done in co-operation with and in support of such civil authorities of the State as are faithful to the Constitution and laws of the United States. The proclamation issued by me, under date of May 26th, 1861,[1] will be strictly maintained. Your houses, families, property, and all your rights, will be religiously respected. We are enemies to none but armed rebels, and those voluntarily giving them aid. All officers of this army will be held responsible for the most prompt and vigorous action in repressing disorder, and punishing aggression by those under their command.

To my great regret, I find that enemies of the United States continue to carry on a system of hostilities prohibited by the laws of war among belligerent nations, and of course far more wicked and intolerable when directed against loyal citizens engaged in the defense of the common Government of all. Individuals and marauding parties are pursuing a guerilla warfare; firing upon sentinels and pickets; burning bridges; insulting, injuring, and even killing citizens because of their Union sentiments, and committing many kindred acts.

I do now, therefore, make proclamation, and warn all persons, that individuals or parties engaged in this species of warfare — irregular in every view which can be taken of it — thus attacking sentries, pickets or other soldiers; destroying public or private property, committing injuries against any of the inhabitants because of Union sentiments or conduct, will be dealt with in their persons and property according to the severest rules of military law.

All persons giving information or aid to the public enemies, will be arrested and kept in close custody; and all persons found bearing arms, unless of known loyalty, will be arrested and held for examination.

Geo. B. McClellan
Maj. Gen. U.S. Army,
Commanding Department

DP, McClellan Papers (B-7:46), Library of Congress. *OR*, Ser. 1, II, p. 196.

1. To the Union Men of Western Virginia, May 26, *supra*.

To the Army of the West

To the Soldiers of the Army of the West:

Head-Quarters, Dep't of the Ohio
Grafton, Va., June 25th, 1861.

You are here to support the Government of your country and to protect the lives and liberties of your brethren, threatened by a rebellious and traitorous foe. No higher and nobler duty could devolve upon you, and I expect you to bring to its performance, the highest and noblest qualities of soldiers — discipline, courage and mercy. I call upon the officers, of every grade to enforce the strictest discipline, and I know that those of all grades, privates and officers, will display in battle cool heroic courage, and will know how to show mercy to a disarmed enemy.

Bear in mind that you are in the country of friends, not of enemies; that you are here to protect, not to destroy. Take nothing, destroy nothing, unless you are ordered to do so by your General officers. Remember that I have pledged my word to the people of Western Virginia, that their rights in person and property shall be respected. I ask every one of you to make good this promise in its broadest sense. We come here to save, not to upturn. I do not appeal to the fear of punishment, but to your appreciation of the sacredness of the cause in which we are engaged. Carry with you into battle the conviction that you are right, and that God is on your side.

Your enemies have violated every moral law — neither God nor man can sustain them. They have without cause rebelled against a mild and paternal Government; they have seized upon public and private property; they have outraged the persons of Northern men merely because they came from the North, and of Southern Union men merely because they loved the Union; they have placed themselves beneath contempt, unless they can retrieve some honor on the field of battle. You will pursue a different course. You will be honest, brave, and merciful; you will respect the right of private opinion; you will punish no man for opinion's sake. Show to the world that you differ from our enemies in the points of honor, honesty and respect for private opinion, and that we inaugurate no reign of terror where we go.

Soldiers! I have heard that there was danger here. I fear now but one thing — that you will not find foemen worthy of your steel. I know that I can rely upon you.

Geo. B. McClellan
Major Gen'l Commanding

DP, McClellan Papers (B-7:46), Library of Congress. *OR*, Ser. 1, II, pp. 196–97.

To Salmon P. Chase

Hon S P Chase
Washington
My dear Sir — Grafton Va June 26 1861

I take pleasure in acknowledging the receipt of your letters of the 19 & 20 which reached me here yesterday. I will send the necessary instructions in reference to the Regiments which Mr Gurley[1] is interested in.

Gov Dennison has in no way interfered with my control of the troops mustered into the U.S. service, all that he has had to do with them was to carry into effect the War Dept orders in regard to changing the 3 mos into 3 year regiments, & on this subject he received instructions from the War Dept I think. In addition to this Gov D. has exerted himself to the fullest extent in providing equipment for the troops — if Ohio has not equipped her contingent quite so rapidly as some other states it is mainly due to the fact that her force was very large. There has been in no respect any conflict between Gov Dennison & myself.

I will take the earliest possible steps to have the necessary pay rolls etc made out — now that I have so large a portion of the active force in front of the enemy I do not think the question of pay will come up for some little time. It may be necessary for me to retain the 3 mos Indiana men in the field beyond the term of their enlistment — I am sure that I can count upon their patriotism. I have 5 of the 3 mos Indiana troops here — well provided in every respect; 5 rgts of 3 years Ohio Vols, 8 rgts Ohio State troops, about 2 Va Regts, 1 Regular Battery, 1 Battery Michigan 3 yrs vols., 1 Ohio State Battery, 1 company Ohio State cavalry, 1 co. Illinois 3 years cavalry, 1 company Regular Artillery serving as Infty, 1 company Illinois Rifles.

These troops are generally well armed & well equipped — I am delayed by non arrival of rations & transportation, but we are adding to the efficiency every day & supplying small deficiencies.

The men are in most excellent spirits & require only careful handling. They will render a good account of themselves, or I am much mistaken. I think we can show that one Southerner is not equal to *more* than 3 Northern men! We have the most magnificent material for an army that was ever brought together — give me three months in a camp of instruction after this little campaign is over & I would not hesitate to put these men at the best of European troops. The officers are not so good as the men, & I beg, Governor, that you will use your influence in giving us educated soldiers for the General Officers & those of the staff.

The Union feeling is strengthening where we are, & I think will grow as we proceed. I find that my proclamations have produced a happy effect. I take the liberty of enclosing a copy of my last, together with my address to the soldiers.

I have fully instructed Capt Rodgers as to the gun boats[2] — my chief difficulty heretofore has been to obtain reliable plans — I have driven some men away in great disgust with my slowness merely because I was not willing to authorize them to go to work until I could ascertain what they intended to do. I feared the loss of time that would be caused by a failure far more than the loss of money. There is pretty good reason to believe that we have Georgia, So Car, & Tenna troops in front of us. Their main force is at the Laurel Mountain between Phillipi & Beverly — I shall move the main column rapidly from Clarksburg on Buckhannon & Beverly to turn that position while the force now at Phillipi slowly advances to distract their attention. I hardly hope that they will be foolish enough to fall into the trap — whether they do so or not I shall then advance on Huttonsville & drive them into & across the mountains. Having accomplished that I will sweep the Kanawha & overrun the country with small columns & assure the Union men.

Begging that you will excuse the length of this, I am respectfully

ALS retained copy, McClellan Papers (A-15:7), Library of Congress. Chase was secretary of the treasury and a former Ohio governor and senator.

1. John A. Gurley, congressman from Ohio. 2. See GBM to Rodgers, May 19, *supra.*

To Winfield Scott [TELEGRAM]

To Lt. Gen. W. Scott Received June 26 1861 From Grafton Va

A letter of Genl Buckner to Gov Magoffin dated Louisville June tenth (10th) has just reached me through the newspapers.[1] It fills me with astonishment. I can scarcely believe what he wrote. It is an entire misconception & is incorrect throughout. The arrangement & stipulations spoken of by him were got within my authority or my imagination.[2] The interview was purely personal solicited by him several times & granted by me mainly in the hope of reclaiming to the cause of the Union an old & intimate friend.[3] My views of the political relations between the General Government & the state of Kentucky were radically different from these attributed to me in his letter. The whole interview was to me inconclusive & unsatisfactory & the only thing in the nature of a stipulation made between us was his voluntary proffer to attack & drive out any secession troops which might enter Kentucky. May I ask that you will explain this fully to the President & cabinet. I write more fully.

G. B. McClellan
Maj Genl

Received copy, Lincoln Papers, Library of Congress.

1. This letter by Maj. Gen. Simon B. Buckner, head of Kentucky's home guard, reported on his meeting with GBM in Cincinnati on the night of June 7–8. Buckner wrote Gov. Magoffin that certain "stipulations" had been agreed to, seemingly guaranteeing Kentucky's neutrality. Frank Moore, ed., *The Rebellion Record* (New York, 1862), II, Documents, p. 163. GBM reported to Col. E. D. Townsend on June 11: "General Buckner came to see me on Friday last. We sat up all night, talking about matters of common interest. Buckner gave me his word that should any Tennessee troops cross the frontier of Kentucky he would use all the force at his disposal to drive them out, and, failing in that, would call on me for assistance." *OR,* Ser. 1, II, p. 674. 2. This garbled passage was presumably meant to read: ". . . were got without my authority or my instigation." 3. Buckner, a Kentuckian, had known GBM since their cadet days at West Point. He joined the Confederate service in September.

To Winfield Scott

Lt Genl Winfield Scott Head Qtrs Dept of the Ohio
General Grafton Va June 26 1861

Since my last letter in regard to the Buckner matter[1] I telegraphed to a friend who was present at a second interview I had with Buckner at Cairo on the 13th & have just received a reply.

I had gone to Cairo on a tour of inspection & while there Buckner arrived with three citizens of Kentucky. The object of his visit was to confer with Genl Prentiss[2] or myself in relation to the cutting down of a secession flag at Columbus by one of our armed boats, & the landing of an armed party into Ky a few days before by Genl P.

Mr. J. M. Douglass[3] of Chicago, well known to the President, was present with me during the whole interview, & the line of conversation pursued was nearly the same (it was shorter) than in the interview of June 8th — the main difference was in the fact that I told these gentlemen that if secession flags were hoisted on the river bank our people would cut them down & I would authorize them to do so, also, that if they did not prevent the outrages committed on Union men our men could not & would not be restrained from aiding them.

I this morning telegraphed Mr. Douglass asking the question whether anything in the Cairo interview justified or confirmed Buckner's letter.

His reply is as follows — "At the Cairo interview etc — [*omitted:* no word was uttered by you bearing the construction published relative to previous interview at Cincinnati — no allusion made to previous treaty or agreements. I was amazed to read the published correspondence touching an agreement which was not of importance enough to mention at Cairo. You distinctly disclaimed any authority to act except as you might be ordered by the government.] "[4]

I submit this to you with the request that you will ask the President his opinion of the intelligence & reliability of Mr. Douglass — then give his reply, General, the weight you think it worth.

Judge Key,[5] who is intimately acquainted with my entire views & action in regard to Ky has written a letter to Secy Chase, which embodies the facts of the case in such a clear form that I cannot do better than to ask you to read it & give it full credence.[6]

This transaction has surprised me beyond expression — my chief fear has been that you, whom I regard as my strongest friend in Washington, might have supposed me to be guilty of the extreme of folly. My personal relations with Buckner, & my high regard for his character, have led me to be more chary perhaps in my expressions than my own interests would warrant — I know that you will appreciate & respect the feeling which has dictated this course.[7] I shall be fully satisfied if I hear from you that you are not displeased with me, & I trust to my actions of the coming week to show to the people that you have not made a mistake in placing me in the position I now occupy.

I am General whatever the result may be your obliged, sincere & respectful friend

Geo B McClellan

ALS retained copy, McClellan Papers (A-15:7), Library of Congress. *OR,* Ser. 1, LII, Part 1, pp. 182–83.

1. Written earlier in the day, the letter elaborated the account of the Buckner interview outlined in GBM's telegram of this date, *supra. OR,* Ser. 1, LII, Part 1, pp. 183–84. 2. Brig. Gen. Benjamin M. Prentiss, in command at Cairo, Ill. 3. John M. Douglas, a lawyer

with the Illinois Central Railroad. **4.** In Douglas to GBM, June 26, McClellan Papers (A-15:7). **5.** Col. Thomas M. Key of GBM's staff, a former Cincinnati commercial court judge. **6.** Key wrote Chase on June 26: "Not one word was said by Gen. McC of any arrangement, stipulation or conclusion whatever. . . ." Key suggested that Buckner's letter to Gov. Magoffin was published to "set a trap for McClellan." Chase Papers, Library of Congress. **7.** A witness to the Cincinnati interview, Samuel Gill, in a telegram to GBM, implied that a somewhat broader understanding was reached with Buckner than GBM suggests in this letter: "I didn't consider . . . that you were stipulating for the Government, but that for the present you would act in accordance with the general views expressed by Simon." Gill to GBM, June 27, McClellan Papers (A-15:7).

To Mary Ellen McClellan

Grafton June 29 [1861]

. . . I am bothered half to death by delays in getting up supplies — unless where I am in person everything seems to go wrong. . . .

I expect in the course of an hour or two to get to Clarksburg — will probably march 12 mi thence today — with Howe's Battery, Mack's & the Chicago Co's., & 1 Co. of cavalry.

I shall have a telegraph line built to follow us up. Look at the maps & find Buckhannon & Beverly — that is the direction of my march. I hope to thrash the infamous scamps before a week is over — all I fear is that I can't catch them. . . .

What a strange performance that of Buckner's was! Fortunately I have secured the testimony of Gill, & Douglass (present at the Cairo interview) that Buckner has entirely misrepresented me. It has annoyed me much, but I hope to do such work here as will set criticism at defiance. . . .

AL copy, McClellan Papers (C-7:63), Library of Congress.

To Mary Ellen McClellan

Clarksburg June 30 [1861]

. . . Again great delays here — will certainly get off by 4 am. tomorrow & make a long march probably 28 mi. After the next march I shall have a large tent, borrowed from the Chicago Rifles; your Father & I will take that, make it reception room, sleeping apartment, mess room &c. . . .

One thing takes up a great deal of time, yet I cannot avoid it — crowds of the country people who have heard of me & read my proclamations come in from all directions to thank me, shake me by the hand, & look at their "liberator, the General"! Of course I have to see them & talk to them. Well, it is a proud & glorious thing to see a whole people here, simple & unsophisticated, looking up to me as their deliverer from tyranny.

AL copy; copy, McClellan Papers (C-7:63/D-10:72), Library of Congress.

To Mary Ellen McClellan

Camp 14 mi south of Clarksburg July 2 [1861]

. . . We start in a few moments to Buckhannon. I have with me 3 Rgts — a battery — 2 cavalry co's — 3 detached co's. Had several heavy rains yesterday. Rosecranz[1] is at Buckhannon, very meek now after a very severe rapping I gave him a few days since.[2] I doubt whether the rebels will fight — it is possible they may, but I begin to think that my successes will be due to manoeuvres, & that I shall have no brilliant victories to record. I would be glad to clear them out of West Virginia & liberate the country without bloodshed if possible. The people are rejoiced to see us.

AL copy, McClellan Papers (C-7 :63), Library of Congress.

1. Brig. Gen. William S. Rosecrans, in command of a brigade. GBM frequently misspelled his name. 2. Rosecrans was reprimanded for allowing some of his troops to camp too far in advance, possibly alerting the enemy to GBM's intentions. *McClellan's Own Story,* draft, McClellan Papers (D-9 :71).

To Jacob D. Cox

[Buckhannon, July 2, 1861]

On receipt of this you will at once assume command of the lst & 2nd Kentucky regiments & the 12th Ohio. Call upon Governor Dennison to supply you with one company of cavalry and six guns. Captain Kingsbury[1] probably has state guns enough to give you.

You will expedite the equipment of those regiments & move them at once to Gallipolis via Hamden & Portland — hiring teams for the supplies of the troops between Portland & Gallipolis, sending Qtr Mst in advance to have teams ready. With the regiment first ready to move proceed to Gallipolis & assume command of the 21st. Cross the river & occupy Point Pleasant; with the regt that next arrives occupy Letart's Falls, & then move the other two regiments to the mouth of ten mile creek, or the point near there where the road from Letart's Falls intersects Kanawha river. Place the last regiment arriving in reserve at Pt Pleasant or any proper point in rear of your line of defence. Entrench two guns at Letart's, four at your advanced position on the Kanawha. Remain on the defensive & endeavor to keep the rebels near Charleston until I can cut off their retreat by movement from Beverly. Should you receive certain intelligence that I am hard pressed seek to relieve me by a rapid advance on Charleston, but place no credit in rumors, for I shall be successful. Use your cavalry as pickets, not exposing them. Punish Ripley if you can. Repress any outbreaks that may occur at Guyandotte or Barboursville.

Remember, my plan is to cut them off, and do all you can to assist that object.[2] Always keep two or three boats on hand. Call on Capt. W.

J. Kountz, at Marietta or Ripley, to supply boats from his fleet. If the two companies of Seventeenth Ohio are still at Ravenswood when you reach Gallipolis, order them to rejoin their regiment, via Parkersburg or Webster. Communicate frequently. A telegraph line follows me out.

Very respectfully, yours,
Geo. B. McClellan
Major General, Commanding

ADf, McClellan Papers (A-17:8), Library of Congress; *OR,* Ser. 1, II, p. 197. Brig. Gen. Cox, Ohio volunteers, was formerly an officer in the state militia. Only the first page of this draft has been found. The last third of the letter is taken from the *Official Records.*

1. Capt. Charles P. Kingsbury, chief of ordnance, Department of the Ohio. 2. Cox stated that this sentence was incomplete as it appeared in the *Official Records.* In his copy it read: "Remember that my present plan is to cut them off by a rapid march from Beverly after driving those in front of me across the mountains, and do all you can to favor that by avoiding offensive movements." Cox, *Military Reminiscences of the Civil War* (New York, 1900), I, p. 60n.

To Thomas A. Morris

Genl T A Morris
Phillipi
General

Head Qtrs Dept of the Ohio
Buckhannon Va July 3 1861

Yours of the 2nd has reached me.[1] After questioning your messenger & hearing his full story I confess that I do not share your apprehensions, & that I am not a little surprised that you feel the defence of Phillipi so hazardous & dangerous an operation. If four thousand (nearly) of our men, in a position selected & fortified in advance — with ample time to examine the ground carefully & provide against any possible plan of attack — are not enough to hold the place against any force these people can bring against it, I think we had better all go home at once. If we cannot fight in position I am much mistaken as to our men.[2]

I have, however, in deference to your views, ordered the 6th Ohio on temporary duty with you, until the crisis has past — although I believe they can be employed to more advantage at other points.

This is all the reinforcement I can now spare — as to the one or two squadrons of efficient cavalry asked for by Captain Benham[3] it seems hardly necessary for me to repeat that I have only one & a half companies — such as they are — & that more important duty is for them here.

You have only to defend a strong position, or at most to follow a retreating enemy. I fear you do not share the confidence I feel in our men, & that you regard their cavalry as more dangerous than I do — I feel that these men of ours can be worked up to any deed of daring, that their leaders can make them cool under fire, & that a couple of good companies of Infantry can drive off all their cavalry in this mountainous country.

I propose taking the really difficult & dangerous part of this work on my own hands — I will not ask you to do anything that I would not be willing to do myself. But let us understand each other, I can give you no more reinforcements — I cannot consent to weaken any further the really active & important column which is to decide the fate of the campaign — if you cannot undertake the defence of Phillipi with the force now under your control I must find some one who will — I have ordered up Latham's company, all of Key's Cavalry that are fit to take the field, & the 6th Ohio — do not ask for further reinforcements — if you do I shall take it as a request to be relieved from your command & to return to Indiana. I have spoken plainly — I speak officially — the crisis is a grave one, & I must have Generals under me who are willing to risk as much as I am, & to be content to risk their lives & reputation with such means as I can give them. Let this be the last of it — give me full details as to the information you obtain — not mere rumors, but facts — & leave it to my judgment to determine what force you need. I wish action now, & determination.

AL retained copy, McClellan Papers (B-7:46), Library of Congress. *OR,* Ser. 1, II, pp. 208–209.

1. Morris wrote that a scouting report "impresses us all here with the fact that there exists a much larger force at Laurel Hill than we have heretofore thought possible.... I confess I feel apprehensive unless our force could equal theirs...." McClellan Papers (B-7:46). 2. In fact, the plan of campaign called for Morris to advance to Laurel Hill and occupy the attention of the enemy force there by threatening an attack. See GBM to Salmon P. Chase, June 26, *supra.* 3. Capt. Benham was chief engineer.

To Mary Ellen McClellan

Buckhannon July 3 [1861]

...We had a pleasant march of 16 mi yesterday, through a beautiful mountain region — magnificent timber, lovely valleys running up from the main valley — the people all out, waving their hdcfs & giving me plenty of bouquets & kind words....

We nearly froze to death last night. I retired, as I thought, at about midnight, intending to have a good night's sleep. About half an hour after I shut up my tent, a colonel in command of a detachment, some 15 miles distant, came to report, so I received him in bed, & fell asleep about six times during the three hours I was talking with him. Finally however he left, & I alternately slept & froze until seven o'clock. This morning I sent Bates[1] on an expedition & raked up a couple of horse blankets, by the aid of which, I hope hereafter to be reasonably comfortable.

I hope to get the trains up tomorrow & make a final start during the day. We have a good many of the scamps to deal with, but my men have the greatest confidence in me & I in most of them. I ordered the Guthrie Grays[2] to Philippi this pm. — to resist a stampede attack that Genl Morris feared. I have not a Brig Genl worth his salt — Morris is a timid old woman — Rosecranz a silly fussy goose — Schleich[3] knows nothing. . . .

I have made your father Inspector Genl of this Army. . . .

AL copy; copy, McClellan Papers (C-7:63/D-10:72), Library of Congress.

1. Bates was GBM's personal servant. 2. 6th Ohio infantry. 3. Brig. Gen. Newton Schleich.

To E. D. Townsend

Col E D Townsend
A.A.G.

Hd Qtrs Dept of the Ohio
Buckhannon Va July 5 1861

Col

You will probably feel as much regret as I do in finding that I am still here — the cause is the difficulty of getting up supplies & arranging transportation. I hope that today's arrivals will enable me to move in the morning. While waiting here I have endeavored to employ our time to advantage.

You will observe that this is the important strategical position in this region — from it I can cover our base of operations & supplies, & move readily by good roads in any desired direction. I have directed the positions on Cheat River, at Grafton, Webster, Clarksburg & Parkersburg to be intrenched, that the necessary garrisons may be reduced as much as possible. The bridges, tunnels etc on the two branches of the RR are now well guarded. The Cheat River (covering the left of our base is guarded by 11 Companies), Grafton by a regiment, Clarksburg some 8 Cos. besides Va recruits, Parkersburg 6 Cos, 2 regts Indiana troops to arrive there today & to be disposable as a reserve where needed. Two other Indiana 3 yrs regts are en route to Bellaire to be sent wherever needed. 6 Cos occupy Wirt County C.H. where Union men have suffered much. 4 Cos at Ravenswood repulsed O. J. Wise[1] night before last; I hope that he determined to renew the attempt, as in that case he will have been cut off by a column of 1200 men, under Col Norton, that were to reach Ripley from Letart at 2 pm. yesterday. I shall not be surprised to learn before this letter is closed that he is captured.[2] In consequence of the threatening aspect of affairs in the Great Kanawha Valley I have ordered 4 Regts there, as explained in my instructions to Genl J D Coxe, a copy of which has been forwarded to you.[3]

Of the troops composing the active army 51 companies & 1 battery are at Phillipi, amusing the enemy who is strongly intrenched with artillery on the Laurel Mountain between that place & Beverly. I have with me here 6 entire regts of Infty, 6 detached Cos, 2 batteries, 2 Cos. of cavalry — two more regiments & some 5 or 6 detached companies of infantry will reach here by tomorrow night. The 7th Ohio occupied Weston some three days since & 4 cos. of the 17th reached Glenville from Parkersburg yesterday — I ordered strong detachments from these commands to move last night on Bull Town & break up a large force of armed rebels congregating there — I can if necessary have them all back with me by tomorrow night. I have sent out frequent small parties to break up the collections of rebels — we have them pretty well under now. One of our parties of 40 last night broke up 200!

The morale of our men is excellent — could not be better. It is difficult to get perfectly accurate information, but we are improving in that respect every day. The feeling of the people here is most excellent — we are acclaimed wherever our men go. It is wonderful to see how rapidly the minds of many of the people become enlightened when they find we can protect them! Fear & ignorance combined have made most of the converts to secession — the reverse process is now going on with great rapidity.

I expect to find the enemy in position on Rich Mountain, just this side of Beverly. I shall if possible turn the position to the south, & then occupy the Beverly road in his rear — if possible I will repeat the manoeuvre of Cerro Gordo.[4]

Assure the General that no prospect of a brilliant victory shall induce me to depart from my intention of gaining success by manoeuvring rather than by fighting; I will not throw these men of mine into the teeth of artillery & intrenchments, if it is possible to avoid it.

Say to the General too that I am trying to follow a lesson long ago learned from him — i.e. — not to move until I know that everything is ready, & then to move with the utmost rapidity & energy. The delays that I have met with have been irksome to me in the extreme — but I felt that it would be exceedingly foolish to give way to impatience & advance before everything was prepared. I think the troops are improving decidedly in their performance of guard & outpost duty & that we are losing nothing in efficiency by the halt at this place. From all that I learn the enemy is still uncertain as to where the main attack is to be made, & is committing the error of dividing his army in presence of superior forces.

If he abandons the position on Laurel Mountain, the troops at Phillipi will press him closely. I shall know tonight with certainty what he has in the pass near Huttonsville. I am told that he has moved all his troops thence towards Beverly. By our present positions we have cut off all his supplies of provisions from this region — so that he must depend almost entirely on Staunton — a long haul over a rough mountain road.

G.B. McClellan
Maj Genl U.S.A.
Comdg Dept

ALS retained copy, McClellan Papers (A-17:8), Library of Congress. *OR*, Ser. 1, II, pp. 198–99.

1. Capt. O. Jennings Wise, CSA. 2. The attempt by Col. Jesse S. Norton's Ohio militia to capture Wise failed, so GBM telegraphed Townsend on July 6, "in consequence of the rapidity with which the rebels fled at the first news of the approach of danger." *OR*, Ser. 1, II, p. 199. 3. GBM to Cox, July 2, *supra*. 4. Winfield Scott's victory at Cerro Gordo, in the Mexican War, was gained by a turning movement.

To Mary Ellen McClellan

Buckhannon July 5 1861

Yesterday was a very busy day with me — reviewing troops all the morning & giving orders all day & pretty much all night....

I realize now the dreadful responsibility on me — the lives of my men — the reputation of the country & the success of our cause. The enemy are in front & I shall probably move forward tomorrow — but not come in contact with them until about the next day. I shall feel my way & be very cautious, for I recognize the fact that everything requires success in my first operations. You need not be at all alarmed as to the result — God is on our side.

This is a beautiful country in which we now are — a lovely valley surrounded by mountains — well cultivated. The people hail our parties as deliverers wherever they go, & we meet with perfect ovations. Yesterday was very hot, & my head almost roasted as I stood bareheaded while the troops passed by in review. We have a nice little camp of our own here — Mack's & Steele's Co's — Howe's Battery next — 2 Co's of cavalry — & 2 well behaved Virginia Co's. When we next go into camp we shall have the German Regt (9th Ohio) with us in camp. I intend having a picked Brigade with me all the time. Lytle's rgt is on the march up from Clarksburg, they signalized their advance into the country by breaking into & robbing a grocery store at Webster![1] The Guthrie Grays are at Philippi; they leave there today & will be here tomorrow night — following us up in reserve, or perhaps overtaking us before we meet the enemy....

AL copy, McClellan Papers (C-7:63), Library of Congress.

1. Col. William H. Lytle commanded the 10th Ohio.

To William Dennison

His Excellency Wm Dennison
Governor of Ohio — Hd. Qrs. Dept. of the Ohio,
Sir: — Buckhannon Va July 6th 1861

I enclose herewith to you copies of Genl. Order No. 19 & of the report of a Court of Inquiry, and of a communication from Brig. Gen'l Rosecrans all relating to Co. C. 19th Regt. O.V.M.[1]

I know that your excellency will deeply regret that a Co. of Ohio Volunteers should be the subject of a proceeding so painful yet I feel assured that your judgment will sustain its propriety and necessity, and that I shall receive your support in maintaining that good order, discipline and regard for private rights, in which I am happy to say the Ohio troops of the Army have been as a body worthy of much commendation.

The protection of the persons, homes, families and property of all peaceful citizens has been by me guaranteed to the people of Western Virginia by the most solomn pledges, and I rejoice to say that since I have entered the State these pledges have been substantially observed by this Army. The beneficial effect of this course has been everywhere apparent. Persons entertaining secession sentiments continually and generally state that they had been deceived and misled as to the purposes of the Government and its course of military action, and the revulsion of feeling and sentiment seems to be very great. I regard such peaceful conquests as very important.

Upon the most mature reflection I have become satisfied that the rule laid down in my general order "holding officers and their commands liable to be ordered home upon the occurrence of such acts as indicate an insubordinate condition of companies or regiments" is the most efficient and practicable method of preserving good order and necessary control.

In the case of Co. C. there appears to prevail among its members very erroneous notions of the purposes of the Government and the duties of soldiers. I therefore advise that the company on its arrival at Columbus be disbanded.

Very Resply yr obt servt
Geo B McClellan
Maj Gen'l Comdg.

Retained copy, McClellan Papers (A-18:8), Library of Congress.

1. Members of Company C, 19th Ohio, were charged with robbing the house of a Virginia secessionist. The case was finally disposed of by the punishment and dismissal of an officer and seven privates of the company. Documents in McClellan Papers (A-17:8, A-18:8).

To Nathaniel Lyon

Genl N Lyon, Missouri — Head Qtrs Dept of the Ohio
General — Buckhannon Va July 6 1861

Yours of the 22d reached me only a few hours ago. In view of the information sent to me by Capt Harding, some days since, of apprehended danger in S.E. Missouri,[1] I directed that three or four of the Illinois Regts should hold themselves in readiness to obey a call from Genl Prentiss, & instructed him (if the report was verified) to move a respectable force from Birds Point upon the place where the rebels were said to be congregating — to enable him to do this I directed Maj McKinstry to provide the requisite wagons & teams. In compliance with other requests from you & your Adjt Genl I have placed two of the Quincy & one Caseyville Regt at your disposal. I have today instructed Genl Pope,[2] comdg at Alton, to place himself & 3 regts at your disposal, for the operation you suggest — the necessity for which I fully recognize.[3] This makes 6 Illinois Regts for service in Missouri in addition to those liable at any moment to move from Cairo.

The exigencies of the service in which I am now personally engaged render it impossible to spare any Indiana or Ohio troops for service in Missouri — in addition to the operations in Western Virginia it is necessary to hold some troops in reserve ready to act in Kentucky when occasion demands — as I believe will be the case before very long. Unless the effect of decisive operations on your part in Missouri, & on mine in Western Virginia, is to intimidate the secession party in Kentucky, it seems to me that there must finally be a collision between the two parties, in Ky, & that we must throw our weight into the scale.

Distant as I am from Missouri — I can only say, General, that so long as it remains attached to my Dept, you may confidently rely upon my giving you all the support in my power.

I do not know what the intention of the Dept was in regard to the Dept of the West, as I have received no instructions beyond the General Order attaching Missouri to the Dept of the Ohio. I presume that the command of the Dept of the West now devolves on Col Alexander.[4]

With my warmest wishes for your continued success

I am General very truly yours
Geo B McClellan
Maj Genl USA Comdg Dept

ALS retained copy, McClellan Papers (A-18:8), Library of Congress. Brig. Gen. Lyon commanded Federal forces in Missouri.

1. Lyon's telegram of June 21 (as it was dated) called on GBM for strong reinforcements. Capt. Chester Harding, Lyon's adjutant, telegraphed on June 27 that Confederate troops were moving into southeastern Missouri "in large numbers. . . . No force here sufficient to meet them. . . . Will you take the matter in hand." McClellan Papers (A-14:6, A-15:7). 2.

Brig. Gen. John Pope. **3.** Lyon planned an advance on Springfield, Mo. **4.** It is not known to whom GBM was referring. Command of the newly formed Western Department went to Maj. Gen. John Charles Frémont.

To E. D. Townsend [TELEGRAM]

Col. E. D. Townsend A.A.G.
Washington D.C.

Head Quarters Department of the Ohio,
Buckhannon Va. July 6th 1861[1]

Newspaper reports say that my department is to be broken up. I hope the General will leave under my control, both the operations on the Mississippi and in Western Virginia. If he cannot do so, the Indiana and Ohio troops are necessary to my success. With these means at my disposal and such resources as I can command in Virginia if the Government will give me ten thousand arms for distribution in Eastern Tennessee I think I can break the backbone of Secession. Please instruct whether to move on Staunton or on Wytheville.[2] I thank the General for his commendation, and hope to deserve it rather in the future than in the past.[3] Please enforce the occupation of Cumberland and Piedmont. The condition of things in that vicinity renders it absolutely necessary to occupy both these points and you will remember that my command does not extend that far. I cannot too strongly impress upon you the necessity of holding these points. The Pennsylvania State troops now in the vicinity of Cumberland will answer the purpose perfectly well.

G. B. McClellan
Major General U.S.A.
Commanding Department

Retained copy, McClellan Papers (C-9 :63), Library of Congress. *OR,* Ser. 1, II, p. 201.

1. The *Official Records* dates this July 7, probably the date it was received. **2.** Townsend replied on July 7: "The General concedes that you are the best judge of your means and the importance of the objects to be gained; but when you speak of extending your operations to Staunton, and even to Wytheville, he fears your line will be too long without intermediate supports. He wishes you to weigh well these points before deciding." *OR,* Ser. 1, II, pp. 201–202. **3.** Townsend had telegraphed GBM on July 6: "General Scott is charmed with your activity, enterprise and success." Records of the Headquarters of the Army, RG 108 (M-857 :6), National Archives.

To Mary Ellen McClellan

Buckhannon July 7 [1861]

I have been obliged to inflict some severe punishments & I presume the Abolition papers of the Western Reserve will be hard down on me for disgracing some of their friends guilty of the small crime of burglary.[1] I believe the Army is beginning to comprehend that they have a master over them who is stern in punishing & means what he says. I fear I shall have to have some of them shot or hung; that may convince some of the particular individuals concerned that they are not in the right track exactly....

I have not told you about our camp at this place. It is in a large grass field on a hill a little out of town; a beautiful grove near by. Your Father & I share the same tent, a very large round one, pitched under a tree. Seth has one near by as an office. Lawrence Williams another as office & mess tent. Marcy, the two Williamses, Judge Key & Lander mess with me; Poe & the rest of the youngsters are in tents near by.[2]...

I had a very complimentary despatch from Genl Scott last night, he said he was "Charmed with my energy, movements & success." Pretty well for the old man! I hope to deserve more of him in the future.

Move at 6 tomorrow morning to overtake adv gd, which consists of 3 rgts, a battery & 1 co cavalry. I take up hd qtrs escort (Mack, Steele, Loomis' battery, Barker's cav, 2 co's. Va infty) & 4 rgts infty — 3 more follow next day. The large supply train up & ready to move. Rob Garnett in command of enemy.[3]

AL copy; copy, McClellan Papers (C-7:63/D-10:72), Library of Congress.

1. See GBM to William Dennison, July 6, *supra*. The case involved the 19th Ohio, a three-month regiment raised in Cleveland. 2. The staff members mentioned are Maj. Marcy, Maj. Seth Williams, Capt. Lawrence A. Williams, Col. Thomas M. Key, Brig. Gen. Frederick W. Lander, and Lt. Orlando M. Poe. 3. Brig. Gen. Robert S. Garnett, CSA.

To Mary Ellen McClellan

Roaring Creek July 10 [1861]

We have occupied the important position on this line without loss. The enemy are in sight & I am about sending out a strong armed reconnaissance to feel him & see what he is. I have been looking at the camps with my glass — they are strongly entrenched, but I think I can come the Cerro Gordo over them.

AL copy, McClellan Papers (C-7:63), Library of Congress.

To Salmon P. Chase [TELEGRAM]

[Roaring Creek, c. July 10, 1861]

Your letter of 7th just received.[1] The movement you suggest meets with my full concurrence. I regard it as the most important that can be undertaken. I have been engaged in maturing its details in my mind & intended preparing for it as soon as through with Western Virginia.

G B. McClellan
Maj Genl USA

Hon S P Chase
Secty of Treasury Washington DC

ALS (telegram sent), McClellan Papers (A-23:11), Library of Congress.

1. In his letter of July 7, Chase described efforts to enlist troops in Kentucky and Tennessee. "You can very materially forward these preparations by your counsel and cooperation: and just as soon as circumstances will allow, you can yourself take the open command of the regiments, and, with your Ohio and Indiana men, march down through the mountain-region, deliver the whole of it, including the mountain districts of North Carolina, Georgia, and Alabama, from the insurrection, and then reach the Gulf at Mobile and New Orleans, thus cutting the rebellion in two." Jacob S. Schuckers, *The Life and Public Service of Salmon Portland Chase* (New York, 1874), pp. 427–28.

To Thomas A. Morris

Hd Qtrs Dept of the Ohio
[Beverly] July 12 1861

Have just gained the enemy's position[1] & occupy the road to Beverly. Rosecrans turned the works by a march of some 7 miles through the mountains. Defeated a large party at Hart's House, taking guns. We now have their intrenchments, all their guns, baggage & some prisoners. Have not lost over 10 men in whole operation. Will send details by another messenger. I move the column to Beverly at once. Do not attack until further orders.[2] I learn that fugitives have retreated towards Laurel Hill.

G B McClellan

Genl T A Morris

ALS copy, in GBM to Ezra A. Carman, Feb. 25, 1880. Civil War Collection, Huntington Library.

1. At Rich Mountain. 2. Morris's brigade faced the main Confederate force under Gen. Garnett at Laurel Hill.

To E. D. Townsend [TELEGRAM]

Col. E. D. Townsend Beverly Va. [July 12] 1861

Success of today is all that I could desire. We captured six brass cannon of which one rifled, all their camp equipage & transportation even to his tents. The number of tents will probably reach two hundred and more than sixty wagons. Their killed & wounded will amount to fully hundred & fifty. At least one hundred prisoners & more coming in constantly. I know already of ten officers killed & prisoners. Their retreat complete. Occupied Beverly by a rapid march. Garnett abandoned his camp early this morning, leaving much of his equipage. He came within a few miles of Beverly but our rapid march turned him back in great confusion and he is now retreating on the road to St George. I have ordered Gen Morris to follow him up closely. I have telegraphed for the two Penna Regts at Cumberland to join Genl Hill[1] at Rowlesburg. The Genl is concentrating all his troops at Rowlesburg [to] cut off Garnett's retreat near West Union or if possible St George. I may say that we have driven out some ten thousand troops strongly entrenched with the loss of eleven killed & thirty five wounded. Provision returns found here show Garnett's force to have been ten thousand men.[2] They were eastern Virginians, Georgians, Tennesseans and I think Carolinians. To-morrow I can give full details as to prisoners &c. Will move on Huttonsville tomorrow and endeaver to seize the Cheat mountain pass where there are now but few troops. I hope that Genl Cox has by this time driven Wise out of the Kanawha Valley.[3] In that case I shall have accomplished the object of liberating Western Virginia. I hope the General will approve my operations.

Geo. B. McClellan
Maj Genl Comdg Dept of Ohio

Received copy, Lincoln Papers, Library of Congress. *OR,* Ser. 1, II, pp. 203–204.

1. Brig. Gen. Charles W. Hill, Ohio militia. 2. GBM included in this figure four regiments intended to reinforce Garnett but which never reached the scene. Garnett's total force was about 5,300 men. 3. Brig. Gen. Henry A. Wise commanded the Confederate forces in the Kanawha Valley.

To Charles W. Hill [TELEGRAM]

Genl C W Hill — Grafton Huttonsville July 13 [1861]

Your dispatch received.[1] I presume mine of last night directing concentration on St George or West Union had not reached you. But a small force now necessary at Clarksburg since depot to be changed to Webster for this column. You can safely diminish garrisons along the line & give Stanley[2] a chance. Look out for Garnett at West Union & try to head him off. Endeavor to get messenger to the rgts at Cumberland so that if they cannot unite with you one of them may at least occupy Piedmont. Do not regard Department lines in cases of emergency. I am at Huttonsville. The advanced guard just moving into the Pass.

Pegram[3] with entire rgt surrendered this morning. Morris was 6 miles in rear of Garrett at last account. Never mind bridges if you can catch Garnett.

G B McClellan
Maj Genl

ALS (telegram sent), McClellan Papers (A-19:9), Library of Congress. Brig. Gen. Hill was charged with the defense of the Baltimore and Ohio Railroad.

1. Dated July 12, Hill's dispatch reported that Confederate cavalry was burning bridges on the railroad to the east. McClellan Papers (A-19:9). 2. Col. T. R. Stanley, 18th Ohio, commanding at Clarksburg. 3. Lt. Col. John Pegram, who had commanded the Confederate detachment at Rich Mountain.

To Mary Ellen McClellan

Huttonsville July 13 [1861]

Since you last heard from me I received from Pegram a proposition to surrender which I granted. L Williams went out with an escort of cavalry & received him — he surrendered with another Col, some 25 offs. and 560 men....

I do not think the enemy in front of us in the Cheat Mtn pass, but that they have fallen back in hot haste — if they are here I will drive them out tomorrow & occupy the pass....

It now appears we killed nearly 200 — took almost 900.

The valley in which we are is one of the most beautiful I ever saw & I am more than ever inclined to make my Head Quarters at Beverly & have you with me. Beverly is a quiet, old fashioned town in a lovely valley; a beautiful stream running by it. A perfectly pastoral scene such as the old painters dreamed of, but never realized. I half think I should be King of it. I find that the prisoners are beyond measure astonished at my humanity towards them. The bearer of the flag from Pegram reached me about 5 this morning. He had been two days without food. I at once gave him some breakfast, & shortly after gave him a drink of whiskey; as he drank it said "I thank you, General — I drink that I may never again be in rebellion against the general government."

AL copy; copy, McClellan Papers (C-7 :63/D-10 :72), Library of Congress.

To Jacob Beyers

Jacob Beyers
Granville Monongalia Co Va

Camp near Huttonsville
July 14 [1861]

Your letter of the 8th inst has been received.[1] No one has any authority to make arrests unless commissioned in the Army of the US or acting under my immediate orders or having such authority from the State Government at Wheeling. It is not intended that such power shall be delegated to private persons by order of officers under my command. Almost all arrests hitherto made have been injudicious and wrong and have operated injuriously to the Union cause. No persons must be arrested except those who are or have been in arms against the US Govt, or have given actual aid or information to armed enemies, or who are especially dangerous as inciting others to take arms, or who attack the persons or property of Union men as such. The arrest of persons not in arms should be very cautiously conducted, but few of these yet made being warranted. All private property whether of secessionists or others must be strictly respected, and no one is to be molested merely because of political opinions.

Yours
G. B. McClellan
Maj Genl Comdg

Retained copy, McClellan Papers (A-19:9), Library of Congress. Beyers was a mustering agent for militia being raised by the newly formed Unionist government of western Virginia.

1. Beyers wrote: "Gen Morris gave me an order to capture or arrest any person in the region of Morgantown who had violated the laws of the United States or in any way aided or abeted the secession army. . . ." He asked if this authority was valid. McClellan Papers (A-18:8).

To Mary Ellen McClellan

July 14 [1861] *Sunday* Huttonsville

Started this morning with a strong advanced guard, supported by 2 rgts to test the question as to whether the rebels were really fortified in the Cheat Mtn pass. I went prepared for another fight — but found that they had scampered. We picked up some of their plunder — but they have undoubtedly gone at least to Staunton. The pass was considerably strong & they might have given us an immense deal of trouble. I went with a few men to Cheat River — the other side of the mtn. . . .

I have made a very clean sweep of it — never was more complete success gained with smaller sacrifice of life — our prisoners will exceed 1000!

On my return I found a telegram from Genl Scott, sent before he had received information as to the full results of my victory. It was "The General in Chief, & what is more the Cabinet, including the Presdt, are charmed with your activity, valour, & consequent success. We do not doubt, that you will in due time, sweep the rebels from West Va, but do not mean to precipitate you, as you are fast enough. Winfield Scott."[1]

I released today on parole, a Dr Walke, on account of his having a sick wife &c. He turned out to have been a student of Father's, knows John very well.[2] He has Father's likeness in his parlor &c. Poor fellow, he felt horribly, & I must confess, that my heart bleeds for these poor misguided men. . . .

Our ride today was truly magnificent, some of the most splendid Mt. views I ever beheld. The Mt we crossed is fully 3000 ft above its base, & the lovely little valleys, the cleared farms, the long ranges of Mountain in the distance all made a varied scene that I cannot describe to you. At the Mt. top was a pretty little farm, neat as neat could be. A very old couple lived there, the old lady, as rosy & cheerful as a cricket. It is sad that war should visit even such sequestered spots as that.

Monday morning [July 15]. After closing my letter last night a courier arrived with the news that the troops I had sent in pursuit of Garnett had caught him, routed his army, captured his baggage, one gun, taken several prisoners — & that Garnett himself lay dead on the field of battle!!![3] Such is the fate of traitors — one of their comdrs a prisoner, the other killed! Their armies annihilated — their cause crushed in this region....

You ask what my plans are — why, you little witch, don't you know that my movements depend much on those of Mons. l'ennemi? I expect to hear in a few hours of the final extermination of the remnants of Garnett's army. Then I am almost hourly awaiting news of Coxe's success in the Kanawha. Should Coxe not be prompt enough I will go down there myself & bring the matter to a close.

West Va being cleared of the enemy I have then to organize & consolidate the army — the time of the 3 mos men is about expiring & they form so large a portion of my force that some delay will ensue....

AL copy; copy, McClellan Papers (C-7:63/D-10:72), Library of Congress.

1. Scott's telegram was dated July 13. *OR,* Ser. 1, II, p. 204. 2. Maj. J. Wistar Walke, surgeon of the 20th Virginia. GBM's father, Dr. George McClellan, had been a founder of Jefferson Medical College in Philadelphia. GBM's brother John H. B. McClellan was also a doctor. 3. Garnett was mortally wounded on July 13 in a rear-guard skirmish against Morris's pursuing Federals.

To Charles W. Hill [TELEGRAM]

Huttonsville, July 14, 1861

Garnetts army completely routed yesterday (13) at 2 p.m. on Cheat River on St George road — baggage captured one gun taken — Garnett killed — his forces demoralized. I charge you to complete our operations by the capture of the remainder of his force. If you have but one regiment attack & check them until others arrive. You may never have such an opportunity again — do not throw it away. Conduct this movement in person & follow them à l'outrance.

G B McClellan
Maj Genl USA

Brig Genl C W Hill
Grafton Va.

ALS (telegram sent), McClellan Papers (A-19:9), Library of Congress. *OR,* Ser. 1, II, p. 227.

To Jacob D. Cox [TELEGRAM]

Huttonsville July 14 1861

In addition to previous success we have routed Garnett's army, captured his baggage & one gun. Garnett killed, his army entirely demoralized. Secession crushed in this direction. Win your spurs by capturing

Wise & occupying Gauley Bridge. I impatiently wait to hear from you that my expectations are justified. Do not fail me but push straight on & complete the first act of our drama.

G B McClellan
Maj Genl USA

Brig Genl J D Coxe
Care Col Smith, Parkersburg

ALS (telegram sent), McClellan Papers (A-19:9), Library of Congress.

To E. D. Townsend [TELEGRAM]

[Huttonsville, July 14, 1861]

Garnett's forces routed — his baggage & one gun taken, his army demoralized — Garnett killed. We have annihilated the enemy in Western Virginia & have lost 13 killed & not more than 40 wounded. We have in all killed at least 200 of the enemy & their prisoners will amount to at least one thousand — have taken 7 guns in all. I still look for the capture of the remnant of Garnett's army by Genl Hill. The troops defeated are the crack regiments of Eastern Virginia, aided by Georgians, Tennesseans & Carolinians. Our success is complete & secession is killed in this country.

G B McClellan
Maj Genl USA

Col E D Townsend
AAG Washington D.C.

ALS (telegram sent), McClellan Papers (A-19:9), Library of Congress. *OR,* Ser. 1, II, p. 204.

To Henry R. Jackson

Hd Qtrs Dept of the Ohio
Camp near Huttonsville Va
July 15 1861

To the Comdg Officer of the Forces
near Staunton[1]
Sir:

I have today received orders from the Comdr in Chief of the U.S. Army respecting the disposition to be made of the prisoners of war now in my hands.[2] These orders are substantially that the non comd officers & privates shall be permitted to return to their homes provided they willingly subscribe an oath or affirmation binding them not to bear arms or serve in any military capacity against the United States, until released from this obligation according to the ordinary usages of war.

The officers to be permitted to return to their homes upon giving a similar parole of honor; from this privilege, however, are excepted such officers as may have recently left the U.S. service with the intention of taking arms against the U.S. Such officers will for the present be sent to Fort McHenry, where they will without doubt be kindly treated.

There are at Beverly some 33 officers, 5 surgeons, & almost 600 non comd offs & privates — there are others at Laurel Hill etc the numbers of whom I do not yet accurately know; with the wounded the number will probably amount to at least 800 men besides officers.

It is my desire to arrange with you for the return to their homes of such of these as may accept the terms offered them.

I would be glad to know what transportation etc you can furnish for them & at what point I may expect it. If no other arrangement will be convenient to you I will provide wagons & tents, as well as rations & cooking utensils for the party, with the understanding that the proper authorities shall undertake to return them to me. The wagons & tents will probably be of those captured at Camp Garnett.[3] Please inform me how many days rations it will be necessary to furnish to the party. I will be glad also to arrange for the return of the wounded as soon as their condition will pemit it — in the mean time their friends may rest assured that every attention will be paid to them.

You will ere this have been informed no doubt of the unhappy fate of Genl Garnett, who fell while acting the part of a gallant soldier — his remains are now at Grafton, preserved in ice, where they will await the instructions of his relations should they desire to remove them to his home.

While I am determined to play my part in this unhappy contest to the utmost of my energy & ability, permit me to assure you of my desire to do all in my power to alleviate its miseries, & to confine its effects to those who constitute the organized armies & meet in battle. It is my intention to cause the persons & property of private citizens to be respected, & to render the condition of prisoners & wounded as little oppressive & miserable as possible.

I trust that I shall be met in the same spirit, & that this contest may remain free from the usual horrible features of civil war.[4]

I am, sir, very respectfully your obedient servant
Geo B McClellan
Maj Genl USA
Comdg Dept of the Ohio

I send this by Lieut R. J. Lipper [Lipford] of the 44th Regt Va Vols who chances to be the captured officer most convenient. I have not yet taken his final parole, but have given him a special one for the purpose of carrying this letter & bringing back an immediate reply. After his return he will be accorded the same parole as the others. For obvious reasons I request that your reply may be transmitted by Lt Lipper.

I will proceed with as little delay as possible to the release of the prisoners, & if ready to forward any before your reply reaches me will take it for granted that you accede to my proposals in regard to the return of the property sent with them.

ALS retained copy, McClellan Papers (A-20:9), Library of Congress. *OR,* Ser. 1, II, pp. 250–51.

1. Brig. Gen. Jackson assumed command of Garnett's forces after that general's death. 2. Dated July 14. *OR,* Ser. 2, III, pp. 9–10. 3. The captured Confederate encampment at Rich Mountain. 4. Jackson replied on July 17 that these arrangements would be satisfactory. In response to GBM's assurances that the wounded would be well cared for, he wrote: "Permit me to add that your well known character as a man had rendered those assurances a matter of supererogation." *OR,* Ser. 1, II, pp. 251–52.

To Mary Ellen McClellan

[Huttonsville] July 15 [1861]

...Nothing from the Kanawha tonight — I fear Coxe is slow. If my generals had obeyed my orders I should before this have captured every rebel in this region but unfortunately I have not a single Brig who is worth his salt.

AL copy, McClellan Papers (C-7:63), Library of Congress.

To Charles W. Hill [TELEGRAM]

Beverly July 16/61

I have just learned of your movement of last night. I think you should have attacked the enemy on Sunday [July 14] when so near their rear guard and that you then allowed the favorable opportunity to pass.[1] I can see no good result likely to follow from your present movement which seems likely to become too extended and is not in the spirit of your instructions which were to cut off the enemy's retreat, not to go into the heart of Virginia unless you are directly on the enemy's track and you are sure to cut him off at once. You will please on receipt of this abandon the pursuit to avoid the possibility of disaster.

G B McC

To Genl Hill

ALS (telegram sent), McClellan Papers (B-20:9), Library of Congress.

1. Hill had taken position at West Union as ordered — see GBM to Hill, July 13, *supra* — but the Confederate column slipped away by another road.

To the Army of the West

Head Quarters
Army of Occupation, Western Virginia,
Beverly, Va., July 16th, 1861

Soldiers of the Army of the West!

I am more than satisfied with you.

You have annihilated two armies, commanded by educated and experienced soldiers, and entrenched in mountain fastnesses fortified at their leisure. You have taken five guns, twelve colors, fifteen hundred stand of arms, one thousand prisoners, including more than forty officers — one of the two commanders of the rebels is a prisoner, the other lost his life on the field of battle. You have killed more than two hundred and fifty of the enemy, who has lost all his baggage and camp equipage. All this has been accomplished with the loss of twenty brave men killed, and sixty wounded on your part.

You have proved that Union men, fighting for the preservation of our Government, are more than a match for our misguided and erring brethren; more than this, you have shown mercy to the vanquished. You have made long and arduous marches, often with insufficient food, frequently exposed to the inclemency of the weather. I have not hesitated to demand this of you, feeling that I could rely on your endurance, patriotism and courage.

In the future, I may have still greater demands to make upon you, still greater sacrifices for you to offer; it shall be my care to provide for you to the extent of my ability; but I know now, that by your valor and endurance, you will accomplish all that is asked.

Soldiers! I have confidence in you, and I trust you have learned to confide in me. Remember that discipline and subordination, are qualities of equal value with courage.

I am proud to say that you have gained the highest reward that American troops can receive — the thanks of Congress, and the applause of your fellow citizens.

Geo. B. McClellan
Major General U.S.A.,
Commanding

DP, McClellan Papers (B-8:47), Library of Congress. *OR*, Ser. 1, II, p. 236.

To Winfield Scott [TELEGRAM]

[Beverly, July 17, 1861]

Will a movement of mine on Staunton facilitate your plans. If so I can probably take that position. I do not know your plan of operations but can move on Staunton if you desire. Please reply at once.[1]

G B McClellan
Maj Genl

Lt Genl Winfield Scott
Washington D.C.

ALS (telegram sent), McClellan Papers (A-23:11), Library of Congress. *OR*, Ser. 1. II, p. 743.

1. On July 16 Brig. Gen. Irvin McDowell's army had advanced from Washington. Scott replied on July 18: "Your suggestions in respect to Staunton would be admirable, like your other conceptions and acts, with support.... If you come to Staunton, and McDowell's

victory at the [Manassas] Junction be complete, he may, with Patterson, give you a hand about Winchester.'' *OR*, Ser. 1, II, p. 743.

To Mary Ellen McClellan [TELEGRAM]

[Beverly, c. July 18, 1861]

Still here awaiting developments. All goes well. Do go to the Springs & remain there until I tell you when & where to meet me.[1] No possible chance of further fighting here at present — no one left to fight with.

I will soon be with you. I hear that I have received the thanks of Congress — the highest honor I could aspire to.[2]

G B McClellan
Maj Genl

Mrs. M E McClellan
Cincinnati

ALS (telegram sent), McClellan Papers, New Jersey Historical Society.

1. Mrs. McClellan, in the seventh month of pregnancy with her first child, would spend much of this summer at the mineral baths at Yellow Springs, near Cincinnati. 2. The Thanks of Congress to GBM and his command was adopted unanimously by joint resolution on July 16.

To Winfield Scott

Unofficial — Head Qtrs Dept of the Ohio
General — Beverly Va July 18 1861

I have received your telegraphic dispatches including that of today.[1]

Knowing how completely your time is occupied, I merely wish to say to you, that I value the commendation, you have been kind enough to bestow upon me, more highly than any reward I can receive from any other source.

All that I know of war I have learned from you, & in all that I have done I have endeavored to conform to your manner of conducting a campaign, as I understand the history of your achievements.

It is my ambition to merit your praise & never to deserve your censure.

Thanking you for your kind expressions

I am, General, truly & respectfully your friend & obdt svt
Geo B McClellan

ALS retained copy, McClellan Papers (A-21:10), Library of Congress.

1. See GBM to Scott, July 17, note 1, *supra*.

To Mary Ellen McClellan

[Beverly] July 19, 1861

I enclose ''Bulletin No 5'' printed with our portable press.[1] You see we have carried civilization with us in the shape of the printing press &

the telegraph; institutions decidedly neglected in this part of the world heretofore & I hear not likely to be paying institutions in this vicinity after we go. The good people here can read but little & have but few ideas & I don't regard them as the most brilliant people in the world. Genl Scott is decidedly flattering to me. I received from him yesterday a despatch beginning "Your suggestion in respect to Staunton would be admirable like your other conceptions & acts." I value that old man's praise very highly & wrote him a short note last night telling him so.[2] I enclose some scraps clipped off a dirty rebel flag captured at Rich Mountain.

Am engaged now in arranging to march home the 3 mos. men to be reorganized & in clearing up matters generally....

I suppose McDowell drove the enemy from Manassas Junction yesterday — if so the way will be pretty well cleared for the present. If any decided movement is made towards Richmond I shall feel sure that they cannot intend to trouble my people here.

AL copy; copy, McClellan Papers (C-7:63/D-10:72), Library of Congress.

1. Probably his address to the Army of the West, July 16, *supra.* 2. See Scott to GBM, July 18, *OR,* Ser. 1, II, p. 743, and GBM to Scott, July 18, *supra.*

To E. D. Townsend [TELEGRAM]

[Beverly, July 19, 1861]

Cox checked on the Kanawha. Has fought something between a victory & a defeat. A wounded Col of ours taken prisoner & a possibility of having lost two Colonels & a Lt Colonel who amused themselves by a reconnaissance beyond the pickets.[1] Have ordered him to remain where he is & will start as soon as possible to cut Wise's rear & relieve our credit. In heaven's name give me some General Officers who understand their profession. I give orders & find some who cannot execute them unless I stand by them. Unless I command every picket & lead every column I cannot be sure of success. Give me such men as Marcy, Stoneman, Sackett, Lander etc & I will answer for it with my life that I meet with no disaster.[2] Had my orders been executed from the beginning our success would have been brief & final.

G B McClellan
Maj Genl

Col E D Townsend
AAG Washington D.C.

ALS (telegram sent), McClellan Papers (A-21:10), Library of Congress. *OR,* Ser. 1, II, p. 288.

1. The wounded officer was Col. Jesse S. Norton, 21st Ohio. The others were Col. Charles A. De Villiers, 11th Ohio, and Col. William E. Woodruff and Lt. Col. George W. Neff,

2nd Kentucky. The skirmish was at Scarey Creek on July 17. 2. Maj. Marcy, Maj. George Stoneman, Lt. Col. Delos B. Sacket, Brig. Gen. Frederick W. Lander.

To Jacob D. Cox [TELEGRAM]

Brig Genl J D Cox
Mouth of Poca via Pomeroy [Beverly, July 19, 1861]

I am entirely disappointed with the result of your operations. You have in front of you but twenty five hundred men badly armed, disciplined and commanded and disaffected to their cause. You should have advanced to the Gauley Bridge without a check. Your Army is nearly as numerous as that which has achieved brilliant results on this line. I see that your Army is demoralized.[1] Encourage your men by telling them that I myself will move upon the enemy's rear and accomplish what ought to have been done without my personal presence. In the mean time hold your own and at least save me the disgrace of a detachment of my Army being routed. In future keep your officers within the line of pickets and impress upon your men that as soon as the long and difficult march before me can be accomplished they will find the road opened for them. The officers taken prisoners are justly punished for their folly and deserve no consideration. I hope it will serve as a useful lesson for the rest.

Geo B McClellan
Maj Genl Comdg

Retained copy, McClellan Papers (A-23:11), Library of Congress.

1. This appraisal of Cox's operations was based on second-hand and inaccurate reports. Cox would presently outflank Henry A. Wise and take both Charleston and Gauley Bridge.

To James Barnett

Col Barnett — Head Quarters Army of Occupation
Col, — Camp near Beverly July 19, 1861

I am aware that the term of service of your command expires in a few days, yet I feel obliged to call upon the patriotism of your officers & men for a short extension of their service. I find it necessary to make one more movement to accomplish the full results we have conferred to ourselves. That movement will probably involve some more fighting & I wish to have your battery in my command.

I feel sure that men who have served their country so gallantly & effectively in the past will not hesitate at the sacrifice of at most 2 or 3 weeks more of their lives but that they will gladly accompany me to the front & avail themselves of the opportunity afforded to add to the reputation they have already gained.[1]

I have to request that you will move your battery to this place tomorrow where you will receive further instructions.

I am respectfully your obd servant
Geo. B. McClellan
Maj Genl Comdg

ALS retained copy, McClellan Papers (A-21:10), Library of Congress. Col. Barnett commanded an Ohio battery of three-month volunteers.

1. Barnett's battery was mustered out on July 27. Other appeals to three-month units by GBM were similarly unavailing.

To Francis H. Peirpoint

F H Peirpoint
Wheeling Va
Your Excellency

Head Qtrs Army of Occupation West Va
Camp near Beverly July 20 1861

I trust you will pardon me for venturing upon a few suggestions in regard to matters in which we both have the deepest & most direct interest. I allude to the military & political reorganization of Western Virginia. I do not regard the purpose of my presence here as being merely the military conquest & occupation of this region — it is to drive out the intruding army, which consisted of troops from Eastern Virginia & from other states, & to afford to the loyal citizens that protection due to them from the Federal Govt while engaged in the task of reorganizing their political affairs, & in the formation of an armed force sufficient to guarantee their safety & independence.

The troops under my command are of course at the service of the people you represent, but in view of the probability of a large portion of them being eventually required in other localities, & of the favorable moral effect that would be produced upon your own people by the consciousness of their possessing the means to protect themselves, I would respectfully urge upon your excellency the propriety, necessity I might say, of prompt & energetic measures being taken to raise troops among the population as we pass through & protect them. Such measures should be well organized & nothing should be left undone to rouse the enthusiasm of the people, who are a race of farmers, of simple habits, not prone to adopt the profession of arms & who seem to need strong urging to induce them to act in their own defence. I think they are somewhat apathetic, & I see no strong disposition manifested to take up arms. Would it not be well that leading & influential citizens should make it their business to traverse the country, address the people, & rouse them to action; this should be followed, on the part of the authorities by vigorous measures to raise regiments for the service. I confess that I am much disappointed by the extreme slowness with which recruiting goes on — cannot something be done at once to expedite matters. Before I left Grafton I made requisitions for arms clothing etc for 10,000 Virginia troops — I begin to fear that my estimate was much too large.

Of no less importance — it may be more — is the vital necessity of establishing the civil authority of the Govt in the counties protected by my troops. I would suggest in regard to this that steps be at once taken to hold elections for minor offices, the opening of the courts, reestablishment of postal facilities, & in fact the placing in operation the whole machinery of Govt.

Is it not important to send to every place occupied by the troops, or covered by their presence, commissioners with authority to enforce the recognition of your Govt by all officials, with power to remove or suspend such as refuse to give the required assurances? I should be pleased to have at my Head Quarters any Commissioner you may deem fit to send, provided he be a gentleman of marked energy & character. Trusting you will appreciate my motives in making these suggestions

I am, Governor, with high respect your obt svt
Geo B McClellan
Maj Genl USA

ALS retained copy, McClellan Papers (A-21:10), Library of Congress. On June 19 a convention meeting in Wheeling had named Peirpoint provisional governor of Unionist Virginia.

To Randolph B. Marcy [TELEGRAM]

Maj R B Marcy
Willard's Hotel Washington D.C.[1] [Beverly, c. July 21, 1861]

I have taken steps to order home all the three months Regts. Cox has been checked on the Kanawha which renders it necessary for me to move there at once with all my available force — so that the Stanton[2] movement is impossible for the present unless I am largely reinforced. Please state this to the Genl in Chief in explanation of my apparent inaction and inform him that the cause of my delay has been the uncertainty of affairs on the Kanawha. Say to him that when I have driven Wise out of the Kanawha I will be ready to execute his final orders — but that I think a movement through Kentucky, Western Tennessee and Northern Alabama would be decisive of the war.

Geo B McClellan
Maj Genl Comdg

Retained copy, McClellan Papers (A-23:11), Library of Congress.

1. Marcy reached Washington on July 18, carrying GBM's report of his western Virginia operations for delivery to Gen. Scott. 2. Staunton, in the Shenandoah Valley.

To Mary Ellen McClellan

Beverly July 21 [1861]

...Were you satisfied with the result? 9 guns taken 12 colors — lots of prisoners — & all this done with so little loss on our side! We found yesterday some more guns abandoned by Garnett — bringing the number taken up to *9*....

Genl Cox has been badly checked in the Kanawha — one wounded Col (Norton) taken prisoner — two others & a Lt Col (Neff) captured while amusing themselves by an insane expedition in advance of the pickets — served them right. Cox lost more men in getting a detachment thrashed than I did in routing two armies. The consequence is I shall move down with a heavy column to take Mr. Wise in rear & hope either to drive him out without a battle or to catch him with his whole force. It is absolutely necessary for me to go in person. I have no one to whom I can entrust the operation. More than that I don't feel sure that the men will fight very well under anyone but myself. They have the utmost confidence in me & will do anything I put them at. I lose about 14 rgts now whose term of service is about expiring & am sorry to say that I have as yet found but few whose patriotism is sufficient to induce them to remain beyond their time.

I expect to get away from here by day after tomorrow at latest. The march to the Kanawha will require about 7 days — I hope to be able to start for Cincinnati in about 2 weeks from tomorrow. I expect the Guthrie Grays here today & will take them with me to the Kanawha.

AL copy, McClellan Papers (C-7:63), Library of Congress.

To Winfield Scott [TELEGRAM]

Beverly 11 p.m. July 21/61

Your telegram of 8 p.m. rec'd.[1] I am much pained at its contents. My 3 months men are homesick & discontented with their officers & determined to return at once. When I suggested the Staunton movement I expected these regiments to unite in it. I should be compelled to fight the enemy now ascertained to be in force at Monterey & should reach Staunton without men enough to accomplish much. McDowell's check would greatly increase my difficulties & render numerous detachments necessary to keep open my communications & protect my flank.

How would it meet your views were I to leave say 4 regts at Huttonsville and in the strong position of Cheat Mountain, 1 at Beverly, send two or three & a better general to reenforce Cox, leaving 1 at Bulltown. Then move with the rest by Railroad to New Creek on B & O R.R., & effect a junction with Patterson near Jamesburg on the road from New Creek to Charlestown?

With this force in addition to such state troops as Penna can furnish we should be able either to defeat Johnston or to separate him from Beauregard & in connection with McDowell fight them in detail.[2]

I shall know early tomorrow the exact condition of the 3 years regiments now in Ohio & Indiana. Depending on that information I can join Patterson with probably 15,000 men besides what Penna can furnish. The time required would be about 7 days, perhaps 6, from the day on which I receive your orders until the junction with Patterson at Jamesburg. This tho' not so brilliant a plan as a movement on Staunton in force, appears to be the sounder & safer one.

Whatever your instructions may be, I will cheerfully do my best to carry them out. I will suspend all further preparations for my projected movement on the Kanawha until I hear from you. Please reply by telegraph at once.

G B McClellan
Maj Genl USA

Lt Genl Winfield Scott

ALS (telegram sent), McClellan Papers (A-22:10), Library of Congress. *OR*, Ser. 1, II, p. 752.

1. Scott's telegram read: "McDowell has been checked. Come down to the Shenandoah Valley with such troops as can be spared from Western Virginia, and make head against the enemy in that quarter...." *OR*, Ser. 1, II, p. 749. 2. GBM was unaware that Brig. Gen. Joseph E. Johnston had evaded Patterson in the Shenandoah Valley and had joined Brig. Gen. P. G. T. Beauregard at Manassas for the battle against McDowell.

To Lorenzo Thomas [TELEGRAM]

To Gen. L. Thomas
Adjt General of U.S.A.
Washington D.C.

Head Quarters Department
of the Ohio
Beverly Va. July 22 1861

Your dispatch of this date has been received.[1] I will make the necessary arrangements for the security of W. Va. & proceed without delay to Washington & report in person at the War Dept. I will take with me three or four Western Regiments.[2]

G B McClellan
Maj Genl U.S.A.

Retained copy, McClellan Papers (A-22:10), Library of Congress.

1. Thomas's telegram read: "Circumstances make your presence here necessary. Charge Rosecrans or some other general with your present department and come hither without delay." *OR*, Ser. 1, II, p. 753. 2. Gen. Scott's reply of this date instructed GBM to bring no troops with him. *OR*, Ser. 1, II, p. 755.

To Jacob D. Cox [TELEGRAM]

Brig Genl J D Cox
via Gallipolis [Beverly, July 22, 1861]

Your telegram of 22nd received.[1] Retain the 21st until you have completed the occupation of the Kanawha Valley. Follow up the retreating enemy. Concentrate all your troops and drive them beyond the Gauley Bridge. I have been ordered to Washington and have turned over command of the department to Genl Rosecrantz who is about to repair to the Kanawha to retrieve your want of success. As his presence is very necessary elsewhere I hope that you will by the vigor of your movements render it unnecessary for him to come to your assistance. I had more confidence in you than in any of my Brig Genls. It is not too late for you to justify my first impression of you. Our Army in the East has met with a great disaster. You must if possible drive Wise beyond the Gauley Bridge. It is no longer possible to take him in rear as I proposed. Communicate with Rosecrantz or myself by way of Parkersburg at least twice a day. Two regts are ordered to Bull Town to feel the enemy in that direction.

Geo B McClellan
Maj Genl USA

Retained copy, McClellan Papers (A-22:10), Library of Congress.

1. Cox reported that the 21st Ohio three-month regiment was agitating to go home. McClellan Papers (A-22:10).

To Mary Ellen McClellan [TELEGRAM]

[Beverly, July 22, 1861]

I am ordered to Washington. Get Larz Anderson[1] to bring you at once to Wheeling at the Machum House. I expect to be there on Wednesday morning [July 24]. Be ready to go with me at least to Philadelphia if your health will permit. It may be that I will reach Wheeling tomorrow. Answer at once.

G B McClellan
Maj Genl

Mrs. M E McClellan
Cincinnati, Ohio

ALS (telegram sent), McClellan Collection, New Jersey Historical Society.

1. Larz Anderson, brother of Robert Anderson, the defender of Fort Sumter, was a friend of the McClellans in Cincinnati.

TWO

THE ARMY OF THE POTOMAC
JULY 27–OCTOBER 31, 1861

THE LARGEST SHARE of General McClellan's correspondence in this three-month period deals with matters of special significance to his wartime career — the organization and training of the Army of the Potomac, and the formulation of a mental picture of the enemy that would stay fixed in his mind for as long as he remained in command. A third major feature of these months was McClellan's struggle against what he regarded as Winfield Scott's baneful influence on the Northern war effort, a struggle that finally concluded on October 31, 1861, when he learned that he would replace Scott as general-in-chief of the Union armies the next day. These themes are revealed with particular clarity in McClellan's letters to his wife, which make up nearly half of the sixty-seven letters and dispatches included here.

Mrs. McClellan, who was expecting their first child, did not accompany the general when he was called to Washington in July but remained instead in Cincinnati, and his frequent letters to her disclose a growing obsession with his enemies, real and imagined, both in the field and on the home front. Editor Prime was at particular pains to censor those he printed in *McClellan's Own Story*. In the case of one especially angry letter, written probably on October 11, in which McClellan savagely characterized the president and most of the Cabinet, Prime eliminated everything of the diatribe but its opening phrase — "I can't tell you how disgusted I am becoming with these wretched politicians. . . ."

The long memorandum of August 2 to President Lincoln, which McClellan characterized for his wife that day as his plan to conduct the war "'En grand' & crush the rebels in one campaign," represented a considerable change in his strategic thinking as first described in his April 27 letter to General Scott. The emphasis was now on making a single major campaign in the eastern theater with a Napoleonic grand army of over a quarter of a million men. By thoroughly defeating the Confederate forces in the field, he wrote, "and pursuing a rigidly protective policy as to private property and unarmed persons, and a lenient course as to common soldiers, we may well hope for the permanent restoration of peaceful Union...."

Less than a week after submitting this plan, McClellan raised the alarm with Scott (August 8) that Washington was in danger of attack by an army of 100,000 men, twice the size of his own forces. Succeeding letters depict the Confederate menace growing ever larger as he worked desperately to ready the Army of the Potomac for the decisive battle. The danger was greatest, by McClellan's reckoning, on September 13, when he warned Secretary of War Simon Cameron, in a letter previously unpublished, that he would be unable to bring more than 60,000 or 80,000 soldiers to the battlefield, while "The enemy probably have 170,000!" In fact, the peak strength of the Confederate field army facing Washington in these months was less than 45,000.

With his August 8 letter to Scott, McClellan invented a crisis and created the delusion of an all-powerful enemy which was only later abetted by the imaginative reports of his intelligence chief, Allan Pinkerton. The letters to Mrs. McClellan clearly demonstrate the strength of the delusion and how desperate he believed his plight to be. At the same time, they demonstrate the strength of his Calvinistic belief in predestination. He was certain he had been called upon by God to save the Union. On October 31, for example, he wrote her, "God will support me & bear me out — he could not have placed me here for nothing," and in that belief he took both comfort and refuge.

In his war against General Scott and others in the government who refused to recognize the gravity of the crisis, McClellan initially had an ally in Edwin M. Stanton, a fellow Democrat and former member of President Buchanan's Cabinet. The draft of McClellan's major strategy paper of October 31 to Cameron reveals that it was written in part by Stanton, at whose Washington house McClellan concealed himself that day (as he told his wife) "To dodge all enemies in shape of 'browsing' Presdt etc." The paper set his conditions for making a campaign before winter against an enemy army facing him "on the Potomac not less than 150 000 strong well drilled & equipped, ably commanded & strongly intrenched." If the Army of the Potomac was raised to parity with the enemy by calling up reinforcements from other theaters and if he was put in overall command, he wrote, he would take the offensive within a month.

To Mary Ellen McClellan

July 27/61 Washington D.C. Saturday

I have been assigned to the command of a Division — composed of Depts of N.E. Va (that under McDowell) & that of Washington (now under Mansfield)[1] — neither of them like it much — especially Mansfield, but I think they must ere long become accustomed to it, as there is no help for it. . . .

I find myself in a new & strange position here — Presdt, Cabinet, Genl Scott & all deferring to me — by some strange operation of magic I seem to have become *the* power of the land. I almost think that were I to win some small success now I could become Dictator or anything else that might please me — but nothing of that kind would please me — *therefore* I *won't* be Dictator. Admirable self denial! I see already the main causes of our recent failure — I am *sure* that I can remedy these & am confident that I can lead these armies of men to victory once more. I start tomorrow very early on a tour through the lines on the other side of the river —it will occupy me all day long & a rather fatiguing ride it will be — but I will be able to make up my mind as to the state of things. Refused invitations to dine today from Genl Scott & four Secy's — had too many things to attend to. . . .

I will endeavor to enclose with this the ''thanks of Congress'' which please preserve. I feel very proud of it. Genl Scott objected to it on the ground that it ought to be accompanied by a gold medal. I cheerfully acquiesce in the Thanks by themselves, hoping to win the medal by some other action, & the sword by some other fait d'éclat.

AL copy; copy, McClellan Papers (C-7:63/D-10:72), Library of Congress.

1. GBM headed the Division of the Potomac, with Brig. Gens. Irvin McDowell and Joseph K. F. Mansfield serving under him, McDowell in command of a division, Mansfield in command of the District of Columbia.

To Allan Pinkerton [TELEGRAM]

To E. J. Allen, Esq.[1]
Cincinnati, Ohio Washington July 30/61

Join me in Washington as soon as possible. Come prepared to stay and bring with you two or three of your best men.[2] Answer by telegraph.

Geo. B. McClellan
Major General

Retained copy, Records of the Office of the Secretary of War, RG 107 (M-504:9), National Archives.

1. Pinkerton customarily employed the nom de guerre E. J. Allen. 2. GBM put Pinkerton in charge of military intelligence-gathering for the Army of the Potomac.

To Mary Ellen McClellan

July 30/61 Washington

. . . Had to work until nearly 3 this morning. . . .

I am getting my ideas pretty well arranged in regard to the strength of my army — it will be a large one. I have been employed in trying to get the right kind of Genl officers. . . .

Have been working this morning at a bill allowing me to appoint as many Aides as I please from civil life & from the army.[1]

I went to the Senate to get it through (the bill increasing number of Aides) & was quite overwhelmed by the congratulations I received & the respect with which I was treated. I suppose half a dozen of the oldest made the remark I am becoming so much used to. "Why how young you look — & yet an old soldier!!" It seems to strike everybody that I am very young. They give me my way in everything, full swing & unbounded confidence. All tell me that I am held responsible for the fate of the Nation & that all its resources shall be placed at my disposal. It is an immense task that I have on my hands, but I believe I can accomplish it. . . .

When I was in the Senate Chamber today & found those old men flocking around me; when I afterwards stood in the library looking over the Capital of our great Nation, & saw the crowd gathering around to stare at me, I began to feel how great the task committed to me. Oh! how sincerely I pray to God that I may be endowed with the wisdom & courage necessary to accomplish the work. Who would have thought when we were married, that I should so soon be called upon to save my country? I learn that before I came on they said in Richmond, that there was only one man they feared & that was McClellan.

AL copy; copy, McClellan Papers (C-7:63/D-10:72), Library of Congress.

1. A bill for the stated purpose was passed by Congress and on Aug. 5 signed into law by the president.

To Abraham Lincoln

Memorandum for the Consideration
of His Excellency the President,
submitted at his request. [Washington, August 2, 1861][1]

The object of the present war differs from those in which nations are usually engaged, mainly in this; that the purpose of ordinary war is to conquer a peace and make a treaty on advantageous terms; in this contest it has become necessary to crush a population sufficiently numerous, intelligent and warlike to constitute a nation; we have not only to defeat their armed and organized forces in the field but to display such an overwhelming strength, as will convince all our antagonists, especially those of the governing aristocratic class, of the utter impossibility of resistance. Our late reverses make this course imperative; had we been successful in the recent battle it is possible that we might have been spared the labor and expense of a great effort; now we have no alternative; their success will enable the political leaders of the rebels to convince the mass of their people that we are inferior to them in force and courage, and to command all their resources. The contest began with a class; now it is with a people. Our military success can alone restore the former issue. By thoroughly defeating their armies, taking their strong places, and pursuing a rigidly protective policy as to private property and unarmed persons, and a lenient course as to common soldiers, we may well hope for the permanent restoration of peaceful Union; but in the first instance the authority of the Government must be supported by overwhelming physical force. Our foreign relations and financial credit also imperatively demand that the military action of the Government should be prompt and irresistible.

The rebels have chosen Virginia as their battle-field — and it seems proper for us to make the first great struggle there; but while thus directing our main efforts, it is necessary to diminish the resistance there offered us, by movements on other points, both by land and water. Without entering at present into details, I would advise that a strong movement be made on the Mississippi, and that the rebels be driven out of Missouri. As soon as it becomes perfectly clear that Kentucky is cordially united with us, I would advise a movement through that state into Eastern Tennessee, for the purpose of assisting the Union men of that region, and of seizing the Railroads leading from Memphis to the East. The possession of those roads by us, in connection with the movement on the Mississippi, would go far towards determining the evacuation of Virginia by the rebels. In the mean time all the passes into Western Virginia from the East should be securely guarded; but I would make no movement from that quarter towards Richmond unless the political condition of Kentucky renders it impossible or inexpedient for us to make the movement upon Eastern Tennessee through that state; every effort should however be made to organize, equip, and arm as many troops as possible in Western Virginia, in order to render the Ohio and Indiana regiments available for other operations.

At as early a day as practicable it would be well to protect and reopen the Baltimore & Ohio Railroad. Baltimore & Fort Monroe should be occupied by *garrisons* sufficient to retain them in our possession.

The importance of Harper's Ferry and the line of the Potomac in the direction of Leesburg will be very materially diminished as soon as our force in this vicinity becomes organized, strong and efficient; because no capable general will cross the river north of this city, when we have a strong army here ready to cut off his retreat.

To revert to the West. It is probable that no very large additions to the troops now in Missouri will be necessary to secure that state. I presume that the force required for the movement down the Mississippi will be determined by its commander and the President.

If Kentucky assumes the right position, not more than 20,000 troops will be needed, together with those that can be raised in that state and Eastern Tennessee, to secure the latter region and its railroads; as well as ultimately to occupy Nashville. The Western Virginia troops with not more than from 5 to 10,000 from Ohio and Indiana should under proper management, suffice for its protection. When we have reorganized our main army here, 10,000 men ought to be enough to protect the Balt. & Ohio R.R. and the Potomac — 5000 will *garrison* Baltimore — 3000 Fort Monroe; and not more than 20,000 will be necessary, at the utmost, for the defence of Washington.

For the main Army of Operations I urge the following composition.

250 Regt's Infantry — say	225,000 men
100 Field Batteries — 600 guns	15,000 "
28 Regts. Cavalry	25,500 "
5 " Engineer troops	7,500 "
Total	273,000 "

This force must be supplied with the necessary engineer and ponton trains, and with transportation for everything save tents. Its general line of operations should be directed that water transportation can be availed of from point to point, by means of the ocean and the rivers emptying into it.

An essential feature of the plan of operations will be the employment of a strong naval force, to protect the movement of a fleet of transports, intended to convoy a considerable body of troops from point to point of the enemy's seacoast; thus either creating diversions and rendering it necessary for them to detach largely from their main body in order to protect such of their cities as may be threatened; or else landing and forming establishments on their coast at any favorable places that opportunity might offer. This naval force should also cooperate with the main army in its efforts to seize the important seaboard towns of the rebels.

It cannot be ignored that the construction of railroads has introduced a new and very important element into war, by the great facilities thus given for concentrating at particular positions large masses of troops from remote sections, and by creating new strategic points and lines of operations. It is intended to overcome this difficulty by the partial operations suggested, and such others as the particular case may require;

we must endeavor to seize places on the railways in the rear of the enemy's points of concentration; and we must threaten their seaboard cities in order that each state may be forced by the necessity of its own defence to diminish its contingent to the Confederate Army.

The proposed movement down the Mississippi will produce important results in this connection. That advance and the progress of the main army at the East will materially assist each other by diminishing the resistance to be encountered by each. The tendency of the Mississippi movement upon all questions connected with cotton are too well understood by the President and Cabinet to need any illustration from me.

There is another independent movement which has often been suggested and which has always recommended itself to my judgment. I refer to a movement from Kansas and Nebraska through the Indian Territory upon Red river and Western Texas, for the purpose of protecting and developing the latent Union and free state sentiment well known to predominate in Western Texas, and which like a similar sentiment in Western Virginia, will, if protected, ultimately organize that section into a free state. How far it will be possible to support this movement by an advance through New Mexico from California is a matter which I have not sufficiently examined to be able to express a decided opinion; if at all practicable, it is eminently desirable as bringing into play the resources and warlike qualities of the Pacific States, as well as identifying them with our cause and cementing the bond of Union between them and the General Government. If it is not departing too far from my province I will venture to suggest the policy of an intimate alliance and cordial understanding with Mexico; their sympathies and interests are with us; their antipathies exclusively against our enemies and their institutions. I think it would not be difficult to obtain from the Mexican Government the right to use, at least during the present contest, the road from Guaymas to New Mexico; this concession would very materially reduce the obstacles of the column moving from the Pacific; a similar permission to use their territory for the passage of troops between the Panuco and the Rio Grande would enable us to throw a column by a good road from Tampico or some of the small harbors north of it upon and across the Rio Grande into the country of our friends, and without risk, and scarcely firing a shot. To what extent if any it would be desirable to take into service, and employ Mexican soldiers is a question entirely political, on which I do not venture to offer any opinion.

The force I have recommended is large — the expense is great. It is possible that a smaller force might accomplish the object in view, but I understand it to be the purpose of this great Nation to reestablish the power of the Government, and to restore peace to its citizens, in the shortest possible time. The question to be decided is simply this; shall we crush the rebellion at one blow, terminate the war in one campaign, or shall we leave it as a legacy for our descendants? When the extent of the possible line of operations is considered, the force asked for, for the main army under my command, cannot be regarded as unduly large. Every mile we advance carries us further from our base of operations and renders detachments necessary to cover our communications; while the enemy will be constantly concentrating as he falls back. I propose with the force which I have requested, not only to drive the enemy out of Virginia and occupy Richmond, but to occupy Charleston, Savannah, Montgomery, Pensacola, Mobile, and New Orleans; in other words to move into the heart of the enemy's country, and crush out this rebellion in its very heart. By seizing and repairing the railroads as we advance, the difficulties of transportation will be materially diminished.

It is perhaps unnecessary to state that in addition to the forces named in this memorandum strong reserves should be formed, ready to supply any losses that may occur. In conclusion, I would submit that the exigencies of the treasury may be lessened by making only partial payments to our troops when in the enemy's country and by giving the obligations of the United States for such supplies as may there be obtainable.

Geo B McClellan
Maj Genl USA

Washington D.C. Aug 2 1861

DS, Lincoln Papers, Library of Congress. *OR,* Ser. 1, V, pp. 6–8.

1. The retained copy of this memorandum bears the endorsement that it was delivered personally to the president by GBM on Aug. 2, and that GBM read it to the Cabinet at 10:00 A.M. the next day. McClellan Papers (A-23:11), Library of Congress.

To Mary Ellen McClellan

[Washington] Aug 2nd/61

Rode over the river, looked at some of the works & inspected 3 or 4 rgts — worked at organizing Brigades — just got thro' with that. I handed to the Presdt tonight a carefully considered plan for conducting the war on a large scale....

I shall carry this thing on "En grand" & crush the rebels in one campaign — I flatter myself that Beauregard has gained his last victory — we need success & must have it — I will leave nothing undone to gain it. Genl Scott has been trying to work a traverse to have Emory made Inspector Genl of *my* army & of *the* army[1] — I respectfully declined the favor & perhaps disgusted the old man, who by the by, is fast becoming very slow & very old. He cannot long retain command I think — when he retires I am sure to succeed him, unless in the mean time I lose a battle — which I do not expect to do....

I have Washn perfectly quiet now — you would not know that there was a regiment here. I have restored order very completely already.

I have on the staff Seth Williams as Adjt Genl, Barnard as Chief Engineer, Van Vliet, Chief Qt Master, H. F. Clarke, Chief Commissary, Barry, Chief of Artillery — Meade will be senior Topog — Dr. Tripler Medical Director.[2] I have applied for Kingsbury as Chief of Ordnance, & for Armstrong & Sweitzer as aides de camp.[3] I dine with the Presdt tomorrow, where I presume I shall meet Prince Napoleon.[4] . . .

You would laugh if you could see the scores of queer letters I receive in these days. I am sorry to say I do not answer any of them, I do no writing myself, except to you. . . .

I was in the saddle nearly 12 hours yesterday. I broke down your Father & sent Seth home half an hour since, neither of them having been out all today.

AL copy; copy, McClellan Papers (C-7:63/D-10:72), Library of Congress.

1. Lt. Col. William H. Emory was not appointed to either position. 2. Majors Seth Williams, John G. Barnard, Stewart Van Vliet, Henry F. Clarke, William F. Barry, Capt. George G. Meade, Maj. Charles S. Tripler. All assumed the posts mentioned except Meade, who would command an infantry brigade. 3. Capts. Charles P. Kingsbury and N. B. Sweitzer were appointed to these positions. The identity of Armstrong is unknown. 4. Napoleon Joseph Charles Paul Bonaparte, cousin of France's Emperor Napoleon III.

To General Officers, Division of the Potomac

[Washington, c. August 4, 1861][1]

Instructions to General Officers

The basis of organization is in the Brigades, & to the Brig Genls the Genl Comdg looks for the instruction, discipline & efficiency of the troops. The Brig Genls will at once establish schools of instruction. They will personally instruct & drill all the field officers, & as many of the Capts & Lts as possible, at least one hour every day. They will require these officers to recite to them in the tactics, regulations, duties of outpost guards & sentinels, forms of parade, inspection, guard mounting, reviews etc; they will instruct them thoroughly as to the various reports & customs required by existing regulations; drill them in the school of the soldier; occasionally drill the companies & battalions, always enforcing the instructions given by their subordinates, & paying especial attention to the drill for skirmishers, that with the bayonet, & target practice. Whenever the Colonels or other regimental officers are already competent the Brig Genls will establish subordinate schools of instruction, always taking care that the company officers & n.c. offs[2] are theoretically instructed every day.

Particular attention is enjoined to the duties of sentinels & the various forms of ceremony etc prescribed by the regulations.

In view of the fact that the greater part of the General Officers are instructed soldiers, the Genl Comdg does not deem it necessary to dwell further upon points of detail, trusting to their soldierly spirit to carry out his wishes, & to perfect the strict discipline & instruction of the troops.

There are, however, some general points to which it is desired to call their attention — i.e.

1. Guards, outposts & sentinels —

The Grand guards will always be posted — their number & position to be determined by circumstances. The outposts & sentinels must be so placed as to render it impossible for any one to pass the lines without being observed, & so as to give ample notice to the grand guards & main body of the approach of the enemy. Sentinels must be obliged to walk their posts constantly & always to be on the alert — in presence of the enemy they will in preference be posted in pairs.

Patrols of infantry & cavalry will be constantly kept out to the front. Sentinels must know that the punishment of death for sleeping, abandoning their arms, or neglecting their duty will be inexorably inflicted.

[2.] *Marches* Frequent military marches will be made for the purpose of instruction, sometimes at night. The trains will accompany the columns, knapsacks will be carried, & all military precautions observed with regard to advanced guards, flankers, rear guard etc. Every place in which an enemy could be concealed will be carefully searched by skirmishers before the main body passes the point, defiles & villages will be searched before & occupied while the main body passes. Every precaution will be taken to render a surprise impossible & to gain intelligence of the position & strength of the enemy in ample time to enable the main body to act as circumstances may require. The composition of the advanced guard will depend upon circumstances — if the country is open cavalry will lead, supported by infantry; if the ground is broken & wooded infantry should lead with only cavalry enough to carry intelligence to the rear. A halt of 15 minutes will be made half an hour after the march is commenced, & one of 10 minutes during every hour, besides a noon halt of at least an hour when circumstances permit. Halts will be made in preference where water & shade can be obtained. Arms will be stacked, not more than one fourth of the men permitted to leave the immediate vicinity of the stacks at the same time, sentinels placed over private houses & gardens, as well as outposts thrown out to prevent a surprise. In no case will the men be allowed to enter houses & gardens, except to obtain water when they cannot obtain it otherwise. The sentinels will always prevent the destruction of property. In marching straggling will be strictly prohibited & the rear guard will have positive orders not to allow any soldier or camp follower to lag behind it. The rear guard will be provided a suitable number of ambulances & a surgeon, who will decide what stragglers should ride — the others will be forced to march in advance of the rear guard.

The men will carry in their knapsacks only a change of underclothing, an extra pair of shoes, towel soap etc. The blanket & shelter tent will form the rest of their load. In winter they will wear the overcoat.

Forty rounds will always be carried in the cartridge boxes. Punctuality in the hour of starting will be always required.

3. *Battles* In regard to *battles* & *affairs* the Genl Officers will receive such specific instructions as the peculiar circumstances may require, the Comdg Genl now desires only to call attention to some general principles which must always be observed.

The orders must be strictly conformed to; no excuse can be received for bringing on an action against or without his instructions, & every Genl Officer, of whatever rank, will be held accountable that the directions given to him are carried out both in the spirit & letter. The Genl Officers must understand that success can only be obtained by carefully observing the orders they receive, & will in no case allow their impulses or individual judgment to induce them to depart from their instructions.

Infantry may act on any kind of ground; in an open country, preferably in column or line; in a broken or wooded country skirmishers should precede, supported by columns — the habitual employment of skirmishers to open the way is advised. Artillery should never be left without a support of both infantry & cavalry, if the ground will permit the employment of the latter, nor should it ever be brought (except in extreme cases) within rifle range of woods or other cover occupied by the enemy; it should always if possible have a clear space of at least 500 or 600 yards in front of it.

Cavalry must be used entirely in an open country, unless its flanks are covered by infantry as it advances; in no case should it be required to act in woods, or along a road skirted by timber.

As a general rule an engagement should be opened by the fire of all the artillery that can be concentrated on the decisive point, when the requisite effect is produced the infantry should advance, supported by the cavalry held ready to follow up their success.

AD, McClellan Papers (A-16:7), Library of Congress

1. This probable date is assigned from the contents of the memorandum, and from an entry of Aug. 4 in the headquarters journal that called all brigade commanders to headquarters "for instructions regarding the duties of their Brigades when formed." McClellan Papers (A-23:11). 2. Noncommissioned officers.

To Mary Ellen McClellan

[Washington] August 4 1861

I dined at the Presdt's yesterday. I suppose some 40 were present — Prince Napoleon & his staff, French Minister, English ditto, Cabinet, some Senators, Genl Scott & myself. Mrs. Lincoln doesn't shine particularly as a hostess. The dinner was not especially interesting; rather long, & rather tedious as such things generally are. I was placed between Col. Pisani,[1] one of the Prince's aides, who spoke no English, & a member of the Legation who laboured under the delusion that he spoke our native tongue with fluency. I had some long talks with the Prince, who speaks English very much as the Frenchmen do in the old English comedies. He is an intelligent man, but not prepossessing. . . .

My horse has at last arrived.[2] I hear there is another one on the way for me, a present from Chicago, I wish some other people would give me two or three more. . . .

It made me feel a little strangely last evening when I went in to the Presdt's with the old General leaning on me — the old veteran (Scott) & his young successor; I could see that many marked the contrast.

Copy, McClellan Papers (D-10:72), Library of Congress.

1. Lt. Col. Camille Ferri Pisani. 2. Presumably Dan Webster, a gift from what GBM called his "railroad friends" in Cincinnati.

To Nathaniel P. Banks [TELEGRAM]

Maj. Genl. N. P. Banks
Comdg in Camp

Head Quarters, Army of the Potomac
Washington, Aug 4 1861 2.30 p.m.

Information has been received which goes to show that the enemy may attack us within the next forty eight hours. Please direct all your guards to exercise the utmost vigilance and hold your command ready to move at the shortest notice, with cooked rations for two days ready.[1] Telegraph to me at least four times each day.

Geo B McClellan
Maj Genl Comdg

Retained copy, McClellan Papers (A-23:11), Library of Congress. Maj. Gen. Banks commanded the Department of the Shenandoah, with headquarters at Sandy Hook, Md., on the upper Potomac.

1. The same alert was sent to all brigade commanders. On Aug. 6 the alert was renewed. *OR*, Ser. 1, V, p. 553.

To Winfield Scott

Lieut. Gen'l Winfield Scott
Comdg U. S. Army
General:

Head Quarters Division of the Potomac
Washington Aug. 8th 1861

Information from various sources, reaching me to-day, through spies, letters and telegrams confirm my impressions derived from previous advices, that the enemy intend attacking our positions on the other side of the river, as well as to cross the Potomac north of us. I have also to-day received a telegram from a reliable agent just from Knoxville Tenn. that large reinforcements are still passing through there to Richmond. I am induced to believe that the enemy has at least 100,000 men in our front. Were I in Beauregard's place, with that force at my disposal, I would attack the positions on the other side of the Potomac and at the same time cross the river above the city in force.

I feel confident that our present army in this vicinity is entirely insufficient for the emergency, and it is deficient in all the arms of the service — Infantry, Artillery, and Cavalry. I therefore respectfully and most earnestly urge that the garrisons of all places in our rear be reduced at once to the minimum absolutely necessary to hold them, and that all the troops thus made available be forthwith forwarded to this city; that every company of regular artillery within reach be immediately ordered here to be mounted; that every possible means be used to expedite the forwarding of new regiments of volunteers to this Capital, without one hour's delay. I urge that nothing be left undone to bring up our force for the defence of this city to 100,000 men before attending to any other point. I advise that at least 8 or 10 good Ohio and Indiana Regiments may be telegraphed for from Western Virginia; their places to be filled at once by the new troops from the same states, who will be at least reliable to fight behind the entrenchments which have been constructed there. The vital importance of rendering Washington perfectly secure, and its *imminent danger,* impel me to urge these requests with the utmost earnestness, and that not an hour be lost in carrying them into execution.[1]

A sense of duty which I cannot resist, compels me to state that in my opinion military necessity demands that the departments of N. E. Viginia, Washington, the Shenandoah, Pennsylvania including Baltimore, and the one including Fort Monroe should be merged into one Department under the immediate control of the Commander of the main army of operations, and which should be known and designated as such.

Very Respty Your obdt servt.
Geo B McClellan
Maj Gen'l Comdg.

"The original of which the foregoing is a copy was delivered to Genl Scott on the day of its date in the usual course of official communications, and a copy of same was on the same day delivered to the President of the United States personally by Thomas M Key — volunteer aid of Genl McClellan."(Attest T M Key)[2]

Retained copy, McClellan Papers (A-24:11), Library of Congress. *OR,* Ser. 1, XI, Part 3, pp. 3–4.

1. Scott responded, to Secretary of War Cameron, on Aug. 9: "I am confident in the opposite opinion; . . . I have not the slightest apprehension for the safety of the Government here." Suffering the infirmities of age and long service, and considering himself undercut by GBM, he asked to be put on the retired list. *OR,* Ser. 1, XI, Part 3, p. 4. 2. With the copy for the president GBM sent a covering letter expressing the hope that Lincoln would

see Key "at once & read attentively the copy of my letter to Genl Scott which he will hand you." William Henry Seward Papers, Rush Rhees Library, University of Rochester.

To Mary Ellen McClellan

[Washington] Aug 8 [1861]

. . . Rose early today (having retired at 3 am) & was pestered to death with Senators etc & a row with Genl Scott until about 4 o'clock, then crossed the river & rode beyond & along the line of pickets for some distance — came back & had a long interview with Seward[1] about my "pronunciamento" against Genl Scott's policy. . . .[2]

How does he think that I can save this country when stopped by Genl Scott — I do not know whether he is a *dotard* or a *traitor!* I can't tell which. He *cannot* or *will* not comprehend the condition in which we are placed & is entirely unequal to the emergency. If he cannot be taken out of my path I will not retain my position, but will resign & let the admn take care of itself. I have hardly slept one moment for the last three nights, knowing well that the enemy intend some movement & fully recognizing our own weakness. If Beauregard does not attack tonight I shall look upon it as a dispensation of Providence — he *ought* to do it. Every day strengthens me — I am leaving nothing undone to increase our force — but that confounded old Genl always comes in the way — he is a perfect imbecile. He understands nothing, appreciates nothing & is ever in my way.

AL copy, McClellan Papers (C-7 :63), Library of Congress.

1. Secretary of State William H. Seward. 2. GBM to Scott, Aug. 8, *supra.*

To Mary Ellen McClellan

Washington Aug 9 [10] 1861 1 am.

I have had a busy day — started from here at 7 in the morning & was in the saddle until about 9 this evening [August 9] — rode over the advanced positions on the other side of the river, was soundly drenched in a hard rain & have been busy ever since my return. Things are improving daily — I received 3 new rgts today — fitted out one new battery yesterday, another today — two tomorrow — about five day after. Within four days I hope to have at least 21 batteries — say 124 field guns — 18 co's. of cavalry & some 70 rgts of infantry. Genl Scott is the great obstacle — he will not comprehend the danger & is either a traitor or an incompetent. I have to fight my way against him & have thrown a bombshell that has created a perfect stampede in the Cabinet — tomorrow [August 10] the question will probably be decided by giving me absolute control independently of him. I suppose it will result in a mortal enmity on his part against me, but I have no choice — the people call upon me to save the country — I *must* save it & cannot respect anything that is in the way.

I receive letter after letter — have conversation after conversation calling on me to save the nation — alluding to the Presidency, Dictatorship &c. As I hope one day to be united with you forever in heaven, I have no such aspirations — I will never accept the Presidency — I will cheerfully take the Dictatorship & agree to lay down my life when the country is saved. I am *not* spoiled by my unexpected & new position — I feel sure that God will give me the strength & wisdom to preserve this great nation — but I tell *you,* who share all my thoughts, that I have no selfish feeling in the matter. I feel that God has placed a great work in my hands — I have not sought it — I know how weak I am — but I know that I mean to do right & I believe that God will help me & give me the wisdom I do not possess. Pray for me, darling, that I may be able to accomplish my task — the greatest, perhaps, that any poor weak mortal ever had to do. . . .

God grant that I may bring this war to an end & be permitted to spend the rest of my days quietly with you. . . .

I met the Prince [Napoleon] at Alexandria today & came up with him.[1] He says that Beauregard's head is turned & that he acts like a fool. That Joe Johnston is quiet & sad, & that he spoke to him in very kind terms of me.

AL copy, McClellan Papers (C-7:63), Library of Congress.

1. On Aug. 8–9 Prince Napoleon and his suite visited the Confederate command at Manassas and toured the Bull Run battlefield.

To Abraham Lincoln

To/ The President — Head Quarters, Division of the Potomac
Sir: — Washington, August 10th 1861

The letter addressed by me under the date of the 8th inst. to Lieutenant General Scott, commanding the United States Army, was designed to be a plain and respectful expression of my views of the measures demanded for the safety of the Government in the imminent peril that besets it at the present hour. Every moment's reflection and every fact transpiring convinces me of the urgent necessity of the measures there indicated, and I felt it my duty to him and to the country to communicate them frankly. It is therefore with great pain that I have learned from you this morning, that my views do not meet with the approbation of the Lieutenant General, and that my letter is unfavorably regarded by him. The command with which I am entrusted, was not sought by me, and has only been accepted from an earnest and humble desire to serve my country in the moment of the most extreme peril. With these views I am willing to do and suffer whatever may be required for that service. Nothing could be further from my wishes than to seek any command or urge any measures not required for the exigency of the occasion, and above all I would abstain from any word or act that could give offense to General Scott or embarrass the President or any Department of the Government.

Influenced by these considerations, I yield to your request, and withdraw the letter referred to. The Government and my superior officer being appraised of what I conceive to be necessary and proper of the defence of the National Capital, I shall strive faithfully and zealously to employ the means that may be placed in my power for that purpose, dismissing every personal feeling or consideration, and praying only the blessing of Divine Providence on my efforts. I will only add that as you requested my authority to withdraw the letter, that authority is hereby given, with the most profound assurances of respect for General Scott and yourself.[1]

Very respectfully your Obd't Serv't
G B McClellan
Maj Gen'l Comdg.

LS, Lincoln Papers, Library of Congress. *OR*, Ser. 1, XI, Part 3, pp. 4–5.

1. Seeking to reconcile his two generals, the president showed this letter to Scott, with the request that he in turn withdraw his letter of resignation sent to Secretary Cameron. Scott, although respecting Lincoln's "patriotic purpose of healing differences," refused, citing the disrespect and neglect of his "ambitious junior" and GBM's dealings with members of the Cabinet "without resort to or consultation with me, the nominal General-in-Chief of the Army." Aug. 12, *OR*, Ser. 1, XI, Part 3, pp. 5–6.

To Gideon Welles

Hon. Gideon Welles
Sec'y U. S. Navy
Sir:

Head Quarters Division of the Potomac
Washington Aug. 12th 1861

I have to day received additional information which convinces me that it is more than probable that the enemy will within a very short time, attempt to throw a respectable force from the mouth of Aquia Creek into Maryland. This attempt will probably be preceded by the erection of batteries at Mathias & White House[1] points. Such a movement on the part of the enemy in connection with others probably designed would place Washington in great jeopardy. I most earnestly urge that the strongest possible naval force be at once concentrated near the mouth of Aquia Creek and that the most vigilant watch be maintained day and night, so as to render such passage of the river absolutely impossible. I recommend that the Minnesota and any other vessels available from Hampton Roads be at once ordered up there,[2] and that a quantity of coal be sent to that vicinity sufficient for several weeks supply. At least one strong war vessel should be kept at Alexandria, and I again urge the concentration of a strong naval force in the Potomac without delay. If the naval Dep't will render it absolutely impossible for the enemy to cross the river below Washington, the security of the Capital will be greatly increased. I cannot too earnestly urge an immediate compliance with these requests.

I am, Sir, very respectfully Your Obdt Servt.
Geo. B. McClellan
Maj. Gen'l Comdg.

"The original of which the foregoing is a copy was upon the day of the date delivered to the Secretary of the Navy by Thomas M Key, volunteer aid of Genl McClellan."(Attest T M Key)

Retained copy, McClellan Papers (A-24:11), Library of Congress. *OR,* Ser. 1, V, p. 47. Welles was secretary of the navy.

1. Presumably GBM meant Whitestone Point, on the lower Potomac upstream from Aquia Creek; Mathias Point is downstream from the creek. 2. The steam frigate *Minnesota* was on blockade duty in Hampton Roads.

To Mary Ellen McClellan

[Washington] Aug 13 [1861]

I am living in Com. Wilkes's house, the N. W. corner of Jackson Square, close to where you used to visit Secy Marcy's family.[1] It is a very nice house. I occupy the three front rooms on the 2nd story, Van Vliet the room in rear of mine, Judge Key behind him, Colburn the story above. I receive the staff every morning until ten & every evening at nine. Quite a levee it makes, & a rather fine looking set they are. Kingsbury arrived last night. Did I tell you that Hudson is one of my regular aides?[2]

Copy, McClellan Papers (D-10:72), Library of Congress.

1. Capt. Charles Wilkes, USN; William L. Marcy, secretary of state under Franklin Pierce and a cousin of Randolph B. Marcy. 2. For GBM's staff, see GBM to Army of the Potomac, Aug. 20, *infra.*

To Mary Ellen McClellan

[Washington] August 15th [14, 1861] midnight

. . . I am almost tired out. I cannot get one minute's rest during the day — & sleep with one eye open at night — looking out sharply for Beauregard, who I think has some notion of making a dash in this direction. Genl Scott is the most dangerous antagonist I have — either he or I must leave here — our ideas are so widely different that it is impossible for us to work together much longer — tant pour cela![1]

My day has been spent much as usual. . . .

Rose at 6 1/2, did any reasonable amount of business — among which may be classed quelling a couple of mutinies among the patriotic volunteers — started on my usual ride at 4 1/2, came home at 9, have been hard at work ever since. As to my mutinous friends — I have ordered 63 of the 2nd Maine rgt to be sent as prisoners to the Dry Tortugas, there to serve out the rest of the war as prisoners at hard labor. I reduced the other gentlemen (79th N.Y.) by sending out a battalion, battery & squadron of regulars to take care of them. The gentlemen at once laid down their arms & I have the ringleaders in irons — they will be tried & probably shot tomorrow — an example is necessary to bring these people up to the mark, & if they will not fight & do their duty from honorable motives, I intend to coerce them & let them see what they have to expect if they pretend to rebel.[2] I deprived the 79th of their colors & have them down stairs — not to be returned to them until they have earned them again by good behavior. The great trouble is the utter worthlessness of the officers of these rgts — we have good material, but no officers.

AL copy, McClellan Papers (C-7 :63), Library of Congress.

1."So much for that." 2. No executions were carried out. The mutinies involved mainly a dispute over whether the regiments' term of service was for three months or three years.

To Elizabeth B. McClellan

My dearest Mother Washington DC Aug 16 [1861]

I enclose some photographs of your wandering son which the artist insisted upon taking by main force & violence. Please give one to Maria, one to Mary, keep one & give the others to Annie Phillips & the "Coxe girls" with my love.[1] I have a weary time here in exile — a load of cares & anxiety on my mind sufficient to crush any one — difficulties to contend against that you cannot imagine. "The Young General" has no bed of roses on which to recline. I try to do my best & trust in God to assist me for I feel full well that I can do nothing in this great crisis without *His* aid.

With my truest love to all ever your affectionate son
Geo McClellan

ALS, McClellan Papers (B-8 :47), Library of Congress. GBM's widowed mother lived in Philadelphia.

1. Maria Eldredge McClellan was the wife of GBM's older brother, John H. B. McClellan. Mary McClellan was GBM's younger sister. The Phillips and Coxe families were maternal relations.

To Mary Ellen McClellan

[Washington, August] 16th [1861]

. . . I am here in a terrible place — the enemy have from 3 to 4 times my force — the Presdt is an idiot, the old General in his dotage — they cannot or will not see the true state of affairs. Most of my troops are demoralized by the defeat at Bull Run, some rgts even mutinous — I have probably stopped that — but you see my position is not pleasant. . . .

I have, I believe, made the best possible disposition of the few men under my command — will quietly await events & if the enemy attacks will try to make my movements as rapid & desperate as may be — if my men will only fight I think I can thrash him notwithstanding the disparity of numbers. As it is I trust to God to give success to our arms — tho' he is not wont to aid those who refuse to aid themselves. . . .

I am weary of all this. I have no ambition in the present affairs — only wish to save my country — & find the incapables around me will not permit it! They sit on the verge of the precipice & cannot realize what they see — their reply to everything is "Impossible! Impossible!" They think nothing possible which is against their wishes.

6 p.m. — . . . Gen. Scott is at last opening his eyes to the fact that I am right & that we are in imminent danger. Providence is aiding me by heavy rains, which are swelling the Potomac, which may be impassable for a week — if so we are saved. If Beauregard comes down upon us soon I have everything ready to make a manoeuvre which will be decisive. Give me two weeks & I will defy Beauregard — in a week the chances will be at least even.

AL copy, McClellan Papers (C-7:63), Library of Congress.

To Charles P. Stone

Letter No. 1 — Head Quarters Division of the Potomac
Washington Aug. 18th 1861

Your letter of Aug 17th 1861 10 pm has been received.[1] Information received from Gen Banks today confirms the belief that the enemy intend crossing the Potomac in your vicinity & move on Baltimore or Washington. There are also strong indications of their intention of attempting the passage of the Potomac south of this city near Aquia Creek (where they are erecting strong batteries), or at some other point. I will recommend to you the utmost vigilance and that you continually bear in mind the necessity of securing your retreat towards Rockville whenever you are unable to prevent the passage of the enemy. Gen Banks will be instructed to move up to your support in case of necessity & will also be instructed to effect his retreat in the same direction in conjunction with you should it become necessary. It is still my wish that the enemies passage of the river & subsequent advance should be opposed & retarded to the utmost of your ability to give me time to make my arrangements & come up to your assistance. A general order has been issued merging the departments of N.E. Va, Shenandoah & Balt. into the Dept of the Potomac under my immediate command.[2] Steps have been taken which will secure us a large reinforcement during the coming week. Give me by next courier the exact strength & disposition of your troops.

Hereafter number your letters in series as they are sent & acknowledge the numbers of those received so that I can be sure you receive all sent.

Very Respt yr obdt servt
G B McClellan
Maj Genl

U.S. Army Brig Gen C. P. Stone

Retained copy, McClellan Papers (A-24:11), Library of Congress. *OR*, Ser. 1, V, pp. 567–68. Brig. Gen. Stone commanded a brigade on the upper Potomac, with headquarters at Poolesville, Md.

1. Stone's dispatch reported his arrival at Poolesville, and that he was "unable as yet to discover the presence of any large force opposite." *OR*, Ser. 1, V, p. 567. 2. Aug. 17, 1861, *OR*, Ser. 1, V, p. 567.

To Mary Ellen McClellan

[Washington, August] 19th [1861]

. . . Beauregard probably has 150,000 men — I cannot count more than 55,000! If this week passes without a battle & reinforcements come in I shall feel sure that a dangerous point is turned.

6 pm. I have been inspecting the defenses over the river & find them quite strong — if they give us a week we shall be so strong on that side that they cannot attack us — or if they do they will be fearfully cut up. We are becoming stronger in our position every day, & I hope for large reinforcements this week.

AL copy, McClellan Papers (C-7:63), Library of Congress.

To the Army of the Potomac

GENERAL ORDERS, No. 1.

HEADQUARTERS ARMY OF THE POTOMAC,
Washington, August 20, 1861.

In accordance with General Order, No. 15, of August 17th, 1861, from the Headquarters of the Army, I hereby assume command of the Army of the Potomac, comprising the troops serving in the former Departments of Washington and Northeastern Virginia, in the valley of the Shenandoah, and in the States of Maryland and Delaware.

The organization of the command into divisions and brigades will be announced hereafter.

The following named officers are attached to the Staff of the Army of the Potomac:

Major S. Williams, Assistant Adjutant General.
Captain A. V. Colburn, Assistant Adjutant General.
Colonel R. B. Marcy, Inspector General.
Col. T. M. Key, Aid-de-camp.
Captain N. B. Sweitzer, 1st Cavalry, Aid-de-camp.
Captain Edward McK. Hudson, 14th Infantry, Aid-de-camp.
Captain Lawrence A. Williams, 10th Infantry, Aid-de-camp.
Major A. J. Meyer, Signal Officer.
Major Stewart Van Vliet, Chief Quartermaster.
Major H. F. Clarke, Chief Commissary.
Surgeon C. S. Tripler, Medical Director.
Major J. G. Barnard, Chief Engineer.
Major J. N. Macomb, Chief Topographical Engineer.
Captain C. P. Kingsbury, Chief of Ordnance.
Brigadier General Geo. Stoneman, Volunteer service, Chief of Cavalry.
Brigadier General W. F. Barry, Volunteer service, Chief of Artillery.

GEO. B. MCCLELLAN,
Major General U. S. Army

DP, McClellan Papers (D-12:74), Library of Congress. *OR*, Ser. 1, V, p. 575.

To Abraham Lincoln

His Excellency
Abraham Lincoln Presdt
Sir Washington D.C. Aug 20 [1861]

I have just received the enclosed dispatch in cypher. Col Marcy knows what he says, & is of the coolest judgment.[1]

I recommend that the Secty of War ascertain at once by telegram how the enlistment proceeds in N.Y. & elsewhere, & that if it is not proceeding with great rapidity drafts be made at once. We must have men without delay.

Very respectfully your obdt svt
Geo B McClellan
Maj Genl USA

ALS, Lincoln Papers, Library of Congress.

1. Marcy's telegram, sent from New York that day, read: "I urge you to instantly make a positive and unconditional demand for an immediate draft of the additional troops you require. Men will not volunteer now, & drafting is the only successful plan. The people will applaud such a course, rely upon it." Lincoln Papers.

To Mary Ellen McClellan

[Washington, August] 20th [1861]

. . . If Beauregard does not attack this week he is foolish — he has given me infinite advantages & you may be sure I have not neglected the opportunity. Every day adds to the strength of my defenses, to the perfection of the organization & some little to our forces. I have now about 80 field guns (there were but 49 at Bull Run) & by Saturday [August 24] will have 112. There were only some 400 cavalry at Bull Run — I now have about 1200, & by the close of the week will have some 3000. I am gaining rapidly in every way — I can now defend Washington with almost perfect certainty. When I came here it could have been taken with the utmost ease. In a week I ought to be perfectly safe & be prepared to defend all Maryland — in another week to advance our positions.

The men were very enthusiastic & looked well. My old State will come out handsomely. . . .

I appeared today for the first time in full tog, chapeau, epaulettes etc — & flattered myself "we" did it well — at least Barry & Kingsbury told me they were quite jealous about what their wives said. I have been much vexed tonight by sundry troublesome things, & fear that I have been very cross; the only comfort has been your Father's arrival, which is a great relief to me — I like to see that cool steady head near me.

AL copy; copy, McClellan Papers (C-7:63/D-10:72), Library of Congress.

To Mary Ellen McClellan

[Washington, August] 23rd [1861]

. . . Yesterday I rode to Alexandria & reviewed 4 Brigades, that is 17 rgts . . .

Beauregard has missed his chance, & I have gained what I most needed — time! . . .

I do not *live* at all. Merely exist, worked & worried half to death. I have no privacy, no leisure, no relaxation, except in reading your letters & writing to you. We take our meals at Wormley's, a "colored gentleman" who keeps a restaurant just around the corner in "I" Street. I take breakfast there pretty regularly; sometimes have it sent over here. As to dinner, it takes its chances, & generally gets no chance at all, as it is often ten o'clock when I get back from my ride & have nothing to eat all day. . . .

Glad to hear that McCook is looking so well. I will try to have his Brigade ordered on here.[1]

AL copy; copy, McClellan Papers (C-7:63/D-10:72), Library of Congress.

1. Probably either Robert L. McCook or his brother, Alexander McD. McCook. Both remained in the western theater.

To Simon Cameron

Head Qtrs Army of the Potomac
[Washington] Aug 24 1861

Respectfully referred to the Hon Secty of War with the recommendation that the request of Gov Andrews be at once granted.[1] I do not think it possible to employ our Army officers to more advantage than in comdg Divisions, Brigades & Regts of new troops, particularly when it is remembered that we have almost *none* of the old troops at our disposal.

Geo B McClellan
Maj Genl USA comdg

ALS, Records of the Adjutant General's Office, RG 94 (M-619:38), National Archives. *OR*, Ser. 3, 1, pp. 444–45.

1. This endorsement is on a letter dated Aug. 22 that GBM received from Gov. John A. Andrew of Massachusetts. Andrew sought the appointment of a regular army officer, Capt. Thomas J. C. Amory, 7th U. S. Infantry, to command the newly formed 17th Massachusetts. The appointment was made.

To Simon Cameron

Head Quarters, Army of the Potomac,
Sir: Washington, August 25th, 1861

I would respectfully suggest that a circular be sent from your Department to the Governors of the several States from which Volunteers have been accepted, requesting that *no* regiments hereafter to be received, whether raised under the authority of the Governors or of the Department, may be uniformed in gray, that being the color generally worn by the enemy.[1]

Very respectfully, your mo. obt. servt.
Geo B McClellan
Major General U.S.A.

Hon. Simon Cameron
Secretary of War.

LS, Records of the Office of the Secretary of War, RG 107 (M-221:193), National Archives. *OR*, Ser. 3, I, p. 453.

1. GBM had made a similar request, following the western Virginia campaign, of the governor of Indiana. GBM to Oliver P. Morton, July 21, McClellan Papers (A-22:10), Library of Congress.

To Mary Ellen McClellan

[Washington] Aug 25 [1861]

Yesterday started at 9 am — rode over Long Bridge & reviewed Richardson's Brigade — then went 3 miles further & at 12 reviewed Blenker's Brigade at Roach's Mills — then rode some 10 miles looking for a position in which to fight a battle to cover Alexandria should it be attacked. I found one which satisfies me entirely, & where I can surely beat M de Beauregard should he arrive to pay his respects. I then returned to Fort Runyon near the head of Long Bridge & reviewed the 21st N.Y. — after which reviewed 4 Batteries of Light Artillery....

This morning telegram from other side announcing enemy advancing in force. Started off Aides & put the wires at work — when fairly started alarm found false....

Friend Beauregard has allowed the chance to escape him. I have now some 65,000 effective men — will have 75,000 by end of week. Last week he certainly had double our force. I feel sure that the dangerous moment has passed.

AL copy, McClellan Papers (C-7 :63), Library of Congress.

To William S. Harney

Brig Gen W S Harney
US Army
General

Head Quarters Army of the Potomac
Washington Aug 30th 1861

I was much surprised and grieved when I received a few moments since, your telegram of to-night. I had understood from several officers that you desired to enter again upon active service, and that it was your wish to serve in the East rather than in the West.[1]

It is probably my misfortune that chance has placed me in command of the main army of the U.S. — supposing that you wished to serve in the field I embraced the earliest opportunity to offer you the highest position in my gift, and took no little trouble to accomplish this purpose.

I did all this in a manner that I thought to be eminently respectful towards you, and having fully in mind the difference between your experience and mine. I wish to say that I was guided by the kindest possible feelings towards you — and that it was my desire to place you in the position I thought you eminently qualified to fill. You have chosen to pursue a very extraordinary course — your telegraphic message is, to say the least of it, difficult to explain.

I have too much respect for your age and rank to comment upon it — & have only to add that I do not feel that you have any longer any claim upon me as a fellow soldier — though I was this morning very anxious to see you.[2]

Very respectfully your obdt servt,
[George B. McClellan]
Maj. Gen'l U.S.A.

Retained copy, Records of U.S. Army Continental Commands, RG 393 (3964: Army of the Potomac), National Archives.

1. Brig. Gen. Harney, third-ranking Federal general at the beginning of the war, had been relieved of command of the Department of the West on May 29. On Aug. 30 GBM wired him an offer of a division in the Army of the Potomac: "I feel sure that in the present emergency you will waive all considerations of previous rank & will cheerfully give to this army the prestige of your name & presence." Harney replied: "Your telegraph is just received. I consider your conduct to say the least of it exceedingly impertinent." McClellan Papers (A-25:11), Library of Congress. 2. Harney played no further role in the war.

To Mary Ellen McClellan

[Washington] Aug 31 [1861]

Drove out yesterday as far as McCall's camp & today down over the river for several hours — have not yet ventured on horseback again — may try it tomorrow.[1] . . .

Our defenses are becoming very strong now & the army is increasing in efficiency & numbers quite rapidly. I think Beauregard has abandoned the idea of crossing the river above us & I learned today again that my movements had entirely disconcerted their plans & that they did not know what to do. They are suffering much from sickness, & I fancy are not in the best possible condition. If they venture to attack us here they will have an awful time of it — I do not think they will dare to attack — we are now ready for them altho' I would much like another week to complete my arrangements. The news from every quarter tonight is favorable — all goes well.

AL copy, McClellan Papers (C-7:63), Library of Congress.

1. GBM had been ill for nearly a week.

To Simon Cameron

Hon Simon Cameron
Secty of War
Sir

Head Quarters Army of the Potomac
Washington Sept. 6, 1861

I have the honor to suggest the following proposition with the request that the necessary authority be at once given me to carry it out: to organize a force of two brigades of five regiments each of New England men, for the general service, but particularly adapted to coast service. The officers and men to be sufficiently conversant with boat service to manage steamers, sailing vessels, launches, barges, surf boats, floating batteries &c. To charter or buy for the command a sufficient number of propellers, or tugboats for transportation of men and supplies, the machinery of which should be amply protected by timber; the vessels to have permanent experienced officers from the merchant service, but to be manned by details from the command. A naval officer to be attached to the staff of the commanding officer. The flank companies of each regiment to be armed with Dahlgren boat guns, and carbines with water proof cartridges; the other companies to have such arms as I may hereafter designate, to be uniformed and equipped as the Rhode Island regiments are. Launches and floating batteries with timber parapets of sufficient capacity to land or bring into action the entire force.

The entire management and organization of the force to be under my control, and to form an integral part of the Army of the Potomac.

The immediate object of this force is for operations in the inlets of Chesapeake Bay and the Potomac; by enabling me to thus put and land troops at points where they are needed; this force can also be used in conjunction with a naval force operating against points on the sea coast. This Coast Division to be commanded by a general officer of my selection. The regiments to be organized as other land forces. The disbursements for vessels &c to be made by the proper departments of the Army upon the requisitions of the general commanding the Division with my approval.

I think the entire force can be organized in thirty days, and by no means the least of the advantages of this proposition is the fact that it will call into the service a class of men who would not otherwise enter the Army. You will immediately perceive that the object of this force is to follow along the Coast, and up the inlets and rivers, the movement of the Main Army when it advances.[1]

I am very respectfully your obt servant
G B McClellan
Maj Genl Comdg

Copy, McClellan Papers (D-7 :69), Library of Congress. *OR,* Ser. 1, V, pp. 586–87.

1. This proposition eventually took the form of the Burnside expedition to the North Carolina coast in February 1862.

To General Officers, Army of the Potomac

Head Quarters, Army of the Potomac,
Genl Orders No [7] Washington, Sept 6, 1861

The Major Genl Comdg desires & requests that in future there may be a more perfect respect for the Sabbath on the part of his command. We are fighting in a holy cause, & should endeavor to deserve the benign favor of the Creator. Unless in the case of an attack by the enemy, or some other extreme military necessity, it is commended to Comdg officers that all work shall be suspended on the Sabbath, that no unnecessary movements shall be made on that day, that the men shall as far as possible be permitted to rest from their labors, that they shall attend divine service after the customary Sunday morning inspection, & that officers & men shall alike use their influence to ensure the utmost decorum & quiet on that day. The Genl Comdg regards this as no idle form — one day's rest in seven is necessary to men & animals; — more than this — we owe at least this small tribute of respect to the God of Mercy & of Battles whom we believe to be on our side.[1]

Geo B McClellan
Maj Genl Comdg

ADfS, McClellan Papers (A-26:12), Library of Congress. *OR*, Ser. 1, LI, Part 1, pp. 472–73.

1. This concluding passage was altered to read (as printed in the *Official Records*), "More than this, the observance of the holy day of the God of Mercy and of Battles is our sacred duty."

To Abraham Lincoln

Confidential

His Excellency
Abraham Lincoln
Sir:

Head Quarters, Army of the Potomac,
Washington, Sept 6, 1861

I sincerely doubt whether the officer you alluded to is exactly the right man for the particular place, although he is invaluable in the duty to which I have assigned him.[1] You well know, Mr. President, that every man has a peculiar fitness for some particular duty — such is the case in this instance. It would *very* seriously impair the efficiency of this army were he to be removed from it. I would suggest for your consideration the name of Genl E. A. Hitchcock, late of the Army (Chief of Genl Scott's staff during the Mexican war), & now a resident of St Louis as probably eminently adapted for the duty in question. I understand that Genl H. has offered his services to the Govt. I think this will be a happy solution of the difficulty. Genl Scott can tell you all about Genl H.[2]

I am sure you will appreciate my motives in being so anxious to retain the services of such officers as Genls Buell,[3] Stoneman etc whose appointment I asked for with special reference to service in this army — on the efficiency of which depends the fate of the nation.

Very respectfully & truly yours
Geo B McClellan
Maj Genl USA

ALS, Lincoln Papers, Library of Congress.

1. Gen. Scott had proposed Brig. Gen. George Stoneman, GBM's chief of cavalry, as chief of staff to Gen. Frémont in the Western Department. Scott to Lincoln, Sept. 5, Lincoln Papers. 2. The post was not filled, and Frémont was relieved on Nov. 2. Ethan Allen Hitchcock was appointed a major general in Feb. 1862. 3. Brig. Gen. Don Carlos Buell was slated to command a division in the Army of the Potomac.

To Mary Ellen McClellan

[Washington, September] 6th/61

I *must* ride much every day for my army covers much space, & unfortunately I have no one on my staff to whom I can entrust the safety of affairs — it is necessary for me to see as much as I can every day, & more than that to let the men see me & gain confidence in me....

I started out about 3 this afternoon & returned at 10 — rode down to the vicinity of Alexandria & on my return (en route) received a dispatch to the effect that the rebels at 6 1/2 this morning were breaking up their camp at Manassas — whether to attack or retreat I do not yet know.[1] If they attack they will in all probability be beaten, & the attack ought to take place tomorrow. I have made every possible preparation & feel ready for them....

AL copy, McClellan Papers (C-7:63), Library of Congress.

1. Randolph Marcy telegraphed GBM on this date: "I am informed that the enemy at Manassas struck their tents and packed their wagons at seven this morning. I send the informer to meet you...." McClellan Papers (A-26:12).

To Mary Ellen McClellan

[Washington, c. September 7, 1861]

...Do not expect Beauregard to attack — will not be ready to advance (ourselves) before November....

AL copy, McClellan Papers (C-7:63), Library of Congress.

To Simon Cameron

Hon Simon Cameron
Secy of War
Sir.

Head Quarters, Army of the Potomac
Washington, September 8th 1861.

Your note of yesterday is received.[1] I concur in your views as to the exigency of the present occasion. I appreciate and cordially thank you for your offers of support and will avail myself of them to the fullest extent demanded by the interests of the Country.

The force of all our arms within the immediate vicinity of Washington is nearly eighty five thousand men. The effective portion of this force is more than sufficient to resist with certain success any attack on our works upon the other side of the river. By calling in the commands of Genls Banks and Stone it will probably be sufficient to defend the City of Washington, from whatever direction it may be assailed. It is well understood that although the ultimate design of the enemy is to possess himself of the City of Washington, his first efforts will probably be directed towards Baltimore, with the intention of cutting our line of communications and supplies as well as to arouse an insurrection in Maryland. To accomplish this, he will no doubt show a certain portion of his force in front of our positions on the other side of the Potomac, in order to engage our attention there and induce us to leave a large portion of our force for the defence of those positions. He will probably also make demonstrations in the vicinity of Aquia Creek, Mathias Point and Occoquan, in order still further to induce us to disseminate our forces. His main and real movement will doubtless be, to cross the Potomac between Washington and Point of Rocks, probably not far from Seneca Falls, and most likely at more points than one. His hope will be so to engage our attention by the diversions already named, as to enable him to move with a large force direct and unopposed on Baltimore. I see no reason to doubt the possibility of his attempting this with a column of at least one hundred thousand effective troops; if he has only one hundred and thirty thousand under arms, he can make all the diversions I have mentioned with his raw and badly armed troops, leaving one hundred thousand effective men for his real movement. As I am now situated, I can by no possibility bring to bear against this column more than seventy thousand and probably not over sixty thousand effective troops.

In regard to the composition of our Active Army, it must be borne in mind, that the very important arms of Cavalry and Artillery had been almost entirely neglected until I assumed command of this Army, and that consequently the troops of these arms, although greatly increased in numbers, are comparatively raw and inexperienced, most of the Cavalry not being yet armed or equipped.

In making the foregoing estimate of numbers I have reduced the enemy's force below what is regarded by the War Department and other official circles as its real strength, and have taken the reverse course as to our own. Our situation then is simply this. If the Commander in Chief of the enemy follows the simplest dictates of the military art, we must meet him with greatly inferior forces. To render success possible, the Divisions of our Army must be more ably led and commanded, than those of the enemy. The fate of the nation and the success of the cause in which we are engaged, must be mainly decided by the issue of the next battle, to be fought by the Army now under my command. I therefore feel, that the interests of the nation demand that the ablest soldiers in the Service should be on duty with the Army of the Potomac, and that contenting ourselves with remaining on the defensive for the present at all other points, this Army should be reinforced at once, by all the disposable troops that the East and West and North can furnish.[2] To ensure present success, the portions of the Army available for active operations should be at least equal to any force which it may be called to encounter. To accomplish this, it is necessary that it should be at once and very largely reinforced. For ulterior results and to bring this war to a speedy close, it will be necessary that our Active Army shall be much superior to the enemy in numbers, so as to make it reasonably certain, that we shall win every battle which we fight and at the same time be able to cover our communications as we advance. I would also urgently recommend, that the whole of the regular army — old and new — be at once ordered to report here, excepting the mounted batteries actually serving in other departments, and the minimum number of companies of Artillery actually necessary to form the nucleus of the garrisons of our most important permanent works. There should be no delay in carrying out this measure. Scattered as the regulars now are, they are nowhere strong enough to produce a marked effect; united in one body, they will ensure the success of this Army.

In organizing the Army of the Potomac, I have selected General and Staff Officers with distinct reference to their fitness for the important duties that may devolve upon them. Any change or disposition of such officers, without consulting the Commanding General, may fatally impair the efficiency of this Army and the success of its operations. I therefore earnestly request, that in future every General Officer appointed upon my recommendation shall be assigned to this Army; that I shall have full control of the officers and troops within this Department; and that no orders shall be given respecting my command, without my being first consulted. It is evident that I can not otherwise be responsible for the success of our arms. In this connection I respectfully insist that Brigadier Generals Don Carlos Buell and J F Reynolds, both appointed upon my recommendation and for the purpose of serving with me, be at once so assigned.[3]

In obedience to your request I have thus frankly stated "in what manner you can at present aid me in the performance of the great duty committed to my charge," and I shall continue to communicate with you in the same spirit.

Very respectfully Your Obt Servt
Geo B McClellan
Maj Genl Comdg

Retained copy, Records of the Adjutant General's Office, RG 94 (M-619:41), National Archives, *OR,* Ser. 1, V, pp. 587–89.

1. Cameron wrote, on Sept. 7: "It is evident that we are on the eve of a great battle — one that may decide the fate of the country. Its success must depend on you, and the means that may be placed at your disposal. Impressed with this belief, and anxious to aid you with all the powers of my Department, I will be glad if you will inform me how I can do so." McClellan Papers (A-26:12), Library of Congress. 2. In a draft for this letter, GBM was more specific: "In view of these facts I respectfully urge that all the available troops in Ohio, Indiana, Michigan, Wisconsin and at least ten thousand Illinois troops (there being fifteen thousand there unarmed) and all those of the Eastern and Northern states be at once directed to report to me for duty. I beg leave to repeat the opinion I have

heretofore expressed that the Army of the Potomac should number not less than three hundred thousand men in order to insure complete success and an early termination of the war.'' McClellan Papers (A-26:12). 3. Buell would soon command a division, and John F. Reynolds a brigade, in the Army of the Potomac.

To Mary Ellen McClellan

[Washington] Sept [11, 1861]

I started early in the day to be present at the presentation of colors to McCall's division by Gov. Curtin.[1] It was long & fatiguing. I then rode over the Chain Bridge & back by Fort Corcoran. When I returned I had a great deal of tedious work to do & fell asleep in the midst of it. This morning I have had a siege with the Sanitary Committee[2] & don't think I will ride out today. How did you learn that Buckner & Smith have joined the rebel army? I can hardly believe it.[3]

You have no idea how the men brighten up now, when I go among them — I can see every eye glisten. Yesterday they nearly pulled me to pieces in one regt. You never heard such yelling. I did not think the Presdt liked it much. Did I tell you that Lawrence Williams has been promoted & leaves my staff? I do not in the least doubt his loyalty.[4] I enclose a card just received from ''A. Lincoln'' — it shows too much deference to be seen outside.[5]

Copy, McClellan Papers (D-10:72), Library of Congress.

1. This review of the Pennsylvania Reserves, on Sept. 10, was attended by President Lincoln and Secretary of War Cameron as well as Pennsylvania's Gov. Curtin. 2. A committee of the U.S. Sanitary Commission, a civilian group organized to promote the welfare of the troops. 3. Simon B. Buckner and Gustavus W. Smith, close army friends of GBM's, had recently entered the Confederate service. 4. Lawrence A. Williams was appointed major of the 6th U.S. Cavalry on Sept. 7. His Virginia background had caused him to be suspected of disloyalty. 5. Probably an undated note from Lincoln reading: ''May I not now appoint [Isaac I.] Stevens a Brig. Genl? I wish to do it.'' McClellan Papers (A-27:12).

To Winfield Scott [TELEGRAM]

To Gen'l W Scott
President Lincoln and Secy War

Smiths Qrs near Chain Bridge
Sep 11 1861

Gen'l Smith[1] made reconnaissance with two thousand men to Lewinsville, remained several hours & completed examination of the ground. When work was completed & the command had started back the enemy opened fire with shell, killing two men & wounding three.

Griffin's battery silenced the enemy's battery.

Our men then came back in perfect order & excellent spirits. They behaved most admirably under fire.

We shall have no more *Bull Run* affairs.

Geo. B. McClellan
Maj Gen'l USA

Received copy, Records of the Office of the Secretary of War, RG 107 (M-504:9), National Archives. *OR*, Ser. 1, V, pp. 167–68.

1. Brig. Gen. William F. Smith.

To Nathaniel P. Banks

Headquarters Army of the Potomac
Washington Sept. 12, 1861

Genl: After full consultation with the President, Secretaries of State, War &c. it has been decided to effect the operation proposed for the 17th.[1]

Arrangements have been made to have a Govt. steamer at Annapolis to receive the prisoners & carry them to their destination.

Some 4 or 5 of the chief men in the affair are to be arrested to-day.[2] When they meet on the 17th you will please have everything prepared to arrest the whole party, and be sure that none escape.

It is understood that you arranged with Genl Dix & Gov. Seward[3] the *modus operandi*. It has been intimated to me that the meeting might take place on the 14th. Please be prepared. I would be glad to have you advise me frequently of your arrangement in regard to this very important matter.

If it is successfully carried out it will go far toward breaking the backbone of the rebellion. It would probably be well to have a special train quietly prepared to take prisoners to Annapolis.

I leave this exceedingly important affair to your tact & discretion & have but one thing to impress upon you — the absolute necessity of secrecy & success.[4]

With the highest regard, I am my dear Genl. your sincere friend
Geo B. Mc.
Maj Genl U.S.A.

Retained copy, McClellan Papers (B-26:12), Library of Congress. The contents indicate Banks as the addressee.

1. On Sept. 11 Banks was notified by Secretary of War Cameron that it was believed that the Maryland legislature, meeting in Frederick, would secretly pass an ordinance of secession. "If necessary all or any part of the members must be arrested," Cameron wrote. *OR*, Ser. 2, I, pp. 678–79. 2. On orders drafted by GBM, these arrests were carried out in Baltimore under the direction of Allan Pinkerton. *OR*, Ser. 2, I, pp. 678, 688. 3. Maj. Gen. John A. Dix, in command at Baltimore; Secretary of State William H. Seward. 4. Banks carried out arrests on Sept. 17. *OR*, Ser. 2, I, pp. 684–85. See also GBM to Samuel S. Cox, Feb. 12, 1864, *infra*.

To Simon Cameron

Hon Simon Cameron
Secy of War. Head Quarters, Army of the Potomac,
Sir Washington, September 13th, 1861 12 PM.

The movement of the enemy so far as discovered by us and information reaching us from many directions and sources all indicate that the enemy intend at a very early day to advance; even that he has already commenced the movement. It is also more than probable that he has been and is now concentrating all his forces in front of us — and that for this purpose he has called to his aid a large portion of the troops formerly operating in Missouri and on the line of the Mississippi — if this be true it is evident that the decisive battle of the War is soon to be fought in this vicinity — it is therefore clear that we must follow the enemy's example and reinforce the Army of the Potomac by all our available troops. I am told that Genl Fremont has some fifty thousand troops in the vicinity of St Louis; if this is the case the safety of the nation requires that twenty five thousand of them be sent here without one day's delay; and that the orders already given for other troops to be sent from the West and East to this Army should be repeated and steps taken to insure immediate compliance with them. Unless the force of the enemy is greatly overrated and all the information I have received concerning it be erroneous it will be found when we meet in the field, that their Active Army outnumbers ours by nearly two to one.

very respectfully your obt servt
Geo B McClellan
Maj Genl USA

[*enclosure*]

Total present for duty in Army of Potomac	122,072
Deduct Genl Dix at Baltimore	7,323
Present on line of Potomac	114,749
deduct Banks & Stone[1]	21,523
Present in vicinity of Washington	93,226
Deduct T. W. Sherman's rgts[2]	8,000
Present at Washington belonging there	84,226[3]
deduct garrison — say	25,000
Leaving here available for active movements	59,226[4]
Add Banks & Stone if rebels cross only to north	21,523
	80,749[5]

The enemy probably have 170,000!

LS (enclosure AD), Cameron Papers, Library of Congress.

1. The commands of Banks and Stone were stationed on the upper Potomac. 2. Brig. Gen. Thomas W. Sherman's expedition was scheduled to attack Port Royal, S.C. 3. This figure should be 85,226. 4. This figure should be 60,226. 5. This total should be 81,749.

To Nathaniel P. Banks

Maj Genl N P Banks — Head Quarters Army of Potomac
Genl, — Washington Sep 16 1861

Your letter of the 15 to the Secy of State has been sent to me. I think you misapprehend the state of affairs.

By General Order No 15 you are, as the Comdr of a division of Vols. entitled to two Aides & one Asst Adjt. Genl. — the Aides to be selected from the company officers of your division, the Adjt. Genl. to be appointed by the President who will no doubt appoint any one you may select. I do not believe it will be possible to give you one of the Regular Adjts. Genls. You have an officer of Topographical Engrs. & a regular Qr. Mr.

No idea has been entertained by me of taking Bests battery from you. On the contrary I had directed that the suggestion be made to you to fill its ranks by details from the volunteers.

As to the regular Cavalry — I have directed all of it to be concentrated in one mass that the numbers in each company may be increased & that I may have a reliable & efficient body on which to depend in a battle.

For all present duty of Cavalry in the upper Potomac volunteers will suffice as they will have nothing to do but carry messages & act as videttes.

Arms will be sent for them as soon as obtained.

Clothing will soon be ready & will be sent at the earliest possible moment. Shoes, socks, underclothing, drawers etc will be sent you at once.

I will send you 800 rifled arms with the supply of stores etc.

I think General that you forget that the present duty of your division is simply to support the division of Genl Stone in opposing any attempt of the enemy to cross the River & that if such an attempt bids fair to succeed I am ready to move up with my large reinforcements & assume command myself.

So long as the purposes of the enemy are uncertain it is necessary for me to hold the mass of the Army concentrated in such a position that it can readily move wherever required.

It may be well for me to state that these measures are taken in consequence of what passed at our interview of Saturday [September 14][1] & are not brought about by your letter to the Hon Secty of State.

If you will fully communicate your wants direct to me through the proper military channel you will find that they will meet the most prompt attention possible, as I feel the same interest in the efficiency of your division that I do in any other portion of the Army under my command

& fully realize that its advanced position renders it necessary that it should in every respect be efficient.

I am General very truly yours
Geo B McClellan
Maj Genl USA

LS, William Henry Seward Papers, Rush Rhees Library, University of Rochester.

1. GBM had met with a number of his field commanders at Rockville, Md., on Sept. 14.

To Simon Cameron

Hd Qtrs Army of the Potomac
Washington Sept 16 1861

I cannot recommend the appointment of General Cadwallader, I do not think it would promote the interests of the country. If he be appointed from any political considerations — which I do not think are proper to be considered in the present exigency — I would respectfully request that he may not be assigned to duty with the Army under my command.[1]

Very respectfully your obt svt
Geo B McClellan
Maj Genl USA

ALS, Cameron Papers, Library of Congress.

1. This is written on the back of a sheet of letters recommending George Cadwalader, a brigadier general of volunteers in the Mexican War and a prominent Philadelphia Democrat, for appointment as a general officer. The president endorsed his approval, and Cameron's endorsement read: "I will be very glad to act in this matter as General McClellan will advise." Cadwalader was not commissioned a major general until April 1862.

To Mary Ellen McClellan

[Washington, c. September 18, 1861]

. . . The enemy keeps very quiet & do not seem disposed to move just now — the arrest of the Maryland Legislature has no doubt taken them by surprise & defeated their calculations. . . .

AL copy, McClellan Papers (C-7:63), Library of Congress.

To William B. Sprague

Rev W B Sprague
Albany
My dear Sir

Head Quarters Army of the Potomac
Washington Sept 27 1861

Dr Thompson has been kind enough to send me your letter to him of the 14 inst.[1]

I confess that I do not appreciate the importance & interest you attach to the autograph of one whose future is so entirely beyond his own control as mine is.

I do not yet realize or comprehend how I am placed in my present position, & — without affectation — I full realize that the future is not in my hands, but in that of the Diety, to whom we all sincerely pray that he may be pleased to give success to our cause, which to us seems righteous.

While I implicitly believe that the good God can cause the weak to overcome the strong, I still feel that it is our duty to avail ourselves of all the mundane advantages we may happen to possess — therefore I have done all in my power to increase the strength, as well as to improve the discipline & morale of the Army that I have the honor to command — & I am sure that you will be pleased to learn that the Army of the Potomac is rapidly becoming a magnificent Army. It is not only becoming organized, disciplined & well instructed — but, more than all, I feel sure that the moral tone of the men is improving.

We have a splendid body of men — their impulses & feelings are just & honorable — I have not been able to detect among them that profanity & irreligion of which they have been often accused — I think that, as a mass, our Army is composed of the best men who ever formed an army.

I ask only for the delay necessary to make a real army of them — that public opinion shall not urge us to premature action — & I feel confident that, with God's blessing, we have seen our last defeat.

If you could witness the enthusiasm of the troops, their subordination, their confidence & desire to meet the enemy — I am sure that you would agree with me in feeling confident of success.

Thanking you for your kind expressions

I am, my dear sir, truly your friend
Geo B McClellan
Maj Genl USA Comdg

ALS, Houghton Library, Harvard University.

1. In a letter dated Sept. 11, Rev. L. S. Thompson, an acquaintance of GBM's from Cincinnati, asked for a signed document of some sort for his friend Rev. William B. Sprague, "a famous autograph collector." GBM probably misstated the date of Sprague's letter to Thompson. McClellan Papers (B-8:47), Library of Congress.

To Mary Ellen McClellan

[Washington] Sept 27 1861

He (the Presdt) sent a carriage for me to meet him & the Cabinet at Genl Scott's office. Before we got through the General "raised a row with me." I kept cool, looked him square in the face, & *rather* I think I got the advantage of him. In the course of the conversation he very strongly intimated that we were no longer friends. I said nothing, merely looked at him, & bowed assent. He tried to avoid me when we left, but I walked square up to him, looked him fully in the eye, extended my hand & said "Good Morning, General Scott." He had to take my hand, & so we parted. As he threw down the glove & I took it up, I presume war is declared — so be it. I do not fear him. I have one strong point; that I do not care one iota for my present position.[1]

Copy, McClellan Papers (D-10:72), Library of Congress.

1. In what Gideon Welles in his diary recalled as an "unpleasant interview," Gen. Scott made objection that he could get no information on the numbers and condition of the Army of the Potomac, and implied that GBM was instead informing members of the Cabinet. *Diary of Gideon Welles*, ed. Howard K. Beale (New York, 1960), I, pp. 241–42.

To Mary Ellen McClellan

[Washington, September 29, 1861]

A most unhappy thing occurred last night, among some of W. F. Smith's raw rgts. They three times mistook each other for the enemy & fired into each other. At least 6 were killed, & several wounded, besides two horses killed.[1] It is dangerous to make night marches on that account, but Smith's march was delayed by causes I could not foresee, & it was necessary to advance at all hazards. The manoeuvring in advance by our flanks alarmed the enemy whose centre at Munson's & Upton's was much advanced.[2] As soon as our pickets informed me that he had fallen back I rushed forward & seized those very important points. We now hold them in strength & have at once proceeded to fortify them. The moral effect of this advance will be great & it will have a bad influence on the troops of the enemy. They can no longer say that they are flaunting their dirty little flag in my face, & I hope they have taken their last look at Washn . . .

Copy, McClellan Papers (D-10:72), Library of Congress.

1. The *National Intelligencer* for Sept. 30 reported the casualties in Brig. Gen. William F. Smith's division as nine killed and twenty-one wounded. 2. Munson's Hill and Upton's Hill, near Falls Church, Va., were Confederate outposts.

To Simon Cameron

The Hon Simon Cameron
Sect of War — Head Quarters, Army of the Potomac
Sir — Washington, Sept 30th, 1861.

I submit for your perusal a report of a reconnaissance made by Genl J. G. Barnard Corps of Engineers as far as Mathias Point.[1] I beg to say that I fully concur in his views.

I have made all the necessary arrangements to send tonight a strong party (4000 men) under Brig Genl D. C. Buell to cut away the timber on Mathias Point. If this meets your views the expedition will be carried out, unless something turns up during the day to make it necessary to move this command in a different direction.[2] Either this same party or a command to be detached by Genl Franklin will do the same thing at White House Point.[3]

Will you be kind enough to signify your approval or disapproval of the measures I have taken.[4]

I am Sir very Respectfully your Obt Servt.
Geo B McClellan
Maj Genl USA

LS, Cameron Papers, Library of Congress.

1. The report of Sept. 28 by Brig. Gen. John G. Barnard, GBM's chief engineer, dealt with a threatened blockade of the lower Potomac by Confederate batteries. *OR,* Ser. 1, V, pp. 606–608. 2. Neither this expedition nor one scheduled subsequently were carried out, and the Confederate blockade was established without opposition. Gustavus V. Fox testimony, *Report of the Joint Committee on the Conduct of the War,* I (1863), pp. 240–41. 3. Brig. Gen. William B. Franklin; no attack was made on Whitestone Point. 4. Cameron replied on this date: "The measures you have taken . . . meet my entire approval." Cameron Papers.

To Mary Ellen McClellan

[Washington] Oct. 2nd [1861]

. . . Genl Gibson's funeral takes place this morning.[1] I have to go, though I can ill afford the time. . . .

I am becoming daily more disgusted with this administration — perfectly sick of it. If I could with honor resign I would quit the whole concern tomorrow; but so long as I can be of any real use to the nation in its trouble I will make the sacrifice. No one seems able to comprehend my real feeling — that I have no ambitious feelings to gratify, & only want to serve my country in its trouble, & when this weary war is over to return to my wife. . . .

AL copy, McClellan Papers (C-7 :63), Library of Congress.

1. Maj. Gen. George Gibson died Sept. 29.

To Mary Ellen McClellan

[Washington] Oct 6 [1861]

. . . I am quite sure that we will spend some time together after your recovery — preparations are slow & I have an infinite deal to do before my army is really ready to fight a great battle. Washington may now be looked upon as quite safe — they cannot attack in front. My flanks are also safe, or soon will be. Then I shall take my own time to make an army that will be sure of success . . .

Genl Scott did try to send some of my troops to Kentucky, but did not succeed — he has become my inveterate enemy! They shall not take any from here if I can help it. The real fighting must be here — that in Ky will be a mere bagatelle — you need not be at all alarmed by any apprehensions you hear expressed. The trouble with Genl Scott has simply arisen from his eternal jealousy of all who acquire any distinction. I have endeavored to treat him with the utmost respect, but it is of no avail; let him do what he chooses. . . .

I do not expect to fight a battle near Washington — probably none will be fought until I advance, & that I will not do until I am fully ready. My plans depend upon circumstances — so soon as I feel that my army is well organized & well disciplined & strong enough, I will advance & force the rebels to a battle on a field of my own selection. A long time must yet elapse before I can do this, & I expect all the newspapers to abuse me for delay — but I will not mind that.

AL copy, McClellan Papers (C-7:63), Library of Congress.

To Mary Ellen McClellan

[Washington] Oct 10 [1861]

I have just time to write a very few lines before starting out. Yesterday I threw forward our right some four miles, but the enemy were not accommodating enough to give me a chance at them, so I took up a new position there & reinforced it by sending McCall over to that side. I am now going over again to satisfy myself as to the state of affairs, & perhaps edge up another mile or so — according to circumstances. When I returned yesterday after a long ride I was obliged to attend a meeting of the Cabinet at 8 pm. & was bored & annoyed. There are some of the greatest geese in the Cabinet I have ever seen — enough to tax the patience of Job. . . .

AL copy, McClellan Papers (C-7:63), Library of Congress.

To Mary Ellen McClellan

[Washington] Friday [c. October 11, 1861]

Yesterday rode to Chain Bridge, thence to Upton's Hill & did not get back until after dark.

I can't tell you how disgusted I am becoming with these wretched politicians — they are a most dispicable set of men & I think Seward is the meanest of them all — a meddling, officious, incompetent little puppy — he has done more than any other one man to bring all this misery upon the country & is one of the least competent to get us out of the scrape. The Presdt is nothing more than a well meaning baboon. Welles is weaker than the most garrulous old woman you were ever annoyed by. Bates[1] is a good inoffensive old man — so it goes — only keep these complimentary opinions to yourself, or you may get me into premature trouble. I believe I have choked off Seward already — & have strong hopes that he will keep himself to his own business hereafter. . . .

AL copy, McClellan Papers (C-7 :63), Library of Congress.

1. Attorney General Edward Bates.

To Mary Ellen McClellan [TELEGRAM]

Mrs. Geo McClellan [Lewinsville, Va.] Oct 12 1861

I thank God you are safe.[1] I am this moment looking after the enemy.[2] Will be in the saddle all day. Telegraph me frequently. All goes well here.

Geo B McClellan

Received copy, McClellan Papers (B-8 :47), Library of Congress.

1. Mrs. McClellan gave birth to a daughter, Mary (or May, as she would be called), that morning. Mary M. Marcy telegram to GBM, Oct. 12, McClellan Papers (B-8 :47). 2. It was believed (wrongly) that the Confederates were readying an attack.

To Mary Ellen McClellan

[Washington] Oct 13th [1861]

I am firmly determined to force the issue with Genl Scott — a very few days will determine whether his policy or mine is to prevail — *he* is for inaction & the defensive, he endeavors to cripple me in every way — yet I see that the newspapers begin to accuse me of want of energy. He has even complained to the War Dept of my making the advance of the last few days. Hereafter the truth will be shown & he will be displayed in his true light. On the 12th while at Porter's camp I heard that the enemy was advancing in force. Spent last night in W F Smith's camp expecting an attack at daylight.

AL copy, McClellan Papers (C-7 :63), Library of Congress.

To Mary Ellen McClellan

[Washington] Oct. 16 1861

I have just been interrupted here by the Presdt & Secty Seward who had nothing very particular to say, except some stories to tell, which were as usual very pertinent & some pretty good. I never in my life met anyone so full of anecdote as our friend Abraham — he is never at a loss for a story apropos of any known subject or incident.

Copy, McClellan Papers (D-10 :72), Library of Congress.

To Thomas A. Scott [TELEGRAM]

Hon. Thos. A. Scott,
Asst. Sec. of War. Camp Griffin [Lewinsville] Oct. 17, 1861

I gave Genl Sherman all the Regts he asked for.[1] At least two of those originally intended for him and promised to me, have been diverted from me. The Artillery promised me to replace Hamilton's Battery has not been given to me. I will not consent to one other man being detached from this Army for that expedition. I need far more than I now have to save this Country and cannot spare any disciplined Regt.

Instead of diminishing this Army true policy would dictate its immediate increase to a large extent. It is the task of the Army of the Potomac to decide the question at issue. No outside expedition can affect the result. I hope that I will not again be asked to detach any body.[2]

Geo. B. McClellan
Maj. Gen. Comd'g.

Received copy, Records of the Office of the Secretary of War, RG 107 (M-473:97), National Archives. *OR*, Ser. 1, VI, p. 179. Scott was assistant secretary of war.

1. Scott telegraphed GBM on this date to ask for the 79th New York regiment for Brig. Gen. Thomas W. Sherman's expedition against Port Royal. *OR*, Ser. 1, VI, p. 179. 2. The 79th New York was in fact assigned to the Port Royal expedition.

To Gideon Welles

Headquarters, Army of the Potomac,
Sir: [Lewinsville] October 18, 1861.

I have this minute received your letter of this date[1] with reference to the navigation of the Potomac, and in reply have the honor to inform you that a command comprised of infantry and cavalry started this morning for different points below here on the Potomac River, accompanied by a staff officer, with orders to examine the country thoroughly to ascertain whether or not it is necessary to erect heavy batteries for the protection of navigation and to accomplish the object asked for in your letter.

I am, sir, very respectfully, your obedient servant,
Geo. B. McClellan,
Major-General

Hon. Gideon Welles,
Secretary of the Navy.

NOR, Ser. 1, IV, p. 727.

1. In his letter Secretary Welles reported that navigation on the lower Potomac was daily and hourly becoming "more dangerous." If the enemy erected batteries to block navigation, he added, the navy would require the army's help to keep the river open. *NOR*, Ser. 1, IV, pp. 726–27.

To Mary Ellen McClellan

[Lewinsville] Oct 19th [1861]

It seems to be pretty well settled that I will be Comdr in Chf within a week. Genl Scott proposes to retire in favor of Halleck. The Presdt & Cabinet have determined to accept his retirement, but *not* in favor of Halleck.[1] The old —— 's antiquity is wonderful & lasting. . . .

The enemy have fallen back on Manassas — probably to draw me into the old error. I hope to make them abandon Leesburg tomorrow.

AL copy, McClellan Papers (C-7:63), Library of Congress.

1. GBM had learned of the decision taken at a Cabinet meeting on Oct. 18 to accept Gen. Scott's resignation. Scott hoped that Maj. Gen. Henry W. Halleck would be named to succeed him as general-in-chief.

To Charles P. Stone [TELEGRAM]

Brig. Gen. C. P. Stone
Edwards Ferry

McClellan's Headquarters
[Washington] October 21, 1861

Is the force of the enemy now engaged with your troops opposite Harrison's Island large?[1] If so, and you require more support than your division affords, call upon General Banks, who has been directed to respond. What force, in your opinion, would it require to carry Leesburg?[2] Answer at once, as I may require you to take it to-day; and, if so, I will support you on the other side of the river from Darnestown.[3]

Geo. B. McClellan
Major General, Commanding

OR, Ser. 1, LI, Part 1, p. 499.

1. The site of the fighting was Ball's Bluff, on the Virginia shore of the Potomac near Leesburg. 2. GBM informed Stone on Oct. 20 that McCall's division had occupied Dranesville, Va., which he hoped would force the Confederates to give up Leesburg, and added: "Perhaps a slight demonstration on your part would have the effect to move them." A. V. Colburn to Stone, *OR*, Ser. 1, V, p. 32. 3. Stone took this ambiguous statement to mean that additional support was available to him from McCall at Dranesville, across the river from Darnestown, Md., the headquarters of Banks's division. Without notifying Stone, however, GBM had already ordered McCall back to the Washington lines. Stone testimony, *Report of the Joint Committee on the Conduct of the War,* II (1863), pp. 488–89.

To Charles P. Stone [TELEGRAM]

[Washington, October 21, 1861]

Call on Banks for whatever aid you need. Shall I push up a Division or two on other side of river. Take Leesburg.

McClellan
Maj Genl

Genl C P Stone

ALS (telegram sent), Records of the Office of the Secretary of War, RG 107 (M-504:65), National Archives. *OR*, Ser. 1, LI, Part 1, p. 500.

To Charles P. Stone [TELEGRAM]

General C. P. Stone
Edwards Ferry

Hd Qrs Army of the Potomac
[Washington] Oct 21, 1861 [10 P.M.]

Hold your position on the Virginia side the Potomac at all hazzards.[1] General Banks will support you with one Brigade at Harrisons Island and the other two at Seneca. Lander[2] will be with you at daylight.

Geo B McClellan
Maj Genl Comdg

Change the disposition of Genl. Banks Division if you think it necessary so as to send two brigades to Harrisons Island instead of one.

Retained copy, McClellan Papers (A-28:12), Library of Congress. *OR*, Ser.. 1, LI, Part 1, p. 500.

1. Stone had two contingents across the river, at Ball's Bluff and at Edwards Ferry, four miles downstream. The fighting was confined to Ball's Bluff. 2. Brig. Gen. Frederick W. Lander commanded a brigade in Stone's division.

To Nathaniel P. Banks [TELEGRAM]

Head Qrs Army of Potomac
[Washington] Oct 21 [1861] 10.45 p.m.

To General N. P. Banks

Push forward your command as rapidly as possible and put as many men over the river to reinforce Genl. Stone as you can before daylight. Genl. Stone is directed to hold his command on the Virginia side the Potomac at all hazzards and informed that you will support him. You will assume command when you join General Stone.

Geo B McClellan
Maj Genl Comdg

Retained copy, McClellan Papers (A-28:12), Library of Congress.

To Abraham Lincoln [TELEGRAM]

Received Oct 22d 1861
From Poolesville 5.30 pm

To President Lincoln

From what I learn here the affair of yesterday was a more serious disaster than I had supposed. Our loss in prisoners & killed was severe. I leave at once for Edwards Ferry.

G B McClellan
Maj Genl USA

Received copy, Lincoln Papers, Library of Congress.

To Division Commanders, Army of the Potomac [TELEGRAM]

[Poolesville, October 24, 1861]

The affair in front of Leesburg on Monday last [October 21] resulted in serious loss to us, but was a most gallant fight on the part of our men, who displayed the utmost coolness & courage. It has given me the utmost confidence in them.

The disaster was caused by errors committed by the immediate Commander[1] — *not* Genl Stone. I have withdrawn all the troops from the other side, since they went there without my orders & nothing was to be gained by retaining them there.

G B McClellan
Maj Genl

Genls McDowell F. J. Porter W. F. Smith Franklin Buell Heintzelman Blenker McCall

ALS (telegram sent), Records of the Office of the Secretary of War, RG 107 (M-504:66), National Archives. *OR*, Ser. 1, V, p. 626.

1. Col. Edward D. Baker, in command at Ball's Bluff. He was killed in the fighting.

To Mary Ellen McClellan

[Washington] Oct 25 [1861]

. . . How weary I am of all this business — case after case — blunder after blunder — trick upon trick — I am well nigh tired of the world, & were it not for you would be fully so.

That affair of Leesburg on Monday last [October 21] was a terrible butchery — the men fought nobly, but were penned up by a vastly superior force in a place where they had no retreat. The whole thing took place some 40 miles from here without my orders or knowledge — it was entirely unauthorized by me & I am in no manner responsible for it.

The man *directly* to blame for the affair was Col Baker who was killed — he was in command, disregarded entirely the instructions he had received from Stone, & violated all military rules & precautions. Instead of meeting the enemy with double their force & a good ferry behind him, he was outnumbered three to one, & had no means of retreat. Cogswell is a prisoner — he behaved very handsomely. Raymond Lee is also taken.[1] We lost 79 killed, 141 wounded & probably 400 wounded & prisoners — stragglers are constantly coming in however, so that the number of missing is gradually being decreased & may not go beyond 300.[2] I found things in great confusion when I arrived there — Genl Banks having assumed command & having done *nothing*. In a very short time order & confidence were restored. During the night I withdrew everything & everybody to this side of the river — which in truth they should never have left.

AL copy, McClellan Papers (C-7:63), Library of Congress.

1. Cols. Milton Cogswell, 42nd New York, and Raymond Lee, 20th Massachusetts. 2. The final casualty list was 49 killed, 158 wounded, and 714 missing, a total of 921. *OR*, Ser. 1, V, p. 308.

To Mary Ellen McClellan

[Washington] Oct 26 [1861]

For the last 3 hours I have been at Montgomery Blair's talking with Senators Wade, Trumbull & Chandler about war matters[1] — they will make a desperate effort tomorrow to have Genl Scott retired at once. Until that is accomplished I can effect but little good — he is ever in my way & I am sure does not desire effective action — I want to get thro' with the war as rapidly as possible. . . .

I go out soon after bkft to review Porter's Divn, about 5 miles from here.

AL copy, McClellan Papers (C-7:63), Library of Congress.

1. Montgomery Blair was postmaster general. The three senators — Benjamin Wade of Ohio, Lyman Trumbull of Illinois, and Zachariah Chandler of Michigan — were Republican radicals.

To Mary Ellen McClellan

[Washington, Oct. 30, 1861]

. . . You remember my wounded friend Col Kelley, whom we met at Wheeling? He has just done a very pretty thing at Romney — thrashed the enemy severely, taken all their guns etc.[1] I am very glad to hear it. You may have heard from the papers etc of the small row that is going on just now between Genl Scott & myself — in which the vox populi is coming out strongly on my side. The affair had got among the soldiers, & I hear that offs & men all declare that they will fight under no one but "our George," as the scamps have taken it into their heads to call me. I ought to take good care of these men, for I believe they love me from the bottom of their hearts. I can see it in their faces when I pass among them. I presume the Scott war will culminate this week — & as it is now very clear that the people will not permit me to be passed over it seems easy to predict the result.

Whatever it may be I will try to do my duty to the army & to the country — with God's help & a single eye to the right I hope that I may succeed. I appreciate all the difficulties in my path — the impatience of the people, the venality & bad faith of the politicians, the gross neglect that has occurred in obtaining arms clothing etc — & also I feel in my innermost soul how small is my ability in comparison with the gigantic dimensions of the task, & that, even if I had the greatest intellect that was ever given to man, the result remains in the hands of God. I do not feel that I am an instrument worthy of the great task, but I *do* feel that I did not seek it — it was thrust upon me. I was called to it, my previous life seems to have been unwittingly directed to this great end, & I know that God can accomplish the greatest results with the weakest instruments — therein lies my hope. I feel too that, much as we in the North have erred, the rebels have been far worse than we — they seem to have deserted from the great cardinal virtues.

AL copy, McClellan Papers (C-7:63), Library of Congress.

1. Brig. Gen. Benjamin F. Kelley took Romney, in western Virginia, on Oct. 26.

To Abraham Lincoln

Head-Quarters, Army of the Potomac,
Washington, Oct 31, 1861

Your Excellency

May I ask you to do me the favor to see Col Kingsbury Chf of Ordnance of my staff, in regard to the purchase of arms.

The matter is of the first importance & unless you interfere in person I see no reason to expect any more arms.

Please accept my apology for not calling in person as I am very hard at work upon the paper I referred to yesterday.[1]

Very respectfully yr obt svt
Geo B McClellan
Maj Genl

Presdt Lincoln

ALS, Lincoln Papers, Library of Congress.

1. See GBM to Simon Cameron, Oct. 31, *infra*.

To Mary Ellen McClellan

[Washington, October 31, 1861]

. . . I have been at work all day nearly on a letter to the Secy of War in regard to future military operations.

I have not been home for some 3 hrs, but am "concealed" at Stanton's[1] to dodge all enemies in shape of "browsing" Presdt etc. . . .

I have been very busy today writing & am pretty thoroughly tired out. The paper is a very important one — as it is intended to place on record the fact that I have left nothing undone to make this army what it ought to be & that the necessity for delay has not been my fault. I have a set of scamps to deal with — unscrupulous & false — if possible they will throw whatever blame there is on my shoulders, & I do not intend to be sacrificed by such people. It is perfectly sickening to have to work with such people & to see the fate of the nation in such hands. I still trust that the all wise Creator does not intend our destruction, & that in his own good time he will free the nation from the imbeciles who curse it & will restore us to his favor. I know that as a nation we have grieviously sinned, but I trust that there is a limit to his wrath & that ere long we will begin to experience his mercy. But it is terrible to stand by & see the cowardice of the Presdt, the vileness of Seward, & the rascality of Cameron — Welles is an old woman — Bates an old fool. The only man of courage & sense in the Cabinet is Blair, & I do not altogether fancy him!

I cannot guess at my movements for they are not within my own control. I cannot move without more means & I do not possess the power to control those means. The people think me all powerful. Never was there a greater mistake — I am thwarted & deceived by these incapables at every turn. I am doing all I can to get ready to move before winter sets in — but it now begins to look as if we are condemned to a winter of inactivity. If it is so the fault will not be mine — there will be that consolation for my conscience, even if the world at large never knows it. . . .

I have one great comfort in all this — that is that I did not seek this position, as you well know, & I still trust that God will support me & bear me out — he could not have placed me here for nothing. . . .

1 am [November 1]. I have just returned from a ride over the river where I went pretty late, to seek refuge in Fitz Porter's camp. You would have laughed if you could have seen me dodge off. I quietly told the little duke (Chartres)[2] to get our horses saddled, & then we slipped off without escort or orderlies & trotted away for Fitz John's camp where we had a quiet talk over the camp fire.

I saw yesterday Genl Scott's letter asking to be placed on the Retired List & saying nothing about Halleck. The offer was to be accepted last night & they propose to make me at once Commander in Chief of the Army. I cannot get up any especial feeling about it — I feel the vast responsibility it imposes upon [me]. I feel a sense of relief at the prospect of having my own way untrammelled, but I cannot discover in my own heart one symptom of gratified vanity or ambition.

AL copy; copy, McClellan Papers (C-7:63/D-10:72), Library of Congress.

1. Edwin M. Stanton. 2. The Duc de Chartres, of the House of Orléans, one of GBM's aides.

To Simon Cameron

To/ The Secretary of War

Sir [Washington, October 31, 1861][1]

In conformity with a personal understanding with the President yesterday I have the honor to submit the following statement of the condition of the Army under my command and the measures required for the preservation of the government and the suppression of the Rebellion.

It will be remembered that in a memorial I had the honor to address to the President soon after my arrival at Washington, and in my communication addressed to Lieutenant General Scott under date of the 8th of August, in my letter to the President authorizing him at his request to withdraw the letter written by me to General Scott and in my letter of the 8th of September answering your note of enquiry of that date my views on the same subject are frankly & fully expressed.[2] In these several communications[3] I have stated the force I regarded as necessary to enable this Army to advance with a reasonable certainty of success, at the same time leaving the Capital & the line of the Potomac sufficiently guarded not only to secure the retreat of the main army in the event of disaster, but to render it out of the enemy's power to attempt a diversion in Maryland.

So much time has passed & the winter is approaching so rapidly that but two courses are left to the Government, viz: Either to go into winter quarters, or to assume the offensive with forces greatly inferior in numbers to the army I regarded as desirable & necessary.

If political considerations render the first course inadvisable the second alone remains. While I regret that it has not been deemed expedient or perhaps possible to concentrate the resources of the nation in this vicinity (remaining on the defensive elsewhere), keeping the attention & efforts of the Govt fixed upon this as the vital point where the issue of the great contest is to be decided, it may still be that by introducing unity of action & design among the various armies of the land, by determining the course to be pursued by the various commanders under one general plan, transferring from the other armies the superfluous strength not required for the purpose in view, & thus reenforcing this main army whose destiny it is to decide the controversy — we may yet be able to move with a reasonable prospect of success before the winter is fairly upon us. The nation feels, & I share that feeling, that the Army of the Potomac holds the fate of the country in its hands. The stake is so vast, the issue so momentous, & the effect of the next battle will be so important throughout the future as well as the present, that I continue to urge, as I have ever done since I entered upon the command of this army, upon the Govt to devote its energies & its available resources towards increasing the numbers & efficiency of the Army on which its salvation depends.

A statement, carefully prepared by the Chiefs of Engineers & Artillery of this Army, gives as the necessary garrison of this city & its fortifications 33,795 men — say 35,000.

The present garrison of Baltimore & its dependencies is about 10,000 — I have sent the Chief of my Staff to make a careful examination into the condition of these troops & to obtain the information requisite to enable me to decide whether this number can be diminished or the reverse.

At least 5000 men will be required to watch the river hence to Harpers Ferry & its vicinity; probably 8000 to guard the lower Potomac.

As you are aware all the information we have from spies, prisoners &c agrees in showing that the enemy have a force on the Potomac not less than 150 000 strong well drilled & equipped, ably commanded & strongly intrenched.[4] It is plain therefore that to ensure success, or to render it reasonably certain, the active army should not number less than 150,000 efficient troops, with 400 guns, unless some material change occurs in the force in front of us, or an aggregate of present & absent of about 240,000 men should the losses by sickness etc not rise to a higher % than at present.

The requisite force for an advance movement by the Army of the Potomac may be thus estimated.

		guns
Column of active operations	150 000	400
Garrison of the City of Washington	35 000	40
To guard the Potomac to Harpers Ferry	5 000	12
To guard the Lower Potomac	8 000	24
Garrison for Baltimore & Annapolis	10 000	12
Total effective force required	208 000	488[5]

Having stated what I regard as the requisite force to enable this Army to advance, I now proceed to give the actual strength of the Army of the Potomac.

The aggregate strength of the Army of the Potomac by the official report on the morning of the 27th inst. was 168,318 officers & men of all grades & arms; this includes the troops at Baltimore, Annapolis, on the upper & lower Potomac, the sick, absent etc. The force present for *duty* was 147,695. Of this number 4268 Cavalry were completely unarmed, 3163 Cavalry only partially armed, 5979 Infantry unequipped making 13410 unfit for the field (irrespective of those not yet sufficiently drilled), & reducing the effective force to 134,285, & the number disposable for an advance to 76,285.[6] The Infantry regiments are to a considerable extent armed with unserviceable weapons.

Quite a large number of good arms which had been intended for this army were ordered elsewhere, leaving the Army of the Potomac insufficiently & in several cases badly armed.

On the 30th October there were with this army 228 field guns ready for the field, so far as arms & equipment are concerned; — some of the batteries are still quite raw & unfit to go into action.

I have intelligence that 8 New York batteries are en route hither, two others are being formed here; when these are ready for the field I will still (if the N.Y. batteries have 6 guns each) be 112 guns short of the number required for the active column, saying nothing for the present of those necessary for the garrisons and corps on the Potomac, which would make a total deficiency of 200 guns.

I have thus briefly stated our present condition & wants; it remains to suggest the means of supplying the deficiencies.

First: That *all* the cavalry & infantry arms as fast as procured, whether manufactured in this country, or purchased abroad, be sent to this army until it is fully prepared for the field.

Second. That the two companies of the 4th Artillery now understood to be en route from Fort Randall to Fort Monroe be ordered to this army to be mounted at once; also that the companies of 3rd Artillery en route from California be sent here. Had not the order for Smead's battery to come here from Harrisburg, to replace the battery I gave Genl Sherman, been so often countermanded I would again ask for it.[7]

Third. That a more effective regulation may be made authorizing the transfer of men from the Volunteers to the regular batteries, infantry & cavalry; that we may make the best possible use of the invaluable regular "skeletons."

Fourth. I have no official information as to the United States forces elsewhere but from the best information I can obtain from the War Department & other sources I am led to believe that the United States troops

in Western Virginia are about	30 000
in Kentucky about	40 000
in Missouri about	80 000
in Fortress Monroe about	11 000
Total	161 000

Besides these I am informed that more than 100,000 are in process of organization in other Northern & Western States.

I would therefore recommend that not interfering with Kentucky there should be retained in Western Virginia and Missouri sufficient force for defensive purposes & that the surplus troops be sent to the Army of the Potomac to enable it to assume the offensive; that the same course be pursued in respect to Fortress Monroe & that no further outside expeditions be attempted until we have fought the great battle in front of us.[8]

Fifth. That every nerve be strained to hasten the enrollment, & organization & armament of new batteries & regiments of Infantry.

Sixth. That all the battalions now raised for the new rgts of regular Infantry be at once ordered to this Army, & that the old Infty & Cavalry en route from California be ordered to this army immediately on their arrival in N.Y.

I have thus indicated in a general manner the objects to be accomplished & the means by which we may gain our ends.

A vigorous employment of these means will in my opinion enable the Army of the Potomac to assume successfully this season the offensive operations which ever since entering upon the command it has been my anxious desire & diligent effort to prepare for and prosecute.[9]

The advance should not be postponed beyond the 25th Nov if possible to avoid it.

Unity in councils, the utmost vigor & energy in action are indispensable. The entire military field should be grasped as a whole not in detached parts; one plan should be agreed upon & pursued; a single will should direct & carry out these plans.

The great object to be accomplished — the crushing defeat of the rebel army at Manassas — should never for one instant be lost sight of; but all the intellect & means & men of the government poured upon that one point. The loyal States possess ample force to effect all this, & more. The rebels have displayed energy unanimity & wisdom worthy of the most desperate days of the French Revolution — should we do less?

The unity of this nation, the preservation of our institutions are so dear to me that I have willingly sacrificed my private happiness with the single object of doing my duty to my country — when the task is accomplished I shall be glad to return to the obscurity from which events have drawn me. Whatever the determination of the Govt may be I will do the best I can with the Army of the Potomac, & will share its fate whatever may be the task imposed upon it.

Permit me to add that on this occasion as heretofore it has been my aim neither to exaggerate nor underrate the power of the enemy nor fail to express clearly the means by which in my judgment that power may be broken; urging the energy of preparation & action which has ever been my choice, but with the fixed purpose by no act of mine to expose this government to hazard by premature movement.[10]

Requesting that this communication may be laid before the President.

ADf (in part in the handwriting of Edwin M. Stanton), McClellan Papers (A-29:13), Library of Congress. *OR*, Ser. 1, V, pp. 9–11.

1. Although this manuscript is undated, Oct. 31 is the only date that fits its contents and the circumstances of its writing as mentioned in the two previous letters. 2. These letters were dated, respectively, Aug. 2, 8, 10, and Sept. 8, 1861, *supra*. 3. The handwriting to this point is that of Edwin M. Stanton, and elaborated GBM's brief original opening: "In various papers submitted to the Presdt & War Dept I have stated . . . ." 4. This sentence is by Stanton, edited by GBM. The Confederate strength figure of 150,000 came from intelligence reports by Allan Pinkerton dated Oct. 28 and by Brig. Gen. Winfield S. Hancock dated Oct. 30. McClellan Papers (A-29:13). 5. Stanton here put figures from GBM's draft into tabular form. 6. This figure was arrived at by subtracting garrison forces of 58,000, as tabulated above, from the effective force of 134,285. The return of "the 27th inst." is that of Oct. 27, 1861. *McClellan's Own Story*, p. 78. 7. The battery of Capt. John R. Smead, 5th U.S. Artillery, in reference to Gen. Thomas Sherman's Port Royal expedition. 8. This point four by Stanton replaced the following phrasing by GBM: "Fourth. That from 6000

to 10 000 good troops be ordered here from Western Va & that the Army there, as well as that in Missouri be reduced as soon as possible to the defensive, that their surplus troops may be sent here without delay to enable us to assume the offensive. That the same principle be applied to the garrison at Fort Monroe. . . .'' **9.** This paragraph is by Stanton. **10.** Stanton rewrote the concluding paragraph from this GBM draft: ''But I wish to have again on record the fact that I have neither underestimated the force of the enemy nor failed to perceive the means by which that force may be broken. I urge as the only means of salvation the energetic course which has ever been my choice. No time is to be lost — we have lost too much already — every consideration requires us to prepare at once, but not to move until we are ready.''

THREE

GENERAL-IN-CHIEF
NOVEMBER 1, 1861–MARCH 11, 1862

THIS SECTION most clearly portrays George McClellan's wartime role as a military executive in detailing the somewhat more than four months he served as both general-in-chief and commander of the Army of the Potomac. New generals were appointed and new initiatives taken. He named Don Carlos Buell to head the Department of the Ohio and Henry W. Halleck to the Department of Missouri. Operations were started, or continued, and plans made to tighten the blockade of the Confederacy's Atlantic coast and to operate against New Orleans from the Gulf of Mexico. At the same time, General-in-Chief McClellan abandoned any previous thought (or promise) of advancing with the Army of the Potomac before the spring of 1862.

The strategy he evolved in this period, described in his letters of instruction, called for forces in every theater of war to act in concert with the Potomac army, still the grand army of his plans. In the western theater, for example, his goal was to seize the Confederates' only direct east-west railroad to prevent them from bringing reinforcements from the west to oppose his spring offensive. Ambrose Burnside's operations on the North Carolina coast were designed to block other reinforcements from reaching the Rebel army in Virginia by cutting the railroads south of Richmond. Once he defeated the enemy in Virginia, it was McClellan's intention to personally command the movement against New Orleans. As for his Potomac army, he devised a new strategy, a turning movement by way of Chesapeake Bay, that was to outflank the Confederates at Manassas near Washington and force them to battle on ground of his own choosing near Richmond. He spelled out his plan in a long letter to the new secretary of war, Edwin Stanton, on February 3, 1862, the most important strategy paper of his Civil War career.

For much of this time, due to the absence of letters to his wife, McClellan's correspondence offers fewer clues than usual to his thoughts and motives. On October 12, 1861, Ellen McClellan had given birth to a daughter, and early in December she and the child joined the general in Washington. They would remain together until he embarked on the Peninsula campaign, and he only wrote her twice, during brief excursions away from Washington. Among the previously unpublished letters that appear here, however, are several that present unique glimpses of his actions, including one offering the Washington command to General John A. Dix (January 14), one to Secretary Stanton (January 26) outlining a plan for shifting the main Federal offensive to Kentucky, and a letter to Chief of Staff Marcy (January 29) confirming McClellan's unusual scheme for gaining the support of the nation's largest newspaper, the *New York Herald*.

Militarily, the most important Union gains of the period were made in Tennessee, in February 1862, when Forts Henry and Donelson were captured and Nashville occupied. McClellan's dispatches illustrate his efforts to coordinate the movements of the forces under Generals Halleck and Buell, his one major venture in operational direction during his time as general-in-chief.

He was meanwhile becoming increasingly bound by controversy, due primarily to his failure to make good with even the smallest operation of the Army of the Potomac. Throughout the winter of 1861–1862 Washington remained virtually blockaded by Confederate forces on the upper and lower Potomac, leaving the capital linked to the rest of the North by only a single rail line, while General McClellan (so his detractors said) did nothing but hold grand reviews of his army. His one effort to break the blockade, at Harper's Ferry in late February, ended in ignominious failure.

His refusal to inform the president of his plans or to take him into his confidence created further problems, and led to what he regarded as interference in operations by the commander-in-chief. McClellan's correspondence demonstrates his ambiguous attitude toward Lincoln. He might describe the president to his wife as "the *original gorrilla*" and unworthy of his office (November 17), yet on the death of young Willie Lincoln of typhoid fever, write him an affecting and apparently heartfelt letter of condolence (February 22). At the beginning of his tenure as general-in-chief McClellan felt confident in his relations with the administration; at the end of it his alienation was almost complete. "If I can get out of this scrape you will never catch me in the power of such a set again," he wrote his wife on his last day in the post.

General Orders No. 19

Head-Quarters, Army of the U.S.
Genl Order No [19] Washington: Nov 1, 1861

In accordance with Genl Order No [94] from the War Dept, I hereby assume command of the Armies of the United States. In the midst of the difficulties which encompass & divide the nation, hesitation & self distrust may well accompany the assumption of so vast a responsibility; but confiding as I do in the loyalty, discipline & courage of our troops, & believing as I do that Providence will favor ours as the just cause, I cannot doubt that success will crown our efforts & sacrifices.

The Army will unite with me in the feeling of regret that the weight of many years & the effect of increasing infirmities, contracted & intensified in his country's service, should just now remove from our head the great soldier of our nation — the hero who in his youth raised high the reputation of his country on the fields of Canada, which he watered with his blood; who in more mature years proved to the world that American skill & valor could repeat, if not eclipse, the exploits of Cortes in the land of the Montezumas; whose whole life has been directed to the service of his country; whose whole efforts have been directed to uphold our honor at the smallest sacrifice of life; a warrior who scorned the selfish glories of the battle field when his great qualities as a statesman could be employed more profitably for his country; a citizen, who in his declining years has given to the world the most shining instance of loyalty in disregarding all ties of birth, & clinging still to the cause of truth & honor. Such has been the career, such the character of Winfield Scott — whom it has long been the delight of the nation to honor both as a man and a soldier. While we regret his loss there is one thing we cannot regret — the bright example he has left for our emulation.

Let us all hope & pray that his declining years may be passed in peace & happiness, and that they may be cheered by the success of the country & the cause he has fought for & loved so well. Beyond all that — let us do nothing that can cause him to blush for us; let no defeat of the Army he has so long commanded embitter his last years — but let our victories illuminate the close of a life so grand.

Geo B McClellan
Maj Genl Comdg USA

ADS, Simon Gratz Autograph Collection, Historical Society of Pennsylvania. *OR*, Ser. 3, I, pp. 613–14.

To John C. Frémont [TELEGRAM]

Hd Qtrs of the Army Wash.
November 1st 1861

I have assumed command of the Armies of the U.S. Please report by telegram in cipher the numbers, position & condition of your troops. Build a telegraph line as your main column advances.[1] State your situation & intentions — the same with regard to the enemy. Report at least once each day by telegram, & by letter. Send me by letter a full account of the state of affairs in your command.[2]

Geo B McClellan
Maj Genl Comdg USA

Maj Genl J C Fremont
Dept of the West

ALS (telegram sent), McClellan Papers, New-York Historical Society. Maj. Gen. Frémont would be relieved of command of the Western Department on Nov. 2.

1. Frémont had advanced to Springfield, Mo. 2. In this period GBM telegraphed all departmental commanders in a similar vein.

To Mary Ellen McClellan

[Washington] November 2/61 1 1/2 am.

I have been at work with scarcely one minute's rest ever since I arose yesterday morning — nearly 18 hours. I find the "Army" just about as much disorganized as was the Army of the Potomac when I assumed command — everything at sixes & sevens — no system, no order — perfect chaos. I *can* & *will* reduce it to order — I *will* soon have it working smoothly.

AL copy, McClellan Papers (C-7 :63), Library of Congress.

To Mary Ellen McClellan

[Washington] Nov 3 [November 2, 1861]

I have already been up once this morning — that was at 4 o'clock to escort Genl Scott to the depot — it was pitch dark & pouring rain — but with most of the staff & a squadron of cavalry I saw the old man off. He was very polite to me — sent various kind messages to you & the baby — so we parted. The old man said that his sensations were very peculiar in leaving Washn & active life — I can easily understand them — & it may be that at some distant day I too shall totter away from Washn — a worn out soldier, with naught to do but make my peace with God. The sight of this morning was a lesson to me which I hope not soon to forget. I saw there the end of a long, active & ambitious life — the end of the career of the first soldier of his nation — & it was a feeble old man scarce able to walk — hardly any one there to see him off but his successor. Should I ever become vainglorious & ambitious remind me of that spectacle. I pray every night & every morning that I may become neither vain nor ambitious — that I may be neither depressed by disaster nor elated by success — & that I may keep one single object in view, the good of my country. At last I am the "Maj Genl Comdg the Army" — I do not feel in the least elated, for I *do* feel the responsibility of the position — & I feel the need for some support. I trust that God will aid me.

AL copy, McClellan Papers (C-7:63), Library of Congress.

To Mary Ellen McClellan

[Washington] Nov 3 1861

. . . After that I came back & received quite a number of congratulatory calls — then went to dine with Andrew Porter,[1] where I had a very pleasant time; Andrew & his wife; her brother; her sister in law, Seth & myself. After dinner Seth & I went to look at some houses; the only one that suited was one formerly occupied by Senator Gwin & once by Senator Aiken, corner of 19th & I — quite an army neighborhood. I think we can make up our minds to residing in Washington for some years.

. . . In the evening a small deputation of 30 waited on me & presented me with that long talked of sword from the city of Phila — it is certainly a very fine one. I listened meekly to a long set speech & replied in my usual way i.e. in very few words. I then had a collation — I abominate the word, it is so *steamboaty*, in the back parlor. Wormley did himself credit on the occasion & got it up very well indeed. The Presdt came in during the proceedings — after I got through with him I was obliged to undergo a "boring operation" from the ——— who talked me almost to death. . . .

Copy, McClellan Papers (D-10:72), Library of Congress.

1. Brig. Gen. Andrew Porter was provost marshal of the Army of the Potomac.

To Thomas A. Scott

Thos A Scott Esq
Asst Sect of War

Head Quarters of the Army
[Washington] Nov 7th 1861

I respectfully request that no more Cavalry regiments be authorized in any part of the country. Those already authorized cannot be armed and equipped for several months & they will be all that will be required this winter.[1]

Very Respectfully Your Obt Srvt
G B McClellan
Maj Gen Comg USA

Retained copy, Records of the Headquarters of the Army, RG 108 (M-857:6), National Archives. *OR*, Ser. 3, I, p. 622.

1. In a report to Secretary of War Edwin M. Stanton on Jan. 29, 1862, GBM sought to reduce further the number of cavalry regiments through disbanding and consolidation. *OR*, Ser. 3, I, p. 873.

To Don Carlos Buell

Brig. Gen. D. C. Buell
General.

Head Quarters of the Army
Washn. Nov. 7 1861

In giving you instructions for your guidance in command of the Department of the Ohio, I do not design to fetter you.[1] I merely wish to express plainly the general ideas which occur to me in relation to the conduct of operations there. That portion of Kentucky west of the Cumberland River is by its position so closely related to the States of Illinois & Missouri that it has seemed best to attach it to the Department of Missouri. Your operations, then, in Kentucky will be confined to that portion of the State east of the Cumberland River. I trust I need not repeat to you that I regard the importance of the territory committed to your care as second only to that occupied by the army under my immediate command. It is absolutely necessary that we shall hold all the State of Kentucky; not only that, but that the majority of its inhabitants shall be warmly in favor of our cause, it being that which best subserves their interests. It is possible that the conduct of our political affairs in Kentucky is more important than that of our military operations. I certainly cannot overestimate the importance of the former. You will please constantly bear in mind the precise issue for which we are fighting,— that issue is the preservation of the Union and the restoration of the full authority of the General Government over all portions of our territory. We shall most readily suppress this rebellion and restore the authority of the Government by religiously respecting the Constitutional rights of all. I know that I express the feelings and opinion of the President when I say that we are fighting only to preserve the integrity of the Union and the Constitutional authority of the General Government.

The inhabitants of Kentucky may rely upon it that their domestic institutions will in no manner be interfered with, and that they will receive at our hands every Constitutional protection. I have only to repeat that you will in all respects carefully regard the local institutions of the region in which you command, allowing nothing but the dictates of military necessity to cause you to depart from the spirit of these instructions.

So much in regard to political considerations. The military problem would be a simple one could it be entirely separated from political influence;— such is not the case. Were the population among which you are to operate wholly or generally hostile, it is probable that Nashville should be your first & principal objective point. It so happens that a large majority of the inhabitants of Eastern Tennessee are in favor of the Union; it therefore seems proper that you should remain on the defensive on the line from Louisville to Nashville, while you throw the mass of your forces by rapid marches, by Cumberland Gap or Walker's Gap on Knoxville, in order to occupy the railroad at that point, & thus enable the loyal citizens of Eastern Tennessee to rise, while you at the same time cut off the railway communication between Eastern Virginia and the Mississippi. It will be prudent to fortify the Pass before leaving it in your rear.

Copy, McClellan Papers (D-7:69), Library of Congress. *OR*, Ser. 1, IV, p. 342.

1. Buell was officially appointed to command the Department of the Ohio on Nov. 9. This letter of instructions may not have been issued, although possibly it was the basis for conversations between the two men that are mentioned in GBM to Buell, Nov. 12, *infra.* In a later report, Buell mentioned receiving only the Nov. 12 instructions. *OR*, Ser. 1, XVI, Part 1, p. 23.

To Samuel R. Curtis [TELEGRAM]

For Gen Curtis Washington Nov. 7, 1861

Arrest the paymaster alluded to in your telegram of today if you find there are grounds for your suspicions, and if you find it necessary to accomplish the object, arrest Fremont. Seize the funds.[1]

Geo B McClellan
Maj Gen

Retained copy, Records of the Office of the Secretary of War, RG 107 (M-504:9), National Archives. Brig. Gen. Curtis commanded the garrison at St. Louis.

1. Curtis's telegram, not found, apparently dealt with suspected fraud by Gen. Frémont's paymaster. Curtis recovered the pay chest without exercising GBM's authorization to arrest Frémont. *OR*, Ser. 1, III, pp. 566–67.

To Mary Ellen McClellan

[Washington] Nov 7 [1861]

I am glad to learn that my order (the military obituary)[1] changed Genl Scott's feelings entirely, & that he now says I am the best man & the best General that ever existed! Such is human nature — the order *was* a little rhetorical — but I wrote it *at* him — for a particular market! It seems to have accomplished the object.

AL copy, McClellan Papers (C-7:63), Library of Congress.

1. General Orders No. 19, Nov. 1, *supra.*

To William T. Sherman [TELEGRAM]

[Washington, November 8, 1861][1]

Your request will be complied with by sending Genl Buell to take command in Kentucky.[2]

G B McClellan
Maj Genl Comdg USA

Brig Genl W T Sherman
Louisville Ky

ALS (telegram sent), Records of the Office of the Secretary of War, RG 107 (M-5 [illegible], National Archives. Brig. Gen. Sherman headed the Department of the Cumberland, with headquarters at Louisville.

1. Dated from an encoded copy. 2. Sherman had telegraphed GBM on Nov. 4: "The publication of Adjutant General Thomas's report impairs my influence. I insist upon being relieved to your army, my old brigade." McClellan Papers (A-30:13), Library of Congress. Lorenzo Thomas's report of Oct. 21 detailed Secretary of War Cameron's interview with Sherman in Louisville five days earlier. Sherman's pessimistic view of events, and his estimate that 200,000 troops would be needed in the western theater, reached the newspapers through a reporter present at the meeting. *OR*, Ser. 1, IV, pp. 313–14. Sherman was assigned a subordinate position in the Department of Missouri.

To Samuel L. M. Barlow

My dear Samuel L. F. X. Q. Q.[1] Washington Nov 8 1861

Better late than never is a pretty good adage — & never better applied in this instance. I am pretty well fagged out, for it is 1 am, & as I have still more work to do, it suggested itself to me that I would refresh myself by an interlude in the way of a few words to an old friend whom I have treated shamefully. First let me thank you for that "carpet bag" which has been the companion of my woes in Western Va & here — I never shave without thinking of you, & religiously determining to write to you before the close of the day — you can therefore judge how little my promises are to be relied upon! Next let me say that that fine blanket you sent me by Van Vliet[2] (our revered & venerable friend) shall comfort me when we advance. Speaking of an advance let me beg of you not to be impatient (I do not know that you are) — do you & all your friends trust implicitly in me — I am more anxious to advance than any other person in this country — there is no one whose interests would be so much subserved by prompt success as myself.

I feel however that the issue of this struggle is to be decided by the next great battle, & that I owe it to my country & myself not to advance until I have reasonable chances in my favor. The strength of the Army of the Potomac has been vastly overrated in the public opinion. It is now strong enough & well disciplined enough to hold Washington against *any* attack — I care not in what numbers. But, leaving the necessary garrisons here, at Baltimore etc — I cannot yet move in force equal to that which the enemy probably has in my front. We are rapidly increasing in numbers & efficiency. My intention is simply this — I will pay no attention to popular clamor — quietly, & quickly as possible, make this Army strong enough & effective enough to give me a reasonable certainty that, if I am able to handle the form, I will win the first battle. I expect to fight a terrible battle — I know full well the capacity of the Generals opposed to me, for by a singular chance they were once my most intimate friends[3] — tho' we can never meet except as mortal foes hereafter — I appreciate too the courage & discipline of the rebel troops — I believe I know the obstacles in our path. I will first be sure that I have an Army strong enough & well enough instructed to fight with reasonable chances of success — I do not ask for perfect certainty. When I am ready I will move without regard to season or weather — I can overcome *these* difficulties. I think that the interests of the country demand the "festina lente"[4] policy. But of one thing you can rest assured — when the blow *is* struck it will be heavy, rapid, & decisive. Help me to dodge the nigger — we want nothing to do with him. *I* am fighting to preserve the integrity of the Union & the power of the Govt — on no other issue. To gain that end we cannot afford to raise up the negro question — it must be incidental & subsidiary. The Presdt is perfectly honest & is really sound on the nigger question — I will answer for it now that things go right with him. As far as you can, keep the papers & the politicians from running over me — that speech that some rascal made the other day that I did *not dare* to advance, & had said so, was a lie — I have always said, when it was necessary to say anything, that I was not yet strong enough — but, did the public service require it, I would *dare* to advance with 10,000 men & throw my life in the balance.

I have said enough for tonight — & must go back to my work. I hope some time next week to have a review of from 30,000 to 50,000 good troops — can you not bring Madame on to it? If you come alone I can certainly accommodate you in my new house (that once occupied by Bayard Smith, corner of H & 15th) — I *think* I will have my ménage so arranged within two days that I shall be glad to have *her* come too. Telegraph me whether she can accompany you, & I will frankly reply whether my *cook* is ready — I *think* I can have everything ready for it. Do write to me often, & don't get mad if I delay replies — for I am rather busy.

Ever your sincere friend
Geo B McClellan

All this is confidential.

I think that it is now best to resign the Presidency of the O & M — Qu'en pensez vous?[5] Do come on here & see me.

ALS, Barlow Papers, Huntington Library.

1. A jape at Barlow's use of initials. 2. Brig. Gen. Stewart Van Vliet was chief quartermaster of the Army of the Potomac. 3. Joseph E. Johnston, P. G. T. Beauregard, Gustavus W. Smith. 4. "Make haste slowly." 5. "What do you think of that?" GBM was still president of the Eastern Division of the Ohio and Mississippi Railroad. See GBM to Barlow, Jan. 18, 1862, *infra*.

To Elizabeth B. McClellan

My dear Mother Washington Nov 9 [1861] 2 am

I enclose with this a copy of the order assigning me to duty as Comdg Genl of the USA, & my own order on assuming command.[1] I have but one thing more that I desire to send to you in the military line — a report of our next victory!

Nell is improving rapidly — she rode out today. I hope she will be able to join me here in less than a month. I have taken a very good house here, & you *must* come on to see us as soon as your new grand daughter is fairly established. Marcy & Arthur are for the present living with me.[2] Arthur is doing very well & will make an excellent soldier. Let me repeat, my own dear Mother, that just as soon as Nell is well & established here you & Mary[3] *must* come on to pay us a visit — I have plenty of room here for you — & I *rather* think that you will enjoy services etc as much as anyone else.

In great haste your affectionate son
Geo McClellan

My best love to Mary — John, Maria & the *other* grand children.[4]

ALS, McClellan Papers (B-9:47), Library of Congress.

1. General Orders No. 19, Nov. 1, *supra*. 2. Chief of Staff Marcy; GBM's brother Arthur, a captain on his personal staff. 3. GBM's sister. 4. GBM's brother John H. B. McClellan and his family.

To Ulysses S. Grant [TELEGRAM]

Washington [November 10, 1861] 10 am

Inform me fully of the number & condition of your command. Tell me your wants & wishes. Give positions numbers & condition of enemy. Your means of transportation by land and water. Size and armament of gun boats. Communicate fully & often.

G B McClellan
Maj Genl Comdg USA

Brig Genl U.S. Grant
Cairo Illinois

ALS (telegram sent), Nicholson Collection, Huntington Library. *OR*, Ser. 1, LIII, p. 507. Brig. Gen. Grant commanded the Military District of Cairo.

To Henry W. Halleck

Maj. Gen. H. W. Halleck, U.S.A.
Comd'g Dept of Missouri — Head Quarters of the Army
General. — Washington, D.C. Nov. 11 1861

In assigning you to the command of the Department of Missouri,[1] it is probably unnecessary for me to state that I have entrusted to you a duty which requires the utmost tact and decision.

You have not merely the ordinary duties of a Military Commander to perform; but the far more difficult task of reducing chaos to order, of changing probably the majority of the personnel of the Staff of the Department, and of reducing to a point of economy consistent with the interests & necessities of the State, a system of reckless expenditure and fraud perhaps unheard of before in the history of the world.

You will find in your Department many General & Staff officers holding illegal commissions & appointments — not recognized or approved by the President or Secretary of War. You will please at once inform these gentlemen of the nullity of their appointment, and see that no pay or allowances are issued to them until such time as commissions may be authorized by the President or Secretary of War.

If any of them give the slightest trouble, you will at once arrest them and send them, under guard, out of the limits of your Department, informing them that if they return they will be placed in close confinement. You will please examine into the legality of the organization of the troops serving in the Department. When you find any illegal, unusual, or improper organizations you will give to the officers and men an opportunity to enter the legal military establishment under general laws & orders from the War Department; reporting in full to these Head Quarters any officer or organization that may decline.

You will please cause competent and reliable Staff Officers to examine all existing contracts immediately, and suspend all payments upon them until you receive the report in each case. Where there is the slightest doubt as to the propriety of the contract, you will be good enough to refer the matter, with full explanation, to these Head Quarters, stating in each case what would be a fair compensation for the services or materials rendered under the contract. Discontinue at once the reception of material or services under any doubtful contract. Arrest and bring to prompt trial all officers who have in any way violated their duty to the Government. In regard to the political conduct of affairs, you will please labor to impress upon the inhabitants of Missouri and the adjacent States, that we are fighting solely for the integrity of the Union, to uphold the power of our National Government, and to restore to the nation the blessings of peace and good order.

With respect to military operations, it is probable, from the best information in my possession, that the interests of the Government will be best served by fortifying and holding in considerable strength Rolla, Sedalia and other interior points; keeping strong patrols constantly moving from the terminal stations; and concentrating the mass of the troops on or near the Mississippi, prepared for such ulterior operations as the public interests may demand.

I would be glad to have you make as soon as possible a personal inspection of all the important points in your Department, and report the result to me. I cannot too strongly impress upon you the absolute necessity of keeping me constantly advised of the strength, condition, and location of your troops, together with all facts that will enable me to maintain the general direction of the Armies of the United States which it is my purpose to exercise. I trust to you to maintain thorough organization, discipline and economy throughout your Department. Please inform me as soon as possible of everything relating to the gunboats now in process of construction, as well as those completed.

The militia force authorized to be raised by the State of Missouri for its defence, will be under your orders.

I am, General, &c, &c.
Geo. B. McClellan
Maj. Gen. Comd'g U.S.A.

Copy, McClellan Papers (D-7:69), Library of Congress. *OR*, Ser. 1, III, pp. 568–69.

1. Halleck was officially appointed to command the Department of Missouri on Nov. 9, in a reorganization superceding Frémont's Western Department.

To Don Carlos Buell

Brig. Gen. D. C. Buell
Comd'g Dept. of the Ohio. — Head Quarters of the Army
General. — Washn. Nov. 12 1861.

Upon assuming command of the Department, I will be glad to have you make as soon as possible a careful report of the condition & situation of your troops, and of the military and political condition of your command. The main point to which I desire to call your attention is the necessity of entering Eastern Tennessee as soon as it can be done with reasonable chances of success, & I hope that you will with the least possible delay organize a column for that purpose, sufficiently guarding at the same time the main avenues by which the rebels might invade Kentucky. Our conversations on the subject of military operations have been so full, and my confidence in your judgment is so great, that I will not dwell further upon the necessity of keeping me fully informed as to the state of affairs, both military and political, & your movements. In regard to political matters, bear in mind that we are fighting only to preserve the integrity of the Union and to uphold the power of the General Government; as far as military necessity will permit religiously respect the constitutional rights of all. Preserve the strictest discipline, among the troops, and while employing the utmost energy in military movements, be careful so to treat the unarmed inhabitants as to contract, not widen, the breach existing between us & the rebels. I mean by this that it is the desire of the Government to avoid unnecessary irritation by causeless arrests & persecution of individuals. Where there is good reason to believe that persons are actually giving aid, comfort, or information to the enemy, it is of course necessary to arrest them; but I have always found that it is the tendency of subordinates to make vexatious arrests on mere suspicion. You will find it well to direct that no arrest shall be made except by your order or that of your Generals, unless in extraordinary cases, always holding the party making the arrest responsible for the propriety of his course. It should be our constant aim to make it apparent to all that their property, their comfort, and their personal safety will be best preserved by adhering to the cause of the Union. If the military suggestions I have made in this letter prove to have been founded on erroneous data, you are of course perfectly free to change the plan of operations.

Copy, McClellan Papers (D-7:69), Library of Congress. *OR*, Ser. 1, IV, pp. 355–56.

To Mary Ellen McClellan

[Washington] November [c. 14] 61

You will have heard the glorious news from Port Royal — our Navy has covered itself with glory & cannot receive too much credit. The thing was superbly done & the chivalry well thrashed — they left in such haste that officers forgot even to carry away their swords. It was true that but one white man was found in Beaufort — & he drunk![1] The negroes came flocking down to the river with their bundles in their hands ready to take passage! There is something inexpressibly mournful to me in that — those poor helpless ignorant beings — with the wide world & its uncertainties before them — the poor serf with his little bundle ready to launch his boat on the wide ocean of life he knows so little of. When I think of some of the features of slavery I cannot help shuddering. Just think for one moment & try to realize that at the will of some brutal master you & I might be separated for ever! It is horrible, & when the day of adjustment comes I will, if successful, throw my sword into the scale to force an improvement in the condition of those poor blacks. I will never be an abolitionist, but I do think that some of the rights of humanity ought to be secured to the negroes — there should be no power to separate families & the right of marriage ought to be secured to them....

I will not fight for the abolitionists....

Early next week I will have a grand review of some 7 divns — say 70,000 men.

AL copy, McClellan Papers (C-7 :63), Library of Congress.

1. The engagement in Port Royal Sound, S.C., took place on Nov. 7. Beaufort was occupied on Nov. 9. Accounts of these victories appeared in Northern newspapers on Nov. 14.

To Simon Cameron

Sir [Washington, c. November 15, 1861]

The command of the Army has devolved upon me so recently that I feel scarcely able to make this report as full as it ought to be, & must ask your indulgence for confining myself to general suggestions.[1]

It is not in observance of a mere form or custom that I express my deep regret that circumstances made it necessary for Lt Genl Scott to retire from active service. Many years spent in the service of his country had so worn down his body that it was no longer equal to the vigor of his mind or to the devotion of his heart every pulsation of which was for the nation. No one could regret more than he that it was no longer possible to give to our sacred cause the benefit of so great an intellect & such varied experience. When the hour arrives for me, in my turn, to commit to other hands the military destinies of this nation, I shall be well contented if my successor looks upon me or my memory with the filial reverence & affection, the deep professional admiration that I feel for Winfield Scott.

I shall be more than contented if he feels as fully as I do the contrast between the experience & reputation of his predecessor & his own.

I feel in the depths of my heart the magnitude of the task committed to me — yet, so great is my confidence in the justice of our cause, &, more than all, in the great mercy of the Creator — that I entertain no doubt as to the result, & have no doubt that I shall be one of the humble instruments employed in the suppression of this unnatural rebellion, & the maintenance of the Union.

During the eventful period that has elapsed since the last annual Report of the Comdg General the rebellion has culminated in open hostilities; skirmishes & battles have been fought with varied results. The most important affair, that of Bull's Run, was a serious reverse for us — this result was plainly due to the fact that our army, raw, unorganized & inexperienced, attacked the enemy in his chosen position — had the case been reversed we should have been successful. The general result of all the affairs that have occurred has been to show that our troops are fully equal, & I am sure, superior to the rebels in courage. The policy of the rebels has been as a general rule to remain on the defensive & receive our attacks in their positions chosen & fortified beforehand. I am glad to advert to the operations in Western Virginia as proving that even behind intrenchments they can readily be beaten if the clear relative proportion of force is maintained to compensate for the advantages of position. Discipline & instruction — mutual confidence between Generals & soldiers — all are necessary to secure success in attacking an enemy strongly intrenched. There is a vast difference between the degree of preparation required to resist an attack successfully, & that needed to assault intrenched positions.

I need not remind you of the fact that since the day when I assumed command of the Army of the Potomac everything had to be created, still less need I call your attention to the rapidity with which the admirable General Officers under my command have accomplished this task.

I ask at the hands of the Administration & the country confidence & patience. So long as I retain my present position I must claim to be the best judge of the time to strike — I repeat, what you already know, that no one is more anxious to terminate speedily this fratricidal war than I am.

One of our chief difficulties consists in the scarcity of instructed staff officers — a want that can only be supplied from the Military Academy. I would therefore urge that the number of Cadets be immediately increased to 400, that being the number for which accommodations can at once be provided; I would also recommend that measures be taken for the prospective increase of the Corps to from 700 to 800.[2]

In the mean time it is absolutely necessary to make some prompt provision to supply the wants of the Staff Depts — it is simply impossible to improvise staff officers — mere intelligence & courage will not answer — a good military education is absolutely necessary. Two plans suggest themselves to me — the one is to modify temporarily the course of instruction at West Point; the other to establish a temporary school independent of the Alma Mater.

ADf, McClellan Papers (A-32:14), Library of Congress.

1. In a calendar of his papers for this period, GBM described this as a "rough draft of report as Genl in Chief." McClellan Papers (A-106:42). He elected not to submit such a report. 2. In another draft, GBM elaborated on this point: "By appointing some 200 additional Cadets & devoting their time to strictly military studies, probably 100 good Infantry officers could be turned out at the end of two months, the other 100 would be fair Artillery & Cavalry officers at the end of four months, & the places of the first one hundred having been at once supplied there would be another 100 ready at the end of the first four months.... The standard of the preliminary examination for these additional Cadets should be very high, & none admitted less than 18 or 19 years of age while the maximum limit might be 25 years. Either Lts of Volunteers should be eligible to these classes, upon the recommendation of the Genls of Brigades, or there should be established a distinct school for volunteer officers of all grades." A bill to enlarge the cadet enrollment at West Point was defeated in Congress in January 1862.

To Mary Ellen McClellan

[Washington] Nov 17 [1861]

. . . I find that today is not to be a day of rest for me. This unfortunate affair of Mason & Slidell has come up, & I shall be obliged to devote the day to endeavoring to get our Govt to take the only prompt & honorable course of avoiding a war with England & France.[1] Our Govt has done wrong in seizing these men on a neutral ship: — the only manly way of getting out of the scrape is a prompt release with a frank avowal of the wrong — before a demand for reparations is made. After our recent successes we can afford to be generous & frank. It is sickening in the extreme & makes me feel heavy at heart when I see the weakness & unfitness of the poor beings who control the destinies of this great country. How I wish that God had permitted me to live quietly & unknown with you — but his will be done!

I will do my best — try to preserve an honest mind — to do my duty as best I may — & will ever, I hope, continue to pray that He will give me that wisdom courage & truth that are so necessary to me now, & so little of which I possess. The outside world may envy me no doubt — they do not know the weight of care that presses on me. . . .

I will try again to write a few lines before I go to Stanton's to ascertain what the Law of Nations is on this Slidell & Mason seizure. . . .

I am very glad you liked the Scott order.[2] I feared you might think it too rhetorical. . . .

I have just returned from Stanton's where I have had a long discussion on the law points of the M & S capture. I am surprised to find that our Govt is fully justified by all the rules of International Law & all the decisions in the highest courts which bear upon the case — so it matters but little whether the English Govt & people make a fuss about it or not, for as we are manifestly & undoubtedly in the right it makes little difference to us, as we can afford to fight in a just cause. . . .

I went to the White House shortly after tea where I found "the *original gorrilla*,"[3] about as intelligent as ever. What a specimen to be at the head of our affairs now! I then went to the Prince de Joinville's[4] — we went up stairs & had a long confidential talk upon politics etc. He showed me some letters from his mother, & his brothers d'Aumale & Nemours, which gave me important information as to the relations of France & England. He, the Prince, is a noble character — one whom I shall be glad to have you know well — he bears adversity so well & so uncomplainingly. I admire him more than almost any one I have ever met with — he is true as steel — like all deaf men very reflective — says but little & that always to the point. . . .

After I left the Prince's I went to Seward's, where I found the "Gorilla" again, & was of course much edified by his anecdotes — ever apropos, & ever unworthy of one holding his high position. I spent some time there & *almost* organized a little quarrel with that poor little varlet Seward by giving him the information I had received from the Prince (without telling the source) — he said he *knew* it was not so. I said I thought I was right — he again contradicted me & I told him that the future would prove the correctness of my story. It is a terrible dispensation of Providence that so weak & cowardly a thing as that should now control our foreign relations — unhappily the Presdt is not much better, except that he is honest & means well. I suppose our country has richly merited some great punishment, else we should not now have such wretched triflers at the head of affairs. . . .

As I parted from the Presdt on Seward's steps he said that it had been suggested to him that it was no more safe for me than for him to walk out at night without some attendants; I told him that I felt no fear, that no one would take the trouble to interfere with me, on which he deigned to remark that they would probably give more for my scalp at Richmond than for his. . . .

AL copy, McClellan Papers (C-7:63), Library of Congress.

1. On Nov. 8 Confederate envoys James M. Mason and John Slidell were taken from the British mail packet *Trent* off Cuba by Capt. Charles Wilkes of the U.S.S. *San Jacinto*. 2. General Orders, No. 19, Nov. 1, *supra*. 3. An epithet for President Lincoln, which GBM had apparently adopted from Edwin M. Stanton. *McClellan's Own Story*, p. 152. 4. Prince de Joinville, of the exiled House of Orléans, was acting as guardian for his nephews, the Duc de Chartres and the Comte de Paris, pretender to the French throne, who were members of GBM's staff.

To Mary Ellen McClellan

[Washington] Nov 18, 1861

I had Genl Sumner & Raymond[1] to dinner — then the Gorrilla came in. Then I tried to take a nap & was *quietly* interrupted by a deputation of twelve ladies & twelve gentlemen (there was *one* very good looking young female in the party) who came on a visit of ceremony, headed by the Governor of Massachusetts.[2] I was as polite as I know how to be; (cross as could be all the time); said something that was intended to be pleasant to all, (especially to the good looking young female — you had better come on soon at that rate), & was delighted to bow them out. Then I had a long interview with David Porter of the Navy, about future plans & operations;[3] then I had to see Mr Astor[4] of N.Y. & appointed him a vol. aide; then I had a long confab with the inevitable McDowell, who left just before I commenced this scrawl & during which interview your Papa as well as Arthur skulked off ignominiously leaving me to bear the brunt of the bathery.

Copy, McClellan Papers (D-10:72), Library of Congress.

1. Brig. Gen. Edwin V. Sumner; Capt. Edward A. Raymond, of GBM's staff. 2. Gov. John A. Andrew. 3. Comdr. David D. Porter. Their discussion concerned an operation against New Orleans. 4. John Jacob Astor, Jr.

To Mary Ellen McClellan

[Washington] Wednesday [November 20, 1861] 8 1/2 pm.

The Grand Review went off splendidly — there were nearly 65,000 men on the ground — not a mistake made, not a hitch. I never saw so large a Review in Europe so well done — I was completely satisfied & delighted beyond expression.

AL copy, McClellan Papers (C-7:63), Library of Congress.

To Mary Ellen McClellan

[Washington] Nov. 21 [1861]

. . . Herr Hermann, "a great Magician" volunteered to give us a private entertainment, so I invited all the staff etc [to] it. The most striking feature of the performance was that the Magician asked the Presdt for his handkerchief — upon which that dignitary replied promptly "You've got me now, I ain't got any"!!!!

AL copy, McClellan Papers (C-7:63), Library of Congress.

To Charles P. Stone [TELEGRAM]

[Washington] Nov 29 [1861]

Please inform Genl Hill[1] that I have no wish to protect robbers & that I will cordially unite in any proper effort to repress marauding. If he will turn these men over to me with the evidence necessary to convict them before a commission they shall be tried & punished in good faith.

Say to him that I have no plea to interpose for men who have disobeyed my orders by stealing, except to recommend the utmost care and reflection in the infliction of a punishment which, although just, may lead to reprisals beyond my power to control & may lend to this contest a degree of ferocity which I desire to avoid.[2]

G B McClellan
Maj Genl Comdg USA

Brig Genl C P Stone
Comdg at Poolesville

ALS (telegram sent), Records of the Office of the Secretary of War, RG 107 (M-504:9), National Archives. *OR*, Ser. 1, V, p. 669.

1. Brig. Gen. D. H. Hill, CSA, stationed at Leesburg, Va. 2. At issue were certain Federal prisoners in Hill's hands. On Dec. 16 Hill received instructions in the matter from Gen.

Joseph E. Johnston: "Let General Hill try and hang our own traitors for murder, robbery, and treason, but the Northern soldiers cannot be dealt with thus summarily." *OR*, Ser. 1, V, pp. 999–1000.

To the Children's Aid Association of Trenton

My dear Children Washington Nov 29 1861

Your very welcome present & your still kinder note reached me today.[1] I feel encouraged & strengthened in the performance of the task imposed upon me when even the children of the land wish me "God speed." Your mothers have taught you that no work can succeed without God's blessing, and our Saviour himself has taught us all not to dispair, but to cherish the purity & innocence of childhood. Of all the unmerited tributes of praise it has fallen to my lot to receive, I assure you, my dear children, your simple prayer has touched me most — I am sure that it comes from your hearts.

I hope & pray that you may preserve through life your present innocence, & that when in years to come you hear that I have passed to another world, you may still be able to wish me "God speed" from the depths of your hearts.

I will do my best ever to deserve your prayers & blessing; do *your* best, dear children, to preserve the right to pray for a soldier who has devoted his honor & life to his country in its greatest need.

I am, dear little ones, your sincere friend
Geo B McClellan
Maj Genl Comdg USA

ALS retained copy, McClellan Papers (B-9:47), Library of Congress.

1. The undated letter, signed with seventeen names, reads: "Will you please accept this small offering from the 'Children's Aid Association of Trenton'? We wish you 'God speed.' " The offering has not been found. McClellan Papers (B-13:49).

To Don Carlos Buell

Brig. Genl. D. C. Buell,
Louisville Washington, Monday night.
My dear Buell: [December 2, 1861]

Your welcome letter of the 27th, reached me this evening.[1] I have just telegraphed you expressing my satisfaction at its contents. I now feel sure I have a "lieutenant" in whom I can fully rely. Your views are right. You have seized the true strategic base and from Lebanon can move where you will. Keep up the hearts of the Tennesseans, make them feel that far from any intention of deserting them, that all will be done to sustain them. Be sure to maintain their ardor, for it will avail you much in the future. I am not as a general rule, at all disposed to scatter troops. I believe in attacks by concentrated masses, but it seems to me, with the little local knowledge I possess, that you *might* attempt two movements, one on Eastern Tenn., say with 15,000 men, and a strong attack on Nashville as you propose with say 50,000 men.

I think we owe it to our Union friends in Eastern Tenn. to protect them at all hazards. First secure that, *then*, if you possess the means, carry Nashville.

If I can ever get the account of the small arms in our possession I can tell you what you may expect, but with the present Chief of Ordnance[2] I scarcely hope for so simple a result. You can count on one thing, viz: that you shall have all I can give you. You have already been informed that 12 regiments have been ordered to you from W. Va. I have also ordered thence to you one regular and one *excellent* volunteer battery. These with the Randall companies will give you 5 batteries equivalent to regulars. Give each of these Captains 3 other batteries and you will soon have your light artillery in good order. I am informed that large supplies of cavalry arms will arrive this week. Telegraph me what you need and I will *try* to supply you. Give me by telegraph and letter the statement of your command by regiments and batteries as soon as possible. I have telegraphed to-day to Halleck for information as to his gun-boats. You shall have a sufficient number of them to perform the operations you suggest. I will place C. F. Smith[3] under your orders and replace his command by other troops.

Inform me some little time before you are ready to move, so that we may move simultaneously. I have also other heavy blows to strike at the same time. I doubt whether all the movements can be arranged so that the grand blows shall be struck in less than a month or six weeks from the present time.

Make the best use of your time in organizing and drilling your command. Unless circumstances render it necessary do not strike until I too am ready. Should I be delayed I will not ask you to wait for me. I will at once take the necessary steps to carry out your views as to the rivers.

In haste truly yours,
Geo B McClellan
Maj Genl

ALS (typewritten copy), Buell Papers, Woodson Research Center, Rice University Library. *OR*, Ser. 1, VII, pp. 457–58 (misdated).

1. Buell's letter described the condition and position of his command, and proposed three possible courses of action: an advance either on Nashville or on East Tennessee, or a simultaneous advance on both. In conjunction with whatever plan was selected he called for two "flotilla columns" to move up the Tennessee and Cumberland rivers. *OR*, Ser. 1, VII, pp. 450–52. 2. Brig. Gen. James W. Ripley. 3. Brig Gen. Charles F. Smith.

To Don Carlos Buell

Brig. Genl. D. C. Buell, Louisville
My dear Buell:

Washington,
December 3d, 1861.

I enclose two letters which were referred to me by the Presdt. and were intended for your eye.[1] I do so feeling sure that you sympathize with me in my *intense* regard for the noble Union men of Eastern Tenn., that you will overlook all mere matters of form, and that you will devote all your energies towards the salvation of men so eminently deserving our protection. I understand your movements and fully concur in their propriety, but I must still urge the occupation of Eastern Tenn. as a *duty* we owe to our gallant friends there who have not hesitated to espouse our cause.

Please send there with the least possible delay troops enough to protect these men. I still feel sure that the best strategical move in this case will be that dictated by the simple feelings of humanity. We *must* preserve these noble fellows from harm. Everything urges us to do that — faith, interest and loyalty. For the sake of these Eastern Tennesseans who have taken part with us I would gladly sacrifice mere military advantages. They deserve our protection, and at all hazards they must have it. I know that your nature is noble enough to forget any slurs they may cast upon you. Protect the true men and you have everything to look forward to. In no event allow them to be crushed out.

I have ordered one regular and one *excellent* volunteer battery to join you. To-day I ordered 10,000 excellent arms to be sent to you at Louisville. I have directed all your requisitions to be filled at once. You may fully rely on my full support in the movement I have so much at heart — the liberation of Eastern Tennessee.

Write to me often, fully and confidentially. If you gain and retain possession of Eastern Tennessee you will have won brighter laurels than any I hope to gain.

With the utmost confidence and firmest friendship, I am truly yours,

Geo B McClellan
Maj Genl Comdg USA

P.S. This letter has been dictated by no doubt as to your movements and intentions, but only by my feelings for the Union men of Eastern Tenn.

McC

ALS (typewritten copy), Buell Papers, Woodson Research Center, Rice University Library. *OR*, Ser. 1, VII, p. 468.

1. These letters, dated Nov. 21 and 25, were written to Tennessee congressman Horace Maynard by Lt. Samuel P. Carter, USN, detailed to the War Department to recruit Tennessee troops for the Union. Carter called for an immediate advance into East Tennessee.

Both letters bore the president's endorsement, "Please read and consider this letter." *OR*, Ser. 1, VII, pp. 468–69.

To Don Carlos Buell

Private Washington —

My dear Buell [December] 5th [1861][1]

I have only time before the mail closes to acknowledge yours of the 30th.[2] Give me at once in detail your views as to the number & armament of gun boats necessary for the water movement — the necessary land forces etc. Would not C F Smith be a good man to command that part of the expedition. When should they move?[3]

Pray do not abandon the Pikeville region. I consider it important to hold that line — your supplies can go by water to Prestonburg. I will also reinforce the Guyandotte region at once.[4] Let me again urge the necessity of sending something into East Tenna as promptly as possible — our friends there have thrown their all into the scale & we must not desert them. I tell the East Tenna men here to rest quiet — that you will take care of them & will never desert them. I ordered today two fully armed regts of cavalry to join you from Dennison[5] — will send you some more inftry from the North West in a day or two.

I will try to write more fully tonight — by all means hold Somerset & London — better entrench both — still better the crossing of the river nearest those points.

In haste truly your friend
McClellan

Genl D. C. Buell

ALS, Buell Papers, Woodson Research Center, Rice University Library. *OR*, Ser. 1, VII, pp. 473–74, 583.

1. As printed in the *Official Records* this letter is tentatively dated Dec. 5, 1861, but a note is inserted changing the date to Feb. 5, 1862. The Dec. 5 date is correct. 2. Buell's letter of Nov. 30 called for "some concert between Halleck's action and mine" and stressed the importance of the advance up the Tennessee and Cumberland rivers that he had proposed. McClellan Papers (B-9:47), Library of Congress. 3. Buell replied on Dec. 10 that 10,000 men would be needed for each of the river movements, but that more information was needed on the enemy posts at Forts Henry and Donelson. He expressed reservations about Charles F. Smith as commander. *OR*, Ser. 1, VII, pp. 487–88. 4. GBM refers here to eastern Kentucky and western Virginia. 5. Camp Dennison, near Cincinnati.

To Henry W. Halleck [TELEGRAM]

For Gen Halleck
St Louis Washington Dec 5, 1861

Please inform me at once the exact number, condition, and armament of the gunboats. If necessary, to complete the crews, detail an unarmed regiment of good men for the purpose. How many troops can you spare from Missouri for an important operation. On receipt of your reply by telegraph I will give you details.[1]

Geo B Mc Clellan
Maj Gen

Retained copy, Records of the Office of the Secretary of War, RG 107 (M-504 :9), National Archives.

1. Halleck telegraphed on Dec. 6 that his forces were untrained and disorganized. ''We are not prepared for any important expedition out of the State; it would imperil the safety of Missouri. Wait till we are ready.'' *OR*, Ser. 1, VIII, p. 408.

To Simon Cameron

Hon Simon Cameron
Secty of War Hd Qtrs of the Army
Sir Washington Dec 9 1861

I have the honor to enclose herewith a copy of the N.Y. Times of Dec 4 1861, containing as you will see a map of our works on the other side of the Potomac, & a statement of the composition of the Divisions in that same locality.

This is clearly giving aid comfort & information to the enemy, & is evidently a case of treasonable action as clear [as] any that can be found. You will remember that this same paper did its best to aid the rebels by publishing full details as to Genl Sherman's expedition before it sailed.[1] I have therefore to represent that the interests of our arms require the suppression of this treasonable sheet, & urgently recommend that the necessary steps to suppress the paper may be taken at once.[2]

Very respectfully yr obdt svt
Geo B McClellan
Maj Genl Comdg USA

ALS retained copy, Records of the Headquarters of the Army, RG 108 (M-857 :6), National Archives.

1. The *New York Times* had published the composition — but not the target — of the Port Royal expedition. J. Cutler Andrews, *The North Reports the Civil War* (Pittsburgh, 1955), p. 143. 2. The *Times* was not suppressed. Editor Henry J. Raymond wrote Cameron on Dec. 13 that both the map and the divisional listing were taken from information released to the press by army headquarters. Raymond Papers, Rare Books and Manuscripts Division, New York Public Library.

To Abraham Lincoln

Confidential

Your Excellency | Washington Dec 10 [1861]

I enclose the paper you left with me — filled as you requested. In arriving at the numbers given I have left the minimum number in garrison & observation.[1]

Information received recently leads me to believe that the enemy could meet us in front with equal forces *nearly* — & I have now my mind actively turned towards another plan of campaign that I do not think at all anticipated by the enemy nor by many of our own people.

Very respectfully your obdt svt
Geo B McClellan
Maj Genl

His Ex the President

ALS, Lincoln Papers, Library of Congress. *OR*, Ser. 1, XI, Part 3, p. 6.

1. Lincoln's memorandum, written about Dec. 1, proposed an immediate advance by the Army of the Potomac to the area of the Occoquan River, to cut the railroad supply line of the Confederate Army at Manassas Junction. In annotating the memorandum, in response to the president's questions, GBM estimated that the movement might take place between Dec. 15 and Dec. 25, with forces totaling 104,000 men. *The Collected Works of Abraham Lincoln,* ed. Roy P. Basler (New Brunswick, N.J., 1953–55), V, pp. 34–35.

To Henry W. Halleck

Maj. Gen. H. W. Halleck,
Commanding Department of Missouri:
General:

Headquarters of the Army
Washington,
December 10, 1861.

Yours of the 6th has this moment reached me.[1] I am obliged to you for the spirit of frankness in which it is written. Let me begin by replying to the last part of your letter.

You will probably remember that soon after General Hunter assumed command of the department he ordered two divisions from Western Missouri to Saint Louis, regarding them as available for other service.[2] My dispatch was predicated on that, and if you had informed me that you had any available troops I intended to propose to you a movement in concert with Buell. His project, though very important, must either be deferred or be carried out in some other way.[3] I have no intention of stripping you of troops when you cannot spare them. I to-day directed General Thomas to telegraph to you that Major Ketchum[4] might remain with you and that I would recommend him as a brigadier-general. I had already determined to try to secure his appointment. I do not understand your statement that four or five of the regular officers you now have are ordered away, but will look into it in the morning. There is some mistake about it, unless you allude to the paroled officers, who cannot under their parole be of any service to you. You are also misinformed as to the number of regular officers on my personal staff. I have two regular aides, instead of the authorized number of three, and one chief of staff; the others apparently are my personal staff, and are really doing their appropriate duties in the line and their respective corps. Even my personal aides are on duty constantly as inspectors.

I am sorry to learn the very disorganized condition of the troops. I appreciate the difficulty of the task before you, and you may rest assured that I will support you to the full extent of my ability. Do not hesitate to use force with the refractory. Can you yet form any idea of the time necessary to prepare an expedition against Columbus or one up the Cumberland and Tennessee rivers, in connection with Buell's movements? I shall send troops to Hunter,[5] to enable him to move into the Indian Territory west of Arkansas and upon Northern Texas. That movement should relieve you very materially. It will require some little time to prepare Hunter, but when he moves you might act in concert with him.

In haste, very truly, yours,
Geo. B. McClellan,
Major-General, Commanding
U.S. Army

OR, Ser. 1, VIII, p. 419.

1. Halleck's letter of Dec. 6 detailed the fraud, corruption, and disorganization of the command he inherited from Frémont, and his lack of troops and instructed officers. *OR*, Ser. 1, VIII, pp. 408–410. 2. Maj. Gen. David Hunter had temporarily commanded the Western Department in place of Frémont. 3. See GBM to Buell, Dec. 2, *supra*. 4. Maj. W. Scott Ketchum, inspector general, Department of Missouri. 5. See GBM to Hunter, Dec. 11, *supra*.

To David Hunter

Unofficial Head Quarters of the Army
General, Washington Decem 11, 1861

Your telegram to General Thomas surprised me exceedingly.[1] Realizing as I do the very trying nature of the circumstances in which you are placed, I have attributed it to momentary irritation which your cooler judgment will at least lead you to regard as unnecessary.

In regard to placing General Halleck in Command of the Department of Missouri, that step was taken from the evident necessity of placing some one there who was in no manner connected, for or against, with the unfortunate state of affairs previously existing in that Department. Immediately after you were assigned to your present Department I requested the Adjutant General to inform you that it was deemed expedient to organize an expedition under your Command to secure the Indian Territory west of Arkansas, as well as to make a descent upon Northern Texas, in connection with one to strike at Western Texas from the Gulf. The General was to invite your prompt attention to this subject, and to ask you to indicate the necessary force and means for the undertaking.

I would again call your attention to this very important subject stating the necessary force shall be placed at your disposal. Three regiments of Wisconsin Infantry have been ordered to report to you, also a battery and two Companies of Cavalry from Minnesota. This is intended only as a commencement and will be followed up by other troops as rapidly as your wants are known and circumstances will permit.

Requesting your early attention to this subject,[2]

Very respectfully yr obt svt
Geo B McClellan
Maj Genl Comdg

LS, Miscellaneous Collections, Huntington Library. *OR*, Ser. 1, VIII, pp. 428–29. Maj. Gen. Hunter was named to the Department of Kansas on Nov. 20.

1. In his dispatch of this date to Lorenzo Thomas, Hunter stated that he was outnumbered ten to one and would be fortunate to keep possession of Kansas. He added that dividing the Western Department into the departments of Missouri and Kansas "was not for the good of the service." *OR*, Ser. 1, VIII, p. 428. 2. Hunter replied on Dec. 19 that at least 20,000 additional troops and a substantial wagon train would be required. *OR*, Ser. 1, VIII, pp. 450–51. See GBM to Edwin M. Stanton, c. Jan. 25, 1862, *infra*.

To Abraham Lincoln

[Washington, c. December 18, 1861]

I would recommend that fifty of the "Coffee Mill" guns be furnished at 20% advance on cost price, which cost may be ascertained by competent Ordnance officers — I think $1200 entirely too high.[1]

Geo. B. McClellan
Maj. Genl. Comg.

Copy, Lincoln Papers, Library of Congress.

1. This copy is in Lincoln's handwriting. GBM apparently wrote the note to the president in response to a letter sent him on Dec. 12 by J. D. Mills, the representative of the maker of this early machine gun. On Dec. 19 Lincoln sent GBM's recommendation to Gen. Ripley, the army's chief of ordnance, with his endorsement: "Let the fifty guns be ordered on the terms above recommended by Gen. McClellan & not otherwise." *Collected Works of Lincoln*, V, p. 75; *Supplement*, p. 115.

To John A. Andrew

His Excellency John A. Andrew,
Governor of Massachusetts
Sir:

Headquarters Army of the Potomac
Washington, December 20, 1861.

A letter addressed to Lieutenant-Colonel Palfrey, commanding Twentieth Regiment Massachusetts Volunteers, signed by Thomas Drew, assistant military secretary, and purporting to have been written by your excellency's authority has just been brought to my notice.[1] In this letter Lieutenant-Colonel Palfrey is directed to convey censure and reprimand to an officer of his regiment for acts performed in the line of his military duty. If the officer referred to had been guilty of any infraction of military law or regulation the law itself points out the method and manner for its own vindication and the channel through which the punishment shall come. Any departure from this rule strikes immediately at the root of all discipline and subordination. The volunteer regiments from the different States of the Union when accepted and mustered into the service of the United States became a portion of the Federal Army and are as entirely removed from the authority of the governors of the several States as are the troops of the regular regiments. As discipline in the service can only be maintained by the strictest observance of military subordination nothing could be more detrimental than that any interference should be allowed outside the constituted authorities.[2]

Trusting that these considerations will commend themselves to your excellency's judgment,

I remain, very respectfully, your obedient servant,

Retained copy, Records of U.S. Army Continental Commands, RG 393 (3964: Army of the Potomac), National Archives. *OR*, Ser. 2, I, pp. 790–91.

1. This letter, dated Dec. 9 and addressed to Lt. Col. Francis W. Palfrey, charged one of Palfrey's officers with "discreditable conduct" in returning fugitive slaves to their Maryland owners "without any observance of even the forms of law, either civil or military." The letter was forwarded to GBM by Charles P. Stone, Palfrey's division commander, who termed it an "unwarranted and dangerous interference" with his command. *OR*, Ser. 2, I, pp. 786–88. 2. While Gov. Andrew and GBM continued to argue the issue of state versus federal authority over volunteer troops (*OR*, Ser. 2, I, pp. 791–93, 796–97), public debate centered on Stone's handling of fugitive slaves, a debate intensified by the investigation of the Joint Committee on the Conduct of the War into Stone's part in the Ball's Bluff defeat.

To Henry W. Halleck

Maj. Gen. H. W. Halleck,
Commanding Department of Missouri:
General:

Headquarters of the Army
Washington, January 3, 1862.

It is of the greatest importance that the rebel troops in Western Kentucky be prevented from moving to the support of the force in front of

General Buell. To accomplish this an expedition should be sent up the Cumberland River, to act in concert with General Buell's command of sufficient strength to defeat any force that may be brought against it. The gunboats should be supported by at least one and perhaps two divisions of your best infantry, taken from Paducah and other points from which they can best be spared. At the same time such a demonstration should be made on Columbus as will prevent the removal of any troops from that place; and, if a sufficient number have already been withdrawn, the place should be taken. It may be well also to make a feint on the Tennessee River, with a command sufficient to prevent disaster under any circumstances.

As our success in Kentucky depends in a great measure on our preventing re-enforcements from joining Buckner and Johnston,[1] not a moment's time should be lost in preparing these expeditions.

I desire that you give me at once your views in full as to the best method of accomplishing our object, at the same time stating the nature and strength of the force that you can use for the purpose and the time necessary to prepare.

Very respectfully,
Geo. B. McClellan
Major-General, Commanding.

OR, Ser. 1, VII, pp. 527–28.

1. Brig. Gen. Buckner in Kentucky served under Gen. Albert Sidney Johnston, Confederate commander in the western theater.

To Don Carlos Buell

Confidential
Brig. Gen. D. C. Buell,
Louisville, Ky.:
My dear General: Washington, Monday, January 6, 1862.

You will have learned ere this that Colonel Cross has been ordered to relieve Colonel Swords,[1] and that two or three active young quartermasters from the Regular Army have been ordered to report to you. Two hundred wagons from Philadelphia have been ordered to you, and Meigs[2] is stirring up the country generally to procure means of transportation for you. There are few things I have more at heart than the prompt movement of a strong column into Eastern Tennessee. The political consequences of the delay of this movement will be much more serious than you seem to anticipate. If relief is not soon afforded those people we shall lose them entirely, and with them the power of inflicting the most severe blow upon the secession cause.

I was extremely sorry to learn from your telegram to the President that you had *from the beginning attached little or no importance* to a movement in East Tennessee.[3] I had not so understood your views, and it develops a radical difference between your views and my own, which I deeply regret.

My own general plans for the prosecution of the war make the speedy occupation of East Tennessee and its lines of railway matters of absolute necessity. Bowling Green and Nashville are in that connection of very secondary importance at the present moment. My own advance cannot, according to my present view, be made until your troops are solidly established in the eastern portion of Tennessee. If that is not possible, a complete and prejudicial change in my own plans at once becomes necessary.

Interesting as Nashville may be to the Louisville interests, it strikes me that its possession is of very secondary importance in comparison with the immense results that would arise from the adherence to our cause of the masses in East Tennessee, West North Carolina, South Carolina, North Georgia, and Alabama, results that I feel assured would ere long flow from the movement I allude to.

Halleck, from his own account, will not soon be in a condition to support properly a movement up the Cumberland. Why not make the movement independently of and without waiting for that?

I regret that I have not strength enough to write a fuller and more intelligible letter, but this is my very first effort at writing for somewhat more than two weeks.[4]

In haste, my dear general, very truly, yours,
Geo. B. McClellan,
Major-General, Commanding.

OR, Ser. 1, VII, p. 531.

1. Maj. Osborn Cross, Col. Thomas Swords. 2. Brig. Gen. Montgomery C. Meigs, the army's quartermaster general. 3. Buell's telegram of Jan. 5 to Lincoln read, in part: "I will confess to your excellency that I have been bound to it [the East Tennessee operation] more by my sympathy for the people of East Tennessee and the anxiety with which you and the General-in-Chief have desired it than by my opinion of its wisdom as an unconditional measure. As earnestly as I wish to accomplish it, my judgment has from the first been decidedly against it...." *OR*, Ser. 1, VII, pp. 530–31. 4. GBM had fallen ill with typhoid fever on Dec. 23, 1861.

To Ambrose E. Burnside

Brig Genl A E Burnside
Comdg Expedn
Genl

Hd Qtrs of the Army
Washington Jany 7 1862

In accordance with verbal instructions heretofore given you, you will after uniting with Flag Officer Goldsborough[1] at Fort Monroe, proceed under his convoy to Hatteras Inlet, when you will in connection with him take the most prompt measures for crossing the Fleet over the "Bulkhead" into the waters of the Sound. Under the accompanying General Order constituting the Dept of North Carolina you will assume the command of the garrison at Hatteras Inlet & make such dispositions in regard to that place as your ulterior operations may render necessary — always being careful to provide for the safety of that very important station in any contingency.

Your first point of attack will be Roanoke Island & its dependencies.

It is presumed that the Navy can reduce the batteries in the marshes & cover the landing of your troops on the main Island, by which — in connection with a rapid movement of the gun boats to the northern extremity as soon as the marsh battery is reduced — it may be hoped to capture the entire garrison of the place.

Having occupied the Island & its dependencies you will at once proceed to the erection of the batteries & defences necessary to hold the position with a small force.

Should the Flag Officer require any assistance in seizing or holding the debouches of the canals from Norfolk, you will please afford it to him.

The Commodore & yourself having completed your arrangements in regard to Roanoke Island & the waters north of it, you will please at once make a descent upon Newbern, having gained possession of which & the RR passing through it, you wil' at once throw a sufficient force upon Beaufort & take the steps necessary to reduce Fort Macon & open that Port. When you seize Newbern you will endeavor to seize the RR as far west as Goldsboro' should circumstances favor such a movement — the temper of the people, the rebel force at hand will go far towards determining the question as to how far west the RR can be safely occupied & held.

Should circumstances render it advisable to seize & hold Raleigh the main north & south line of RR passing through Goldsboro' should be so effectually destroyed for considerable distances north & south of that point as to render it impossible for the rebels to use it to your disadvantage. A great point would be gained, in any event, by the effectual destruction of the Wilmington & Weldon R.R.

I would advise great caution in moving so far into the interior as upon Raleigh. Having accomplished the objects mentioned the next point of interest would probably be Wilmington, the reduction of which may require that additional means shall be afforded you.

I would urge great caution in regard to proclamations — in no case would I go beyond a moderate joint proclamation with the Naval Comdr, which should say as little as possible about politics or the negro — merely state that the true issue for which we are fighting is the preservation of the Union & upholding the laws of the Genl Govt, & stating that all who conduct themselves properly will as far as possible be protected in their persons & property.

You will please report your operations as often as an opportunity offers itself.

With my best wishes for your success

I am, General, sincerely your friend
Geo B McClellan
Maj Genl Comdr in Chief

P.S. Any prisoners you take should be sent to the most convenient northern post — you can however exchange any of them for any of your own men who may be taken.

Geo B McC

ALS, Records of the Adjutant General's Office, RG 94 (159: Burnside Papers), National Archives. *OR*, Ser. 1, IX, pp. 352–53. Brig. Gen. Burnside had been assigned command of the Roanoke Island expedition, with headquarters at Annapolis, Md., on Oct. 23, 1861.

1. Flag Officer Louis M. Goldsborough, commander of the North Atlantic Blockading Squadron.

To Nathaniel P. Banks [TELEGRAM]

[Washington, January 7, 1862]

Say to Genl Lander[1] that I might comment very severely on the tone of his dispatches but abstain. Give him positive orders to repair at once to Romney & carry out the instructions I have sent already to fall back on the Railway.

It would be folly to cross the river at Hancock under present circumstances, except with a small corps of observation, but not to follow up the enemy.

Genl Lander is too suggestive & critical.[2]

G B McClellan
Maj Genl Comdg

Maj Genl N P Banks
Frederick

ALS (telegram sent), McClellan Papers (A-35:15), Library of Congress.

1. Brig. Gen. Lander commanded a division under Banks in the upper Potomac area. 2. Presumably GBM referred to Lander's dispatches of Jan. 6 to Banks that called for a prompt crossing of the Potomac to attack the Confederates under Maj. Gen. Thomas J. Jackson, who were raiding such targets as the Baltimore and Ohio Railroad; and of Jan. 7 to Banks that read: "I now demand direct orders" to cross the river. McClellan Papers (A-35:15, B-10:47).

To Alexander D. Bache

Prof A D Bache
Supt Coast Survey — Hd Qtrs of the Army
My dear Sir — Washington Jany 10 1862

I regret to learn that the House of Reps. have decided to suspend work in the Coast Survey during the war.

This decision has caused me great concern, & not knowing whom else to address I have determined to write to you, asking you to make any use you can of my views.

With the exception of the results of the Govt Expeditions on the Plains etc the only reliable topographical information we have of our country is derived from the Coast Survey.

Without the Coast Survey maps it would certainly have been very difficult, if not impossible, to have arranged & carried out most of our military operations. The only maps of any value that we possess of the country on the other side of the Potomac is the result of the labors of the Coast Survey.

Far from suspending the operations of the Coast Survey, I would strongly urge that military necessity demands that its work be pushed with the greatest vigor, & that its field of work be extended as far inland as possible.

The money expended upon the Coast Survey will be repaid an hundred fold in our time of need.[1]

I am very truly & respectfully your obdt svt
Geo B McClellan
Maj Genl Comdg USA

ALS, Rhees Collection, Huntington Library. Bache was superintendent of the United States Coast Survey.

1. Bache replied on the same date that no one "would doubt the terrible blow your letter will deal to the enemies of the Coast Survey." He wrote again on Jan. 16 that GBM's letter "will I feel certain determine Congress against the suspension of the Coast Survey." The Survey's operations did not cease during the war. McClellan Papers (B-9:47, B-10:47), Library of Congress.

To Don Carlos Buell

Brig. Gen. D. C. Buell, — Headquarters of the Army,
Commanding Department of the Ohio: — Washington,
My dear General: — January 13, 1862.

Your telegram asking for six more batteries is received. I have taken measures to have them ordered to you at once, and will endeavor to order two more to you to-morrow. I hope you will ere long receive the two regular companies from Fort Randall.

You have no idea of the pressure brought to bear here upon the Government for a forward movement. It is so strong that it seems absolutely necessary to make the advance on Eastern Tennessee at once. I incline to this as a first step for many reasons. Your possession of the railroad there will surely prevent the main army in my front from being re-enforced and may force Johnston[1] to detach. Its political effect will be very great. Halleck is not yet in condition to afford you the support you need when you undertake the movement on Bowling Green. Meigs has sent to you the 400 wagons for which requisition was made. Should the supply of Government wagons be insufficient, I would recommend hiring private teams. If the people will not freely give them, why then, seize them. It is no time now to stand on trifles. I think Ohio can now give you five or six new regiments, that can at least guard your communications, and are probably about as good as the mass of the troops opposed to you.

I am now quite well again, only somewhat weak. Hope to be in the saddle in a very few days.

In haste, truly, yours,
Geo B. McClellan
Major-General, Commanding.

OR, Ser. 1, VII, p. 547.

1. Albert Sidney Johnston, commanding the western Confederate army.

To Abraham Lincoln

Washington Tuesday [January 14, 1862]

I enclose for your Excellency's perusal copies of letters from Genl Halleck which will explain themselves.[1]

I have replied to him in regard to my letter of the 3rd that he had not read it carefully.[2] In it I told him what I wanted done & asked his views, as well as the number of troops he could spare for the purpose.

Will your Excellency be good enough to return me the enclosed when you have got through with them. All goes well. I worked until after midnight yesterday, & that with a good deal of work today has fatigued me so much that I will hardly be able to call upon you today.

Very respectfully & truly
Geo B McClellan

I am rapidly getting matters in hand again & will carry out the promise I made to you yesterday.[3]

ALS, Lincoln Papers, Library of Congress.

1. Probably Halleck's dispatches to GBM of Jan. 9 and 10. *OR*, Ser. 1, VII, pp. 539–40, 543. 2. GBM to Halleck, Jan. 3, *supra*. Halleck had replied on Jan. 9: "If a sufficient

number of troops are to be withdrawn from Missouri at the present time to constitute an expedition up the Cumberland..., we must seriously peril the loss of this State.'' **3.** At a military conference at the White House on Jan. 13, GBM refused to reveal his plans for the Army of the Potomac, but agreed (in Lincoln's words) to ''press the advance in Kentucky.'' Montgomery C. Meigs, ''General M. C. Meigs on the Conduct of the Civil War,'' *American Historical Review*, 26:2 (Jan. 1921), p. 293.

To John A. Dix

Confidential — Hd Qtrs of the Army
My dear General — Washington Jany 14 1862

It will soon become necessary for me to make a movement in advance with the main army; when the advance takes place the safety of the Capital becomes a matter of vital interest & must be confided to sure hands.

Circumstances which I will explain to you when we meet will render the task doubly interesting.

After full consideration I have determined to ask you to take upon yourself this very delicate & responsible position.

I write to you thus early to invite your attention to the choice of your successor in the immediate command at Baltimore (which will remain under your control) as well as to enable you quietly to make your arrangements for the change in your station.

Very soon after I am able to get into the saddle again I shall ask you to come here to go over all the ground with me, that we may have a complete understanding, & that you may know the purpose of all I have done in the last few months. The plan of campaign I shall probably follow will be such as to make your position doubly responsible.[1]

Begging that this communication may be regarded as most strictly confidential & asking your views as to the proper person to command at Baltimore

I am sincerely & respectfully your friend
Geo B McClellan
Maj Genl

Maj Genl J A Dix
Comdg at Baltimore

ALS, Dix Papers, Rare Book and Manuscript Library, Columbia University. Maj. Gen. Dix commanded the garrison at Baltimore.

1. Dix did not assume the Washington command. He was appointed to head the Department of Virginia, with headquarters at Fort Monroe, on June 1.

To Abraham Lincoln

Head-Quarters, Army of the Potomac,
Your Excellency Washington, Jany 15 1862

I am so much better this morning that I am going before the Joint Committee. If I escape alive I will report when I get through.[1]

I think Halleck is a little premature but that Buell will check his feint until the proper time arrives.[2] It is singular that H. has not received the 11,000 arms.

Very truly & respectfully
Geo B McClellan
Maj Genl

His Ex the Presdt

ALS, Lincoln Papers, Library of Congress.

1. The Joint Committee on the Conduct of War. GBM told a newspaperman the next day that the session went well, and that the committee was fully satisfied with his testimony. Malcolm Ives to Frederic Hudson, Jan. 16, 1862, James Gordon Bennett Papers, Library of Congress. Senator Zachariah Chandler, however, reported that committee members were blunt in questioning the Army of the Potomac's inactivity. Detroit Post and Tribune, *Zachariah Chandler: An Outline Sketch of His Life and Public Services* (Detroit, 1880), pp. 224–26. 2. Halleck had ordered a demonstration toward Columbus, Ky., to divert attention from Buell's proposed advance on East Tennessee. *OR*, Ser. 1, VII, pp. 539–40.

To Samuel L. M. Barlow

My dear Barlow Washington Jany 18 [1862]

I owe you replies to about a dozen notes & thanks for at least the same number of acts of kindness, not forgetting *these* boots! Let me thank you in a lump & assure you that my thanks are none the less sincere for being crowded together in this style. I am quite well now but still weak — the trouble is that they don't give me time to recover — but allow me not one minute of rest when I need it most. If I *could* pass a day or two at 229[1] I *know* I should recover — but I shall not see N.Y. until either I have thrashed Joe Johnston or he has whipped me — should the latter unhappily prove to be the case I don't think I will care to show my face in N.Y.!!

I sent my resignation direct to Alsop the other day — so I am no longer a RR man[2] — but strongly suspect that I will go back to some occupation in civil life when this rebellion is over.

Stanton's appointment was a most unexpected piece of good fortune, & I hope it will produce a good effect in the North.[3]

There is somebody after me! So I must close.

My wife sends her kindest regards to Mrs. B & yourself — present mine also.

In haste ever your friend
Geo B McClellan

S L M Barlow Esq

ALS, Barlow Papers, Huntington Library.

1. 229 Fifth Avenue, Barlow's New York residence. 2. GBM's resignation as president of the Eastern Division of the Ohio and Mississippi Railroad was dated Jan. 9. 3. Edwin M. Stanton was confirmed as secretary of war on Jan. 15.

To Mary M. Marcy

[Washington] Thursday evng
[January 23, 1862]

My dear Grandmama

Prince[1] & I have been looking into our domestic affairs this evng & find part of the family in a sad condition. Poor Nell wanted to go out to a party this evng & found that she was absolutely in the condition of Miss Flora McFlimsey! Nell talks about economy — but that is nonsense.

So please get her *at least one* very handsome silk for an evening dress — some color that will become her — red (not brick dust) is my favorite, but she has one already — get her a *very* handsome one.

If you think she ought to have two now, please get them. I don't know whether there ought to be any flowers for the hair to go with silk dresses — if yes get them also.

Please get the young woman also a *wreath* of *rose color* to match the white (trimmed with pink) dress she had made here — she says you will know the color & had better go to Haldimans unless you can happen in upon some smart auction store where partially injured articles are going cheap.

Get me also a wreath of roses for myself — I think I'll come out in a new way. Please send *Nell's* rose colored wreath by Adams Express — I'm not in so great a hurry for mine.

The baby is splendid — laughs inordinately & so loudly that it is almost a nuisance — converses intelligently in 3 languages — & when missed day before yesterday was found strolling around Willard's Hotel after a search of an hour or two.

Nell has behaved very well considering! She patronizes the "thing" [*illegible*] extensively, & I manage to pass a peaceable & quiet time in the day time by staying at the office from breakfast time until 6 o'clock. Poor Nell — bears her disappointment tonight like a young angel. Nothing new here — except that the mud is almost two feet deeper than when you left.

Tell Fan[2] to pay particular attention to spelling at school — it does not look well for a young lady of 16 (?) to write, or spell, "Highdrewfoebiah" "Dearexshun" "Miss Dar Meaner" eatsetthera eatsetthera. Tell her I wish to impress upon her the fact that spelling is equally important with callisthenics. Tell her that if she will wash her face regularly, not drink too much coffee, & whistle occasionally she will be happy.

My paper is out — like your patience. Love to miserable Grandpapa & tell him to festina lente[3] — love also to Fanny. All well here except Prince who is disgusted this evng.

With much love to all from Nell & myself
Your affectionate son
G B McC

Give love to all the family. Tell the Dr that I braved to their faces about a dozen alopaths in the Sanitary Comm today![4] Say to Emma that I learn that Raymond only uses words beginning with *D*. Whether they end with a vowel or consonant I have not yet learned.

ALS, McClellan Papers (B-40:60), Library of Congress. Mrs. Marcy, GBM's mother-in-law, was in New York with Randolph Marcy during his recuperation from typhoid fever.

1. The McClellans' dog. 2. Fanny Marcy, GBM's sister-in-law. 3. Make haste slowly. 4. Dr. Erastus E. Marcy, a homeopathic physician who was caring for his brother Randolph Marcy, had also treated GBM for his typhoid. A contingent from the U.S. Sanitary Commission, including practitioners of more conventional allopathic medicine, called on GBM that day to seek reform of the army's medical service. *The Diary of George Templeton Strong: The Civil War, 1860–1865,* eds. Allan Nevins and Milton H. Thomas (New York, 1952), p. 203.

To Edwin M. Stanton

Hon E. M. Stanton
Secretary of War
Sir.

Head Quarters of the Army
Washington January 24, 1862.

Many complaints have reached me through Division commanders and otherwise as to the manner in which vacancies among the Officers of Volunteer Regiments are filled by the Governors of States in many instances. Instead of promoting meritorious Officers non-commissioned Officers and Soldiers who have shown a fitness for their position and have acquired a certain amount of experience and confidence, it is too often the case that such persons are passed over and superceded by men entirely raw and untried appointed from political or personal considerations, and altogether unfit for their duties.

I would respectfully beg leave to invite your attention to this great evil and to suggest for your consideration the propriety of asking from Congress the passage of a law regulating the system of promotion and supplying vacancies in the Volunteer Regiments.

I think also that when a vacancy occurs it should be filled by the next in rank, if fit for the position and that the lower grades should to a great extent be filled by capable non-commissioned Officers. I would also suggest that the troops of each State should be considered as a unit for the purpose of promotion, viz. if the Colonel of a New York Regiment dies then the senior Lieutentant Colonel of the State of New York would, if competent, be promoted to the place.

Some system of this kind would, I am sure, remedy many evils now existing.[1]

I enclose herewith the project of an order from the War Department in regard to inscribing on the Colors of Regiments &c the names of Battles. I spoke to the Secretary about this and submit the order for his consideration.[2]

There are cases of Regiments raised under the direct authority of the War Department, independently of the State authorities — difficulties exist still in regard to some of these. I would suggest that, if the consolidation of the troops from each State, for purposes of promotion, be favorably considered, these independent Regiments be merged in the organization of *some* State, for there are cases where a Regiment is composed of companies from various States.[3]

I am, Sir, very respectfully Your Obdt Servant

Retained copy, Records of the Headquarters of the Army, RG 108 (M-857:6), National Archives.

1. Congress did not act on this proposal. 2. This order was issued on Feb. 22, 1862. *OR*, Ser. 3, I, p. 898. 3. An order to this effect was issued on Feb. 21, 1862. *OR*, Ser. 3, I, p. 898.

To Edwin M. Stanton

[Washington, c. January 25, 1862]

I think that no expedition of 30,000 men, as proposed, is either practicable or advisable at present. From recent information it seems certain that forage cannot be found between Ft Leavenworth & Fort Scott even for the force proposed by Genl Lane.[1] It would be next to impossible & very expensive to transport it from Illinois etc. The true line of supply would seem to be by the Pacific RR &c, keeping north of the Osage, direct to Fort Scott.

I recommend that the expedition in question be at least kept within the numbers asked for by Genl Lane; that the Qtr Mr Gl be instructed to ascertain if it is practicable to send the necessary supplies, & the cavalry asked for, over the route I suggest, at a reasonable cost in the present season; and that the movement of all troops now under orders or en route for Leavenworth be at once suspended until either supplies have been sent in advance or the possibility of obtaining forage in the country is demonstrated. If the expedition asked for by Genl Hunter is necessary, or if it proves to be the case that forage must be transported for the smaller force asked by Genl Lane, I would advise that the expedition be at least deferred until the season is so far advanced that the grass is up.[2]

Very respectfully
Geo B McClellan
Maj Genl Comdg USA

Hon E M Stanton
Secty of War

ALS, Records of the Adjutant General's Office, RG 94 (M-619:36), National Archives. This endorsement by GBM appears on Montgomery C. Meigs to Stanton, Jan. 24.

1. Quartermaster Meigs analyzed the supply needs of two alternative proposals: that of Maj. Gen. Hunter for 30,000 men carrying all their own supplies, and that of Brig. Gen. James H. Lane for 20,000 men living largely off the country. The expedition was to march southwest from Fort Leavenworth through Kansas and Indian Territory toward northern Texas. See GBM to Hunter, Dec. 11, 1861, *supra*. 2. On Jan. 31 Lincoln wrote to Stanton of this expedition: "I have not intended, and do not now intend that it shall be *a great exhausting affair*; but a snug, sober column of 10,000 or 15,000." *Collected Works of Lincoln*, V, pp. 115–16. The expedition was not undertaken.

To Edwin M. Stanton

Confidential

My dear Stanton [Washington] Sunday — [January 26, 1862]

Have you anything from Scott as to the means we can command in the way of moving troops westward by rail & water.[1] My mind is more & more tending in that direction, tho' not fully committed to it. But there should be no delay in ascertaining precisely *what we can do* should it prove advisable to move in that direction.

Please put the machinery in motion to ascertain exactly how many troops we can move per diem hence to Kentucky, how many days the transit would occupy etc.[2] Should we change the line I would wish to take about 70,000 infantry, 250 guns, 2500 cavalry — at least 3 bridge trains.[3]

truly yours
Geo B McClellan

ALS, Stanton Papers, Library of Congress.

1. Assistant Secretary of War Thomas A. Scott was then making a study of army transportation. Scott to Stanton, Jan. 23, 1862, *OR*, Ser. 3, I, pp. 807–808. 2. Acting on Stanton's instructions dated Jan. 29, Scott was sent to the Midwest to examine this question, and on Feb. 1 sent his first report to Stanton on shifting troops from the Army of the Potomac to Kentucky. Stanton Papers. 3. This suggests that GBM intended to command personally any shift of the main advance to the western theater. Neither he nor any troops from the Army of the Potomac went to Kentucky, however. See GBM to Scott, Feb. 20, *infra*.

To Henry W. Halleck

Maj. Gen. H. W. Halleck, Saint Louis
My dear General: Washington, January 29, 1862.

I have recommended A. J. Smith for brigadier-general, as you requested, and when his name is acted upon will assign him to duty with you. I have also recommended General Hitchcock, as you desire.[1] Your welcome letter in regard to future operations is received.[2] I will reply in full in a day or two. In the mean time get your force in hand and study the ground. I will try to-day to send you some more infantry arms. Cavalry arms are terribly scarce. I have had to take to lances here to supply deficiencies. I like your views as to the future. They fully agree with my own ideas from the beginning, which has ever been against a movement in force down the Mississippi itself. The news from the Burnside expedition is by no means so unfavorable as the telegram reports. He had terrible gales while crowded in a small harbor. The only real evil of consequence is the delay.

I will try to devote this afternoon to you and Buell, to give you my views and intentions in full.

Can you spare Stanley to Buell as chief of cavalry, or shall I look elsewhere to get him one? He (Buell) has not asked for him, but I know him to be a first-rate officer.[3]

While I think of it, do you not think it would be well to try one of those mortar floats thoroughly with 50 or 100 discharges before arming them all? Je m'en doute un peu.[4] It is very desirable to move all along the line by the 22d February, if possible.[5]

In haste, sincerely, your friend,
Geo. B. McClellan

OR, Ser. 1, VII, pp. 930–31.

1. Col. A. J. Smith, Halleck's chief of cavalry, was named brigadier general on Mar. 17. Ethan Allan Hitchcock was named major general on Feb. 10. 2. Written Jan. 20, Halleck's letter proposed an end to a scattered "pepper-box strategy" in favor of a concentrated operation of 60,000 men along the line of the Cumberland and Tennessee rivers. The Mississippi, he wrote, "is not a proper line of operations...." *OR*, Ser. 1, VIII, pp. 508–511. 3. Brig. Gen. David S. Stanley became a division commander under Gen. Pope. 4. "I have my doubts about them." 5. On Jan. 27 President Lincoln had issued his General War Order No. 1, calling for "a general movement" by land and naval forces on Feb. 22. *Collected Works of Lincoln*, V, pp. 111–12.

To Don Carlos Buell [TELEGRAM]

[Washington, January 29, 1862]

A deserter just in from the rebels says that Beauregard had not left Centreville four days ago but that as he was going on picket he heard officers say that Beauregard was under orders to go to Kentucky with 15 regts from the Army of Potomac.[1]

G B McClellan
Maj Genl

Brig Genl D. C. Buell
Louisville Ky

ALS (telegram sent), Records of the Office of the Secretary of War, RG 107 (M-473 :10), National Archives. *OR*, Ser. 1, VII, p. 571. The same telegram was sent to Halleck.

1. Beauregard left Centreville, Va., for Kentucky on Feb. 2 to be second-in-command to Albert Sidney Johnston. He took no troops with him from the Confederate Army of the Potomac, but acting largely on the strength of this telegram Halleck approved Gen. Grant's plan to attack Fort Henry, on the Tennessee River, before it could be reinforced. *OR*, Ser. 1, VII, p. 572.

To Randolph B. Marcy

[Washington] Wednesday (Evening)
[January 29, 1862]

My dear Marcy

I am glad to hear that you are improving — do not hurry back until you are perfectly restored[1] — the weather has been so bad here that you would have faired illy had you been here.

I am getting on very well — Stanton's appointment has helped me infinitely thus far, & will still more in the future.

I wish you would see Mr Bennett or Hudson (the former if possible) & ask him which (*if either*) is his *confidential agent* Dr Ives or Hanscom![2] The Secty & myself are both puzzled a little to know "t'other from which" — Ives intimates that Hanscom is not the "confidential" man, & H intimates that Ives is not.[3]

I would like to know which one Mr B. wishes me to communicate fully & unreservedly with — I am anxious to keep Mr B. well posted & wish to do it fully — ask how far I can go in communicating important matters to either.[4]

Roads horrid — I think I can arrange my pleasure party very satisfactorily.[5]

Love to Grandma & Fanny — Nell will add a line.

Yours affectionately
Geo B McC

My kindest regards to the Dr & family.

ALS, McClellan Papers (A-106 :42), Library of Congress.

1. Chief of Staff Marcy was still in New York recuperating from typhoid fever. 2. James Gordon Bennett, owner of the *New York Herald*; Frederic Hudson, his managing editor; Malcolm Ives and Simon P. Hanscom, *Herald* reporters. 3. On Jan. 28 Hanscom told Stanton that Ives was not the newspaper's accredited Washington correspondent. Ives to Bennett, Jan. 29, Bennett Papers, Library of Congress. 4. Ives wrote Bennett on Jan. 15 that Stanton

had introduced him to GBM the previous evening. GBM told him, according to Ives: "... I am now going to convey through you to Mr Bennett and *Mr Hudson*; I am going to give you *all* the knowledge I possess myself, with no reserve...." Bennett Papers. GBM continued to brief the reporter, but Ives soon ran afoul of Stanton and was imprisoned for some three months for violating censorship regulations. Andrews, *The North Reports the Civil War,* pp. 57–58. 5. Presumably his plan for a flanking movement against the Confederates by water. See GBM to Stanton, [Feb. 3], *infra.*

To John M. Brannan

Brig. Gen. John M. Brannan: Headquarters of the Army,
General: Washington, January 30, 1862.

So soon as arrangements have been perfected for the necessary supplies and ordnance you will please proceed at once to your destination, and on your arrival assume command of the Department of [Key West]. Your first and most important duty will be to place Forts Jefferson and Taylor on the war footing and in a thorough condition for defense, assigning the troops and distributing the guns and material at your disposal between the forts to the best of your judgment, and constructing such temporary batteries and defenses as, upon consultation with the engineer officer, may seem advisable. Cause your men to be well instructed in the service of heavy guns. Preserve the strictest vigilance as to the admission of vessels of all kinds into the harbors, and allow no persons to visit the forts, except those in Government employ, without a pass from the commanding officer. Repress all disunion movements in Key West, arresting any citizens whose presence is manifestly dangerous to the Government or who may give aid and comfort to the rebels, if necessary sending them under guard to the North. In fine, exercise all the vigilance and precaution usual in time of war, bearing in mind that your greatest danger is from surprise, and that you are not likely to receive warning of the breaking out of hostilities. You will please afford such protection as may be in your power to the Light-House Board in reestablishing and maintaining the lights most necessary for navigation in those waters, and cover the operations of the Coast Survey so far as may be done without risk. Should the commanders of Forts Pickens and Ship Island call upon you in an emergency you will lend them such assistance as you can without risk to the security of your own posts. Should the state of affairs render it advisable to occupy Tampa for the purpose of procuring supplies of fresh beef for the army and navy forces in the Gulf, you are authorized to seize and hold it, calling upon the naval commander in the vicinity for the necessary assistance. I hope to send you at an early day at least one steamer and one or more schooners. When you have transportation you must use your discretion as to any movements upon Cedar Keys or Apalachicola. No movement on the former would be necessary, unless for a mere foray, except in case of the occupation of Fernandina by Sherman;[1] on the latter, advisable only to seize cotton and prevent contraband trade. You are authorized to occupy such land as may be necessary for the erection of batteries and defenses or for the encampment of your troops, and to take possession of any buildings which may be required for the preservation and security of public stores. As your command might suffer from the want of fresh water before the requisite condensers can be furnished, you are also authorized, in case of emergency, to take such supplies of it as may have been collected for sale to naval and other vessels.

I am, &c.
Geo. B. McClellan,
Major-General, U.S. Army,
Commanding.

OR, Ser. 1, LIII, pp. 74–75. Brig. Gen. Brannan was named head of the Department of Key West on Jan. 11.

1. Brig. Gen. Thomas W. Sherman, commander of the Port Royal expedition.

To Frederick W. Lander [TELEGRAM]

Head Quarters, Army of the Potomac,
General F. W. Lander Washington, Feb. 2 1862

Ohio regiments & battery ordered temporarily to New Creek. In attacking Romney you must use your discretion & be certain that the enemy is not reinforced from Winchester. Do not advance beyond Romney. Banks needs time to prepare to cooperate & you would be in danger East of Romney if he were not in position to distract enemy.[1]

If you gain Romney look out for return of Jackson, whom I know to be a man of vigor & nerve, as well as a good soldier.

Geo. B. McClellan
Maj General Comdg

Retained copy, Records of the Office of the Secretary of War, RG 107 (M-473:11), National Archives. *OR*, Ser. 1, LI, Part 1, p. 523.

1. Confederate Thomas J. "Stonewall" Jackson had occupied Romney, Va., on Jan. 10. He would withdraw to Winchester, Va., on Feb. 7.

To Edwin M. Stanton

Hon E M Stanton
Secty of War Head Quarters of the Army
Sir: Washington January 31st [February 3] 1862[1]

I ask you indulgence for the following paper, rendered necessary by circumstances.

I assumed command of the troops in the vicinity of Washington on Saturday July 27 1861, 6 days after the battle of Bull Run.

I found no army to command, a mere collection of regiments cowering on the banks of the Potomac, some perfectly raw, others dispirited by their recent defeat.

Nothing of any consequence had then been done to secure the southern approaches to the Capital by means of defensive works; nothing whatever had been undertaken to defend the avenues to the city on the northern side of the Potomac.

The troops were not only undisciplined, undrilled & dispirited — they were not even placed in military positions — the city was almost in a condition to have been taken by a dash of a single regiment of cavalry.

Without one day's delay I undertook the difficult task assigned to me — the task the Hon Secty knows was given to me without my solicitation or foreknowledge. How far I have accomplished it will best be shown by the past & present. The Capital is secure against attack — the extensive fortifications erected by the labor of our troops enable a small garrison to hold it against a numerous army; the enemy have been held in check; the State of Maryland is securely in our possession; the detached counties of Virginia are again within the pale of our laws, & all apprehension of trouble in Delaware is at an end; the enemy are confined to the positions they occupied before 21 July; — more than all this, I have now under my command a well drilled & reliable Army to which the destinies of the country may be confidently committed. This Army is young, & untried in battle, but it is animated by the highest spirit, & is capable of great deeds. That so much has been accomplished, & such an Army created in so short a time from nothing will hereafter be regarded as one of the highest glories of the Administration & the nation.

Many weeks, I may say many months, ago this Army of the Potomac was fully in condition to repel any attack; — but there is a vast difference between that & the efficiency required to enable troops to attack successfully an Army elated by victory, and entrenched in a position long since selected, studied, & fortified. In the earliest papers I submitted to the Presdt I asked for an effective movable force far exceeding the aggregate now on the banks of the Potomac — I have not the force I asked for. Even when in a subordinate position I always looked beyond the operations of the Army of the Potomac; I was never satisfied in my own mind with a barren victory, but looked to combined & decisive operations.

When I was placed in command of the Armies of the U.S. I immediately turned my attention to the whole field of operations — regarding the Army of the Potomac as only *one,* while the most important, of the masses under my command.

I confess that I did not then appreciate the absence of a general plan which had before existed, nor did I know that utter disorganization & want of preparation pervaded the western armies. I took it for granted that they were nearly, if not quite, in condition to move towards the fulfillment of my plans — I acknowledge that I made a great mistake.

I sent at once, with the approval of the Executive, officers I considered competent to command in Kentucky & Missouri — their instructions looked to prompt movements. I soon found that the labor of creation & organization had to be performed there — transportation, arms, clothing, artillery, discipline — all were wanting; these things required time to procure them; the Generals in command have done their work most creditably — but we are still delayed. I had hoped that a general advance could be made during the good weather of December — I was mistaken.

My wish was to gain possession of the Eastern Tennessee Railroads as a preliminary movement, — then to follow it up immediately by an attack on Nashville & Richmond as nearly at the same time as possible.

I have ever regarded our true policy as being that of fully preparing ourselves & then seeking for the most decisive results; — I do not wish to waste life in useless battles, but prefer to strike at the heart.

Two bases of operations seem to present themselves for the advance of the Army of the Potomac. —

I. That of Washington — its present position — involving a direct attack upon the enemy's entrenched positions at Centreville, Manassas etc, or else a movement to turn one or both flanks of those positions, or a combination of the two plans.

The relative force of the two Armies will not justify an attack on both flanks.

An attack on his left flank alone involves a long line of wagon communication & cannot prevent him from collecting for the decisive battle all the detachments now on his extreme right & left.

Should we attack his right by the line of the Occoquan & a crossing of the Potomac below the Occoquan & near his batteries, we could perhaps prevent the junction of the enemy's extreme right with his centre (we *might* destroy the former), we would remove the obstructions to the navigation of the Potomac, reduce the length of wagon transportation by establishing new depots at the nearest points of the Potomac, & strike more directly his main railway communication.

The fords of the Occoquan below the mouth of Bull Run are watched by the rebels, batteries are said to be placed on the heights in rear (concealed by the woods), & the arrangement of his troops is such that he can oppose some considerable resistance to a passage of the stream. Information has just been received to the effect that the enemy are entrenching a line of heights extending from the vicinity of Sangster's (Union Mills?) towards Evansport. Early in Jany. Sprigg's ford was occupied by Genl Rhodes with 3600 men & 8 guns; there are strong reasons for believing that Davis' Ford is occupied.[2]

These circumstances indicate, or prove, that the enemy anticipate the movement in question & are prepared to resist it.

Assuming for the present that this operation is determined upon, it may be well to examine briefly its probable progress.

In the present state of affairs our columns (for the movement of so large a force must be made in several columns, at least 5 or 6) can reach the Accotinck without danger; during the march thence to the Occoquan our right flank becomes exposed to an attack from Fairfax Station, Sangster's & Union Mills; — this danger must be met by occupying in some force either the two first named places, or, better, the point of junction of the roads leading thence to the village of Occoquan — this occupation must be continued so long as we continue to draw supplies by the roads from this city, or until a battle is won.

The crossing of the Occoquan should be made at all the fords from Wolf's Run to the mouth, the points of crossing not being necessarily confined to the fords themselves.

Should the enemy occupy this line in force we must, with what assistance the flotilla can afford, endeavor to force the passage near the mouth, thus forcing the enemy to abandon the whole line or be taken in flank himself.

Having gained the line of the Occoquan, it would be necesary to throw a column by the shortest route to Dumfries, partly to force the enemy to abandon his batteries on the Potomac, partly to cover our left flank against an attack from the direction of Acquia, & lastly to establish our communication with the river by the best roads, & thus give us new depots.

The enemy would by this time have occupied the line of the Occoquan above Bulls Run, holding Brentsville in force & perhaps extending his lines somewhat further to the S.W.

Our next step would be to prevent the enemy from crossing the Occoquan between Bull Run & Broad Run, to fall upon our right flank while moving on Brentsville; this might be effected by occupying Baconrace Church & the cross roads near the mouth of Bull Run, or still more effectually by moving to the fords themselves & preventing him from debouching on our side. These operations would probably be resisted, & would require some time to effect them. As nearly at the same time as possible we should gain the fords necessary to our purposes above Broad Run.

Having secured our right flank it would become necessary to carry Brentsville at any cost, for we could not leave it between our right flank & main body. The final movement on the Railroad must be determined by circumstances existing at the time.

This brief sketch brings out in bold relief the great advantage possessed by the enemy in the strong central position he occupies, with roads diverging in every direction, & a strong line of defence enabling him to remain on the defensive with a small force on one flank, while he concentrates everything on the other for a decisive action. Should we place a portion of our force in front of Centreville while the rest crosses the Occoquan we commit the error of dividing our Army by a very difficult obstacle & by a distance too great to enable the two portions to support each other, should either be attacked by the masses of the enemy while the other is held in check.

I should perhaps have dwelled more decidedly on the fact that the force left near Sangster's must be allowed to remain somewhere on that side of the Occoquan, until the decisive battle is over, to cover our retreat in the event of disaster, unless it should be decided to select & entrench a new base somewhere near Dumfries — a proceeding involving much time.

After the passage of the Occoquan by the main Army, this covering force could be drawn in to a more central & less exposed position, say Brimstone Hill or nearer the Occoquan.

In this latitude the weather will for a considerable period be very uncertain, & a movement commenced in force on roads in tolerably firm condition will be liable, almost certain, to be much delayed by rains & snow. It will therefore be next to impossible to surprise the enemy, or take him at a disadvantage by rapid manoeuvres; — our slow progress will enable him to divine our purposes & take his measures accordingly.

The probability is, from the best information we possess, that he has improved the roads leading to his lines of defence, while we must work as we advance.

Bearing in mind what has been said, & the present unprecedented & impassable condition of the roads, it will be evident that no precise period can be fixed upon for the movement on this line, nor can its duration be closely calculated; it seems certain that many weeks *may* elapse before it is possible to commence the march.

Assuming the success of this operation & the defeat of the enemy as certain, the question at once arises as to the importance of the results gained.

I think these results would be confined to the possession of the field of battle, the evacuation of the line of the upper Potomac by the enemy, & the moral effect of the victory — important results it is true, but not decisive of the war, nor securing the destruction of the enemy's main Army; for he could fall back upon other positions, & fight us again & again, should the condition of his troops permit.

If he is in no condition to fight us again out of range of the entrenchments at Richmond we would find it a very difficult & tedious matter to follow him up there — for he would destroy the railroad bridges & otherwise impede our progress through a region where the roads are as bad as they well can be; & we would probably find ourselves forced at last to change the entire theatre of war, or to seek a shorter land route to Richmond with a smaller available force & at an expenditure of much more time than were we to adopt the short line at once.

We would also have forced the enemy to concentrate his forces & perfect his defensive measures at the very points where it is desirable to strike him where least prepared.

II. The second base of operations available for the Army of the Potomac is that of the lower Chesapeake Bay, which affords the shortest possible land routes to Richmond, & strikes directly at the heart of the enemy's power in the East.

The roads in that region are passable at all seasons of the year.

The country now alluded to is much more favorable for offensive operations than that in front of Washington (which is *very* unfavorable) — much more level — more cleared land — the woods less dense — soil more sandy — the spring some two or three weeks earlier.

A movement in force on that line obliges the enemy to abandon his entrenched position at Manassas, in order to hasten to cover Richmond & Norfolk.

He *must* do this, for should he permit us to occupy Richmond his destruction can be averted only by entirely defeating us in a battle in which he must be the assailant.

This movement if successful gives us the Capital, the communications, the supplies of the rebels; Norfolk would fall; all the waters of the Chesapeake would be ours; all Virginia would be in our power; & the enemy forced to abandon Tennessee & North Carolina.

The alternatives presented to the enemy would be to beat us in a position selected by ourselves; disperse; — or pass beneath the Caudine Forks.[3] Should we be beaten in a battle, we have a perfectly secure retreat down the Peninsula upon Fort Monroe, with our flanks perfectly secured by the fleet. During the whole movement our left flank is covered by the water, our right is secure for the reason that the enemy is too distant to reach us in time — he can only oppose us in front; we bring our fleet into full play.

After a successful battle our position would be — Burnside forming our left, Norfolk held securely, our centre connecting Burnside with Buell, both by Raleigh & Lynchburg, Buell in Eastern Tennessee & Northern Alabama, Halleck at Nashville & Memphis.

The next movement would be to connect with Sherman on the left, by reducing Wilmington & Charleston; to advance our centre into South

Carolina & Georgia; to push Buell either towards Montgomery, or to unite with the main army in Georgia; to throw Halleck southward to meet the Naval Expedition at New Orleans.

We should then be in a condition to reduce at our leisure all the southern seaports; to occupy all the avenues of communication; to use the great outlet of the Mississippi; to reestablish our Govt & arms in Arkansas, Louisiana & Texas; to force the slaves to labor for our subsistence instead of that of the rebels; — to bid defiance to all foreign interference.

Such is the object I have ever had in view; this is the general plan which I have hoped to accomplish. For many long months I have labored to prepare the Army of the Potomac to play its part in the programme; from the day when I was placed in command of all our armies, I have exerted myself to place all the other armies in such a condition that they too could perform their allotted duties. Should it be determined to operate from the lower Chesapeake, the point of landing which promises the most brilliant results is Urbana on the lower Rappahannock.

This point is easily reached by vessels of heavy draught, it is neither occupied nor observed by the enemy; it is but one long march from West Point, the key to that region, & thence but two marches to Richmond.

A rapid movement from Urbana would probably cut off Magruder[4] in the *Peninsula,* & enable us to occupy Richmond before it could be strongly reinforced. Should we fail in that we could, with the cooperation of the Navy, cross the James & throw ourselves in rear of Richmond, thus forcing the enemy to come out & attack us — for his position would be untenable, with us on the southern bank of the river.

Should circumstances render it not advisable to land at Urbana we can use Mob Jack Bay, — or — the worst coming to the worst — we can take Fort Monroe as a base, & operate with complete security, altho' with less celerity & brilliancy of results, up the Peninsula.

To reach whatever point may be selected as the base, a large amount of cheap water transportation must be collected — consisting mainly of canal boats, barges, wood boats, schooners etc towed by small steamers — all of a very different character from those required for all previous expeditions. This can certainly be accomplished within 30 days from the time the order is given.

I propose, as the best possible plan that can, in my judgment, be adopted, to select Urbana as the landing place of the first detachments. To transport by water four (4) Divisions of Infantry, with their batteries, the Regular Infty, a few wagons, one bridge train & a few squadrons of Cavalry — making the vicinity of Hooker's position the place of embarkation for as many as possible.[5] To move the Regular Cavalry, & Reserve Artillery, the remaining bridge trains, & wagons to a point somewhere near Cape Lookout, then ferry them over the river by means of North River ferry boats, march them over to the Rappahannock (covering the movement by an Infantry force placed near Heathsville), cross the Rappahannock in a similar way.

The expense & difficulty of the movement will thus be much diminished (a saving of transportation of about 10,000 horses!), & the result none the less certain.

The concentration of the Cavalry etc in the lower counties of Maryland can be effected without exciting suspicion, & the movement made without delay from that cause.

This movement, if adopted, will not at all expose the city of Washington to danger.

The total force to be thrown upon the new line would be (according to circumstances) from 110,000 to 140,000. I hope to use the latter number, by bringing fresh troops into Washington, & still leaving it quite safe.

I fully realize that, in all projects offered, time is probably the most valuable consideration — it is my decided opinion that in that point of view the 2nd plan should be adopted. It is possible, nay highly probable, that the weather & state of the roads may be such as to delay the direct movement from Washington, with its unsatisfactory results & great risks, far beyond the time required to complete the second plan. *In the first case,* we can fix no definite time for an advance — the roads have gone from bad to worse — nothing like their present condition has ever been known here before — they are impassable at present, we are entirely at the mercy of the weather. In the second plan, we can calculate almost to a day, & with but little regard to the season.

If at the expense of 30 days delay we can gain a decisive victory which will probably end the war, it is far cheaper than to gain a battle tomorrow that produces no final results, & may require years of warfare & expenditure to follow up.

Such, I think, is precisely the difference between the two plans discussed in this long letter. A battle gained at Manassas will result merely in the possession of the field of combat — at best we can follow it up but slowly, unless we do what I now propose, viz: — change the line of operations.

On the Manassas line the rebels can, if well enough disciplined (& we have every reason to suppose that to be the case) dispute our advance, over bad roads, from position to position.

When we have gained the battle, if we do gain it, the question will at once arise — "What are we to do next?" —

It is by no means certain that we can beat them at Manassas.

On the other line I regard success as certain by all the chances of war.

We demoralize the enemy, by forcing him to abandon his prepared position for one which we have chosen, in which all is in our favor, & where success must produce immense results. My judgment as a General is clearly in favor of this project.

Nothing is *certain* in war — but all the chances are in favor of this movement.

So much am I in favor of the southern line of operations, that I would prefer the move from Fort Monroe as a base, as a certain, tho' less brilliant movement than that from Urbana, to an attack on Manassas.

I know that his Excellency the President, you & I all agree in our wishes — & that our desire is to bring this war to as prompt a close as the means in our possession will permit. I believe that the mass of the people have entire confidence in us — I am sure of it — let us then look only to the great result to be accomplished, & disregard everything else.

In conclusion I would respectfully, but firmly, advise that I may be authorized to undertake at once the movement by Urbana.

I believe that it can be carried into execution so nearly simultaneously with the final advance of Buell & Halleck that the columns will support each other.

I will stake my life, my reputation on the result — more than that, I will stake upon it the success of our cause.

I hope but little from the attack on Manassas; — my judgment is against it. Foreign complications may entirely change the state of affairs, & render very different plans necessary. In that event I will be ready to submit them.

I am very respectfully your obedient servant
Geo B McClellan
Maj Genl Comdg USA

ALS, Lincoln Papers, Library of Congress. *OR,* Ser. 1, V, pp. 42–45.

1. The dating of this letter requires clarification. As printed in GBM's *Report on the Organization of the Army of the Potomac* (Washington, 1864) and reprinted in the *Official Records,* it is dated Feb. 3, and several paragraphs near the end in the original manuscript are omitted. According to GBM's *Report* (pp. 42–43), it was prepared in response to the President's Special War Order No. 1 of Jan. 31, which called for the Army of the Potomac to advance in the area of the Occoquan River against the communications of the Confederate army at Manassas Junction. After receiving this order, GBM wrote, he went to the president with his objections and obtained permission to present his case in writing. On Feb. 3 he submitted his letter to Secretary of War Stanton, but before Stanton forwarded it to the president GBM received Lincoln's own thoughts on the issue, dated Feb. 3. Lincoln contrasted his Occoquan plan with GBM's Urbanna plan by means of a series of questions:

"1st. Does not your plan involve a greatly larger expenditure of *time,* and *money* than mine?

"2nd. Wherein is a victory *more certain* by your plan than mine?

"3rd. Wherein is a victory *more valuable* by your plan than mine?

"4th. In fact, would it not be *less* valuable, in this, that it would break no great line of the enemie's communications, while mine would?

"5th. In case of disaster, would not a safe retreat be more difficult by your plan than by mine." *Collected Works of Lincoln,* V, pp. 115, 118–19.

GBM assumed these questions were "substantially answered" by his letter to Stanton — possibly the letter was forwarded to Lincoln at his request — and he made no further reply. Portions of a draft of GBM's letter preserved in the McClellan Papers (A-39:16), Library of Congress, suggest the letter originated somewhat differently. Marked-out phrases indicate that it was originally intended for Lincoln and was drafted in response to an earlier meeting with the president, probably about the third week in January, at which at Stanton's suggestion he presented his Urbanna plan verbally (*Report,* p. 42). At one point the draft reads: "Such I think is precisely the difference between the two plans discussed this morning"; "this morning" is crossed out and replaced by "in this long letter." An undated Lincoln memorandum on his Occoquan plan is almost certainly related to this conference (*Collected Works,* V, p. 119).

After receiving Lincoln's War Order No. 1 on Friday, Jan. 31, and obtaining permission to respond, GBM spent the weekend revising and expanding the draft he had prepared earlier. As indicated in note 2 below, one change involved incorporating new intelligence information that was only received on Feb. 1. He then copied the revised draft, making further changes and rearranging material, and submitted it to Stanton on Monday, Feb. 3, without making a fair copy for his files.

Why he dated it Jan. 31 is unclear. Perhaps he intended it to be a direct response to the president's war order of that date; perhaps he had started the first pages of the finished copy that day. From its contents, however, it is certain that much of it was written on or after Feb. 1. As a whole, the letter responds more directly to Lincoln's earlier Jan. memorandum than to the Feb. 3 questions, but in any event the questions are answered, if only indirectly.

When GBM's *Report* was being prepared a year or so later, the copyist apparently found only the draft of this letter to work from. The paragraphs omitted from the *Report* printing are in fact in the draft, but in a different place and marked for repositioning, a process the copyist may not have understood. This would explain the omissions in the printed versions. 2. A telegram dated Feb. 1 from Gen. McDowell noted that according to an informant "the enemy are fortifying a range of hills from Sangsters to Evansport." A second intelligence report supplying data current "until February 1st" gave the size and armament of Brig. Gen. Robert Rodes's command. McClellan Papers (A-39:16). 3. The narrow defile in Italy where a Roman army was captured by the Samnites in 321 B.C. and forced to pass under a yoke of crossed spears. 4. Maj. Gen. John B. Magruder, commanding the Confederate Department of the Peninsula. 5. Brig. Gen. Joseph Hooker was posted in lower Maryland on the Potomac.

To Henry W. Halleck

Private — Head Quarters, Army of the Potomac,
My dear General — Washington, Feby 6, 1862

I received your letters in regard to Siegel & at once showed them to Secty Stanton who requests me to say to you from him that *you can rely upon his full & cordial support.*[1] He thinks that the power of the Germans by no means equals their wishes, & that you will find means to keep order. You may rely upon it that you have the confidence of all here — I need not repeat to you that you have mine.

The roads being impassable between Buell & his opponents it now becomes a question whether we cannot throw all our available force by the two rivers[2] upon Nashville — can we move there *now* in that manner? I will try tonight to write you my views more fully.

In great haste truly yours
Geo B McClellan

Maj Genl H W Halleck

ALS, Civil War Collection, Huntington Library. *OR,* Ser. 1, VII, p. 937.

1. Halleck's letter of Feb. 2, enclosing intelligence reports, outlined an alleged plot by German-born officers and German-language newspapers in St. Louis to displace Halleck with Brig. Gen. Franz Sigel, paving the way for a return to power of Frémont and his abolitionist supporters. *OR,* Ser. 1, VIII, pp. 828–29. 2. The Cumberland and Tennessee rivers.

To Don Carlos Buell [TELEGRAM]

[Washington, February 6, 1862, 7 P.M.]

Halleck telegraphs that Fort Henry largely reinforced from Columbus & Bowling Green.[1] If roads so bad in front had we not better throw all available force on Fort Henry & Fort Donelson? What think you of making that the main line of operations? Answer quick.[2]

G B McClellan
Maj Genl

Brig Genl D. C. Buell
Louisville Ky

ALS (telegram sent), Records of the Office of the Secretary of War, RG 107 (M-473:11), National Archives. *OR,* Ser. 1, VII, p. 587.

1. Halleck warned on this date that the Fort Henry garrison might become too strong for Grant's troops and Flag Officer Andrew H. Foote's gunboats. *OR,* Ser. 1, VII, pp. 586–87. 2. Buell replied at midnight that he agreed, although the operation would be hazardous. *OR,* Ser. 1, VII, pp. 587–88.

To Henry W. Halleck [TELEGRAM]

Maj. Gen. H. W. Halleck
Saint Louis, Mo.:

Headquarters Army [Washington],
February 7, 1862 — 7.15 p.m.

Dispatch received.[1] I congratulate you upon the result of your operations. They have caused the utmost satisfaction here. I would not undertake a dash at Columbus now. Better devote everything towards turning it; first collecting a sufficient force near Forts Henry and Donelson to make success sure.

Either Buell or yourself should soon go to the scene of operations. Why not have Buell take the line of Tennessee and operate on Nashville, while your troops turn Columbus? Those two points gained, a combined movement on Memphis will be next in order. The bridges at Tuscumbia and Decatur should at all hazards be destroyed at once.[2]

Please number telegraphic dispatches and give hour of transmittal. Thank Grant, Foote, and their commands for me.

Geo. B. McClellan
Major General, Commanding

OR, Ser. 1, VII, p. 591.

1. Halleck telegraphed that day: "Fort Henry is ours. The flag of the Union is re-established on the soil of Tennessee. It will never be removed." *OR*, Ser. 1, VII, p. 590. 2. Railroad bridges over the Tennessee River in northern Alabama.

To Andrew Porter

Brig Genl Andrew Porter
Provost Marshall — Hd Quarters of the Army
General — Washn Feby 8th 1862

You will please at once arrest Brig Genl Chas P Stone U.S. Volunteers & retain him in close custody, sending him under suitable escort by the first train to Fort Lafayette[1] there to be placed under charge of the comdg officer [*crossed out:* to await trial]. See that he has [no] communication with any one from the time of his arrest.[2]

Very respectfully yours
Geo B McClellan
Maj Genl

[*verso*]

Comdg officer Fort Lafayette
Sir

This will be handed to you by the officer sent in charge of Brig Genl Chas P Stone who is under close arrest.

You will please confine Genl Stone in Fort Lafayette, allowing him the comforts due his rank, & allowing him no communication with any one by letter or otherwise except under the usual inspection.

ALS retained copy, McClellan Papers (A-40:16), Library of Congress. *OR*, Ser. 1, V, pp. 341–42.

1. A fort in New York Harbor used as a military prison. 2. GBM was acting under instructions from Secretary of War Stanton dated Jan. 28. *OR*, Ser. 1, V, p. 341. In its investigation of the Ball's Bluff defeat, the Joint Committee on the Conduct of the War heard testimony impugning Gen. Stone's loyalty. He would be neither tried nor formally charged, however, and after 189 days' imprisonment was released. See GBM to Stone, Dec. 5, 1862, *infra*.

To Albert S. White

Hon Albert White
Dear Sir

Hd Qtrs of the Army
Washn Feby 8 1862

Your letter of the 7th is received.

The last arrest of Mr Dickins was made very reluctantly on my part, & after a most careful examination of the evidence against him.[1]

That evidence was to the effect that he was in the habit of communicating with the rebels; rendering them aid & comfort; giving them information of our movements, of the position of our pickets etc.

There is no one for whose patriotism & feelings I have more regard than yourself, so that I could not bring myself to ordering the arrest of your brother in law, until I could give my personal attention to the evidence against him.

I transmitted the case to the Secty of War before deciding upon his arrest.

I am compelled to believe that the presence of Mr F. A. Dickins between our lines & those of the enemy is very dangerous to our cause, & that it is absolutely necessary that he should be held in custody until he can no longer do injury to our cause.

I am very truly yours
Geo B McClellan
Maj Genl Comdg USA

ALS, Francis A. Dickins Papers, Southern Historical Collection, University of North Carolina Library. White was a congressman from Indiana.

1. Francis A. Dickins of Annandale, Va., was arrested as a spy on Jan. 14 on the testimony of his slave and of neighbors, and was confined to Old Capitol Prison in Washington. He was paroled on Mar. 28. Allan Pinkerton to GBM, Jan. 28, 1862, McClellan Papers (A-38:16), Library of Congress; *OR,* Ser. 2, II, pp. 238, 277.

To Abraham Lincoln

His Excellency the President
Dear Sir

[Washington] Saturday evng
[February 8, 1862]

Your note was received by me very late this evening.[1]

I had a long conversation with Genl Hooker about the roads etc in the region we were speaking of, & would beg until Monday morning [February 10] to give a final opinion.

I have not yet heard from the canal boats above.

The experiment of arranging the two will be completed on Monday, when I can make the necessary calculations with exactness.[2]

I have nothing new from Halleck or Buell tonight. Apologizing for the delay

I am most respectfully & truly yours
Geo B McClellan
Maj Genl

ALS, Lincoln Papers, Library of Congress.

1. In his note of this date Lincoln called for news "from the West" and "from the Canal-boats," and asked: "Have you determined, as yet, upon the contemplated movement we have talked of?" *Collected Works of Lincoln,* V, p. 130. 2. GBM refers here to a plan he had discussed with Lincoln to attack the Confederate batteries on the Potomac from Gen. Hooker's position across the river at Liverpool Point in lower Maryland. It was proposed to use canal boats as troop carriers, linked in pairs by timber platforms to increase their capacity. The idea was abandoned. Hooker to Seth Williams, Feb. 17, *OR,* Ser. 1, V, pp. 723–24.

To Ambrose E. Burnside

Private

My dear old Burn Washn Feby 10 1862

Your dispatches of 29th Jan & 3d Feby received yesterday — together with your private notes.[1] I feel for you in your troubles — but you have borne yourself nobly in difficulties more trying than any that remain to you to encounter — & the same energy & pluck that has carried you through up to the present will take you through to the end.

We hear various rumors today about firing at Roanoke Island — I hope to hear tomorrow that you have taken it. In any event I shall feel sure that you have done all that a gallant & skilful soldier can accomplish. We are in status quo here — have gained a great point in Tenna by the capture of Fort Henry — which opens the road to us into Tenna.

Everything is bright — except the roads. Madame, Marcy & his wife all send their kindest. God bless you old fellow & give you success.

Ever yours
Geo B McClellan

Genl A E Burnside

ALS, Records of U.S. Army Continental Commands, RG 393 (3964: Army of the Potomac), National Archives. *OR,* Ser. I, IX, p. 360.

1. Burnside detailed the obstacles he faced in getting his expedition into Pamlico Sound and in condition to attack Roanoke Island. *OR,* Ser. 1, IX, pp. 356–57, 358–59. In a private note dated Jan. 31 he wrote of "elements of a decided failure looking me square in the face.... I think you have overestimated my ability, but shall try not to disappoint you." McClellan Papers (B-40:60), Library of Congress.

To William H. Seward

Hon W H Seward
Secty of State
Dear Sir:

Hd Qtrs of the Army
Washn Feby 11 1861 [1862]

I have had an interview with Col Cluseret, late of the Italian Army, introduced to me by Capt Mohain of the suite of the Prince de Joinville. Col C. also brought me a letter of introduction from Genl Garibaldi. Col C, whose "etat de service" is good, informs me that he resigned his commission as Col in the Italian Army upon the instance of Mr Marsh, who had corresponded with the late Secty of War & yourself upon the subject. That he resigned after receiving what he regarded as a promise that he should have the grade of General of Brigade in our service.[1]

He seems to be a gentleman & good soldier. He has been waiting here many weeks, so that his slender means have become exhausted. May I ask you to inform me whether your records throw any light on the case & whether the good faith of the Govt is pledged to this officer.[2]

The Secty of War being absent from his office it seemed better to address you direct without delay as Col C has been waiting a long time.

Very truly & respectfully
Geo B McClellan
Maj Genl Comdg USA

ALS, William Henry Seward Papers, Rush Rhees Library, University of Rochester.

1. French soldier of fortune Gustave Paul Cluseret had supported Orléanist rule in 1848 and fought in the Crimea before casting his lot with Garibaldi. He was recruited for American service by George P. Marsh, envoy to Sardinia, with the apparent approval of Secretaries Cameron and Seward. 2. Seward replied the next day that in order to conciliate European opinion it would be "good policy" to accommodate Cluseret. Seward Papers. In his memoirs GBM recalled Cluseret less favorably. "I did not like his appearance and declined his services," he wrote, adding that even after Secretary Stanton appointed him a staff colonel in the Army of the Potomac, "I still declined to have anything to do with him. . . ." *McClellan's Own Story,* p. 143. Cluseret allied himself with Gen. Frémont and led a checkered Civil War career before resigning in 1863.

To Edwin M. Stanton

Hon E. M. Stanton
Secretary of War
Sir.

Head Quarters of the Army
Washington Feby 11, 1862

I would respectfully submit to you the following extracts taken from the Report of Major A. Baird, Assistant Inspector General, U.S. Army on the inspection of the Kansas troops, viz.

"If the practice of seizing and confiscating the private property of rebels which is now extensively carried on by the troops known as "Lanes

Brigade'' is to be continued, How may it be managed so as to prevent the troops being demoralized and the Government defrauded?

This practice has become so fixed and general that I am convinced that orders arresting it would not be obeyed and that the only way of putting a stop to it would be to remove the Kansas troops to some other field of action.''[1]

The fact that the property of Citizens is seized and confiscated by the troops engaged in the service of the U.S. is substantiated by both official and reliable private evidence, and from the frequent repetition of these acts the Commanding Officers in Kansas appear to have assumed its legality. The authority under which it is done is unknown to me further than such destruction of private property as is unavoidable from a state of war conducted according to the established usages of civilized nations. I would therefore request the policy of the Government for my guidance in dealing with questions of this nature.[2]

To what extent can the right of confiscation legally be carried? And by what tribunal civil or military are the questions that will naturally arise, to be decided, that the innocent will not suffer while punishing the guilty and that the dignity and justice of the Government may not be at the mercy of individuals governed by cupidity or revenge? This question has assumed such proportions that it will require vigorous means and well defined authority to suppress or direct its applications.

I am Sir very respectfully Your obt Servant
[George B. McClellan]
Maj Genl Commdg U.S.A.

Retained copy, Records of the Headquarters of the Army, RG 108 (M-857:6), National Archives. *OR,* Ser. 1, VIII, pp. 552–53.

1. Maj. Absalom Baird's inspection was undertaken in connection with the so-called Lane expedition. See GBM to Stanton, c. Jan. 25, *supra*. 2. The brigade raised by Kansas senator James H. Lane was notorious. ''Their principal occupation for the last six months,'' Halleck wrote Stanton on Mar. 25, ''seems to have been the stealing of negroes, the robbing of houses, and the burning of barns, grain, and forage. The evidence of their crimes is unquestionable.'' *OR,* Ser. 1, VIII, p. 642. At GBM's direction, the Kansas forces, including the units in Lane's brigade, were reorganized. *OR,* Ser. 1, VIII, pp. 615–17.

To Ambrose E. Burnside

Brig Genl A E Burnside
Comdg Dept of North Carolina
General

Hd Qtrs of the Army
Washn Feby 12 1862

We are all rejoiced to hear, through rebel sources, the gallant capture of Roanoke Island & the rebel gun boats[1] — I hope to receive your account of it in a day or two, & take it for granted that your success has been at least as decisive & brilliant as indicated & assured by the rebel accounts.

I am glad to see that Comdr Goldsborough & yourself have pushed the enemy so rapidly & so far — I hope that the effect has been produced of drawing the attention of the rebels towards Norfolk &c, so that, after having fully secured what you have gained, you will by a rapid countermovement be enabled to make the second attack with every chance of success.[2] I still hope that you will be able to seize & hold Goldsboro, as well as gaining possession of the seaport in view.

You will have heard of our marked success in Tennessee — the capture of Fort Henry & the trip of our gun boats into Alabama.

Everything goes well with us but your success seems to be the most brilliant yet — I expect still more from you. While in the Sound please gain all possible information as to the possibility of attacking Norfolk from the south — that *may* prove to be the best blow to be struck. Although as I am not yet quite prepared to secure it as it should be, it may be our best policy to defer that until you have accomplished all the original objects of the expedition, when, with suitable reinforcements you may attack Norfolk to great advantage.

I regret that the special messenger is waiting & that I must close this.

Very truly yours
Geo B McClellan
Maj Genl Comdg USA

ALS, Records of U.S. Army Continental Commands, RG 393 (3964: Army of the Potomac), National Archives. *OR,* Ser. 1, IX, pp. 362–63.

1. These actions were fought on Feb. 7–8. 2. Burnside's objectives were New Bern and Beaufort, to the south.

To Thomas W. Sherman

Brig. Gen. T. W. Sherman
Comd'g at Port Royal, &c — Head Qrs of the Army
General. — Washington, Feb. 14 1862

Your despatches in regard to the occupation of Dafuskie Island[1] &c. were received to-day. I saw also to-day for the first time your requisition for a siege train for Savannah.

After giving the subject all the consideration in my power, I am forced to the conclusion that, under present circumstances, the siege and capture of Savannah do not promise results commensurate with the sacrifices necessary. When I learned that it was possible for the gunboats to reach the Savannah River above Fort Pulaski, two operations suggested themselves to my mind as its immediate result. *First;* — the capture of Savannah by a "coup de main," — the result of an instantaneous advance and attack by the Army & Navy. The time for this has passed, & your letter indicates that you are not accountable for the failure to seize the propitious moment, but that, on the contrary, you perceived its advantages.[2] *Second;* — to isolate Fort Pulaski, cut off its supplies, and at least facilitate its reduction by a bombardment. Although we have a long delay to deplore, the second course still remains open to us; and I strongly advise the close blockade of Pulaski, and its bombardment as soon as the 13 in. mortars and heavy guns reach you. I am confident you can thus reduce it. With Pulaski, you gain all that is really essential. You obtain complete control of the harbor, you relieve the blockading fleet, and render the main body of your force disposable for other operations.[3]

I do not consider the possession of Savannah worth a siege after Pulaski is in our hands. But the possession of Pulaski is of the first importance. The expedition to Fernandina is well, and I shall be glad to learn that it is ours.

But, after all, the greatest moral effect would be produced by the reduction of Charleston and its defences. There the rebellion had its birth; — there the unnatural hatred of our Government is most intense; there is the centre of the boasted power and courage of the rebels. To gain Fort Sumter and hold Charleston is a task well worthy of our greatest efforts, and considerable sacrifices. That is the problem I would be glad to have you study. Some time must elapse before we can be in all respects ready to accomplish that purpose. Fleets are en route and armies in motion which have certain preliminary objects to accomplish, before we are ready to take Charleston in hand. But the time will before long arrive when I shall be prepared to make that movement.[4] In the meantime, it is my advice and wish that no attempt be made upon Savannah, unless it can be carried with certainty by a "coup de main."

Please concentrate your attention and forces upon Pulaski and Fernandina. St. Augustine might as well be taken by way of an interlude, while awaiting the preparations for Charleston. Success attends us everywhere at present.

Very truly yours
Geo. B. McClellan
Maj. Gen. Comdg. U.S.A.

Copy, McClellan Papers (D-7 :69), Library of Congress. *OR*, Ser. 1, VI, p. 225.

1. Daufuskie Island is at the mouth of the Savannah River. 2. In a Feb. 5 dispatch Sherman attributed this delay to the navy. *OR*, Ser. 1, VI, p. 221. 3. Fort Pulaski would be bombarded into surrender on Apr. 11. 4. Sherman replied on Mar. 8 that he believed Charleston "can be carried with much more ease than I anticipated. . . ." He would not play a role in the extended operations against Charleston, however. *OR*, Ser. 1, VI, p. 240.

To Henry W. Halleck

Maj Genl H. W. Halleck
Commdg Dept of Missouri — Head Quarters of the Army
General. — Washington Feby 14, 1862.

I have just received your gratifying dispatch that our forces occupy Springfield[1] and are in hourly expectation of having similar news in regard to Fort Donelson.

Your proposition in regard to the formation of a Western Division has one fatal obstacle, viz. that the proposed Commander of the new Department of Missouri ranks you![2] I would be glad to hear from you in detail as to the troops from your Department now on the Tennessee and Cumberland rivers.

Do you learn anything as to Beauregard's whereabouts and what troops (if any) he took with him?

What disposition do you intend to make of Hitchcock?[3] If you do not go in person to the Tennessee & Cumberland I shall probably write Buell to take the line of the Tennessee so far as Nashville is concerned — if his advance on Bowling Green must be done, it may well be necessary to throw a large portion of his troops up the Tennessee in which case he is entitled to their command.

Burnside has been very successful. All seems to be well.

Very truly yours
[George B. McClellan]
Maj Genl Commdg U.S.A.

Retained copy, Records of the Headquarters of the Army, RG 108 (M-857:6), National Archives. *OR,* Ser. 1, VII, p. 614.

1. Federal forces occupied Springfield, Mo., on Feb. 13. 2. Halleck wrote GBM on Feb. 8 proposing himself for overall command in a reorganized Western Division, with Buell, Ethan Allen Hitchcock, and David Hunter as his departmental lieutenants. Hunter's commission as a major general of volunteers predated Halleck's as a major general in the regular army by six days. *OR,* Ser. 1, VII, p. 595. In his reply on Feb. 19 Halleck wrote: "It was decided in the Mexican war that regulars ranked volunteers, without regard to dates. This decision, if sustained, makes everything right for the Western Division." *OR,* Ser. 1, VII, p. 636. 3. Hitchcock declined the appointment.

To Frederick W. Lander [TELEGRAM]

[Washington] 10 p.m. Feby 14 [1862]

Telegram received. Your conduct is just like you. Don't talk about resigning. If your health makes it necessary for you to be relieved of course you shall be.[1] I advise, in view of probable movements, that you quietly rest at Cumberland & endeavor to recruit your health before making another move. If you can recover more rapidly here I will arrange to relieve you & give you other work as soon as you are well enough.[2] Give my thanks to the gallant officers & men under your command, & accept my own yourself.

G B McClellan
Maj Genl Comdg USA

Brig Genl F W Lander
Paw Paw etc

ALS (telegram sent), Records of the Office of the Secretary of War, RG 107 (M-473:11), National Archives. *OR,* Ser. 1, LI, Part 1, p. 531.

1. Lander reported on this date that he had personally led a successful assault on a "rebel nest" at Bloomery Gap in western Virginia. Suffering the aftereffects of a wound received at Ball's Bluff, he asked to be relieved. *OR,* Ser. 1, V, pp. 405–406. 2. Lander was stricken with pneumonia and died on Mar. 2.

To Ulysses S. Grant [TELEGRAM]

[Washington] Saturday [February] 15 [1862] 10 p.m.

Telegraph in full the state of affairs with you.[1]

G B McClellan
Maj Genl

Brig Genl U S Grant
Fort Henry

ALS (telegram sent), Records of the Office of the Secretary of War, RG 107 (M-473:11), National Archives. *OR,* Ser. 1, LII, Part 1, p. 212.

1. This telegram was not received until March 3. Grant, *Personal Memoirs* (New York, 1885), I, p. 326.

To Henry W. Halleck [TELEGRAM]

For Halleck [Washington] Feby 15/62 [11 P.M.]

Yours of 8 pm received. Your idea is in some respects good but if Buell can rapidly advance on Nashville he will take it and cut off the enemy who are near Fort Donelson if they do not retreat immediately.[1] His advance in force beyond Bowling Green will at once relieve Grant. His orders are to reinforce Grant if he cannot reach Nashville in time. The immediate possession of Nashville is very important. It can best be gained by the movement I have directed. The possession of Decatur will not necessarily cause the rebels to evacuate Nashville. You must also threaten to occupy Stevenson to accomplish that.[2] I do not see that Buell's movement is bad strategy for it will relieve the pressure upon Grant and leads to the results of first importance. If the destruction of the railroad is so extensive as to make the operation impracticable or very difficult and slow I have provided for the alternative in my instructions to Buell.[3]

Enable Grant to hold his own and I will see that Buell relieves him. The Decatur movement and the one on Memphis are the next steps in my programme. I am arranging to talk with Buell and yourself over the wires tomorrow morning and would be glad to have you at the telegraph office when all is ready. Buell will also be in Louisville office and we can come to a full understanding.

McClellan

Retained copy, Records of the Office of the Secretary of War, RG 107 (M-473 :11), National Archives. *OR,* Ser. 1, VII, pp. 617–18.

1. In a dispatch of this date Halleck described an advance on Nashville by Buell as "bad strategy," arguing instead that Buell should assist Grant's operations against Fort Donelson and then advance on Decatur, Ala., to cut the Memphis and Charleston Railroad. "Nashville would then be abandoned, precisely as Bowling Green has been, without a blow." *OR,* Ser. 1, VII, p. 617. 2. Stevenson, Ala., marked the junction of the second of the two railroads linking Nashville with the Memphis and Charleston line. 3. In a dispatch of this date, GBM instructed Buell to send a column beyond Bowling Green. "If Nashville is open the men could carry their small rations and bread, driving meat on the hoof." *OR,* Ser. 1, VII, p. 626.

To Edwin M. Stanton

Dear Stanton [Washington, February 16, 1862]

I enclose copy of dispatch to Navy Dept which speaks for itself. I shall be able to *talk* over the crisis with Buell and Halleck some time today & arrange all things. We have a brilliant chance to bag Nashville. I have no fears for the ultimate fall of Donelson notwithstanding Foote's drubbing.[1] As soon as I know the exact state of things I will inform you.

I have taken such steps as will make Grant safe & I think force the evacuation of Donelson or its surrender.

Truly yours
McClellan

ALS, Records of the Office of the Secretary of War, RG 107 (M-473 :96), National Archives.

1. Flag Officer Foote's gunboats were repulsed by the Fort Donelson batteries on Feb. 14.

To Elizabeth B. McClellan

My dear Mother Washn Feby 16 [1862]

It is so long since we have heard from any of you at home that I am half inclined to think you must have "seceded" & gone over to the enemy — but I know you are not fond of stage riding & am sure that I have not signed any passport for you, so that unless you & Mary[1] have assumed the name of Jones or Brown, you are probably still in the peaceful city of Phila. I am so glad to know that Mary has recovered from her illness as I was sorry to hear of her attack.

We have good news again today in the shape of the taking of a portion of Fort Donelson — the rest will soon come — it seems to be merely a matter of time now.

My friend Burnside has so far done splendidly, & I am sure will continue in the same path. In truth the rebellion has received some hard blows of late, & we can hope that it will have some harder cracks yet before long. Nelly sends her best love & wishes to know whether you ever received a letter from her some time ago asking you & Mary to come on & pay us a visit as soon as Mary had recovered sufficiently.

I cannot see much of you when you do come for I have but little spare time on my hands — but we would both be very glad if you would come on before I start South. We have a room ready for you at all times.

So one of the juvenile Coxes has taken unto himself a wife — he began early, did he not? Is it not almost time for Brinton & the girls? I presume Eckley is still in Europe — deep down in mines, occasionally refreshing himself by revisiting the upper air & sitting on a coal heap. Give my kindest love to all the Coxes — from the Judge down. If the Phillips are yet in the land of the Union give our love to them too — is it true that Annie has grown thin as Holmes & wears blue spectacles? I did not believe it when I heard it, & attribute it to the malicious abolitionists.[2] The last I heard from Maria[3] was that she had 4 Latin, 6 arithmetic, 3 spelling, & one whipping lesson to give when she called on some friend of hers in Phila. What does Mary do in these days? — keep her usual early hours? Please let us know when to expect you on here. With kindest love to Mary, John, Maria & the children we are your affectionate children

The McCs

Arthur[4] is well except a plaster on one side of his face. The baby has got so far as to have her photograph taken & very pretty.

ALS, McClellan Papers (B-41:61), Library of Congress.

1. GBM's younger sister. 2. References are to members of the Coxe and Phillips families, relations of Mrs. McClellan's in Philadelphia. 3. GBM's sister-in-law. 4. GBM's younger brother.

To the Army of the Potomac

Head Quarters, Army of the Potomac,
General Orders, No.[1] Washington, Feby 17 1862

Soldiers of the Army of the Potomac!

I announce to you glorious victories gained by our fellow soldiers in the west & south. The names of Mill Spring, Roanoke, Fort Henry & Fort

Donelson will hereafter be the pride of all true Americans, & will cause the hearts of all loyal men to throb with joy. None can rejoice in these successes, my comrades, more than we do; but, if I judge aright by taking my feelings as yours — and I know that one common impulse actuates us — there is awakened in your minds another sentiment, — the desire to eclipse these noble deeds of our brethren.

You wish to strike *your* blow, & to show that the Army of the Potomac strikes hard & true, & that it is equal to the great hopes reposed in it by the nation.

I have long held you back my comrades, at first that from a mass of brave but undisciplined citizens I might cement you into an Army — equal to any task that might be imposed upon you. I have restrained you for another reason also. I wished you to strike when the time arrived to give the death blow to this accursed rebellion.

The task of discipline is completed — I am satisfied with you. The time has well nigh arrived when your mission is to be accomplished.

When I place you in front of the rebels remember that the great God of Battles ever favors the just cause, remember that you are fighting for all that men hold dearest. You have battles to win, fatigues to endure, sufferings to encounter, but remember that they will conduct you to a goal from which you will return, covered with glory, to your homes, & that each one of you will bear through life the proud honor of being one of the men who crushed the most wicked rebellion that ever threatened free institutions & a beneficent government.

AD, McClellan Papers (A-41:17), Library of Congress.

1. This address was not issued. See GBM's address to the Army of the Potomac, Mar. 14, 1862, *infra*.

To Henry W. Halleck [TELEGRAM]

Washn. Feby 18 1862 1.30 pm

I am directed by the Secty of War to instruct you that no arrangements either by equivalents or otherwise will be made for the exchange of the rebel Generals Johnson Buckner, Pillow & Tillman, nor for that of prisoners who had served in our regular army without special orders from these Head Quarters.[1]

G B McClellan
Maj Genl Comdg USA

General Halleck

ALS (telegram sent), Records of the Office of the Secretary of War, RG 107 (M-473:11), National Archives. *OR*, Ser. 2, III, p. 275. The same telegram was sent to Generals Buell, Rosecrans, and John E. Wool.

1. Of the Confederate generals named — Bushrod Johnson, Simon B. Buckner, Gideon Pillow, and Lloyd Tilghman — only Buckner and Tilghman were in fact captured at Forts Henry and Donelson. When prisoner exchange was later agreed to, Confederate officers and men formerly in U.S. service were included, and both generals were exchanged.

To Thomas A. Scott [TELEGRAM]

T A Scott [Washington, February 20, 1862]

Telegram received.[1] Increase rolling stock on Nashville Railway. At present no troops will move from East. Ample occupation for them here. Rebels hold firm at Manassas Junction.

McClellan

ALS (telegram sent), Records of the Office of the Secretary of War, RG 107 (M-473:12), National Archives. *OR,* Ser. 1, VII, p. 641.

1. Assistant Secretary of War Scott telegraphed GBM from Louisville on Feb. 19: "Buell immediately needs re-enforcements. Will they come?" *OR,* Ser. 1, VII, p. 635.

To Don Carlos Buell [TELEGRAM]

Buell [Washington, February 20, 1862]

Halleck says Columbus reinforced from New Orleans & steam up on their boats ready for move probably on Cairo. Wishes to withdraw some troops from Donelson.[1] I tell him improbable that rebels reinforced from New Orleans or attack Cairo. Think will abandon Columbus. What force have you in Bowling Green what in advance of it and where today. How soon can you be in front of Nashville & in what force. What news of the rebels. If the force in West can take Nashville or even hold its own for the present I hope to have Richmond and Norfolk in from three to four weeks. Answer fully.

McClellan

ALS (telegram sent), Records of the Office of the Secretary of War, RG 107 (M-473:11), National Archives. *OR,* Ser. 1, VII, p. 640.

1. In his telegram of Feb. 19, Halleck also called for reinforcements from Buell, who he predicted would be unable to advance on Nashville "for two or three weeks." *OR,* Ser. 1, VII, pp. 636–37.

To Don Carlos Buell [TELEGRAM]

Head-Quarters, Army of the Potomac,
Washington, Feby 21, 1862 1 am

Telegraph me at least once every day the position of your own troops — that of the rebels & the state of affairs. Unless I have this detailed information I cannot tell whether it is necessary or not to suspend or abandon my own plans here. Neither Halleck nor yourself give me as much detailed information as is necessary for me. This is the critical period & I must be constantly informed of the condition of your affairs.

G B McClellan
Maj Genl

Brig Genl D. C. Buell
Louisville or Bowling Green

ALS (telegram sent), Records of the Office of the Secretary of War, RG 107 (M-473:12), National Archives. *OR*, Ser. 1, VII, p. 645. A similar dispatch was sent on this date to Halleck.

To Henry W. Halleck [TELEGRAM]

Head Quarters Army of the Potomac
Halleck St. Louis Washington, D.C. Feb. 21 1862

Buell at Bowling Green knows more of the state of affairs than you at St. Louis. Until I hear from him I cannot see necessity of giving you entire command.

I expect to hear from Buell in a few minutes. I do not yet see that Buell cannot control his own line. I shall not lay your request before the Secretary until I hear definitely from Buell.[1]

McClellan

Retained copy, Records of the Office of the Secretary of War, RG 107 (M-473:12), National Archives. *OR*, Ser. 1, VII, p. 645.

1. Halleck had telegraphed on Feb. 20: "I must have command of the armies in the West. Hesitation and delay are losing us the golden opportunity. Lay this before the President and Secretary of War. May I assume the command? Answer quickly." *OR*, Ser. 1, VII, p. 641.

To John E. Wool [TELEGRAM]

Gen J E Wool
Fortress Monroe [Washington] Feb 21 '62 [4 P.M.]

The iron clad steamer Monitor and a large frigate will be at Hampton Roads within the time you specify.[1] Do you need troops to replace those intended for Genl Butler?[2] If so how many? With the cooperation of the navy how many additional troops do you need to take Yorktown, and how many by a subsequent operation to take Norfolk? Send me your best map of Norfolk and vicinity. Please communicate fully. Let me hear from you every day. Can you take the Sewells Point battery?[3] If so do it and spike the guns.

G B McClellan
Major Genl Comdg USA

Retained copy, Records of the Office of the Secretary of War, RG 107 (M-473:12), National Archives. *OR,* Ser. 1, IX, pp. 15–16. Maj. Gen. Wool commanded the Department of Virginia, with headquarters at Fort Monroe.

1. In a Feb. 21 dispatch to GBM, Wool reported the intelligence that the *Merrimack,* a steam frigate captured at Norfolk by the Confederates and converted into an ironclad, would lead an attack on Newport News within five days. *Confidential Correspondence of Gustavus Vasa Fox,* eds. Robert M. Thompson and Richard Wainwright (New York, 1920), I, p. 428. The new Federal ironclad *Monitor* was then undergoing trials at New York. 2. These troops at Fort Monroe were slated for operations against New Orleans. See GBM to Benjamin F. Butler, Feb. 23, *infra.* 3. The Sewell's Point battery guarded the approach to Norfolk.

To Abraham Lincoln

Private

My dear Sir Washn Feby 22 1862

I have not felt authorized to intrude upon you personally in the midst of the deep distress I know you feel in the sad calamity that has befallen you & your family — yet I cannot refrain from expressing to you the sincere & deep sympathy I feel for you.[1]

You have been a kind true friend to me in the midst of the great cares & difficulties by which we have been surrounded during the past few months — your confidence has upheld me when I should otherwise have felt weak. I wish now only to assure you & your family that I have felt the deepest sympathy in your affliction.

I am pushing to prompt completion the measures of which we have spoken, & I beg that you will not allow military affairs to give you one moment's trouble — but that you will rest assured that nothing shall be left undone to follow up the successes that have been such an auspicious commencement of our new campaign.

I am very sincerely & respectfully your friend & obt svt

Geo B McClellan

His Excellency Abraham Lincoln
Presdt, US.

ALS, Lincoln Papers, Library of Congress.

1. The president's eleven-year-old son, Willie, had died of typhoid fever on Feb. 20.

To Benjamin F. Butler

Maj Genl B. F. Butler
U.S. Army — Head Quarters of the Army
General — [Washington] February 23d 1862

You are assigned to the command of the land forces destined to co-operate with the Navy in the attack upon New Orleans.[1] You will use every means to keep your destination a profound secret, even from your staff officers, with the exception of your chief of staff, and Lt Weitzel[2] of the Engineers.

The force at your disposal will consist of the first thirteen regiments named in your memorandum handed to me in person,[3] the 21st Indiana, 4th Wisconsin & 6th Michigan (old and good regiments from Baltimore); these three regiments will await your orders at Fort Monroe. Two companies of the 21st Indiana are well drilled at heavy artillery. The Cavalry force already en route for Ship Island, will be sufficient for your purposes. After full consultation with officers well acquainted with the country in which it is proposed to operate I have arrived at the conclusion that 3 light batteries fully equipped and one without horses will be all that are necessary.

This will make your force about 14,400 Infantry, 275 Cavalry, 580 Artillery — total 15,255 men.

The Comdg Genl of the Dept of Key West is authorized to loan you temporarily, 2 regiments. Fort Pickens can probably give you another, which will bring your force to nearly 18,000. The object of your expedition is one of vital importance — the capture of New Orleans. The route selected, is up the Mississippi River & the first obstacle to be encountered (perhaps the only one) is in the resistance offered by Forts St Philip & Jackson. It is expected that the Navy can reduce the works, in that case you will after their capture leave a sufficient garrison in them to render them perfectly secure, & it is recommended that on the upward passage a few heavy guns, and some troops be left at the Pilot Station (at the forks of the river) to cover a retreat in the case of a disaster (the troops and guns will of course be removed as soon as the Forts are captured).

Should the Navy fail to reduce the works, you will land your forces, & siege train, and endeavor to breach the works, silence their fire, and carry them by assault.

The next resistance will be near the English bend, where there are some earthen batteries; here it may be necessary for you to land your troops to cooperate with the naval attack, altho' it is more than probable that the Navy unassisted can accomplish the result. If these works are taken the city of New Orleans necessarily falls.

In that event it will probably be best to occupy Algiers with the mass of your troops. Also the Eastern bank of the river above the city — it may be necessary to place some troops *in* the city to preserve order tho' if there appears sufficient Union sentiment to control the city it may be best for purposes of discipline to keep your men out of the city.

After obtaining possession of New Orleans, it will be necessary to reduce all the works guarding its approaches from the East, and particularly to gain the Manchac Pass.

Baton Rouge, Berwick Bay & Fort Livingston will next claim your attention.

A feint on Galveston may facilitate the objects we have in view. I need not call your attention to the necessity of gaining possession of all the rolling stock you can, on the different railways, and of obtaining control of the roads themselves. The occupation of Baton Rouge by a combined naval and land force should be accomplished as soon as possible after you have gained New Orleans. Then endeavor to open your communication with the Northern column of the Mississippi, always bearing in mind the necessity of occupying Jackson Miss. as soon as you can safely do so, either after or before you have effected the junction. Allow nothing to divert you from obtaining full possession of *all* the approaches to New Orleans. When that object is accomplished to its fullest extent, it will be necessary to make a combined attack on Mobile, in order to gain possession of the harbor and works, as well as to control the railway terminus at the city. In regard to this I will send more detailed instructions as the operations of the Northern column develop themselves. I may simply state that the general objects of the expedition are *first* the reduction of New Orleans and all its approaches, then Mobile and all its defenses, then Pensacola, Galveston etc. It is probable that by the time New Orleans is reduced it will be in the power of the Government to reinforce the land forces sufficiently to accomplish all these objects; in the mean time you will please give all the assistance in your power to the Army and Navy commanders in your vicinity, never losing sight of the fact that the great object to be achieved is the capture and firm retention of New Orleans.

Very Respectfully Your Obt Sevt
Geo B McClellan
Maj Genl Comdg USA

LS, Butler Papers, Library of Congress. *OR,* Ser. 1, VI, pp. 694–95. Maj. Gen. Butler was appointed to command of the Department of the Gulf on this date.

1. On Jan. 25 GBM had recommended that the proposed army-navy operation against New Orleans, which he suggested would require 30,000 to 50,000 troops, be suspended. *OR,* Ser. 1, VI, pp. 677–78. At that time he anticipated commanding any such expedition himself. Malcolm Ives to James Gordon Bennett, Jan. 15, 1862, Bennett Papers, Library of Congress. 2. Lt. Godfrey Weitzel, Corps of Engineers. 3. Probably a memorandum dated Feb. 12. *OR,* Ser. 1, VI, p. 687.

To Joseph Hooker [TELEGRAM]

Washn Feb 23 [1862]

We can count upon the assistance of the iron clad steamer Erricson, armed with 2 eleven inch guns during the present week.[1] Will it in your judgment be better to wait for her or to adopt the original plan?[2] It seems to me that the safest plan is to use the Erricson, supported by the whole flotilla & a heavy force prepared to land. I can furnish here the means of landing at any point from 10,000 to 15,000 men in addition to your command. Answer by telegram.[3]

G B McClellan
Maj Genl Comdg

Brig Genl J Hooker
Budd's Ferry

ALS (telegram sent), Records of the Office of the Secretary of War, RG 107 (M-473:12), National Archives. *OR,* Ser. 1, LI, Part 1, p. 536.

1. The *Monitor,* designed by John Ericsson. She did not reach Hampton Roads until Mar. 8. 2. The plan for assaulting the Confederate batteries on the lower Potomac from Maryland. 3. Hooker replied on this date that he was ready to proceed without waiting for the *Monitor,* and recommended expanding the operation to include the seizure of Fredericksburg. *OR,* Ser. 1, V, pp. 726–27.

To Henry W. Halleck [TELEGRAM]

Head Quarters Army of the Potomac,
Halleck, St. Louis Washington, D.C. Feb. 24th 1862

Cullum telegram in regard to reconnaissance of Columbus received.[1] Buell will be in front of Nashville tomorrow evening. Best cooperate with him to the full extent of your power, to secure Nashville beyond a doubt. Then by a combined movement of troops and gun boats seize Decatur. Buell will be directed to occupy and hold in force the railroad junctions in vicinity of Chattanooga and to reestablish the railroads from Nashville to Decatur and Stevenson. This will very nearly isolate A. S. Johnston from Richmond.

The next move should be either a direct march in force upon the rear of Memphis or else first upon the communications and rear of Columbus, depending entirely on the strength and movements of the Rebels. In the mean time it would be well to amuse the garrison of Columbus with our mortar boats as soon as a sufficient number of them can be spared with gun boats from the Tennessee and Cumberland rivers.

The early possession of Humboldt in force is of importance, but should not be undertaken until Nashville is securely ours.

The possession of Grand Junction will complete the isolation of the rebels. It may be better to occupy Corinth instead of Decatur after Chattanooga is firmly in our possession. Please communicate fully and frequently.

McClellan

Retained copy, Records of the Office of the Secretary of War, RG 107 (M-473:12), National Archives. *OR,* Ser. 1, VII, p. 661.

1. Brig. Gen. George W. Cullum, Halleck's chief of staff, reported on Feb. 23 that Columbus, Ky., was still held by the enemy. *OR*, Ser. 1, VII, p. 658.

To Edwin M. Stanton [TELEGRAM]

Hon E M Stanton [Sandy Hook, Md.] Feb. 26 [1862, 10:20 P.M.]

The bridge was splendidly thrown by Captain Duane, assisted by Lieutenants Babcock, Reese, and Cross.[1] It was one of the most difficult operations of the kind ever performed. I recommend Captain Duane to be made a major by brevet for his energy and skill in this matter, also Lieutenants Babcock, Reese, and Cross, all of the Corps of Engineers, to be captains by brevet. We have 8500 infantry, eighteen guns, and two squadrons of cavalry on the Virginia side. I have examined the ground and seen that the troops are in proper positions and are ready to resist any attack. Loudon and Bolivar Heights as well as Maryland Heights are occupied by us. Burns' brigade will be here in a couple of hours and will cross at day break. Four more squadrons of cavalry and several more guns pass here. Reports that G W Smith[2] with fifteen thousand men is expected at Winchester.

Colonel Geary[3] deserves praise for the manner in which he occupied Virginia and crossed after the construction of the bridge. We will attempt the canal boat bridge tomorrow. The spirit of the troops is most excellent. They are in the mood to fight anything. It is raining hard but most of the troops are in houses.

G B McClellan

Retained copy, Records of the Office of the Secretary of War, RG 107 (M-473:12), National Archives. *OR*, Ser. 1, V, p. 727.

1. Capt. James C. Duane, Lts. Orville E. Babcock, Chauncey B. Reese, Charles E. Cross. For the plan of operations, see GBM to War Department, c. Mar. 1, *infra*. 2. Maj. Gen. Gustavus W. Smith, CSA. 3. Col. John W. Geary, 28th Pennsylvania.

To Mary Ellen McClellan

Sandy Hook near Harper's Ferry
Thursday am Feby 27 1862

...Here I still am — I crossed the river as soon as the bridge was finished & watched the troops pass. It was a magnificent spectacle — one of the grandest I ever saw. As soon as my horse & escort got over I rode out to the line of pickets & saw for myself that everything was right & ready for an attack. The position is a superb one.

I got over about 12 guns & 8000 infty before dark — also a squadron of cavalry. I heard in the p.m. a rumor that G. W. Smith was expected at Winchester with 15,000 men — altho' I did not fully credit it I nevertheless took all the military precautions necessary & felt perfectly secure during the night. The enemy are not now in sight, but I have sent out cavalry patrols that may bring in intelligence of value. It was after dark & raining hard when I recrossed the bridge. The narrow road was so completely blocked up that it was a very difficult matter to make one's way among the wagons.

It rained hard & was very cold during the night. . . .

The rest of us slept in a car — I was up most of the night, telegraphing etc. This morning it is blowing a hurricane, but the bridge stands well thus far. Burns' Brigade came up during the night. I left them in the cars & crossed them this morning early. The wagons have gone over, a regt of cavalry is now crossing, another battery will follow, & I will have everything well cleared up before the arrival of Abercrombie's Brigade, which should be here by 2 o'clock. I will get it over before dark, also the heavy artillery & regular cavalry if it arrives. I hope to be able to occupy Charleston tomorrow & get Lander to Martinsburg. It will then require but a short time to finish matters here. The roads on the other side are good — the country more open than near Washn. You have no idea how the wind is blowing now — a perfect tornado — it makes the crossing of the river very difficult & interferes with everything. I am anxious about our bridge. . . .

AL copy, McClellan Papers (C-7:63), Library of Congress.

To Edwin M. Stanton [TELEGRAM]

Hon. E. M. Stanton
Secretary of War Sandy Hook 3 1/2 p.m. Feby 27th 1862

The lift lock is too small to permit the canal boats to enter the river so that it is impossible to construct the permanent bridge as I intended.[1] I shall probably be obliged to fall back upon the safe and slow plan of merely covering the reconstruction of the Railroad. This will be done at once but will be tedious. I cannot as things now are be sure of my supplies for the force necessary to seize Winchester which is probably reinforced from Manassas. The wiser plan is to rebuild the Railroad Bridge as rapidly as possible and then act according to the state of affairs.

G. B. McClellan
Maj Gen'l

Received copy, Records of the Office of the Secretary of War, RG 107 (M-473:98), National Archives. *OR*, Ser. 1, V, p. 728.

1. These canal boats, intended as piers for the bridge, had been floated to the site in the Chesapeake and Ohio Canal paralleling the Potomac.

To Randolph B. Marcy [TELEGRAM]

Gen R B Marcy Sandy Hook [February 27, 1862] 8 pm

Revoke Hooker's authority in accordance with Barnard's opinion.[1] Immediately on my return we will take the other plan and push on vigorously.[2]

G B McClellan

Received copy, Records of the Office of the Secretary of War, RG 107 (M-504 :9), National Archives. *OR,* Ser. 1, V, p. 728.

1. In a Feb. 27 telegram Brig. Gen. John G. Barnard, chief engineer of the Army of the Potomac, expressed opposition to Hooker's plan for attacking the batteries on the lower Potomac from Maryland. *OR,* Ser. 1, LI, Part 1, p. 542. 2. The "other plan" was an advance on the Virginia side of the Potomac against the batteries.

To Abraham Lincoln [TELEGRAM]

For A Lincoln, President [Sandy Hook, February 28, 1862]

It is impossible for many days to do more than supply the troops now here & at Charlestown. We could not supply and move to Winchester for many days, & had I moved more troops here they would have been at a loss for food on the Virginia side. I know that I have acted wisely & that you will cheerfully agree with me when I explain. I have arranged to establish depots on that side so we can do what we please. I have secured opening of the road.

G B McClellan
Maj Genl Comdg

ALS (telegram sent), McClellan Papers (C-10 :63), Library of Congress. *OR,* Ser. 1, V, p. 730.

To the War Department

[Washington, c. March 1, 1862][1]

When I started for Harper's Ferry I plainly stated to the Presdt & the Secty of War that the chief object of the operation would be to open the Baltimore & Ohio Railroad, by crossing the river in force at Harper's Ferry. That I had collected the material for making a permanent bridge by means of canal boats, that from the nature of the river it was doubtful whether such a bridge could be constructed, that if it could not I would at least occupy the ground in front of Harper's Ferry, in order to cover the rebuilding of the R.R. bridge, & finally when the communications were perfectly secure move on Winchester.

When I arrived at the place I found the Bateau Bridge nearly completed — the holding ground proved better than had been anticipated — the weather was favorable, there being no wind. I at once crossed over the two brigades which had arrived, & took steps to hurry up the other two, belonging respectively to Banks' & Sedgwick's Divisions. The difficulty of crossing supplies had not then become apparent. That night I telegraphed for a regt of regular cavalry & four batteries of heavy artillery to come up the next day (Thursday) [February 27]; besides directing Keyes Division of Infantry to be moved up on Friday.

Next morning the attempt was made to pass the canal boats through the lift lock in order to commence at once the construction of a permanent bridge — it was then found for the first time that the lock was too small to permit the passage of the boats, it having been built for a class of boats running on the Shenandoah Canal, & too narrow by some 4 or 6 inches for the canal boats. The lift locks above & below are all large enough for the ordinary boats — I had seen that at Edward's Ferry thus used — it had always been represented to the Engineers by the railway employees & others that the lock *was* large enough, & the difference being too small to be detected by the eye, no one had thought of measuring it, or suspecting any difficulty. I thus suddenly found myself unable to build the permanent bridge; — a violent gale had arisen which threatened the safety of our only means of communication; — the narrow approach to the bridge was so crowded & clogged with wagons that it was very clear that under existing circumstances nothing more could be done than to cross over the baggage & supplies of the four brigades; of these instead of being able to cross both during the morning, the last arrived only in time to go over just before dark. It was evident that the troops under orders would only be in the way should they arrive, & that it would not be possible to subsist them for a rapid march on Winchester. It was therefore deemed necessary to countermand the order, content ourselves with covering the reopening of the R.R. for the present, & in the mean time use every exertion to establish as promptly as possible depots of forage & subsistence on the Virginia side to supply the troops & enable them to move on Winchester independently of the bridge. The next day — Friday — I sent a strong reconnaissance to Charleston, & under its protection went there myself. I then determined to hold that place, & to move the troops composing Lander's & Williams' commands at once on Martinsburg & Bunker Hill — thus effectually covering the reconstruction of the R.R.

Having done this, & taken all the steps in my power to ensure the rapid transmittal of supplies over the river I returned to this City well satisfied with what had been accomplished. While up the river I learned that the Presdt was dissatisfied with the state of affairs, but on my return have understood from the Secty of War that upon learning the whole state of the case the Presdt was fully satisfied. I contented myself therefore with giving to the Secty a brief statement, about as I have written it here — he did not even require that much of me. He was busy — I troubled him as little as possible, & immediately went to work at other important affairs.[2]

AD copy, McClellan Papers (A-43:17), Library of Congress. *OR,* Ser. 1, V, pp. 48–49.

1. Although this manuscript bears a later endorsement, not by GBM, describing it as a "copy of letter to the War Department written somewhere about Feb 1862 on the movement at Harper's Ferry," its contents indicate that it was written no earlier than Mar. 1, the day GBM returned to Washington. The original has not been found. The concluding sentences further suggest that it might better be described as a memorandum or notes based on the original. 2. GBM wrote in his memoirs that in fact Stanton "deceived" him and never showed the statement to the president. *McClellan's Own Story,* p. 195.

Memorandum on Potomac Batteries

[Washington, March 1, 1862]

Barnard, McDowell, Franklin, Hooker & Heintzelman to meet say tomorrow to prepare & propose a plan for opening the lower Potomac batteries on the following basis —

To occupy Dumfries (some 9 miles from Colchester) in sufficient force to draw off the enemy in the vicinity & thus enable detachments to move down to the batteries and thoroughly destroy them. A part of this plan will be to occupy Fairfax C.H., Vienna (?), Drainsville (?), Fairfax or perhaps still better Sangster's Station & strongly secure Wolf Run shoals, while a sufficient force crosses at Occoquan & Colchester, throwing out parties to the right to cover its flank & secure the retreat. The landing of a Division[1] near Freestone Point would materially facilitate the passage of the Occoquan & might form the advance guard on the march to Dumfries. The cooperation of the flotilla including the Erricson[2] will form a necessary part of the plan.[3]

AD, McClellan Papers (A-88:35), Library of Congress.

1. Hooker's division, from lower Maryland. 2. The *Monitor*. 3. Attached calculations by GBM specified a force of over 118,000 men for the proposed operation.

To Henry W. Halleck

Private & strictly confidential

My dear Halleck Washington March 3 1862

Yours of the 24th arrived while I was up the river.[1]

I went there to superintend the passage of the river & decide as to the ulterior movements of the troops. The passage was a *very* difficult one, but the Engineer Troops under Duane did wonders. I found it impossible to supply a large body of troops without first establishing depots on the Virginia side — which we are rapidly doing. So I contented myself for the present with occupying Charleston etc in order to cover the reopening of the B & O RR. I have also occupied Martinsburg & will tomorrow throw out a strong force to Bunker Hill. We are thus in position to attack Winchester as soon as our supplies are collected.

I hope to open the Potomac this week — provided the weather permits — it will require a movement of the whole Army in order to keep "Manassas" off my back — I cannot count upon any effective cooperation on the part of the Navy. As soon as I have cleared the Potomac I shall bring here the water transportation now ready (at least it will be in four or five days) & then move by detachments of about 55,000 men for the region of sandy roads & short land transportation. When you have asked me for 50,000 men from here, my dear fellow, you have made one of two mistakes — either you have much overrated my force or you have thought that I intended to remain inactive here.[2]

I expect to fight a desperate battle somewhere near Richmond — the most desperate of the war — for I am well assured that the army of Manassas remains intact & that it is composed of the best armed & best disciplined troops that the rebels have — with the prestige of Bull's Run in their favor. I have, or expect to have, one great advantage over you, as the result of my long & tedious labors — troops that will be demoralized neither by success nor disaster. I feel that I can count upon this Army of mine, & shall gladly venture my life in the scale.

If you had been as long in command you would have had as good, or perhaps a better, army than this of which I feel very proud — but that has been your bad luck & my good fortune. You have done all that could have been done with the means at your disposal — the fate of war is yet to decide whether I shall prove as skilful as you have been — I am sure that I have your good wishes & prayers.

I hardly know what to say as to your proposition about new grades. Why change the European order in the military hierarchy & make a "General" junior to a "Lieut General"? I see no especial reason for it.

I had determined to bide my time — content with my present rank for the present, & hoping that Congress would give another grade after marked success. I have ever felt that higher grades than that of Maj Genl are necessary in so large an Army as that we now have — but I have felt great delicacy in alluding to it. But very few weeks will elapse before the questio vexata will be decided — suppose we let it wait until then & then say what we think? I am willing however to defer to your judgment in the matter & will do all I can to carry out the plan. I don't think *I* can do anything now — I have but few friends in Congress — the abolitionists are doing their best to displace me & I shall be content if I can keep my head above water until I am ready to strike the final blow. You have no idea of the undying hate with which they pressure me — but I take no notice of them, & try to keep Warren Hasting's motto in mind — mens aequa in arduis![3] I sometimes become quite angry, but generally contrive to keep my temper. Do write me fully your views as to future movements in the West — I think the first thing to be done is to separate Johnson[4] from Memphis by seizing Decatur — Buell must then force Chattanooga & you can then with perfect safety operate on Memphis etc & open your communications with the combined expedition which ought to gain New Orleans within three weeks from this date. Butler will have about 16,000 men — the naval fleet is tremendous in power. Nothing new from Sherman — he & Dupont are not on good terms — they neutralize each other.[5]

Burnside is doing well.

Very sincerely your friend
Geo B McClellan

Maj Genl H W Halleck
St Louis

ALS, James S. Schoff Collection, William L. Clements Library, University of Michigan. *OR*, Ser. 1, XI, Part 3, pp. 7–8.

1. Halleck's letter of Feb. 24 proposed a plan to frustrate the "abolition party" from promoting its favorites over GBM by creating "the rank of *General* between the Major Genl & Lieut Genl, and leave the latter as it now is, for brevet only." Only he and GBM would be named to the new rank. "Of course you will get the Brevet Lt Genlship as soon as Richmond is taken, and . . . I will try to come in for a Brevet at the close of the war." He noted "attempts of the abolition press to create jealousies between us. . . . I have too high a regard for your character & military skill to permit any thing of that kind." McClellan Papers (A-42:17), Library of Congress. 2. In an interview with Assistant Secretary of War Scott, Halleck had called for 50,000 reinforcements from the Army of the Potomac. Scott to Stanton, Feb. 17, 1862, Stanton Papers, Library of Congress. 3. Warren Hastings, governor-general of India, advised an even temper in adversity as the lesson of his acquittal in 1795 after a seven-year impeachment trial. 4. Gen. Albert Sidney Johnston. 5. Flag Officer Samuel F. Du Pont was Gen. Thomas Sherman's naval counterpart in the Port Royal expedition.

To Henry W. Halleck [TELEGRAM]

Washn March 3/62 6 pm

Your dispatch of last evening received.[1]

The future success of our cause demands that proceedings such as Grant's should at once be checked. Generals must observe discipline as well as private soldiers. Do not hesitate to arrest him at once if the good of service requires it, & place C F Smith in command. You are at liberty to regard this as a positive order if it will smooth your way. I appreciate the difficulties you have to encounter & will be glad to relieve you from troubles as far as possible.[2]

G B McClellan
Maj Genl Comdg USA

Maj Genl H W Halleck
St Louis

ALS (telegram sent), Records of the Office of the Secretary of War, RG 107 (M-473:50), National Archives. *OR*, Ser. 1, VII, p. 680. This dispatch is endorsed "Approved Edwin M. Stanton Sec of War."

1. Halleck telegraphed that he had received no word from Grant in more than a week, and that he "richly deserves" censure for "this neglect and inefficiency." *OR*, Ser. 1, VII, pp. 679–80. 2. The difficulty was resolved — it was later traced to a communications breakdown — and Grant was not arrested.

To John A. Dix [TELEGRAM]

Wash Sunday March 9 [1862] 11 am

Merrimac sank the Cumberland, the Congress surrendered. Minnesota & St. Lawrence ran aground in approaching scene of contest. At half past eight last night Merrimac had retired to Craney Island. Please be fully on alert. See that Fort Carroll[1] is placed in a condition for defense as rapidly as possible in case Merrimac should run by Fort Monroe. Until further orders stop passage of army transports passing from Phila to Annapolis & Perryville by Canal.[2] What is condition of Fort Carroll.

G B McClellan
Maj Genl Comdg USA

Maj Genl J A Dix
Baltimore Md

ALS (telegram sent), Records of the Office of the Secretary of War, RG 107 (M-473:50), National Archives. *OR*, Ser. 1, LI, Part 1, p. 549. GBM sent similar warnings to fort commanders at Philadelphia, New York, Newport, New London, Boston, and Portland. *OR*, Ser. 1, IX, p. 19.

1. Fort Carroll guarded the Patapsco River approach to Baltimore. 2. The canal linking the Delaware River with Chesapeake Bay.

To John E. Wool [TELEGRAM]

[Washington] March 9 [1862] 1 p.m.

If the rebels obtain full command of the water it would seem impossible for you to hold Newport News. You are therefore authorized to evacuate that place, drawing the garrison in upon Fort Monroe which I need not say to so brave an officer is to be held at all hazards, as I will risk everything to sustain you should you be attacked by superior forces. From indications here I suspect an intention of the enemy to fall back nearer to Richmond that they may better concentrate their forces. An attack upon you is not improbable. If the fifteen inch gun is at Newport News I would suggest its immediate removal to either Fort Monroe or Fort Calhoun, unless it will enable you to retain possession of Newport News.

By authorizing you to withdraw from Newport News I do not mean to give you the order to do so, but to relieve you from that grave sense of responsibility which every good officer feels in such a case — I would only evacuate Newport News when it became clear that the rebels would certainly obtain complete control of the water & render it untenable. Do not run the risk of placing its garrison under the necessity of surrendering. You will also please inform me fully of your views & wishes — the practicality & necessity of reinforcing you &c. The performances of the Merrimac place a new aspect upon everything, & may very probably change my whole plan of campaign, just on the eve of execution.[1]

G B McClellan
Maj Genl Comdg

Maj Genl John E Wool
Fort Monroe

ALS (telegram sent), Records of the Office of the Secretary of War, RG 107 (M-473 :50), National Archives. *OR,* Ser. 1, IX, p. 23.

1. Wool replied on Mar. 10: "If I can get the number of men and batteries asked for, I think I will be able to keep Newport News, that is, if no accident happens to the *Monitor.*" *NOR,* Ser. 1, VII, p. 84.

To Edwin M. Stanton

Private Head-Quarters, Army of the Potomac,
My dear Sir Washington [March 9, 1862]

The preparation of the boats etc to be sunken in the Potomac is being carried out. As fast as enough are prepared for one tug boat they will go down to Wyman.[1]

Very truly yours
Geo B McClellan

Hon E M Stanton
Secty of War

I think we will find the danger less as we learn more, & am less & less inclined to apprehend that the Merrimac will venture out — nevertheless we must take it for granted that the worst will happen.

McC

ALS, McClellan Papers, New-York Historical Society.

1. Stanton had ordered scows loaded with stone in preparation for blocking the channel should the *Merrimack* venture up the Potomac toward Washington. Lt. Robert H. Wyman commanded the Potomac flotilla. The plan was soon canceled.

To Abraham Lincoln, Edwin M. Stanton [TELEGRAM]

[Hall's Hill, Va., March 9, 1862]

We have Sangster's Station & Fairfax Court House. I am arranging to move forward to push the retreat of rebels as far as possible.[1] I have ordered railway & telegraph repairs to be pushed tomorrow. I shall return late tonight & start out early in morning.

G B McClellan
Maj Genl

A Lincoln Presdt
E M Stanton Secty of War

ALS (telegram sent), McClellan Papers (A-50:20), Library of Congress.

1. It was reported on this date that the Confederates had withdrawn from Manassas Junction and Centreville.

To Edwin M. Stanton [TELEGRAM]

[Hall's Hill, March 10, 1862, 1 A.M.]

You have entirely misunderstood me, & the idea I intended to convey was simply that I could not under the pressure of the new aspect of affairs immediately carry out the Presdt's order as to the formation of Army Corps.[1] It is absolutely necessary that I should at once move Divisions as they stand — if you require me to suspend movements until Army Corps can be formed I will do so, but I regard it as a military necessity that the Divisions should move to the front at once without waiting for the formation of Army Corps. If it is your order to wait until the Corps can be formed I will of course wait. I will comply with the Presdt's order as soon as possible. I intended to do so tomorrow, but circumstances have changed. If you desire it I will at once countermand all the orders I have given for an advance until the formation of Army Corps is completed. I have only to add that the orders I have given tonight to advance early tomorrow morning were dictated solely by the present position of affairs.

If the leave to suspend the order be granted there will be no unreasonable delay in the formation of Army Corps. I await your reply here, that I may countermand my orders at once. Please reply at once.[2]

G. B. McClellan
Maj Genl Comdg

ALS (telegram sent), McClellan Papers (A-52:20), Library of Congress. *OR,* Ser. 1, V, pp. 740–41.

1. In his General War Order No. 2 of Mar. 8, the president ordered the divisions of the Army of the Potomac to be grouped into army corps, under Generals Irvin McDowell,

Edwin V. Sumner, Samuel P. Heintzelman, Erasmus D. Keyes, and Nathaniel P. Banks. On Mar. 9 GBM requested the order be suspended until his movement toward Manassas was made. Stanton responded that "it is the duty of every officer to obey the President's orders." *OR,* Ser. 1, V, pp. 18, 739. 2. Stanton replied on this date: "Move just as you think best now, and let the other matter stand until it can be done without impeding movements." *OR,* Ser. 1, V, p. 741.

To Edwin M. Stanton [TELEGRAM]

Head-Quarters of the Army,
Fairfax C.H. March 11, 1862 8.30 p.m.

I have just returned from a ride of more than forty miles. Have examined Centreville, Union Mills, Blackburns ford, Manassas, the battle field etc. The rebels have left all their positions & from the information obtained during our ride today I am satisfied that they have fallen behind the Rapidan holding Fredericksburg & Gordonsville. Their movement from here was very sudden — they left many wagons, some caissons, clothing, ammunition, personal baggage, etc. Their winter quarters were admirably constructed, many not yet quite finished. The works at Centreville are formidable — more so than Manassas.

Except the turnpikes the roads are horrible — the country entirely stripped of forage & provisions. Having fully consulted with Genl McDowell I propose occupying Manassas by a portion of Banks's command, & then at once throwing all the forces I can concentrate upon the line agreed upon last week.[1] The Monitor justifies this course. I telegraphed this morning to have the transports brought to Washington to start from there — I presume you will approve this course. Circumstances may keep me out here some little time longer.

Geo B McClellan
Maj Genl Comdg USA

Hon E M Stanton
Secty of War Washington

ALS (telegram sent), Records of the Office of the Secretary of War, RG 107 (M-504:66), National Archives. *OR,* Ser. 1, V, p. 742.

1. A council of war meeting on Mar. 8 had approved an advance on Richmond by way of the lower Chesapeake.

To Randolph B. Marcy [TELEGRAM]

Fairfax CH [March 11, 1862] 9 pm

Dispatch received.[1] It is impossible for me to come in tonight — I am completely tired out. Besides I think the less I see of Washington the better. Be careful to have copies of all my dispatches of any importance sent to Secty & President. See Secty about ordering transports to Washington.

G B McClellan
Maj Genl

Genl R B Marcy
Washington

ALS (telegram sent), Records of the Office of the Secretary of War, RG 107 (M-504:66), National Archives. *OR,* Ser. 1, LI, Part 1, p. 550.

1. Marcy telegraphed on this date that he had seen former Ohio governor William Dennison, and urged GBM to inform the administration "what you propose to do & are now doing. Come to Washn tonight.... Dennison desires to see you before you see any one else." McClellan Papers (B-10:47), Library of Congress. Dennison had been delegated to explain to GBM the decision taken that day to remove him as general-in-chief and limit him to the command of the Army of the Potomac while it was on campaign.

To Mary Ellen McClellan

Fairfax C.H. March 11 1862

...None of our wagons came up until after I rode out this morning, so we got along as best we could last night. Some one lent me some blankets, & somebody else a cot, so I was very well off — tonight I have my own bed. I started at about 9 this morning, & rode first to Centreville. We found there quite a formidable series of works, which would have been somewhat uncomfortable for new troops to carry by storm. Thence I rode over horrid roads to the celebrated Manassas, which we found also abandoned. Thence to the battle field of last July, & over pretty much the whole of it. Thence home via Stone Bridge & Centreville reaching here about 8 1/2. I rode Kentuck today & as the rascal was fretful he fatigued me very much — so that it is impossible for me to go to Washn tonight, notwithstanding your father's pressing telegram.

I regret that the rascals are after me again. I had been foolish enough to hope that when I went into the field they would give me some rest, but it seems otherwise — perhaps I should have expected it. If I can get out of this scrape you will never catch me in the power of such a set again — the idea of persecuting a man behind his back. I suppose they are now relieved from the pressure of their fears by the retreat of the enemy & that they will increase in virulence. Well — enough of that — it is bad enough for me to be bothered in that without annoying you with it.

The country thru' which we passed today was very desolate. I think Manassas is the most desolate & forbidding spot I ever beheld. They have not destroyed many of their winter quarters, which are very well built & comfortable — far more so than I expected to see them. From the great number of camps scattered about it is evident that they had a very large force here. They must have left in a great hurry, for they abandoned a great deal of baggage, tents, stores, ammunition, caissons, wagons etc.

It seems that the order was given very suddenly — they left on Sunday [March 9], except a rear guard. It is said by *"intelligent contrabands"* & others that the men were very much disgusted & disheartened. . . .

AL copy, McClellan Papers (C-7 :63), Library of Congress.

FOUR

THE PENINSULA CAMPAIGN
MARCH 12–MAY 30, 1862

ON MARCH 12, 1862, General McClellan made the decision to base his grand campaign against Richmond at Fort Monroe, the Union-held position at the tip of the peninsula between the James and York rivers, seventy-five miles southeast of the Confederate capital. Fort Monroe had been the "worst coming to the worst" option in his February 3 plan of operations for the Army of the Potomac; now it was forced on him by the sudden actions of the enemy.

On March 8 the Rebel ironclad *Merrimack* had steamed into Hampton Roads from Norfolk and decimated the Federal blockading squadron. Although the Union's *Monitor* fought her to a draw the next day, the *Merrimack* remained a threat to McClellan's supply line in the Chesapeake and also blocked any Federal advance on Richmond by way of the James. At the same time, General Joseph E. Johnston withdrew his army from Manassas to a position behind the Rappahannock River. His move frustrated McClellan's long-matured plan for a surprise landing at Urbanna on the Rappahannock and any hope he might have had for getting between Johnston's army and Richmond. Operating from Fort Monroe was now his only alternative to an overland advance on Richmond from Washington. Once he was assured that the *Monitor* could at least hold the *Merrimack* in check, he put the scheme to a vote of his corps commanders, who approved it unanimously, and on March 17 the first contingents sailed for Fort Monroe. The correspondence reproduced here covers planning for the movement and the first two months of the Peninsula campaign, taking McClellan to the eve of the final battle for Richmond.

On the evidence of such letters as that of March 28 to General Totten of the engineers, it is obvious that he went to the Peninsula predisposed to siege operations. His first experience in war had been at the siege of

Vera Cruz in the Mexican War, and he had made a close study of the siege lines at Sevastopol when he was in the Crimea in 1855. It was a form of warfare he felt he had mastered, and his decision to put Yorktown under siege was made more decisively than most of his military actions. By contrast, at Williamsburg on May 5 he waited nearly the entire day to be called to the field despite the continuing sound of heavy firing indicating that a pitched battle was in progress.

These letters and dispatches demonstrate an increasing remoteness from factual reality. Running through McClellan's correspondence in these months, for example, is the positive and recurring assertion that he was greatly outnumbered by the enemy. He telegraphed Secretary Stanton on April 7 from Yorktown that within a matter of days he expected to be facing 100,000 Rebel troops. On May 14 he warned President Lincoln that with his 80,000 men he would have to attack an enemy entrenched in numbers double his own; "I beg that you will cause this Army to be reinforced without delay by all the disposable troops of the Government."

The logic of these calculations seemed to General McClellan obvious. An opponent who had confronted him at Washington in August of 1861 with 100,000 men (as he himself had estimated) and then raised that count to 150,000 by the end of October would hardly make the final defense of his capital with a lesser number. In truth, on his arrival before Yorktown on April 5 and for some days afterward he was bluffed by a force about one-fifth the size of his own. When he insisted to the president on May 14 that he was confronting some 160,000 enemy soldiers, General Johnston could muster but 62,500 to contest his advance. From first to last, McClellan's military decisions on the Peninsula were based on his belief in a phantom Confederate army.

A second important thread running through the correspondence here is his conviction that the administration in Washington was failing to support him, and was in fact acting deliberately to insure his defeat. "History will present a sad record of these traitors who are willing to sacrifice the country & its army for personal spite & personal aims," he wrote his wife on April 11. This belief was as illusory as his picture of the enemy. The truth of the matter is that when he was finally ready to make his final advance on Richmond, the government had put more troops at his disposal than his plans had called for.

To Mary Ellen McClellan [TELEGRAM]

For Mrs. Genl McClellan *Fairfax C.H. March 12/62*

Do not be at all worried by what has occurred & say nothing about it. I have meant well for my country — & God will not desert me.[1] Am very well today.

G B McClellan
Maj Genl

Retained copy, McClellan Papers (C-11:63), Library of Congress.

1. Marcy had telegraphed GBM that an order relieving him as general-in-chief was printed in the *National Intelligencer* that morning. McClellan Papers (A-45:18).

To Gustavus V. Fox [TELEGRAM]

For G V Fox Fort Monroe Fairfax CH Mar 12 '62

Can I rely on the Monitor to keep the Merrimac in check so that I can take Fort Monroe as a base of operations.[1]

Geo. B. McClellan
Maj Genl

Please answer at once.

Retained copy, McClellan Papers (C-11:63), Library of Congress. *OR,* Ser. 1, IX, p. 27. Fox was assistant secretary of the navy.

1. Fox replied on Mar. 13: "The Monitor may, and I think will, destroy the Merrimac in the next fight; but this is hope, not certainty." *OR,* Ser. 1, IX, p. 27.

To Gustavus V. Fox [TELEGRAM]

Received March 12, 1862
To Secy Fox Ft Monroe From Fairfax Court House

Is it possible to block up the channel from Hampton roads to Norfolk some where between Sewalls Point and Craney Island by sinking hulks loaded with stone so that the Merrimac cannot get out if so how soon can it be done using every exertion. Please let me know at the earliest possible moment.[1]

G B McClellan

Received copy, Lincoln Papers, Library of Congress.

1. Gen. Wool replied to Secretary of War Stanton on Mar. 13 that to block the mouth of the Elizabeth River as GBM proposed would require the *Monitor* to reduce the enemy batteries on Sewall's Point and Craney Island. Both he and Flag Officer Goldsborough opposed this "lest she should become crippled. She is our only hope against the Merrimac." *OR,* Ser. 1, IX, p. 30.

To Abraham Lincoln

Unofficial

His Excellency Abraham Lincoln
President
My dear Sir:

Head-Quarters Army of Potomac
Fairfax C.H. March 12 1862

I have just seen Gov. Dennison who has detailed to me the conversations he held with you yesterday & today.

I beg to say to you that I cordially endorse all he has said to you in my behalf, and that I thank you most sincerely for the official confidence & kind personal feelings you entertain for me. I believe I said to you some weeks since, in connection with some western matters, that no feeling of self interest or ambition should ever prevent me from devoting myself to your service — I am glad to have the opportunity to prove it, & you will find that under present circumstances I shall work just as cheerfully as ever before, & that no consideration of self will in any manner interfere with the discharge of my public duties.[1]

Again thanking you for the official & personal kindness you have so often evinced towards me

I am most sincerely & respectfully your friend
Geo B McClellan

ALS, Lincoln Papers, Library of Congress.

1. On Mar. 14 Dennison wrote GBM: "Have just left the President. He is very much gratified with your letter and says my construction of the order as I gave it to you is exactly correct. You command the Army of the Potomac wherever it may go. Everything is right — move quick as possible." McClellan Papers (A-46:18), Library of Congress.

To Edwin M. Stanton [TELEGRAM]

Hon Sect of War

Head-Quarters, Army of the Potomac,
Flint Hill 6.15 pm March 13th 1862

Your dispatch was received at 6.10 pm at this place, about three miles from Fairfax CH where I am reviewing a Division. The members of the council together with myself were unanimous in favoring the plan which was presented to you by Gen McDowell.[1]

Steps have already been taken so that if the plan meets your approval the movement can commence early tomorrow morning. I will communicate more fully as soon as I return to my camp. Your speedy action will facilitate the movement.[2]

G B McClellan
Maj Genl

Retained copy, McClellan Papers (A-46:18), Library of Congress.

1. Stanton's dispatch sought clarification of the plan approved that day by a council of corps commanders for an advance on Richmond via the Virginia Peninsula. *OR,* Ser. 1, V, pp. 55–56, 750. 2. Stanton telegraphed that evening that the president approved the plan provided that Washington and Manassas Junction were strongly garrisoned, and that the advance be made "at once" to Fort Monroe "or anywhere between here and there...." *OR,* Ser. 1, V, p. 56.

To Lorenzo Thomas [TELEGRAM]

Head-Quarters of the Army,
Fairfax C.H. March 13 1862 8.30 pm

In the uncertainty as to General Burnside's position & how far he may now be engaged in his final operations it is difficult to give him very precise orders at present.[1] I think it would be well that he should not engage himself further inland than at Newbern & should at once reduce Beaufort. Leaving there a sufficient garrison in Fort Macon he should at once return to Roanoke Island ready to cooperate with all his available force either by way of Winton or by way of Fort Monroe as circumstances may render necessary. I advise this on the supposition that Capt Fox is correct in his opinion that Burnside will have Newbern this week.[2] If he has become fairly engaged in the movement I would not stop him.

G B McClellan
Maj Genl

L Thomas
Adjt Genl

ALS (telegram sent), Records of the Office of the Secretary of War, RG 107 (M-504 :66), National Archives. *OR,* Ser. 1, V, p. 751.

1. Thomas had been instructed by Stanton to ascertain GBM's plans for cooperating with Burnside's Roanoke Island expedition. War Board minutes, Mar. 14, Stanton Papers, Library of Congress. 2. Gustavus V. Fox to GBM, Mar. 13, *OR,* Ser. 1, IX, p. 27.

To Edwin M. Stanton [TELEGRAM]

Fairfax C.H. March 13 [1862] 9.40 pm

I would respectfully suggest that the Secretary of the Navy be requested to order to Fort Monroe whatever force Dupont can now spare, as well as any available force that Goldsborough can send up as soon as his present operations are completed.[1]

G B McClellan
Maj Genl

Hon E M Stanton
Secty of War

ALS (telegram sent), Records of the Office of the Secretary of War, RG 107 (M-504 :66), National Archives. *OR,* Ser. 1, V, p. 751.

1. Flag Officers Du Pont and Goldsborough commanded, respectively, naval forces with the Port Royal and Roanoke Island expeditions. Gideon Welles wrote Stanton on Mar. 14 that the navy would gladly cooperate in capturing Norfolk — "always a favorite measure of this Department" — but he was otherwise reluctant to weaken his blockading squadrons. *OR*, Ser. 1, V, pp 758–59.

To Gustavus V. Fox

Private Head-Quarters of the Army,
My dear Fox Fairfax C.H. March 14 1 A.M. 1862.

From all accounts received I have such a lively faith in the gallant little Monitor that I feel that we can trust her — so I have determined on the Fort Monroe movement. A part of this programme will be the reduction of Yorktown & Gloucester — to effect this rapidly we shall need your help. Can you not under present circumstances bring up some of Dupont's force, as well as some of Goldsborough's gunboats? I shall probably commence embarking today, & by tomorrow be under full headway, so no time is to be lost & I hope you will be able to give us powerful aid.

If you will pardon me for talking about a matter may I venture to repeat a suggestion made to me by the Prince de Joinville this afternoon — probably nothing new — viz that the Monitor should take a long cable (hemp) in tow & by running around the Merrimac endeavor to foul her propeller! To a landsman it seems a good idea. Can't we do something in the way of blocking up the Channel to Norfolk?[1]

Congratulating you on Worden's gallant action[2]

I am ever your friend
Geo B McClellan

P.S. How soon will the Mystic iron clad ship be finished?[3]

ALS, Fox Papers, New-York Historical Society.

1. Fox replied on this date that Joinville's idea was a good one, "but too much risk to the Monitor should she back herself." The Norfolk channel could be blocked, he added, only after the batteries guarding it were taken. McClellan Papers (A-46:18), Library of Congress. 2. Lt. John L. Worden had commanded the *Monitor* against the *Merrimack*. 3. The *Galena*, an ironclad under construction in Mystic, Conn. Fox reported that she "will not be ready in time."

To Edwin M. Stanton

Hon E. M. Stanton
Secretary of War. Head-Quarters, Army of the Potomac,
My Dear Sir. Fairfax Court House March 14th 1862

The situation of the Army of the Potomac at present is about as follows: Keyes' Division in reserve at Prospect Hill, with a Regiment of Cavalry

(Rush) in advance; McCall at Hunter's Mills; Smith at Flint Hill; Porter & Franklin at this place; McDowell in advance towards Centreville; Blenker near the Railroad, in advance of Burke's Station; Cooke's Cavalry Brigade between Blenker & Fairfax Station; Sumner at Union Mills & Manassas, with one regiment thrown forward to guard Stoneman's forage train, — General Stoneman being en route to the Rappahannock with ten squadrons of Cavalry.

The orders of Gen. Stoneman are to capture or drive in any force he may find on this side of the Rappahannock, and to reconnoitre that river. Heintzelman in reserve near Alexandria. One of Banks's Divisions is ordered to move at once to Centreville, — the majority of another to follow it. I propose placing the mass of Banks's Army Corps near Manassas (to cover the approaches to Washington) leaving detachments adequate to guard the Manassas Gap Railway, Strasburg and Winchester. I think the result of Gen. Stoneman's advance will be the destruction (by the rebels) of the railway bridge over the Rappahannock, thus making Manassas safe. I propose giving General Banks a large Cavalry force to enable him to scour the country completely in front of Manassas, & in the valley of the Shenandoah. From all the information I have received, I have no doubt that the mass of the rebels have retired to Gordonsville, leaving a force on the Rappahannock. I am well assured of the fact that the true reasons for their evacuation of their works were twofold — 1st My advance from Harper's Ferry — 2nd The intimation that I intended to turn their right flank. Most accounts substantially agree in this, & my information is very full. They have expended a very large amount of labor upon their works at Centreville and Manassas. I would be glad if you could find it convenient to visit these places yourself. You would then be sure that it would have been a desperate affair to have attacked Centreville.

The slaves are being taken South as rapidly as possible. A levy of 80,000 men seems to have been ordered in this State, & I shall be much mistaken if we have not a severe battle to fight before reaching Richmond. Of the result of this, however, I feel very sure, for I have the utmost confidence in the spirit & discipline of our men.

I have been arranging the multitude of details necessary to take up the new line, and anxiously await certain information as to the transports.

I shall have the Army well in hand & ready for anything that occurs.

I am Very Respectfully & Truly
Geo B McClellan
Maj Genl USA

LS, Lincoln Papers, Library of Congress.

To the Army of the Potomac

SOLDIERS OF THE ARMY OF THE POTOMAC! — Headquarters Army of the Potomac, *Fairfax Court House, Va., March 14, 1862.*

For a long time I have kept you inactive, but not without a purpose: you were to be disciplined, armed and instructed; the formidable artillery you now have, had to be created; other armies were to move and accomplish certain results. I have held you back that you might give the death-blow to the rebellion that has distracted our once happy country. The patience you have shown, and your confidence in your General, are worth a dozen victories. These preliminary results are now accomplished. I feel that the patient labors of many months have produced their fruit; the Army of the Potomac is now a real Army, — magnificent in material, admirable in discipline and instruction, excellently equipped and armed; — your commanders are all that I could wish. The moment for action has arrived, and I know that I can trust in you to save our country. As I ride through your ranks, I see in your faces the sure presage of victory; I feel that you will do whatever I ask of you. The period of inaction has passed. I will bring you now face to face with the rebels, and only pray that God may defend the right. In whatever direction you may move, however strange my actions may appear to you, ever bear in mind that my fate is linked with yours, and that all I do is to bring you, where I know you wish to be, — on the decisive battlefield. It is my business to place you there. I am to watch over you as a parent over his children; and you know that your General loves you from the depths of his heart. It shall be my care, as it has ever been, to gain success with the least possible loss; but I know that, if it is necessary, you will willingly follow me to our graves, for our righteous cause. God smiles upon us, victory attends us, yet I would not have you think that our aim is to be attained without a manly struggle. I will not disguise it from you: you have brave foes to encounter, foemen well worthy of the steel that you will use so well. I shall demand of you great, heroic exertions, rapid and long marches, desperate combats, privations, perhaps. We will share all these together; and when this sad war is over we will all return to our homes, and feel that we can ask no higher honor than the proud consciousness that we belonged to the ARMY OF THE POTOMAC.

GEO. B. MCCLELLAN
Major General Commanding

DP, McClellan Papers (A-46:18), Library of Congress.

To Nathaniel P. Banks

[Washington, March 16, 1862]

Genl Banks to post his command in the vicinity of Manassas — to entrench himself there and to throw his cavalry pickets well out to the front. His first care to be the rebuilding of the railway from Washington to Manassas & Strasburg in order to open his communications with the valley of the Shenandoah.

As soon as the Manassas Gap RR is in order Genl B. to entrench a brigade of Infantry (say 4 regiments) with a couple of batteries at or near the point where the M.G. RR crosses the Shenandoah. Something like 2 regts of cavalry should be left in that vicinity to occupy Winchester & thoroughly scout the country south of the R.R. & up the Shenandoah valley — as well as through Chester (?) Gap which might perhaps be advantageously occupied by a detachment of Infty well entrenched. Blockhouses to be built at the RR bridges.

Warrenton Junction, or the *place* (Warrenton) itself to be occupied — also some still more advanced point on the O & A RR by a Grand Guard as soon as the RR bridges repaired. Great activity to be observed by the Cavalry — besides the two regts at Manassas. Another regt of Cavalry will be at the Genl's disposition to scout towards the Occoquan & probably a 4th towards Leesburg.

The important points are —

1st A strong force well entrenched in the vicinity Manassas — perhaps even Centreville — another force (a brigade) near Strasburg — also well entrenched.

2nd Block houses at RR bridges.

3rd Constant employment of Cavalry well to the front.

4th Grand guards at Warrenton & in advance as far as Rappahannock if possible.

5th Great care to obtain full & early information as to enemy.

6th General object to cover line of Potomac & Washington.

ADf, McClellan Papers (A-50:20), Library of Congress. *OR*, Ser. 1, V, p. 56. This draft order is in GBM's handwriting. As issued it was signed by his adjutant, Seth Williams.

To Edwin M. Stanton

Hon E M Stanton
Secty of War
Sir:

Hd Qtrs Army of Potomac
Washn March 16 1862

In order to carry out the proposed object of this Army it has now become necessary that its Commander should have the entire control of affairs around Fort Monroe. I would respectfully suggest that the simplest method of effecting this would be to merge the Dept of Virginia into that of the Potomac, the name of which might properly be changed to that of the Dept of the Chesapeake; in carrying this into effect I would respectfully suggest that the present Comdr of the Dept Virginia be assigned to some other command.[1] Genl Mansfield can take temporary charge of Fort Monroe & its dependencies until the Army arrives there.

I am very respectfully yr obt svt
Geo B McClellan
Maj Genl USA

ALS, Lincoln Papers, Library of Congress. *OR,* Ser. 1, XI, Part 3, pp. 8–9.

1. The presence of John E. Wool at the head of the Department of Virginia created a touchy command situation. The seventy-eight-year-old Wool, a major general by brevet since the Mexican War, considered himself GBM's superior. On Mar. 18, however, he agreed to Stanton's proposal "to waive the exercise of your authority temporarily in his [GBM's] favor." Wool was transferred to the command of the Middle Department on June 1. *OR,* Ser. 1, IX, p. 29; XI, Part 3, pp. 14, 207.

To Samuel L. M. Barlow

My dear Barlow Washington March 16 1862

I am here for a few hours only, my Hd Qtrs being on the other side of the river.

I came back last night from Fairfax C.H. — en route for the decisive battle. My movements gave us Manassas with the loss of one life — a gallant cavalry officer — history will, when I am in my grave, record it as the brightest passage of my life that I accomplished so much at so small a cost. It will appear in the future that my advance from Harper's Ferry, & the preparation for turning their right flank have induced them to give up what Halleck & the newspapers would call "the rebel stronghold of the East."

I shall soon leave here on the wing for Richmond — which you may be sure I will take. The Army is in magnificent spirits, & I think are half glad that I now belong to them alone.

Mrs McC joins me in kindest regards to Mrs B & yourself. Do not mind the abolitionists — all I ask of the papers is that they should defend me from the most malicious attacks — tho' to speak frankly I do not care to pay much attention to my enemies.

My wife received your note & desires her thanks for it.

The President is all right — he is my strongest friend.

In haste sincerely yours
Geo B McClellan

S L M Barlow Esq

ALS, Barlow Papers, Huntington Library.

To Edmund C. Stedman

My dear Sir Hd Qtrs Seminary [Alexandria] March 17 1862

I cordially thank you for your kind letter & your efforts in my behalf.[1] Kind words are so seldom heard by me of late that I do indeed appreciate them. I know now fully the value of true & disinterested friends.

I believe that we are now on the eve of the success for which we have been so long preparing — yet I have felt for several days that there was a strong probability that I should be denied the satisfaction of leading the Army of the Potomac to victory & of sharing the fruit of the work of many months. I now begin to hope for better things. If permitted to retain command of this Army I feel assured of the result, & trust that end will justify the great confidence that you & so many other friends have placed in me. Again thanking you for your friendship

I am very truly yours
Geo B McClellan

E C Stedman Esq.
Washington

ALS retained copy, McClellan Papers (B-10:48), Library of Congress. Stedman was the Washington correspondent for the *New York World.*

1. With his letter of this date Stedman enclosed a clipping, from the previous day's *World,* of an article he wrote in support of GBM, and assured him: "We have watched and sustained your efforts from the first and . . . shall continue to counteract your detractors as best we may." McClellan Papers (B-10:48).

To Edwin M. Stanton [TELEGRAM]

Hon E M Stanton,
Secy of War Alexandria 1.15 pm March 18th [1862]

Please have McCallum[1] provide Engines and Cars sufficient to transport supplies only for an army of one hundred and thirty thousand men, including twenty thousand horses over the West Point and Richmond Railway.[2] The road is about twenty eight miles long. The only trouble at present is in regard to horse transports. If shall arrive promptly, we shall have rapid & glorious results.

G. B. McClellan
Maj Gen

Received copy, Records of the Office of the Secretary of War, RG 107 (M-473:98), National Archives. *OR,* Ser. 1, XI, Part 3, pp. 15–16.

1. Col. Daniel C. McCallum, director of military railroads. 2. The Richmond and York River Railroad, connecting Richmond with West Point, where the Mattapony and Pamunkey rivers join to form the York.

To Edwin M. Stanton

Hon E. M. Stanton
Secty of War — Head Quarters Army of the Potomac
Sir — Theological Seminary Va. March 19 1862

I have the honor to submit the following notes on the proposed operations of the active portion of the Army of the Potomac.

The proposed plan of campaign is to assume Fort Monroe as the first base of operations taking the line by Yorktown and West Point upon Richmond as the line of operations, Richmond being the objective point. It is assumed that the fall of Richmond involves that of Norfolk and the whole of Virginia; also that we shall fight a decisive battle between West Point and Richmond, to give which battle the rebels will concentrate all their available forces, understanding as they will that it involves the fate of their cause. It therefore follows —

1st. That we should collect all our available forces, and operate upon adjacent lines, maintaining perfect communications between our columns.

2d. That no time should be lost in reaching the field of battle.

The advantages of the Peninsula between the York and James Rivers are too obvious to need explanation. It is also clear that West Point should as soon as possible be reached and used as our main depot, that we may have the shortest line of land transportation for our supplies, and the use of the York River.

There are two methods of reaching this point —

1st. By moving directly from Fort Monroe as a base and trusting to the roads for our supplies, at the same time landing a strong corps as near Yorktown as possible in order to turn the rebel lines of defence south of Yorktown. Then to reduce Yorktown and Gloucester by a siege in all probability, involving a delay of weeks perhaps.

2d. To make a combined naval and land attack upon Yorktown, the first object of the campaign. This leads to the most rapid and decisive results. To accomplish this the Navy should at once concentrate upon the York River all their available and most powerful batteries. Its reduction should not in that case require many hours: a strong corps would be pushed up the York under cover of the Navy directly upon West Point immediately upon the fall of Yorktown and we could at once establish a new base of operations at a distance of some twenty five miles from Richmond — with every facility for developing and bringing into play the whole of our available force on either or both banks of the James.

It is impossible to urge too strongly the absolute necessity of the full cooperation of the Navy, as a part of this programme. Without it the operations may be prolonged for many weeks and we may be forced to carry in front several strong positions which by their aid could be turned without serious loss of either time or men.

It is also of first importance to bear in mind the fact already alluded to, that the capture of Richmond necessarily involves the prompt fall of Norfolk — while an operation against Norfolk if successful at the beginning of the campaign facilitates the reduction of Richmond merely by the demoralization of the rebel troops involved, and that after the fall of Norfolk we should be obliged to undertake the capture of Richmond, by the same means which would have accomplished it in the beginning having mean while afforded the rebels ample time to perfect their defensive arrangements — for they would well know from the moment the Army of the Potomac changed its base to Fort Monroe that Richmond must be its ultimate object.

It may be summed up in few words that for the prompt success of this campaign it is absolutely necessary that the Navy should at once throw its whole available force, its most powerful vessels, against Yorktown. There is the most important point — there the knot to be cut. An immediate decision upon the subject matter of this communication is highly desirable, and seems called for by the exigencies of the occasion.

I am, Sir, Very Respectfully Your Obt Servant
Geo B McClellan
Maj Gen'l

Copy, McClellan Papers (D-7 :69), Library of Congress. *OR,* Ser. 1, V, pp. 57–58.

To Randolph B. Marcy

Confidential — Memorandum[1] [Alexandria, March 22, 1862]

For operations against Yorktown, Richmond &c where we will probably find exterior earthworks heavily garrisoned, we shall require the means of overwhelming them by a vertical fire of shells.

I should therefore be glad to have disposable at Fort Monroe —

I.	1st	20 10″ mortars complete
	2nd	20 8″ " "
II.		20 8″ siege howitzers
III.		20 (?) 4 1/2″ wrought iron siege guns
IV.		40 20 pdr Parrotts
V.		__ 24 pdr siege guns

The 20 pdr Parrotts with the batteries will of course be counted as available.

I do not know number of 4 1/2 guns available, if not so many as I have indicated, something else should be substituted.

I wish Genl Barry and Col Kingsbury to consult with Genl Marcy, to make such suggestions as occur to them, and ascertain at once to what extent this memorandum can be filled.

It is possible we cannot count upon the Navy to reduce Yorktown by their independent efforts, we must therefore be prepared to do it by our own means.[2]

There are said to be at Yorktown from 27 to 32 heavy guns, at Gloucester 14 Columbiads. The probable armament of Yorktown, when exterior guns are drawn in, will be from 40 to 50 heavy guns, from 24 pdrs to 8″ and perhaps 10″ Columbiads.

Copy, McClellan Papers (A-48:19), Library of Congress.

1. This memorandum was sent to Chief of Staff Marcy on Mar. 22 with the notation: "The matter is an important one and should be attended to without delay." 2. Marcy replied on this date that eighteen siege pieces were then aboard ship, and an additional fifty-six had been ordered from various military arsenals. McClellan Papers (A-48:19).

To Nathaniel P. Banks [TELEGRAM]

Head Quarters, Army of the Potomac,
Seminary March 24 11 am 1862

Dispatch received.[1] Your course was right. As soon as you are strong enough push Jackson hard & drive him well beyond Strasburg pursuing at least as far as Woodstock & if possible with Cavalry to Mount Jackson. Strasburg should then be held in force & the repairs of the Railway bridge over the Shenandoah pushed forward as rapidly as possible. The very moment the thorough defeat of Jackson will permit it, resume the movement on Manassas, always leaving the whole of Shields' command at or near Strasburg & Winchester until Manassas Gap Railway is fully repaired. Call on Sedgwick for aid if you require it — but not unless necessary. Communicate fully & frequently & act vigorously.

G B McClellan
Maj Genl

Maj Genl N P Banks
Comdg 5th Corps Winchester

ALS (telegram sent), Records of the Office of the Secretary of War, RG 107 (M-504:66), National Archives. *OR*, Ser. 1, XII, Part 3, p. 16.

1. Banks telegraphed on this date that Brig. Gen. John Sedgwick's division was standing by in the wake of Stonewall Jackson's repulse at Kernstown the previous day by Brig. Gen. James Shields's command. *OR*, Ser. 1, XII, Part 3, p. 16.

To Joseph G. Totten

Unofficial & Private Hd Qtrs Army of Potomac
My dear General[1] Seminary March 28 1862

I learn that you are very anxious to get two Engineers from this Army for service on Permanent Fortifications; I fully appreciate your anxiety & necessities but would beg to lay before you a few considerations which will I hope induce you to allow the matter to lay over for a few weeks.

You know that the Army is being embarked as rapidly as possible for Fort Monroe — the first operation will be the capture of Yorktown & Gloucester, this *may* involve a siege (at least I go prepared for one) in case the Navy is not able to afford the means for destroying the rebel batteries at these points. Again it is probable that we may have some siege operations to undertake against Richmond, & perhaps finally, against Norfolk. I do not expect to go through *all* the regular operations of a siege against all these places, but *do* expect to be obliged to establish batteries & perhaps open some trenches — operations which will require the services of a number of Engineer officers. I would therefore ask you to endeavor to postpone your call for two more Engineer officers until these operations are accomplished — which cannot involve a delay of more than a very few weeks. If I can even keep them until the question of Yorktown is disposed of I shall feel better satisfied.[2]

I feel sure that the good of the service & the Corps will be best served by the course I propose — asking your views in reply to this

I remain very sincerely your friend
Geo B McClellan
Maj Genl Comdg

ALS, Pierpont Morgan Library. Brig. Gen. Totten headed the Corps of Engineers.

1. Although the addressee is not named, this letter is clearly in response to a request by Totten for engineers to work on the fortifications of Northern coastal cities. War Board minutes, Mar. 18, 19, 1862, Stanton Papers, Library of Congress. 2. The Army of the Potomac retained these engineers.

To Samuel P. Heintzelman [TELEGRAM]

Bg Gen S P Heintzelman Hd Qrs Seminary
Comdg 3d Corps — Ft Monroe Mch 28/62 [11:45 A.M.]

Your telegram of yesterday morning received only last night.[1] I hope the movement on Big Bethel was well considered in view of my wish not to prematurely develop our plans to the enemy. If the destruction of their batteries and your subsequent return confirms the idea that we are after Norfolk all is well except the mere fact of falling back. If this reaches you in time it would be well to hold the position of Big Bethel if its reoccupation by the enemy can give us any trouble. You on the ground can best judge of this.

G. B. McClellan
Maj Gen Comdg

Retained copy, McClellan Papers (C-10 :63), Library of Congress. *OR*, Ser. 1, XI, Part 3, p. 43.

1. Heintzelman's telegram of Mar. 27 reported on reconnaissances sent out that day from Fort Monroe. *OR*, Ser. 1, XI, Part 3, p. 42.

To Edwin M. Stanton [TELEGRAM]

Seminary [March 28, 1862] 9.30 pm

I have instructed Genl Williams to telegraph Mr. Morley[1] to procure at Baltimore the lumber requisite to rebuild the Manassas Railway bridge over the Shenandoah. I would advise that Mr McCallum at once look into the practicability of connecting Winchester with Strasburg by a railway. If this can be done within a reasonable time it will be of immense advantage to us in a military point of view.

The repairs of the Manassas Gap Railway being completed & this new road built we would have easy control of that entire region.[2]

I would ask immediate attention to this very important matter.

G B McClellan
Maj Genl

Hon E M Stanton
Secty of War

ALS (telegram sent), Records of the Office of the Secretary of War, RG 107 (M-504 :66), National Archives. *OR*, Ser. 1, XII, Part 3, p. 26.

1. Capt. R. F. Morley, general manager of military railroads. 2. GBM proposed to complete a railroad line running the length of the Shenandoah Valley by linking the Manassas Gap and Winchester and Potomac railroads. The proposal was not carried out.

To Abraham Lincoln

Private

My dear Sir Washington March 31/62

Your note in regard to Genl Blenker's Division has reached me just as I am on the point of leaving for Alexandria.[1]

I need not say that I regret the loss of Blenker's Division first because they are excellent troops — second — because I know they are warmly attached to me.

I fully appreciate, however, the circumstances of the case, & hasten to assure you that I cheerfully acquiesce in your decision without any mental reservation.

Recognizing implicitly as I ever do the plenitude of your power as Commander in Chief, I cannot but regard the tone of your note as in the highest degree complimentary to me, & as adding one more to the many proofs of personal regard you have so often honored me with.

I shall do my best to use all the more activity to make up for the loss of this Division, & beg again to assure you that I will ever do my very best to carry out your views & support your interests in the same frank spirit you have always shown towards me.

I am very respectfully and sincerely your friend
Geo B McClellan

His Excellency Abraham Lincoln
Presdt

ALS, Lincoln Papers, Library of Congress.

1. The president wrote on this date: "This morning I felt constrained to order Blenker's Division to Fremont; and I write this to assure you that I did so with great pain, understanding that you would wish it otherwise. If you could know the full pressure of the case, I am confident you would justify it — even beyond a mere acknowledgment that the Commander-in-chief, may order what he pleases." *Collected Works of Lincoln,* V, pp. 175–76. Brig. Gen. Louis Blenker's division was sent as reinforcement to Frémont's Mountain Department, in western Virginia.

To Nathaniel P. Banks

Maj. Gen. N. P. Banks
Comdg. 5th Corps
General,

Hd. Qtrs. Army of the Potomac.
Onboard the Commodore [Alexandria],
April 1/62

The change in affairs in the valley of the Shenandoah has rendered necessary a corresponding departure — temporarily at least — from the plan we some days since agreed upon.[1] In my arrangements I assume that you have with you a force amply sufficient to drive Jackson before you, provided he is not re-inforced largely. I also assume that you may find it impossible to detach anything towards Manassas for some days, probably not until the operations of the main Army have drawn all the rebel forces towards Richmond.

You are aware that Genl. Sumner has for some days been at Warrenton Junction, with two Divisions of Infantry, 6 batteries, & two Regts. of Cavalry; & that a reconnaissance to the Rappahannock forced the enemy to destroy the railway bridge at Rappahannock station on the Orange & Alexandria R.R. Since that time our Cavalry have found nothing on this side of the Rappahannock in that direction, and it seems clear that we have no reason to fear any return of the rebels in that quarter. Their movements near Fredericksburg also indicate a final abandonment of that neighborhood. I doubt whether Johnston will now re-inforce Jackson with a view to offensive operations, — the time has probably passed when he could have gained anything by doing so. I have ordered in one of

Sumner's Divisions (that of Richardson,[2] late Sumner's) to Alexandria for embarkation; Blenker's has been detached from the Army of the Potomac, & ordered to report to Genl. Fremont.

Abercrombie is probably at Warrenton Junction today, — Geary at White Plains.[3]

Two regts. of Cavalry have been ordered out & are now on the way to relieve the two regts. of Sumner.

Four thousand infantry & one battery leave Washington at once for Manassas, some 3000 more will move in one or two days, & soon after some 3000 additional.

I will order Blenker to march on Strasburg, & to report to you for temporary duty, so that should you find a large force in your front, you can avail yourself of his aid. As soon as possible please direct him on Winchester, thence to report to the Adjt. Genl. of the Army for orders — but keep him until you are sure what you have in front.

In regard to your own movements — the most important thing at present is to throw Jackson well back & then to assume such a position as to enable you to prevent his return. As soon as the railway communications are re-established it will be probably important & advisable to move on Staunton, but this would require secure communications, & a force of from 25,000 to 30,000 for active operations. It should also be nearly coincident with my own move on Richmond, — at all events not so long before it as to enable the rebels to concentrate on you & then return on me. I fear that you cannot be ready in time, — altho' it may come in very well, with a force less than that I have mentioned, after the main battle near Richmond.

When Genl. Sumner leaves Warrenton Junction, Genl. Abercrombie will be placed in immediate command of Manassas & Warrenton Junction, under your general orders.

Please inform me frequently by telegraph and otherwise as to the state of things in your front.

I am very truly yours
Geo B McClellan
Maj. Gen. Comdg.

P.S. From what I have just learned, it would seem that the two Regts of Cavalry intended for Warrenton Junction have gone to Harper's Ferry. Of the four additional regts. placed under your orders, two should as promptly as possible move by the shortest route on Warrenton Junction.

I am respectfully your obdt. servt.
G. B. McClellan
Maj. Genl. Comdg.

Retained copy, McClellan Papers (A-50:20), Library of Congress. *OR*, Ser. 1, V, pp. 59–60.

1. See GBM to Banks, Mar. 16, *supra*. 2. Brig. Gen. Israel B. Richardson. 3. Brig. Gen. John J. Abercrombie, Col. John W. Geary.

To Lorenzo Thomas

Brigadier General L. Thomas
Adjutant General U.S. Army
General:

Head-Quarters, Army of the Potomac,
Steamer Commodore, April 1, 1862

I have to request that you will lay the following communication before the Hon. Secretary of War.

The approximate numbers and positions of the troops left near and in the rear on the Potomac are about as follows.

Genl. Dix has, after guarding the railroads under his charge, sufficient troops to give him 5000 for the defence of Baltimore, and 1988 available for the Eastern shore, Annapolis &c. Fort Delaware is very well garrisoned by about 400 men.

The garrisons of the forts around Washington amount to 10,600 men; other disposable troops now with Genl. Wadsworth[1] being about 11,400 men.

The troops employed in guarding the various railways in Maryland amount to some 3359 men. These it is designed to relieve, being old regiments, by dismounted Cavalry, and to send forward to Manassas.

Gen. Abercrombie occupies Warrenton with a force, which including Col. Geary at White Plains and the Cavalry to be at his disposal, will amount to some 7780 men, with 12 pieces of Artillery. I have the honor to request that all the troops organized for service in Pennsylvania & New York, and in any of the Eastern States, may be ordered to Washington. I learn from Governor Curtin that there are some 3500 men now ready in Pennsylvania. This force I should be glad to have sent at once to Manassas. Four thousand men from Genl. Wadsworth I desire to be ordered to Manassas. The troops with the railroad guards above alluded to will make up a force under the command of Genl. Abercrombie to something like 18,639 men.

It is my design to push Genl. Blenker's division from Warrenton upon Strasburg. He should remain at Strasburg long enough to allow matters to assume a definite form in that region before proceeding to his ultimate destination.

The troops in the valley of the Shenandoah will thus, — including Blenker's Division, 10,028 strong with 24 pieces of Artillery, Banks' 5th Corps which embraces the command of Genl. Shields, 19,687 strong with 41 guns, some 3652 disposable Cavalry, and the Railroad guards, about 2100 men, — amount to about 35,467 men.

It is designed to relieve General Hooker by one regiment, say 850 men; leaving with some 500 Cavalry, 1350 men on the Lower Potomac.

To recapitulate, —	at Warrenton there is to be,	7,780	men
	at Manassas, say	10,859	"
	In the valley of the Shenandoah	35,467	"
	On the lower Potomac,	1,350	"
	In all,	55,456	men

There would thus be left for the garrisons, and the front of Washington under Genl. Wadsworth, some 18,000 men — exclusive of the batteries under construction.

The troops organizing or ready for service in New York, I learn will probably number more than four thousand. These should be assembled at Washington subject to disposition where their services may be most needed.

I am very Respectfully your obedient servant
Geo. B. McClellan
Maj. Genl. Comdg.

Copy, Lincoln Papers, Library of Congress. *OR*, Ser. 1, V, pp. 60–61.

1. Brig. Gen. James S. Wadsworth commanded the Washington defenses.

To Mary Ellen McClellan

Steamer Commodore April 1 1862 Potomac River

4.15 pm. As soon as possible after reaching Alexandria I got the Commodore under weigh & "put off" — I did not feel safe until I could fairly see Alexandria behind us. I have brought a tug with us to take back dispatches from Budd's Ferry, where I shall stop a few hours for the purpose of winding up everything. I feared that if I remained at Alexandria I would be annoyed very much & perhaps be sent for from Washn. Officially speaking, I feel very glad to get away from that sink of iniquity....

8 pm. I have just returned from a trip in one of the naval vessels with Capt Wyman to take a look at the rebel batteries (recently abandoned) at Shipping Point etc. They were pretty formidable & it would have given us no little trouble to have taken possession of them had they held firm. It makes only the more evident the propriety of my movements by which Manassas was forced to be evacuated & their batteries with it. The trip was quite interesting....

AL copy, McClellan Papers (C-7:63), Library of Congress.

To Ambrose E. Burnside

Headquarters Army of the Potomac
Steamer Commodore,
April 2, 1862.

Maj. Gen. Ambrose E. Burnside,
Commanding Department of North Carolina:
General:

I expect to reach Fort Monroe to-day, to take control of active operations from that point. The line of operations will be up the Peninsula, resting our line on the York River and making Richmond the objective point. In the course of events it may become necessary for us to cross the James below Richmond and move on Petersburg. It has now become of the first importance that there should be frequent communication between us, and that I should be informed of the exact state of things with you and in your front. Four additional regiments should have reached you by this time.

I am entirely in the dark as to the condition of your operations against Beaufort, the force of the enemy there and at Goldsborough. Will you please at once inform me fully, stating how soon you expect to be in possession of Fort Macon,[1] what available troops you will then have for operating on Goldsborough, what can, in your opinion, be affected there in the way of taking possession of it, of neutralizing a strong force of the enemy there, and of doing something toward preventing the enemy's retreat from Richmond. On the other hand, please inform me what you can do in the way of a demonstration at Winton on Suffolk.

You will readily understand that if I succeed in driving the enemy out of Richmond I will at once throw a strong force on Raleigh and open the communication with you via Goldsborough; after which I hope to confide to you no unimportant part of subsequent operations.

Taking all things into consideration, it appears probable that a movement in the direction of Goldsborough would be the best thing for you to undertake, as you can make it in larger force than that on Winton, for as soon as you have possession of Fort Macon nearly all your force will be available. Great caution will, however, be necessary, as the enemy might throw large forces in that direction. The main object of the movement would be to accomplish that, but it would not do for you to be caught. We cannot afford any reverse at present. I wish your opinion in regard to the whole affair.

Very truly, yours,
Geo. B. McClellan

OR, Ser. 1, IX, p. 374.

1. Fort Macon guarded the approach to Beaufort.

To Mary Ellen McClellan [TELEGRAM]

Fort Monroe April 2 11 1/2 pm /62

Have arrived here all well. Navy fully prepared to sink the Merrimac. I only hope she may appear tomorrow. The grass will not grow under my feet.

G B McClellan

Mrs. McClellan
Washington

ALS (telegram sent), Records of the Office of the Secretary of War, RG 107 (M-504 :66), National Archives.

To Mary Ellen McClellan

Steamer Commodore April 3 [1862] Hampton Roads 1 1/2 pm.

. . . I have been up to my eyes in business since my arrival. We reached here about 4 yesterday pm. — ran in to the wharf & unloaded the horses, then went out & anchored. Marcy & I at once took a tug & ran out to the flag ship Minnesota to see Goldsborough where we remained until about 9, taking tea with him.

On our return we found Genl. Heintzelman — soon followed by Porter & Smith — all of whom remained here all night. I sat up very late arranging movements, & had my hands full. I have been hard at work all the morning & not yet been on shore. Dine with Genl Wool today at 4 — & go thence to our camp. We move tomorrow a.m. Three Divisions take the direct road to Yorktown, & will encamp at Howard's Bridge. Two take the James River road & go to Young's Mills. The Reserve goes to Big Bethel, where my Hd Qtrs will be tomorrow night. My great trouble is the want of wagons — a terrible drawback — but I cannot wait for them. I hope to get possession before tomorrow night of a new landing place some 7 or 8 miles from Yorktown, which will help us very much. It is probable that we shall have some fighting tomorrow — not serious — but we may have the opportunity of drubbing Magruder. You need not be at all anxious about me — I shall be in reserve as tomorrow will be merely an affair of advanced guards. The harbor here is very crowded — facilities for landing are bad — Van Vliet (as usual) has not arrived — ever late when most needed. I hope to get possession of Yorktown day after tomorrow. Shall then arrange to make the York River my line of supplies. The eclat of taking Yorktown will cover a delay of the few days necessary to get everything in hand & ready for action. The great battle will be (I think) near Richmond as I have always hoped & thought. I see my way very clearly — & with my trains once ready will move rapidly. . . .

AL copy, McClellan Papers (C-7 :63), Library of Congress.

To Louis M. Goldsborough

Flag Officer Goldsborough
Comdg Squadron — Head-Quarters of the Army of Potomac
Dear Sir — Hampton Roads April 3 1862.

I find that I have wagons sufficient to move the greater part of the force now here & have accordingly concluded to advance towards York tomorrow morning.

Unless delayed by an obstinate resistance on the part of the enemy our advanced guard ought to be in rear of the Ship's Point Battery at about 2 o'clock tomorrow afternoon, & in possession of it by from 3 to 3 1/2 o'clock.

I propose on the next day (5th) to invest Yorktown, throwing a sufficient force above it to prevent the escape of the Garrison by land, unless they abandon the place on our approach. So many days would elapse before I could collect the transports necessary to land a force on the Gloucester side, that I have thought it more prudent to advance upon Yorktown without waiting for the movement on the other side. I would now respectfully ask for such assistance in the way of gun boats as you can properly afford.

A couple (or more of) gun boats) tomorrow *afternoon* near Ship's Point battery would be of great use to us.

If you can send all your available force — after providing for the other objects you have in view — so as to reach the vicinity of Yorktown day after tomorrow, I think we can make short work of it.

If we can arrange matters so that I can get in rear of Yorktown before you open fire we ought very soon to get the place.

I shall have troops at Howards Bridge tomorrow by midday, & we might arrange to communicate there; but I expect to have the telegraph completed to my Hd Quarters tomorrow evening & can then tell you the exact state of affairs, & the time when I shall probably reach the rear of Yorktown. If at all possible I will come out to see you this evening, but in the mean time let me ask the favor that you will inform me what I can probably count upon at Ships's Point & Yorktown in the way of Naval assistance.

very truly yours
Geo B McClellan
Maj Genl Comdg

ALS, Office of Naval Records and Library, RG 45 (M-625:85), National Archives. *NOR*, Ser. 1, VII, pp. 195–96.

To Edwin M. Stanton [TELEGRAM]

Head-Quarters,
Army of the Potomac,
Fort Monroe April 3, 1862

Hon. E. M. Stanton
Secretary of War Washington D.C.

I expect to move from here tomorrow morning on Yorktown, where a force of some fifteen thousand of the rebels are in intrenched position, and I think it quite probable they will attempt to resist us.

No appearance of the Merrimac as yet.

Commodore Goldsborough is quite confident he can sink her when she comes out.

Geo. B. McClellan
Maj Genl Comdg

Retained copy, McClellan Papers (C-10 :63), Library of Congress. *OR*, Ser. 1, XI, Part 3, p. 64. The same telegram was sent to Gen. Sumner.

To Irvin McDowell

Headquarters Army of the Potomac,
Fort Monroe, April 4, 1862.

Maj. Gen. I. McDowell,
Commanding First Corps:
General:

The information I have obtained here has induced me to move forward the troops for whom I have wagons, in order to invest Yorktown.

I still think that it will be advisable for you to land at least one division on the Severn, in order to insure the fall of Gloucester. I have therefore telegraphed to Franklin and Rucker[1] to get your First Division embarked as soon as possible (supposing you will be here by this morning) to make this movement.

I hope to turn the battery at Ship Point this afternoon or early to-morrow morning and to get in rear of Yorktown to-morrow. I can therefore tell to-morrow what is the best disposition to make of your corps. It will probably be best to land one division on the Severn and to hold the others ready to move up the York River immediately upon the fall of Yorktown. My headquarters will be at Big Bethel to-night.

I had a full conversation with Flag-Officer Goldsborough and Captain Missroon[2] last evening, and would be glad if you will see them also.

You know that we are substantially weakened to the extent of two divisions; first, by the loss of Blenker; next, by the rescinding of the order placing this fort and its dependencies under my command.[3]

If you can get up to Big Bethel I can take care of you to-night and make you comfortable. Should I miss you, I will write fully, as events develop themselves.

Very truly, yours
Geo. B. McClellan
Major-General

OR, Ser. 1, XI, Part 3, p. 68.

1. Col. Daniel H. Rucker, quartermaster's department. 2. Comdr. John S. Missroon headed the naval force at Hampton Roads assigned to cooperate with GBM. 3. On Apr. 4 Gen. Wool wrote Stanton: "I will with my force occupy the stations abandoned by the rebels as the general advances. This will protect . . . his rear and left flank, which was suggested by myself, which the general readily assented to. . . ." *OR,* Ser. 1, XI, Part 3, p. 66.

To Mary Ellen McClellan

Big Bethel April 4 [1862] 8 1/2 pm.

. . . Everything has worked well today — I have gained some strong positions without fighting & shall try some more manoeuvring tomorrow. . . .

I shall try to invest Yorktown tomorrow & may have a fight.

AL copy, McClellan Papers (C-7 :63), Library of Congress.

To Abraham Lincoln [TELEGRAM]

Hon A. Lincoln, President   Near Yorktown, [April 5, 1862] 7.30 p.m.

The Enemy are in large force along our front and, apparently, intend making a determined resistance. A reconnaissance just made by Genl. Barnard, shows that their line of works extends across the entire Peninsula from Yorktown and Warwick river. Many of these are formidable. Deserters say that they are being reinforced daily from Richmond, and from Norfolk.

Under these circumstances I beg that you will reconsider the order detaching the first Corps from my Command.[1] In my deliberate judgment the success of our cause will be imperilled[2] when it is actually under the fire of the enemy, and active operations have commenced. Two or three of my Divisions have been under fire of Artillery most of the day. I am now of the opinion that I shall have to fight all of the available force of the Rebels not far from here. Do not force me to do so with diminished numbers. But whatever your decision may be, I will leave nothing undone to obtain success. If you cannot leave me the whole of the first Corps, I urgently ask that I may not lose Franklin and his Division.

G B McClellan
Maj General

Received copy, Lincoln Papers, Library of Congress. *OR,* Ser. 1, XI, Part 3, p. 71.

1. Announced by a telegram sent on Apr. 4 but just received. In a letter of Apr. 4 Adj. Gen. Thomas wrote GBM: "The President, deeming the force to be left in front of Washington insufficient to insure its safety, has directed that McDowell's army corps should be detached from the forces operating under your immediate direction." *OR,* Ser. 1, XI, Part 1, p. 10, Part 3, p. 66. 2. At this point the phrase "by so greatly reducing my force" was omitted, apparently inadvertently, from the copy of the telegram given to the president.

To Louis M. Goldsborough

Head-Quarters of the Army of Potomac
My dear Flag Officer 5 miles from Yorktown April 5 1862 10.30 PM

The rebels are close in my front & we have had sharp cannonading most of the afternoon — with but little loss on our side — some 8 or 10 killed. Our neighbors are in a very strong position, their left at Yorktown (strongly entrenched, with numerous guns), thence extending along the line of the Warwick River to its mouth. This river is some seven feet deep to a point near Lee's Mills, banks marshy & almost impassable; from point to point they have batteries. The roads are infamous & I have had great difficulty in moving. Tomorrow I shall spend in making reconnaissances, in repairing the roads, getting up supplies, & establishing my depots at Ship Point. I cannot turn Yorktown without a *battle,* in which I must use heavy artillery & go through the preliminary operations of a siege. The reconnaissances of tomorrow will enable me to form a pretty correct judgment of what I have to meet & the best way of overcoming the difficulties before me. Naval cooperation seems to me more essential than ever, I can best give you my ideas by tomorrow night. I learn that the Mystic[1] has reached you — will you be able to put her at the Yorktown batteries if I find it necessary?

If I find the position as strong as I now anticipate I will probably propose to you that I shall put my siege guns & mortars in battery to open simultaneously with the action of such naval vessels as you can spare.

Reinforcements are said to be arriving from Richmond & Norfolk.

I fear our Severn expedition may be impracticable — I received this evening a dispatch from the Adjt General informing me that McDowell's Corps (some 35,000 men) has been withdrawn from my command. I need not tell you that nothing could have astonished me more — I received the dispatch while listening to the rebels guns, & when well assured that I required all the force I had counted upon. I shall send this through Missroon & ask him to read it.

Do let me hear from you occasionally — as often as your duties will permit.[2]

I can tell you better tomorrow evening about the Severn & will ask Missroon to come & see me tomorrow.

Ever your friend
Geo B McClellan
Maj Genl Comdg

Flag Officer Goldsborough
Comdg Squadron

ALS, Office of Naval Records and Library, RG 45 (M-625 :85), National Archives. *NOR*, Ser. 1, VII, pp. 205–206.

1. The ironclad *Galena*. 2. Goldsborough replied on Apr. 6 that he did not expect the *Galena* "for some time to come. Until the guns on Gloucester Point be turned by the movement up the Severn it will be wholly impracticable, in my judgment, for the small naval force I can now detail to assist you to attack the forts at Yorktown and Gloucester with any prospect of success.... I dare not leave the Merrimac and consorts unguarded." *OR*, Ser. 1, XI, Part 3, p. 80.

To Mary Ellen McClellan

Near Yorktown April 6 [1862] 1 am.

...I find the enemy in strong force & in a very strong position but will drive him out. Fitz John is in the advance on the right, Baldy on the left[1] — they are doing splendidly. Their Divisions have been under fire all the afternoon [April 5] — have lost only about 5 killed in each & have punished secesh badly. Thus far it has been altogether an artillery affair. While listening this pm. to the sound of the guns, I received the order detaching McDowell's Corps from my command — it is the most infamous thing that history has recorded. I have made such representations as will probably induce a revocation of the order — or at least save Franklin to me. The idea of depriving a General of 35,000 troops when actually under fire! Tomorrow night I can tell you exactly what I intend doing.

We have no baggage tonight — our wagons being detained by the bad roads. Have taken possession of a *hut* in a deserted secesh camp — found a table therein — & sleep on a horse blanket if I find time to "retire." Colburn is copying a long letter — Seth, standing by the fire, looking *very* sleepy![2] He wakes up & sends his kindest regards, in which Colburn asks to participate — I am sorry to say that your Father is snoring loudly in a corner.

AL copy; copy, McClellan Papers (C-7 :63/D-10 :72), Library of Congress.

1. Brig. Gens. Fitz John Porter and William F. Smith. 2. Lt. Col. A. V. Colburn and Brig. Gen. Williams, of GBM's staff.

To Abraham Lincoln [TELEGRAM]

Head Quarters Army of the Potomac
A. Lincoln Presdt [Before Yorktown] April 6th 1862 [11 A.M.]

The order forming new Departments, if rigidly enforced deprives me of the power of ordering up wagons and troops absolutely necessary to enable me to advance to Richmond.[1] I have by no means the transportation I must have to move my army even a few miles. I respectfully request I may not be placed in this position, but that my orders for wagons — trains, ammunition and other material that I have prepared & necessarily left behind, as well as Woodbury's brigade,[2] may at once be complied with. The Enemy is strong in my front, & I have a most serious task before me, in the fulfillment of which I need all the aid the Government can give me.[3] I again repeat the urgent request that Genl Franklin & his division may be restored to my command.

G. B. McClellan Maj Genl

Received copy, Records of the Office of the Secretary of War, RG 107 (M-473 :99), National Archives. *OR*, Ser. 1, XI, Part 3, pp. 73–74.

1. This order, of Apr. 4, created the Department of the Shenandoah, under Banks, and the Department of the Rappahannock, under McDowell. *OR*, Ser. 1, XI, Part 3, pp. 67–68. 2. Brig. Gen. Daniel P. Woodbury commanded a brigade of engineering troops. 3. Lincoln replied by telegraph on this date: "Sec. of War informs me that the forwarding of transportation, amunition, & Woodburys, brigade, under your orders, is not, and will not be interfered with." *Collected Works of Lincoln*, V, p. 182.

To William B. Franklin [TELEGRAM]

Near Yorktown Apr 6th 1862

I have twice urgently telegraphed the Presdt requesting that you & your Division might be restored to my command.

Do all you can to accomplish it. Heaven knows I need you here.[1]

McClellan

Gen W B Franklin
Alexandria

ALS (telegram sent), McClellan Papers (A-50 :20), Library of Congress.

1. On Apr. 7 Franklin replied: "I was so entirely taken by surprise, and so entirely powerless in the matter that I was unable to do anything to stave the thing off. . . . McDowell told me that it was intended as a blow at you. That Stanton had said that you intended to work by strategy, and not by fighting, that all of the opponents of the policy of the administration centred around you — in other words that you had political aspirations." McClellan Papers (A-50 :20).

To Edwin M. Stanton [TELEGRAM]

Head-Quarters, Army of the Potomac,
In front of Yorktown April 7 7 pm 1862

Your telegram of yesterday[1] arrived here while I was absent examining the enemy's right which I did pretty closely.

The whole line of the Warwick which really heads within a mile of Yorktown is strongly defended by detached redoubts & other fortifications armed with heavy & light guns. The approaches except at Yorktown are covered by the Warwick over which there is but one or at most two passages, both of which are covered by strong batteries. It will be necessary to resort to the use of heavy guns & some siege operations before we can assault. All the prisoners state that Gen J. E. Johnston arrived in Yorktown yesterday with strong reinforcements. It seems clear that I shall have the whole force of the enemy on my hands, probably not less than one hundred thousand (100,000) men & possibly more. In consequence of the loss of Blenkers Division & the First Corps my force is possibly less than that of the enemy, while they have all the advantage of position.

I am under great obligation to you for the offer that the whole force and material of the Govt. will be as fully and speedily under my command as heretofore, or as if the new departments had not been created.

Since my arrangements were made for this campaign at least fifty thousand (50,000) men have been taken from my command.

Since my dispatch of the 5th Inst.[2] five divisions have been in close observation of the enemy and frequently exchanging shots.

When my present command all joins I shall have about eighty five thousand 85,000 men for duty, from which a large force must be taken for guards, escorts &c. With this Army I could assault the enemys works and perhaps carry them — but were I in possession of their entrenchments and assailed by double my numbers I should have no fears as to the result.

Under the circumstances that have been developed since we arrived here I feel fully impressed with the conviction that here is to be fought the great battle that is to decide the existing contest. I shall of course commence the attack as soon as I can get up my siege train and shall do all in my power to carry the enemys works but to do this with a reasonable degree of certainty requires in my judgment that I should if possible have at least the whole of the 1st Army Corps to land upon the Severn River and attack Gloucester in the rear. My present strength will not admit of a detachment sufficient for this purpose without materially impairing the efficiency of this column.

Flag Officer Goldsborough thinks the works too strong for his available vessels unless I can turn Gloucester. I send by mail copies of his letter and one of the commander of the gun boats here.[3]

Geo. B. McClellan
Maj Genl

AL (in part) retained copy, McClellan Papers (A-50:20), Library of Congress. *OR,* Ser. 1, XI, Part 1, pp. 11–12. Only the first third of this dispatch is in GBM's handwriting.

1. Stanton explained that the "force under Banks and Wadsworth was deemed . . . much less than had been fixed by your corps commanders as necessary to secure Washington. . . . Your advance on Yorktown gratified me very much, and I hope you will press forward and carry the enemy's works and soon be at Richmond." *OR,* Ser. 1, XI, Part 3, p. 73. 2. GBM to Lincoln, Apr. 5, *supra.* 3. Letters from Goldsborough and Missroon to GBM, Apr. 6, *OR,* Ser. 1, XI, Part 3, pp. 80, 81–82.

To Abraham Lincoln [TELEGRAM]

To the President
Washington

Head-Quarters of the Army of the Potomac
[Before Yorktown] April 7 1862 [11 P.M.]

Your telegram of yesterday received.[1] In reply I have the honor to state that my entire force for duty only amounts to about eighty five thousand (85,000) men. General Wool's command as you will observe from the accompanying order has been taken out of my control, although he has most cheerfully cooperated with me.

The only use that can be made of his command is to protect my communications in rear of this point. At this time only fifty three thousand (53,000) men have joined me, but they are coming up as rapidly as my means of transportation will permit.

Please refer to my dispatch to the Secretary of War of tonight for the details of our present situation.[2]

G. B. McClellan
Maj. Genl.

[*verso*]

Return of March 31st 1862 shows men for duty —			171,602
Deduct —	1st Corps Inft & Arty	32,119	
	Blenker	8,616	
	Banks	21,759	
	Wadsworth	19,308	
	Cavalry of 1st Corps — say	1,600	
	" Blenker	800	
	Van Alen & Wyndham	1,600	
		85,792[3]	85,792
For duty —			85,810[4]
Officers about		3,900	
Total absent from whole command		23,796	

Retained copy (verso AD), McClellan Papers (A-50:20), Library of Congress. *OR*, Ser. 1, XI, Part 1, p. 11.

1. Lincoln telegraphed, in part: "You now have over one hundred thousand troops, with you independent of Gen. Wool's command. I think you better break the enemies' line from York-town to Warwick River, at once. They will probably use *time*, as advantageously as you can." *Collected Works of Lincoln*, V, p. 182. 2. GBM to Stanton, Apr. 7, *supra*. The president responded on Apr. 9: "Your despatches complaining that you are not properly sustained, while they do not offend me, do pain me very much.... I think it is the precise time for you to strike a blow. By delay the enemy will relatively gain upon you — that is, he will gain faster, by *fortifications* and *re-inforcements*, than you can by re-inforcements alone. And, once more let me tell you, it is indispensable to *you* that you strike a blow. *I* am powerless to help this.... The country will not fail to note — is now noting — that the present hesitation to move upon an intrenched enemy, is but the story of Manassas repeated. I beg to assure you that I have never written you, or spoken to you, in greater kindness of feeling than now, nor with a fuller purpose to sustain you.... *But you must act.*" *Collected Works of Lincoln*, V, pp. 184–85. 3. This figure should be 85,802. 4. This figure should be 85,800.

To Mary Ellen McClellan

[Before Yorktown] April 8 [1862] 8 am.

Raining hard all night & still continues to do so. Am now encamped about 5 mi from Yorktown — have been here 2 or 3 days. Have now visited both the right & left, & in spite of the heavy rain must ride to Ship Point & our right immediately after breakfast & all I care for about the rain is the health & comfort of the men. They are more fond of me than ever — more enthusiastic than I deserve — wherever I go it seems to inspire the fullest confidence....

I have raised an awful row about McDowell's Corps — & have I think rather scared the authorities that be. The Presdt very coolly telegraphed me yesterday that he thought I had better break the enemy's lines at once! I was much tempted to reply that he had better come & do it himself.

AL copy, McClellan Papers (C-7:63), Library of Congress.

To Edwin M. Stanton [TELEGRAM]

Head Quarters, Army of the Potomac,
Near Yorktown April 11 12.30 am 1862

The reconnaissances of today [April 10] prove that it is necessary to invest & attack Gloucester Point. Give me Franklin's & McCall's Divisions under command of Franklin & I will at once undertake it.

If circumstances of which I am not aware make it impossible for you to send me two Divisions to carry out the final plan of campaign I will run the risk & hold myself responsible for the results if you will give me

Franklin's Division. If you still confide in my judgment I entreat that you will grant this request — the fate of our cause depends upon it.

Although willing under the pressure of necessity to carry this through with Franklin alone, I wish it to be distinctly understood that I think two Divisions necessary. Franklin & his Division are indispensable to me. Genl Barnard concurs in this view. I have determined upon the point of attack & am at this moment engaged in fixing the position of the batteries.

G B McClellan
Maj Genl

Hon E M Stanton
Secty of War

ALS (telegram sent), McClellan Papers (A-51:20), Library of Congress. *OR*, Ser. 1, XI, Part 3, p. 86.

To Mary Ellen McClellan

[Before Yorktown] April 11 [1862] 8 am.

I am just recovering from a terrible scare. Early this morning I was awakened by a dispatch from Fitz John's Hd Qtrs, stating that Fitz had made an ascension in the balloon this morning, & that the balloon had broken away & come to the ground some 3 miles S.W. — which would be within the enemy's lines! You can imagine how I felt! I at once sent off to the various pickets to find out what they knew, & try to do something to save him — but the order had no sooner gone, than in walks Mr. Fitz just as cool as usual — he had luckily come down near my own camp, after actually passing over that of the enemy!! You may rest assured of one thing: you won't catch me in the confounded balloon nor will I allow any other Generals to go up in it!...[1]

Dont worry about the wretches — they have done nearly their worst & can't do much more. I am sure that I will win in the end, in spite of all their rascality.

History will present a sad record of these traitors who are willing to sacrifice the country & its army for personal spite & personal aims. The people will soon understand the whole matter & then woe betide the guilty ones.

AL copy; copy, McClellan Papers (C-7:63/D-10:72), Library of Congress.

1. Thaddeus S. C. Lowe, the army's chief aeronaut, remarked of Porter's experience: "I found it difficult for a time to restore confidence among the officers as to the safety of this means of observation on account of this accident...." *OR*, Ser. 3, III, p. 274.

To Winfield Scott

Head-Quarters, Army of the Potomac,
Dear General; Camp Winfield Scott April 11 1862

I find myself with a siege before me, and as I entertain strong hopes that the result of the operations now impending will be decisive of the present contest, I have taken the liberty to give to this Camp the name of the General under whom I first learned the art of war and whom I have ever regarded as my sincere friend. I hope, General, that the operations emanating from this Camp will not be unworthy of the approbation of the great General whose name it now bears.

When I moved from Fort Monroe, I was deceived by the maps laid before me and supposed that Yorktown could be turned and its garrison cut off by two rapid marches. I therefore moved the Divisions F. J. Porter and Hamilton by the road from Hampton and Big Bethel to Howard's Bridge, throwing a strong advance guard far enough to the front to force the evacuation of Ship Point; at the same time, I moved the Divisions Smith (W. F.) and Couch from Newport News on Young's Mill; with Sedgwick's Division, the regular Infantry and Cavalry and the Artillery Reserve, I moved to Big Bethel. The orders for the next day's march were for the left column to move rapidly to "Halfway House"—6 miles from Yorktown on the Williamsburg road, in order to cut the communications of the garrison of York; the right column to move upon York and invest it. I moved the reserves to a point 5 miles from Yorktown, whence I could direct it to the support of either column, supposing that the left would most require its aid.

It proved, however, to be the case that the topography of the country was very different from what had been supposed and that the enemy had occupied and strongly entrenched the right bank of the Warwick River, which heads about one-half a mile from Yorktown. The works are formidable, the Artillery pretty heavy. The bed of the Warwick is next to impassable owing to its marshy nature and numerous inundations. The defences of Yorktown itself and of Gloucester are truly formidable. The water batteries are so heavy as to deter the gun-boats from attacking them. The roads have been infamous—we are working energetically upon them—are landing our siege guns, and leaving nothing undone.

We are forced to the use of mortars and heavy guns, although I do not expect, at present, to be obliged to resort to the tedious operations of a formal siege. Franklin's Division has just been restored to me. With it, I shall attack Gloucester Point.

The "Mystic," iron-clad, has been promised me. I shall try to have her run through the passage between York and Gloucester, in order to cut off the supplies and reinforcements constantly received by the rebels by way of York River, and at the same time take their water batteries in reverse.

You are probably aware, General, that, since I commenced this movement, my Army has been weakened by detachments to the extent of nearly 50,000 men. Of these, Franklin's Division (say 11,000) has today been restored to me.

Excuse me, General, for troubling you with this long and hasty letter; but I feel assured that you entertain a strong interest in the movements of this Army; so much so, that I will take the liberty of occasionally writing to you, if it is not disagreeable to you.

I send, with this, a map which will give you a general idea of the position. Tomorrow, I can send you a clear and good one. Only two or three of the enemy's numerous batteries are marked on this.

I am General your sincere & attached friend,
Geo. B. McClellan
Major General

Lt. Genl. Winfield Scott,
U.S. Army

Copy, McClellan Papers (A-51:20), Library of Congress.

To Edwin M. Stanton [TELEGRAM]

[Camp Winfield Scott, April 12, 1862, noon]

Your telegram received. I thank you most sincerely for the reinforcements sent to me.[1]

Franklin will attack on the other side. The moment I hear from Missroon I will state point of rendesvous. I am confident as to results now.

G B McClellan
Maj Genl Comdg

Hon E M Stanton
Secty of War

ALS (telegram sent), McClellan Papers (A-51:20), Library of Congress. *OR*, Ser. 1, XI, Part 3, p. 92.

1. Stanton telegraphed Apr. 11: "Franklin's division is marching to Alexandria to embark. McCall's will be sent if the safety of this city will permit." *OR*, Ser. 1, XI, Part 3, p. 90.

To Gustavus V. Fox

Private Head-Quarters, Army of the Potomac,
My dear Fox Camp Winfield Scott April 14, 1862.

Wyman[1] is here & I will send this by him. I fear friend Missroon is not the man for the place exactly, he is a little too careful of his vessels, & has as yet done us no good — not even annoyed the enemy.

Can't you possibly arrange the matter so as to put Wyman or some one like him in command? It would of course be a great advantage that the Army & Navy Comdrs should know each other & understand each other, so as to secure perfect cooperation — put Wyman in command & I feel perfectly sure that the thing will work out right. I received this morning a dispatch from Missroon as follows — "The enemy are increasing troops in rear of picket station abreast the ships today" — I replied "Won't you shell them out?" — Have received no reply, but have heard no shells. I have an indistinct idea that it would not be disagreeable to Missroon to go on Ordnance duty — a duty of great importance in these times. Do give me Wyman if you can — I like him & feel by instinct that he is a first rate officer for the work.[2]

Effective naval cooperation will shorten this affair by weeks. Don't forget to let me have the Mystic. I shall soon open trenches.

The work before us is rum but I can see the way to gain new and brilliant success.

Give my kindest regards to Judge Blair & say to him that I received his letter & will not fail to act upon his suggestions.[3]

If Wyman comes here can you not send the Anacosta & Badger with him?[4]

In haste very truly your friend
Geo B McClellan

Hon G V Fox
Asst Secty

ALS, Fox Papers, New-York Historical Society.

1. Commander of the Potomac flotilla. 2. On Apr. 30 Missroon was replaced by Comdr. William Smith. 3. Montgomery Blair, Fox's brother-in-law, wrote GBM on Apr. 9: "Whilst a bloody battle & a dear bought victory will not place you higher in the estimation of men of professional skills, it will perhaps do more to raise you in the estimation of people generally than successes achieved by strategy merely.... I hope for your own sake & that of the country that you now feel that it is both necessary & proper to fight at once." McClellan Papers (A-50:20), Library of Congress. 4. The gunboat *Anacostia,* commanded by Lt. Oscar C. Badger.

To Abraham Lincoln [TELEGRAM]

Head Quarters, Army of the Potomac,
Camp Winfield Scott April 14 8.40 pm 1862

I have seen General Franklin & beg to thank you for your kindness & consideration. I now understand the matter, which I did not before.[1]

Our field guns annoyed the enemy considerably to day. Roads & bridges now progressing rapidly — siege guns & ammunition coming up very satisfactorily — shall have nearly all up tomorrow. The tranquility of Yorktown is nearly at an end.

G B McClellan
Maj Genl Comdg

A Lincoln
President Washington

ALS (telegram sent), McClellan Papers (A-51:20), Library of Congress. *OR,* Ser. 1, XI, Part 3, p. 98.

1. Franklin had been summoned to the White House and told (so Gen. McDowell learned from the president) "to acquaint General McClellan with the reasons, which were purely of a public character," for retaining McDowell's corps at Washington. *OR,* Ser. 1, XII, Part 1, p. 277.

To Mary Ellen McClellan

Camp Winfield Scott April 14 [1862] 11 p.m.

. . . I believe I now know who instigated the attack upon me & the country.[1] . . .

So Fox told you all about our troubles[2] — they *were* severe for some time, but we are pretty well over the worst of them. . . .

I do not expect to lose many men, but to do the work mainly with artillery, & so avoid much loss of life. Several brave fellows have already gone to their long home, but not a large number.

I can't tell you how soon I will attack, as it will depend upon the rapidity with which certain preliminary work can be done & the heavy guns brought up. I do not fear a repulse — I shall not quit this camp until I do so to continue the march on Richmond. If I am repulsed once, will try it again & keep at it until we succeed — but I do not anticipate a repulse — am confident of success. . . .

I received today a very kind letter from old Mr. Blair, which I enclose for you to keep for me.[3] . . .

Remained at home this morning doing office work, but rode out all the p.m., rode to the front & took another look at secesh. . . .

AL copy, McClellan Papers (C-7:63), Library of Congress.

1. GBM had just talked with Gen. Franklin, who was persuaded of Stanton's perfidy, and this is perhaps a reference to the secretary of war. See GBM to Franklin, Apr. 6, *supra,*

note 1. 2. Assistant Navy Secretary Fox had visited GBM on Apr. 9. 3. Francis P. Blair wrote GBM on Apr. 12: "If you can accomplish your object of reaching Richmond by a slower process than storming redoubts & batteries in earth works, the country will applaud the achievement which gives success to its arms, with greatest parsimony of the blood of its children." McClellan Papers (A-51:20).

To Mary Ellen McClellan

[Camp Winfield Scott] April 18th [1862] 1.15 am.

... About 1/2 hr ago the accustomed intermittent sound of artillery was varied in its monotony by a very heavy & continued rattle of musketry with the accompaniment of a very respectable firing of artillery. I started at once for the telegraph office & endeavored in vain for some ten or fifteen minutes to arouse the operators at the stations in the direction of the firing. So I ordered twenty of the escort to saddle up, & started off Hudson, Sweitzer & the Duc de Chartres to learn the state of the case. The firing has ceased now for some minutes & I am still ignorant as to its whereabouts & cause. Of course I must remain up, until I know what it is. I had had Arthur, Wright, Hammerstein, Radowitz & the Count de Paris as well as Colburn also up, with some of the escort ready to move or carry orders, as the case may be, but just now told them to lie down until I sent for them.[1] It is a beautiful moonlight night clear & pleasant, almost too much so for sleeping....

Have not ridden out today [April 17], but have found plenty of work at home. Have arranged tonight for the commencement of 5 batteries tomorrow — mounting 41 guns — this is a mere preliminary & as soon as I get the roads & bridges finished I will commence several more....

Poor Wagner of the Topogs, lost an arm this afternoon by the bursting of a shell — he is doing well however. Merrill was severely, but not dangerously wounded in the arm yesterday.[2]

In Smith's affair yesterday [April 16] we lost I fear nearly 200 killed & wounded.[3] The object I proposed had been fully accomplished with the loss of about 20 — when after I left the ground a movement was made in direct violation of my orders, by which the remainder of the loss was uselessly incurred. I do not yet know the details nor who is responsible. We have a severe task before us, but we will gain a brilliant success....

The great trouble I have is in the want of good staff officers — Colburn is my stand by — so true & faithful. Many of my aides are excellent but the trouble is in the Chfs of Depts whose lack of experience I am obliged to supply by personal labor. No Genl ever labored under greater disadvantages, but I will carry it through in spite of everything. I hope Franklin will be here tomorrow or next day. I will then invest Gloucester & attack it at the same time I do York. When the Galena arrives I will cause it to pass the batteries, take them in reverse & cut off the enemy's communications by York River. As I write I hear our guns constantly sounding, & the bursting of shells in Secessia.

9 am. The firing of last night was caused by the attempt of a part of the enemy to cross the stream in Smith's front. They were repulsed at once; tried it later & were again driven back.

AL copy; copy, McClellan Papers (C-7 :63/D-10 :72), Library of Congress.

1. All members of GBM's staff: Edward McK. Hudson, N. B. Sweitzer, Arthur McClellan, Edward H. Wright, Herbert Hammerstein, Paul Von Radowitz, A. V. Colburn, and the two young Frenchmen, the Duc de Chartres and the Comte de Paris. 2. Lts. Orlando G. Wagner, Topographical Engineers, and William E. Merrill, Corps of Engineers. Wagner's wound was mortal. 3. A sortie involving the division of Brig. Gen. William F. Smith.

To Edwin M. Stanton [TELEGRAM]

Head-Quarters, Army of the Potomac,
Camp Winfield Scott April 18 1862 10 pm.

Dispatch received.[1] I cannot hope such good fortune as that the enemy will take the offensive. I am perfectly prepared for any attack the enemy may make. He will do nothing more than sorties. I beg that the Presdt will be satisfied that the enemy cannot gain anything by attacking me — the more he does attack the better I shall be contented.

All is well. I am glad to hear of Banks good fortune.

G B McClellan
Maj Genl

Hon E M Stanton
Secty of War

ALS (telegram sent), McClellan Papers (A-52 :20), Library of Congress. *OR*, Ser. 1, XI, Part 3, p. 108.

1. Stanton telegraphed on this date that the president "directed me to ask you whether the indications do not show that the enemy are inclined to take the offensive." *OR*, Ser. 1, XI, Part 3, p. 107.

To Abraham Lincoln [TELEGRAM]

Confidential & in cipher

Head Quarters, Army of the Potomac,
Camp Winfield Scott
April 18 11.30 pm 1862

If compatible with your impressions as to the security of the Capital & not interfering with operations of which I am ignorant I would be glad to have McCall's Division so as to be enabled to make a strong attack upon West Point to turn position of the enemy. After all that I have heard of things which have occurred since I left Washington & before I would prefer that Genl McDowell should not again be assigned to duty with me. [*crossed out:* Better that some other field of action should be given him.]

G B McClellan
Maj Genl Comdg

His Excellency A Lincoln
Presdt

ALS (telegram sent), McClellan Papers (A-52:20), Library of Congress. *OR,* Ser. 1, LI, Part 1, p. 578.

To Ambrose E. Burnside

Private Head-Quarters, Army of the Potomac,
My dear Burn Camp Winfield Scott April 19 1862

Your welcome letter of the 17th has just reached me, together with your dispatch.[1]

You are too modest in regard to your report — I do not find too many men in these days who *will* tell the truth — but I will not bore you by expressing my thanks again — I can never forget the debt I owe you for your manly truth. I feel, Burn, as you an implicit trust that God will carry me through — at all events that he will order things for the best. Now that such vast responsibility is upon me — the lives of thousands — the happiness of tens of thousands — the honor & salvation of a Govt, I more than ever feel the necessity of the aid of God — I pray that we may have his arm on our side.

I think you are making the best use of your time & hope to hear soon that Macon is in your hands — I will suggest to the Secty the propriety of sending to you some of the siege material rendered disposable by the fall of Pulaski.[2] I will do all in my power to get for you the regiment of cavalry & the two batteries you ask for — you should have them.

As soon as Macon falls you can undertake some forward movement — but whether that should be in the direction of Goldsborough or Winton must depend upon the state of affairs here at the time.

I find myself brought up all standing by a formidable line of earth works with a marshy river in front — I am building siege batteries & shall attack the town itself in spite of its strength. I have had great difficulties arising from the weather & the roads — most of them are now overcome & we are fairly started with the preparations for opening fire. The batteries I am now building are mostly concealed from view — about the time they are armed I will commence the first parallel & exposed batteries — we will have lively times here & have difficulties to overcome but I feel confident of success.

Barnard has just come in to discuss tomorrow's operations so I must stop.

Remember me most kindly to Parke, Foster & Reno — *how* handsomely they have acted! Give my regards also to Williamson & any other of my friends that are with you.[3]

McC

I have just telegraphed to the Secty of War requesting that the Rhode Island Cavalry & two good batteries 1st N.Y. Artillery under Lt Col Turner be sent to you at once.

McC

ALS, Records of the Adjutant General's Office, RG 94 (159: Burnside Papers), National Archives.

1. Burnside's letter of Apr. 17 detailed operations against Fort Macon. *OR,* Ser. 1, IX, pp. 377–78. 2. Fort Pulaski, at Savannah, was captured Apr. 11. 3. Brig. Gens. John G. Parke, John G. Foster, and Jesse L. Reno, brigade commanders under Burnside; and Capt. Robert S. Williamson, Topographical Engineers.

To Mary Ellen McClellan

[Camp Winfield Scott] April 19 [1862] 10 1/2 pm.

... Today it has been very quiet — our batteries have merely fired enough to keep the enemy entirely silent at his works in front of Smith & at Wynn's Mill. Last night we commenced a Battery at Farenholdt's house for 5 100 pdr Parrotts & 1 200 pdr Parrott — also one for 15 heavy guns about 2000 yds from the enemy's main defenses, another for 6 & one for 5 close by. Another for 6 was armed today, & kept down the enemy's fire at Wynn's Mill. Tomorrow morning we commence batteries for 13″ mortars. About Monday night [April 21] we will construct the first parallel & several other batteries in exposed positions, leaving those already commenced to cover the work & render it more safe. We shall soon be raining down a terrible tempest on this devoted place. Today the enemy sent a flag of truce to Smith, asking a suspension of hostilities to bury the killed of the 16th. The officer who met Sweitzer acknowledged that their loss was very severe & the bearing of our men admirable. I recd today a letter from Burnside which I enclose....

Franklin arrived yesterday & spent the night in my tent — he is at Ship Point tonight — I expect his Divn tomorrow....

Don't be at all discouraged — all is going well — the more there are in Yorktown the more decisive will the results be. I know exactly what I am about & am quite confident that with God's blessing I shall utterly defeat them. I can't go "*with a rush*" over strong posts. I must use heavy guns & silence their fire — all that takes much time & I have not been longer than the usual time for such things — much less than the usual in truth....

I can't tell you when Yorktown is to be attacked, for it depends on circumstances that I cannot control. It shall be attacked the first moment I can do so successfully — but I don't intend to hurry it — I cannot afford to fail. I have a little over 100,000 effective men including Franklin's Division. . . .

I may have the opportunity of carrying the place next week — or may be delayed a couple of weeks — much of course depends on the rapidity with which the heavy guns & ammunition arrive. Never mind what such people as Wade[1] say — they are beneath contempt. I telegraphed the Presdt last night requesting that McDowell might *not* again be assigned to duty with me.[2]

I will put in a leaf of holly from the bower some of the men have made in front of my tent today; they have made quite an artistic thing of it — holly & pine — it adds much too, to my comfort, as it renders the tent more private & cool.

AL copy; copy, McClellan Papers (C-7:63/D-10:72), Library of Congress.

1. Senator Benjamin F. Wade, chairman of the Joint Committee on the Conduct of the War. 2. GBM to Lincoln, Apr. 18, *supra*.

To Abraham Lincoln

Private

His Excellency The President — Head-Quarters, Army of the Potomac,
My dear Sir — Camp Winfield Scott April 20 1862

I enclose herewith a copy of the first reliable map we have prepared of this vicinity — it will give you a good general idea of positions. In a day or two we will have one on a larger scale which will be more satisfactory to you. I will soon send you one of the immediate front of Yorktown on which I will mark the batteries now being entrenched & send such information as will enable you to put down the new works as they progress.

We are now actually at work, & nearly through, with 6 batteries for guns, have commenced a series for 10 13″ mortars, & commence tomorrow morning another gun battery. As soon as these are armed we will open the first parallel & other batteries for 8″ & 10″ mortars & some heavy guns. Everything is going on admirably & we shall soon open with a terrific fire. I hope to hear hourly of the arrival of Franklin's Division, & shall lose no time in placing him in position. I hope the Galena will be here to assist us very soon.

Genl Robt Lee is in command in our front — Johnston is *under him*![1] I learn that there has been quite a struggle on the subject between Davis & his Congress, Davis insisting upon Johnston. I prefer Lee to Johnston — the former is *too* cautious & weak under grave responsibility — personally brave & energetic to a fault, he yet is wanting in moral firmness when pressed by heavy responsibility & is likely to be timid & irresolute in action.

The difficulties of our position are considerable, that is the enemy is in a very strong position — but I never expected to get to Richmond without a hard fought battle, & am just as willing to fight it here as elsewhere — I am confident of success, not only of success but of brilliant success. I think that a defeat here substantially breaks up the rebel cause.

They are making great efforts — enforcing the conscription with the utmost vigor, & now have their regiments full — whether the infusion of raw & perhaps unwilling men will benefit them remains to be seen. I doubt whether it is a disadvantage to us.

I am, Sir, most respectfully and sincerely your friend
Geo B McClellan

ALS, Lincoln Papers, Library of Congress.

1. On Mar. 13 Gen. Robert E. Lee was called to Richmond and, "under the direction of the President,... charged with the conduct of military operations in the armies of the Confederacy," a position that in effect made him chief of staff of the Confederate army. *OR*, Ser. 1, V, p. 1099.

To Mary Ellen McClellan

[Camp Winfield Scott] April 23 [1862] 11 1/2 pm.

...Have been working hard all day, but not in the saddle — it has been head work in my tent today. I am getting on splendidly with my *slow* preparations — the Prince[1] is delighted & thinks my work gigantic — I *do* believe that I am avoiding the faults of the Allies at Sebastopol & quietly preparing the way for a great success. I have brought *40* heavy guns in battery — tomorrow night I hope to have 12 more guns & 5 to 10 heavy mortars in battery.

I begin in the morning the redoubts to cover the flank of the 1st Parallel which will be constructed tomorrow night. I will not open fire unless the enemy annoys us — hoping to get all the guns in battery & the trenches well advanced before meeting with serious opposition. We have done much more than they suspect. Have ordered a forced reconnaissance of a dangerous point in the morning — it may cost several lives, but I have taken all possible precautions & hope to gain the information necessary with but little loss — there is no other choice than to run the risk. I think I see the way clear to success & that at no distant day....

Everything is as quiet now as if there were no enemy within a hundred miles of us. The Galena, under Rodgers,[2] will be here the day after tomorrow — in a day or two after she arrives you will hear of a blow struck that will surprise secesh & delight the country — I *may* delay it for a few days if I meet with any delays in my preparations, but it will soon come in a way secesh does not expect.

AL copy, McClellan Papers (C-7:63), Library of Congress.

1. Prince de Joinville. 2. Comdr. John Rodgers.

To Abraham Lincoln

Head-Quarters, Army of the Potomac,
Private & confidential [Camp Winfield Scott]
Your Excellency: April 23 midnight 1862

I am well aware of the firm friendship & confidence you have evinced for me, & instead of again thanking you for it will endeavor to assure you that it is not misplaced.

Do not misunderstand the apparent inaction here — not a day, not an hour has been lost, works have been constructed that may almost be called gigantic — roads built through swamps & difficult ravines, material brought up, batteries built. I have tonight in battery & ready for action 5 100 pdr Parrott guns, 10 4 1/2″ Ordnance guns, 18 20 pdr Parrotts, 6 Napoleon guns & 6 10 pdr Parrotts — this not counting the batteries in front of Smith & on his left — 45 guns. I will add to it tomorrow night 5 30 pdr Parrotts, 6 20 pdr Parrotts, from 5 to 10 13″ mortars, & (if it arrives in time) 1 200 pdr Parrott. Before sundown tomorrow I will essentially complete the redoubts necessary to strengthen the left of the 1st Parallel; & will construct that Parallel as far as Wormley's Creek from the left, & probably all the way to York River tomorrow night. I will then be secure against sorties. It has become necessary to make tomorrow morning early a "forced reconnaissance" to gain some information as to the ground on the left flank of the proposed 1st Parallel — this ground is strongly held by the enemy's pickets, is swampy & covered with thick brush & timber — I cannot now tell what facilities they possess for crossing the stream in force — to gain this information I have ordered Col Gove[1] to move with his Regt, the 22nd Massachusetts, early in the morning — I have taken all possible precautions, so that the object *may* be gained without loss — yet it is possible that many lives *may* be lost — there is no other way of accomplishing the object, & I merely wish to state beforehand what the purpose is, in order that the result may be understood. I do not propose to open fire at present unless the enemy attempt to interfere with the construction of the 1st Parallel & the new batteries which will be commenced at once. If he will permit it I will at once build a battery at close range for 5 more 100 pdrs & another 200 pdr rifle, batteries for the 10 & 8 inch mortars, 8″ howitzers, & additional 30 & 20 pounder Parrotts, in the mean time pushing the approaches forward as rapidly as possible. I still hope that we will not be seriously interfered with until I can open an overwhelming fire & give the assault from a reasonable distance under its cover. My course must necessarily depend to a great extent upon that of the enemy — but I see the way clear to success & hope to make it brilliant, although with but little loss of life. I expect great aid from the Galena — Franklin will probably land as soon as she arrives — his preparations ought to be completed tomorrow.

I am most respectfully & truly your friend
Geo B McClellan

His Excellency the President

ALS, Lincoln Papers, Library of Congress.

1. Col. Jesse A. Gove.

To Edwin M. Stanton

Hon E.M.S. — Head Quarters, Army of the Potomac,
Sir — Before Yorktown [c. April 27, 1862]

I received today a note from Asst Secty Watson enclosing an extract from a letter the author of which is not mentioned.[1] I send a copy of the extract with this.

I hope that a copy has also been sent to Genl McDowell, whom it concerns more nearly perhaps than it does me.

At the risk of being thought obtrusive I will venture upon some remarks which perhaps my position does not justify me in making, but which I beg to assure you are induced solely by my intense desire for the success of the Govt in this struggle.

You will, I hope, pardon me if I allude to the past, not in a captious spirit, but merely so far as may be necessary to explain my own course & my views as to the future.

From the beginning I had intended, so far as I might have the power to carry out my own views, to abandon the line of Manassas as the line of advance — I ever regarded it as an improper one; my wish was to adopt a new line, based upon the waters of the lower Chesapeake. I always expected to meet with strong opposition on this line, the strongest that the rebels could offer, but I was well aware that after overcoming this opposition the result would be decisive, & pregnant with great results.

Circumstances, among which I will now only mention the uncertainty as to the power of the Merrimac, have compelled me to adopt the present line, as probably safer, tho' far less brilliant than that by Urbana. When the movement was commenced I counted upon an active & disposable force of nearly 150,000 men, & intended to throw a strong column upon West Point either by York River, or, if that proved to be impracticable, by a march from the mouth of the Severn — expecting to turn in that manner all the defences of the Peninsula. Circumstances have proved that I was right & that my intended movements would have produced the desired results.

After the transfer of troops had commenced from Alexandria to Fort Monroe, but before I started in person, the Division Blenker was detached from my command — a loss of near 10,000 men.

As soon as the mass of my troops were fairly started I embarked myself. Upon reaching Fort Monroe I learned that the rebels were being rapidly reinforced from Norfolk & Richmond — I therefore determined to lose no time in making the effort to invest Yorktown, without waiting for the arrival of the Divisions Hooker, Richardson & the 1st Corps; intending to employ the 1st Corps in mass to move upon West Point, reinforcing it as circumstances might render necessary.

The advance was made on the morning of the second day after I reached Fort Monroe. When the troops reached the immediate vicinity of Yorktown the true nature of the enemy's position was for the first time developed — while my men were under fire I learned that the 1st Corps was removed from my command — no warning had been given me of this, nor was any reason then assigned. I should also have mentioned that the evening before I left Fort Monroe I received a telegraphic dispatch from the War Dept informing me that the order placing Fort Monroe & its dependent troops under my command was rescinded, no reason was given for this, nor has it been to this day — I confess that I have no right to know the reason.

This order deprived me of the support of another Division which I had been authorized to form for active operations from among the troops near Fort Monroe. Thus when I came under fire, I found myself weaker by five Divisions (near 50,000 men) than I had expected when the movement commenced. It is more than probable that no General ever was placed in such a position before. Finding myself thus unexpectedly weakened & with a powerful enemy strongly entrenched in my front I was compelled to change my plans & become cautious. Could I have retained my original force I confidently believe that I would now have been in front of Richmond instead of where I now am — the probability is that that city would now have been in our possession.

But the question now is in regard to the present & the future rather than the past.

The enemy, by the destruction of the bridges of the Rappahannock has deprived himself of the means of a rapid advance on Washington. Lee will never venture upon a bold movement on a large scale.

The troops I left for the defence of Washington, as I fully explained to you in the letter I wrote the day I sailed,[2] are ample for its protection.

Our true policy is to concentrate our troops on the fewest possible lines of attack — we have now too many, & an enterprising enemy could strike us a severe blow. I have every reason to believe that the main portion of the rebel forces are in my front — they are *not* "drawing off" their troops from Yorktown.

Give me McCall's Division & I will undertake a movement on West Point which will shake them out of Yorktown. As it is I will win — but I must not be blamed if success is delayed — I do not feel that I am answerable for the delay of victory.

I do not feel authorized to venture upon any suggestions as to the disposition of the troops in other Depts, but content myself with stating the least that I regard as essential to prompt success here — If circumstances render it impossible to give what I ask, I still feel sure of success — but more time will be required to achieve the result.

AL retained copy, McClellan Papers (A-88:35), Library of Congress.

1. This extract, enclosed with Assistant Secretary of War Peter H. Watson's letter of Apr. 25, suggested that Jefferson Davis was successfully detaining GBM at Yorktown while drawing off troops from there to fall on McDowell's forces at Fredericksburg. *OR,* Ser. 1, XI, Part 3, p. 121. 2. GBM to Lorenzo Thomas, Apr. 1, *supra.*

To Mary Ellen McClellan

[Camp Winfield Scott] April 27 [1862] midnight

. . . Was engaged with Barnard, Porter etc until about one, when I rode to the trenches. Then of course had to walk — a good deal was muddy so it was tiresome. Went over the whole extent & saw everything with care. The enemy have fired a good deal today, but the men are now so well covered that no one has been hurt today. Commenced today batteries for 15 10″ mortars, & tonight another battery for heavy guns — another for 10 mortars tomorrow morning — an extension of the parallel on the left commenced tonight. By tomorrow night the parallel should be finished in all its details, as well as the two covering redoubts on the left. Some time day after tomorrow I hope to have 35 mortars in battery. Tomorrow night will open a boyau in advance leading to a new gun battery — fast getting ready to blow secesh up & he will have a bad time of it after we open. Think he will find Yorktown very uncomfortable. Have news this evening via Richmond that New Orleans is in our possession. I presume it is true — so the work goes bravely on. . . .

Yesterday [April 27] made Fitz Porter "Director of the Siege" — a novel title but made necessary by the circumstances of the case. I give all my orders relating to the siege through him — making him at the same time comdt of the siege operations & a chief of staff for that portion of the work. It not being *M*'s[1] specialty he cannot assist me in siege operations. This new arrangement will save me much trouble, relieve my mind greatly & save much time. In going over the line of trenches yesterday I found so many blunders committed that I was very thankful to put Porter on duty at once. . . .

Be careful to say not one word about Stanton, McDowell or any of my enemies, let us present a contrast with those people & show by no word or act that we care what they say or do.

The good fellow (Colburn) never leaves me — wherever I ride, he sticks close after me. He is one of the very best men I ever knew; so thoroughly honest & reliable. His judgment is excellent & he is perfectly untiring. Day and night are about the same to him & he will start out on a long ride at midnight in a pitch dark or rainy night with as much good humour as at midday. Kentuck is still at Fort Monroe sick, will rejoin in a few days I hope — Marsh is with him, & I am sometimes half wicked enough to suspect that Marsh finds Fort Monroe more comfortable than camp would be.

AL copy; copy, McClellan Papers (C-7:63/D-10:72), Library of Congress.

1. Chief of Staff Marcy.

To Mary Ellen McClellan

[Camp Winfield Scott] April 30th [1862] am.

Had a quiet night — very little firing — drove them out of an orchard where they had been annoying us, & pushed them still further in towards their works. A good deal of firing on their part yesterday — did very little harm — killing some 3 & wounding 4 or 5 of our people. Scarcely a gun fired today as yet — we are working like horses & will soon be ready to open. It will be a tremendous affair when we do begin & will I hope make short work of it. . . .

Have put the Regulars in the exposed portions of the work — they work so much better. A raw disagreeable day — I fear it will rain — unless it snows — wind from east. . . .

10.30 p.m. After I got thro' my morning work went down to see the opening of Battery No. 1 — it worked handsomely — drove all the rebel schooners away from the wharf & made a general scatteration. The effect was excellent. Shall not open the general fire for some *four* days.

Next morning. Another wet drizzly uncomfortable sort of a day. Good deal of firing during the night. I shall be very glad when we are really ready to open fire & then finish this confounded affair. I am tired of public life — & even now when doing the best I can for my country in the field I know that my enemies are pursuing me more remorselessly than ever, & "kind *friends*" are constantly making themselves agreeable by informing me of the pleasant predicament in which I am — the rebels on one side, & the abolitionists & other scoundrels on the other — I believe in my heart & conscience, however, that I am walking on the ridge between the two gulfs, & that all I have to do is to try to keep the path of honor & truth & that God will bring me safely through — at all events I am willing to leave the matter in his hands & will be content with the decision of the Almighty.

AL copy, McClellan Papers (C-7 :63), Library of Congress.

To Abraham Lincoln [TELEGRAM]

Head Quarters, Army of the Potomac,
Camp Winfield Scott May 1 1862 9.30 pm

I asked for the Parrott guns from Washington for the reason that some expected had been two weeks nearly on the way & could not be heard from.[1] They arrived last night. My arrangements had been made for them & I thought time might be saved by getting others from Washington. My object was to hasten not procrastinate. All is being done that human labor can accomplish.

G B McClellan
Maj Genl

His Excellency the President
Washington D C

ALS (telegram sent), McClellan Papers (A-55 :22), Library of Congress. *OR*, Ser. 1, LI, Part 1, p. 589.

1. The president telegraphed on this date: "Your call for Parrott guns from Washington alarms me — chiefly because it argues indefinite procrastination. Is anything to be done?" *Collected Works of Lincoln*, V, p. 203.

To Louis M. Goldsborough [TELEGRAM]

Head Quarters, Army of the Potomac,
Confidential Camp Winfield Scott May 2 [1862] 9.30 pm

It is probable that I will be able to open a very heavy fire on Monday morning [May 5], certainly by Tuesday morning. I think the gun boats can pass the batteries any dark night — they certainly can after a day's firing on our part. I have proposed to Capt Smith that he shall run by the night after we open. Rogers will I suppose be available for the same purpose.[1] I think the effect of such a movement will be to enable me to gain possession of Yorktown on the 2d or 3d day. Can you spare for this decisive attack some more vessels? It is all important to make this blow a sure one.

G B McClellan
Maj Genl

Flag Officer L M Goldsborough
Hampton Roads

ALS (telegram sent), McClellan Papers (A-55:22), Library of Congress. *OR*, Ser. 1, LI, Part 1, p. 591.

1. Comdr. William Smith, of the gunboat flotilla; Comdr. Rodgers, of the ironclad *Galena*.

To Mary Ellen McClellan

[Camp Winfield Scott] May 3 [1862] 12.30 am.

After the hot firing of today [May 2] everything is so unusually still that I am a little suspicious that our friends may intend a sortie — so I have taken all the steps necessary to be ready for them & am sitting up for a while to await developments. I feel much better satisfied when they are firing than when they are silent — today they have wasted almost a thousand rounds & have done us no harm worth speaking of — except (Irish) bursting one of their own guns. We are now nearly ready to open — shall begin I think on Monday morning [May 5], certainly by Tuesday. If all works well it is not impossible that we shall have Yorktown by Wednesday or Thursday. The task is a difficult one, yet I am sure we have taken the right way to accomplish our purpose & that we will soon win. I fear that we are to have another storm tonight — we want no more rain, but will make the best of it if it comes. Had plenty of work to do at home all the morning, & in the afternoon rode down to "Shield's House" to meet the new comdr. of the flotilla — Capt Smith — he is a great improvement on Mr. Missroon & will do something I hope. . . .

I don't half like the perfect quietness which reigns now — I have given orders to take advantage of it & push our approaches as far forward as possible — it don't seem natural — it looks like a sortie or an evacuation — if either I hope it may be the former. I do not want these rascals to get away from me without a sound drubbing, which they richly deserve & which they will be sure to get if they remain. . . .

I need rest — my brain is taxed to the extreme — I feel that the fate of a nation depends upon me, & I feel that I have not one single friend at the seat of Govt — any day may bring an order relieving me from command — if such a thing should be done our cause is lost. If they will simply let me alone I feel sure of success — but, will they do it?

Saturday [May 3] am. All quiet — nothing unusual has occurred — no more at present.

AL copy, McClellan Papers (C-7:63), Library of Congress.

To Edwin M. Stanton [TELEGRAM]

Head Quarters, Army of the Potomac,
Camp Winfield Scott May 4 1862

Yorktown is in our possession.

G B McClellan
Maj Genl

Hon E M Stanton
Secty of War

ALS (telegram sent), McClellan Papers (C-13:64), Library of Congress. *OR,* Ser. 1, XI, Part 3, p. 133.

To Edwin M. Stanton [TELEGRAM]

Headquarters, Army of the Potomac,
Camp Winfield Scott May 4 1862 9 am

We have the enemy's heavy guns ammunition camp equipage etc — hold the entire line of his works which the Engineers report as being very strong. I have thrown all my cavalry & horse artillery in pursuit, supported by Infantry.

I move Franklin & as much more as I can transport by water up to West Point today. No time shall be lost. Gun boats have gone up York River. I omitted to state that Gloucester is also in our possession. I shall push the enemy to the wall.

G B McClellan
Maj Genl

Hon E M Stanton
Secty of War

ALS (telegram sent), McClellan Papers (A-55:22), Library of Congress. *OR,* Ser. 1, XI, Part 3, p. 134.

To Winfield Scott [TELEGRAM]

Lieut. Genl. Winfield Scott
Brevort House New York

Head-Quarters, Army of the Potomac,
Yorktown Va May 4 1862

The enemy abandoned Yorktown last night in great haste. Our parallels were pushed within eleven hundred yards of their strong-hold. They abandoned eighty heavy guns, with a large amount of ammunition, their tents, camp equipage &c &c. I am pushing forward to overtake them and one of our columns has come up with their rear.

I am also sending a large force on transports up York River to cut off the retreat.

Their works here were very formidable and could not have been carried without shelling which I was today prepared to commence.

The rebel forces are represented by deserters to be greatly demoralised. Their numbers are stated to be from 100,000 to 120,000, with large light artillery force.

Geo. B. McClellan
Maj. Genl.

Retained copy, McClellan Papers (A-55:22), Library of Congress.

To Edwin M. Stanton [TELEGRAM]

Head Quarters, Army of the Potomac,
Yorktown May 4 — 7 pm. 1862

Our cavalry & horse artillery came up with enemy's rear guard in their entrenchments about (2) two miles this side of Williamsburg. A brisk fight ensued. Just as my aide left Smith's Division of Infantry arrived on the ground & I presume carried the works tho' I have not yet heard. The enemy's rear guard is strong but I have force enough up there to answer all purposes.

We have thus far (82) eighty two heavy guns, large amounts of tents, ammunition etc all along the line.

Their works prove to have been most formidable & I am now fully satisfied of the correctness of the course I have pursued. Our success is brilliant & you may rest assured that its effects will be of the greatest importance.

There shall be no delay in following up the rebels.

The rebels have been guilty of the most murderous & barbarous conduct in placing torpedoes *within* the abandoned works, near wells & springs, near flag staffs, magazines, telegraph offices, in carpet bags, barrels of flour etc. Fortunately we have not lost many men in this manner — some 4 or 5 killed & perhaps a dozen wounded.

I shall make the prisoners remove them at their own peril.

G B McClellan
Maj Genl Comdg

Hon E M Stanton
Secty of War

ALS (telegram sent), McClellan Papers (A-55:22), Library of Congress. *OR,* Ser. 1, XI, Part 3, pp. 134–35.

To Mary Ellen McClellan [TELEGRAM]

Head Quarters, Army of the Potomac,
Yorktown May 4 — 7 pm 1862

Dear Nell. Results glorious — (82) eighty two heavy guns and large amounts of stores taken.

Stoneman[1] brought their rear guard to bay in their works within two (2) miles of Williamsburg, & I expect every moment to hear that Smith has carried the works.

All well & in splendid spirits. The enemy's works of very great strength. He must have been badly scared to have abandoned them in such a hurry.

G B McClellan
Maj Genl

Mrs. G B McClellan
5th Avenue Hotel N.Y. City[2]

ALS (telegram sent), McClellan Papers (C-13 :64), Library of Congress.

1. Brig. Gen. George Stoneman commanded the advance guard. 2. Mrs. McClellan had left Washington in April and would stay for varying periods, over the next five months, in New York City; North Orange, N.J.; and Hartford, New London, and Middletown, Conn.

To Edwin M. Stanton [TELEGRAM]

Head-Quarters, Army of the Potomac,
Yorktown May 5 9 am 1862

Raining hard now & most of the night — roads consequently infamous. Enemy still at Williamsburg — heavy firing now going on. The weather has delayed Franklin — I hope to overcome all obstacles today & throw a sufficient force up the York to cut the enemy's line of retreat. Several of our batteries are actually stuck fast in the mud. The men have done all that could be done.

No signs of cessation of rain.

G B McClellan
Maj Genl

Hon E M Stanton
Secty of War

ALS (telegram sent), McClellan Papers (A-56 :22), Library of Congress. *OR,* Ser. 1, XI, Part 3, p. 139.

To Mary Ellen McClellan

[Before Yorktown] May 5 [1862] 9 1/2 am.

. . . You will have learned ere this that Yorktown is ours — it is a place of immense strength & was very heavily armed — it so happened however that our preparations for the attack were equally formidable, so that Lee, Johnston & Davis confessed that they could not hold the place — they evacuated it in a great hurry, leaving their heavy guns, baggage etc. I sent the cavalry after them at once — & our advance is now engaged with them at Wmsburg. The weather is infamous — it has been raining all night & is still raining heavily — no signs of stopping — roads awful. I hope to get to West Point today — altho' the weather has delayed us terribly — it could not well be worse — but we will get through nevertheless. The villains (secesh) have scattered torpedoes everywhere — by springs, wells etc etc — it is the most murderous & barbarous thing I ever heard of.

AL copy, McClellan Papers (C-7:63), Library of Congress.

To Edwin M. Stanton [TELEGRAM]

Hon E M Stanton In front of Williamsburg
Secy of War, Washington [May 5] 1862 [10 P.M.]

After arranging for movement up York River I was urgently sent for here. I find Joe Johnston in front of me in strong force, probably greater a good deal than my own & very strongly entrenched. Hancock has taken two redoubts & repulsed Early's Brigade[1] in a real charge with the bayonet taking one color & one hundred & fifty prisoners, killing at least two Colonels & as many Lieut Colonels and many privates. His conduct was brilliant in the extreme. I do not know our exact loss but fear Hooker has lost considerably on our left. I learn from prisoners that they intend disputing every step to Richmond. I shall run the risk of at least holding them in check here while I resume the original plan. My entire force is undoubtedly considerably inferior to that of the Rebels, who still fight well, but I will do all I can with the force at my disposal.

Geo B McClellan
Maj Genl Comdg

Received copy, Stanton Papers, Library of Congress. *OR*, Ser. 1, XI, Part 1, pp. 448–49.

1. Brig. Gen. Winfield S. Hancock, Brig. Gen. Jubal A. Early, CSA.

To Mary Ellen McClellan [TELEGRAM]

Williamsburg May 6/62 11 pm. [A.M.]

The battle of Wmsburg has proved a brilliant victory. We have the enemy's strong works, the town & all sick & wounded of the enemy etc. None of your friends injured though our loss considerable. That of the enemy severe. The Quaker Army is doing very well. Hancock was superb yesterday. I am in Joe Johnston's Hd Qtrs of yesterday. This is a beautiful little town & quite old & picturesque.

G B McC

ALS copy (telegram sent), McClellan Papers (C-7 :63), Library of Congress.

To Mary Ellen McClellan

Williamsburg May 6 1862

I telegraphed you this morning that we had gained a battle — every hour its importance is proved to be greater. On Sunday [May 4] I sent Stoneman in pursuit, with the cavalry & 4 batteries of Horse Artillery; he was supported by the Divisions Hooker, Smith, Couch, Casey & Kearny[1] — most of which arrived on the ground only yesterday. Unfortunately I did not go with the advance myself — being obliged to remain to get Franklin & Sedgwick started up the River for West Point.

Yesterday I received pressing private messages from Smith & others begging me to go to the front. I started with half a dozen aides & some 15 orderlies & found things in a bad state. Sumner had proved that he was even a greater fool than I had supposed & had come within an ace of having us defeated. Hancock was engaged with a vastly superior force some 2 miles from any support. Hooker fought nearly all day without assistance, & the mass of the troops were crowded together where they were useless. I found everybody discouraged — officers & men — our troops in wrong positions, on the wrong side of the woods — no system, no cooperation, no orders given, roads blocked up etc. As soon as I came upon the field the men cheered like fiends & I saw at once that I could save the day. I immediately reinforced Hancock, & arranged to support Hooker — advanced the whole line across the woods — filled up the gaps & got everything in hand for whatever might occur. The result was that the enemy saw that he was gone if he remained in his position & scampered during the night.

His works were very strong — but his loss was very heavy. The roads are in such condition that it is impossible to pursue except with a few cavalry — it is with the utmost difficulty that I can feed the men, many of whom have had nothing to eat for 24 hours & more. I had no dinner yesterday, no supper, a cracker for breakfast & no dinner yet.

I have no baggage — was out in the rain all day & until late at night — still in my clothes & boots, & could not even wash my face & hands. I, however, expect my ambulance up pretty soon, when I hope for better things. I have been through the hospitals, where are many of our own men & of the rebels. One Virginian sent for me this morning & told me that I was the only General from whom they expected any humanity etc. I corrected his mistake. This is a beautiful little town — several very old houses & churches, pretty gardens etc. I have taken possession of a very fine house which Jo Johnston occupied as his Hd Qts — it has a lovely flower garden & conservatory — if you were here I would be much inclined to spend some weeks here. *G.W.* was one of the whipped community — also Jo Johnston, Cadmus Wilcox, A. P. Hill, D. H. Hill, Longstreet, Jeb Stuart, Early (badly wounded) & many others that we know.[2] We have *all* their wounded, 8 guns so far — in short we have given them a tremendous thrashing — & I am not at all ashamed of the conduct of the Army of the Potomac. Had I been on the field five hours earlier I think we would have taken 20,000 prisoners — but the utter stupidity & worthlessness of the Corps Comdrs came near making it a defeat. Heaven alone can help a General with such commanders under him....

AL copy, McClellan Papers (C-7 :63), Library of Congress.

1. Brig. Gens. Joseph Hooker, William F. Smith, Darius N. Couch, Silas Casey, and Philip Kearny. 2. Williamsburg was defended by the division of Maj. Gen. James Longstreet, supported by Maj. Gen. Daniel H. Hill's division. The brigades of Brig. Gens. Cadmus M. Wilcox, Ambrose P. Hill, Jubal A. Early, and J. E. B. Stuart (cavalry) were engaged. Maj. Gen. G. W. Smith was not on the field.

To Edwin M. Stanton [TELEGRAM]

Hon E M Stanton
Secy War Williamsburg May [8] 1862

I respectfully ask permission to [reorganize] the Army Corps. I am not willing to be held responsible for the present arrangement experience having proved it to be very bad & it having very nearly resulted in a most disastrous defeat. I wish either to return to the organization by Divisions or else be authorized to relieve incompetent Commanders of Army Corps. Had I been one half hour later on the field on the fifth we would have been routed & would have lost everything.

Notwithstanding my positive orders I was informed of nothing that had occurred & I went to the field of Battle myself upon unofficial information that my presence was needed to avoid defeat. I found there the utmost confusion & incompetency, the utmost discouragement on the part of the men. At least a thousand lives were really sacrificed by the organization into Corps. I have too much regard for the lives of my comrades & too deep an interest in the success of our cause to hesitate for a moment. I learn that you are equally in earnest & I therefore again request full & complete authority to relieve from duty with this army Commanders of Corps or Divisions who prove themselves incompetent.[1]

G B McClellan
Maj Genl Comdg

Received copy, Stanton Papers, Library of Congress. *OR*, Ser. 1, XI, Part 3, pp. 153–54.

1. Lincoln's reply on May 9 (sent over Stanton's name) gave GBM permission to suspend the corps organization "in the Army now under your immediate command, and adopt any you see fit until further orders." The president wrote him privately on May 9: "I now think it indispensable for you to know how your struggle against it [the corps organization] is received in quarters which we cannot entirely disregard. It is looked upon as merely an effort to pamper one or two pets, and to persecute and degrade their supposed rivals. . . . I am constantly told . . . that you consult and communicate with nobody but General Fitz John Porter, and perhaps General Franklin. . . . But . . . are you strong enough, even with my help — to set your foot upon the necks of Sumner, Heintzelman, and Keyes all at once? This is a practical and very serious question for you." *Collected Works of Lincoln,* V, pp. 207–209. GBM retained the corps organization, but added two additional corps, under Porter and Franklin, on May 18.

To Edwin M. Stanton [TELEGRAM]

Head-Quarters, Army of the Potomac,
Williamsburg May 8 12.30 pm 1862

Your two telegrams received.[1] I have sent cavalry to Jamestown to endeavor to communicate with Rogers. Genl Stoneman is some fourteen or fifteen miles in advance, & may be able to communicate with Franklin tonight. I shall start Smith's Division this afternoon, & I hope three others tomorrow morning. The difficulties arising from the roads are very great but I will manage to surmount them. If I can effect the junction with Franklin I shall consider our next step gained — it is a delicate matter but can be done. I think that the time has arrived to bring all the troops in Eastern Virginia into perfect cooperation. I expect to fight another and very severe battle before reaching Richmond & with all the troops the Confederates can bring together, & therefore should have all the reinforcements that can be given me. It is of course possible that the enemy may abandon Richmond without a battle but we have no right to take that for granted. All the troops on the Rappahannock, & if possible those in the Shenandoah should take part in the approaching battle. We ought immediately to concentrate everything, & not run the risk of engaging a desperate enemy with inferior numbers. All minor considerations should be thrown to one side & all our energies & means directed towards the defeat of Johnston's Army in front of Richmond.

G B McClellan
Maj Genl Comdg

Hon E M Stanton
Secty of War

ALS (telegram sent), McClellan Papers (A-56:22), Library of Congress. *OR,* Ser. 1, XI, Part 3, pp. 150–51.

1. Stanton's telegrams of May 7 dealt with a naval expedition on the James River, led by Comdr. Rodgers in the *Galena,* and reports that Norfolk would soon be abandoned. *OR,* Ser. 1, XI, Part 3, pp. 147, 148.

To Mary Ellen McClellan

[Williamsburg] Thursday [May 8, 1862] 1 pm.

. . . I hope to get Smith's Divn off this afternoon — followed by others in the morning. Stoneman is some 15 miles in advance & will I hope communicate with Franklin tonight — although I am not yet sure that the enemy may not still be between the two. I shall start tomorrow morning & overtake Smith.

I have ordered up Hd Qtrs & the accompanying paraphernalia at once — so I hope to get within a few miles of my tooth brush in a day or two — it is not very pleasant — this going entirely without baggage — but it could not be helped. I find that the results of my operations are beginning to be apparent — the rebels are evacuating Norfolk I learn. Your two letters of Sunday & Monday reached me last night. I do not think you overmuch rejoiced at the results I gained. I really thought that you would appreciate a great result gained by pure skill & at little cost more highly than you seem to.

It would have been easy for me to have sacrificed 10,000 lives in taking Yorktown, & I presume the world would have thought it more brilliant — I am content with what I have done, & history will give me credit for it. I am sorry that you do not exactly sympathize with me in the matter. The battle of Williamsburg was more bloody — had I reached the field three hours earlier I could have gained far greater results & have saved a thousand lives — it is perhaps well as it is, for the officers & men feel that I saved the day. . . .

I don't know when the next battle will occur. I presume on the line of the Chickahominy — or it may be tomorrow in effecting a junction with Franklin. It may suit the views of the masses better as being more bloody — *I* hope not, & will make it as little so as possible. . . .

AL copy, McClellan Papers (C-7 :63), Library of Congress.

To Edwin M. Stanton [TELEGRAM]

Hon. E. M. Stanton Ewells Farm May 10 1862
Secretary of War 3 miles from Williamsburg 5 A.M.

From the information reaching me from every source, I regard it as certain that the enemy will meet us with all his force, on, or near the Chickahominy. They can concentrate many more men than I have, and are collecting troops from all quarters, especially, well disciplined troops from the South. Casualties, sickness, garrisons and guards have much reduced our numbers, and will continue to do so. I shall fight the Rebel army, with whatever force I may have, but duty requires me to urge that every effort be made to reinforce me, without delay, with all the disposable troops in Eastern Virginia, and that we concentrate all our forces, as far as possible to fight the great battle now impending, and to make it decisive.

It is possible that the enemy may abandon Richmond without a serious struggle, but I do not believe he will, and it would be unwise to count upon anything but a stubborn and desperate defense, — a life and death contest. I see no other hope for him than to fight this battle, — and we must win it. I shall fight them, whatever their force may be; but I ask for every man that the Department can send me. No troops now should be left unemployed. Those who entertain the opinion that the Rebels will abandon Richmond without a struggle, are, in my judgment, badly advised, and do not comprehend their situation, which is one requiring desperate measures.

I beg that the President and Secretary will maturely weigh what I say, and leave nothing undone to comply with my request. If I am not reinforced, it is probable that I will be obliged to fight nearly double my numbers, stronger entrenched. I do not think it will be at all possible for me to bring more than seventy thousand men upon the field of battle.

George B. McClellan
Major General

Received copy, Stanton Papers, Library of Congress. *OR*, Ser. 1, XI, Part 1, p. 26.

To Edwin M. Stanton [TELEGRAM]

Head Quarters, Army of the Potomac,
Camp 19 miles from Williamsburg May 10 — 5 pm. 1862

I have fully established my connection with the troops near West Point & the dangerous moment has passed. The West Point Railway is not very much injured — materials for repairs, such as rails etc, cars & engines may now be sent to me. Should Norfolk be taken & the Merrimac destroyed I can change my line to the James River & dispense with the Railroad.

I shall probably occupy New Kent in force tomorrow, & then make my final preparations for battle. As it is my troops are in advance of their supplies & I must so arrange my depots that I can follow up success.

When at New Kent I will be in position to make a thorough examination of the country so as to act understandingly.

Genl Johnston cannot well be in front of Fremont for two reasons — first he has no business there — second, I know that I fought him on Monday [May 5] & that he is now on the Chickahominy.[1] I have used his vacated Head Quarters from day to day. He is certainly in command here with all the troops he can gather. Two or three more of the cavalry regiments I left on the Potomac would be very acceptable — I am overworking what I have.

G B McClellan
Maj Genl Comdg

Hon E M Stanton
Fort Monroe

ALS (telegram sent), McClellan Papers (A-57:22), Library of Congress. *OR,* Ser. 1, XI, Part 3, pp. 160–61.

1. Stanton telegraphed on this date: "Frémont thinks that Johnston with a large force is in front of him." *OR,* Ser. 1, XI, Part 3, p. 160. The general in question was Brig. Gen. Edward Johnson, of Jackson's command.

To Mary Ellen McClellan

May 10 [1862] Saturday 11.45 pm.
Camp 19 miles from Williamsburg

... Am encamped now at an old wooden church, & in easy communication with Franklin, Porter &c. Fitz came over to see me this afternoon & I go over to see him & Franklin tomorrow. Tomorrow being Sunday I give the men a rest — merely closing up some of the troops in rear. I begin to find some Union sentiment in this country....

I expect to fight a very severe battle on the Chickahominy, but feel no doubt as to the result. All my officers & men have unlimited confidence in me — I saw the effect of my presence the other day in front of Wmsburg — & the men all felt the change — they behaved superbly & will do better if possible next time. Tomorrow I will get up supplies — reorganize — arrange details & get ready for the great fight — feeling that I shall lose nothing by respecting Sunday as far as I can. Secesh is gathering all he can in front of me — so much the better — I will finish the matter by one desperate blow. I have implicit confidence in my men & they in me! What more can I ask....

Sunday [May 11] 8 am. As I told you last night I am giving my men some rest today — they need it much — for they have for some time been living on long marches, short rations & rainy bivouacs....

My cavalry were within 6 miles of the upper Chickahominy yesterday. Norfolk is in our possession, the result of my movements....

Monday [May 12] pm. While I write the 2nd Dragoon band is serenading & about 50 others are playing tattoo at various distances — a grand sound this lovely moonlight night. My camp is at an old frame church in a grove — I differ from most of the Generals in preferring a tent to a house — I hope not to sleep in a house again until I see you....

Are you satisfied now with my bloodless victories? Even the abolitionists seem to be coming around — judging at least from the very handsome Resolution offered by Mr. Lovejoy in the House.[1] I look upon that Resolution as one of the most complimentary I know of — & that too offered by my bitterest prosecutors — but the union of civic merit with military success is what pleases me most — to have it recognized that I have saved the lives of my men & won success by my own efforts is to me the height of glory. I hope that the result in front of Richmond will cause still greater satisfaction to the country. I still hope that the God who has been so good to me will continue to smile upon our cause, and enable me to bring this war to a speedy close, so that I may at last have the rest I want so much. . . .

I do need rest — you know I have had but little in my life. But the will of God be done — what is given me to do I will try to do with all my might. . . .

I think one more battle here will finish the work. I expect a great one, but feel that confidence in my men & that trust in God which makes me very sanguine as to the result. They will fight me in front of Richmond I am confident — defeat there is certain destruction to them & I think will prove the ruin of their wretched cause. They are concentrating everything for the last death struggle — my government, alas, is not giving me any aid! But I will do the best I can with what I have & trust to God's mercy & the courage of my men for the result. . . .

We march in the morning for Cumberland — gradually drawing nearer to Richmond.

AL copy, McClellan Papers (C-7 :63), Library of Congress.

1. Owen Lovejoy, an abolitionist congressman from Illinois. The House resolution, adopted May 9, tendered thanks "to Major-General George B. McClellan, for the display of those high military qualities which secure important results with but little sacrifice of human life."

To Edwin M. Stanton [TELEGRAM]

Camp 19 m from Williamsburg May 11 — 9 am [1862]

I congratulate you from the bottom of my heart upon the destruction of the Merrimac.[1] I would now most earnestly urge that our gun boats & the iron clad boats be sent as far as possible up the James River without delay. This will enable me to make our movements much more decisive.

G B McClellan
Maj Genl Comdg

Hon E M Stanton
Secty of War Fort Monroe

ALS (telegram sent), McClellan Papers (A-57 :22), Library of Congress, *OR*, Ser. 1, XI, Part 3, p. 164.

1. Drawing too much water to reach Richmond, the *Merrimack* was destroyed by her crew on this date.

To Salmon P. Chase

Hon. S. P. Chase
Secretary of the Treasury
Washington

Hd. Qtrs Army of the Potomac
Camp at Cumberland [Landing],
New Kent Co. Va. May 14, 1862

I beg to call your attention to the subject of opening trade with this Peninsula and its adjacent waters as rapidly as our land & naval forces establish our flag. The country is very destitute of all the necessaries of life, and many of its families are suffering for food. An order authorizing commerce under such restrictions as you may deem proper, would serve of humanity, promote our political interests, and even contribute to the comfort of some of our own forces, especially sick & wounded men.[1]

Very Resp. Your obt servt.
Geo. B. McClellan
Maj. Genl. Comdg.

Copy, McClellan Papers (A-57:22), Library of Congress.

1. Chase responded by telegraph on May 16: "Whatever the law allows to be done will be done as promptly as possible to give effect to your suggestions." McClellan Papers (A-57:22).

To Abraham Lincoln [TELEGRAM]

His Excellency Abraham Lincoln
President of the United States

Camp at Cumberland,
May 14th [1862]

I have more than twice telegraphed to the Secretary of War,[1] stating that, in my opinion, the enemy were concentrating all their available force to fight this army in front of Richmond, and that such ought to be their policy. I have received no reply whatever to any of these telegraphs. I beg leave to repeat their substance to your Excellency and to ask that kind consideration which you have ever accorded to my representations and views. All my information from every source accessible to me, establishes the fixed purpose of the rebels to defend Richmond against this Army by offering us battle with all the troops they can collect from East, West, and South, and my own opinion is confirmed by that of all my commanders whom I have been able to consult.

Casualties, sickness, garrisons, and guards have much weakened my force and will continue to do so. I cannot bring into actual battle against the enemy more than eighty thousand men at the utmost, and with them I must attack in position, probably entrenched, a much larger force, perhaps double my numbers. It is possible that Richmond may be abandoned without a serious struggle but the enemy are actually in great strength between here and there and it would be unwise and even insane for me to calculate upon anything except a stubborn and desperate resistance. If they should abandon Richmond it may well be that it is done with the purpose of making the stand at some place in Virginia south or west of there, and we should be in condition to press them without delay. The Confederate leaders must employ their utmost efforts against this Army in Virginia, and they will be supported by the whole body of their military officers, among whom there may be said to be no Union feeling, as there is also very little among the higher class of citizens in the seceding states. I have found no fighting men left in this Peninsula. All are in the ranks of the opposing foe. Even if more troops than I now have should prove unnecessary for the purposes of military occupation our greatest display of imposing force in the Capital of the Rebel Government will have the best moral effect. I most respectfully and earnestly urge upon your Excellency that the opportunity has come for striking a fatal blow at the enemies of the Constitution and I beg that you will cause this Army to be reinforced without delay by all the disposable troops of the Government. I ask for every man that the War Department can send me. Sent by water, they will soon reach me. Any commander of the reinforcements whom your Excellency may designate will be acceptable to me, whatever expression I may have heretofore addressed to you on the subject.[2] I will fight the enemy, whatever their force may be, with whatever force I may have, and I firmly believe that we shall beat them, but our triumph should be made decisive and complete. The soldiers of this Army love their Government and will fight well in its support. You may rely upon them. They have confidence in me as their General and in you as their President. Strong reinforcements will at least save the lives of many of them. The greater the force, the more perfect will be our combinations and the less our loss.

For obvious reasons, I beg you to give immediate consideration to this communication and to inform me fully, at the earliest moment, of your final determination.[3]

Geo. B. McClellan
Major General Comdg

Retained copy, McClellan Papers (A-57:22), Library of Congress. *OR,* Ser. 1, XI, Part 1, pp. 26–27.

1. See GBM to Stanton, May 8, 10, *supra.* 2. See GBM to Lincoln, Apr. 18, *supra.* 3. Lincoln telegraphed on May 15: "Have done, and shall do, all I could and can to sustain you. . . . I am still unwilling to take all our force off the direct line between Richmond and here." *Collected Works of Lincoln,* V, p. 216. On May 17 McDowell's First Corps was ordered to join the Army of the Potomac by the overland route.

To Henry Wilson, Francis P. Blair, Jr.

Hon H. Wilson, Chairman Mil. Com. U.S. Senate. Camp near
Hon. F. P. Blair, " " " " H.R. Cumberland, Va.
Gentlemen, May 15, 1862

The legislation in relation to the corps of Engineers and Topographical Engineers, which I requested last winter as a measure required by the good of the service, I have greatly felt the need of during the siege of Yorktown. These officers, with very insufficient numbers, have performed laborious and highly important duties, which have resulted in the bloodless reduction of the place, — bloodless, so far as the Army in general is concerned, but costly enough for them. Each corps has lost a valuable officer, — one killed, and the other dangerously wounded — and this from a total of only seventeen. They have fairly earned the favorable consideration of Congress.

Legislation is greatly needed to effect three practical objects immediately:

1st To unite the Corps of Engineers and Topographical Engineers, and thus to do away with a complicated and faulty organization.

2nd To provide a proper means for filling the numerous and increasing vacancies, — a matter which is becoming embarrassing. My Engineer officers have been greatly overworked, and in fact crippled, from the want of the young officers, who, if the bill submitted last winter had become a law, would now be actively engaged. These vacancies (about thirty) cannot be properly filled without legislation.

3d To give the rank — at least temporary — which is demanded by every principle of equity and expediency.

I have a battalion of three companies of regular Engineer troops. It is commanded by a *captain,* an officer of fourteen years' invaluable experience, who may well feel aggrieved at not having even the rank to which his actual command would entitle him in any regiment of the line. Each of these companies is commanded by a lieutenant, upon whom the same relative injustice is inflicted. This is all the more galling to the officers of these two corps, because they are habitually and necessarily refused permission to accept the command of volunteer regiments, on the ground that their professional services cannot be spared.

I therefore earnestly hope that a bill providing for these three needs of the service may very speedily become a law. The necessity for it is injuriously felt every day. The bill submitted by these corps last winter, had and still has, my full approval; but if Congress is unwilling to increase so largely the permanent rank, the provisions for temporary rank during the war, added as an amendment to the bill reported by the

Military Committee of the Senate, will provide for the immediate and pressing needs of the service.[1]

Geo. B. McClellan
Maj. Gen. Comdg.

Copy, Miscellaneous Manuscripts Collection, American Antiquarian Society. Sen. Wilson of Massachusetts and Rep. Blair of Missouri were chairmen, respectively, of the Senate and House military affairs committees.

1. Legislation merging the Topographical Engineers into the Corps of Engineers was enacted on Mar. 3, 1863.

To Mary Ellen McClellan

Cumberland May 15 [1862] 2.30 pm.

Another wet horrid day! It rained a little yesterday morning, more in the afternoon, much during the night & has been amusing itself in the same manner very persistently all day. I had expected to move Hd Qtrs to White House today — but this weather has put the roads in such condition that I cannot do more than get Franklin & Porter there today. Hd Qtrs cavalry & Hunt[1] will move there tomorrow — perhaps one or two other Divisions as well. We had quite a visitation yesterday, in the shape of Secy Seward, Gideon Welles, Mr. Bates, Fred Seward, Dahlgren, Mrs. Goldsborough & one of her daughters, Mrs. Fred Seward & some other ladies whose names I did not catch.[2] I went on board their boat — then had some ambulances harnessed up & took them around camp — was very glad when I got thro' with them — such visits are always a nuisance.

We are just about 25 miles from Richmond here — the advance considerably nearer. I don't yet know what to make of the rebels — I do not see how they can possibly abandon Virginia & Richmond without a battle — nor do I understand why they abandoned & destroyed Norfolk & the Merrimac unless they also intended to abandon all of Virginia! There is a puzzle there somewhere which will soon be solved....

I am heartily tired of this life I am leading — always some little absurd thing being done by those gentry in Washington. I am every day more & more tired of public life & earnestly pray that I may soon be able to throw down my sword & live once more as a private gentleman....

I confess I find it difficult to judge whether the war will soon be at an end or not — I think that the blows the rebels are now receiving & have lately received ought to crush them up — but one can do no more than speculate. Yes I *can* imagine peace & quietness reigning once more in this land of ours — it is just what I am fighting for!...

Still raining hard & dismally — an awful time for the men — the only comfort is that they all have plenty to eat.

9 pm. ... Have received today the official copy of the Resols of the House.[3] I learn that the abolitionists begin to think that I am not such a wretch after all, or else that it is best to say so.

It was all a humbug about my being struck by a piece of a shell at Wmsburg. That reminds me of a joke some of the youngsters played upon Billy Palmer[4] at Yorktown. They sent him to see an immense "shell" that had fallen in our Head Qtrs camp. He found it, but it proved to be a large *oyster* shell....

I send you a photograph which I have just received from Genl Blume Chief of Artillery in the Prussian Army. I knew him abroad, & the old gentleman writes to me occasionally.

AL copy; copy, McClellan Papers (C-7:63/D-10:72), Library of Congress.

1. Col. Henry J. Hunt, artillery reserve. 2. Secretary of State Seward, Secretary of the Navy Welles, Attorney General Bates, Secretary Seward's son Frederick and his wife, Capt. John A. Dahlgren of the Washington Navy Yard, and the wife and daughter of Flag Officer Goldsborough. 3. See GBM to his wife, May 10, *supra*. 4. Capt. William R. Palmer, Topographical Engineers.

To Edwin M. Stanton [TELEGRAM]

Head Quarters, Army of the Potomac,
White House May 17 [1862] — 10.45 pm

After a careful consideration of the meager accounts I have received of the gun boat operations on the James River I am inclined to think that we ought not to be discouraged.[1] They were caught in very adverse circumstances & I think their repulse will prove to be due to the fact that they were subjected to a close musketry fire they could not reply to.

I would urge the necessity of perfect cooperation between all the Army & Navy forces in Eastern Virginia. I have not one word of official information as to the objects to be attained by any of them.

G B McClellan
Maj Genl

Hon E M Stanton

ALS (telegram sent), McClellan Papers (A-57:22), Library of Congress. *OR*, Ser. 1, XI, Part 3, p. 177.

1. On May 15 a Federal flotilla, including the *Monitor*, was defeated by batteries at Drewry's Bluff, eight miles short of Richmond.

To Mary Ellen McClellan

White House May 18th [1862] Sunday 6 pm.

... We leave here in the morning — Porter & Franklin march at 4 & 8 am — Hd Qtrs at 7. We will go to Tunstall's, or perhaps a little beyond it, & will now soon close up on the Chickahominy & find out what secesh is doing. I think he will fight us there, or in between that & Richmond — & if he is badly thrashed (as I trust he will be) incline to believe that he will begin to cry peccavi & say that he has enough of it — especially if Halleck beats him at Corinth.

Midnight ... I start early in the morning....

Those hounds in Washington are after me again. Stanton is without exception the vilest man I ever knew or heard of.

AL copy, McClellan Papers (C-7 :63), Library of Congress.

To Ambrose E. Burnside

Maj. Gen. Ambrose E. Burnside,
Commanding Department
of North Carolina: Headquarters of the Army
My dear Burn: Tunstall's Station, May 21, 1862

Your dispatch and kind letter received. I have instructed Seth to reply to the official letter[1] and now acknowledge the kind private note. It always does me good, in the midst of my cares and perplexities, to see your wretched old scrawling. I have terrible troubles to contend with, but have met them with a good heart, like your good old self, and have thus far struggled through successfully. Our progress has been slow, but that is due to ignorance of the country (we have to feel our way everywhere; the maps are worthless), the narrowness, small number, and condition of the roads, which become impassable for trains after a day's rain, of which we have had a great deal.

I feel very proud of Yorktown; it and Manassas will be my brightest chaplets in history; for I know that I accomplished everything in both places by pure military skill. I am very proud and grateful to God that he allowed me to purchase such great success at so trifling a loss of life. We came near being badly beaten at Williamsburg. I arrived on the field at 5 p.m. and found that all thought we were whipped and in for a disaster. You would have been glad to see, old fellow, how the men cheered and brightened up when they saw me. In five minutes after I reached the ground a possible defeat was changed into certain victory. The greatest moral courage I ever exercised was that night, when, in the face of urgent demands from almost all quarters for re-enforcements to hold our own, I quietly *sent back* the troops I had ordered up before I reached the field. I was sure that Johnston would leave during the night if he understood his business, or that I could be able to thrash him in the morning by a proper use of the force I had. It turned out that Jo. left! Hancock conducted himself magnificently; his charge was elegant!

I expect to fight a desperate battle in front of Richmond, and against superior numbers, somewhat intrenched. The Government have deliberately placed me in this position. If I win, the greater the glory. If I lose, they will be damned forever, both by God and men.

Well, I have bored you long enough, old fellow. I will merely add that my light troops have crossed the Chickahominy at Bottom's Bridge this morning, 10 miles from Richmond, and that the advanced guard, under Stoneman, has driven in everything upon New Bridge (on my right), 6 miles from Richmond. The crisis cannot long be deferred. I pray for God's blessing on our arms, and rely far more on his goodness than I do on my own poor intellect. I sometimes think now that I can almost realize that Mahomet was sincere. When I see the hand of God guarding one so weak as myself, I can almost think myself a chosen instrument to carry out his schemes. Would that a better man had been selected....

If I thrash these rascals we will soon be in direct communication, and I shall then wish to give you a command from this army to add to the noble men you now have.

Good-by, and God bless you, Burn. With the sincere hope that we may soon shake hands,

I am, as ever, your sincere friend,
McClellan

OR, Ser. 1, IX, p. 392.

1. Seth Williams's reply of this date to Burnside's May 17 request for instructions was based on a GBM memorandum reading in part: "I would therefore think that cautious yet bold advance on Goldsboro as soon as transportation arrives would produce a better effect than anything else that can be done and would have the effect to neutralize a larger portion of the enemys force." McClellan Papers (A-108:43), Library of Congress; *OR,* Ser. 1, IX, pp. 389, 393.

To Abraham Lincoln [TELEGRAM]

Hd Qurs. Army of the Potomac
Camp near Tunstall's Station Va.
May 21, 1862 11 p.m.

His Excellency Abraham Lincoln
President of the United States.

Your dispatch of yesterday respecting our situation and the batteries at Fort Darling was rec'd while I was absent with the advance, where I have also been all this day.[1] I have communicated personally with Capt. Goldsborough & by letter with Capt. Smith. The vessels can do nothing without cooperation on land, which I will not be in position to afford for several days. Circumstances must determine the propriety of a land attack.

It rained again last night, and rain on this soil soon makes the roads incredibly bad for army transportation. I personally crossed the Chickahominy today at Bottom's bridge ford and went a mile beyond, the enemy being about half a mile in front. I have three Regts on the other bank guarding the rebuilding of the bridge. Keyes' Corps is on the New Kent road, near Bottom's bridge. Heintzelman is on the same road, within supporting distance. Sumner is on the R.R. connecting right with left. Stoneman with advanced guard is within one mile of New bridge. Franklin with two Divisions is about two miles this side of Stoneman. Porter's Division with the Reserve of Infantry & Artillery is within supporting distance. Head Quarters will probably be at Coal [Cold] Harbor tomorrow, one mile this side of Franklin. All the bridges over the Chickahominy are destroyed.

The enemy are in force on every road leading to Richmond, within a mile or two west of the stream. Their main body is on the road from New bridge encamped along it for four or five miles, spreading over the open ground on both sides. Johnston's Head Quarters are about two miles beyond the bridge.

All accounts report their numbers as greatly exceeding our own. The position of the rebel forces, the declarations of the Confederate authorities, the resolutions of the Virginia legislature, the action of the City Govt., the conduct of the citizens, and all other sources of information accessible to me, give positive assurance that our approach to Richmond, involves a desperate battle between the opposing armies.

All our Divisions are moving towards the foe. I shall advance steadily & carefully & attack them according to my best judgment, and in such manner as to employ my greatest force.

I regret the state of things as to Genl. McDowell's command. We must beat the enemy in front of Richmond. One Division added to this Army for that effort would do more to protect Washington than his whole force can possibly do anywhere else in the field. The rebels are concentrating from all points for the two battles at Richmond & Corinth. I would still most respectfully suggest the policy of our concentrating here by movements on water. I have heard nothing as to the probabilities of the contemplated junction of McDowell's force with mine. I have no idea when he can start, what are his means of transportation, or when he may be expected to reach this vicinity. I fear there is little hope that he can join me overland in time for the coming battle. Delays on my part will be dangerous. I fear sickness & demoralization. This region is unhealthy for northern men, and unless kept moving I fear that our soldiers may become discouraged. At present our numbers are weakening from disease, but the men remain in good heart.

I regret also the configuration of the Department of the Rappahannock. It includes a portion even of the City of Richmond. I think that my own Department should embrace the entire field of active military operations designed for the capture of that city.

Again, I agree with your Excellency that one bad General is better than two good ones. I am not sure that I fully comprehend your orders of the 17th inst. addressed to myself & Genl McDowell.[2] If a junction is effected before we occupy Richmond, it must necessarily be east of the RR to Fredericksburg, & within my Department. This fact, my superior rank, & the express language of the 62d Article of War will place his command under my orders unless it is otherwise specially directed by your Excellency. I consider that he will be under my command except that I am not to detach any portion of his forces, or give any order which can put him out of position to cover Washington. If I err in my construction I desire to be at once set right. Frankness compels me to say, anxious as I am for an increase of force, that the march of McDowell's column upon Richmond by the shortest route, will in my opinion uncover Washington as to any interposition by it, as completely as its movement by water. The enemy cannot advance by Fredericksburg on Washington. Should they attempt a movement, which to me seems utterly improbable, their route would be by Gordonsville & Manassas. I desire that the extent of my authority over Genl. McDowell may be clearly defined, lest misunderstandings & conflicting views may produce some of those injurious results which a divided command has so often caused. I would respectfully suggest that this danger can only be surely guarded against by explicitly placing Genl. McDowell under my orders in the ordinary way, & holding me strictly responsible for the closest observance of your instructions. I hope, Mr. President, that it is not necessary for me to assure you that your directions would be observed in the utmost good faith, & that I have no personal feelings which could influence me to disregard them in any particular.[3]

I believe that there is a great struggle before this Army, but I am neither dismayed nor discouraged. I wish to strengthen its force as much as I can, but in any event I shall fight it with all the skill, caution, & determination that I possess, & I trust that the result may either obtain for me the permanent confidence of my Government, or that it may close my career.

Geo B McClellan
Maj Genl Comdg

Retained copy, McClellan Papers (A-58:23), Library of Congress. *OR,* Ser. 1, XI, Part 1, pp. 28–29.

1. Lincoln's telegram asked if any action could be taken against the Fort Darling batteries at Drewry's Bluff. *Collected Works of Lincoln,* V, p. 224. 2. A copy of Stanton's May 17 instructions to McDowell, "By order of the President," was sent to GBM, and read in part: "While seeking to establish as soon as possible a communication between your left wing and the right wing of General McClellan, you will hold yourself always in such position as to cover the capital of the nation against a sudden dash of any large body of the rebel forces." *OR*, Ser. 1, XI, Part 1, p. 28. 3. The president replied on this date: "You will have just such control of Gen. McDowell and his force as you therein indicate. . . . By land he can reach you in five days after starting, whereas by water he would not reach you in two weeks, judging by past experience." *Collected Works of Lincoln*, V, p. 226.

To Abraham Lincoln [TELEGRAM]

Head Quarters A of P
Coal Harbor,[1] May 22 —
12.30 p.m. 1862

His Excellency A Lincoln *Presdt*

Your dispatch just rec'd.[2] The discipline of the army will not permit the restoration of General Hamilton to his division. Since the matter is pressed as it is I feel obliged to state what I did not care to before viz. that Gen. Hamilton is not fit to command a division. The task before me is too serious to permit me to hesitate when called upon to express an opinion. The cause of his removal from this army was ample to justify me in the course I pursued. You cannot do anything better calculated to injure my army and diminish the probabilities of success in the approaching battle now imminent than to restore Gen Hamilton to his Division. I earnestly protest against any such action and I trust that after this statement you will not think of sending Gen Hamilton back to this army.[3]

G. B. McClellan
Maj Genl Comdg

Retained copy, Records of the Office of the Secretary of War, RG 107 (M-504 :66), National Archives. *OR*, Ser. 1, XI, Part 3, pp. 185–86.

1. Cold Harbor. 2. In his telegram of May 21, Lincoln reported receiving a petition signed by twenty-three senators and eighty-four representatives calling for the reinstatement of Brig. Gen. Charles S. Hamilton, relieved from duty during the Yorktown siege. *Collected Works of Lincoln*, V, p. 227. 3. Hamilton did not again serve with the Army of the Potomac.

To Mary Ellen McClellan

May 22 [1862] 6 1/2 pm.
Camp near Chickahominy

I can't tell you how often I have thought of you today, & how often my thoughts have reached to two years ago. At *two* exactly I wrote a dispatch to you which you will understand.[1] I have just returned from a ride to the front where I have taken a good look at the rebel lines. I suppose I must have ridden some 30 miles today. Some one just brought me a bouquet of wild white flowers — a negro at that — I clutched it most eagerly, as reminding me of one, who two years ago became my wife. It is on the table in front of me as I write; in a tin tumbler, to be sure, but none the less pure & white.

[May] 23rd pm. Soon after I finished the last page I was taken quite sick & continued so most of the night. I have remained in my tent all day feeling quite miserable — but will be all right & able to ride out in the morning. . . .

The occurrences of the next few days are quite uncertain. I have secured one passage of the Chickahominy & hope to get two more tomorrow. I have been within 6 miles of the rebel capital, & our balloonists have been watching it all day. The intentions of the enemy are still doubtful. I go on prepared to fight a hard battle, but I confess that the indications are not now that he will fight. Unless he has some deep laid scheme that I do not fathom, he is giving up great advantage in not opposing me on the line of the Chickahominy — he could give me a great deal of trouble & make it cost me hundreds or thousands of lives. If he fights now he must do so in the very outskirts of Richmond, which must in that event suffer terribly, & perhaps be destroyed. I do not know that I can control fully this army of volunteers if they enter the city on the heels of the enemy after an assault. I will do my best to prevent outrage & pillage, but there are bad men in all armies & I hope that I shall not be forced to witness the sack of Richmond. God knows I am sick of this civil war — altho' no feeling of the kind unsteadies my hand or ever makes me hesitate or waver — it is a cruel necessity. I am very glad that the Presdt has come out as he did about Hunter's order — I feared he would not have the moral courage to do so. I can't think how Hunter could have done such a thing without authority from some one.[2] . . .

If I succeed in getting the two additional passages of the River tomorrow I will move next day — in fact I hope to have a strong advanced guard within a couple of miles of Richmond tomorrow evening. Then I shall be able to examine the enemy's positions & arrange for the battle. I will not fight on Sunday if I can help it. If I am obliged to do so I will have faith that God will defend the right, & trust that we have the right on our side. How freely I shall breathe when my long task of months is over & Richmond is ours! I know the uncertainty of all human events — I know that God may even now deem best to crush all the high hopes of the nation & this army — I will do the best I can to insure success & will do my best to be contented with whatever result God sees fit to terminate our efforts. I have long prayed that I might neither be elated by success nor unduly cast down by defeat. I hope my prayers may be granted. I am here on the eve of one of the great historic battles of the world — one of those crises in a nation's life that occurs but seldom — far more than my fate is involved in the issue. I have done the best I could. I have tried to serve my country honestly & faithfully — all I can now do is to commit myself to the hands of God & pray that the country may not be punished for my sins & shortcomings.

11 pm. . . . Have had some skirmishes & cannonading today — successful in all.

AL copy; copy, McClellan Papers (C-7:63/D-10:72), Library of Congress.

1. May 22 was the McClellans' wedding anniversary. His telegram read: "I send this only to show you that I remember about occurrences exactly two years ago. The most fortunate moment of my life. I cannot celebrate it in Richmond but hope soon to be there. . . . " Records of the Office of the Secretary of War, RG 107 (M-504:66), National Archives. 2.

On May 19 the president disavowed an order issued by Maj. Gen. David Hunter that abolished slavery in South Carolina, Georgia, and Florida.

To Abraham Lincoln [TELEGRAM]

Head-Quarters, Army of the Potomac,
Coal Harbor May 24 [1862] 8.30 pm

Telegram of four PM received.[1] I will make my calculations accordingly.

G B McClellan
Maj Genl Comdg

The President Washington D.C.

ALS (telegram sent), McClellan Papers (A-58:23), Library of Congress. *OR*, Ser. 1, XI, Part 3, p. 190.

1.The president's telegram read: "In consequence of Gen. Banks' critical position I have been compelled to suspend Gen. McDowell's movement to join you. The enemy are making a desperate push upon Harper's Ferry, and we are trying to throw Fremont's force & part of McDowell's in their rear." *Collected Works of Lincoln*, V, p. 232.

To Mary Ellen McClellan

May 25 [1862] Sunday 3 1/2 pm. Coal Harbor

...Have been rather under the weather the last three days — had to ride out in the rain yesterday & was kept up very late last night — so I was not so well as I might have been this morning....

It cleared off about sunset yesterday, & today has been bright & pleasant — drying up the roads rapidly — they have been so cut & bad as to prevent any movements in force or with rapidity — fortunately the ground dries rapidly here & will soon be in such condition that we can move anywhere. I have this moment received a dispatch from the Presdt who is terribly scared about Washington — & talks about the necessity of my returning in order to save it![1] Heaven save a country governed by such counsels! I must reply to his telegram & finish this by & by!

5 pm. Have just finished my reply to his Excellency![2] It is perfectly sickening to deal with such people & you may rest assured that I will lose as little time as possible in breaking off all connection with them — I get more sick of them every day — for every day brings with it only additional proofs of their hypocrisy, knavery & folly — well, well, I ought not to write in this way, for they may be right & I entirely wrong, so I will drop the subject....

I feel much better this afternoon, quite myself again....

If I should find Washn life as bad after the war as it was when I was there I don't think I could be induced to remain in the army after peace.

10 pm. ...It seems from some later dispatches I have received that

Banks has been soundly thrashed & that they are terribly alarmed in Washn. A scare will do them good, & may bring them to their senses. . . .

I have a fire in my tent tonight.

AL copy, McClellan Papers (C-7 :63), Library of Congress.

1. The president telegraphed on this date that the enemy was advancing in the Shenandoah Valley "in sufficient force to drive Banks before him. . . . I think the movement is a general and concerted one, such as could not be if he was acting upon the purpose of a very desperate defence of Richmond. I think the time is near when you must either attack Richmond or give up the job and come to the defence of Washington." *Collected Works of Lincoln*, V, pp. 235–36. 2. GBM to Lincoln, May 25, *infra*.

To Abraham Lincoln [TELEGRAM]

Head-Quarters, Army of the Potomac
Coal Harbor May 25 [1862] 5 p.m.

Telegram received. Independently of it the time is very near when I shall attack Richmond. The object of enemy's movement is probably to prevent reinforcements being sent to me. All the information obtained from balloons, deserters prisoners & contrabands agrees in the statement that the mass of rebel troops are still in immediate vicinity of Richmond ready to defend it.

I have no knowledge of Banks's position & force, nor what there is at Manassas, therefore cannot form a definite opinion as to force against him. I have two Corps across Chickahominy within six miles of Richmond — the others on this side at other crossings within same distance & ready to cross when bridges completed.

G B McClellan
Maj Genl Comdg

His Excellency A. Lincoln
Presdt

ALS (telegram sent), McClellan Papers (A-58 :23), Library of Congress. *OR*, Ser. 1, XI, Part 1, p. 32.

To Mary Ellen McClellan [TELEGRAM]

Head Quarters, Army of the Potomac,
Camp near New Bridge May 26 1862 1.30 pm

Have reached my new Camp. All quite well although it is raining again. The net is quietly closing & some fish will soon be caught.

G B McClellan
Maj Genl Comdg

Mrs G B McClellan
Care N Shipman Esq
Hartford Connecticut

ALS (telegram sent), McClellan Papers (C-13:64), Library of Congress.

To Abraham Lincoln [TELEGRAM]

Head-Quarters, Army of the Potomac,
Camp near New Bridge May 26 [1862] 7.30 pm

Have arranged to carry out your last orders.[1] We are quietly closing in upon the enemy preparatory to the last struggle. Situated as I am I feel forced to take every possible precaution against disaster & to secure my flanks against the probably superior force in front of me. My arrangements for tomorrow are very important, & if successful will leave me free to strike on the return of the force detached.

G B McClellan
Maj Genl Comdg

His Excellency A Lincoln
Presdt

ALS (telegram sent), McClellan Papers (A-58:23), Library of Congress. *OR*, Ser. 1, XI, Part 1, p. 33.

1. These orders presumably referred to cutting railroads north of Richmond.

To Mary Ellen McClellan

May 26 [1862] 8 pm. Camp near New Bridge.

. . . We broke up the last camp about 2 & moved to this place which is quite on the banks of the Chickahominy & very near New Bridge. It *of course* commenced raining about an hour after we started — but as it was not a very heavy rain we got on very well. . . .

I have been troubled by the old Mexican complaint, brought on I suppose by exposure to the wet etc, but I am really substantially well again.[1] . . .

Fitz starts off in the morning on a trip that will take a day to go & one to return — the object being to cut off & disperse a force of the enemy threatening my right & rear — also to destroy the RR bridges — when this is done I will feel very comfortable in that direction & shall be quite ready to attack. My men are in such excellent condition & such good spirits that I cannot doubt the result. I feel that we must beat the rebels & I hope end the war — from all that I can learn the gaining of this battle will insure the return of Virginia to her allegiance — the people here have not much Union feeling but are becoming heartily tired of the war — especially as they now feel its evils in their midst — a fate from which I pray that God may deliver our own Northern states.

My camp is about 4 1/2 to 5 miles from Richmond. I fancy secesh is becoming rather disturbed — he don't know exactly what I am about. I could not help laughing this afternoon when I received from the Secy of War a copy of a dispatch from McDowell which proves them all to have been a precious lot of fools & that I have been right all the time.[2] Had the instructions I left for Banks & Wadsworth been complied with we should have been spared the shame of Banks' stampede. It will prove that Banks ran away from a small force & needlessly evacuated the part of Va. in possession of which I placed him. Some of the Presdt's dispatches for the last two days have been amazing in the extreme. I cannot do justice to them so I shall not attempt to describe them. I feared last night that I would be ordered back for the defense of Washington! You can imagine the course I had determined to pursue in such a contingency.

AL copy, McClellan Papers (C-7:63), Library of Congress.

1. GBM's ''old Mexican complaint'' was malaria, contracted during the Mexican War. 2. McDowell's dispatch, dated May 25, reported intelligence that Confederate forces were ordered ''back to Richmond to take part in the great battle now about to take place there.'' *OR*, Ser. 1, XII, Part 3, p. 233.

To Edwin M. Stanton [TELEGRAM]

New Bridge May 27 1862 2.30 pm

Very severe storm last night & this morning has converted everything into mud again & raised Chickahominy. Richmond papers urge Johnston to attack now he has us away from gun boats. I think he is too able for that. I communicated with gun boats yesterday by a small party. Am not yet ready to cooperate with them. Every day is making our result more sure & I am wasting no time. Rather heavy firing in direction of Porter from whom I expect good news in a few hours. What about Banks? Will answer in a few minutes about arms. Am obliged for the promised reinforcements.[1]

G B McClellan
Maj Genl Comdg

Hon E M Stanton
Secty of War

ALS (telegram sent), McClellan Papers (A-58:23), Library of Congress. *OR*, Ser. 1, XI, Part 3, p. 193.

1. Stanton telegraphed on this date that two regiments of infantry and one of artillery would be sent for garrison duty. *OR*, Ser. 1, XI, Part 3, p. 193.

To Edwin M. Stanton [TELEGRAM]

Hon E. M. Stanton
Secy of war McClellans May 27, 1862 8.30 p.m.

I find some of the newspapers publish letters from their Correspondents with this Army, giving important information concerning our movements, positions of troops &c. in positive violation of your orders. As it is impossible for me to ascertain with certainty who these anonymous writers are I beg to suggest that another order be published holding the Editors responsible for its infraction.[1]

G. B. McClellan
Maj Genl.

Retained copy, Records of the Office of the Secretary of War, RG 107 (M-504:65), National Archives. *OR*, Ser. 1, XI, Part 3, p. 194.

1. In a second telegram on this subject, sent three hours later, GBM wrote: "Notwithstanding the trouble, I would be glad to have them required to submit all letters as well as telegraphs to these headquarters." *OR*, Ser. 1, XI, Part 3, p. 194.

To Edwin M. Stanton [TELEGRAM]

Hanover CH May 28 [1862] 4 pm

Porter's action of yesterday was truly a glorious victory — too much credit cannot be given to his magnificent Division & its accomplished leader. The rout of the rebels was complete — not a defeat but a complete rout. Prisoners are constantly coming in — two companies have this moment arrived with excellent arms.

There is no doubt that the enemy are concentrating everything on Richmond. I will do my best to cut off Jackson, but am doubtful whether I can.

It is the policy & duty of the Govt to send me by water all the well drilled troops available. I am confident that Washington is in no danger.

Engines & cars in large numbers have been sent up to bring down Jackson's command. I may not be able to cut them, but will try. We have cut all but the F & R RR.[1] The real issue is in the battle about to be fought in front of Richmond — all our available troops should be collected here, not raw regiments but the well drilled troops. It cannot be ignored that a desperate battle is before us — if any regiments of good troops remain unemployed it will be an irreparable fault committed.

G B McClellan
Maj Genl Comdg

Hon E M Stanton
Secty of War

P.S. our total loss in the battle of Hanover C.H. is 397 (three hundred & ninety-seven) killed, wounded & missing, of which (53) fifty three killed. The loss of enemy at least (1000) one thousand & totally disorganized.

ALS (telegram sent), McClellan Papers (A-59:23), Library of Congress. *OR*, Ser. 1, XI, Part 1, p. 35.

1. The Richmond, Fredericksburg and Potomac Railroad.

To Mary Ellen McClellan [TELEGRAM]

Mrs. G. B. McClellan — Hanover CH
Care N Shipman Hartford Conn — [May] 28 [1862] 4.15 pm

I am on Fitz field of battle. His success of yesterday was a glorious victory. The old rascal has done all that I could ask. The rebels are completely routed. It is a fair presage of the great victory which awaits us at Richmond. God bless you.

G B McClellan
Maj Genl

Received copy (War Dept.), Records of the Office of the Secretary of War, RG 107 (M-504:65), National Archives.

To Edwin M. Stanton [TELEGRAM]

New Bridge May 30 [1862] — am

From tone of your dispatches & President's I do not think that you at all appreciate the value & magnitude of Porter's victory.[1] It has entirely relieved my right flank which was seriously threatened, routed & demoralized a considerable portion of the rebel force, taken over 750 (seven hundred & fifty) prisoners, killed & wounded large numbers, one gun, many small arms & much baggage taken. It was one of the handsomest things of the war both in itself & its results. Porter has returned & my Army is again well in hand. Another day will make the probable field of battle passable for artillery. It is quite certain that there is nothing in front of Genl McDowell (Fredericksburg). I regard the burning of S Anna bridges as least important result of Porter's movement.

G B McClellan
Maj Genl Comdg

Hon E M Stanton
Secty of War

ALS (telegram sent), McClellan Papers (A-59:23), Library of Congress. *OR*, Ser. 1, XI, Part 1, p. 37.

1. In response to incomplete information sent to Washington, Lincoln telegraphed on May 28 to express puzzlement that a key railroad bridge over the South Anna River was not destroyed by Porter. The bridge was subsequently burned. *Collected Works of Lincoln*, V, pp. 244–45.

To Edwin M. Stanton [TELEGRAM]

Head-Quarters, Army of the Potomac,
New Bridge May 30 [1862] 9.30 pm

A contraband reports that Beauregard arrived in Richmond day before yesterday, with troops & amid great excitement.

I cannot vouch for the truth of this but give it for what it may be worth in connection with evacuation of Corinth.

Terrible storm this afternoon & tonight — roads again frightful. Need more ambulances.

G B McClellan
Maj Genl

Hon E M Stanton
Secty of War

ALS (telegram sent), McClellan Papers (A-59:23), Library of Congress. *OR*, Ser. 1, XI, Part 3, p. 201.

FIVE

THE BATTLE FOR RICHMOND

MAY 31–JULY 2, 1862

THE BATTLE OF Fair Oaks, on May 31 and June 1, 1862, and the Seven Days' battles that opened on June 25 severely tested General McClellan as a battlefield commander. How he met the test is revealed with unusual clarity in the letters and dispatches that follow, especially in the considerable number — thirty-six of the total of seventy-eight — that appear here for the first time or (in the case of those to his wife) for the first time as they were originally written.

During the month following the Yorktown siege, McClellan had edged his army up to the Chickahominy River and crossed his left wing — Heintzelman's Third Corps and Keyes's Fourth — to the south bank of that stream and to within six miles of Richmond. When Joe Johnston struck at this wing at Fair Oaks on May 31, McClellan was lying ill at his headquarters north of the river with what he termed his "Mexican disease," a recurrent malarial fever he had first contracted during the Mexican War. He was able to do little beyond ordering up reinforcements, and only reached the battlefield on June 1 when the fighting was over. His men beat off the uncoordinated Rebel attacks, leaving the two sides about where they were when the battle began.

General Johnston was badly wounded at Fair Oaks, and on June 1 Robert E. Lee took command of the Army of Northern Virginia. In his letter of April 20 to the president McClellan had written that as a commander General Lee was "likely to be timid & irresolute in action," a judgment that proved signally unprophetic. Although Lee succeeded in massing some 85,000 men to defend Richmond, the largest army he would ever command, it was a count far short of the 200,000 McClellan credited him with on the eve of the Seven Days. Thinking himself outnumbered by two to one, his intended tactic against this host, described in his letter of June 15 to Mrs. McClellan, was to use his advantage in artillery to make Richmond and its defenders hostage to his heavy siege guns.

When the armies moved up the Peninsula, the Confederates were forced to destroy the *Merrimack*, which drew too much water to fall back to Richmond, but McClellan did not take advantage of this to shift his line to the James. Instead he continued to make his line of communications the York and Pamunkey rivers to White House, from where the 600 tons of supplies he needed daily, and his siege guns, could be carried directly to the front over the York River Railroad. Lee determined to strike at this supply line, and Fitz John Porter's Fifth Corps guarding it, with a turning movement. He was taking a calculated risk, leaving fewer than 30,000 men to defend Richmond against the four Federal corps south of the Chickahominy should McClellan counterattack.

On the evidence of his June 26 telegram to his wife, McClellan at first gave thought to exactly that tactic — "I give you my word that I believe we will surely win & that the enemy is falling into a trap," he told her — but then failed to act on the opportunity. He surrendered the initiative to his opponent, and when Lee's series of assaults on Porter finally succeeded at Gaines's Mill on June 27, he admitted defeat and put his army in retreat toward the James, where it could be protected by the navy's gunboats.

In the month spent on the Chickahominy line the Federals had linked their positions by field telegraph, and consequently there is a remarkably full telegraphic record of the first days of the Seven Days' fighting, before the Army of the Potomac retreated. The telegrams McClellan wrote during the Gaines's Mill battle, for example, reveal his belief that he was under attack that day south of the Chickahominy as well as north of it, a measure of how successfully the Richmond defenders stage-managed their operation while Lee was carrying out his offensive.

These telegrams form the background for McClellan's aberrant dispatch of June 28 to Secretary of War Stanton, in which he insisted he had been defeated "because my force was too small" and accused the administration of deliberately attempting to sacrifice his army. Unaware that the dispatch was censored by the supervisor of military telegrams in Washington before it was shown to Stanton, McClellan took the secretary's failure to respond to his charge of treason as a silent admission of guilt. That he made the accusation intentionally is evident from his letter of June 29 to General Dix, in which he repeated the charge and called on Dix, should the campaign claim his life, to make the letter public.

The record here of the fighting during the retreat to the James is less full, primarily because McClellan played only a limited role in it. During the critical action at Glendale on June 30 he was aboard a gunboat in the James. He only witnessed the next day's fighting at Malvern Hill from a distance, and directed none of it. Having already elected to continue the retreat to Harrison's Landing, he gave no thought to taking advantage of the incisive Federal victory at Malvern Hill with a counteroffensive of his own.

To Samuel P. Heintzelman [TELEGRAM]

General Heintzelman, Headquarters Army of the Potomac,
Commanding Left Wing: New Bridge, May 31, 1862 — 5 p.m.

You have done what I expected of you in retrieving the disaster of Casey.[1] With the remaining five divisions you should hold your own. I will post everything during the night, so as to be able to cross at New Bridge to-morrow. Tell Kearny, Hooker, and [Couch] that I expect them to hold firm and repulse every and any attack. Recapture, if possible, any guns taken. Keep me fully informed of all that passes. Let me send to Washington as soon as possible the news that all is right.

Geo. B. McClellan
Major-General

OR, Ser. 1, XI, Part 3, p. 203.

1. The Battle of Fair Oaks opened with an attack on Gen. Casey's division.

To Randolph B. Marcy [TELEGRAM]

Genl R B Marcy Head Quarters, Army of the Potomac
Chief of Staff [Tyler House] 31st of May 1862 9.20 p.m.

Have rations cooked & ammunition issued to all the commands tonight & have the men ready for action tomorrow without fatiguing them too much tonight. Have the works & approaches to all possible bridges pushed to the utmost tonight, so that as many as possible may be practicable in the morning. Have the Trains ready to park. I have sent to Heintzelman and Keyes & will communicate with you. Select carefully the positions for parking the Trains & have Stoneman & the command at Mechanicsville well in hand.

If the Engineers cannot build the bridges tonight, commit the work to Porter & Franklin. I am sure Duane can do it. If they cannot, the sooner we get rid of the Corps of Engineers the better — communicate this to Barnard. It is absolutely necessary that several bridges be practicable for Artillery in the morning.

G B McClellan
Maj Genl

ALS (telegram sent), McClellan Papers, New-York Historical Society. *OR*, Ser. 1, LI, Part 1, p. 647.

To Edwin M. Stanton [TELEGRAM]

Headquarters Army of the Potomac
June 1 [1862] 12 M — Field of Battle

We have had a desperate battle in which the Corps of Sumner, Heintzelman & Keyes have been engaged against greatly superior numbers. Yesterday at one the enemy taking advantage of a terrible storm which had flooded the valley of the Chickahominy attacked our troops on the right bank of that river. Casey's Division which was in first line gave way unaccountably & discreditably. This caused a temporary confusion during which some guns & baggage were lost. But Heintzelman & Kearny most gallantly brought up their troops, which checked the enemy.

At the same time Sumner succeeded by great exertions in bringing across Sedgwick's & Richardson's Divisions, who drove back the enemy at the point of the bayonet, covering the ground with his dead. This morning the enemy attempted to renew the conflict but was every where repulsed. We have taken many prisoners, among whom Genl Pettigrew and Col. Long.[1] Our loss is heavy, but that of the enemy must be enormous. With the exception of Casey's Division our men have behaved splendidly — several fine bayonet charges have been made. The Second Excelsior[2] made two today.

G B McClellan
Maj Genl

Hon E M Stanton
Secty of War — Washington

ALS (telegram sent), McClellan Papers, New-York Historical Society. *OR*, Ser. 1, XI, Part 1, p. 749.

1. Brig. Gen. J. Johnston Pettigrew, Lt. Col. John O. Long. 2. The 71st New York regiment.

To Edwin M. Stanton [TELEGRAM]

Head Quarters, Army of the Potomac,
New Bridge June 2 1862 12.30 pm

I am delighted to hear of Halleck's success.[1] I have sent to learn numbers of killed, wounded & prisoners — it will take some time to ascertain details. The attack was a sudden one by the enemy in large force on Casey on Saturday [May 31]. Casey's pickets rushed in without attempting a stand & the camp was carried by the enemy. Heintzelman moved up at once with Kearny's Divn & checked the enemy. A portion of Hooker's arrived about dark. As soon as informed of the state of affairs I ordered Sumner across the Chickahominy. He displayed the utmost energy in bringing his troops into action, & handled them with the utmost courage in action. He repulsed every attack of the enemy, & drove him wherever he could get at him.

The enemy attacked in force & with great spirit yesterday morning, but were everywhere most signally repulsed with great loss. Our troops charged frequently on both days & uniformly broke the enemy.

The result is that our left is now within four (4) miles of Richmond. I only wait for the river to fall to cross with the rest of the force & make a general attack. Should I find them holding firm in a very strong position I may wait for what troops I can bring up from Fort Monroe — but the morale of my troops is now such that I can venture much & do not care for odds against me. The victory is complete & all credit is due to the gallantry of our officers & men.

G B McClellan
Maj Genl

Hon E M Stanton

ALS (telegram sent), McClellan Papers (C-13:64), Library of Congress. *OR*, Ser. 1, XI, Part 1, pp. 749–50.

1. Stanton telegraphed on this date: "Dispatches from General Halleck represent the rebel army from Corinth retreating in great disorder to Okolona. General Pope is pursuing and harassing them with 50,000 men. . . . " *OR*, Ser. 1, XI, Part 3, p. 209.

To the Army of the Potomac

SOLDIERS OF THE ARMY OF THE POTOMAC!

Head-Quarters, Army of the Potomac,
Camp near New Bridge, Va., June 2d, 1862.

I have fulfilled at least a part of my promise to you: you are now face to face with the rebels, who are at bay in front of their Capital. The final and decisive battle is at hand. Unless you belie your past history, the result cannot be for a moment doubtful. If the troops who labored so patiently, and fought so gallantly at Yorktown, and who so bravely won the hard fights at Williamsburg, West Point, Hanover Court House and Fair Oaks, now prove worthy of their antecedents, the victory is surely ours. The events of every day prove your superiority; wherever you have met the enemy you have beaten him; wherever you have used the bayonet he has given way in panic and disorder. I ask of you now one last crowning effort. The enemy has staked his all on the issue of the coming battle. Let us meet and crush him here in the very centre of the rebellion.

Soldiers! I will be with you in this battle, and share its dangers with you. Our confidence in each other is now founded upon the past. Let us strike the blow which is to restore peace and union to this distracted land. Upon your valor, discipline and mutual confidence that result depends.

Geo. B. McClellan,
Major General Commanding

DP, McClellan Papers (D-12:74), Library of Congress. *OR*, Ser. 1, XI, Part 3, p. 210.

To Mary Ellen McClellan [TELEGRAM]

Mrs. G B McClellan
Care N Shipman Hartford Conn

McClellan's [June] 2 [1862]
6.30 [P.M.]

Your two dispatches received. I said that none of your acquaintances killed & none that I know of wounded. Battle desperate & loss heavy but success complete. One more & we will have Richmond & I shall be there with Gods blessing this week. It is possible that yesterday's victory will open Richmond to us without further fighting. The result is very glorious for my gallant troops. I am quite well. Sleeve buttons not yet rec'd. Have not had time to write.

G B McClellan

Received copy (War Dept.), Records of the Office of the Secretary of War, RG 107 (M-504:66), National Archives.

To Mary Ellen McClellan

June 2 [1862] 8 pm. New Bridge

It has been impossible for me to write to you for the last two or three days. I was quite sick on Friday [May 30] & Saturday — on the last day rose from my bed & went to the field of battle — remained on horseback most of the time until Sunday evening. I came back perfectly worn out & exhausted — laid down at once & tho' I could not sleep much I got some rest. I think tonight will bring me quite up again — as I am not anxious.[1]

The Chickahominy is now falling & I hope we can complete the bridges tomorrow. I can do nothing more until that is accomplished. The enemy attacked on Saturday & Sunday with great ferocity & determination — their first attack alone was successful — Casey's Division broke & ran — losing most of their guns & their camp. As the other Divisions came up they checked the enemy & we gradually got the better of him — he was badly handled before night. On Sunday morning he renewed the attack & was everywhere repulsed in disorder & with heavy loss. We had regained all the ground lost & more last night — today we are considerably in advance of the field of battle. It is certain that we have gained a glorious victory. I only regret that the rascals were smart enough to attack when the condition of the Chickahominy was such that I could not throw over the rest of the troops to follow up the success — but the weather now seems settled & I hope the river will be low enough tomorrow to enable me to cross. I expect to fight another battle, but trust it will be a decisive one. I feel sure of success — so good is the spirit of my men & so great their ardor. But I am tired of the sickening sight of the battlefield, with its mangled corpses & poor suffering wounded! Victory has no charms for me when purchased at such cost. I shall be only too glad when all is over, & I can return where I best love to be....

I think the Richmond question will be settled this week....

Your Father is quite well — so are all the Staff. I don't think any of your friends were hurt in the battle — several colonels killed & some wounded.

AL copy, McClellan Papers (C-7 :63), Library of Congress.

1. GBM was suffering from malaria.

To Edwin M. Stanton [TELEGRAM]

Head Quarters, Army of the Potomac,
New Bridge June 3 6 pm 1862

Some firing today — nothing serious. Hard at work upon the bridges, removing wounded etc.

I expect at White House tonight six regiments ordered up from Fort Monroe.[1] These will at once be distributed among the old Brigades. The next leap will be the last one.

G B McClellan
Maj Genl Comdg

Hon E M Stanton
Secty of War Washington

ALS (telegram sent), McClellan Papers (A-60 :24), Library of Congress. *OR*, Ser. 1, XI, Part 3, p. 212.

1. On June 1 the Fort Monroe garrison was put under GBM's control. *OR*, Ser. 1, XI, Part 3, p. 207.

To Abraham Lincoln [TELEGRAM]

Head Quarters, Army of the Potomac,
New Bridge June 4 [1862] 1 p.m.

Terrible rain storm during the night & morning — not yet cleared off. Chickahominy flooded, bridges in bad condition — are still hard at work at them. I have taken every possible step to insure the security of the Corps on the right bank, but I cannot reinforce them from here until my bridges are all safe as my force is too small to insure my right & rear should the enemy attack in that direction, as they may probably attempt. I have to be very cautious now. Our loss in the late battle will probably exceed (5000) five thousand. I have not yet full returns. On account of the effect it might have on our own men & the enemy I request that you will regard this information as confidential for a few days. I am satisfied that the loss of the enemy was very considerably greater — they were terribly punished.

I mention these facts now merely to show you that the Army of the Potomac has had serious work & that no child's play is before it. You must make your calculations on the supposition that I have been correct from the beginning in asserting that the serious opposition was to be here.

G B McClellan
Maj Genl Comdg

A Lincoln President

ALS (telegram sent), McClellan Papers (A-61:24), Library of Congress. *OR*, Ser. 1, XI, Part 1, p. 45.

To Abraham Lincoln [TELEGRAM]

Head Quarters, Army of the Potomac,
New Bridge June 5 1862 [4 P.M.]

May I again invite your Excellency's attention to the great importance of occupying Chattanooga & Dalton by our western forces. The evacuation of Corinth would appear to render this very easy — the importance of this move in force cannot be exaggerated.[1]

G B McClellan
Maj Genl Comdg

His Excellency A Lincoln
Presdt Washington

ALS (telegram sent), McClellan Papers (C-13:64), Library of Congress. *OR*, Ser. 1, XI, Part 3, p. 215.

1. The president forwarded this dispatch to Halleck, who replied on June 7 that he was already advancing toward Chattanooga. *OR*, Ser. 1, X, Part 1, p. 670.

To Mary Ellen McClellan

[New Bridge] June 6th [1862] 10 pm.

. . . Have been as usual very quiet today — lying down almost all the time & leaving my tent scarcely at all. . . .

It has at last cleared up, & for some days I think. . . .

It is now quite certain that Joe Johnston was severely wounded last Saturday [May 31] — now said to be in the shoulder by a rifle ball — I think there is little doubt but that it is so. That places Smith G. W. in command.[1] I have drawn 9 rgts from Fort Monroe — the first use I made of the command given me of that place[2] — the last of them will be up tomorrow; these will go far towards filling our ranks. The losses in the late battle were almost 5500 — of course we have lost many by disease. I am promised either McCall's or King's Division in a very few days. If I hear tomorrow that they will surely be here in three or four days I will wait for them, as it would make the result certain & less bloody. I can't afford to have any more men killed than can be avoided. . . .

June 7 8.30 am. . . . The sun is struggling very hard this morning with the clouds — thus far the latter have rather the better of him, but I hope the old fellow will persevere & beat them out in an hour or two. I presume the mystery of the two telegraphic messages has been cleared up before this. I said that *none* of your acquaintances were killed. The operator must have been unmanned by excitement, for my official dispatch was terribly bungled in many ways. One of the two similar dispatches must have been sent on the operator's own account. I think I sent you but two altogether that day. Did not that solution occur to you?

AL copy, McClellan Papers (C-7:63), Library of Congress.

1. G. W. Smith led the army for a matter of hours. Gen. Lee took command of the Army of Northern Virginia on June 1. 2. When the Department of Virginia was put under GBM on June 1, Gen. Dix replaced Gen. Wool at Fort Monroe.

To Edwin M. Stanton [TELEGRAM]

Hon. E M Stanton
Secy War McClellan's [June] 7 [1862] 1 pm

Your dispatch of twelve thirty pm today recd & I must confess that its contents have not only struck me with astonishment but have given me much pain.[1] The care of our sick & wounded has tasked the unremitted energies of the whole medical corps in this army as well as occupied a great share of my attention from other important duties & I feel conscious that everything has been done for their comfort that human efforts could accomplish. The White House of the rebel Gen Lee referred to is a small frame building of six rooms worth probably fifteen hundred dollars & the medical director states that it would not accommodate more than 30 patients. He has tents where the patients are comfortable & he has therefore never conceived it necessary to call for the use of the house as a hospital. As to the story about thirsty wounded suffering soldiers having to buy a glass of water its only foundation probably originated in the fact that some civilian who was too indolent to go for the water himself may have paid a negro for bringing it to him. The following extract from a dispatch just recd from Col R Ingalls[2] the chief Q M in charge at White House will give you some light upon this subject & perhaps satisfy you as to the motive of the individuals who make the urgent complaints in question. "No one here has ever had cause to suffer for water unless he was too drunk or sick to drink it. We have water in unnecessary abundance. The springs are numerous the water is very fine & no prohibition has ever been placed on the free & unlimited use of it. The author of any report to the contrary of this statement must be a simpleton or a malicious knave." I have given special directions to protect the property of the White House from any unnecessary injury or destruction because it was once the property of Gen Washington & I cannot believe that you will regard this a cause for rebuke or censure. I protect no house against use when they are needed for sick or wounded soldiers. Persons who endeavor to impose upon you such malicious & unfounded reports as those alluded to are not only enemies of this army but the cause in which we are now fighting.[3]

Geo B McClellan
Maj Gen

Received copy, Records of the Office of the Secretary of War, RG 107 (M-473 :102), National Archives.

1. Stanton telegraphed: "Very urgent complaints are being made from various quarters respecting the protection afforded to the Rebel General Lee's property, called the 'White House,' instead of using it as a hospital for the care of wounded soldiers. It is represented that they have even to purchase a glass of water. . . . " Stanton Papers, Library of Congress. 2. Lt. Col. Rufus Ingalls. 3. Stanton replied the next day: "I am glad that your explanation will enable me to correct this misapprehension. Neither you nor I can hope to correct all such stories, but so far as it is in my power I shall labor to do so." Stanton Papers. See GBM to Barlow, June 23, *infra*.

To Edwin M. Stanton [TELEGRAM]

Hon Edwin M. Stanton
Secy of War McClellan's June 7th 4.40 pm 1862

In reply to your dispatch of two pm today[1] I have the honor to state that the Chickahominy River has risen so as to flood the entire bottoms to the depth of three & four feet. I am pushing forward the bridges in spite of this and the men are working night and day up to their waists in water to complete them. The whole face of the country is a perfect bog entirely impassable for artillery or even cavalry except directly in the narrow roads which renders any general movement either of this or the rebel army utterly out of the question at present until we have more favorable weather. I am glad to learn that you are pressing forward reinforcements so vigorously. I shall be in perfect readiness to move forward to take Richmond the moment that McCall reaches here & the ground will admit the passage of artillery. I have advanced my pickets about a mile today driving off the rebel pickets and securing a very advantageous position. The rebels have several batteries established commanding the debouches from two of our bridges & fire upon our working parties continually but as yet they have killed but very few of our men.

G B McClellan

Received copy, Records of the Office of the Secretary of War, RG 107 (M-473 :102), National Archives. *OR*, Ser. 1, XI, Part 1, p. 46.

1. Stanton telegraphed that McCall's division plus seven regiments would be sent as reinforcements. "Please state whether you will feel sufficiently strong for your final movement when McCall reaches you." *OR*, Ser. 1, XI, Part 3, p. 219.

To Robert E. Lee

Head Quarters Army of the Potomac
General. [New Bridge] June 8th 1862

I have the honor to acknowledge the receipt of Major General A. P. Hill's letter of to day[1] and to express my thanks for the prompt compliance with my request in regard to Lieut Perkins. I would beg to apologize for failing to send Lieut Throneburg or Bohannon with this, they were sent to Fort Monroe inadvertently. I have directed that one be returned at once, and have no doubt that he can be delivered to you by day after to-morrow morning. I fully agree that a general exchange or cartel would be preferable and should it be agreeable to you, would be very glad to designate a General or Staff Officer to meet one to be selected by you for the purpose of endeavoring to arrange the cartel.

It has reached me that circumstances have rendered it inconvenient for you to supply our wounded with all the necessary stores; while thanking you for the kind treatment which has been extended to wounded and prisoners taken from the Army under my command since it entered the Peninsula, may I ask permission to send such supplies as may be required by men in your possession, in such manner as may be designated by you.

A reply to this would reach me most conveniently by way of Meadow Bridge, where the officer commanding my picket will be instructed to receive it.[2]

I am Sir Very Respectfully Your Obt Servant
[George B. McClellan]
Maj General Comdg

To the Officer Commanding the Army of Northern Virginia[3]
Richmond, Va.

Copy, Records of U.S. Army Continental Commands, RG 393 (3964: Army of the Potomac), National Archives. *OR*, Ser. 2, III, p. 663.

1. Gen. Hill's letter dealt with prisoner exchange. *OR*, Ser. 2, III, p. 662. 2. Lee replied on June 11 that he had designated Brig. Gen. Howell Cobb to arrange for a general exchange of prisoners, and added: "I am not aware that your wounded in our hospitals are suffering

for the want of medical stores, but can assure you that they will receive the same attention as our own." *OR*, Ser. 2, III, pp. 674–75. See GBM to Stanton, June 15, *infra*. 3. The following letter shows that GBM believed G. W. Smith commanded the Army of Northern Virginia.

To Mary Ellen McClellan

[New Bridge, June 9, 1862] Monday morning

. . . A large dose of Spaniards yesterday — Genl Prim[1] & staff arrived & are quartered on us — some seven in all — a rather inconvenient addition to the mess. On the other hand, however, they are very gentlemanly & a very nice set of people. Genl Prim speaks only French & Spanish — he is a dark-faced, black-haired, bright, young looking man of 45 — I like him much. His Chief of Staff — Genl Milans — is a perfect old trump who speaks English & looks for all the world like a French Marquis of the stage. His hair & beard iron gray — his moustache of the most approved pattern of the Spanish Cavaliers of old — a cane suspended to his button hole — red pants tucked in high boots — a loose green coat covered with silver embroidery — the funniest little hat imaginable — on the whole a most peculiar picture; such as I never saw before. They are delighted with what they have seen (I hear the funny little fellow's voice now — "Gd mornin Sir — 'Hope yr well") fully appreciate the great difficulties under which we have been laboring & will do much I think towards giving a just idea in Europe of the difficulties we have to contest against in this most singular of all campaigns. . . .

I had a telegram from your friend McDowell last evening stating that he was ordered down here with his command & assuring me that he received the order with great satisfaction!![2] I have not replied to it, nor shall I — the animal probably sees that the tide is changing & that I am not entirely without friends in the world. The Secy & Presdt are also becoming quite amiable of late — I am afraid that I am a little cross to them & that I do not quite appreciate their sincerity & good feeling — "Timeo Danaos et dona ferentes." How glad I will be to get rid of the whole lot. I had another letter from our friend *A.P.H.* yesterday in reply to mine to Jo Johnston — so I am now confident that Jo is badly wounded. In my reply sent this morning I ignore Hill entirely & address mine to the "Comdg Genl etc." So G.W. will have to come out this time. I hope to arrange for a general exchange of prisoners & thus relieve our poor fellows who have been so long confined. I must do secesh the justice to say that they now treat our wounded & prisoners as well as they can. . . .

AL copy, McClellan Papers (C-7 :63), Library of Congress.

1. Gen. Juan Prim y Prats. 2. In his telegram of June 8 McDowell wrote: "In view of the remarks made with reference to my leaving you and my not joining you before by your

friends, and of something I have heard as coming from you on that subject, I wish to say that I go with the greatest satisfaction, and hope to arrive with my main body in time to be of service." *OR*, Ser. 1, XI, Part 3, pp. 220–21.

To Maria E. McClellan

My dear Maria Camp near New Bridge June 9th 1862

I have time only to write a line or two to thank you for your kind letter of Wednesday. I am very glad to hear that you are all well and that John is so busy. Wistar,[1] who is still here, told me that John had been away from home for some days cutting off some unhappy man's leg. There have been only too many surgical cases among these poor fellows of mine of late, & I fear that there are to be a good many more before Richmond is reached. They have determined to give one more battle I am confident. Perhaps it is best that they should be made to suffer still more that the war may the sooner be over.

We are tolerably quiet here — waiting for the Chickahominy to become practicable & the ground to dry enough for artillery to pass over it. A little musketry firing & the occasional exchange of artillery shots relieve the monotony — some artillery firing is going on now as I write.

You are mistaken about Nelly & the baby holding levees in Hartford[2] — they are there to rest & are resting most quietly. I have Genl Prim & his staff on my hands just now — a good set, but it is rather a bore to take care of so many at such a time.

My breakfast is ready so I will stop. With love to all

Your affectionate brother
Geo B McClellan

Mrs J H B McC

ALS, McClellan Papers (B-11:48), Library of Congress. Maria Eldredge McClellan, GBM's sister-in-law, was the wife of John H. B. McClellan.

1. Caspar Wistar, a family friend from Philadelphia. 2. Mrs. McClellan and daughter May were then staying with friends in Hartford, Conn.

To Mary Ellen McClellan

[New Bridge] June 10 [1862] 7 1/2 am.

It is again raining hard & has been for several hours! I feel almost discouraged — that is I would do so did I not feel that it must all be for the best, & that God has some just purpose in view through all this. It is certain that there has not been for years & years such a season — it does not come by chance. I am quite checked by it — first the Chickahominy is so swollen & the valley so covered with water that I cannot establish safe communication over it — then again the ground is so muddy that we cannot use our artillery — the guns sink up to their axle trees.

I regret all this extremely — but take comfort from the thought that God will not leave so great a struggle as this to mere chance — if he ever interferes with the destinies of men & nations this would seem to be a fit occasion for it.

Whenever I feel discouraged by adverse circumstances, I do my best to fall back on this great source of confidence & almost always find that it gives me strength to bear up against anything that may occur. I do not see how anyone can fill such a position as I do without being constantly forced to think of higher things & the Supreme Being. The great responsibility — the feeling of personal weakness & incompetency — of entire dependence on the will of God — the thousand circumstances entirely beyond our control that may defeat our best laid plans — the sight of poor human suffering — all these things *will* force the mind to seek rest above. . . .

I feel quite well today — by far better than at any time before — I think that if I can stand the test of this rainy day all must be right. I will not go out while it rains if I can help it. . . .

The Spaniards are still here, & I fear will remain some time unless this rain drives them off. Prim is very well, but it is a nuisance to be obliged to be polite when one's head is full of more important things. . . .

Still raining very hard — I don't know what *will* become of us!

AL copy; copy, McClellan Papers (C-7:63/D-10:73), Library of Congress.

To Edwin M. Stanton [TELEGRAM]

[New Bridge] June 10 [1862] 3.30 pm

I have again information that Beauregard has arrived & that some of his troops are to follow him. No great reliance, perhaps none whatever, can be attached to this, but it is possible & ought to be their policy.

I am completely checked by the weather.

The roads and fields are literally impassable for Artillery, almost so for Infantry. The Chickahominy is in a dreadful state — we have another rain storm on our hands. I shall attack as soon as the weather & ground permit, but there will be a delay — the extent of which no one can foresee, for the season is altogether abnormal.

In view of these circumstances I present for your consideration the propriety of detaching largely from Halleck's Army to strengthen this, for it would seem that Halleck has now no large organized force in front of him, while we have.

If this cannot be done, or even in connection with it, allow me to suggest the movement of a heavy column from Dalton upon Atlanta. If but the one can be done it would better conform to military principles to strengthen this army; & even although the reinforcements might not arrive in season to take part in the attack upon Richmond the moral effect would be great, & they would furnish valuable assistance in ulterior movements.[1]

I wish it to be distinctly understood that whenever the weather permits I will attack with whatever force I may have, although a larger force would enable me to gain much more decisive results. I would be glad to have McCall's Infantry sent forward by water at once without waiting for his Artillery & Cavalry.

If Genl Prim returns via Washington please converse with him as to the condition of affairs here.

G B McClellan
Maj Genl Comdg

Hon E M Stanton
Secty of War

ALS (telegram sent), McClellan Papers (A-62:24), Library of Congress. *OR*, Ser. 1, XI, Part 1, pp. 46–47.

1. Stanton forwarded this proposal to Halleck, who replied on June 12 rejecting "the supposition that Beauregard or any considerable part of his force has gone to Richmond." He added, on June 16: "Should our forces be too much weakened here by detachment I have no doubt Beauregard would immediately march back and attack us." *OR*, Ser. 1, XVI, Part 2, pp. 8, 14, 26.

To Mary Ellen McClellan

June 11 [1862] New Bridge am.

. . . Am very well today & the weather is good & will start in half an hour or so for the other side of the river — it threatens rain again, so that I do not believe I can make the entire tour — probably only on Smith & Sumner — do the rest tomorrow. Besides I do not care to ride too far today — as I have not been on horseback before since the day of the battle. I must be careful for it would be utter destruction to the army were I to be disabled so as not to be able to take command — Sumner would ruin things in about two days. . . .

Burnside left yesterday, thinks there is a great deal of Union feeling in North Carolina & that our gaining possession of Richmond will at once bring N.C. back into the Union. . . .

I half doubt whether there is much Union feeling south of N.C. . . .

McCall's Division has commenced arriving — some of them reached the White House last night. This relieves me very much.

AL copy, McClellan Papers (C-7:63), Library of Congress.

To Mary Ellen McClellan

June 12 [1862] 8 am. New Bridge

. . . Am about to break up this camp & move over the Chickahominy to Dr Trent's house — to its vicinity at least, for I abominate houses when in the field. In addition have to take a farewell ride some 7 or 8 miles up this side of the river to look again at the ground & give the last instructions to Porter & Franklin for their guidance on this side of the river. I took quite a ride yesterday — the first since the battle & got through with it nicely. I am about as nearly well now as I expect to be in this climate — bright & strong enough to fight a much better battle than any yet. I had a wonderful telegram from the Secy of War last night — he declares that he is & ever has been my best friend![1] By the way did you ever criticize Stanton, McDowell or any of that tribe in talking with Sturgis?[2] I don't believe you ever did say much to such people & denied it strongly. But do be very careful what you say — I apprehend Sturgis is a Jesuit. The fact is that you & I cannot be too careful how we talk — but perhaps it don't make much difference, because people put words in our mouths. I think we will have good weather now — it *seems* to have changed for the better.

AL copy, McClellan Papers (C-7 :63), Library of Congress.

1. Stanton had telegraphed on June 11: "Be assured, general, that there never has been a moment when my desire has been otherwise than to aid you with my whole heart, mind, and strength since the hour we first met; and whatever others may say for their own purposes, you have never had, and never can have, any one more truly your friend, or more anxious to support you. . . . " *OR*, Ser. 1, XI, Part 1, p. 47. 2. Brig. Gen. Samuel E. Sturgis held a command in the Washington defenses.

To Edwin M. Stanton [TELEGRAM]

Hon E M Stanton
Secy of War

Head-Quarters, Army of the Potomac,
[Camp Lincoln] June 12 1862

In your telegram respecting reinforcements you inform me that Genl McDowell with the residue of his command will proceed overland to join me before Richmond.[1] I beg leave to suggest that the destruction of the RR bridges by flood & fire cannot probably be remedied in under 4 weeks, that an attempt to employ wagon transportation must involve great delay and may be found very difficult of accomplishment. An extension of my right wing to meet him may involve serious hazard to my flank and my line of communications and may not suffice to rescue him from any peril in which a strong movement of the enemy may involve him. I would advise that his forces be sent by water. Even a portion thus sent would by reason of greater expedition and security and less complications of my movements probably be more servicable in the operations before Richmond. The roads throughout the region between the Rappahannock and the James can not be relied upon and may become execrable even should they be in their best condition. The junction of his force with the extension of my right flank can not be made without derangement of my plans and if my recent experience in moving troops be indicative of the difficulties incident to McDowell's march the exigencies of my present position will not admit of the delay. I have ordered back all the transports used in bringing McCall's Division, that they may be ready for service if you deem it best to employ water transportation. I have to day moved my Head Quarters across the Chickahominy to a central position so that I can readily reach any point of attack or advance. The enemy are massing their troops near our front, throwing up earthworks on all the approaches to Richmond and giving every indication of fight.

Geo B. McClellan
Maj Genl

Retained copy, McClellan Papers (A-62:25), Library of Congress. *OR*, Ser. 1, XI, Part 3, p. 225.

1. Stanton's telegram was dated June 11. *OR*, Ser. 1, XI, Part 1, p. 47.

To Edwin M. Stanton [TELEGRAM]

Hon E. M. Stanton
Sec. of War

Head-Quarters, Army of the Potomac,
[Camp Lincoln] June 14, 11 a.m. 1862

A rebel force of Cavalry and Artillery variously estimated at from one to five thousand came around our right flank last evening, attacked and drove in a picket guard of two squadrons of Cavalry stationed at Old Church. Thence they proceeded to a landing three miles above White House where they burned two forage schooners and destroyed some wagons. Thence they struck the Rail Road at Tunstalls station — fired into a train of cars killing some five or six.

Then they met a force of Infantry which I sent down to meet them, where they ran off.

I have several Cavalry detachments out after them and hope to punish them. No damage has been done to the Rail Road.[1]

Geo. B. McClellan
Major General

Retained copy, McClellan Papers (A-63:25), Library of Congress. *OR*, Ser. 1, XI, Part 1, p. 1005.

1. Brig. Gen. J. E. B. Stuart's cavalry force completed its circuit of the Federal army on June 16.

To Edwin M. Stanton [TELEGRAM]

Head-Quarters, Army of the Potomac,
Camp Lincoln June 14 [1862] midnight

All quiet in every direction. The stampede of last night has passed away.

Weather now very favorable. I hope two days more will make the ground practicable.

I shall advance as soon as the bridges are completed & the ground fit for artillery to move. At the same time I would be glad to have whatever troops can be sent to me — I can use several raw regiments to advantage.

It ought to be distinctly understood that McDowell & his troops are completely under my control. I received a telegram from him requesting that McCall's Division might be placed so as to join him immediately upon his arrival.[1] That request does not breathe the proper spirit — whatever troops come to me must be disposed of so as to do the most good. I do not feel that in such circumstances as those in which I am now placed Genl McD should wish the general interests to be sacrificed for the purpose of increasing his command. If I cannot fully control all his troops I want none of them, but would prefer to fight the battle with what I have & let others be responsible for the results. The Department lines should not be allowed to interfere with me, but Genl McD & all troops sent to me should be placed completely at my disposal to do with them as I think best. In no other way can they be of assistance to me.

[*Crossed out*: I doubt whether he will ever reach me by land & I shall not count upon his aid, but if he does come] I therefore request that I may have entire & full control of all the troops that are sent to me. The stake at issue is too vast to allow personal considerations to be entertained — you know that I have none.

G B McClellan
Maj Genl Comdg

Hon E M Stanton
Secty of War

The indications are from our balloon reconnaissances & from all other sources that the enemy are entrenching, daily increasing in force & determination to fight desperately.

McC

ALS (telegram sent), McClellan Papers (A-63:25), Library of Congress, *OR*, Ser. 1, XI, Part 1, pp. 47–48.

1. McDowell telegraphed on June 12: "My third division McCalls has embarked and is now on the way. Please do me the favor to so place it that it may be in position to join the others as they come down from Fredericksburg." McClellan Papers (A-62:25).

To Edwin M. Stanton [TELEGRAM]

Hon E. M. Stanton — Head Quarters Army of the Potomac
Secy of War — [Camp Lincoln] June 15 7.40 pm. 1862

Another rain set in about 3 p.m. today and has continued up to the present time. This will retard our operations somewhat, as a little rain causes the ground in this section to become soft and boggy rendering it impossible to move Artillery except directly in the travelled roads. In this arm especially consists our great superiority over the enemy, and as we will have to cut out several roads through new ground for the Army to advance on, it is absolutely necessary that we should have some few days of dry weather to make the ground firm enough to sustain horses & guns.

Our bridges are progressing rapidly and we shall very soon be ready to strike the final blow.

Colonel Key has had an interesting interview with Howell Cobb today, the particulars of which I will explain to you by letter.[1] It proves among other things most conclusively that they will defend Richmond to the last extremity. The interview was arranged for the purpose of bringing about an exchange of prisoners, but in the course of the conversation other matters were introduced and discussed.

Six prisoners just captured from the 1st N. Carolina state troops say their Regt. arrived in Richmond a few days ago from Goldsborough with the 3rd N. Carolina, 30th Virginia, 44th & 49th Georgia troops.

I think it important in view of this to hurry on transportation to Burnside.

Geo. B. McClellan
Maj Genl

Retained copy, McClellan Papers (A-64:25), Library of Congress. *OR*, Ser. 1, XI, Part 3, pp. 229–30.

1. GBM forwarded Col. Key's report on June 17. His conversation with Gen. Cobb ranged into political affairs, and Key gave his impressions: "That the rebels are in great force at Richmond, and mean to fight a general battle in defense of it; . . . that there is little hope of reconstruction so long as the rebels have a large army in the field anywhere; that it may be found necessary in particular States, if not in all, to destroy the class which has created this rebellion, by destroying the institution which has created them." *OR*, Ser. 1, XI, Part 1, pp. 1052–56.

To Mary Ellen McClellan

June 15 [1862] 10.15 p.m. Camp Lincoln

. . . We have had several skirmishes — the rebels have attacked our pickets on several points, but were everywhere beaten back with the loss of several killed & respectable number of prisoners. . . .

The worst interruption of all, was a "party" of ladies & gentlemen that Van Vliet had no more sense than to insist upon coming up here. Senator [Harris][1] & a lot of others. All of whom I was really glad to see, although this was no place for them. I am sorry to say that when I heard of their arrival, I *swore* a little *internally* & sent Russell[2] flying out of my tent, declaring that I would not see any of them. But soon afterwards Senator [Harris] came here & he was so kind & friendly that I was at once mollified. I talked to him some time & he went back to Van Vliet's tent. I then gave to Averell[3] my orders for a "surprise party" tomorrow, to repay Secesh for his raid of day before yesterday. Then went over to call on Mrs. ——. Then I *was* in for it. I was presented to all the ladies, listened to Mrs. [Ricketts's][4] version of her trip to Richmond, & very rapidly beat a retreat, giving business as an excuse. Charles got up a lunch for the party, a rainstorm coming on in the meanwhile. When they were nearly through, I took Averell over & talked with them for a while. Then we adjourned to my tent, where I was *rather* victimized. The two dear old Mesdames were just as good & *fat* as they could be; can I say more? When they left, they asked me to give them sprigs from the bower in front of my tent, so I send you one too.

Of one thing you may rest assured — I will do all that is in my power to bring us together again. There is no happiness or contentedness for me when away from you. I fear that I do not yet fully appreciate our dear little baby, for she is always a secondary consideration. I do love her — bless her sweet little self! But I am free to say that she does not yet rival her Mother.

I do not think our rain of today will do much harm. The chances now are that I will make the first advance on Tuesday [June 17] or Wednesday. By that time I think the ground will be fit for the movements of artillery & that all our bridges will be completed. I think the rebels will make a desperate fight, but I feel sure that we will gain our point. Look on the maps I sent you a day or two ago & find "Old Tavern" on the road from New Bridge to Richmond — it is in that vicinity that the next battle will be fought. If we gain that the game is up for Secesh — I will then have them in the hollow of my hand. I think they see it in that light & that they are fully prepared to make a desperate resistance. I shall make the first battle mainly an artillery contest — I think I can bring some 200 guns to bear & sweep everything before us. As soon as I gain possession of the "Old Tavern" I will push them in upon Richmond & behind their works — then I will bring up my heavy guns — shell the city & carry it by assault. I speak very confidently but if you could see the faces of the troops as I ride among them you would share my confidence. They will do anything I tell them to do.

I could not help laughing when on the day of the last battle I was riding along in front of Keyes Corps, *with Keyes* (!) a man jumped out in an interval of the cheering & addressed me quite familiarly, saying "Hallo George — how are you? You are the only one of the whole crowd of Genls that is worth a ——." I won't fill up the last word, but will only say that the whole command shouted "that's so!"

. . . I think there is scarcely a man in this whole army who would not give his life for me & willingly do whatever I ask. I have tried them more than once & whenever I am near they never fail me. The next battle will doubtless be a very desperate one, but I think that I can so use our artillery as to make the loss of life on our side comparatively small. . . .

AL copy; copy, McClellan Papers (C-7:63/D-10:72), Library of Congress.

1. In copying this paragraph, GBM's daughter left this name and others blank. Mrs. McClellan's father wrote her on this date that a party headed by New York Senator Ira Harris visited army headquarters, and Gen. Heintzelman also mentioned the party in his diary. Randolph B. Marcy to Mary Ellen McClellan, McClellan Papers (B-10:48); Samuel P. Heintzelman diary, June 15, 1862, Library of Congress. **2.** Maj. W. W. Russell, of GBM's staff. **3.** Col. William W. Averell, 3rd Pennsylvania cavalry. **4.** Mrs. James B. Ricketts, the wife of an officer wounded and captured at First Bull Run, had nursed her husband during his imprisonment in Richmond.

To Edwin M. Stanton [TELEGRAM]

Hon E M Stanton
Secy of War

Head-Quarters, Army of the Potomac,
Camp Lincoln June 15, 1862 11 pm.

In the battle of Fair Oaks the division of Gen Casey was broken in such manner as to show that its commander had failed to infuse proper morale into his troops. In the action he behaved with personal gallantry but he does not command the confidence of his soldiers. He is a most excellent tactician of infantry, having written a manual on the subject and would be very useful in the camp of instruction of Annapolis. I suggest that he be at once assigned to duty there; but in such manner not to convey reproach.[1]

G. B. McClellan
Maj Genl

Retained copy, McClellan Papers (A-64:25), Library of Congress.

1. Stanton replied on June 19 that new troops "will have to go into the field as fast as they can be raised so that there can be no occasion for the general's services in the way you propose." McClellan Papers (A-65:26). On June 23 Casey was assigned to command the supply base at White House, and later transferred to a training command.

To Abraham Lincoln [TELEGRAM]

His Excellency Abraham Lincoln Camp Lincoln June 18th 62

I have the honor to acknowledge the receipt of your dispatch of today.[1] Our army is well over the Chickahominy except the very considerable forces necessary to protect our flanks and communications. Our whole line of pickets in front runs within six miles of Richmond. The rebel line runs within musket range of ours. Each has heavy supports at hand. A general engagement may take place any hour. Any advance by us involves a battle more or less decisive. The enemy exhibit at every point a readiness to meet us. They certainly have great numbers and extensive works. If ten or fifteen thousand men have left Richmond to reinforce Jackson it illustrates their strength and confidence . After tomorrow we shall fight the rebel army as soon as Providence will permit. We shall await only a favorable condition of the earth and sky & the completion of some necessary preliminaries.

Geo. B. McClellan
Maj Genl Comdg

Retained copy, McClellan Papers (C-10 :63), Library of Congress. *OR*, Ser. 1, XI, Part 3, p. 233.

1. In response to reports from GBM and elsewhere that 10,000 to 15,000 reinforcements were going to Jackson in the Shenandoah Valley, Lincoln wrote: "If this is true, it is as good as a re-inforcement to you of an equal force. I could better dispose of things if I could know about what day you can attack Richmond. . . . " *Collected Works of Lincoln*, V, p. 276.

To Ambrose E. Burnside [TELEGRAM]

General A. Burnside — Head-Quarters, Army of the Potomac,
New Berne N.C. — [Camp Lincoln] June 20 1862 12.30 pm

How many troops could you bring to White House and leave everything secure in your present position and what time would it require to get the disposable troops to Fort Monroe.

What is the earliest moment you can move with your present transportation on Goldsborough.

Answer at once.[1]

Geo. B. McClellan
Major General

Care of General J. A. Dix Fort Monroe to be sent forward without delay.

Geo B. McClellan
Maj. Genl.

Retained copy, McClellan Papers (A-66 :26), Library of Congress. *OR*, Ser. 1, XI, Part 3, p. 237.

1. Burnside replied on June 23 that within five days he could land 7,000 men at Norfolk, or advance that many against Petersburg from the south, or in two and a half days move against Goldsboro, N.C., with 10,000 men. McClellan Papers (C-11 :63).

To Abraham Lincoln [TELEGRAM]

Head Quarters, Army of the Potomac,
Camp Lincoln June 20 1862 2 pm

Your Excellency's dispatch of 11 am received also that of Genl Sigel.[1] I have no doubt that Jackson has been reinforced from here. There is reason to believe that Genl R S Ripley has recently joined Lee's Army with a Brigade or Division from Charleston. Troops have arrived recently from Goldsboro'.

There is not the slightest reason to suppose that the enemy intends evacuating Richmond; he is daily increasing his defenses.

I find him everywhere in force & every reconnaissance costs many lives. Yet I am obliged to feel my way foot by foot at whatever cost — so great are the difficulties of the country. By tomorrow night the defensive works covering our position on this side of the Chickahominy should be completed. I am forced to this by my inferiority in numbers so that I may bring the greatest possible numbers into action & secure the Army against the consequences of unforeseen disaster. I would be glad to have permission to lay before your Excellency by letter or telegram my views as to the present state of military affairs throughout the whole country. In the mean time I would be pleased to learn the dispositions as to numbers & position of the troops not under my command in Virginia and elsewhere.[2]

G B McClellan
Maj Genl Comdg

His Ex A Lincoln
Presdt

ALS (telegram sent), McClellan Papers (C-13:64), Library of Congress. *OR*, Ser. 1, XI, Part 1, p. 48.

1. Lincoln's telegram, and Gen. Sigel's of June 19 from the Shenandoah Valley, dealt with "the proposition that Jackson is being re-inforced from Richmond. This may be reality, and yet may only be contrivance for deception; and to determine which, is perplexing." *Collected Works of Lincoln*, V, pp. 277–78; *OR*, Ser. 1, XII, Part 3, p. 411. 2. The president replied on June 21 that he was concerned about security in sending such correspondence, and on June 22 GBM telegraphed that he would postpone the matter. *Collected Works of Lincoln*, V, p. 279; *OR*, Ser. 1, XI, Part 1, p. 48. See GBM to Lincoln, July 7, 1862, *infra*.

To Mary Ellen McClellan

[Camp Lincoln] June 22 [1862] Sunday 3 pm.

I had no letter from you this morning, & no telegram yesterday or today!! I have telegraphed you every day & fear the dispatches don't go well to Orange.[1] . . .

The only pleasant thing I look forward to, is our reunion. All that I care to live for is to be with you & our sweet child. It is too bad that I should lose so much of you both. . . .

I almost envy you the rest & quiet you must be now enjoying & am very anxious to have you tell me how the place looks; what the surroundings are, & what the house.

By an arrival from Washn today (Allen)[2] I learn that Stanton & Chase have fallen out; that McDowell has deserted his friend C & taken to S!! That Seward & Blair stand firmly by me — that Honest A has again fallen into the hands of my enemies & is no longer a cordial friend of mine! Chase is evidently desirous of coming over to my side! Alas poor country that should have such rulers. I tremble for my country when I think of these things, but still can trust that God in his infinite wisdom will not punish us as we deserve, but will in his own good time bring order out of chaos & restore peace to his unhappy country. His will be done — whatever it may be. I am as anxious as any human being can be to finish this war, yet when I see such insane folly behind me I feel that the final salvation of the country demands the utmost prudence on my part & that I must not run the slightest risk of disaster, for if anything happened to this army our cause would be lost. I feel too that I must not unnecessarily risk my life — for the fate of my army depends upon me & they all know it. . . .

I got up some heavy guns today & hope to give secesh a preliminary pounding tomorrow & to make one good step next day. The rascals are very strong & outnumber me very considerably — they are well intrenched also & have all the advantages of position — so I must be prudent — but I will yet succeed notwithstanding all they do & leave undone in Washington to prevent it. I would not have on my conscience what those men have for all the world. I am sorry to say that I shall lose the dear old Prince de Joinville in a few days — he is obliged to return to Europe. Genl Prim has sent me his photograph. . . .

It is quite hot this afternoon. . . .

It is almost time for our evening skirmish — secesh has been very quiet today — scarcely fired a shot. I am very glad of it as it enabled me to give my men a good quiet rest for Sunday. It is stated that GW[3] has again been afflicted with a paralytic stroke. . . .

AL copy; copy, McClellan Papers (C-7 :63/D-10 :72), Library of Congress.

1. Mrs. McClellan was staying with her uncle, Dr. Erastus E. Marcy, in North Orange, N.J. 2. Allan Pinkerton, employing the nom de guerre E. J. Allen. 3. Maj. Gen. G. W. Smith, CSA.

To Samuel L. M. Barlow

Head-Quarters, Army of the Potomac,
My dear Barlow [Camp Lincoln] June 23 1862

I have only time to thank you for your kind letter of the 17th,[1] as well for the great kindness Mrs B & you have shown to my wife.

By a recent arrival from Washington I hear that Chase & Stanton have parted company, & that McDowell has attached himself to Stanton!

They have got themselves into a nice scrape with their White House business — I have written to Frank Blair requesting him to call for my letter to the Secty on the topic.[2]

Never was there a more groundless slander & never a malicious lie more thoroughly exposed than this will be when all is known about it. The worst of it is that Stanton knew the facts *before* the subject was agitated in Congress & did not choose to explain — my letter has incorporated in it what had passed between S & myself & will expose his treachery most completely!

We are making slow progress here — but I dare not risk this Army on which I feel the fate of the nation depends. I will succeed, but for the sake of the cause must make a sure thing of it.

Considerable skirmishing this afternoon — even as I write — must break off to look after it.

In great haste, & with my kindest regards to Mrs. Barlow

Sincerely your friend
Geo B. McClellan

S L M Barlow Esq
N.Y.

ALS, Barlow Papers, Huntington Library.

1. "Supposing . . . that the final struggle is now close at hand," Barlow wrote, "I cannot refrain from telling you how hearty & unanimous the whole people are in your favor & if the War Dept. does its duty I am sure of your success. I was in Washington last week. Saw Blair. He is your friend. He said among other things, 'If Chase & the others don't let McClellan alone, they will make him president.' I told him that I thought no one had less political ambition than yourself." McClellan Papers (A-65:26), Library of Congress. 2. See GBM to Stanton, June 7, *supra*. GBM's letter to Francis P. Blair, Jr., has not been found, but his correspondence relating to the White House affair was laid before Congress on July 8.

To Mary Ellen McClellan

Hd Qtrs Trent's House June 23 [1862] 10 1/2 pm.

. . . You may be sure that no man in this army is so anxious as its General to finish the campaign — every poor fellow that is killed or wounded almost haunts me! My only consolation is that I have honestly done my best to save as many lives as possible & that many others might have done less towards it.

I have had a rather anxious day — the movements of the enemy being mysterious — but I have gained something, & am ready for any eventuality I think. I have a kind of presentiment that tomorrow will bring forth *something* — *what* I do not know — we will see when the time arrives. I expect to be able to take a decisive step in advance day after tomorrow, & if I succeed will gain a couple of miles towards Richmond. It now looks to me as if the operations would resolve themselves into a series of partial attacks, rather than a general battle.

[June] 24th 10 am. I was interrupted just here by some stampede telegrams that kept me up until 1 1/2 or 2 this morning — in the mean time a terrible storm came up, & blew this unhappy sheet into the mud & rain. I send it as it is however, as a slight specimen of the "sacred soil." Also because I am about starting out on a ride from which I am not likely to return before the mail leaves camp. Nothing of any interest this morning — all quiet — weather cloudy & may rain today again. If it rains hard I will come home early. I think nothing will be done today on either side of the river — so we will probably be quiet.

AL copy, McClellan Papers (C-7:63), Library of Congress.

To John Rodgers [TELEGRAM]

Head Quarters, Army of the Potomac,
Camp Lincoln June 24 6 pm 1862

Dispatch received. If you can effectually destroy the bridge in question the sooner it is done the better.[1] They cannot replace a bridge of that length for many weeks & I am about to commence decisive measures. Circumstances force me to begin my attack at some distance from the James River — in a few days I hope to gain such a position as to enable me to place a force above Ball's & Drewry's Bluffs, so that we can remove the obstructions & place ourselves in communication with you so that you can cooperate in the final attack. In the mean time please keep some gun boats as near Drewry's Bluff as prudence will permit. Within the next two or three days I hope to be within range of Richmond.

By that time I hope to see you in person to arrange our movements. I will inform you fully how I progress.

G B McClellan
Maj Genl

Comdr Jno Rodgers
U.S. Steamer Galena off Jamestown

ALS (telegram sent), McClellan Papers (C-13:64), Library of Congress. *OR*, Ser. 1, XI, Part 3, p. 250.

1. Rodger's dispatch of this date described a plan to burn the Swift Creek bridge, on the railroad between Petersburg and Richmond. The attempt, on June 29, failed. *OR*, Ser. 1, XI, Part 3, p. 250; *NOR*, Ser. 1, VII, p. 524.

To Samuel P. Heintzelman [TELEGRAM]

Head Quarters, Army of the Potomac,
Camp Lincoln 6.30 pm [June] 24th 1862

Dispatch of 6 pm received. If it is a possible thing take advantage of the weakness of the enemy & push your pickets at least to the edge of the next clearing. Please give your personal attention to this & arrange with Genl Sumner so that he may maintain constant connection.

I have been all over the right today & will open with heavy guns tomorrow. Tomorrow night I hope to gain possession of the Garnett field, & by another day of the Old Tavern & some ground in advance. It will be chiefly an Artillery & Engineering affair. Keep your command as fresh as possible, ready for another battle — I cannot afford to be without Heintzelman, Kearny & Hooker in the next effort. I have satisfactory communications from the gun boat fleet in James River.

The enemy have done an immense amount of work on our right but seem to be deceived as to our intentions. All looks well.

G B McClellan
Maj Genl

Genl S P Heintzelman
Comdg 3rd Corps

ALS (telegram sent), McClellan Papers (C-13:64), Library of Congress. *OR*, Ser. 1, XI, Part 3, pp. 250–51.

To Edwin M. Stanton [TELEGRAM]

Head-Quarters, Army of the Potomac
[Camp Lincoln] June 24 12 pm 1862

A very peculiar case of desertion has just occurred from the enemy. The party states that he left Jackson, Whiting & Ewell[1] fifteen Brigades at Gordonsville on the 21st. That they were moving to Frederickshall & that it was intended to attack my rear on the 28th.

I would be glad to learn at your earliest convenience the most exact information you have as to the position and movements of Jackson as well as the sources from which your information is derived that I may better compare it with what I have.[2]

G B McClellan
Maj Genl

Hon E M Stanton
Secty of War

ALS (telegram sent), McClellan Papers (A-67:27), Library of Congress. *OR*, Ser. 1, XI, Part 1, p. 49.

1. Brig. Gen. W. H. C. Whiting and Maj. Gen. Richard S. Ewell commanded divisions under Jackson. 2. "We have no definite information as to the numbers or position of Jackson's force," Stanton telegraphed on June 25. After reviewing the conflicting intelligence, he concluded: "I think, therefore, that while the warning of the deserter to you may also be a blind, it could not safely be disregarded." *OR*, Ser. 1, XI, Part 1, p. 49.

To Edwin M. Stanton [TELEGRAM]

Headquarters Army of the Potomac
Redoubt No 3 June 25 [1862] 3.15 pm

Enemy are making desperate resistance to advance of picket lines. Kearny & one half of Hooker's are where I want them. Have this moment reinforced Hooker's right with a Brigade & a couple of guns & hope in a few minutes to finish the work intended for to day. Our men are behaving splendidly — the enemy fighting well also. This is not a battle merely an affair of Heintzelman's Corps supported by Keyes. Thus far all goes well & we hold every foot we have gained. If we succeed in what we have undertaken it will be a very important advantage gained. Loss not large thus far. The fighting up to this time done by Hooker's division which has behaved as usual — that is most handsomely.[1] On our right Porter has silenced the enemy's batteries in his front.

G B McClellan
Maj Genl Comdg

Hon E M Stanton
Secty of War

ALS (telegram sent), McClellan Papers, New-York Historical Society. *OR*, Ser. 1, XI, Part 1, p. 50.

1. This action at Oak Grove was the first of the Seven Days' battles.

To Edwin M. Stanton [TELEGRAM]

Camp Lincoln June 25 [1862] 6.15 pm

I have just returned from the field and find your dispatch in regard to Jackson.[1]

Several contrabands just in give information confirming supposition that Jackson's advance is at or near Hanover CH & that Beauregard arrived with strong reinforcements in Richmond yesterday. I incline to think that Jackson will attack my right & rear. The rebel force is stated at (200,000) two hundred thousand including Jackson & Beauregard. I shall have to contend against vastly superior odds if these reports be true. But this Army will do all in the power of men to hold their position & repulse any attack.

I regret my great inferiority in numbers but feel that I am in no way responsible for it as I have not failed to represent repeatedly the necessity of reinforcements, that this was the decisive point, & that all the available means of the Govt should be concentrated here. I will do all that a General can do with the splendid Army I have the honor to command & if it is destroyed by overwhelming numbers can at least die with it & share its fate.

But if the result of the action which will probably occur tomorrow or within a short time is a disaster the responsibility cannot be thrown on my shoulders — it must rest where it belongs.

Since I commenced this I have received additional intelligence confirming the supposition in regard to Jackson's movements & Beauregard's arrival. I shall probably be attacked tomorrow — & now go to the other side of the Chickahominy to arrange for the defense on that side.

I feel that there is no use in my again asking for reinforcements.[2]

G B McClellan
Maj Genl

Hon E M Stanton
Secty of War

ALS (telegram sent), McClellan Papers (A-68:27), Library of Congress. *OR*, Ser. 1, XI, Part 1, p. 51.

1. See GBM to Stanton, June 24, note 2, *supra.* 2. Lincoln replied on June 26 that this dispatch "suggesting the probability of your being overwhelmed by 200,000, and talking of where the responsibility will belong, pains me very much. I give you all I can, and act on the presumption that you will do the best you can with what you have, while you continue, ungenerously I think, to assume that I could give you more if I would. I have omitted and shall omit no opportunity to send you re-enforcements whenever I possibly can." *OR*, Ser. 1, XI, Part 3, p. 259.

To Ambrose E. Burnside [TELEGRAM]

[Camp Lincoln] Head Qrs
June 25 [1862, 7 P.M.]

To Maj Gen A. E. Burnside

Reports from contrabands and deserters today make it probable that Jackson's forces are coming to Richmond and that a part of Beauregard's force have arrived at Richmond. You will please advance on Goldsborough with all your available forces, at the earliest practicable moment. I wish you to understand that every minute in this crisis is of great importance. You will therefore reach Goldsborough as soon as possible destroying all the RR communications in the direction of Richmond in your power. If possible destroy some of the bridges on the Raleigh & Gaston RR and threaten Raleigh.[1]

G. B. McClellan

Copy, Records of the Office of the Secretary of War, RG 107 (M-473:103), National Archives. *OR*, Ser. 1, XI, Part 3, pp. 252–53.

1. The Goldsboro operation was abandoned in favor of reinforcing the Army of the Potomac. See GBM to John A. Dix, June 28, *infra*.

To Randolph B. Marcy [TELEGRAM]

Porter's Hd Qtrs June 25 [1862] 10 pm.

Urge Sumner & Heintzelman to cut as much timber as possible in front of their positions tonight & in the morning. Be sure to have the (8) eight inch howitzers all in position & well supplied with ammunition before morning. Also the four (4) Napoleon guns intended for the redoubts. Impress upon Sumner & especially Heintzelman that if an attack is made in force it must be awaited in the line of entrenchments — that the pickets are only to give warning & should be supported only sufficiently to prevent them from being driven in by a small force. If attacked by a large force they must at once fall back on the entrenchments, taking care to leave full play for the Artillery & as far as possible for the musketry as they retire. Sumner should occupy the rifle pits between Naglee's right & Hooker just before daylight by a sufficient force to hold against first attacks. The different parts of the line should be occupied so as to leave near one half the force disposable as reserves to strengthen the parts most vigorously attacked. I think that the mass of Birney's & Palmer's Brigades, as well as De Russy's two guns should at once be drawn behind the entrenchments if Heintzelman is confident that the enemy will attack in force in the morning — leaving merely the picket lines with rather more than the usual supports to hold the ground against any new attack by skirmishers & to observe the enemy.[1]

You cannot too strongly impress upon the Generals the fact that I wish to fight behind the lines if attacked in force, & that the force in front should be only sufficient to watch & resist heavy skirmishers.

Be sure that the timber is cut as much as possible tonight. Get a specific reply to this & be sure they understand it.

Geo B McClellan
Maj Genl Comdg

Genl R B Marcy
Chief of Staff

ALS (telegram sent), McClellan Papers (A-68:27), Library of Congress.

1. GBM had four army corps — those of Keyes, Heintzelman, Sumner, and Franklin — on the south, or Richmond, side of the Chickahominy, leaving only Porter's corps north of the river.

To Edwin M. Stanton [TELEGRAM]

Porter's Hd Qtrs [June 25, 1862] 10.40 pm

The information I receive on this side tends to confirm impression that Jackson will soon attack our right & rear. Every possible precaution is being taken. If I had another good Division I could laugh at Jackson. The task is difficult but this Army will do its best & will never disgrace the country. Nothing but overwhelming forces can defeat us. Indications are of attack on our front tomorrow. Have made all possible arrangements.

G B McClellan
Maj Genl

Hon E M Stanton
Secty of War

ALS (telegram sent), McClellan Papers (A-68:27), Library of Congress. *OR*, Ser. 1, XI, Part 3, p. 254.

To Stewart Van Vliet [TELEGRAM]

Camp Lincoln June 25 [1862] 10.45 pm[1]

Please be sure to push up all the provisions, grain & ammunition you can tonight & tomorrow.

We need much more ammunition for the (4 1/2) four & a half inch — say (600) six hundred rounds each & as much for Parrott (30) thirty pounders.

Leave nothing undone to accomplish this. Tell Kingsbury[2] to arrange to have a good supply of assorted ammunition afloat on James River with the provisions & forage.

G B McClellan
Maj Genl

Genl S Van Vliet
Chf Qtr Mr Head Qtrs

ALS (telegram sent), McClellan Papers (A-68:27), Library of Congress.

1. This telegram was actually sent from Gen. Porter's headquarters north of the Chickahominy River. 2. Col. Charles P. Kingsbury, chief of ordnance.

To Edwin M. Stanton [TELEGRAM]

Head Quarters, Army of the Potomac,
Camp Lincoln June 26 — 12m 1862

I have just heard that our advanced cavalry pickets on left bank of Chickahominy are being driven in — it is probably Jackson's advanced guard. If this be true you may not hear from me for some days as my communications will probably be cut off. The case is perhaps a difficult one but I shall resort to desperate measures & will do my best to out manoeuvre & outwit & outfight the enemy. Do not believe reports of disaster & do not be discouraged if you learn that my communications are cut & even Yorktown in possession of the enemy. Hope for the best & I will not deceive the hopes you formerly placed in me.

G B McClellan
Maj Genl

Hon E M Stanton
Secty of War

ALS (telegram sent), McClellan Papers (C-13:64), Library of Congress. *OR*, Ser. 1, XI, Part 1, pp. 51–52.

To Mary Ellen McClellan

June 26 [1862] 2 pm. Trent's

If you knew how tired I am you would not blame me if I did not write, but I cannot rest contented until I do write, if only a few lines. I telegraphed you yesterday twice & today.

We had quite a little affair yesterday. I wished to advance our picket line & met with a good deal of opposition. We succeeded fully however & gained the point with but little loss. The enemy fought pretty hard but our men did better. I was out there all day taking a personal direction of affairs & remained until about 5 1/2 pm. when I returned to camp, & met on my way the news that Stonewall Jackson was on his way to attack my right & rear. I rode over to Porter's soon after I reached camp & returned about 2 1/2 am. At 3 I started off again & went to the front where an attack was expected by some — finding all quiet I rode all along the line & returned here. You may imagine that I am *rather* tired out. I think that Jackson is en route to take us in rear — have just received the positive information that Jackson is en route to take us in rear — you probably will not hear for some days but do not be at all worried. . . .

AL copy; copy, McClellan Papers (C-7:63/D-10:72), Library of Congress.

To Louis M. Goldsborough [TELEGRAM]

Head-Quarters,
Department Army of Potomac
Flag Officer L. M. Goldsborough [Camp Lincoln] June 26th 1862.

Dispatch received. I take it for granted that Commander Rodgers will execute the service you alluded to before he visits me. On my return from the field yesterday I saw your reply to Genl Van Vliet. I regret your completely misunderstanding of the meaning of Genl Van Vliet's telegram & cannot understand how you could possibly draw from it the inference you did. I did send copies to Secretaries of Navy & War with the request that orders may be given to you that will insure a prompt complyance with such reasonable requests as I may make. The case of the Provision Transports in James River is a matter of vital importance to the safety of this Army & you will please pardon me for saying that I do not think this is a time for searching for points of etiquette & that the tone of your dispatch surprises me exceedingly — it has ever been my endeavor to treat you with the utmost deference & politeness, but my situation is at present too serious to permit me to stand on trifles.[1] I again request that the request made in my name by Genl Van Vliet in regard to transports in James River may be complied with. It is a matter of vital importance & may involve the existence of this Army.

Very Respy
Geo B McClellan
Maj Genl Comdg

Received copy, Office of Naval Records and Library, RG 45 (M-625 :86), National Archives. *NOR*, Ser. 1, VII, p. 510.

1. This contretemps grew out of Flag Officer Goldsborough's offense at the tone of a dispatch addressed to him by Quartermaster Van Vliet on June 23. While pledging his full cooperation with the army, Goldsborough wrote Secretary of the Navy Welles on June 27 that he hoped GBM might be enjoined on "the propriety of inculcating better official manners of addressing me as his equal in rank; and . . . not permitting an officer under his command to address me as a subordinate and refuse to confer upon me the denomination given me by law." *NOR*, Ser. 1, VII, pp. 500, 511–12.

To Fitz John Porter [TELEGRAM]

Camp Lincoln June 26 [1862] 3.15 pm

From all the information you give me it would seem best to hold your position at least until after dark.

I will hold everything in readiness here to move all available troops to your support when needed. We must save all baggage & guns. Keep me constantly informed & instruct your pickets etc to give you constant information. Let me know where Stoneman[1] is & in what direction he will retreat so that I may at once give the necessary orders to the troops at Tunstalls & White House. Give me your views in full & all you know as to the force of enemy now about to attack you. Tell me whether position of affairs is such that an attack on Old Tavern by Franklin would aid you.[2] Be prepared to throw everything over the Chickahominy if possible — better send your heavy baggage over as soon as possible. What is appearance of things near Mrs Prices' etc.

G B McClellan
Maj Genl Comdg

Genl F J Porter
Comdg 5th Corps

ALS (telegram sent), McClellan Papers (A-69 :27), Library of Congress.

1. Gen. Stoneman commanded the cavalry screening Porter's position. 2. A position south of the Chickahominy in the Confederate lines defending Richmond.

To Mary Ellen McClellan [TELEGRAM]

To Mrs. McClellan, Camp Lincoln June 26 [1862]
North Orange New Jersey 4.30 pm

Dear Nell. I may not be able to telegraph or write to you for some days. There will be great stampedes but do not be alarmed. I think the enemy are making a great mistake, if so they will be terribly punished. There will be severe fighting in a day or two but you may be sure that your husband will not disgrace you and I am confident that God will smile upon my efforts & give our arms success. You will hear that we are cut off, annihilated etc. Do not believe it but trust that success will crown our efforts. I tell you this darling only to guard against the agony you would feel if you trusted the newspaper reports. I give you my word that I believe we will surely win & that the enemy is falling into a trap. I shall allow the enemy to cut off our communications in order to ensure success.

G. B. McC

Eckert: Send to her in cipher if cant send it some way privately & regard strictly confidential. Answer.[1]

Retained copy, McClellan Papers (C-10 :63), Library of Congress.

1. Maj. Thomas T. Eckert, supervisor of military telegrams, replied that evening: "I will forward your message to Mrs. McClellan confidentially & from time to time send her such information as I know would receive your sanction. She shall not suffer for want of news in your temporary exile. . . . " McClellan Papers (A-107 :42).

To Edwin M. Stanton [TELEGRAM]

Head Quarters, Army of the Potomac,
Porters Hd Qtrs June 26 1862 7.40 pm

A very heavy engagement in progress just in front of me. McCall & (2) two Brigades of Morell are fighting gallantly against superior numbers so far with marked success.[1] There is no longer any doubt as to the strength of attack on this (left) bank of Chickahominy. My men are behaving superbly. But you must not expect them to contest too long against great odds. The engagement is very serious & is just below Mechanicsville.[2] You may rely upon this Army doing all that men can do. I still keep communication with White House but it may be cut any moment & I cannot prevent it.

G B McClellan
Maj Genl

Hon E M Stanton

ALS (telegram sent), McClellan Papers (A-69 :27), Library of Congress. *OR*, Ser. 1, XI, Part 3, p. 259.

1. Brig. Gens. George A. McCall and George W. Morell commanded two of Porter's divisions.
2. The fighting this day would be termed the Battle of Mechanicsville.

To Edwin M. Stanton [TELEGRAM]

Hon E M Stanton
Sec of War Porter's June 26 8 pm 1862

Engagement still continues with great vigor. The enemy have not gained a foot & McCall is doing splendidly. He is showing that his Division is equal to the veterans of the Army of Potomac. Rebel forces very large but our position good & our men as brave as can be. The stragglers are all to the front. Not one to the rear. Morell's men just as McCall's. Dispatch as to reinforcements this moment read.[1] I thank you for them. I am rejoiced that the troops in front of Washington are to be placed under one command. Keep at that & all will be well. I will answer for it that this Army will do all that the Country expects of it.

G B McClellan
Maj. Genl.

Retained copy, McClellan Papers (A-69 :27), Library of Congress. *OR*, Ser. 1, XI, Part 3, p. 260.

1. Stanton's telegram of this date promised 5,000 reinforcements. "They will be followed by more, if needed. McDowell's, Banks', and Fremont's force will be consolidated as the Army of Virginia, and will operate promptly in your aid by land." *OR*, Ser. 1, XI, Part 1, p. 52.

To Mary Ellen McClellan [TELEGRAM]

Head Quarters, Army of the Potomac,
[Porter's Headquarters] June 26 8.15 pm. 1862

We have again whipped secesh badly. McCall & Morell are the heroes of the day. Stonewall Jackson is the victim this time.

G B McClellan
Maj Genl

Mrs. G B McClellan
Care Dr E E Marcy North Orange New Jersey

ALS (telegram sent), McClellan Papers (A-69:27), Library of Congress.

To Randolph B. Marcy [TELEGRAM]

Head Quarters, Army of the Potomac,
Porters 9 pm [June 26] 1862

We have completely gained the day — not lost a single foot of ground.
McCall has done splendidly as well as Morell.

Tell our men on your side that they are put to their trumps & that with such men disaster is impossible.

Geo B McClellan

Genl R B Marcy
Chf Staff

ALS (telegram sent), McClellan Papers (A-69:27), Library of Congress.

To Edwin M. Stanton [TELEGRAM]

Head Quarters, Army of the Potomac,
Porter's Bivouac June 26 1862 9 pm

The firing has nearly ceased. I have nearly everything in the way of impediments on the other side of Chickahominy & hope to be ready for anything tomorrow. Please see that Goldsborough complies promptly with my requests. Victory of today complete & against great odds. I almost begin to think we are invincible.

G B McClellan
Maj Genl

Hon E M Stanton
Secty of War

ALS (telegram sent), McClellan Papers (A-69:27), Library of Congress. *OR*, Ser. 1, XI, Part 3, p. 260.

To Edwin M. Stanton [TELEGRAM]

Head-Quarters, Army of the Potomac,
Camp Lincoln [June] 27 10 am 1862

The night passed quietly. During it we brought all wagons, heavy guns etc to this side and at day break drew in McCall's Division about three miles. This change of position was beautifully executed under a sharp fire with but little loss.

The troops on the other side are now well in hand & the whole Army so concentrated that it can take advantage of the first mistake made by the enemy.

White House as yet undisturbed. Success of yesterday complete.

G B McClellan
Maj Genl

Hon E M Stanton
Secty of War

ALS (telegram sent), McClellan Papers (A-70:28), Library of Congress. *OR,* Ser. 1, XI, Part 3, p. 264.

To Edwin M. Stanton [TELEGRAM]

Camp Lincoln June 27 [1862] 12m

My change of position on other side just in time. Heavy attack now being made by Jackson & two other Divisions.[1] Expect attacks also on this side.

G B McClellan
Maj Genl

Hon E M Stanton
Secty of War

ALS (telegram sent), McClellan Papers (A-70:28), Library of Congress, *OR,* Ser. 1, XI, Part 3, p. 264.

1. The fighting on June 27 would be called the Battle of Gaines's Mill.

To Mary Ellen McClellan [TELEGRAM]

Mrs. G B McClellan [Camp Lincoln, June 27, 1862]
Care Dr E E Marcy North Orange NJ 1:15 pm

Dispatch rec'd. Heavy firing in all directions. So far we have repulsed them everywhere. I expect wire to be cut every moment. All well & very busy. Cannot write today.

G B McClellan

Received copy (War Dept.), Records of the Office of the Secretary of War, RG 107 (M-504:66), National Archives.

To Edwin M. Stanton [TELEGRAM]

Head-Quarters, Army of the Potomac,
[Camp Lincoln] June 27 1 pm 1862

Your dispatch of noon received. I thank you for it.

We are contending at several points against superior numbers. The enemy evince much desperation but as we have no choice but to win you may be sure that we will do all that can be expected. Thus far we have been successful but I think the most severe struggle is to come. The enemy neglects White House thus far & bestows his whole attention on us. If I am forced to concentrate between the Chickahominy & James I will at once endeavor to open communications with you. All reinforcements should for the present go to Fort Monroe to which point I will send orders. It is absolutely certain that Jackson, Ewell & Whiting are here. As this may be the last dispatch I send you for some time I will beg that you put some one General in command of the Shenandoah & of all the troops in front of Washington. For the sake of the country secure unity of action & bring the best men forward. Good bye & present my respects to the President.

G B McClellan
Maj Genl

Hon E M Stanton
Secty of War

ALS (telegram sent), McClellan Papers (A-70:28), Library of Congress, *OR*, Ser. 1, XI, Part 3, pp. 264–65.

To William B. Franklin [TELEGRAM]

Brig. Gen W B Franklin [Camp Lincoln] June 27th 1862

If you see a chance to go over the Duane bridge and take the enemy in flank please do it. I will support you with something.[1]

G B McClellan
Maj Genl

Retained copy, McClellan Papers (A-70:28), Library of Congress.

1. Franklin replied that crossing the Chickahominy for a flank attack was impossible, for he had destroyed the bridge when the enemy threatened to capture it. McClellan Papers (A-70:28).

To Fitz John Porter [TELEGRAM]

To Genl F J Porter Camp Lincoln [June 27, 1862] 3.25 pm

Slocum is now crossing Alexander's Bridge with his whole command. Enemy have commenced on Infantry attack on Smith's left.[1] I have ordered down Sumner & Heintzelmans reserves & you can count on the whole of Slocum. Go on as you have begun.

G B McClellan
Maj Genl

ALS (telegram sent), McClellan Papers (A-48:19), Library of Congress. *OR,* Ser. 1, XI, Part 1, p. 58.

1. Brig. Gen. Henry W. Slocum commanded a division in Franklin's corps. Franklin's other division, under Brig. Gen. William F. Smith, remained south of the Chickahominy.

To Fitz John Porter [TELEGRAM]

To Brig Genl F J Porter [Camp Lincoln] June 27th 1862

Gen Slocum's Division has gone over to support you. If the enemy are retiring and you are a chasseur, pitch in.[1]

G B McClellan
Maj Genl

Retained copy, McClellan Papers (A-70:28), Library of Congress.

1. This may have been sent in response to a report from Capt. George A. Custer that there was a pause in the attack on Porter and the enemy appeared to be retiring. GBM to Franklin, McClellan Papers (A-70:28).

To Fitz John Porter [TELEGRAM]

General Fitz John Porter,
Commanding Fifth Corps: Camp Lincoln, June 27, 1862 — 4.30 p.m.

Your dispatch of 4.10 received.[1] Send word to all your troops that their general thanks them for their heroism, and says to them that he is now sure that nothing can resist them. Their conduct and your own has been magnificent, and another name is added to their banners. Give my regulars a good chance. I look upon to-day as decisive of the war. Try to drive the rascals and take some prisoners and guns. What more assistance do you require?

Ever yours
McClellan

OR, Ser. 1, XI, Part 3, p. 265.

1. Probably Porter's message that he had "just returned from the whole front and found everything most satisfactory.... Our men have behaved nobly and driven back the enemy many times, cheering them as they retired...." McClellan Papers (A-69:27), Library of Congress.

To Fitz John Porter [TELEGRAM]

To Genl F J Porter Camp Lincoln 5.30 pm [June 27] 1862

Hold your own.[1] Eight regts from Sumner move at once to your support. Probably a Brigade from Smith, & certainly one from Couch. You must beat them if I move the whole Army to do it & transfer all on this side.

G B McClellan
Maj Genl

ALS (telegram sent), McClellan Papers (A-69:27), Library of Congress.

1. About 5:00 P.M. Porter telegraphed: "I am pressed hard, very hard. About every Regiment I have has been in action," and added that without assistance "I am afraid I shall be driven from my position." McClellan Papers (A-69:27).

To Edwin M. Stanton [TELEGRAM]

Camp Lincoln June 27 8 p.m. 1862

Have had a terrible contest — attacked by greatly superior numbers in all directions. On this side we still hold our own, though a very heavy fire is still kept up.

On the left bank of Chickahominy the odds have been immense. We hold our own very nearly. I may be forced to give up my position during the night, but will not if it is possible to avoid it. Had I (20,000) twenty thousand fresh & good troops we would be sure of a splendid victory tomorrow. My men have fought magnificently.

G B McClellan
Maj Genl

Hon E M Stanton
Secty of War

ALS (telegram sent), McClellan Papers (A-70:28), Library of Congress. *OR*, Ser. 1, XI, Part 3, p. 266.

To Mary Ellen McClellan [TELEGRAM]

Mrs. McClellan Camp Lincoln 8 pm June 27th [1862]

Have had a terrible fight against vastly superior numbers. Have generally held our own & we may thank God that the Army of the Potomac has not lost its honor. It is impossible as yet to tell what the result is. I am well but tired out. No sleep for two nights & none tonight. God bless you.

G. B. McC

Retained copy, McClellan Papers (C-10:63), Library of Congress.

To Samuel P. Heintzelman [TELEGRAM]

To Brig Genl S P Heintzelman [Camp Lincoln] June 27 1862

On the other side of the Chickahominy the day is lost. You must hold your position at all cost.

G B McClellan
Maj Genl Comdg

Retained copy, McClellan Papers (A-70:28), Library of Congress.

To Louis M. Goldsborough [TELEGRAM]

Flag Officer Goldsborough
Norfolk

Head Quarters, Army of the Potomac,
[Camp Lincoln] June [27] 1862 10.30 pm

I desire you will send some light draft gun boats at once up the Chickahominy as far as possible, and also that you will forthwith instruct the gun boats on the James River to cover the left flank of this Army. I should be glad to have the gun boats proceed as far up the river as may be practicable, & hope they may get in as far as the vicinity of Newmarket.

We have met a severe repulse to day having been attacked by vastly superior numbers, and I am obliged to fall back between the Chickahominy and the James River.

I look to you to give me all the support you can, in covering my flanks as well as in giving protection to my supplies afloat in James River.[1]

G. B. McClellan
Maj Gen

Retained copy, McClellan Papers (A-71:28), Library of Congress. *OR*, Ser. 1, XI, Part 3, p. 267.

1. Goldsborough replied at 1:00 A.M. on June 28: "Without a moment's delay instructions shall be communicated to Commander Rodgers to comply immediately with all you desire." *OR*, Ser. 1, XI, Part 3, pp. 268–69.

To Edwin M. Stanton [TELEGRAM]

Savage Station June 28 [1862] 12.20 am

I now know the full history of the day [June 27]. On this side of the river — the right bank — we repulsed several very strong attacks. On the left bank our men did all that men could do, all that soldiers could accomplish — but they were overwhelmed by vastly superior numbers even after I brought my last reserves into action. The loss on both sides is terrible — I believe it will prove to be the most desperate battle of the war. The sad remnants of my men behave as men — those battalions who fought most bravely & suffered most are still in the best order. My regulars were superb & I count upon what are left to turn another battle in company with their gallant comrades of the Volunteers. Had I (20,000) twenty thousand or even (10,000) ten thousand fresh troops to use tomorrow I could take Richmond, but I have not a man in reserve & shall be glad to cover my retreat & save the material & personnel of the Army.

If we have lost the day we have yet preserved our honor & no one need blush for the Army of the Potomac. I have lost this battle because my force was too small. I again repeat that I am not responsible for this & I say it with the earnestness of a General who feels in his heart the loss of every brave man who has been needlessly sacrificed today. I still hope to retrieve our fortunes, but to do this the Govt must view the matter in the same earnest light that I do — you must send me very large reinforcements, & send them at once.

I shall draw back to this side of the Chickahominy & think I can withdraw all our material. Please understand that in this battle we have lost nothing but men & those the best we have.

In addition to what I have already said I only wish to say to the Presdt that I think he is wrong, in regarding me as ungenerous when I said that my force was too weak.[1] I merely reiterated a truth which today has been too plainly proved. I should have gained this battle with (10,000) ten thousand fresh men. If at this instant I could dispose of (10,000) ten thousand fresh men I could gain the victory tomorrow.

I know that a few thousand men more would have changed this battle from a defeat to a victory — as it is the Govt must not & cannot hold me responsible for the result.

I feel too earnestly tonight — I have seen too many dead & wounded comrades to feel otherwise than that the Govt has not sustained this Army. If you do not do so now the game is lost.

If I save this Army now I tell you plainly that I owe no thanks to you or any other persons in Washington — you have done your best to sacrifice this Army.[2]

G B McClellan

Hon E M Stanton

ALS (telegram sent), McClellan Papers (A-71:28), Library of Congress. *OR*, Ser. 1, XI, Part 1, p. 61.

1. See GBM to Stanton, June 25, 6:15 P.M., note 2, *supra*. 2. Shocked by this concluding paragraph, Edward S. Sanford, head of the War Department's telegraphic office, had the deciphered telegram recopied without the offending sentence before delivering it to Stanton. David H. Bates, *Lincoln in the Telegraph Office* (New York, 1907), pp. 108–109. The president replied on this date: "Save your Army at all events. Will send re-inforcements as fast as we can.... I have not said you were ungenerous for saying you needed re-inforcement. I thought you were ungenerous in assuming that I did not send them as fast as I could. I feel any misfortune to you and your Army quite as keenly as you feel it yourself. If you have had a drawn battle, or a repulse, it is the price we pay for the enemy not being in Washington. We protected Washington, and the enemy concentrated on you...." *Collected Works of Lincoln*, V, pp. 289–90.

To Mary Ellen McClellan [TELEGRAM]

Mrs. McClellan [Savage's Station] June 28 '62

Dear Nell. We are well tonight. I fear your uncle has been seriously hurt in the terrible battle of yesterday. They have outnumbered us every where but we have not lost our honor. The Army has acted magnificently. I thank my friends in Washn for our repulse. Clitz is badly wounded.[1]

Geo. B. McClellan

Retained copy, McClellan Papers (C-10 :63), Library of Congress.

1. Maj. Henry B. Clitz, 12th U.S. Infantry.

To John A. Dix [TELEGRAM]

Gen. J. A. Dix Fort Monroe [Savage's Station, June 28, 1862]

Please send a message to Gen. Burnside not to move on Goldsboro' but to have everything ready to move to Fort Monroe. Col. Ingalls Q.M. and Cap. Bell[1] Commissary will go to Fort Monroe. Please direct them to push up supplies to the gun boats on James River.

Geo. B. McClellan
Maj. Gen.

Copy, Fitz John Porter Papers, Library of Congress. Gen. Dix took command at Fort Monroe on June 3.

1. Capt. George Bell.

To John A. Dix

Head Quarters, Army of the Potomac,
In field June 29 1862, 2 o'clock PM

This will be sent by Genl Keyes who is on our left. Please send up to the front he occupies a large number of entrenching tools — viz axes, shovels & picks. Send up also whatever reinforcements arrive.

We have had desperate work & a most terrible battle, but I hope by tonight to have my line based on James River. Thus far I have saved all the heavy guns & hope to save all my wagons. I need all the reinforcements that can be sent. Pray take good care of Yorktown — that must be made perfectly secure at once. If necessary abandon Williamsburg & let the troops now there fall back on Yorktown. This army has behaved nobly. We are all worn out & tired to death but retain strength enough to take Richmond. May God forgive the men who have caused the loss this army has experienced.

It is now clear beyond a doubt that 20,000 more men would have given us a glorious victory. I for one can never forget nor forgive the selfish men who have caused the lives of so many gallant men to be sacrificed. I have at least one proud consolation & that is that the Army of the Potomac has preserved its honor. We may not yet be safe & the whole of this army may be sacrificed — but I have at least the satisfaction of a clear conscience.

If we get through this it will be better for you to keep this to yourself as confidential — if I lose my life make such use of it as you deem best.

Ever your friend,
McClellan
Maj Genl

Genl J A Dix

ALS, Dix Papers, Rare Book and Manuscript Library, Columbia University.

To Mary Ellen McClellan

Head Quarters, Army of the Potomac
In the field June 29 [1862] 3 pm.

My own dear Nelly

I send you only this line to say that I still think God is with us. We have fought a terrible battle against overwhelming numbers. We held our own & history will know that I have done all that man can do. Your uncle is killed.[1] I fear my telegraph about that has not reached you.

Please break the news to Frank & Maria as gently as you can & say to them that you & I will stand in the place of their father & husband. Poor fellow, he died gallantly & like a true soldier. I feel now that I will still retrieve our fortunes & that God will smile upon me. We will trust him.

Your loving husband,
Geo

ALS, McClellan Papers (B-11:48), Library of Congress.

1. Maj. Nathan B. Rossell, U.S. 3rd Infantry.

To Randolph B. Marcy

June 30, 1862
Haxall's house Turkey Island[1]

Please bring Hd Qrs down here. The wagons have been down towards Harrison's bar — 6 miles below here. Navy men say we must occupy a point below City Pt in order to enable us to use transports. Let all the Engineers & Topo Engrs go to work to examine the point on which we must take up our new position. The probability is we must take up a new line parallel to that we now hold and come down the River below City Point. Send back to Smith and ascertain how much more of the train is yet to move. Also ascertain what roads exist leading from our present position e.g. from White Oak bridge to Long Bridge & Jones Bridge.

G B McClellan
Maj Genl

ALS, McClellan Papers (A-71:28), Library of Congress.

1. On the James River, behind Malvern Hill.

To Edwin M. Stanton [TELEGRAM]

Hon Edwin M. Stanton Turkey Bridge June 30th [1862] 7 pm[1]

Another day of desperate fighting.[2] We are hard pressed by superior numbers. I fear I shall be forced to abandon my material to save my men under cover of the Gun Boats. You must send us very large reinforcements by way of Fort Monroe and they must come very promptly. My Army has behaved superbly and have done all that men could do. If none of us escape we shall at least have done honor to the country. I shall do my best to save the Army. Send more Gun Boats.[3]

G. B. McClellan
Maj Genl Commanding

Received copy, Lincoln Papers, Library of Congress. *OR*, Ser. 1, XI, Part 3, p. 280.

1. Telegrams from this period were delivered by navy vessels for sending over the Fort Monroe line. 2. The fighting on June 30 took place at Glendale. 3. President Lincoln replied on July 1: "It is impossible to re-inforce you for your present emergency. If we had a million of men we could not get them to you in time.... Maintain your ground if you can; but save the Army at all events, even if you fall back to Fortress-Monroe. We still have strength enough in the country, and will bring it out." *Collected Works of Lincoln*, V, p. 298.

To Mary Ellen McClellan [TELEGRAM]

Headquarters Army of the Potomac
Turkey Bridge 7 pm. June 30 [1862]

I am well but worn out — no sleep for many days. We have been fighting for many days & are still at it. I still hope to save the army.

None of our especial friends lost except your poor uncle who was killed on Friday [June 27] in the battle of Gaines Mill. We have fought every day for five days. Good bye dear Nell & God bless you.

G B. McClellan
Maj Genl

Mrs G B McClellan
Care Dr E E Marcy
South Orange New Jersey

ALS (telegram sent), McClellan Papers (B-11:48), Library of Congress.

To Lorenzo Thomas [TELEGRAM]

Turkey Island July 1st [1862] 2.40
L. Thomas, Adjt Genl Tuesday morning[1]

Another desperate combat today [June 30]. Our reinforcements repulsed the enemy. I was sending orders to renew the combat tomorrow [July 1], fearing the consequences of further retreat in the exhausted condition of the reinforcements, & being as willing to stake the last chance of battle in that position as any other under the circumstances, when I learned that the right had fallen back, after dark, & that the centre was following. I have taken steps to adopt a new line, the left resting on Turkey Island, & thence along a ridge parallel to James River as far as I have the force to hold it. Rodgers will do all that can be done to cover my flanks. I will probably be obliged to change the line in a few days, when I have rested the men, for one lower down & extending from the Chickahominy to the James River. If it is the intention of the Government to reinforce me largely, it should be done promptly, and in mass. I need fifty thousand *50,000* more men, and with them I will retrieve our fortunes. More would be well, but that number sent at once, will, I think enable me to assume the offensive. I cannot too strongly urge the necessity of prompt action in this matter. Even a few thousand fresh men within the next twenty four or forty eight hours, will do much towards relieving & encouraging this wearied army, which has been engaged in constant combat for the last five or six days. I must apologize for the incoherency of this letter. I am exhausted by want of sleep and constant anxiety for many days.[2]

Very Respcty Yours
Geo B McClellan
Maj Genl

Received copy, Records of the Office of the Secretary of War, RG 107 (M-473:50), National Archives. *OR,* Ser. 1, XI, Part 3, p. 281.

1. This dispatch was written on Malvern Hill about midnight on June 30, and later marked for sending from army headquarters on the James. 2. On July 2 Lincoln replied, in part: "Allow me to reason with you a moment. When you ask for fifty thousand men to be promptly sent you, you surely labor under some gross mistake of fact. . . . All of Fremont in the valley, all of Banks, all of McDowell, not with you, and all in Washington, taken together do not exceed, if they reach sixty thousand. . . . Thus, the idea of sending you fifty thousand, or any other considerable force promptly, is simply absurd. . . . If you think you are not strong enough to take Richmond just now, I do not ask you to try just now. Save the Army, material and personal; and I will strengthen it for the offensive again, as fast as I can." *Collected Works of Lincoln,* V, p. 301.

To Mary Ellen McClellan

July 1 [1862] Haxall's Plantation

... The whole army is here — worn out & war worn — after a week of daily battles. I have still very great confidence in them & they in me — the dear fellows cheer me as of old as they march to certain death & I feel prouder of them than ever.

I am completely exhausted — no sleep for days — my mind almost worn out — yet I *must* go through it. I still trust that God will give me success & I cheerfully entrust to his will....

AL copy, McClellan Papers (C-7 :63), Library of Congress.

To Lorenzo Thomas [TELEGRAM]

Brig Genl L Thomas
Adjt Genl USA
Genl

Hd Qtrs Army of Potomac
Haxall's Plantation July 1/62

My whole army is here with all its guns & material. The battle of yesterday was very severe — but the enemy were repulsed & severely punished. After dark the troops retired to this position. My men are completely exhausted & I dread the result if we are attacked today by fresh troops. If possible I shall retire tonight to Harrison's Bar where the gun boats can render more aid in covering our positions. Permit me to urge that not an hour should be lost in sending me fresh troops. More gun boats are much needed. I hope that the enemy was so severely handled yesterday as to render him careful in his movements today — I now pray for time. My men have proved themselves the equals of any troops in the world — but they are worn out. Our losses have been very great. I doubt whether more severe battles have ever been fought — we have failed to win only because overpowered by superior numbers.

Very truly yours
Geo B McClellan
Maj Genl

ALS, James S. Schoff Collection, William L. Clements Library, University of Michigan. *OR*, Ser. 1, XI, Part 3, p. 282.

To John A. Dix

Genl J A Dix
Comdg at Fort Monroe
My dear General

Hd Qtrs Army Potomac
Haxhall's Plantation July 1/62

Will you do me the favor to urge forward with the utmost rapidity whatever reinforcements arrive for this Army — we need them much, &

the arrival of even a thousand fresh men would do much towards reviving the worn out men under my command. They have fought every day for a week — are exhausted by want of food & sleep — & long marches.

Urge Casey & all others who command reinforcements to bring them up to Harrison's Bar at once.

My whole command is here — we have preserved our material & guns — but my men are in no condition to fight without 24 hours rest — I pray that the enemy may not be in condition to disturb us today. If left quiet I will move tonight to Harrison's Bar where the gun boats can render more efficient aid.

Very truly your friend
Geo B McClellan
Maj Genl

ALS, Dix Papers, Rare Book and Manuscript Library, Columbia University.

To Abraham Lincoln [TELEGRAM]

Berkeley, Harrison's Bar
Hon A Lincoln President US July 2nd [1862] 5.30 pm

I have succeeded in getting this Army to this place on the banks of the James River. I have lost but one gun which had to be abandoned last night because it broke down. An hour and a half ago the rear of the wagon train was within a mile of Camp and only one wagon abandoned. As usual we had a severe battle yesterday and beat the Enemy badly, the men fighting even better than before.[1] We fell back to this position during the night and morning. Officers and men thoroughly worn out by fighting every day and working every night for a week. They are in good spirits and after a little rest will fight better than ever. If not attacked during this day I will have the men ready to repulse the Enemy tomorrow. General Ferry is here.[2] Our losses have been very heavy for we have fought every day since last Tuesday. I have not yielded an inch of ground unnecessarily but have retired to prevent the superior force of the Enemy from cutting me off — and to take a different base of operations.

I thank you for the reinforcements. Every thousand men you send at once will help me much.[3]

G B McClellan
Maj Genl

Received copy, Lincoln Papers, Library of Congress. *OR,* Ser. 1, XI, Part 3, pp. 287–88.

1. The Battle of Malvern Hill. 2. Brig. Gen. Orris S. Ferry brought 5,000 reinforcements from Alexandria, the vanguard of Gen. Shields's division from the Shenandoah Valley. 3. Lincoln replied on July 3: "I am satisfied that yourself, officers and men have done the best you could. All accounts say better fighting was never done. Ten thousand thanks for

it. . . . We hope you will have help from him [Burnside] soon. To day we have ordered Gen. Hunter to send you all he can spare. At last advices Halleck thinks he can not send reinforcements, without endangering all he has gained.'' *Collected Works of Lincoln,* V, p. 303.

To Mary Ellen McClellan

July 2 [1862] 11 pm. Steamer Ariel

. . . I will now take a few moments from the rest which I really need & write at least a few words. . . .

We have had a terrible time. On Wednesday [June 25] the serious work commenced. I commenced driving the enemy on our left & by hard fighting gained my point. Before that affair was over I received news that Jackson was probably about to attack my right. I galloped back to camp, took a fresh horse & went over to Porter's camp where I remained all night making the best arrangements I could, & returned about daybreak to look out for the left. On Thursday afternoon Jackson began his attack on McCall, who was supported by Porter. Jackson being repulsed, I went over there in the afternoon & remained until 2 or 3 am. I was satisfied that Jackson would have force enough next morning to turn Porter's right, so I removed all the wagons, heavy guns etc during the night & caused Porter to fall back to a point nearer the force on the other side of the Chickahominy. This was most handsomely effected — all our material being saved. The next day Porter was attacked in his new position by the whole force of Jackson, Longstreet, Ewell, Hill & Whiting. I sent what supports I could — but was at the same time attacked on my own front & could only spare 7 Brigades. With these we held our own at all points after most desperate fighting. It was on this day that your poor uncle was gallantly leading his rgt — he was struck in the breast & died in a few hours. Clitz fell that day also.

John Reynolds[1] was taken prisoner. I was forced that night to withdraw Porter's force to my side of the Chickahominy & therefore to make a very dangerous & difficult movement to reach the James River. I *must* say good night now, for I am very tired, & may require all my energies tomorrow.

AL copy, McClellan Papers (C-7:63), Library of Congress.

1. Brig. Gen. John F. Reynolds, a brigade commander in McCall's division.

SIX

HARRISON'S LANDING
JULY 3–AUGUST 23, 1862

DURING THE seven weeks that followed the Army of the Potomac's arrival at Harrison's Landing, the Federal war effort in the East remained stalled on dead center. These were weeks of waiting and frustration for McClellan. He spent his time trying to restore the morale and strength of his army and debating with the government the proper strategy for pressing the war. In numerous private letters — thirty-four of the seventy-seven pieces of correspondence in this section — he excused the failure of his Peninsula campaign and, in increasingly vitriolic terms, laid blame for the failure on the administration in Washington.

Since reducing McClellan to the command of only the Army of the Potomac, President Lincoln and Secretary of War Stanton had attempted to manage the war without a general-in-chief. In the wake of the defeat before Richmond they found themselves in need of professional military advice, and on July 11 Lincoln named Henry Halleck to be general-in-chief. When he assumed the position on July 23, Halleck found a situation he regarded as highly dangerous.

General John Pope's Army of Virginia, newly assembled from the various forces that fought unsuccessfully against Stonewall Jackson in the Shenandoah Valley earlier in the year, was posted in northern Virginia with responsibility for guarding Washington. McClellan's army on the James, some twenty-five miles from Richmond, was well beyond supporting distance of Pope. Between them was Lee's Army of Northern Virginia, its strength appraised by McClellan at 200,000 men. Foreseeing that with a force that great Lee could strike at first one and then the other of the two widely separated Federal armies, Halleck ordered McClellan to evacuate the Peninsula and combine his army with Pope's. A primary reason for his decision was McClellan's letter to him of July 26, which in its demand for 50,000 to 55,000 reinforcements more than doubled the number McClellan had agreed at their Harrison's Landing meeting would meet his needs.

In his anger and disgust at the situation, General McClellan expressed his views of men and events with more candor and force than at probably any other time during the war. His famous Harrison's Landing letter to Lincoln (July 7) gave an exposition of his political stance on war issues that was outspoken enough to become a widely distributed campaign document during his 1864 presidential bid. Letters to Samuel Barlow, the New York Democratic leader, were unsparing in their attacks on the Lincoln administration. Letters to his wife were filled with equally unsparing opinions of Secretary Stanton and of Generals Pope and Halleck.

A recurring theme in the letters to Mrs. McClellan that summer was his frequent musing on the will of God. To George McClellan, all fortune, whether ill or good, was an expression of God's will. His reverses on the battlefield and the slurs he suffered at the hands of his enemies on the home front must have, he believed, some ultimately wise purpose, and it led him to conclude (July 10), "If I had succeeded in taking Richmond now the fanatics of the North might have been too powerful & reunion impossible. However that may be I am sure that it is all for the best." He did admit (August 22) that with so many contrary events taking place, "it is often difficult to understand the ways of Providence. . . ."

The pace at which the Army of the Potomac evacuated the Peninsula would become a matter of heated controversy. The underlying but unstated element in the correspondence between McClellan and Halleck on the subject is the differing perspectives of the two men. Halleck, expecting an attack on Pope at any moment, wanted an immediate and steady flow of reinforcements from the Army of the Potomac. McClellan, expecting the Rebels' attack to fall on him if he made the least slip during his retreat down the Peninsula, hoarded his forces for defense throughout his preparations. He then withdrew virtually the entire army from Harrison's Landing in one movement, with consequent delays in shipping the troops northward. It was yet one more result of his belief in overwhelming Confederate numbers.

To Edwin M. Stanton

Hon E M Stanton
Secty of War
Sir:

Head Quarters Army of Potomac
Harrison's Bar July 3 1862

In order to ensure a perfect understanding of the exact condition of this Army I have directed my Chief of Staff, Genl R B Marcy, to repair to Washington & give you full explanations of the events of last few weeks.

A simple summary is that this Army has fought every day for a week against superior numbers, holding its own, at least, often repulsing the enemy by day, then retiring at night. Our light & heavy guns are saved, with the exception of one; all the wagons are now within the line of pickets — & I hope will all be saved. The Army is thoroughly worn out & requires rest & very heavy reinforcements.

Our losses have been very great — for the fighting has been desperate, & officers and men have behaved heroically.

I am in hopes that the enemy is as completely worn out as we are; he was certainly very severely punished in the last battle; the roads are now very bad — for these reasons I hope that we shall [have] enough breathing space to reorganize & rest the men, & get them into position before the enemy can attack again. I have ordered Burnside to bring up all his available force, & leave to your judgment the question of evacuating Newbern & its dependencies so as to bring every available man to reinforce this Army. It is of course impossible to estimate as yet our losses — but I doubt whether there are today more than 50,000 men with their colors.

To accomplish the great task of capturing Richmond & putting an end to this rebellion reinforcements should be sent to me rather much over than much less than 100,000 men.

I beg that you will be fully impressed by the magnitude of the crisis in which we are placed — we require action on a gigantic scale — one commensurate with the view I expressed in a memorandum to the Presdt submitted early last August[1] — when first ordered to command the Army of the Potomac. The safety of the country & the preservation of its honor demand the utmost energy & intelligence.[2]

I am very respectfully your obdt svt
Geo B McClellan
Maj Genl Comdg

ALS, Houghton Library, Harvard University. *OR*, Ser. 1, XI, Part 3, pp. 291–92.

1. GBM to Lincoln, Aug. 2, 1861, *supra*. 2. The president wrote GBM on July 4: "I understand your position as stated in your letter, and by Gen. Marcy. To reinforce you so as to enable you to resume the offensive within a month, or even six weeks, is impossible.... Under these circumstances the defensive, for the present, must be your only care.

Save the Army — first, where you are, if you *can;* and secondly, by removal, if you must. . . . P.S. If, at any time, you feel able to take the offensive, you are not restrained from doing so.'' *Collected Works of Lincoln,* V, pp. 305–306.

To Randolph B. Marcy [TELEGRAM]

Head-Quarters Berkeley July 4 62

After I left you I went at once to the front & found chaos. I rode in advance of the troops halted everything — selected the positions for myself. Moved Smith at double quick to seize the key point & rapidly got the troops in position. The positions are now occupied by three Corps, two in reserve — the ground is in advance of Barnard's line & is partly on the dangerous hills beyond Herring Creek. I am now ready to fight. In twenty hours more shall be secure. Troops in splendid spirits. All now goes well. Had a long telegram from the Presdt[1] which quite discourages me as it shows a fatal want of appreciation of the glorious achievements of this Army, & of the circumstances of the case, as well as of the causes which led to it. I will save this Army & lead it to victory in spite of all enemies in all directions.

G B. McClellan

Brig Genl R B Marcy Washington
Care Stager or Eckert[2]

ALS (telegram sent), McClellan Papers (A-72:29), Library of Congress.

1. See GBM to Lorenzo Thomas, July 1, 1862, note 2, *supra,* 2. Anson Stager and Thomas T. Eckert, of the military telegraph office.

To Mary Ellen McClellan

July 4 [1862] Berkeley's

. . . You will understand before this reaches you the glorious yet fearful events which have prevented me from writing. . . .

We have fine weather today, which is drying the ground rapidly. I was quite stampeded yesterday just before your Father left — a report came to me that the enemy were advancing in overwhelming numbers, & that none of my orders for placing the troops in position & reorganizing them had been carried out. I at once rode through the troops, clear in front of them — to let them see there was no danger — they began to cheer as usual, & called out that they were all right & would fall to the last man ''for little Mac''! I saw at once where the trouble was — halted all the commands — looked at the ground, & made up my mind what the true position was — started Smith at a double quick to seize the key point, followed by a Battery of Horse Artillery at a gallop — they went up most beautifully — opened on the enemy, drove him off after 18 rounds & finally held the place. I pushed Slocum's Divn up in support — hurried off Heintzelman's Corps to take its position on Franklin's left, supported by Keyes still further to the left, & came back to camp a little before dark with a light heart for the first time in many days. I am ready for an attack now — give me 24 hours even & I will defy all Secessia — if they will let my men rest 3 days I will begin to press them. The movement has been a magnificent one — I have saved all our material, have fought every day for a week & marched every night.

You can't tell how nervous I became — everything seemed the opening of artillery, & I had no rest, no peace except when in front with my men. The duties of my position are such as often to make it necessary for me to remain in the rear — it is an awful thing.

I believe now we are all right. I have reinstituted the playing of bands, beating the calls etc by way of keeping the men in good spirits, & have ordered the national salutes to be fired today at noon from the camp of each corps. I have some more official letters to write, so I must close this & must soon start to ride around the lines.

AL copy, McClellan Papers (C-7:63), Library of Congress.

To John A. Dix

Head Qrs dept of Virginia
My dear General: July 4, 1862

I beg to acknowledge the receipt of your letter of yesterday. The necessity of maintaining Fortress Monroe and Yorktown is a primary consideration. I think myself sufficiently strong here; and if the enemy will abstain from attack for twenty four hours more, I shall be able to maintain myself against any force that the enemy can bring against me. Even now, I have no fears as to the issue of an attack. I do not advise therefore that you further strip yourself of troops to send to me. I have ordered to Genl. Burnside to join me with all his disposable force. It would be well to hold Suffolk if possible — and if indispensable to the defence the railroad bridges there might be destroyed. But I hope no such necessity will arise, inasmuch as our line of advance may be on that side.

The result of the affair of the 27th ulto which was so serious in its consequences to the army is already known to you. Superior bodies of the enemy overwhelmed my right wing which was only saved from destruction by the good conduct and obstinate resistance of the troops. Cut off from my base at the White House, I had to take Richmond or find another base on the James River. With a marked success on the 27th, I could have, by crossing the right wing, concentrated my forces, and on the succeeding day been in Richmond. As it was, the only course was to concentrate and change my base to this point. Having decided upon the movement I threw bridges across the White Oak Swamp, brought the right wing across the Chickahominy the night after the battle, withdrew the left and the right through the Swamp; and after sustaining a battle and winning it with the centre, withdrew it also through the Swamp, on the night of the 29th ulto.

On the 30th ulto, the whole army marched to the James River at Turkey Island, being engaged on the flanks and in rear, during the day, in battles each of which from the numbers engaged and the fierceness of the conflicts will have its separate place in our military annals. We repulsed the enemy at each attack. The day succeeding we sustained a combined attack of the pursuing columns of the enemy, and drove them off with great loss.

Turkey Island not having however the requisites for security as a base and the safety of the army now so reduced rendering it imperative to retire to this place, the army moved hither with celerity and entire success on the night of the 2nd inst, bringing with us our artillery and trains.

Nothing of consequence, in all this important movement, fell into the hands of the enemy, subsistance for some few days, and a quantity of reserve ammunition having been destroyed.

The operations of this army have not unfortunately been such as to produce the results so anxiously hoped for by my countrymen — though happily the end is not frustrated, and I have been able to extricate my army from difficulties sudden, unanticipated and almost overwhelming. In a military point of view, neither the country nor the profession to which we belong, have any cause for complaint of this army or its leader.

I tender you, my dear General, my grateful acknowledgments for the patriotic and self sacrificing spirit which you have evinced in responding to my calls for troops &c. It has been potent in sustaining me.

I am very truly your friend
Geo B McClellan
Maj Genl

Maj Gen J. A. Dix
Comdg Ft. Monroe

12 M. *July 4.* The national salute is firing — bands are playing. The troops are in fine spirits.

LS, Dix Papers, Rare Book and Manuscript Library, Columbia University.

To Abraham Lincoln [TELEGRAM]

Head-Quarters, Army of the Potomac,
To the President Harrison's Bar, James River. July 4th 1862 [noon]

I have the honor to acknowledge the receipt of your dispatch of the 2d inst.[1] I shall make a stand at this place and endeavor to give my men the repose they so much require.

After sending my communication on Tuesday [July 1], the enemy attacked the left of our lines and a fierce battle ensued lasting until night — they were repulsed with great slaughter. Had *their* attack succeeded the consequence would have been disastrous in the extreme. This closed the hard fighting which had continued from the afternoon of the 26th ult. in a daily series of engagements wholly unparalleled on this continent for determination and slaughter on both sides. The mutual loss in killed and wounded is enormous; that of the enemy certainly greatest. On Tuesday evening — the 1st — our Army commenced its movement from Haxall's to this point, our line of defence there being too extended to be maintained by our weakened forces. Our train was immense, and about 4 am on the 2d a heavy storm of rain began which continued during the entire day and until the forenoon of yesterday. The roads became horrible. Troops, Artillery and wagons moved on steadily and our whole Army, men and material, was finally brought safe into this camp. The last of the wagons reaching here at noon yesterday. The exhaustion was very great but the Army preserved its morale, and would have repelled any attack which the enemy was in condition to make.

We now occupy a line of heights about two miles from the James, a plain extending from there to the river. Our front is about three miles long. These heights command our whole position and must be maintained. The gun boats can render valuable support upon both flanks. If the enemy attack us in front, we must hold our ground as we best may and at whatever cost [*crossed out*: because the loss of the heights involves the total destruction of the Army]. Our positions can be carried only by overwhelming numbers. The spirit of the Army is excellent. Stragglers [*crossed out*: of whom there was a vast number] are finding their regiments, and the soldiers exhibit the best results of discipline. Our position is by no means impregnable, especially as a morass extends on this side of the high ground, from our center to the James on our right. The enemy may attack in vast numbers and if so, our front will be the scene of a desperate battle which if lost will be decisive. Our Army is fearfully weakened by killed, wounded & prisoners. I can not now approximate to any statement of our losses, but we were not beaten in any conflict. The enemy was unable to by their utmost efforts, to drive us from any field. Never did such a change of base, involving a retrograde movement, and under incessant attacks from a most determined and vastly more numerous foe, partake so little of [*crossed out*: the character of a rout or result in so] disorder. We have lost no guns except 25 in the field of battle — 21 of which were lost by the giving way of McCall's Division under the onset of superior numbers.

Our communications by the James river are not secure. There are points where the enemy can establish themselves with cannon or musketry and command the river and where it is not certain that our gun boats can drive them out. In case of this or in case our front is broken I will still make every effort to preserve at least the personnel of the Army and the events of the last few days leave no question that the troops will do all that their country can ask. Send such reinforcements as you can. I will do what I can.

We are shipping our wounded and sick — and landing supplies. The Navy department should cooperate with us to the extent of its resources. Capt Rodgers is doing all in his power, in the kindest and most efficient manner.

When all the circumstances of the case are known, it will be acknowledged by all competent judges that the movement just completed by this Army is unparalleled in the annals of war. Under the most difficult circumstances we have preserved our trains, our guns, our material — & above all our honor.

Geo. B. McClellan
Maj Genl

AL (in part) retained copy, McClellan Papers (A-72:29), Library of Congress. *OR*, Ser. 1, XI, Part 1, pp. 71–72.

1. See GBM to Lorenzo Thomas, July 1, 1862, note 2, *supra*.

To Abraham Lincoln [TELEGRAM]

Hd Qrs Army of Potomac
The President Harrisons Bar James River July 4 [1862] 1 pm

I have the honor to acknowledge the receipt of your dispatch of yesterday afternoon.[1] I thank you for your expression of satisfaction with the conduct of this army & myself. On yesterday I ordered Genl Burnside to send me such reinforcements as he could afford. I thank you for the order to Genl Hunter to send me all the troops he can spare. I regret that Genl Halleck considers all his force necessary to maintain position. I do not wish to endanger in any way the secure occupation of what has been gained in the southwest. I will do the best I can with such force as I have & such aid as you can give me. I think that the Army of Virginia should keep out strong cavalry reconnaissances in the direction of Richmond less the enemy should prefer an advance to Washn to attacking this Army. I wish to be advised fully of all matters in front of that Army. If the Capital should be threatened I will move this Army at whatever hazard in such direction as will best divert the enemy. Our whole Army is now drawn up for review in its positions, bands playing, salutes being fired & all things looking bright.[2]

Geo B McClellan
Maj Genl Comdg

Received copy, Lincoln Papers, Library of Congress, *OR* Ser. 1, XI, Part 3, p. 294.

1. See GBM to Lincoln, July 2, 1862, note 3, *supra*. 2. Lincoln telegraphed on July 5: "A thousand thanks for the relief your two despatches of 12 & 1 P.M. yesterday — give me. Be assured the heroism and skill of yourself, officers, and men, are, and forever will be appreciated. If you can hold your present position, we shall '*hive*' the enemy yet." *Collected Works of Lincoln,* V, p. 307.

To the Army of the Potomac

Head-Quarters, Army of the Potomac,
Camp near Harrison's Landing, Va.,
July 4th, 1862.

Soldiers of the Army of the Potomac!

Your achievements of the last ten days have illustrated the valor and endurance of the American Soldier! Attacked by vastly superior forces, and without hope of reinforcements, you have succeeded in changing your base of operations by a flank movement, always regarded as the most hazardous of military expedients. You have saved all your material, all your trains, and all your guns, except a few lost in battle, taking in return guns and colors from the enemy. Upon your march you have been assailed day after day with desperate fury by men of the same race and nation, skillfully massed and led; and under every disadvantage of numbers, and necessarily of position also, you have in every conflict beaten back your foes with enormous slaughter. Your conduct ranks you among the celebrated armies of history. No one will now question that each of you may always say with pride: "I belonged to the Army of the Potomac!" You have reached this new base, complete in organization and unimpaired in spirit. The enemy may at any moment attack you. We are prepared to receive them. I have personally established your lines. Let them come, and we will convert their repulse into a final defeat. Your Government is strengthening you with the resources of a great people. On this our Nation's Birthday we declare to our foes, who are rebels against the best interests of mankind, that this Army shall enter the Capital of their so-called Confederacy; that our National Constitution shall prevail; and that the Union which can alone insure internal peace and external security to each State must and shall be preserved, cost what it may in time, treasure and blood.

Geo. B. McClellan
Major-General Commanding

DP, McClellan Papers (B-11:48), Library of Congress. *OR,* Ser. 1, XI, Part 3, p. 299.

To Mary Ellen McClellan [TELEGRAM]

Head-Quarters, Army of the Potomac,
Berkeley's July 5 3.30 pm 1862

Dear Nelly. All is bright. The Army is safe & we will soon be after secesh. I hope they may attack — it will be their ruin if they do. I am very well & not so much fatigued for my mind is at rest.

G B McClellan
Maj Genl

Mrs G B McClellan
Care Dr E E Marcy North Orange New Jersey

ALS (telegram sent), Records of the Office of the Secretary of War, RG 107 (M-504:65), National Archives.

To Mary Ellen McClellan

[Berkeley] July 6 [1862] Sunday morning 2.15

Early in the evening [July 5] I received the intelligence that secesh was in full force in front of me. I have just completed my arrangements to meet him & believe that with God's blessing we will defeat him terribly. I go into this battle with the full conviction that our honor makes it necessary for me to share the fate of my army. My men are confident & I have no doubt as to our success unless the Creator orders otherwise. I believe we will give them a tremendous thrashing & I still hope that from my universal anxieties I will yet find repose — may God grant it thus! Whatever the result may be I am sure that you will never have cause to blush for me — therefore my conscience is quite clear — God has done far more for me than I had any right to expect — I trust, most humbly, that unworthy as I am he will not desert me now. I yet believe that there is in store for us the supreme happiness of being together once more. If this cannot be in this world, I trust I may be forgiven for my many faults & sins & be permitted to rejoin in Heaven the one who has made my life so happy....

Tomorrow [July 6] will probably determine the fate of the country — I expect to be attacked by greatly superior numbers & hope to beat them.[1]

AL copy; copy, McClellan Papers (C-7:63/D-10:72), Library of Congress.

1. No enemy attack was made that day.

To Mary Ellen McClellan

[Berkeley] Monday [July 7, 1862] 7.30 am.

I had a good refreshing night's sleep....

We are to have another *very* hot day — it is already apparent — I am writing in my shirt sleeves, with tent walls raised etc....

Our army has not been repulsed — we fought every day against greatly superior numbers & were obliged to retire at night to new positions that we could hold against fresh troops. The army behaved magnificently — nothing could have been finer than its conduct....

You need not be ashamed of your husband or his army — we have accomplished one of the grandest operations of Military History....

I don't think the enemy will now attack us here — we are strengthening our position very rapidly & will with God's help surely beat them if they do attack.

AL copy, McClellan Papers (C-7:63), Library of Congress.

To Abraham Lincoln [TELEGRAM]

Headquarters, Army of the Potomac,
Berkeley, July 7 [1862] 8.30 am

As boat is waiting I have only time to acknowledge receipt of dispatches by Genl Marcy. Enemy have not attacked — my position is very strong & daily becoming more so — if not attacked today I shall laugh at them.

I *have* been anxious about my communications.[1] Had long consultation about it with Flag Officer Goldsborough last night — he is confident he can keep river open. He should have all gun boats possible. Will see him again this morning. My men in splendid spirits & anxious to try it again.

Annoy yourself as little as possible about me & don't lose confidence in this army.

G B McClellan
Maj Genl

A Lincoln Presdt.

ALS (telegram sent), Records of the Office of the Secretary of War, RG 107 (M-473:50), National Archives. *OR,* Ser. 1, XI, Part 1, p. 73.

1. In his letter of July 4, the president gave it as his opinion that the Army of the Potomac could hold its position "provided, and so long as, you can keep the James River open below you. If you are not tolerably confident you can keep the James River open, you had better remove as soon as possible." *Collected Works of Lincoln,* V, p. 306.

To Edwin M. Stanton

To the Hon Edwin M Stanton
Sec'y of War
Sir.

Head Quarters Army of the Potomac
Camp near Harrison's Landing,
July 7th 1862.

The energy, ability, gallantry and good conduct displayed throughout the eventful period of this campaign through which we have just passed by Brig Genl F. J. Porter, desires the marked notice of the Executive and the nation.

From the very commencement his unwearied assiduity in his various duties, his intelligent and efficacious assistance which he has rendered me under all circumstances, his skilful management of his command on the march, in the siege and on the field of battle and his chivalric and soldierly bearing under fire, have combined to render him conspicuous among the many faithful and gallant spirits of this Army.

I respectfully therefore recommend that Brig Genl Fitz-John Porter receive the brevet of Brigadier General in the regular Army for Hanover Court House and the brevet of Major General in the regular Army for the battle of Gaines Mills.

If there were another grade to add I would ask for it for the battle of Malvern. The latter eclipses in its results any other engagement in the campaign, and too much credit cannot be given to Genl Porter for his skill, gallantry, and conduct on the occasion.

If there be any vacancy among the General Officers in the regular Army I ask one for him. I saw myself the dispositions he made and the gallantry he displayed. I do not speak from hearsay, but from personal observation; would that the country had more General Officers like him.[1]

I have the honor to be, Sir, very respectfully your obt servant
Geo B McClellan
Maj Genl Commanding

LS retained copy, McClellan Papers (C-6:63), Library of Congress. *OR*, Ser. 1, XII, Part 2 supplement, p. 1111.

1. Porter was named a brigadier general by brevet in the regular army, to date from June 27, and major general of volunteers, to date from July 4.

To John Pope

Major General John Pope
Comd'g Army of Virginia
General

Head Quarters Army of the Potomac
Camp near Harrison's Bar, Va.
July 7th 1862

I have to acknowledge the receipt of your letter of the 4th instant and to thank you for your offers of co-operation and assistance.[1] I cordially approve your project of concentrating your troops. The departure from this wise principle has been the cause of all our troubles in front of Washington. I cannot too strongly represent to you the pressing necessity there is for the rapid concentration of your forces, for it is not yet determined which policy the enemy intend to pursue, whether to attack Washington or to bestow his entire attention upon this Army. I am in a very strong natural position, rendered stronger every day by the labor of the troops and which in a few days will be impregnable. I hope in the course of tomorrow to seize a position on the right bank of the James which will enable me to use either bank of that river at will. I am pushing up supplies as rapidly as possible in order to be perfectly independent of the navigation of the river until strong reinforcements can reach me. The Army is in admirable spirits and discipline. It would fight better tomorrow than it ever did before. I shall carefully watch for any fault committed by the enemy and take advantage of it. As soon as Burnside arrives, I will feel the force of the enemy and ascertain his exact position. If I learn that he has moved upon you I will move upon Richmond, do my best to take it and endeavor to cut off his retreat.

If you are not molested I would urge that you lose not a day in the concentration of your troops and at least push your cavalry so far forward as to partially divert the attention of the enemy from this Army. The Army of the Potomac has lost heavily in killed and wounded during the series of desperate battles which it has given during the past two weeks but I repeat it is in no way disheartened. Its morale, discipline and desire to fight are not only unimpaired but increased. Although to insure success it is absolutely necessary that we promptly receive heavy reinforcements, the spirit of this Army is such that I feel unable to restrain it from speedily resuming the offensive unless reconnaissances should develop so overwhelming a force of the enemy in front as to render it out of the question. Even in that event we will endeavor to find some weak point in the enemy's lines which we will attack in order to break it.

I would be glad to be in daily communication with you both by telegraph and by letter.

I may say in conclusion that so far as my position is concerned, I feel abundantly able to repulse any attack. I feel only for the other side of the river and for my communications. To preserve the morale of my men I must maintain my present position as long as it is possible. Therefore I shall not fall back unless absolutely forced to do so.

Again thanking you for your cordial offer of support

I am, very sincerely yours,
Geo. B. McClellan
Maj Genl Comdg

Retained copy, McClellan Papers (C-6:63), Library of Congress. *OR,* Ser. 1, XI, Part 3, p. 306. Maj. Gen. John Pope commanded the newly formed Army of Virginia.

1. Pope's letter detailed the strength, location, and condition of his forces. It was his general design, he wrote, "to cut off any force which may penetrate into the valley of the Shenandoah from the direction of Richmond, and at the same time be able to concentrate my whole force with little delay in front of Washington in case of necessity." *OR,* Ser. 1, XI, Part 3, pp. 295–97.

To Abraham Lincoln

(Confidential) Head Quarters, Army of the Potomac
Mr President Camp near Harrison's Landing, Va. July 7th 1862[1]

You have been fully informed, that the Rebel army is in our front, with the purpose of overwhelming us by attacking our positions or reducing us by blocking our river communications. I can not but regard our condition as critical and I earnestly desire, in view of possible contingencies, to lay before your Excellency, for your private consideration, my general views concerning the existing state of the rebellion; although they do not strictly relate to the situation of this Army or strictly come within the scope of my official duties. These views amount to convictions and are deeply impressed upon my mind and heart.

Our cause must never be abandoned; it is the cause of free institutions and self government. The Constitution and the Union must be preserved, whatever may be the cost in time, treasure and blood. If secession is successful, other dissolutions are clearly to be seen in the future. Let neither military disaster, political faction or foreign war shake your settled purpose to enforce the equal operation of the laws of the United States upon the people of every state.

The time has come when the Government must determine upon a civil and military policy, covering the whole ground of our national trouble. The responsibility of determining, declaring and supporting such civil and military policy and of directing the whole course of national affairs in regard to the rebellion, must now be assumed and exercised by you or our cause will be lost. The Constitution gives you power sufficient even for the present terrible exigency.

This rebellion has assumed the character of a War; as such it should be regarded; and it should be conducted upon the highest principles known to Christian Civilization. It should not be a War looking to the subjugation of the people of any state, in any event. It should not be, at all, a War upon population; but against armed forces and political organizations. Neither confiscation of property, political executions of persons, territorial organization of states or forcible abolition of slavery should be contemplated for a moment. In prosecuting the War, all private property and unarmed persons should be strictly protected; subject only to the necessities of military operations. All private property taken for military use should be paid or receipted for; pillage and waste should be treated as high crimes; all unnecessary trespass sternly prohibited; and offensive demeanor by the military towards citizens promptly rebuked. Military arrests should not be tolerated, except in places where active hostilities exist; and oaths not required by enactments — Constitutionally made — should be neither demanded nor received. Military government should be confined to the preservation of public order and the protection of political rights.

Military power should not be allowed to interfere with the relations of servitude, either by supporting or impairing the authority of the master; except for repressing disorder as in other cases. Slaves contraband under the Act of Congress, seeking military protection, should receive it. The right of the Government to appropriate permanently to its own service claims to slave labor should be asserted and the right of the owner to compensation therefor should be recognized. This principle might be extended upon grounds of military necessity and security to all the slaves within a particular state; thus working manumission in such state — and in Missouri, perhaps in Western Virginia also and possibly even in Maryland the expediency of such a military measure is only a question of time. A system of policy thus constitutional and conservative, and pervaded by the influences of Christianity and freedom, would receive the support of almost all truly loyal men, would deeply impress the rebel masses and all foreign nations, and it might be humbly hoped that it would commend itself to the favor of the Almighty. Unless the principles governing the further conduct of our struggle shall be made known and approved, the effort to obtain requisite forces will be almost hopeless. A declaration of radical views, especially upon slavery, will rapidly disintegrate our present Armies.

The policy of the Government must be supported by concentrations of military power. The national forces should not be dispersed in expeditions, posts of occupation and numerous Armies; but should be mainly collected into masses and brought to bear upon the Armies of the Confederate States; those Armies thoroughly defeated, the political structure which they support would soon cease to exist.

In carrying out any system of policy which you may form, you will require a Commander in Chief of the Army; one who possesses your confidence, understands your views and who is competent to execute your orders by directing the military forces of the Nation to the accomplishment of the objects by you proposed. I do not ask that place for myself. I am willing to serve you in such position as you may assign me and I will do so as faithfully as ever subordinate served superior.

I may be on the brink of eternity and as I hope forgiveness from my maker I have written this letter with sincerity towards you and from love for my country.

Very respectfully your obdt svt
Geo B McClellan
Maj Genl Comdg

His Excellency A Lincoln
Presdt U.S.

LS, Lincoln Papers, Library of Congress. *OR,* Ser. 1, XI, Part 1, pp. 73–74.

1. GBM handed this letter to the president upon his arrival at Harrison's Landing on July 8. It is probable, however, that he had drafted it, at least in general outline, as early as June 20. See GBM to Lincoln, June 20, 1862, *supra.*

To Mary Ellen McClellan

[Berkeley] July 8 [1862]

I have only time before your father starts on his return to Washington to say two words to you. It is terribly hot & has been so for the last two days — almost overpowering — but we manage to worry through it. There is nothing new here — we are strengthening our position daily — the enemy waiting for something or other a few miles off. I hardly know what they will try next — probably to cut off our supplies — but I have quite a large amount here now & I do not think they can trouble us much in that way....

The day is insufferably hot — intense — so much so that I have suspended all work on the part of the men. I have written a strong frank letter to the Presdt, which I send by your father[1] — if he acts upon it the country will be saved. I will send you a copy tomorrow, as well as of other important letters which I wish you to keep as my record. They will show, with the others you have, that I was true to my country, that I understood the state of affairs long ago, & that had my advice been followed we should not have been in our present difficulties....

My conscience is clear — I have done the best I could — God has disposed of events as to him seemed best. I submit to his decrees with perfect cheerfulness, & as sure as he rules I believe that all will yet be for the best....

How I have longed to see you in the midst of my troubles. The thought of you has been an immense consolation & support to me. How perfectly happy I shall be if God sees fit to permit me to be with you once more. I will never leave you again if it is in the power of humanity to avoid it. No rank, nor wealth, nor honors can reconcile me to absence from you.

AL copy; copy, McClellan Papers (C-7:63/D-10:72), Library of Congress.

1. GBM to Lincoln, July 7, *supra.* Lincoln's arrival at Harrison's Landing later this day made it unnecessary to send the letter to Washington by Gen. Marcy.

To Edwin M. Stanton

Head Quarters, Army of the Potomac
Dear Sir Camp near Harrison's Landing, Va. July 8th 1862

Your letter of the 5th instant by General Marcy has made a deep impression on my mind.[1] Let me in the first place express my sympathy with you in the sickness of your child, which I trust may not prove fatal.

I shall be better understood by you and our friendly relations will become more fixed if I am permitted to recur briefly to the past.

When you were appointed Secretary of War I considered you my intimate friend and confidential adviser; of all men in the nation you were my choice for that position. It was the unquestionable prerogative of the President to determine the military policy of the administration and to select the commanders who should carry out the measures of the government. To any action of this nature I could of course take no personal exception. But from the time you took office, your official conduct towards me as commander in chief of the Army of the U.S. and afterwards as commander of the Army of the Potomac was marked by repeated acts done in such manner as to be deeply offensive to my feelings and calculated to affect me injuriously in public estimation. After commencing the present campaign your concurrence in the withholding of a large portion of my force, so essential to the success of my plans, led me to believe that your mind was warped by a bitter personal prejudice against me. Your letter compells me to believe that I have been mistaken in regard to your real feelings and opinions and that your conduct so unaccountable to my own fallible judgment, must have proceeded from views and motives which I did not understand.

I have made this frank statement, because I thought that it would best accord with the spirit of your communication.

It is with a feeling of great relief that I now say to you that I shall at once resume on my part the same cordial confidence which once characterized our intercourse. You have more than once told me that together we could save this country, it is yet not too late to do so.

To accomplish this, there must be between us the most entire harmony of thought and action and such I offer you. The crisis through which we are passing is a terrible one. I have briefly given in a confidential letter to the President my views (Please ask to see it.) as to the policy which ought to govern this contest on our part.[2] You and I during last Summer so often talked over the whole subject that I have only expressed the opinions then agreed upon between us. The nation will support no other policy. None other will call forth its energies in time to save our cause, for none other will our Armies continue to fight. I have been perfectly frank with you. Let no cloud hereafter arise between us.

Very respectfully your obdt sevt
Geo B McClellan
Maj Genl Comdg

Hon E M Stanton
Secty of War

LS retained copy, McClellan Papers (A-72:29), Library of Congress.

1. Stanton's letter read, in part: "There is no cause in my heart or conduct for the cloud that wicked men have raised between us for their own base and selfish purposes. No man had ever a truer friend than I have been to you and shall continue to be. You are seldom absent from my thoughts and I am ready to make any sacrifice to aid you." McClellan Papers (A-72:29). 2. GBM to Lincoln, July 7, *supra*.

To Mary Ellen McClellan

July 9 [1862] 9 1/2 pm. Berkeley

I telegraphed you briefly this afternoon that I thought secesh had retired — this opinion seems to be fully confirmed — at least to the extent of his having fallen back a certain distance — he is not within 6 or 7 miles of us even with his cavalry & considerably further with his infantry. I am not sorry on the whole that he has gone, for the reason that it will enable my men to rest tranquilly — just what they need. I do not expect to receive many reinforcements for some time — even Burnside's men are halted at Ft Monroe by order of the Presdt! His Excellency was here yesterday & left this morning. He found the army anything but demoralized or dispirited — in excellent spirits. I do not know to what extent he has profited by his visit — not much I fear, for he really seems quite incapable of rising to the height of the merits of the question & the magnitude of the crisis. I will enclose with this a copy of a letter I handed him, which I would be glad to have you preserve carefully as a very important record.

I thank you a thousand times for your kind & loving sympathy you have evinced for me in my trials. I can't tell you what a comfort it is to have your sweet sympathy. I do feel that God has ordered all these later events for some wise purpose. I am sure of it.

My camp is now immediately on the bank of the James River, in the woods. . . .

AL copy; copy, McClellan Papers (C-7:63/D-10:72), Library of Congress.

To Mary Ellen McClellan

[Berkeley, July] 10th [1862] 7 am.

Rose a little before six etc. . . .

I do not know what paltry trick the administration will play next — I did not like the Presdt's manner — it seemed that of a man about to do something of which he was much ashamed. A few days will however show, & I do not much care what the result will be. I feel that I have already done enough to prove in history that I am a General, & that the causes of my want of success are so apparent that no one except the Chandler tribe can blame me hereafter.[1] My conscience is clear at least to *this* extent — viz: that I have honestly done the best *I* could; I shall leave it to others to decide whether that was the best that *could* have been done — & if they find any who can do better am perfectly willing to step aside & give way. I would not for worlds go through that horrid work again — when with my heart full of care I had to meet everyone with a cheerful smile & look as light hearted as tho' nothing were at stake! . . .

9.30 pm. . . . I have not done splendidly at all — I have only tried to do my duty & God has helped me, or rather he has helped my army & our country — & we are safe. I think I begin to see his wise purpose in all this & that the events of the next few days will prove it. If I had succeeded in taking Richmond now the fanatics of the North might have been too powerful & reunion impossible. However that may be I am sure that it is all for the best.

AL copy, McClellan Papers (C-7:63), Library of Congress.

1. Zachariah Chandler of Michigan delivered a strong attack on GBM in the Senate on July 7.

To Randolph B. Marcy [TELEGRAM]

[Berkeley] July 10th 1862

Enemy has fallen back. I shall get fuller information today & know what I can do if Burnside joins me. Use your judgment about Keyes etc. I must modify some staff departments to ensure success. If Barry & Kingsbury can be placed on other duty I can get on better. Same for Barnard.[1] All quite well. Note received & in every respect attended to.

G B McClellan
Maj Genl

Brig Genl R B Marcy
Chief of Staff Washington D.C.

ALS (telegram sent), McClellan Papers (A-72:29), Library of Congress.

1. Gen. Keyes retained his corps command, but did not serve again under GBM in the field. Artillerists William F. Barry and Charles P. Kingsbury were appointed to other duties. Gen. Bernard was put in command of the Washington fortifications.

To Lorenzo Thomas [TELEGRAM]

Brig. General L. Thomas
Adjutant General USA
General

Head Quarters Army of the Potomac
Berkeleys Landing July 10th 1862

I would beg leave to call your attention most urgently to the necessity of taking immediate measures for filling up to the regulation standard all the regiments and batteries of the regulars and volunteers composing this Army. This system is by far preferable, in every respect to that of raising new regiments and batteries.

If it can be done in no other way I would suggest consolidating the old regiments into a small number of companies for each, and receiving the number of entire companies necessary to raise the regiments to the maximum standard. If it be possible to fill up the existing skeleton companies it would be preferable, but it is probable that much valuable time would be gained by following the course first suggested.

I do not believe that any *general* system of recruiting for volunteers will succeed. It must be attempted for particular regiments and companies in the localities where they originated. Recruits scattered among the veteran regiments would soon become efficient; while a long time would be required to render raw recruits reliable. The regular batteries (I may say the same of the volunteer) are very deficient in men.

Commending this subject to the immediate attention of the department, I am

very respectfully your obedient servant
G. B. McClellan
Maj Gen Comdg

Retained copy, McClellan Papers (C-6:63), Library of Congress. *OR*, Ser. 1, XI, Part 3, p. 310.

To Edwin M. Stanton

Hd Qtrs Army of Potomac
Berkeley July 10 1862[1]

Desiring to obtain all possible information in regard to rifled guns, I sent, in December last, one of my aides (Col Hudson)[2] who is an excellent Artillery officer to witness experiments made with the *new* James projectile & guns. The result was about as follows—

The batteries withdrawn from service by Genl Barry were old six pounders rifled—the new gun is of a different model, though the same calibre.

The projectile (James) used before these guns (old batteries) were withdrawn was very objectionable—the new projectile is entirely different & free from the defects which rendered the other useless. With the new projectile the old guns would doubtless be available, tho' probably inferior to the new model.

Col H. did not see the steel guns, but they were represented by Mr James as superior to the others which Col H. regarded as superior to any others in use.

I have that opinion of Col H's judgment in such matters that induces me to attach weight to his opinions. I *know* from personal observation that the projectiles furnished by the Ordnance Dept for the 20 & 30 pdr

Parrotts, & the 3″ gun, as well as some of those for the 10 pdr Parrott are worthless, & have not infrequently killed our own men.

The Schenkl is far better — the best so far — but I am decidedly in favor of trying anything which promises to be better than the wretched ammunition which has so often been furnished this Army by the Ordnance Dept. I would also add that no reliance could be placed on the 4 1/2″ guns until we found the Schenkl ammunition.

It is full time to throw prejudice to one side & seek only the true interests of the service.[3]

Very respectfully
Geo B McClellan
Maj Genl Comdg

Hon E M Stanton
Secty of War Washington

ALS, Houghton Library, Harvard University.

1. This letter is written on the back of Brig. Gen. James W. Ripley's letter of July 7 to GBM, in which Ripley, chief of the Ordnance Department, objected on the basis of earlier trials to purchasing three batteries of bronze and steel guns from Charles T. James. 2. Lt. Col. Edward McK. Hudson. 3. A limited number of James guns saw service with the Army of the Potomac.

To Mary Ellen McClellan

[Berkeley] Friday [July] 11th [1862] 7 am.

Am a little belated for it has been raining all the morning & most of the night, so that I rather overslept myself. . . .

There is now strong reason to believe that Clitz is not dead — I hope for the best for the gallant fellow.[1] . . .

You have no idea of the number of general officers applying to go off on sick leave — nearly 20 — more than that including those who have already gone! I do not interpose many obstacles — for I want none but willing ones. . . .

I have commenced receiving letters from the North urging me to march on Washington & assume the Govt!! . . .

AL copy, McClellan Papers (C-7 :63), Library of Congress.

1. Maj. Henry B. Clitz had been wounded and captured at the Battle of Gaines's Mill on June 27.

To Abraham Lincoln [TELEGRAM]

Berkeley July 11th [1862] 8 am

The enemy have certainly retreated — but it has been in good order & with a fair amount of wagons. Our Cavalry follow their rear guard closely & have taken a few prisoners but have made no decided impression.

None of the enemy appear to have crossed the Long Bridge — but all to have gone in direction of Richmond — some crossing White Oak Swamp. None towards mouth of Chickahominy now. Considerable force of enemy at Haxalls yesterday — probably Cavalry almost entirely.

Stonewall Jackson not dead. Prisoners all state that I had (200,000) two hundred thousand enemy to fight — a good deal more than two to one, & they knowing the ground.

G B McClellan
Maj Genl Comdg

A Lincoln
Presdt

ALS (telegram sent), McClellan Papers (A-72:29), Library of Congress. *OR,* Ser. 1, XI, Part 3, p. 315.

To Hill Carter

Hill Carter, Esqr
Shirley

Head Quarters, Army of the Potomac
July 11/62

My dear Sir

Your letter of yesterday is received. Allow me to express my thanks to you for the humane and Christian conduct you and your family have displayed towards my helpless sick & wounded; my attention had already been called to this subject.

Without pausing to inquire or desiring to learn whether you are friend or foe to the cause I have the honor to serve, it was my intention to do all in my power to alleviate in your case the sufferings caused by the inevitable exigencies of this unhappy war.

Permit me here to state that it ever has been, and ever shall be, my constant effort to confine the effects of this contest to the armed masses and political organization directly concerned in carrying it on. I have done my best to secure protection to private property, but I confess that circumstances beyond my control have often defeated my purposes. I have not come here to wage war upon the defenseless, upon non-combatants, upon private property, nor upon the domestic institutions of the land. I and the Army I command are fighting to secure the Union & to maintain its Constitution & laws — for no other purpose.

I regret the losses you have suffered, & the inconveniences you have endured.

I send this by a confidential officer of my Staff who is instructed to ascertain from you what kind of a safeguard will best secure your person and property, how I can best indemnify you for your losses, & in what manner the other requests you make can best be carried out.

Again expressing my thanks for the noble spirit of humanity you have shown towards men whom you probably regard as bitter foes

I am sir, with the highest respect your obedient servant
Geo B McClellan
Maj Genl USA Comdg

Copy, McClellan Papers (B-11:48), Library of Congress. *OR*, Ser. 1, XI, Part 3, p. 316. Carter was the proprietor of the James River plantation Shirley.

To Abraham Lincoln [TELEGRAM]

Berkeley July 12 [1862] 7.15 am

Hill and Longstreet crossed into New Kent County via Long Bridge. I am still ignorant what road they afterwards took but will know shortly. Nothing else of interest since last dispatch.

Rain ceased & everything quiet. Men resting well, but beginning to be impatient for another fight.

I am more & more convinced that this Army ought not to be withdrawn from here — but promptly reinforced & thrown again upon Richmond. If we have a little more than half a chance we can take it. I dread the effects of any retreat upon the morale of the men.

G B McClellan
Maj Genl Comdg

A Lincoln
Presdt

ALS (telegram sent), McClellan Papers (A-72:29), Library of Congress. *OR*, Ser. 1, XI, Part 1, pp. 74–75.

To Ira Harris

Head Quarters Army of the Potomac
My Dear Sir. Berkeley, Va. July 12th 1862

I perceive by the newspaper reports of congressional proceedings that there has been considerable discussion on the subject of requiring Military Commanders to receive Negroes seeking protection in their camps and to employ them in suitable labor connected with Military Service. It may be well for the fact to be made known that all Negroes, male and female, who have come into the camps of the Army of the Potomac on this peninsula, have been protected and set to work at wages, in performing offices which would otherwise have devolved upon our soldiers. The supply of these operatives has thus far been insufficient for our wants.

I am my dear Senator Very truly your friend
Geo B McClellan
Maj Genl Commanding

Hon Ira Harris
N.Y. Senator

Retained copy, McClellan Papers (C-6 :63), Library of Congress. Harris was a senator from New York.

To Mary Ellen McClellan

[Berkeley, July] 13th [1862] Sunday 7.45 am.

It is a little hard that I cannot see my own baby or her dear Mother, but I trust it is all for the best, & how happy we will be when we do meet. I am so glad little May is such a comfort to you. God was good when he gave you the dear little thing. How lonely you would be without her in my absence. I wish indeed I could see her, & *some body else too.*

I hope to get rid of Barnard in a few days — he has nearly exhausted my troops. I have ordered all labor suspended today, to give the men a chance to think of what they have gone through. We are to have service today by the chaplain of Gregg's rgt Penna cavalry. Next Sunday I think I will invite Mr. Neal to preach for us, provided there is any attendance today.

I enclose this in an envelope with some others I send you. One from Bishop McIlvaine, which will gratify you, I know; another from some poor fellow in Indiana, who has named his child after me. If you choose to send out some little present for it, well and good.

1:30 pm. . . . Had service this morning by the chaplain of Gregg's rgt, the Rev. Mr. Egan, an Episc. clergyman of Phila. . . .

There never was such an army, but there have been plenty of better generals. When I spoke about being repulsed, I meant our failure to take Richmond — in no *battle* were we *repulsed.* We always at least held our own on the field if we did not beat them. . . .

I still hope to get to Richmond this summer — unless the Govt commits some *extraordinarily* idiotic act — but I have no faith in the administration & shall cut loose from public life the very moment my country can dispense with my services. Don't be alarmed about the climate — it is not at all bad yet & we are resting splendidly — the men look better every day. So you want to know how I feel about Stanton, & what I think of him now? I will tell you with the most perfect frankness. I think that he is the most unmitigated scoundrel I ever knew, heard or read of; I think that (& I do not wish to be irreverent) had he lived in the time of the Saviour, Judas Iscariot would have remained a respected member of the fraternity of the Apostles, & that the magnificent treachery & rascality of E. M. Stanton would have caused Judas to have raised his arms in holy horror & unaffected wonder — he would certainly have claimed & exercised the right to have been the Betrayer of his Lord & Master, by virtue of the same merit that raised Satan to his "bad eminence." I *may* do the man injustice — God grant that I may be wrong — for I hate to think that humanity *can* sink so low — but my opinion is just as I have told you. He has deceived me once — he never will again. Are you satisfied now — lady mine? I ever will, hereafter, trust your judgment about men — your woman's tact & your pure heart make you a better judge than my dull apprehension. I remember what you thought of Stanton when you first saw him — I thought you were wrong — I now know you were right. Enough of the creature — it makes me sick to think of him! Faugh!!

Since I reached here I have received about 8500 or 9000 fresh troops — my losses in the battles will not be over 12,000. Burnside has 8000 (about) at Ft Monroe, where he was detained by order of the Presdt — he has been in Washn & will probably be here *himself* tonight when I will know the views of the Presdt. The probability is that I will attack again very soon — as soon as some losses are supplied — such as canteens & some small things necessary for the comfort of the men. I also must first get off all the sick & wounded. I'll give them a hard fight this time.

11 1/2 pm. Have just been at work dictating my report of the recent operations — got as far as bringing Porter back across the Chickahominy & quit in disgust. . . .

Please reply to Mr —— & say that I thank him & feel deeply grateful for his trust & kind feeling, & that I am glad to say that there is no reason for despondency on account of my present position. I flatter myself that this army is a greater thorn in the side of the rebellion than ever & I most certainly (with God's blessing) intend to take Richmond with it. . . .

I trust that we have passed through our darkest time & that God will smile upon us & give us victory. . . .

I do not want to be Secy of War — but of course will do anything that will be useful to my country. I am glad to know that my countrymen still love me — *I* have honestly done my best to save my country & I trust will yet save it.

I would give up most cheerfully all the reputation I have gained, or may yet acquire, all the hold I have upon the love of the people; everything would I gladly give up just to be with you & our little child. I don't think I would ever want to see anybody else, or talk to anybody else. You are all I care for in the wide world, yet I am deprived of the society of those I cherish most. Well, well, we must not complain. I presume it is all for the best & I hope that in after years we will look upon these dreary months of separation as the foundation of our true happiness. I must say good bye now & finish some blessed official letters. You must take this note as lubie[1] & not look upon it as a letter. Love to all. Kiss my little May a dozen times for me.

AL copy; copy, McClellan Papers (C-7:63/D-10:72), Library of Congress.

1. An odd or whimsical notion.

To Randolph B. Marcy [TELEGRAM]

Head-Quarters, Army of the Potomac,
Berkeley July 13 1862 [8 A.M.]

Dispatch received. Am sorry you are not well. This is no place to recuperate so do not return until you are strong. Nothing new, except that Lee is giving me my wounded and sick. All is going on well & quietly. I am better than for months & ready for any work. Watch my new friend — I fear he is in collusion with that vile fellow Chandler, at least I am so informed.[1]

G B McClellan
Maj Genl Comdg

Genl R B Marcy
Washington D.C.

ALS (telegram sent), McClellan Papers (A-72:29), Library of Congress.

1. This is apparently a reference to Gen. Pope. Marcy replied that day: "Your new friend is all right and not in cahoots with the member from Michigan, so wise ones believe." McClellan Papers (A-73:29).

To Robert E. Lee

Head-Quarters, Army of the Potomac,
July 13th 1862

General,

I have the honor to inform you that I have received official information that the Secretary of War has invested Major General John A Dix with authority "to negotiate for a general exchange of all prisoners taken and held on both sides. The exchange to be on the principles of the Cartel between the United States and Great Britain in the last war with that power." If your views on this subject remain as heretofore expressed it is presumed that there will be little difficulty in bringing the negotiation to a satisfactory conclusion. General Dix is under my command and will meet any representative whom you may appoint at such place in the vicinity and not within our lines as you may designate. It will be necessary for you to give me 36 hours notice of the time and place that General Dix may be enabled to meet the appointment.[1] I have the honor to be, General

Very Respectfully, Your obt svt
Geo B McClellan
Maj Genl Commanding

General R E Lee
Comdg Army of Northern Va.

Retained copy, John A. Dix Papers, Rare Book and Manuscript Library, Columbia University. *OR,* Ser. 2, IV, pp. 189–90.

1. Gen. Lee designated Maj. Gen. D. H. Hill to negotiate with Dix, and an agreement on prisoner exchange was signed on July 22. *OR,* Ser. 2, VI, pp. 210, 266–68.

To Abraham Lincoln [TELEGRAM]

Head Quarters, Army of the Potomac,
To the President, [Berkeley] July 14th 1862

Your telegram of yesterday has been received.[1] The difference between the effective force of troops and that expressed in returns is considerable in every army. All commanders find the actual strength less than strength represented on paper. I have not my own returns for the trimonthly periods since arriving at Fortress Monroe, at hand at this moment, but even on paper I will not, I am confident, be found to have received 160,000 officers and men present — although present and absent my returns will be accountable for that number.

You can arrive at the number of absentees, however, better by my returns of July 10, which will be ready to send shortly. I find from official reports that I have present for duty,

Officers 3215. Enlisted men 85,450. In all present for duty, 88,665. Absent by authority 34,472; without authority 3778. Present and absent 144,407.[2]

The number of officers and men present sick is 16,619.

The Medical Director will fully explain the cause of the amount of sickness, which I hope will begin to decrease shortly.

Thus the number of men really absent is 38,250. Unquestionably of the number reported present, some are absent, say 40,000 will cover the absentees.

I quite agree with you that more than one half these men are probably fit for duty to day.

I have frequently called the attention lately of the War Department to the evil of absenteeism.

I think that the exciting of the public press to persistent attacks upon officers and soldiers absent from the Army; the employment of deputy marshals to arrest and send back deserters; summary dismissals of officers whose names are reported for being absent without leave and the publication of those names will exhaust the remedies applicable by the War Department. It is to be remembered that many of those absent by authority and those who have got off either sick or wounded or under pretense of sickness or wounds, and having originally pretext of authority, are still so reported absent by authority. If I could receive back the absentees, could get my sick men up I would need but small reinforcements to enable me to take Richmond.

After the battle of Williamsburg, Fair Oaks, &c &c most of these men got off. Well men got on board hospital boats taking care of sick etc, etc. There is always confusion and haste in shipping and taking care of wounded after a battle. There is no time for nice examination of permits to pass here or there.

I can now control people getting away better, for the natural opportunities are better. Leakages by desertion occur in every Army — and will occur here of course but I do not at all, however, anticipate anything like a recurrence of what has taken place.[3]

Geo B McClellan
Maj Genl Comdg

Retained copy, McClellan Papers (C-12:64), Library of Congress. *OR,* Ser. 1, XI, Part 3, pp. 321–22.

1. The president had been told, he wrote on July 13, that over 160,000 men were in the Army of the Potomac on the Peninsula, yet by his calculations he found "45,000 of your Army still alive, and not with it. I believe half, or two thirds of them are fit for duty today.... If I am right, and you had these men with you, you could go into Richmond in the next three days. How can they be got to you? and how can they be prevented from getting away in such numbers for the future?" *Collected Works of Lincoln,* V, p. 322. 2. Included in this total, but unlisted by GBM, are the Fort Monroe garrison and the quartermaster guard. *OR,* Ser. 1, XI, Part 3, p. 312. 3. See also GBM to Lorenzo Thomas, Sept. 28, 1862, *infra.*

To Mary Ellen McClellan

[Berkeley] July 15 [1862] 7.30 am.

... I was amused at a couple of telegrams yesterday urging me to the offensive as if I were unwilling to take it myself!! It is so easy for people to give advice — it costs nothing! But it is a little more difficult for poor me to create men & means, & to wipe out by mere wishes the forces of the enemy. I confess that I sometimes become provoked. I have *16,600* men sick in camp!!! and but 85,000 for duty. I could not bring 70,000, at most 75,000, into battle — & it *is so easy to attack* from 150,000 to 170,000 brave men entrenched with that number!!

I had quite an adventure in a small way last night, that was rather ludicrous. I yesterday sent a flag of truce after some wounded men, Sweitzer going on the boat. Well, it appears that he & the doctor on board, between them, allowed a young English nobleman to come down with them, and Raymond was discreet enough to bring him up to Hd Qtrs & was apparently quite proud of his prize — wished me to see him &c. Upon inquiry, I found that he came from Richmond, had no papers or passports, save a pass from the secesh Secy of War & acknowledged that he had surreptitiously slipped into Richmond a couple of weeks ago. This was a pretty kettle of fish! I did not like to hang the young rascal for a spy, for fear of getting up a row with England — I determined he *should not* go through & so I this morning sent him back to Secessia & told him to try it again at his peril. The young man was exceedingly disgusted & has, I presume, by this time, come to the conclusion that the fact of being an Englishman is not everywhere a sufficient passport.

AL copy; copy, McClellan Papers (C-7:63/D-10:72), Library of Congress.

To Randolph B. Marcy [TELEGRAM]

[Berkeley] July 15 8 am 1862

Your proposition is easily enunciated but not so readily carried out.[1] You may rest assured that it is not necessary to urge me from a distance — I on the spot am quite as anxious to finish this agreeable game as any of my disinterested friends away from here. I get neither men nor a policy. I doubt my new friend.

G B McClellan
Maj Genl

Genl R B Marcy
Washington D.C.

ALS (telegram sent), McClellan Papers (A-73:29), Library of Congress.

1. Marcy telegraphed on July 13: "It is very generally thought that an advance on Richmond at an early period would be received with more enthusiasm now than at any time since the war commenced. The people seem to demand it...." McClellan Papers (A-73:29).

To Nathaniel S. Berry

His Excellency, the Governor of New Hampshire,
Concord
Sir, Berkeley, July 15th 1862.

I am sure that in the present emergency you will pardon me for venturing upon a few suggestions as to the most useful manner of increasing the strength of this Army.

The greatest benefit that can be conferred upon it would be to fill to the maximum the old regiments which have so nobly sustained the honor of the Union and their State; I would prefer 50,000 recruits for my old regiments to 100,000 men organized into new regiments, and I cannot too earnestly urge the imperative necessity of following this system.

By far the best arrangements would be to fill up all the old companies; if that cannot be done, the next best thing is to consolidate the old companies and add new ones to each regiment. We have here the material for making excellent officers in the regiments; these men, tried and proved in many hard fought battles, all infinitely to be preferred to any new appointments. More than that they have won their promotion; policy and gratitude alike demand that their claims should be recognized.

With the old regiments thus filled up the whole Army would in a very few weeks be ready for any service. New regiments would require several months to fit them for service, and they would be brought into action with untried, and in many cases unfit officers.

Again, I would earnestly impress upon you the great mistake of bringing men into the field for a less period than three years or the War; the contact of such troops with those enlisted for three years would soon breed dissatisfaction among the latter, while the term of service of the former would expire about the time they became valuable to the service. I would also urge the propriety, necessity rather, of sending recruits to their regiments as rapidly as enlisted. They will become Soldiers here in one tenth of the time they could in the home depots, and would have all the advantages of contact with the veterans who now compose this Army.

I have also to ask your attention to the many officers and men who are now in the north on sick leave, etc. Many thousands of these are fit for duty, and should at once be made to join their regiments. May I ask the earnest efforts of your excellency to secure this very important end. I would also request that no officer who has resigned from this Army be commissioned in another regiment unless furnished with a special recommendation to that effect from the Commander of his Division or Army Corps. I regret to say that many officers have resigned to avoid the consequence of cowardly conduct, inefficiency etc — it is a melancholy fact, that, while many noble exceptions are to be found, the officers of Volunteers are as a mass (perhaps I should say, were, for the worst are sifted out) greatly inferior to the men they command.

Trusting that you will pardon me for the liberty I have taken in making these suggestions and that you will be good enough to give them your careful consideration,

I have the honor to be Sir Most Respectfully, your obdt servant
Geo B McClellan
Maj Genl Comdg

LS, Houghton Library, Harvard University. The same letter was sent to other Northern governors.

To Samuel L. M. Barlow

Head-Quarters, Army of the Potomac,
My dear Barlow July 15 Berkeley 1862

Your kind letter of the 6th reached me a day or two since — but I have been too busy to reply to it, & now can only scrawl off a few brief lines. There was truly propriety in your mingled feelings "of sadness & joy" upon receiving the news of recent events here — joy that the Army behaved with such heroism, so worthily of its country — sadness that so many brave & good men have fallen victims to the stupidity & wickedness at Washington which have done their best to sacrifice as noble an Army as ever marched to battle. I cannot express to you my admiration of the superb conduct of my men — their heroic gallantry, extreme patience, great endurance & excellent discipline. You will have learned ere this that Clitz is *not* dead — but that we may soon hope to have him again among us. He was severely but not dangerously wounded. I do not care if they *do* remove [me] from this Army — except on account of the Army itself. I have lost all regard & respect for the majority of the Administration, & doubt the propriety of my brave men's blood being spilled to further the designs of such a set of heartless villains.

I do not believe that Stanton will go out of office — he will not willingly, & the Presdt has not the nerve to turn him out — at least so I think. Stanton has written me a most abject letter — declaring that he has ever been my best friend etc etc!![1] Well, burn this up when you have read it. Give my kindest regards to the Madame & believe me truly your friend

Geo B McClellan

S L M Barlow Esq

I will write you fully in a day or two — we are doing well here — waiting!

ALS, Barlow Papers, Huntington Library.

1. See GBM to Stanton, July 8, note 1, *supra*.

To Abraham Lincoln [TELEGRAM]

Head-Quarters, Army of the Potomac,
Berkeley July 17 — 8 am 1862

I have consulted fully with Genl Burnside & would commend to your favorable consideration the General's plan for bringing (7) seven additional regiments from North Carolina by leaving Newburn to the care of the gun boats.

It appears manifestly to be our policy to concentrate here everything we can possibly spare from less important points to make sure of crushing the enemy at Richmond, which seems clearly to be the most important point in rebeldom. Nothing should be left to chance here. I would recommend that Genl Burnside with all his troops be ordered to this Army to enable it to assume the offensive as soon as possible.[1]

Very respectfully
G B McClellan
Maj Genl Comdg

A Lincoln
Presdt

ALS (telegram sent), McClellan Papers (A-73:29), Library of Congress. *OR*, Ser. 1, XI, Part 1, p. 75.

1. On July 15 Burnside wrote GBM from Fort Monroe: "I've much to say to you. . . . The President has ordered me to remain here for the present. . . . I dont know what it means; but I do know my dear Mac that you have lots of enemies, but you must keep cool; dont allow them to provoke you into a quarrel. . . ." McClellan Papers (A-73:29).

To Mary Ellen McClellan

[Berkeley] July 17 [1862] am.

Genl Dix & Burnside are both here. . . .

Burnside is very well & if the Presdt permits will bring me large (respectably) reinforcements. . . .

Am quite well today — a little disgusted at the stupidity of people in Washington. You need not be at all alarmed as to my being deceived by them. I *know* that they are ready to sacrifice me at any moment & are only restrained by fear of the people. I shall not be at all surprised to have some other Genl made Comdr of the whole army, or even to be superseded here — & to tell you the truth I don't care how soon they do it. I have lost confidence in the Govt, & would be glad to be out of the scrape — keep this to yourself. . . .

7 pm. . . . You ask me when I expect to reach Richmond & whether I shall act on the offensive this summer. I am at the mercy of the Govt — after the first 9000 or 10,000 men sent to me they have withheld all further reinforcements. Burnside is halted at Ft Monroe — with his own troops & those of Hunter he can bring me some 20,000 troops — but I have no idea of the intentions of the Govt — if I am reinforced to that extent I will try again, with the least possible delay — I am not at all in favor of baking on the banks of this river, but am anxious to bring matters to an issue. I agree with you that a certain eminent individual *is* "an old stick" — & of pretty poor timber at that.[1] I confess that I do not at all appreciate his style of friendship. The army did *not* give him an enthusiastic reception — I *had to order* the men to cheer & they did it very feebly — this you can keep to yourself, it is a "jurer mon secret." You need not be at all alarmed lest any of these people *flatter* me into the belief that they are my friends — it's mighty little flattery or comfort I get out of any of them in these days, I assure you. . . .

Don't think much about the war. I think the crisis will soon be upon us. If the adm conducts the war on right principles it will soon be over — if it adopts those radical & inhuman views to which it seems inclined, & which will prolong the struggle over a great length of time, I cannot well in conscience serve the Govt any longer. . . .

So you like my letter to the Presdt?[2] I feel that I did my duty in writing it tho' I apprehend it will do no good whatever — but it clears my conscience to have spoken plainly at such a time. You do not feel one bit more bitterly towards those people than I do; I do not say much about it — but I fear they have done all that cowardice, folly & rascality can do to ruin our poor country — & the blind people seem not to see it, but to submit like serfs to the lash. It makes my blood boil when I think of it. I cannot resign so long as the fate of the Army of the Potomac is entrusted to my care — I owe a great duty to this noble set of men — & that is the only feeling that sustains me. I fear that my day of usefulness to the country is past — at least under this administ — I have no respect for any member of it & *our* opinions do not differ in the slightest. I hope & trust that God *will* watch over guide & protect me — I accept most resignedly all the adversity he has brought upon me — perhaps I have really brought it on myself, for while striving conscientiously to do my best, it may well be that I have made great mistakes, that my vanity does not permit me to perceive — when I see so much self blindness around me, I cannot arrogate to myself greater clearness of vision & self examination. I *did* have a terrible time during that week — for I stood alone, without *anyone* to help me — I felt that on me rested everything & I felt how weak a thing poor mortal erring man is! I felt it sincerely & shall never I trust forget the lesson — it will last me to my dying day. . . .

I *am* very well now — perfectly well & ready for any amount of fatigue that can be imagined.

AL copy, McClellan Papers (C-7:63), Library of Congress.

1. The reference is to President Lincoln. 2. GBM to Lincoln, July 7, *supra.*

To Abraham Lincoln [TELEGRAM]

Head Quarters, Army of the Potomac,
Berkeley July 18 8 am 1862

No change worth reporting in the state of affairs. Some (20,000) twenty to (25,000) twenty five thousand of enemy at Petersburg, & others thence to Richmond. Those at Petersburg say they are part of Beauregard's Army. New troops arriving via Petersburg. Am anxious to learn determination of Govt that no time may be lost in preparing for it. Hours are very precious now, & perfect unity of action necessary.

G B McClellan
Maj Genl Comdg

A Lincoln
Presdt

ALS (telegram sent), McClellan Papers (C-15:64), Library of Congress. *OR,* Ser. 1, XI, Part 1, p. 75.

To Mary Ellen McClellan

July 18 [1862] Berkeley Friday 9 pm.

... I have my head half occupied with the idea of making another last appeal to the Presdt to endeavor to beat some sense into his head....

I am inclined now to think that the Presdt will make Halleck comdr of the Army[1] & that the first pretext will be seized to supersede me in command of this army — their game seems to be to withold reinforcements & then to relieve me for not advancing — well knowing that I have not the means to do so. If they supersede me in command of the Army of the Potomac I will resign my commission at once; if they appoint Halleck Comg Genl I will remain in command of this army as long as they will allow me to, provided the army is in danger & likely to play an active part. I cannot remain as a subordinate in the army I once commanded any longer than the interests of my own Army of the Potomac require. I owe no gratitude to any but my own soldiers here — none to the Govt or to the country. I have done my best for my country — I expect nothing in return — they are my debtors, not I theirs....

My letter to Stanton was fairly "diplomatic" & if you read it carefully you will see that it is bitter enough — politely expressed, but containing much more than is on the surface.[2] ...

If things come to pass as I anticipate I shall leave the service with a sad heart for my country, but a light one for myself. I am tired of being dependent on men I despise from the bottom of my heart. I cannot express to you the infinite contempt I feel for these people; but one thing keeps me at my work — love for my country & my army. Surely no General had ever better cause to love his men than I have to love mine. Unhappily the men are too often better than their officers.

Smith W. F. went off today. I don't think he intends returning, & don't think he was as sick as many who remained — he had not even the decency to bid me good bye after all I have done for him! Such is gratitude — I no longer expect such a feeling. I don't care to have him come back.

AL copy, McClellan Papers (C-7 :63), Library of Congress.

1. GBM's surmise was correct. On July 11 Halleck was ordered to the post of general-in-chief. The appointment was reported in the press on July 20, and he assumed command on July 23. 2. GBM to Stanton, July 8, *supra.*

To Randolph B. Marcy [TELEGRAM]

Head-Quarters, Army of the Potomac,
Berkeley July 19 — 8 am 1862

Dispatch of (17) seventeenth received.[1] No change whatever. Not a man since you left. Not a word from Gomorrah. Burn[2] not under my orders and do not know whether he will be. The event cannot occur without stupid insanity on my part until I have tools to work with & I am surprised that it is alluded to under the circumstances. You need not hurry. Will inform you the moment I receive any help or know anything. I do not know what to expect.

G B McClellan
Maj Genl

Brig Genl R B Marcy
North Orange New Jersey

ALS (telegram sent), McClellan Papers (A-73:29), Library of Congress.

1. This dispatch, not found, presumably dealt with an advance by the Army of the Potomac.
2. Gen. Burnside.

To William H. Aspinwall

Confidential Head-Quarters, Army of the Potomac,
My dear Mr Aspinwall Berkeley July 19th 1862

I again find myself in a position such that I may ere long have to tax your friendship.

I have reason to believe that Genl Halleck is to be made Comdr in Chief of the Army, &, if I am not mistaken, I think I detect the premonitory symptoms of still further changes.

I can get no replies from Washington to any of my dispatches — Burnside and his troops are taken out of my hands — I receive no reinforcements & no hope of them is held out to me; — the game apparently is to deprive me of the means of moving, & then to cut my head off for not advancing — in other words it is my opinion that I will be removed from the command of this Army in a short time. The present policy is, I think, merely a continuation of the inveterate persecution that has pursued me since I landed on the Peninsula — weakening my command so as to render it inadequate to accomplish the end in view, & then to hold me responsible for the results. I am quite weary of this.

If I am superseded in the command of the Army of the Potomac I shall resign my commission in the service — feeling that I can no longer be of use — on the contrary only in the way.

Looking forward to that event, my main object in writing to you is to ask you to be kind enough to cast your eyes about you to see whether there is anything I can do in New York to earn a respectable support for my family — I have no exaggerated ideas or expectations, all I wish is some comparatively quiet pursuit — for I really need rest. Pretty much everything I had has been sacrificed in consequence of my reentering the service, & when I leave it I must commence anew & work for my support — that I am quite willing to do.

I *know* that I need not apologize for troubling you in regard to this matter.

Please regard this as confidential except with Mr Alsop & Mr Bartlett.[1]

I am, my dear sir, most sincerely your friend
Geo B McClellan

Wm H Aspinwall Esq
New York City

ALS retained copy, McClellan Papers (A-73:29), Library of Congress. Aspinwall, a New York buinessman and financier, had hired GBM for the Ohio and Mississippi Railroad in 1860.

1. Joseph W. Alsop and Edwin Bartlett, executives with the Ohio and Mississippi. Alsop wrote GBM on July 24: "Dont think of resigning. The Country will follow you. In the end *Truth* will be made manifest and those in power will be unable to make you bear the burthen of their inequities." On the same day, Aspinwall wrote: "Your sphere whilst the war lasts, is the army — you have no right to entertain any idea of a return to civil life just now ... weigh well the political bearing of advice which may be given you to the contrary." McClellan Papers (A-73:29).

To Abraham Lincoln [TELEGRAM]

Head-Quarters, Army of the Potomac,
Berkeley July 20 1.30 pm 1862

I have again heard from returned prisoners that Jackson's troops commenced leaving Richmond about one week ago by rail either towards Gordonsville or Fredericksburg, & that the movement continued for some three (3) days by night & day. This comes through so many sources that I feel obliged to call your close attention to it.

I also learn that large numbers of conscripts are constantly arriving in Richmond from the south. My cavalry scouts are today amusing themselves with the enemy at Malvern Hill.

Jackson's movement may be against Buell — the fact of his taking the Gordonsville route would in that case be accounted for by the necessity of their keeping the Petersburg & Danville roads free for the transit of wounded, recruits and supplies. In any event I beg to urge concentration of the masses of troops in front of Washington, & the sending of cavalry far to the front. If I am to have Burnside's troops I would be glad to avail myself of at least a portion of them to occupy a point on the south bank of James River.

Health of the command improving a little. I should be glad to hear daily from Pope's outposts — it is important that I should do so.

G B McClellan
Maj Genl Comdg

A Lincoln
Presdt

ALS (telegram sent), McClellan Papers (A-73:29), Library of Congress. *OR*, Ser. 1, XI, Part 3, pp. 328–29.

To Mary Ellen McClellan

[Berkeley] July 20 [1862] pm.

...Which dispatch of mine to Stanton did you allude to — the telegraphic one in which I told him that if I saved the army I owed no thanks to anyone in Washn, & that he had done his best to sacrifice my army?[1] It was pretty frank & quite true. Of course they will never forgive me for that — I knew it when I wrote it, but as I thought it possible that it might be the last I ever wrote it seemed better to have it exactly true. The Presdt was entirely too smart to give my correspondence to the public — it would have ruined him & Stanton forever. Of course he has not replied to my letter, & never will — he *cannot*.[2] His reply may be, however, to avail himself of the first opportunity to cut my head off.

I see it reported in this evening's papers that Halleck is to be the new Genl in Chief. Now let them take the next step & relieve me & I shall once more be a free man....

Later ...I believe it is now certain that Halleck is comdr in chief — I have information this evening from Washn from private sources which seems to render it quite certain — so you will have to cease directing your letters to me as Comdg US Army & let the address be "Comdg the Army of the Potomac" — quite as proud a title as the other, at all events. I shall have to remove the three stars from my shoulders & put up with two — Eh bien — it is all for the best I doubt not. I hope Halleck will have a more pleasant time in his new position than I did when I held it. This of course fixes the future for us — I cannot remain permanently in the army after this slight. I must of course stick to this army so long as I am necessary to it, or until the Govt adopts a policy in regard to the war that I cannot conscientiously affirm — the moment either of these events comes to pass I shall leave the service....

No position in the gift of the country can ever tempt me into public life again — my experience in it has been sad enough, but I have learned a useful lesson. I have tried to do my best, honestly & faithfully, for my country — that I have to a certain extent failed I do not believe to be my fault — tho' my self conceit probably blinds me to many errors that others see. But one useful lesson I have learned — to despise earthly honors & popular favor as vanities — I am content — I have not disgraced my name, nor will my child be ashamed of her father — thank God for that. I shall try to get something to do which will make you comfortable & it will be most pleasant & in the best taste for me that we should lead hereafter a rather quiet & retired life — it will not do to parade the tattered remnants of my departed honors to the gaze of the world. Let us try to live for each other & our child, & to prepare for the great change that sooner or later must overtake us all. I have enough of earthly honors & place — I have drained the goblet nearly to the dregs, & found it poison. I believe I can give up all, & retire to privacy once more, a better man than when we gave up our dear little home with wild ideas of serving the country — I feel that I have paid all that I owe her — I am sick & weary of this business — I am tired of serving fools & knaves. God help my country — he alone can save it.

It *is* grating to have to serve under the orders of a man whom I know by experience to be my inferior — but so let it be — God's will be done. My conscience is clear & all will turn out for the best. My trust *is* in God & I cheerfully submit to his will. . . .

AL copy, McClellan Papers (C-7 :63), Library of Congress.

1. GBM to Stanton, June 28, 1862, *supra*. 2. This is probably a reference to GBM's Harrison's Landing letter to Lincoln of July 7, *supra*.

To Mary Ellen McClellan

[Berkeley] July 22 [1862] 7 1/2 am.

. . . While I think of it be very careful what you telegraph & tell your father the same thing. *I have the proof that the Secy reads all my private telegrams.* If he has read my private letters to you also his ears must have tingled somewhat. I am more & more convinced that he is the most depraved hypocrite & villain that I have ever had the bad fortune to meet with. . . .

I am about doing a thing today which will I suppose cause the abolitionists & my other *friends* to drive the last nail in my official coffin! You know that our sick & wounded in Richmond are suffering terribly for want of proper food, medicines, hospital supplies etc — well — I have ordered a boat load of all such things (lemons, tea, sugar, brandy, underclothing, lint, bandages, chloroform, quinine, ice etc etc) to be sent up to Genl Lee today to be used at his discretion for the sick & wounded of *both* armies. I know he would not, & could not, receive them for our men alone, therefore I can only do it in the way I propose, & trust to his honor to apply them properly — half & half.[1] I presume I will be accused now of double dyed treason — giving aid & comfort to the enemy etc. What do *you* think of it? Am I right or wrong? . . .

I see that the Pope bubble is likely to be suddenly collapsed — Stonewall Jackson is after him, & the paltry young man who wanted to teach me the art of war will in less than a week either be in full retreat or badly whipped. He will begin to learn the value of "*entrenchments, lines of communication & of retreat,* bases of supply etc" — they will learn bye & bye.[2]

Pm. It is a lovely afternoon, bright & sunny, a pleasant breeze blowing, & everything charming to the eye. The old river looks beautiful today — as bright as when John Smith, Esq, & my dusky ancestress Madame Pocahontas Rolfe neé Powhatan paddled her canoe & children somewhere in this vicinity. If it were not for the accompaniments & present surroundings it would delight me beyond measure to have you here, to see the scenery & some of the fine old residences, which stud its banks. The old rascals of two or three generations ago, must have lived in great state & comfort here, when abolitionists were not dreamed of & pestiferous wooden nutmeg, psalm singing yankees were animals as rare as camelopards & black swans. I suspect they had a pretty good time, interrupted only by the chills & fever, bad luck in gambling & horse racing & the trouble of providing for their woolly headed dependents.

6 pm. ... I see that the fickle press (& I presume the people) are beginning to turn & worship Halleck as the rising star — as soon as Stanton & the Presdt feel that they can safely do so they will either supersede me or do something to put me out of service. I shall surely take care not to let them put me in the wrong....

I do not like the political turn that affairs are taking....

AL copy; copy, McClellan Papers (C-7:63/D-10:72), Library of Congress.

1. On July 23 Gen. Lee replied to GBM that these supplies were unnecessary, in view of the prisoner exchange agreement made the previous day. *OR*, Ser. 2, IV, p. 269. 2. On July 14, in an address to his Army of Virginia, Gen. Pope announced: "I have come to you from the West, where we have always seen the backs of our enemies.... I desire you to dismiss from your minds certain phrases, which I am sorry to find so much in vogue amongst you. I hear constantly of 'taking strong positions and holding them,' of 'lines of retreat,' and of 'bases of supplies.' Let us discard such ideas...." *OR*, Ser. 1, XII, Part 3, pp. 473–74.

To Samuel L. M. Barlow

My dear Barlow Berkeley Wednesday [July] 23 [1862]

Your two kind letters received, the last this evening.[1]

I will briefly reply to both at once. I have *not* been in any manner consulted as to Halleck's appointment & it is intended as "a slap in the face." I do not think it best to reply to the lies of such a fellow as Chandler — he is beneath my notice, & if the people are so foolish as to believe aught he says I am content to lose their favor & to wait for history to do me justice. I am in my own mind satisfied that I will be relieved from the command of this Army, & shall then leave the service.

I am weary, very weary, of submitting to the whims of such *"things"* as those now over me — I have suffered as much for my country as most men have endured, & shall be inexpressibly happy to be free once more.

If relieved from command of this Army I shall ask Halleck for a leave of absence for a month or so to give me time to think — will go with my wife & child to some very quiet place where not a human being knows me & try to rest — for I need repose.

Stanton's statement that I outnumbered the rebels is simply false — they had more than two to one against me. I could *not* have gone into Richmond with my left.

However I will not discuss these things now.

From a remark in your last letter I infer that you think that Burnside's troops are under my control — they are *not,* he having been withdrawn from my control by the order of the Presdt — I have several times asked for him but cannot get him.

I have not received 10,000 fresh troops since I reached this place — have had none for a long time, am receiving none, & see no chance of getting any except Burnside's. When the Presdt was here he asked for no explanations, expressed no dissatisfaction — treated me with no confidence, & did not ask my opinion except in *three* questions —

1st. "How many troops have you left?"

2nd. "How many did you lose in the late actions?"

3rd. "Can you move this Army still further in retreat?"

You see pretty well how the case stands. If I go north I may possibly see you for a few moments altho' I shall avoid N.Y. & all crowded places.

With my kindest regards to Madame

Ever your friend
McClellan

S L M Barlow Esq

My regards to Meagher.[2] Excuse the brevity of this but I am pressed for time.

ALS, Barlow Papers, Huntington Library.

1. Barlow's letter of July 18 read, in part: "When the history of this war is written, the fault will be thrown upon Stanton and I think upon no one else. . . . I think I do him no injustice when I say that no intelligent man knows Stanton without knowing that he is the greatest hypocrite alive. . . . I hope this change [Halleck's appointment] has been made with your knowledge & sanction. If not, if it totally intercedes as a slap in the face, I still hope that you will not resign. . . . I have always believed that through you we may win this war & restore our government & that it is your duty under almost all circumstances to stand by the country." He suggested that if GBM would "give the facts in a paper" his friends would "say all that is necessary" to counter the attacks of Senator Chandler. Barlow Papers. 2. Brig. Gen. Thomas F. Meagher, on leave in New York.

To Mary Ellen McClellan

[Berkeley] July 24 [1862]

. . . Your Father arrived this evening. . . .

Took a long ride in the sun today. Our men look better than ever — like real veterans now — tough, brown & fearless. . . .

I have nothing yet from Washn, & must confess that I am as indifferent as possible to what they do. If they reinforce me I am ready to fight harder than ever & will give secesh a sharp rub for his capital. If they make it necessary for me to resign I am quite ready to do so. . . .

I presume I shall learn something tomorrow about the destination of Burnside — I can then enable you to guess how matters will go — I am yet in complete ignorance — being no longer taken into the confidence of the "powers that be." . . .

You ask me whether my self respect will permit me to remain longer in the service after Halleck's appt?[1] It will permit me to remain only so long as the welfare of the Army of the Potomac demands — no longer. Don't mind these things — I have done the best I could, history will justify me — I bide my time. Whatever God sends me, be it defeat & loss of rank — or be it success & honor — I will cheerfully submit to & try neither to be unduly depressed by the one, or too much elated by the other — may God help me in this.

I do not see whither events are tending, & the poor country does seem to be under a terrible cloud — but God's will be done — he will in his own good time bring all this to the best termination. . . .

I presume I shall hear something today from that council of military pundits who have been about in Washn — there is not a handful of brains among them all & a nice mess they will make of it.

AL copy, McClellan Papers (C-7:63), Library of Congress.

1. Mrs. McClellan had written, on July 22: "To have a man put over you without even *consulting* with you is rather more than I can endure — & if you do not resign I will!! . . . You know there was a consultation of Cabinet & *General* officers & probably Pope. McD[owell] & Wadsworth were the Officers. I am *indignant*. What *is* this country coming to, darling? We are certainly under a terrible cloud." McClellan Papers (B-11:48).

To Joseph W. Alsop

Head Quarters Army of the Potomac
Berkeley July 26 1862

My dear Mr Alsop

Your kind note of the 24th as well as that of Mr Aspinwall reached me this morning.[1] I do not (nor have I for a moment) considered Halleck's appointment as a reason for resigning. My fate is linked with that of the Army of the Potomac, and so long as I can be useful with it I must remain with it. I have seen Halleck and believe that he will act with me in good faith.[2] . . .

Your sincere friend
Geo B McClellan

J. W. Alsop Esq
New York

Copy, McClellan Papers (A-73:29), Library of Congress.

1. See GBM to Aspinwall, July 19, note 1, *supra*. 2. Gen. Halleck conferred with GBM at Harrison's Landing on July 25–26.

To Henry W. Halleck

Maj Genl H W Halleck
Comdg U.S. Army — Head Quarters Army of the Potomac
General — Berkeley July 26th 1862

I have seen to day nearly a thousand of our sick & wounded just returned from Richmond; some refugees have also arrived, & a number of surgeons and chaplains taken prisoners at Bull Run. All of these who have enjoyed any opportunities of observation unite in stating, that reinforcements are pouring into Richmond from the South.

Dr L H Stone (U.S.A.) saw at Charlotte from 7000 to 8000 troops en route to Richmond; he & others unite in stating that it is quite positive that the troops on James Island (Charleston) have arrived in Richmond, & that the Southern States are being drained of their garrisons to reinforce the Army in my front. It is said that the troops of Beauregards old Army are also en route hither — this last is not positive, & I hope to learn the truth in regard to it tomorrow.

3 rgts (1 So Ca, 1 No Ca, 1 Georgia) reached Richmond yesterday; supplies are being rapidly pushed in by all routes.

It would appear that Longstreet is in front of Richmond, on this side of the James; D. H. Hill at Fort Darling & vicinity.

Our cavalry pickets on Charles City Road were driven in today by a heavy force of cavalry & some artillery — Averell started after them with a sufficient force — I have not yet heard the result.

Allow me to urge most strongly that *all* the troops of Burnside & Hunter[1] — together with all that can possibly be spared from other points — be sent to me at once. I am sure that you will agree with me that the true defence of Washington consists in a rapid & heavy blow given by this Army upon Richmond.

Can you not *possibly* draw 15,000 or 20,000 men from the West to reinforce me temporarily? They can return the moment we gain Richmond. Please give weight to this suggestion — I am sure it merits it.

I have to be, General, very respectfully Your obedient Svt
Geo B McClellan
Maj Genl USA

ALS, Records of the Adjutant General's Office, RG 94 (159: Halleck Papers), National Archives. *OR*, Ser. 1, XI, Part 3, pp. 333–34.

1. The troops in these two commands totaled some 35,000.

To Lorenzo Thomas [TELEGRAM]

Brig Gen L Thomas
Adjt Genl USA

Head-Quarters, Army of the Potomac,
[Berkeley] July 27 1862

I respectfully apply for permission to send an officer from each regiment to the place where it was raised, with authority to bring on every officer and man he can find fit for duty whether on leave of absence or not, no matter from what source the leave may be granted. I have official assurance that the number of people absent on leave is having an injurious effect on the recruiting service. Absentees tell such exaggerated stories of the hardships and sufferings of campaign life and of the carnage of the battle field that they deter recruits from enlisting. The leaves might be revoked by an order from the Adjt's Genl's office, except where the case is that of bona fide sick and wounded unable to join.

The officers I propose to send from each regiment should report at your office; and receive orders (such is my application) to visit all hospitals and places where soldiers may be detained, whether on extra duty or otherwise, no matter by what order or whose authority and bring them here to their regiments. The recruiting service or important duty of course will be excepted. I am satisfied that the most fertile source of increase to the diminished ranks of the regiments is to get back the absentees from the army. There are two well men absent to one really sick man.[1]

G B McClellan
Maj Genl Cmdg

LS (telegram sent), McClellan Papers, New-York Historical Society. *OR*, Ser. 1, XI, Part 3, p. 338.

1. General Orders No. 92, issued July 31 by Stanton, addressed the problem of absentees, relying on civil authorities for enforcement. *OR*, Ser. 3, II, pp. 286–87.

To Mary Ellen McClellan

[Berkeley] July 27 [1862] Sunday

When the mail came, & my package of letters was handed me, my heart sank way down to the toes of my slippers, was rapidly wearing a hole through one of them, for there was no letter from you. In about twenty minutes, Seth[1] gladdened my heart, saved my slippers & put me generally in a good humour with the whole world by handing me your glorious & splendid five pager. I tell you, I took the first chance to read it, & have just finished it. "Tired of it"? You knew when you wrote it, that you were acting on Mr. Weller's[2] principle & stopped short to make me "wish there was more of it"; its brevity was the only thing that disgusted me....

We feel alike about these trials. I do feel that God does what is right

& that my interests, my troubles are & ought to be nothing in comparison with the general good. I will do my best to continue to act unselfishly & solely with an honest heart & am sure that if we do not find peace & happiness in this world we *will* be rewarded in the great eternity. My prayer to God is, that he will permit us to be together in the next world, & that we may pass through eternity hand in hand, heart joined to heart, looking back with a smile to the ephemeral troubles on this poor sinful earth.

I can't tell you how glad I am that I went to see all those poor wounded men yesterday. Another batch will come tonight, & I will if possible go to see all of them tomorrow morning. I regard it as a duty I owe the poor fellows — rather a hard one to perform, but still one that cannot be neglected. I am sorry that no other General officer does the same — it would do the men good. . . .

You ask me whether I advised the Presdt to appoint Halleck — the letter of which I sent you a copy[3] is all that ever passed on the subject, either directly or indirectly — not another word than is there written. We never conversed on the subject — I was never informed of his views or intentions, & even now have not been officially informed of the appt. I only know it through the newspapers. In all these things the Presdt & those around him have acted so as to make the matter as offensive as possible — he has not shown the slightest gentlemanly or friendly feeling & I cannot regard him as in any respect my friend — I am confident that he would relieve me tomorrow if he dared do so. His cowardice alone prevents it. I can never regard him with other feelings than those of thorough contempt — for his mind, heart & morality. I can assure you that my regard for the A of P is the only feeling that induces me to remain in the service. . . .

I can't say that I think that the Presdt is very fortunate in his military advisers. I hope Halleck will scatter them to the four winds. McDowell is morally dead — he has no longer one particle of influence & is despised by all alike. . . .

Fitz Porter has, on the contrary, stuck through it all most nobly — he is all that I thought him & more. Nothing has depressed him; he is always cheerful, active & ready, & is much more efficient than all put together. . . .

AL copy; copy, McClellan Papers (C-7:63/D-10:72), Library of Congress.

1. Seth Williams, of GBM's staff. 2. Samuel Weller, in Dickens's *The Pickwick Papers*. 3. GBM to Lincoln, July 7, *supra*.

To Henry W. Halleck [TELEGRAM]

Head-Quarters, Army of the Potomac,
Berkeley July 28 8 am 1862

Nothing especially new except corroboration of reports that reinforcements reaching Richmond from South. It is not confirmed that any of Bragg's troops are yet here.[1] My opinion is more & more firm that here is the defence of Washington & that I should be at once reinforced by all available troops to enable me to advance.

Retreat would be disastrous to the Army & the cause — I am confident of that.

G B McClellan
Maj Genl

Maj Genl H W Halleck
Comdg US Army Washington D.C.

ALS (telegram sent), McClellan Papers (A-73:29), Library of Congress. *OR,* Ser. 1, XI, Part 1, p. 75.

1. Braxton Bragg had replaced Beauregard in command of the Confederate Army of Tennessee.

To Mary Ellen McClellan

[Berkeley] July 29 [1862]

. . . I have nothing as yet from Washn, & begin to believe that they intend & hope that I & my army may melt away under the hot sun — if they leave me here neglected much longer I shall feel like taking my rather large military family to Washn to seek an explanation of their course — I fancy that under such circumstances I should be treated with rather more politeness than I have been of late. . . .

Secesh is very quiet of late — scarcely even a cavalry skirmish — he is almost too quiet for good & must be after some mischief — may be we *will* have a visit from monster Merrimac No 2![1] What a row it would create among the transports — such a scampering. I am in hopes that I will receive orders of *some kind* from Washn this evening — I am getting dreadfully tired of sucking my thumbs & doing nothing. I begin to feel the want of a little quiet excitement. I could rest at home away from my men — but the idea of remaining quietly in camp, with an army about me, & an active enemy at some mischief or other, is a very very different thing.

10 1/2 pm . . . Nothing tonight from Washn, so that I am yet completely in the dark as to the intentions of our benign Govt.

AL copy, McClellan Papers (C-7:63), Library of Congress.

1. The Confederate ironclad *Richmond.* She was not completed before the Army of the Potomac evacuated the Peninsula.

To Henry W. Halleck

Maj Genl H W Halleck
Cmdg US Army — Head-Quarters, Army of the Potomac,
General — Berkeley July 30 1862

There is nothing new of any interest to give you. The Cavalry scouts are daily extending their beats, & meet with less resistance during the last few days. The enemy still at Malvern, its vicinity rather, in small force — probably a brigade with a battery. Nothing seems to be doing on the other side of the James — if I had even a part of Burnside's command I could beat them up on that bank of the James, as well as stir them up at Malvern. I am very weak in Cavalry — not more than 3800 for duty — could not Williams' Regt from Port Royal, & Mix' from Newbern both be ordered up here. A large part of my Cavalry was taken from me when I left Washington for Fort Monroe — I feel the want of it very much.

It is not true (my information goes) that either of the Hills or Longstreet are with Jackson near Gordonsville — nor does it seem probable that J's force is more than 30,000 to 35,000 — altho' it is possible that I may be deceived about the latter point. Heavy reinforcements have arrived in Richmond and are still coming.

I still feel that our true policy is to reinforce this Army by every available means & throw it again upon Richmond.

Should it be determined to withdraw it I shall look upon our cause as lost, & the demoralization of this Army certain — I sincerely hope that *some* decision may be promptly arrived at, & that it may be in accordance with the views I have so frequently expressed.

I am very respectfully your obdt svt
Geo B McClellan
Maj Genl Cmdg

ALS, Records of the Adjutant General's Office, RG 94 (159: Halleck Papers), National Archives. *OR*, Ser. 1, XI, Part 3, p. 342.

To Samuel L. M. Barlow

My dear Barlow — Berkeley July 30 1862

Yours of the 26 received. You are right *to this extent at least* — it has only been the fear of the effect upon my men, & partly perhaps of public opinion, that has prevented my being removed from the command of the Army of the Potomac. The command was for two days persistently pressed upon a General Officer, who happened to be a true friend of mine, & declined the offer.[1] I *know* that the rascals will get rid of me as soon as they dare — they all know my opinion of them. They are aware that I have seen through their villainous schemes, & that if I succeed my foot will be on their necks.

I do not believe there is one honest man among them — & I know what I say — I fear none of them wish to save the Union — they prefer ruling a separate Northern Confederacy — God will yet foil their abominable designs & mete out to them the terrible punishment they deserve.

Don't trust *McD*,[2] or anything he says or writes — he is wily & specious — but is not true.

Halleck remained but a few minutes (comparatively) here & saw *nothing* of the Army — departed just as wise as he came.

I get no reinforcements & no information — until Halleck came I had no word from Washington, since he left I have received nothing. I know nothing, absolutely nothing as to the plans & intentions of the Govt — but I have strong reason to believe that they literally have *no* plans, but are halting in a wretched state of indecision — trembling at the storm they themselves have conjured & not knowing how to quiet it.

Much obliged to you for the copy of Meagher's speech — give him my regards & tell him that I am very anxious for his success — we want many more "wild Irishmen."

If this Army is retired from here I abandon all hope — our cause will be lost. It ought *not* to yield an inch — here is the true defense of Washington.

If I hear anything today or tomorrow I will let you know.

In the mean time, with my kindest regards to Mrs Barlow,

believe me sincerely your friend
Geo B McClellan

S L M Barlow Esq
N.Y.

ALS, Barlow Papers, Huntington Library.

1. Gen. Burnside. 2. Gen. McDowell.

To Mary Ellen McClellan

[Berkeley] July 30 [1862] 10.15 pm.

. . . Another day elapsed & nothing from Washn. I have positive information today that the command of this army was pressed upon Burnside & that he peremptorily refused it. I learn that Meigs is very anxious for it — much good may it do him. I still think from all that comes to me that the chances are at least even that I will be superseded. . . .

We were relieved today by a little excitement — the gun boats reported that 6 rebel gun boats (including Mr. Merrimac No 2) were on the way down — so we were for some hours considerably brightened up by the prospect of seeing a shindy — but it turned out to be a false report. . . .

I see among other lies, that the papers say that the enemy drove off 500 of our beef cattle the other day — a lie cut of whole cloth....

I am sorry to say that I hear that too much faith must not be rested in Halleck — I hope it is not so — but will be very careful how far I trust him, or any other man in these days. He has done me *no good yet.* As a counterpart to what you say Alsop said of H's conversation in the cars (that McC was the ablest soldier in the world)[1] he told some one else (that is *H.* did) that *I* was too dilatory. The adm. have proclaimed a policy that I will not carry out. As soon as I receive the official copy of the Presdt's Proclamation I shall issue orders directly opposite to Pope's — then there will be a furious row![2]

AL copy, McClellan Papers (C-7:63), Library of Congress.

1. Mrs. McClellan had recently visited Joseph W. Alsop and his wife in New York. Alsop had related the same story to GBM in his letter of July 24: "Mr. Lord (of the Illinois C.) is here.... He said to me this (which I immediately noted down) that in a conversation had with Genl Halleck on Monday last [July 21] in the cars, he (the General) said *that McClellan was the ablest military man in the world.* This delighted me." McClellan Papers (A-73:29). 2. The president's proclamation of July 25 promulgated the recently enacted Second Confiscation Act. *Collected Works of Lincoln,* V, p. 341. GBM's response was to issue General Orders No. 154 on Aug. 9, which read, in part: "The general commanding takes this occasion to remind the officers and soldiers of this army... that we are not engaged in a war of rapine, revenge, or subjugation; that this is not a contest against populations, but against armed forces and political organizations; that it... should be conducted by us upon the highest principles known to Christian civilization." *OR,* Ser. 1, XI, Part 3, pp. 362–64.

To Mary Ellen McClellan

[Berkeley] July 31 [1862]

... This morning I visited the Genl Hospital not far from here, & went through it all — finding the patients comfortable & all improving in health. They are nearly all in hospital tents & are well provided for — in truth they are about as well off as they could be away from home, & many of them doubtless better off than they would be there. I find the men more contented than the officers — the truth is that if the officers were in their sphere one tenth as good as the men in theirs we should have the finest army in the world. I confess that the men enlist my sympathies much more warmly than the officers — they are so patient & devoted — they have generally entered the service too from higher & more unselfish motives. Poor fellows — I can never willingly break the link that unites me to them & shall always be very proud of them & of their love for me — even if it is not decreed by Providence that I am to lead them to Richmond. After the long time that has elapsed without my hearing anything from Washn I can hardly hope to learn anything by today's mail — but I assure you that we are all becoming very impatient at the long delay here, so unnecessary as it seems to us.

I commenced turning over a new leaf today — that is neither writing or telegraphing to Washn & have about determined to draw back into my shell until the oracle deigns to speak. I have said all I well can — I have told them about all I think & know — have pointed out to them what I regard as the genl effects of the course I fear they are likely to adopt — words can no further go — by saying more & repeating what has already said I should only render myself ridiculous & a bore — so I will be silent & if they send me the order I dread (that of withdrawing this army) I will make one last desperate appeal before obeying it & then let matters take their course — confident that I have honestly endeavored to do the best I could, altho' I may not have done as well as others could. There is a great consolation in feeling that one has tried to do right, & not been actuated by selfish motives — of the last I *know* that I am free, & would say so were I even on my death bed....

To tell the truth (which it will not be necessary for you to repeat to ——) I have quite enough civilians on my staff — they are of little or no use to me, & are a great deal more trouble than they are worth. I manage to employ those I have in writing & in carrying unimportant orders — but the really serious work, especially under fire, has to be done by Colburn, Sweitzer, Hudson, Radowitz, Hammerstein, Wright (who has picked up a good deal), Lowell & some youngsters I have caught. The most useless thing imaginable is one of these "highly educated" civilians — it takes them a long time to learn the fact that they know nothing & they are very apt to give offense by their assumption of manner etc. I have raked mine down so that they are now pretty regulated, but I would not for the world have any new ones....

I told you the result of the interview with Halleck — thus far practically nothing — not a word have I heard from Washn since his return there. I shall not write or telegraph another word until I hear from them, unless something of great importance occurs. I shall stand on what is left of my dignity now!!...

I cannot feel that I have any intentional error to reproach myself with, & I feel prepared to meet with a brave heart, firm will & clear brain anything that may occur.

1 am. [August 1] As I was just about comfortably asleep about 3/4 of an hour ago I was awakened by a tremendous shelling — the rascals (not you — but secesh) opened on us with field guns from the other side of the river & kept up a tremendous fire. It is now pretty much over, but still going on — no shells have burst nearer than 300 or 400 yds to my camp so I am quite indifferent. It took me about 5 minutes to wake Marcy — he did not hear a single shot....

Still some firing — now heavy again — gun boats at work — they were very slow in getting ready. A queer thing this writing a letter to my wife at this time of night to the music of shells — I fear they must have done some harm. Now they are quiet again — there goes a *whopper* from the gun boats! Queer times these!

1 1/2 [A.M.] Pretty quiet now — only an occasional shot, apparently from the gun boats — there goes one! Now another! Marcy & I have just been discussing (another) people in Washn & conclude that they are "a mighty trifling set" — indeed it is very criminal to leave me thus without one word of information as to their plans & purposes. If any lives have been lost tonight the guilt (another shot) is on their shoulders — for I told them that I desired to occupy with Burnside's troops the very point where this firing has come tonight — another shot — but I begin to believe that they wish this army to be destroyed — the wretches! How sick & tired I am of serving such a set of incompetent knaves — I do not believe that any nation was ever accursed with such a set of people as those who now rule in Washn.

2.45 [A.M.] Tired of waiting for Hammerstein's return with the news of the damage done. . . .

Well! He has just returned — it was so dark that no one could tell what the damage was — one man at Fitz Porter's Hd Qtrs had his leg shot off — no vessels set on fire — the camps all quiet.

8 am. All quiet & comfortable — no harm done by all that firing except the one poor fellow hit in the leg. . . .

AL copy, McClellan Papers (C-7 :63), Library of Congress.

To Henry W. Halleck

Confidential and unofficial Head-Quarters, Army of the Potomac,
My dear General; Berkeley August 1st 1862

Your kind and very welcome letter of the 30th reached me this morning.[1]

My own experience enables me to appreciate most fully the difficulties and unpleasant features of your position. I have passed through it all and most cordially sympathize with you; for I regard your place, under present circumstances as one of the most unpleasant under the Government.

Of one thing, however, you may be sure, and that is of my full and cordial support in all things. Had I been consulted as to who was to take my place, I would have advised your appointment. So far as you are concerned, I feel towards you, and shall act, precisely as if I had urged you for the place you hold. There is not one particle of feeling or jealousy in my heart towards you. Set your mind perfectly at rest on that score. No one of your old and tried friends will work with you more cordially and more honestly than I shall.

If we are permitted to do so, I believe that together we can save this unhappy country and bring this war to a comparatively early termination; the doubt in my mind is whether the selfish politicians will allow us to do so. I fear the results of the *civil* policy inaugurated by recent Acts of Congress and practically enunciated by General Pope in his series of orders to the Army of Virginia.[2]

It is my opinion that this contest should be conducted by us as a *War,* and as a War between civilized nations; that our efforts should be directed towards crushing the armed masses of the rebels, not against the people; but that the latter should, as far as military necessities permit, be protected in their constitutional, civil, and personal rights.

I think that the question of slavery should enter into this war solely as a *military* one; that while we do our best to prevent the rebels from making military uses of their slaves, we should avoid any proclamations of general emancipation, and should protect inoffensive citizens in the possession of that, as well as of other kinds of property. If we do not actively *protect* them in this respect, we should at least, avoid taking an active part on the other side and let the negro take care of himself.

The people of the South should understand that we are not making war upon the institution of slavery, but that if they submit to the Constitution and Laws of the Union they will be protected in their constitutional rights of every nature. I think that pillaging and outrages to persons ought not to be tolerated; that private persons and property should enjoy all the protection we can afford them, compatible with the necessities of our position. I would have the conduct of the Union troops present a strong contrast with that of the rebel Armies and prove by our action, that the Government is, as we profess it to be, benign and beneficent; that, wherever its power extends, protection and security exist for all who do not take an active part against us.

Peculiar circumstances may force us to depart from these principles in exceptional cases, but I would have these departures the exceptions, not the rule.

I and the Army under my command are fighting to restore the Union and the supremacy of its laws, not for revenge; I therefore deprecate, and view with infinite dread, any policy which tends to render impossible the reconstruction of the Union and to make this contest simply a useless effusion of blood.

We need more men: the old regiments of this Army should be promptly filled — by immediate drafting, if necessary. We should present such an overwhelming force as to render success certain, be able to follow it up, and to convince the *people* of the South that resistance is useless.

I know that our ideas as to the concentration of forces agree perfectly. I believe that the principles I have expressed in this letter accord with your own views. I sincerely hope that we do not differ widely. You see I have met you in your own spirit of frankness, and I would be glad to have your views on these points, that I may know what I am doing. We *must* have a full understanding on all points, and I regard the civil or political question as inseparable from the military, in this contest.

It is unnecessary for me to repeat my objections to the idea of withdrawing this Army from its present position. Every day's reflection but serves to strengthen my conviction that the true policy is to reinforce this Army, at the earliest possible moment, by every available man, and to allow it to resume the offensive with the least possible delay.

I am, General, your sincere friend,
Geo. B. McClellan

Major General H. W. Halleck,
Commanding U.S. Army

Retained copy, McClellan Papers (A-73:29), Library of Congress. *OR,* Ser. 1, XI, Part 3, pp. 345–46.

1. Halleck wrote on July 30: "I have always had strong personal objections to mingling in the politico-military affairs of Washington.... There seemed to be a disposition in the public press to cry down any one who attempted to serve the country instead of party. This was particularly the case with you, as I understand.... There was no one in the Army under whom I could serve with greater pleasure, and I now ask from you that same support and co-operation and that same free interchange of opinions as in former days." *OR,* Ser. 1, XI, Part 3, p. 343. 2. In addition to the Second Confiscation Act, GBM refers to a series of harsh orders issued by Gen. Pope relating to Southern civilians living in the war zone. *OR,* Ser. 1, XII, Part 2, pp. 50–52.

To Mary Ellen McClellan

[Berkeley] Aug 2 [1862]

...Circumstances have made it unavoidable for me to send out two important expeditions & a large working party, altho' it is Sunday [August 3]. One of the expeditions goes to Malvern, the other on the other side of the James River....

I had quite an interesting visit on the other side today — the place we burned up yesterday was a very handsome one — it was a rather hard case to be obliged to do it, but it could not be avoided.[1] ...

I had (as usual) not a single word from Washn today from any one, nor anything from Burnside. If the latter is really under orders for the Rappahannock there is something very strange in his failure to communicate with me — not even giving me the slightest hint of it; therefore I am disposed to discredit Com. Wilkes' report[2] & to think that he must be mistaken in regard to it — for I *know* Burnside to be true to me — there can be no doubt about *that.* If he *is* ordered to the Rappahannock I believe that this army will be withdrawn from here, & then the cup of misery of this country will be full indeed....

When you contrast the policy I urge in my letter to the Presdt[3] with that of Congress & Mr. Pope you can readily agree with me that there can be little mutual confidence between the Govt & myself — we are the antipodes of each other & it is more than probable that they will take the earliest opportunity to relieve me from command & get me out of sight. I shall endeavor to pursue the plain path of duty — as I have often told you my mind is prepared to endure anything that a man of honor can — but I shall consult my own sense of right & my own judgment — not deferring to that of others when my own convictions are strong. There are *some* things to which I cannot submit & to which nothing can induce me to yield. . . .

7.30 am. Aug. 3rd . . . One of my expeditions of last night failed[4] — had to come back because the guides lost the way — will try again tonight or tomorrow. The other one not yet heard from, but has I hope met with better luck than the first. . . .

Everything quiet during the night — no firing & no stampede of any kind. . . .

AL copy, McClellan Papers (C-7 :63), Library of Congress.

1. The place from which Confederate field guns had shelled the Harrison's Landing camp on the night of July 31–Aug. 1. 2. Commodore Charles Wilkes had replaced John Rodgers in command of the James River flotilla. Burnside's command was ordered to the Rappahannock on Aug. 1. 3. GBM to Lincoln, July 7, *supra*. 4. To Malvern Hill.

To Henry W. Halleck [TELEGRAM]

Head-Quarters, Army of the Potomac,
Berkeley August 4 12m 1862

Your telegram of last evening is received.[1] I must confess that it has caused me the greatest pain I ever experienced, for I am convinced that the order to withdraw this Army to Acquia Creek will prove disastrous in the extreme to our cause — I fear it will be a fatal blow.

Several days are necessary to complete the preparations for so important a movement as this & while they are in progress I beg that careful consideration may be given to my statements.

This Army is now in excellent discipline & condition; we hold a debouche on both banks of the James River, so that we are free to act in any direction, & with the assistance of the gun boats I consider our communications as now secure. We are (25) twenty five miles from Richmond & are not likely to meet the enemy in force sufficient to fight a battle until we have marched (15) fifteen to (18) eighteen miles, which brings us practically within (10) ten miles of Richmond. Our longest line of land transportation would be from this point, (25) twenty five miles; but with the aid of the gun boats we can supply the Army by water, during its advance, certainly to within (12) twelve miles of Richmond. At Acquia Creek we would be (75) seventy five miles from Richmond, with land transportation all the way.

From here to Fort Monroe is a march of about (70) seventy miles, for I regard it as impracticable to withdraw this Army and its material except by land.

The result of the movement would thus be to march (145) one hundred and forty five miles to reach a point now only (25) twenty five miles distant, & to deprive ourselves entirely of the powerful aids of the gun boats & water transportation.

Add to this the certain demoralization of this Army which would ensue, the terribly depressing effect upon the people of the North, & the strong probability that it would influence foreign Powers to recognize our adversaries, & these appear to me sufficient reasons to make it my imperative duty to urge in the strongest terms afforded by our language that this order may be rescinded, & that far from recalling this Army it be promptly reinforced to enable it to resume the offensive.

It may be said that there are no reinforcements available — I point to Burnside's force, to that of Pope not necessary to maintain a strict defensive in front of Washington & Harper's Ferry, to those portions of the Army of the West not required for a strict defensive there. Here, directly in front of this Army, is the heart of the rebellion; it is here that all our resources should be collected to strike the blow which will determine the fate of this nation.

All points of secondary importance elsewhere should be abandoned & every available man brought here — a decided victory here and the military strength of the rebellion is crushed — it matters not what partial reverses we may meet with elsewhere. Here is the true defence of Washington, it is here on the banks of the James that the fate of the Union should be decided.

Clear in my conviction of right, strong in the consciousness that I have ever been and still am actuated solely by love for my country, knowing that no ambitious or selfish motives have influenced me from the commencement of this war — I do now what I never did in my life before — I entreat that this order may be rescinded.

If my counsel does not prevail I will, with a sad heart, obey your orders to the utmost of my power, directing to the movement, which I clearly foresee will be one of the utmost delicacy & difficulty, whatever skill I may possess.

Whatever the result may be, and may God grant that I am mistaken in my forebodings, I shall at least have the internal satisfaction that I have written & spoken frankly, & have sought to do the best in my power to avert disaster from my country.[2]

G B McClellan
Maj Genl Comdg

Maj Genl H W Halleck
Comdg US Army

ALS (telegram sent), McClellan Papers (A-74:29), Library of Congress. *OR,* Ser. 1, XI, Part 1, pp. 81–82.

1. Halleck telegraphed on Aug. 3: "It is determined to withdraw your army from the Peninsula to Aquia Creek. You will take immediate measures to effect this, covering the movement the best you can." *OR,* Ser. 1, XI, Part 1, pp. 80–81. 2. In Halleck's reply on Aug. 6 he wrote, in part: "You, general, certainly could not have been more pained at receiving my order than I was at the necessity of issuing it." He referred to GBM's estimate that Lee had 200,000 men at Richmond, while Pope had 40,000 and the Army of the Potomac 90,000. "You are 30 miles from Richmond and General Pope 80 or 90, with the enemy directly between you, ready to fall with his superior numbers upon one or the other, as he may elect. Neither can re-enforce the other in case of such an attack.... If you or any one else had presented a better [plan] I certainly should have adopted it, but all of your plans require re-enforcements, which it is impossible to give you." *OR,* Ser. 1, XII, Part 2, pp. 9–11.

To Mary Ellen McClellan

Berkeley Aug 4 [1862] 6 1/2 pm

...I was off on the other side of the river all day yesterday — where I had a hot & fatiguing tramp on foot, besides getting a little damp in the rain. Our enterprise on that side of the river was quite successful. I found a splendid position to cover that bank, so as to enable us to cross the army if necessary as well as to prevent any more midnight serenades like that of last week. I now hold the other shore with a sufficient number of troops to prevent a surprise. Averell went out with 3 squadrons, met & thrashed an entire regiment, drove them to & through their camp, which he captured & leisurely destroyed — thus making the 13th Va Cavalry exceedingly uncomfortable last night, for all their tents, provisions, cooking utensils & baggage were effectually burned up! He got some prisoners & sabred a respectable number — having only two wounded himself — the 5th Regular Cavalry & the 3rd Penna Cavalry did the work....

11 1/2 pm. I had a note from Burnside this evening — he has been ordered to the Rappahannock & has I presume started — not one word have I heard on that subject from Wash. Halleck has begun to show the cloven foot already — he will kill himself in less than two weeks....

So Genl Scott told Aspinwall that he had not lost confidence in me! I am quite sure that I owe Halleck's appointment to him!![1] ...

I have a large expedition out tonight — a couple of Divns of Infty & some 2000 Cavalry to try to catch the secesh who are at Malvern Hill. Shall not hear from them before tomorrow noon. Colburn has gone with them....

7 am [August 5]. Pretty sharp cannonading has been going on in my front this morning — Hooker's command at Malvern — they are still

cracking away pretty sharply — have not heard details, but will ride out in that direction as soon as I get my bkfst. . . .

AL copy, McClellan Papers (C-7 :63), Library of Congress.

1. On July 31 Mrs. McClellan wrote GBM: "Genl Scott told Mr. Aspinwall that his confidence in you was *undiminished* & Mr. Alsop seemed to think every thing is going on well & that all these little trials & annoyances will only redound to your good in the end. . . ." McClellan Papers (B-11 :48).

To Randolph B. Marcy

Aug 5 [1862] — Malvern Hill 1 pm

. . . Hooker has been entirely successful in driving off the enemy — took about 100 prisoners, killed & wounded several. The mass escaped under cover of a thick fog. Hooker's dispositions were admirable & nothing but the fog prevented complete success. We have lost 3 killed & 11 wounded — among the latter 2 officers. I shall retain the command here tonight. Keep all things ready to move out should we be attacked. I shall not return before dark & may remain all night — will send in for my blankets & ambulance if I stay. I am now starting to look over the ground. I have sent a party to communicate with Averell — directing him to take post tonight near Nelson's farm. Will send in again as soon as I return from my ride.

Excuse the illegibility of this, as it is written on horseback & the flies trouble Dan. The enemy in strong force at New Market. Better send a special dispatch to Halleck & tell him that I hate to give up this position. Secesh is under cover, & tho' he is in strong force I can beat him if they will give me reinforcements.[1] Send this to Nell if I do not get back in time for mail.

AL copy, McClellan Papers (C-7 :63), Library of Congress.

1. Marcy's dispatch of this date to Halleck, sent over GBM's name, read, in part: "This is a very advantageous position to cover an advance on Richmond and only 14 3/4 miles distant, and I feel confident that with re-enforcements I could march this army there in five days." *OR,* Ser. 1, XI, Part 1, pp. 77–78.

To Joseph Hooker

Hd Quarters Army of Potomac
Berkeley Aug 6 [1862] 10 pm

My dear General

I find it will not be possible to get the whole Army in position before some time tomorrow afternoon, which will be too late to support you & hold the entire position should the enemy attack in large force at day break, which there is strong reason to suppose he intends doing. Should we fight a general battle at Malvern it will be necessary to abandon the whole of our works here & run the risk of getting back here should the enemy prove too strong for us.

Under advices I have received from Washington I think it necessary for you to abandon the position tonight, getting everything away before day light.[1]

Please leave cavalry pickets at Malvern with orders to destroy the Turkey Creek Bridge when they are forced back.

The roads leading in to Haxall's from the right should be strongly watched & Haxall's, at least, held by strong cavalry force & some light batteries as long as possible.

I leave the manner of the withdrawal entirely to your discretion.

Please signal to the fleet when the withdrawal is almost completed.

Report frequently to these Head Quarters. Genl Sumner was ordered up to support you, but will halt when this passes him & will inform you where he is.

Truly yours
Geo B McClellan
Maj Genl

Genl. J. Hooker
Comdg at Malvern Hill

ALS, McClellan Papers (A-74:29), Library of Congress. *OR,* Ser. 1, XI, Part 1, p. 79.

1. Before Halleck's letter of Aug. 6 reached him (see GBM to Halleck, Aug. 4, note 2, *supra*), GBM received a telegram from the general-in-chief on Aug. 5 informing him that the order to withdraw from the Peninsula would not be rescinded. At 3 A.M. on Aug. 6 Halleck telegraphed: "I have no re-enforcements to send you." *OR,* Ser. 1, XI, Part 1, pp. 82, 78.

To Mary Ellen McClellan

Aug 8 [1862] Saturday [Friday] Berkeley

I can't convey an idea of the heat today — it has been intense — not a breath of air stirring. I got through with the ordinary business of receiving Generals, decided on papers &c about 12. Then took the ambulance & drove down to see Fitz about some business matters, remained there until three when I came home, made an attempt to take a nap, but it was so terribly hot, that I was lamentably unsuccessful & pretty soon got up in disgust; went out under the trees in light costume, & smoked cigarettes until dark, when we dined. Then, I had quite a host of visitors; first a naval officer on duty; then Allen just back from Washington; then, Ingalls, Brooks, Sykes, Porter & Franklin[1] — the latter having returned tonight. After they had all gone I had a long talk with Allen, who gave me the last news & present state of affairs in Washington. Then I had a talk with Marcy & dictated an order to Key. Then, I read the defense of my course in the N.Y. World of yesterday;[2] then received some reports from Pleasonton[3] that the enemy were pressing him hard near Malvern Hill, & gave the necessary orders. . . .

I am in strong hopes that the enemy will be foolish enough to drive Pleasonton in & attack me in this position — I have ordered P. to draw them on if possible, & if they come in sight will try to keep my men concealed & do my best to induce them to attack me. Should they be so foolish as to do that I will surely beat them & follow them up to Richmond but I fear they are too smart for that. I can hardly hope for so much good luck — if it is a possible thing to humbug them into an attack I will do it.

I will issue tomorrow an order giving *my* comments on Mr. Jno Pope[4] — I will strike square in the teeth of all his infamous orders & give directly the reverse instructions to my army — forbid all pillaging & stealing & take the highest Christian ground for the conduct of the war — let the Govt gainsay it if they dare. I am willing to fall in such a cause. I will not permit this army to degenerate into a mob of thieves, nor will I return these men of mine to their families as a set of wicked & demoralized robbers — I will not have that sin on my conscience. . . .

I have received my orders from Halleck — I cannot *tell* you what they are, but if you will bear in mind what I have already written to you, you can readily guess them when I say that they are as bad as they can be, & that I regard them as almost fatal to our cause. I have remonstrated as warmly as I know how to do — but to no avail. My only hope now is that I can induce the enemy to attack me. I shall of course obey the orders unless the enemy gives me a very good opening — which I should at once avail myself of. I hear thru private sources that they have not yet determined how to dispose of me — personally. Their game is to force me to resign — mine will be to force them to place me on leave of absence, so that when they begin to reap the whirlwind that they have sown I may still be in position to do something to save my country. With all their faults I *do* love my countrymen & if I can save them I will yet do so. . . .

I had another letter from Halleck tonight — I strongly suspect him of being a "scallawag."[5]

AL copy; copy, McClellan Papers (C-7:63/D-10:72), Library of Congress.

1. Allan Pinkerton, Rufus Ingalls, W. T. H. Brooks, George Sykes, Fitz John Porter, William B. Franklin. 2. In an editorial published Aug. 7, editor Manton Marble of the *New York World* wrote, in part: "The failure of this campaign, the profitless expenditure of hundreds of millions of treasure, and of tens of thousands of lives, were due, not to any want of capacity, nor courage, nor energy, nor forethought of Gen. McClellan; . . . but . . . were the direct, natural and necessary result of the suicidal policy which deprived the general-in-chief of a part of his command, and transferred the control of our armies, and conduct of the war, to an irresponsible committee [the Joint Committee on the

Conduct of the War] and an incompetent civilian [Secretary of War Stanton].'' 3. Brig. Gen. Alfred Pleasonton had commanded the cavalry in the Malvern Hill expedition. 4. General Orders No. 154, Aug. 9. See GBM to his wife, July 30, note 2, *supra*. 5. Probably Halleck's letter of Aug. 6. See GBM to Halleck, Aug. 4, note 2, *supra*.

To Mary Ellen McClellan

[Berkeley] Aug 10 [1862] 8 am

. . . Halleck is turning out just like the rest of the herd — the affair is rapidly developing itself, & I see more clearly every day their settled purpose to force me to resign. I am trying to keep my temper & force *them* to relieve me or dismiss me from the service. I have no idea that I will be with this army more than two or three weeks longer & should not be surprised any day or hour to get my ''walking papers.'' I have a strong idea that Pope will be thrashed during the coming week — & very badly whipped he will be & ought to be — such a villain as he is ought to bring defeat upon any cause that employs him. . . .

4 pm. . . . I am inclined to believe that Pope will catch his Tartar within a couple of days & be disposed of. The absurdity of Halleck's course in ordering the army away from here is that it cannot possibly reach Washn in time to do any good, but will necessarily be too late — I am sorry to say that I am forced to the conclusion that H. is very dull & very incompetent — alas poor country! I hope to be ready tomorrow afternoon to move forward in the direction of Richmond — I will try to catch or thrash Longstreet & then if the chance offers follow in to Richmond while they are lamming away at Pope. It is in some respects a desperate step, but it is the best I can do for the nation just now & I would rather even be defeated than retreat without an effort to relieve Washn in the only way at all possible. If I fail — why well & good. I will fall back. If I win I shall have saved my country & will then gratefully retire to private life. . . .

I am getting the sick away quite rapidly now — but they are in large numbers & it is at best a slow process. The heavy baggage is all being stored on board ships so that in whatever direction we move it will be comparatively unencumbered. I shall send off all that I have except a carpet bag & pair of blankets — change my large tent for a ''wall tent'' & go about as light as any of them. I half apprehend that they will be too quick for me in Washn & relieve me before I have the chance of making the dash. If so — well & good. I am satisfied that the dolts in Washn are bent on my destruction if it is possible for them to accomplish it — but I believe that Providence is just enough to bring their own sins upon their heads & that they will before they get through taste the dregs of the cup of bitterness. The more I hear of their wickedness the more am I surprised that such a wretched set are permitted to *live* much less to occupy the positions they do. It is no doubt all for the best & Providence has some wise purpose to fulfil thro' them....

The next few days will probably be decisive. If I succeed in my coup everything will be changed in this country so far as we are concerned & my enemies will be at my feet. It may go hard with some of them in that event, for I look upon them as the enemies of the country & of the human race....

Midnight. I received a very harsh & unjust telegram from Halleck this evening & a very *friendly private* letter from the same individual — blows hot & cold.[1] I replied to his telegram — closing by quietly remarking "The present moment is probably not the proper one for me to refer to the unnecessarily harsh & unjust tone of your telegrams of late. It will however make no difference in my official action."[2] Under the circumstances I feel compelled to give up the idea of my intended attack upon Richmond & must *retrace my steps.* Halleck *writes* that all the forces in Virginia including Pope, Burnside etc are to be placed under my command — I doubt it, but will accept no less place. They are committing a fatal error in withdrawing me from here — & the future will show it. I believe that I could take Richmond were I to advance tomorrow. I think the result of their machinations will be that Pope will be badly thrashed within two days & that they will be very glad to turn over the redemption of their affairs to me. I won't undertake it unless I have full & entire control....

AL copy, McClellan Papers (C-7:63), Library of Congress.

1. In his letter of Aug. 7, Halleck wrote: "I fully agree with you in regard to the manner in which the war should be conducted, and I believe the present policy of the President to be conservative.... I deeply regret that you cannot agree with me as to the necessity of reuniting the old Army of the Potomac. I, however, have taken the responsibility of doing so, and am to risk my reputation on it. As I told you when at your camp, it is my intention that you shall command all the troops in Virginia as soon as we can get them together; and with the army thus concentrated I am certain that you can take Richmond. I must beg of you, general, to hurry along this movement.... " His telegram of Aug. 10 read: "The enemy is crossing the Rapidan in large force.... There must be no further delay in your movements. That which has already occurred was entirely unexpected, and must be satisfactorily explained." *OR,* Ser. 1, XI, Part 3, pp. 359–60, Part 1, p. 86. 2. GBM to Halleck, Aug. 10, *OR,* Ser. 1, XI, Part 1, p. 86.

To Henry W. Halleck [TELEGRAM]

Genl Halleck Berkeley Aug 12 [1862] 4 pm

Information from various sources received within a few days past goes to corroborate the evidence you have rec'd that the rebel army at Richmond has been much weakened by detachments sent to Gordonsville & that the remaining forces have been so much dispersed between Richmond & this place on both sides James River as to render it doubtful if they can be concentrated again rapidly. D. H. Hill with a division or more is in the vicinity of Petersburg, others are along the south bank of James River back of Fort Darling & I am quite certain that Longstreet with about eighteen thousand men now occupies an intrenched position which can probably be turned & is about three miles above Malvern Hill. I can in forty eight hours advance on him & either drive him into the works around Richmond or defeat & capture his forces. Should I succeed in accomplishing the latter I see but little difficulty if my information is correct in pushing rapidly forward into Richmond. This would involve the cooperation of all my available forces but the question would soon be decided & if successful I should require reinforcements to maintain my communications. This effort would it seems to me have the effect to draw back the forces now before Genl Pope & thus relieve Washington from all danger. One of my general officers who for five days past has held a position near Malvern Hill in a letter just received says The enemy before us is weak. From all I can learn there is not thirty six thousand men between this & Richmond nor do I believe they can get more before we can whip them. I have good guides etc.[1] Genl Barnard, Chief of my Engineers, is decidedly in favor of this movement at this time. Under these circumstances I consider it my duty to present the foregoing information & for your consideration, as under existing orders I do not feel authorized to make the movement. I shall continue to forward reinforcements & sick as rapidly as transports arrive & have given the necessary instructions to insure no delay in moving the army.

Geo. B. McClellan
Maj Genl Comdg

Retained copy, McClellan Papers (C-10:63), Library of Congress. *OR,* Ser. 1, XI, Part 3, pp. 372–73.

1. Quoted from a dispatch by Gen. Pleasonton to Gen. Marcy, Aug. 11. *OR,* Ser. 1, XI, Part 3, p. 369.

To Henry W. Halleck [TELEGRAM]

Berkeley August 12 [1862] 11 pm

Your dispatch of noon today received.[1] It is positively the fact that no more men could have embarked hence than have gone & that no unnecessary delay has occurred. Before your orders were received Col Ingalls directed all available vessels to come from Monroe. Officers have been sent to take personal direction. Have heard nothing here of Burnside fleet. There are some vessels at Monroe such as Atlantic & Illinois which draw too much to come here. Hospital accommodations exhausted this side New York.

Propose filling Atlantic & Illinois with serious cases for New York &

to encamp slight cases for the present at Monroe. In this way can probably get off the (3400) thirty four hundred sick still on hand by day after tomorrow night. I am sure that you have been misinformed as to availability of vessels on hand. We cannot use heavily loaded supply vessels for troops or animals & such constitute the mass of those here which have been represented to you as capable of transporting this Army.

I fear you will find very great delay in embarking troops & material at Yorktown & Monroe both from want of vessels & of facilities for embarkation. At least two additional wharves should at once be built at each place — I ordered two at the latter some (2) two weeks ago, but you countermanded the order.

I learn that wharf accommodations at Acquia are altogether inadequate for landing troops & supplies to any large extent — not an hour should be lost in remedying this. Great delays will ensue there from shallow water.

You will find a vast deficiency in horse transports. We had nearly (200) two hundred when we came here. I learn of only (20) twenty provided now. They carry about (50) fifty horses each.

More hospital accommodations should be provided. We are much impeded here because our wharves are used night & day to land current supplies. At Monroe a similar difficulty will occur. With all the facilities at Alexandria & Washington (6) six weeks about were occupied in embarking this Army & its material. Burnside's troops are not a fair criteria for rate of embarkation — all his means were in hand, his outfit specially prepared for the purpose & his men habituated to the movement. There shall be no unnecessary delay — but I cannot manufacture vessels.

I state these difficulties from experience & because it appears to me that we have lately been working at cross purposes because you have not been properly informed by those around you who ought to know the inherent difficulties of such an undertaking. It is not possible for any one to place this Army where you wish it ready to move in less than a month. If Washington is in danger now this Army can scarcely arrive in time to save it — it is in much better position to do so from here than from Acquia.

Our material can only be saved by using the whole Army to cover it if we are pressed.

If seriously weakened by detachments the result might be the loss of much material & many men.

I will be at the telegraph office tomorrow morning to talk with you.[2]

G B McClellan
Maj Genl

Maj Genl H W Halleck
Washn DC

ALS (telegram sent), McClellan Papers (A-74:29), Library of Congress. *OR*, Ser. 1, XI, Part 1, pp. 87–88.

1. Halleck telegraphed: "The Quartermaster-General informs me that nearly every available steam vessel in the country is now under your control.... Burnside moved nearly 13,000 troops to Aquia Creek in less than two days, and his transports were immediately sent back to you. All vessels in the James River and the Chesapeake Bay were placed at your disposal, and it was supposed that 8,000 or 10,000 of your men could be transported daily.... The bulk of your material on shore it was thought could be sent to Fort Monroe, covered by that part of the army which could not get water transportation.... " *OR*, Ser. 1, XI, Part 1, p. 87. 2. In reply to GBM's two telegrams of this date, Halleck replied, on Aug. 14: "There is no change of plans. You will send up your troops as rapidly as possible. There is no difficulty in landing them. According to your own accounts, there is now no difficulty in withdrawing your forces." *OR*, Ser. 1, XI, Part 1, p. 89.

To Henry W. Halleck [TELEGRAM]

Head Quarters, Army of the Potomac,
Berkeley Aug 14 11 pm 1862

Movement has commenced by land & water. All sick will be away by tomorrow night.

Everything being done to carry out your orders. I don't like Jackson's movements — he will suddenly appear when least expected. Will telegraph fully & understandingly in the morning.

G B McClellan
Maj Genl

Maj Genl H W Halleck
Washington DC

ALS (telegram sent), McClellan Papers (C-15:64), Library of Congress. *OR*, Ser. 1, XI, Part 1, p. 89.

To Fitz John Porter [TELEGRAM]

Barrett's Ferry Aug 17 [1862] 12.30 pm

Your dispatches of last evening & 8.20 this morning just received. You were misinformed as to Franklin having arrived here, no troops of consequence have yet arrived since your own left. As things are it is probably well that you have moved on, but the consequences might be very serious should the enemy attack in force. I do not think we shall be troubled but will not feel entirely safe until all the wagons are over the bridge. My wish was to have had everything in hand until getting the wagons past Williamsburg. As it is now you could not return in time & had better continue the movement. If there are transports at Monroe embark your command at once & proceed to Acquia Creek, leaving some suitable officer to bring up the wagons as soon as transportation is ready.[1]

G B McClellan
Maj Genl Comdg

Maj Genl F J Porter
Comdg 5th Corps Williamsburg Va

ALS (telegram sent), McClellan Papers (A-74:29), Library of Congress.

1. See GBM to Porter, Dec. 19, 1862, *infra*.

To Henry W. Halleck

Private

General Barrett's Ferry Chickahominy Aug 17 2.30 pm / 62

I have had this morning a full conversation with General Burnside. To be perfectly frank with you I must say that I did think from some of your recent telegrams that you were not disposed to treat me in a candid or friendly manner — this was the more grating to me because I was conscious that although I differed from you in opinion I had done so with entire frankness & loyalty, and that I had not delayed one moment in preparing to carry out your orders [*crossed out:* while I availed myself of the unavoidable delay to urge upon you my own view of the case]. I am glad to say that Burnside has satisfied me that you are still my friend — in return I think he can satisfy you that I have loyally carried out your instructions, altho' my own judgment was not in accordance with yours.

Let the past take care of itself — so long as I remain in command of this Army I will faithfully carry out the new progamme [*crossed out:* but I will make no more suggestions unless you ask for them]. I feel quite confident that I will have everything across the Chickahominy by daylight. If all is then quiet I will regard my command as reasonably safe & feel justified in moving it solely with reference to its speedy embarkation.[1]

Very respectfully yours
Geo B McClellan
Maj Genl Comdg

Maj Genl H W Halleck
Comdg US Army Washn D.C.

ALS retained copy, McClellan Papers (A-74:29), Library of Congress. *OR*, Ser. 1, XI, Part 3, p. 378.

1. Halleck replied on Aug. 20: "When I felt that the safety of Washington depended on the prompt and rapid transfer of your army it is very probable that my messages to you were more urgent and pressing than guarded in their language. I certainly meant nothing harsh, but I did feel that you did not act as promptly as I thought the circumstances

required. . . . That Lee is moving on Pope with his main army I have no doubt. . . . Under these circumstances you must pardon the extreme anxiety (and perhaps a little impatience) which I feel. Every moment seems to me as important as an ordinary hour.'' *OR*, Ser. 1, XI, Part 3, pp. 379–80.

To Mary Ellen McClellan

Aug 17 [1862] 3 pm. Barrett's Ferry, Chickahominy

. . . I have the greater part of the army over now, & if we are not disturbed for six hours more all will be well. I have abandoned neither men nor material, & the *"retreat"* has been conducted in the most orderly manner, & is a perfect success so far as so disgusting an operation can be. I learn that all the troops in Va. are to be placed under my command. Burnside came down to assure me from Halleck that he (H.) is really my friend — qu'il soit! I begin to think that I may still be master of the situation. . . .

I hope to get everything over tonight & will be at my old Hd Qtrs at Williamsburg tomorrow evening. Next day at Yorktown. If all is then quiet I will go thence by water to Ft. Monroe & complete the arrangements for embarking. . . .

I took a savage satisfaction in being the last to leave my camp at Berkeley yesterday! . . .

AL copy, McClellan Papers (C-7:63), Library of Congress.

To Mary Ellen McClellan

Aug 18 [1862] pm. Williamsburg

. . . Am pretty well tired out, for I have been much in the saddle lately & have been very anxious — besides having slept very little. . . .

I crossed the Chickahominy yesterday & remained there today until all the troops had crossed & moved several miles in advance. When I left the Bridge was taken up & nothing but a few worthless stragglers left behind — they will all be brought over tonight I think — tho' so far as they are concerned individually I would much prefer that secesh should capture them all. I have made a remarkably successful retreat — left absolutely *nothing* behind — secesh can't find one dollar's worth of property if he hunts a year for it. I have not seen the enemy since we started, & I rather doubt whether he knows where we are now. Shall go to Yorktown in the morning — remain there one or two days, then go to Ft. Monroe. . . .

It will take a long time to embark this army & have it ready for action on the banks of the Potomac. . . .

The men all know that I am not responsible — I have remained constantly with the rear guard — was the very last one to leave our camp at Berkeley, remained on the Chickahominy until the bridge was removed & still have the proud satisfaction of hearing the cheers of the men as I pass, seeing their faces brighten up....

Strange as it may seem the rascals have not I think lost one particle of confidence in me & love me just as much as ever.

I am glad to inform you that your friend Pleasonton has done *splendidly.* I placed him in command of the rear guard. The little fellow (Pleasonton) brightened up very much this morning when he came to report. I looked very sternly at him & told him that I had a very serious complaint to make against him. He looked rather wild, injured, & disgusted, & wished to know what it was. I replied that he had entirely disappointed me, that he had not created a single stampede, nor called for any reinforcements. That such heinous conduct was something I did not at all look for, & that if it was persisted in, I must send him to Pope. The little fellow began to grin & was well pleased. He *is* a most excellent soldier & has performed a very important duty most admirably.

I have felt every moment that I was conducting a false movement, & which was altogether against my own judgment & that of the army. I have done it without demoralizing the army....

AL copy; copy, McClellan Papers (C-7 :63/D-10 :72), Library of Congress.

To Henry W. Halleck [TELEGRAM]

Head-Quarters, Army of the Potomac,
[Williamsburg] August 18, 11 pm. 1862

Please say a kind word to my Army that I can repeat to them in Genl Orders in regard to their conduct at Yorktown, Williamsburg, West Point, Hanover C.H. & on the Chickahominy — as well as in regard to the (7) seven days, & the recent retreat. No one has ever said anything to cheer them but myself. Say nothing about me — merely give my men & officers credit for what they have done. It will do you much good & will strengthen you much with them if you issue a handsome order to them in regard to what they have accomplished — they deserve it.[1]

G B McClellan
Maj Genl

Maj Genl Halleck
Comdg USA Washington D.C.

ALS (telegram sent), McClellan Papers (A-74 :30), Library of Congress. *OR,* Ser. 1, XI, Part 1, pp. 91–92.

1. Halleck made no reply to this telegram.

To Ambrose E. Burnside

Confidential

Maj. Gen. Ambrose E. Burnside: Fort Monroe, Va.,
My dear Burn: August 20, 1862.

You will have learned ere this that our movement in retreat was most successfully accomplished, without loss and without abandoning any property.

Since my arrival here I have received a couple of telegrams from Halleck, indicating that Pope was in danger, and urging that re-enforcements be sent on as rapidly as possible.

I am pushing everything; not a moment is being lost, and it shall not be my fault if the troops do not arrive in time.

Yesterday and to-day I have received intelligence from confidential sources leading me to think it probable that Halleck either will not or cannot carry out his intentions in regard to my position, as expressed to you. This shall make no difference with me. I shall push on everything just as if I were to remain in command. Please keep me posted as to all you know.

I shall remain here until the whole or the mass of this army is embarked, unless I receive orders to the contrary in the mean time.

I send this by a special messenger.

Ever your friend,
Geo. B. McClellan,
Major-General

OR, Ser. 1, XII, Part 3, p. 605.

To Mary Ellen McClellan

Aug 21 [1862] 8 pm. Fort Monroe (camp)

I believe I have triumphed!! Just received a telegram from Halleck stating that Pope & Burnside are very hard pressed — urging me to push forward reinforcements, & to *come myself as soon as I possibly can!*[1] I am going to the Fortress now to hurry on my arrangements — shall put Hd Qtrs on board a vessel tomorrow morning & probably go myself in a fast boat tomorrow afternoon. Now they are in trouble they seem to want the "Quaker," the "procrastinator," the "coward" & the "traitor"! Bien — my ambulance is ready & I must go. I will write more when I come back.

AL copy, McClellan Papers (C-7:63), Library of Congress.

1. Telegram of this date. *OR*, Ser. 1, XI, Part 1, p. 92.

To Henry W. Halleck [TELEGRAM]

Head Quarters, Army of the Potomac,
Fort Monroe Aug 21 10.25 pm 1862

I have ample supplies of ammunition for Infantry & Artillery & will have it up in time.

I can supply any deficiencies that may exist in Genl Pope's Army.

Quite a number of rifled field guns are on hand here. The forage is the only question for you to attend to — please have that ready for me at Acquia. I want many more schooners for cavalry horses — they should have water on board when they come here.

If you have leisure & there is no objection please communicate to me fully the state of affairs & your plans — I will then be enabled to arrange details understandingly.

G B McClellan
Maj Genl

Maj Genl Halleck
Washington

ALS (telegram sent), McClellan Papers (C-15 :64), Library of Congress. *OR,* Ser. 1, XI, Part 1, p. 92.

To Fitz John Porter [TELEGRAM]

Head Quarters, Army of the Potomac,
Fort Monroe Aug 21 10.40 pm 1862

Tell your men & those of Heintzelman when they arrive that I will leave here tomorrow & will be with them when they are engaged. I am pushing everything forward.

Franklin is here & embarking tonight. Sumner arrives in the morning. I am forwarding ample supplies of everything except forage for which I have called on Washington. Whatever occurs hold out until I arrive.[1]

G B McClellan
Maj Genl

Maj Genl F J Porter
Acquia Creek

ALS (telegram sent), McClellan Papers (C-15 :64), Library of Congress. *OR,* Ser. 1, XII, Part 3, pp. 615–16.

1. Porter replied on Aug. 22: "I guess we shall have no trouble to hold out for five or six days." Lincoln Papers, Library of Congress.

To Mary Ellen McClellan

[Fort Monroe] Aug 22 [1862] 10 am.

... I did not get back from the Fort until sometime after midnight & too tired to write....

I shall go to the Fort pretty soon & as soon as the tents are dry move everything on board the vessels so that I shall be ready to start at a moment's notice. I have two Corps off & away.

Franklin ought to have been off nearly by this time, but he & Smith have so little energy that I fear they will be very slow about it. They have disappointed me terribly — I do not at all doubt Franklin's loyalty now, but his efficiency is very little — I am very sorry that it has turned out so. The main, perhaps the only cause is that he has been & still is sick — & one ought not to judge harshly of a person in that condition. I presume I ought also to make a great deal of allowance for Smith also on the same account — so will try to be as charitable as we can under all these circumstances. I think they are pretty well scared in Washn & probably with good reason. I am confident that the disposition to be made of me will depend entirely upon the state of their nerves in Washn. If they feel safe there I will no doubt be shelved — perhaps placed in command here vice Genl Dix. I don't care what they do — would not object to being kept here for a while — because I could soon get things in such condition that I could have you here with me....

Their sending for me to go to Washn only indicates a temporary alarm — if they are at all reassured you will see that they will soon get rid of me. I shall be only too happy to get back to quiet life again — for I am truly & heartily sick of the troubles I have had & am not fond of being a target for the abuse & slander of all the rascals in the country. Well, we will continue to trust in God & feel certain that all is for the best — it is often difficult to understand the ways of Providence — but I have faith enough to believe that nothing is done without some great purpose. But enough of my troubles!...

I feel so sick & tired of human nature that I am already wary of being brought in contact with it. To think that a man whom I so sincerely admired, trusted & liked as I did Stanton turning against *me* as he has — & that without any cause that I am aware of! Pah — it is too bad!...

AL copy, McClellan Papers (C-7:63), Library of Congress.

To Mary Ellen McClellan

Aug 23 [1862] 3 pm. Steamer City of Hudson

I am off at last & on the way to Acquia....

9 1/2 pm. We are pounding along up the Potomac now, & as the boat is a fast one are passing anything we find....

We will reach Acquia sometime after midnight. Early in the morning I will telegraph to Halleck informing him of my arrival & asking for orders. I have no idea what they will be, nor do I know what has been happening on the Rappahannock yesterday & today. I take it for granted that my orders will be as disagreeable as it is possible to make them — unless Pope is beaten, in which case they may want me to save Washn again. Nothing but their fear will induce them to give me any command of importance or to treat me otherwise than with discourtesy. Bah! We will know tomorrow what it is to be — in the mean time I am perfectly cool & not in the slightest degree excited. . . .

AL copy, McClellan Papers (C-7:63), Library of Congress.

SEVEN

SECOND BULL RUN
AUGUST 24–SEPTEMBER 4, 1862

DURING THE twelve-day period covered here, the tone of General McClellan's correspondence ranges between extremes as varied as his fortunes. On arriving at Aquia Landing on August 24 from the Peninsula, he anticipated being "master of the situation" (as he told his wife) and in command of both the Army of the Potomac and the Army of Virginia. Moving his headquarters to Alexandria, he witnessed instead his troops taken away unit by unit to be fed into General Pope's Second Bull Run operations until he, the highest ranked general in the Federal service, commanded no more than a few staff officers and orderlies. Finally, called to Washington in the first days of September to salvage the wreck of yet another Union defeat, he had not only his own army returned to him but Pope's as well. "A terrible & thankless task . . . ," he wrote his wife on September 2. "I only consent to take it for my country's sake & with the humble hope that God has called me to it. . . ."

At the first evidence of the Army of the Potomac's withdrawal from the Peninsula, General Lee had shifted his forces northward to strike at Pope's Army of Virginia before McClellan's forces could combine with it. When he was unable to bring the Federals to battle on the line of the Rappahannock, Lee sent a column under Stonewall Jackson on a long flanking march to cut Pope's communications by striking at his main supply depot at Manassas Junction. Jackson's vanguard seized the depot on the night of August 26, just as McClellan reached Alexandria. The raiders also cut Pope's telegraphic link with Washington, and many of the dispatches McClellan exchanged with General-in-Chief Halleck in the days following reveal their uncertainty as to what was happening at the front.

As Pope called in his scattered commands and turned back to search out the raiders, Jackson took position on the old Bull Run battlefield of 1861. On August 28 he revealed his location by assaulting one of Pope's passing columns. The next day Pope opened the Second Bull Run fighting with an attack on Jackson. His dispatch written on the morning of August 30, his first to reach Washington in four days, predicted victory. That afternoon, however, with his army again united, Lee counterattacked and drove Pope from the field. The campaign ended at Chantilly on September 1, when Lee's attempt to turn the flank of the retreating Federals fell short.

The majority of McClellan's dispatches written during this time dealt with the disposition of the two Army of the Potomac corps — Sumner's Second and Franklin's Sixth, 25,000 men in all — that were under his direct control at Alexandria. In common with the Harrison's Landing withdrawal, he and General Halleck viewed the issue from very different perspectives. Halleck saw Franklin's and Sumner's troops as essential reinforcements for Pope, and he telegraphed on August 28 that they must reach the front without delay, "ready or not ready. If we delay too long to get ready there will be no necessity to go at all, for Pope will either be defeated or be victorious without our aid."

Considering Pope incompetent and anticipating his defeat, McClellan viewed the case as throwing good money after bad, and exposing Washington to capture if its defenders were weakened by the smallest amount. He urged that Pope be ordered not to give battle but instead fall back to the Washington lines. As he telegraphed the president on August 29, using a particularly unfortunate turn of phrase, the course he obviously favored was "To leave Pope to get out of his scrape & at once use all our means to make the Capital perfectly safe."

Acting on this conviction, McClellan held back the two corps for as long as possible in the face of Halleck's orders. Sufficient artillery had finally arrived from the Peninsula to enable both Franklin and Sumner to have reached the field in time to take part in the second day's fighting at Bull Run, but in fact they arrived only in time to cover Pope's retreat. McClellan argued that the enemy was present in such force as to endanger the reinforcements on their way to the front. "Reports numerous from various sources," he warned Halleck on August 28, indicated that the entire Army of Northern Virginia, 120,000 strong, was on the scene. This figure, more than twice the actual size of Lee's army and based on rumor rather than credible evidence, was another reflection of the illusory picture of the enemy that General McClellan had carried in his mind for more than a year.

The president's decision to place him in charge of Washington's defenses and then in command of the combined armies, described in McClellan's letters to his wife on September 2, was based on two realities of the situation — McClellan's known skills as an organizer and administrator, and the concern that in the crisis the demoralized troops would fight for no other general. Lincoln was candid in admitting to his cabinet that McClellan suffered from the "slows" and was "good for nothing for an onward movement," yet for defending the capital at that moment he was the best available.

To Mary Ellen McClellan

Aug 24 [1862] Sunday 9.30 am. Acquia Creek

We reached here during the night — sent a dispatch about 6 to Halleck informing him that I had arrived here & awaited orders; also sent one to Burnside. . . .

I have no reply as yet to my dispatches & am not at all impatient. I learn that all my troops are ordered to Alexandria for embarkation — so I presume they will be merged in Pope's army. If that is the case I will (if I find it proper) try for a leave of absence! . . .

I learn nothing whatever of the state of affairs — not even whether Pope is still falling back, or whether there has been any fighting — so I suppose it is all right. I fancy that Pope is in retreat — tho' this is only a guess of mine without anything to base it on. I don't see how I can remain in the service if placed under Pope — it would be too great a disgrace, & I can hardly think that Halleck would permit it to be offered me. . . .

I am glad you like the last order — it seems to have knocked Mr. Pope & the administration.[1] . . .

I expect Porter & Burnside here in a few minutes & then will know something of the state of affairs I hope. This is a wretched place — utterly unfit for the landing & supplying of a large body of troops — they have at last found it out, tho' *H.* insisted upon it that there were ample facilities here for all purposes. . . .

12.15 pm. I have seen Burnside & Porter & gained some information from them. Pope ran away from the Rappahannock last night, shamefully abandoning Porter & Burnside without giving them one word of warning. They only found it out this morning by sending a cavalry patrol there, who found everything deserted. It was most infamous conduct & he deserves hanging for it. They will extricate themselves however. I have not one word yet from Washn & am quietly waiting here for something to turn up. I presume they are discussing me now — to see whether they can get along without me. . . .

They will suffer a terrible defeat if the present state of affairs continues. I *know* that with God's help I can save them. . . .

AL copy, McClellan Papers (C-7:63), Library of Congress.

1. General Orders No. 154, Aug. 9. See GBM to his wife, July 30, 1862, note 2, *supra*.

To Henry W. Halleck [TELEGRAM]

Head Quarters, Army of the Potomac,
Acquia Creek Aug. 24 2 pm 1862

Your telegram received.[1] Morrell's scouts report Rappahannock station burned & abandoned by Pope without any notice to Morrell or Sykes. This was telegraphed you some hours ago. Reynolds Reno & Stevens are supposed to be with Pope as nothing can be heard of them today.[2] Morrell & Sykes are near Morrisville Post Office watching the lower fords of Rappahannock with no troops between them & Rappahannock station which is reported abandoned by Pope. Please inform me immediately exactly where Pope is & what doing. Until I know that I cannot expedite Porter's movements; he is much exposed now & decided measures should be taken at once. Until I know what my command & position are to be, & whether you still intend to place me in the command indicated in your first letter to me, & orally through Genl Burnside at the Chickahominy I cannot decide where I can be of most use. If your determination is unchanged I ought to go to Alexandria at once. Please define my position & duties.[3]

G B McClellan
Maj Genl

Maj Genl H W Halleck
Comdg USA Washington DC

ALS (telegram sent), McClellan Papers, New-York Historical Society. *OR*, Ser. 1, XI, Part 1, pp. 93–94.

1. Halleck telegraphed at 12:30 P.M. on this date: "Porter and Reno should hold the line of the Rappahannock below Pope, subject for the present to his orders. I hope by to-morrow to be able to give some more definite directions. You know my main object, and will act accordingly." *OR*, Ser. 1, XII, Part 3, p. 645. 2. Maj. Gen. George Morell, Brig. Gen. George Sykes, and Brig. Gen. John F. Reynolds commanded divisions in Porter's Fifth Corps. Maj. Gens. Jesse L. Reno and Isaac I. Stevens commanded divisions in Burnside's Ninth Corps. 3. Halleck replied that night: "You ask me for information which I cannot give. I do not know either where General Pope is or where the enemy in force is. These are matters which I have all day been most anxious to ascertain." *OR*, Ser. 1, XI, Part 1, p. 94.

To Henry W. Halleck [TELEGRAM]

Maj Genl H W Halleck Falmouth Va. 12.45 am Aug 25 '62

The only additional information I hear from Pope is from a multitude of his stragglers who say that he abandoned Rappahannock Station & retreated towards Warrenton Station carrying off the Artillery from the lower fords to some unknown point. You have no doubt taken all possible means to ascertain the exact position of Pope and I hope you will soon be able to give me definite information. All the means possible to gain it on this line have been used. In the meantime you may be sure of my hearty cooperation.

Geo B McClellan
Maj Genl

Received copy, Records of the Office of the Secretary of War, RG 107 (M-473 :50), National Archives. *OR*, Ser. 1, XII, Part 3, p. 659.

To Mary Ellen McClellan

Aug 27 [1862] am. Alexandria

We arrived here last night — rose early — reported to Washn that I had arrived & am waiting for something to turn up. It seems that some 500 of the enemy's cavalry made a dash last night & burned the Bull Run RR bridge. I fear this will cause much inconvenience as the troops in front are mainly dependent on the RR for supplies. My troops are getting pretty well into position — Porter between Fredericksburg & Rappahannock Station — Heintzelman at Rappk Sta. — Franklin near this place — Sumner landing at Acquia Creek. I have heard nothing new today & don't know what is going on in front — am terribly ignorant of the state of affairs & therefore somewhat anxious to know. . . .

I find all going on well enough here. Davis[1] has just returned from selecting a camp for Hd Qtrs — he has picked out a place between the Seminary (*our* old camp) & the river, about 1/2 or 3/4 mile from the Seminary. I shall go into my tent this time & not trouble a house. With the exception of the 2 or 3 days I passed at Wmsburg on our upward march & one night at Ft. Monroe I have not slept in a house since I left you. I know nothing definite yet in regard to my fate. . . .

10.30 [A.M.] Have been again interrupted by telegrams requiring replies. Halleck is in a disagreeable situation — can get no information from the front either as to our own troops or the enemy. I shall do all I can to help him loyally & will trouble him as little as possible, but render all the assistance in my power without regard to myself or my own position. . . .

Our affairs here now much tangled up & I opine that in a day or two your old husband will be called upon to unsnarl them. In the mean time I shall be very patient — do to the best of my ability whatever I am called upon to do & wait my time. I hope to have my part of the work pretty well straightened out today — in that case I shall move up to Washn this evening. . . .

Have just heard that it is probable that a general engagement will be fought today or tomorrow near Warrenton. . . .

AL copy, McClellan Papers (C-7 :63), Library of Congress.

1. Maj. Nelson H. Davis, of GBM's staff.

To Henry W. Halleck [TELEGRAM]

Head-Quarters, Army of the Potomac,
Alexandria Aug 27 10.20 am 1862

Telegram this moment received.[1] I have sent orders to Franklin to prepare to march with his Corps at once, & to repair here in person to inform me as to his means of transportation.

Kearny was yesterday at Rappahannock Station — Porter at Bealeton, Kelly's, Barnett's etc. Sumner will commence reaching Falmouth to day. Williams' Massachusetts cavalry will be mostly at Falmouth today. I loaned Burnside my personal escort — (1) one squadron (4th) fourth regulars to scout down Rappahannock. I have sent for Couch's Division to come at once.

As fast as I gain any information I will forward it altho' you may already have it.[2]

G B McClellan
Maj Genl

Maj Genl H W Halleck
Washington D.C.

ALS (telegram sent), Records of the Office of the Secretary of War, RG 107 (M-504:65), National Archives. *OR,* Ser. 1, XI, Part 1, p. 95.

1. Halleck telegraphed at 10:00 A.M.: "I can get no satisfactory information from the front.... There seems to have been great neglect and carelessness about Manassas. Franklin's corps should march in that direction as soon as possible." *OR,* Ser. 1, XI, Part 1, p. 95. 2. Halleck replied: "Take entire direction of the sending out of the troops from Alexandria. Determine questions of priority in transportation, and the places they shall occupy." *OR,* Ser. 1, XI, Part 1, p. 95.

To Henry W. Halleck [TELEGRAM]

Head-Quarters, Army of the Potomac,
Alexandria Aug 27 11.20 am 1862

In view of Burnside's dispatch[1] just received would it not be advisable to throw the mass of Sumner's Corps here to move out with Franklin to Centreville or vicinity?

If a decisive battle is fought at Warrenton a disaster would leave any troops on lower Rappahannock in a dangerous position — they would do better service in front of Washington.[2]

G B McClellan
Maj Genl

Maj Genl Halleck
Washington D.C.

ALS (telegram sent), Records of the Office of the Secretary of War, RG 107 (M-504:65), National Archives. *OR,* Ser. 1, XII, Part 3, p. 689.

1. Burnside's telegram of this date included dispatches from Porter announcing that a battle was imminent. *OR,* Ser. 1, XII, Part 3, p. 701. 2. Halleck telegraphed at 1:50 P.M. that he approved bringing Sumner's corps to Alexandria. *OR,* Ser. 1, XII, Part 3, p. 691.

To Henry W. Halleck [TELEGRAM]

Head-Quarters, Army of the Potomac,
Alexandria Aug 27 12M 1862

I have just learned through Genl Woodbury[1] that it was stated in your office last night that it was very strange that with (20,000) twenty thousand men here I did not prevent the raid upon Manassas. This induces me to ask whether your remark in your telegram today that there had been great neglect about Manassas was intended to apply to me.[2] I cannot suppose it was, knowing as you do that I arrived here without information & with no instructions beyond pushing the landing of my troops. The bridge was burned before my arrival, I knew nothing of it till this morning. I ask as a matter of justice that you will prevent your staff from making statements which do me such gross injustice at a time when the most cordial cooperation is required.[3]

G B McClellan
Maj Genl

Maj Genl H W Halleck
Washington D.C.

ALS (telegram sent), Records of the Office of the Secretary of War, RG 107 (M-504:65), National Archives. *OR,* Ser. 1, XII, Part 3, p. 690.

1. Brig. Gen. Daniel P. Woodbury, engineer brigade. 2. See GBM to Halleck, Aug. 27, 10:20 A.M., note 1, *supra.* 3. Halleck replied on this date that no censure of GBM was intended. "Indeed, I did not blame any particular person, but merely said there must have been neglect somewhere." *OR,* Ser. 1, XII, Part 3, p. 690.

To Henry W. Halleck [TELEGRAM]

Head Quarters, Army of the Potomac,
Alexandria Aug 27 1.15 pm 1862

Franklin's Artillery have no horses except for (4) four guns without caissons.[1] I can pick up no cavalry. In view of these facts will it not be well to push Sumner's Corps here by water as rapidly as possible. To make immediate arrangements for placing the works in front of Washington in an efficient condition of defense. I have no means of knowing the enemy's force between Pope & ourselves. Can Franklin without his Artillery or Cavalry effect any useful purpose in front. Should not Burnside at once take steps to evacuate Falmouth & Acquia at the same time covering the retreat of any of Pope's troops who may fall back in that direction. I do not see that we have force enough in hand to form a connection with Pope whose exact position we do not know. Are we safe in the direction of the valley?

G B McClellan
Maj Genl

Maj Genl Halleck
Washington

ALS (telegram sent), McClellan Papers (C-15:64), Library of Congress. *OR*, Ser. 1, XI, Part 1, p. 96.

1. In a telegram sent at noon, Halleck gave the positions of units of the Army of Virginia. "Porter reports a general battle imminent. Franklin's troops should move out by forced marches, carrying three or four days' provisions, and to be supplied as far as possible by railroad." *OR*, Ser. 1, XI, Part 1, p. 94.

To Henry W. Halleck [TELEGRAM]

Head Quarters, Army of the Potomac,
Alexandria Aug 27 1.35 pm 1862

I learn that Taylor's Brigade[1] sent this morning to Bulls Run Bridge is either cut to pieces or captured. That the force against them had many guns & about (5000) five thousand Infantry — receiving reinforcements every moment. Also that Gainesville is in possession of enemy. Please send some Cavalry out towards Dranesville via Chain Bridge to watch Lewinsville & Dranesville & go as far as they can. If you can give me even one squadron of good Cavalry here I will ascertain state of case. I think our policy now is to make these works perfectly safe, & mobilize a couple of Corps as soon as possible, but not to advance them until they can have their Artillery & Cavalry. I have sent for Col Tyler[2] to place his artillery men in the works.

Is fort Marcy securely held?

McClellan

Genl Halleck

Some of Cox's troops were also engaged with another force of enemy.[3]

ALS (telegram sent), McClellan Papers (C-15:64), Library of Congress. *OR*, Ser. 1, XII, Part 3, p. 690.

1. Brig. Gen. George W. Taylor's brigade of the Sixth Corps. 2. Col. Robert O. Tyler commanded the Army of the Potomac's siege train. 3. Brig. Gen. Jacob D. Cox commanded four regiments of the Kanawha Division, newly arrived from western Virginia.

To Henry W. Halleck [TELEGRAM]

Maj Genl H. W. Halleck Alexandria, August 27, 1862. 2.30 pm.

Sumner has been ordered to send here all of his Corps that are within reach. Orders have been sent to Couch to come here from Yorktown with the least possible delay. But one squadron of my cavalry has arrived, that will be disembarked at once and sent to the front. If there is any cavalry in Washington it should be ordered to report to me at once.

I still think that we should first provide for the immediate defence of Washington on both sides of the Potomac. I am not responsible for the past and cannot be for the future, unless I receive authority to dispose of the available troops according to my judgment. Please inform me at once what my position is. I do not wish to act in the dark.[1]

G. B. McClellan
Maj Genl

Retained copy, McClellan Papers (A-75:30), Library of Congress. *OR*, Ser. 1, XI, Part 1, pp. 96–97.

1. Halleck replied that afternoon: "From your knowledge of the whole country about here you can best act.... As you must be aware, more than three-quarters of my time is taken up with the raising of new troops and matters in the West. I have no time for details. You will therefore, as ranking general in the field direct as you deem best.... " *OR*, Ser. 1, XII, Part 3, p. 691.

To Henry W. Halleck [TELEGRAM]

Maj. Genl. H W Halleck
Comdr. in Chief U.S.A.
Washington D.C.

Head Quarters, Army of the Potomac,
Alexandria August 27 1862 6 p.m.

I have just received the copy of a dispatch from Genl. Pope to you dated 10 a.m. this morning in which he says: All forces now sent forward should be sent to my right at Gainesville.[1]

I now have at my disposal here about ten thousand (10,000) men of Franklin's Corps, about twenty eight hundred (2800) of Genl Tyler's Brigade, and Col. Tyler's[2] 1st Conn. Artillery, which I recommend should be held in hand for the defence of Washington.

If you wish me to order any part of this force to the front it is in readiness to march at a moments notice to any point you may indicate.

In view of the existing state of things in our front I have deemed it best to order Genl. Casey[3] to hold his men for Yorktown in readiness to move but not to send them off till further orders.

Geo. B. McClellan
Maj Genl

Retained copy, McClellan Papers (C-15:64), Library of Congress. *OR*, Ser. 1, XI, Part 1, p. 97.

1. *OR*, Ser. 1, XII, Part 3, p. 684. 2. Brig. Gen. E. B. Tyler, Col. Robert O. Tyler. 3. Gen. Casey headed a training command for new troops.

To Mary Ellen McClellan

Aug 28th [1862] 9 1/2 am. Steamer Ariel

I am just about starting back for Alexandria. I came up here (Washington) last night — reached Halleck's house about midnight & remained talking with him until 3. . . .

I have a great deal of hard work before me now but will do my best to perform it. I find Halleck well disposed, he has had much to contend against. I shall keep as clear as possible of the Presdt & Cabinet — endeavor to do what must be done with Halleck alone — so I shall get on better. Pope is in a bad way — his communications with Washn cut off & I have not yet the force at hand to relieve him. He has nearly all the troops of my army that have arrived. I hope to hear better news when I reach Alexdra.

AL copy, McClellan Papers (C-7:63), Library of Congress.

To Amiel W. Whipple [TELEGRAM]

Alexandria Aug 28 [1862] 2.30 pm

I think you had better send the guns & artillerists to Fort Buffalo & Ramsay at once. Can you send enough reliable infantry to complete the garrisons? As soon as I know whether I must move my men to the front or not I can decide as to sending a division or two to the point in question. I think they should be held in force. Please reply.

G B McClellan
Maj Genl

Brig Genl Whipple
Arlington

ALS (telegram sent), Records of the Office of the Secretary of War, RG 107 (M-504:65), National Archives. Brig. Gen. Whipple commanded Washington's defenses on the Virginia side of the Potomac.

To Henry W. Halleck [TELEGRAM]

Maj Genl H. W. Halleck
Genl in Chief Alexandria Va Aug 28th 1862

From a full conversation with Col Scammon[1] I am satisfied that the enemy is in large force between us & Pope. One of his surgeons who was taken & released saw Jackson, A. P. Hill & three other Generals. At about five p.m. yesterday there was heavy cannonading in direction of Manassas. It is my opinion that any movement made from here must be in force with Cavalry & Artillery or we shall be beaten in detail. Can you find a squadron to go to Vienna via Lewinsville & ascertain whether enemy there. The right of our line of works on this side the river should be most carefully watched & pickets well out on all roads. Videttes should extend at least to Lewinsville & Prospect Hill. If possible to Meridian Hill & on the ridge thence to Dranesville. It is of vital importance to know what there is near Vienna at once. The impressions I receive from Scammon are corroborated from other sources. I dont see how McDowell can well be at Gainesville. Have this moment received intelligence from a prisoner captured the other night & just escaped that he saw Jackson, Stewart & Minke[2] — that enemy were 30,000 strong in vicinity of Manassas & being reinforced constantly. I suggest that you take into consideration the propriety of Pope's falling back via Davis, Spriggs & Bradleys fords etc between the Occoquan & Potomac & rejoining via Wolfs run Shoals, Occoquan etc. Our best troops here advancing say tomorrow morning or tonight if ready so far as Fairfax, Brimstone Hill & Wolfs run Shoals to cover the movement. I do not think it now worthwhile to attempt to preserve the Railway. The great object is to collect the whole Army in Washington ready to defend the works & act upon the flank of any force crossing the upper Potomac. If Pope makes this movement steps must be taken at once to build Pontoon Bridges over the Occoquan.

Geo. B. McClellan
Maj Genl Comdg

Received copy, Records of the Office of the Secretary of War, RG 107 (M-473:50), National Archives. *OR*, Ser. 1, XII, Part 3, p. 708.

1. Col. E. P. Scammon had made a reconnaissance along the Orange and Alexandria Railroad to Bull Run. 2. Stonewall Jackson and J. E. B. Stuart; "Minke" is no doubt a telegrapher's error for Richard S. Ewell.

To Henry W. Halleck [TELEGRAM]

Head-Quarters, Army of the Potomac,
Hd Qtrs Camp near Alexandria Aug 28 4.10 pm 1862

General Franklin is with me here. I will know in a few minutes the condition of Artillery & Cavalry. We are not yet in condition to move.[1] May be by tomorrow morning. Pope must cut through today or adopt the plan I suggested. I have ordered troops to garrison the works at Upton's Hill. They must be held at any cost. As soon as I can see the way to spare them I will send a Corps of good troops there. It is the key to Washington, which cannot be seriously menaced as long as it is held.

G B McClellan
Maj Genl

Maj Genl Halleck
Washn D.C.

ALS (telegram sent), Records of the Office of the Secretary of War, RG 107 (M-504:65), National Archives. *OR*, Ser. 1, XI, Part 1, p. 97.

1. At 12:40 P.M. on this date Halleck had ordered Franklin by telegraph "to move with your corps to-day toward Manassas Junction, to drive the enemy from the railroad." At 1:00 P.M. GBM replied: "The moment Franklin can be started with a reasonable amount of artillery he shall go." *OR*, Ser. 1, XII, Part 3, pp. 707, 708.

To Henry W. Halleck [TELEGRAM]

Camp near Alexandria Aug 28 [1862] 4.45 p.m.

Your dispatch received.[1] Neither Franklin's nor Sumner's Corps are now in condition to move & fight a battle — it would be a sacrifice to send them out now. I have sent aides to ascertain the condition of the Commands of Cox & Tyler,[2] but I still think that a premature movement in small force will accomplish nothing but the destruction of the troops sent out. I repeat that I will lose no time in preparing the troops now here for the field, & that whatever orders you give after hearing what I have to say will be carried out.

G B McClellan
Maj Genl

Maj Genl Halleck
Washington

ALS (telegram sent), Records of the Office of the Secretary of War, RG 107 (M-504:65), National Archives. *OR*, Ser. 1, XII, Part 3, p. 709.

1. At 3:30 P.M. Halleck had telegraphed: "Not a moment must be lost in pushing as large a force as possible toward Manassas, so as to communicate with Pope before the enemy is re-enforced." *OR*, Ser. 1, XII, Part 3, p. 709. 2. Brig. Gens. Cox and E. B. Tyler.

To Henry W. Halleck [TELEGRAM]

Genl H. W. Halleck
Genl in Chief U.S.A.
Washington D.C.

Head-Quarters, Army of the Potomac,
Alexandria Aug. 29 [28] 1862. 10 pm.

Your dispatch received.[1]

Franklin's Corps has been ordered to march at 6 o'clock tomorrow morning.

Sumner has about fourteen thousand Infantry without Cavalry or Artillery here.

Cox's Brigade of four Regiments is here with two batteries of Artillery. Men of two Regts much fatigued — came in today. Tyler's Brigade of three new regiments but little drilled is also here.

All these troops will be ordered to hold themselves ready to march tomorrow morning — and all except Franklin's to await further orders.

If you wish any of them to move toward Manassas please inform me.

Colonel Wagner[2] 2d N. York Vol. Artillery has just come in from the front. He reports strong Infantry & Cavalry force of rebels near Fairfax Ct. House.

Reports numerous from various sources, that Lee & Stuart with large forces are at Manassas. That the enemy with 120,000 men intend advancing on the forts near Arlington and Chain Bridge, with a view of attacking Washington & Baltimore.

Genl. Barnard[3] telegraphs me tonight that the length of the line of fortifications on this side of the Potomac requires 2000 additional Artillery men, and additional troops to defend intervals, according to circumstances. At all events he says an old regiment should be added to the force at the Chain Bridge, and a few Regts distributed along the lines to give confidence to our new troops.

I agree with him fully and think our fortifications along the upper part of our line on this side the river very unsafe with their present garrisons — and the movements of the enemy seems to indicate an attack upon those works.

Geo. B. McClellan
Maj Genl

Retained copy, McClellan Papers (A-75:30), Library of Congress. *OR,* Ser. 1, XII, Part 3, p. 710.

1. At 7:40 P.M. Halleck had telegraphed: "There must be no further delay in moving Franklin's corps toward Manassas. They must go to-morrow morning, ready or not ready. If we delay too long to get ready there will be no necessity to go at all, for Pope will either be defeated or be victorious without our aid." *OR,* Ser. 1, XII, Part 3, p. 710. **2.** Col. Gustav Waagner. **3.** Gen. Barnard now commanded the Washington defenses.

To John G. Barnard [TELEGRAM]

Genl J. G. Barnard
Washington D.C.

Head-Quarters, Army of the Potomac,
Alexandria Aug. [29] 1862 2 a.m.

Your dispatch received.[1]

I have ordered two Regiments and a Battery to proceed at once up this side of the river to the Chain Bridge, and I have told the officer who sends them (Genl. Sumner) that you would have an officer there to post them.

I would advise you to hold the works as long as you can with safety and at the same time be prepared to destroy the Bridge at short notice.

Geo. B. McClellan
Maj Genl

Retained copy, Records of the Office of the Secretary of War, RG 107 (M-504:65), National Archives. *OR,* Ser. 1, XII, Part 3, p. 725.

1. In his telegram, sent forty minutes earlier, Barnard called for reinforcements at the Chain Bridge, on the Potomac some three miles upstream of the city. At about the same time Halleck telegraphed: "I think you had better place Sumner's corps as it arrives near the fortifications, and particularly at the Chain Bridge. The principal thing to be feared now is a cavalry raid into this city. . . . " *OR,* Ser. 1, XII, Part 3, p. 725, XI, Part 1, p. 97.

To Henry W. Halleck [TELEGRAM]

Camp near Alexandria Aug 29 10.30 am 1862

Franklin's Corps is in motion — started about (6) six am. I can give him but two squadrons of cavalry. I propose moving Genl Cox to Upton's Hill to hold that important point with its works & to push cavalry scouts to Vienna via Freedom hill & Hunter's Lane. Cox has (2) two squadrons cavalry. Please answer at once whether this meets your approval. I have directed Woodbury with the Engineer Brigade to hold Fort Lyon. Sumner detached last night two regiments to vicinity of Forts Ethan Allen & Marcy. Meagher's brigade is still at Acquia. If he moves in support of Franklin it leaves us without any reliable troops in & near Washington, yet Franklin is too weak alone.[1] What shall be done? No more cavalry arrived — have but (3) three squadrons. Franklin has but (40) forty rounds of ammunition & no wagons to move more. I do not think Franklin is in condition to accomplish much if he meets with serious resistance. I should not have moved him but for your pressing order of last night. What have you from Vienna & Dranesville.[2]

G B McClellan
Maj Genl

Maj Genl Halleck
Washington DC

ALS (telegram sent), Records of the Office of the Secretary of War, RG 107 (M-504 :65), National Archives. *OR,* Ser. 1, XI, Part 1, pp. 97–98.

1. Presumably GBM refers here to Sumner's Second Corps, of which Gen. Meagher's brigade was a part. 2. Halleck replied at noon: "Upton's Hill arrangements all right. We must send wagons and ammunition to Franklin as fast as they arrive. Meagher's brigade ordered up yesterday. . . . I have nothing from Dranesville." *OR,* Ser. 1, XI, Part 1, p. 98.

To Henry W. Halleck [TELEGRAM]

Head-Quarters, Army of the Potomac
Camp near Alexandria Aug 29 1 pm 1862

I anxiously await reply to my last dispatch in regard to Sumner.[1] Wish to give the orders at once. Please authorize me to attach new regiments permanently to my old Brigades. I can do much good to old & new troops in that way.

I shall endeavor to hold a line in advance of Forts Allen & Marcy at least with strong advanced guards. I wish to hold the line through Prospect Hill, Mackall's, Minor's & Hall's Hills. This will give us timely warning. Shall I do as seems best to me with all the troops in this vicinity, including Franklin who I really think ought not under present circumstances to advance beyond Annandale.[2]

G B McClellan
Maj Genl

Genl Halleck

ALS (telegram sent), Records of the Office of the Secretary of War, RG 107 (M-504:65), National Archives. *OR,* Ser. 1, XI, Part 1, p. 99.

1. GBM had telegraphed at noon, proposing to post Sumner's corps to cover the approaches to Washington. *OR,* Ser. 1, XI, Part 1, p. 99. 2. Halleck replied at 3:00 P.M.: "Dispose of all troops as you deem best. I want Franklin's corps to go far enough to find out something about the enemy. Perhaps he may get such information at Annandale as to prevent his going farther; otherwise he will push on toward Fairfax. Try to get something from the direction of Manassas.... Our people must move more actively and find out where the enemy is. I am tired of guesses." *OR,* Ser. 1, XII, Part 3, p. 722.

To Abraham Lincoln [TELEGRAM]

Head Quarters, Army of the Potomac,
Camp near Alexandria Aug 29, 2.45 pm 1862

The last news I received from the direction of Manassas was from stragglers to the effect that the enemy were evacuating Centreville & retiring towards Thorofare Gap.[1] This by no means reliable. I am clear that one of two courses should be adopted — 1st To concentrate all our available forces to open communication with Pope — 2nd To leave Pope to get out of his scrape & at once use all our means to make the Capital perfectly safe. No middle course will now answer. Tell me what you wish me to do & I will do all in my power to accomplish it. I wish to know what my orders & authority are — I ask for nothing, but will obey whatever orders you give.

I only ask a prompt decision that I may at once give the necessary orders. It will not do to delay longer.[2]

G B McClellan
Maj Genl

A Lincoln Presdt
& copy to Genl Halleck

ALS (telegram sent), McClellan Papers (C-15:64), Library of Congress. *OR,* Ser. 1, XI, Part 1, p. 98.

1. At 2:30 P.M. the president had telegraphed: "What news from direction of Mannassas Junction? What generally?" *Collected Works of Lincoln,* V, p. 399. 2. The president replied at 4:10 P.M.: "I think your first alternative to wit 'To concentrate all our available forces to open communication with Pope' is the right one but I wish not to control. That I now leave to Genl Halleck aided by your counsels." McClellan Papers (A-30:75).

To Mary Ellen McClellan

[Alexandria] Aug 29 [1862] 3 pm.

. . . I was awake all last night & have not had one moment until now to write to you. I have a terrible task on my hands now — perfect imbecility to correct. No means to act with, no authority — yet determined if possible to save the country & the Capital. I find the soldiers all clinging to me — yet I am not permitted to go to the post of danger! Two of my Corps will either save that fool Pope or be sacrificed for the country. I do not know whether I will be permitted to save the Capital or not — I have just telegraphed very plainly to the Presdt & Halleck what I think ought to be done — I expect merely a contemptuous silence. . . .

I am heart sick with the folly & ignorance I see around me — God grant that I may never pass through such a scene again. . . .

AL copy, McClellan Papers (C-7:63), Library of Congress.

To Henry W. Halleck [TELEGRAM]

Maj Genl H W Halleck
Comdg US Army

Head-Quarters, Army of the Potomac,
[Alexandria] August 29th 1862 5.25 p.m.

Before receiving the President's message[1] I had put Sumner's Corps in motion towards Arlington and the Chain Bridge, not having received any reply from you. The movement is still under your control in either direction though now under progress as stated.

G B McClellan
Maj Genl

I think that one of the two alternatives should be fully carried out.

Retained copy, Records of the Office of the Secretary of War, RG 107 (M-504:65), National Archives. *OR,* Ser. 1, XII, Part 3, p. 723.

1. See GBM to Lincoln, Aug. 29, note 2, *supra.*

To Henry W. Halleck [TELEGRAM]

Head Quarters, Army of the Potomac,
Camp near Alexandria 8 pm Aug 29 1862

By referring to my telegrams of 10.30 am, 12 m, 1 pm together with your reply of 2.48 you will see why Franklin's Corps halted at Annandale.[1] His small cavalry force, all I had to give him was ordered to push on as far as possible towards Manassas. It was not safe for Franklin to move beyond Annandale under the circumstances until we knew what was at Vienna. Genl Franklin remained here until about 1 pm endeavouring to arrange for supplies for his command. I am responsible for both these circumstances & do not see that either was in disobedience to your orders. Please give distinct orders in reference to Franklin's movements of tomorrow. I have sent to Col Haupt[2] to push out construction & supply trains as soon as possible — Genl Tyler to furnish the necessary guards.

I have directed Genl Banks' supply trains to start out to night at least as far as Annandale, with an escort from Genl Tyler.

In regard to tomorrow's movements I desire definite instructions as it is not agreeable to me to be accused of disobeying orders when I have simply exercised the discretion you committed to me.

G B McClellan
Maj Genl

Maj Genl Halleck
Washington D.C.

ALS (telegram sent), McClellan Papers (C-15:64), Library of Congress. *OR*, Ser. 1, XI, Part 1, pp. 99–100.

1. At 7:50 P.M. Halleck had telegraphed: "I have just been told that Franklin's corps stopped at Annandale.... This is all contrary to my orders; investigate and report the facts of this disobedience. That corps must push forward, as I directed.... " *OR*, Ser. 1, XII, Part 3, p. 723. See GBM's telegrams of this date, 10:30 A.M. and 1:00 P.M., *supra;* his telegram of noon dealt with allocating forces for the defense of Washington: *OR*, Ser. 1, XI, Part 1, p. 99. Halleck's "reply of 2.48" is probably his 3:00 P.M. telegram; see GBM to Halleck, Aug. 29, 1:00 P.M., note 2, *supra*. 2. Col. Herman Haupt was the Army of Virginia's chief of construction and transportation.

To Mary Ellen McClellan

[Alexandria] Aug 29 [1862] 9 1/2 pm.

I have been terribly busy since reaching here — not a moment have I had to myself. I found everything in the most terrible confusion — apparently inextricably so, but affairs are now better. The works on this side the river are in condition for defense....

I see the evening paper states that I have been placed in command of all the troops in Va. — this is not so — I have no command at present — that is to say I have none of the Army of the Potomac with me & have merely "turned in" on my own account to straighten out whatever I catch hold of. By tomorrow evening I hope to have the works etc in fair condition of defense....

Pope has been in a tight place, but from the news received this evening I think the danger is pretty much over. Tomorrow will tell the story.

I am terribly crippled by the want of cavalry. None of mine have arrived except 3 small squadrons. I hope for more tonight. There was a terrible scare in Washn last night. A rumor got out that Lee was advancing rapidly on the Chain Bridge with 150,000 men — & such a stampede! I did not get 5 minutes consecutive sleep all night — so thick were the telegrams!...

I have seen neither the Presdt nor the Secy since I arrived here — have been only once to Washn & hope to see very little of the place — I abominate it terribly....

I have no faith in anyone here & expect to be turned loose the moment their alarm is over. I expect I got into a row with Halleck tonight — he sent me a telegram I did not like & I told him so very plainly. He is not a refined person at all, & probably says rough things when he don't mean them....

AL copy, McClellan Papers (C-7 :63), Library of Congress.

To Mary Ellen McClellan

Aug 30 [1862] 8 am Camp near Alexandria

...Was awakened last night by a few scattering shots that no doubt came from some of those *very* raw troops that are about here. Shall start soon after bkfst & ride to Upton's Hill — thence to the Chain bridge & along the line of Forts. I want to see all on this side of the river today if I can. No one in Washington appears to know the condition of matters, & I have a fancy for finding them out for myself. If I once get matters reasonably straight I shall not trouble myself much more. What I am doing now is rather a volunteer affair — not exactly my business, but you know that I have a way of attending to most other things than my own affairs.

I had a very funny letter yesterday from the Duc de Chartres which I will enclose with this, as it may amuse you — the *English* is *superb*!

1 1/2 pm. ...I expected to start out on a long ride, but have thus far been detained by various matters which have kept me very busy....

There has been heavy firing going on all day long somewhere beyond Bull Run. I have sent up every man I have, pushed everything, & am left here on the flat of my back without any command whatever. It is dreadful to listen to the cannonading & not be able to take any part in it — but such is my fate....

I must close now for I have some more orders to give.

9.15 pm. ...I feel too blue & disgusted to write any more now, so I will smoke a cigar & try to get into a better humor. They have taken *all* my troops from me — I have even sent off all my personal escort & camp guard & am here with a few orderlies & the aides. I have been listening to the distant sound of a great battle in the distance — my men engaged in it & I away! I never felt worse in my life.

AL copy; copy, McClellan Papers (C-7 :63/D-10 :72), Library of Congress.

To Ambrose E. Burnside [TELEGRAM]

Head-Quarters, Army of the Potomac,
Camp near Alexandria Aug 30 1862 8.20 am

Telegram of midnight received.[1] Use your discretion about the cavalry — I have only three squadrons two of which with Franklin — I expect some today. Do not strip yourself of anything. Your information about Pope substantially confirmed from this side. His troops are at Centreville. Supplies have gone to him by rail & by wagon. Secesh has missed his first coup. We will soon see what his second is to be.

G B McClellan
Maj Genl

Maj Genl Burnside
Falmouth

ALS (telegram sent), Records of the Office of the Secretary of War, RG 107 (M-504:65), National Archives. *OR,* Ser. 1, XII, Part 3, p. 758.

1. Burnside's telegram reported on the situation at Falmouth and the disposition of his forces. *OR,* Ser. 1, XII, Part 3, pp. 757–58.

To Henry W. Halleck

Major General H. W. Halleck
General in Chief U.S.A.,
Washington D.C. Head Quarters Army of the Potomac,
General: [Alexandria] August 30, 1862 [11:30 A.M.][1]

Ever since General Franklin received notice that he was to march from Alexandria he has been using every effort to get transportation for his extra ammunition, but he was uniformly told by the Quarter Masters here that there was none disposable and his command marched without wagons.[2] After the departure of his Corps at 6 A.M. yesterday, he procured twenty wagons to carry a portion of his ammunition by unloading some of General Banks' supply train for that purpose.

General Sumner was one entire day in endeavoring by application upon Quarter Masters and others to get a sufficient number of wagons to transport his reserve ammunition but without success, and was obliged to march without it.

I have this morning sent all my Head Quarters train that is landed to be at once loaded with ammunition for Sumner and Franklin, but they will not go far toward supplying the deficiency.

Eighty-five wagons were got together by the Quarter Master last night, loaded with subsistence, and sent forward, under an escort at 1 A.M. via Annandale.

Every effort has been made to carry out your instructions promptly.

The difficulty seems to consist in the fact that the greater part of the transportation on hand at Alexandria and Washington has been needed for current supplies of the garrisons. At all events such is the state of the case as represented to me by the Quarter Masters, and it appears to be true.

I take it for granted that this has not been properly explained to you.

I am very respectfully your obt servt
Geo B McClellan
Maj Genl USA

LS, Records of the Adjutant General's Office, RG 94 (159: Halleck Papers), National Archives. *OR,* Ser. 1, XII, Part 3, pp. 744–45.

1. A retained copy of this communication indicates it was originally intended to be a telegram. McClellan Papers (A-75:30), Library of Congress. 2. Halleck had telegraphed at 9:40 A.M.: "I am by no means satisfied with General Franklin's march of yesterday. Considering the circumstances of the case, he was very wrong in stopping at Annandale. Moreover, I learned last night that the Quartermaster's Department could have given him plenty of transportation, if he had applied for it, any time since his arrival at Alexandria. He knew the importance of opening communication with General Pope's army, and should have acted more promptly." *OR,* Ser. 1, XII, Part 3, p. 744.

To Henry W. Halleck [TELEGRAM]

Maj Genl H W Halleck
Comdg USA

Head Qtrs Army Potomac
[Alexandria] August 30th 1862

Sumners command was fully in motion by 2 1/2 pm & Franklins was past Fairfax at 10 am. All moving forward as rapidly as possible.[1] I have sent the last cavalry man I have to the front. Also every other soldier in my Command except a small camp guard.

G B McClellan
Maj Genl

The firing in front has been extremely heavy for the past hour.

Retained copy, Records of the Office of the Secretary of War, RG 107 (M-504:65), National Archives. *OR*, Ser. 1, XII, Part 3, pp. 747–48.

1. Halleck had telegraphed at 2:10 P.M.: "Franklin's and all of Sumner's corps should be pushed forward with all possible dispatch. They must use their legs and make forced marches. Time now is everything...." *OR*, Ser. 1, XII, Part 3, p. 747.

To Henry W. Halleck [TELEGRAM]

Head Quarters, Army of the Potomac,
Camp near Alexandria Aug 30 10.30 pm 1862

I have sent to the front all my troops with the exception of Couch's Division & have given the orders necessary to ensure its being disposed of as you directed.[1] I hourly expect the return of one of my aides who will give authentic news from the field of battle. I cannot express to you the pain & mortification I have experienced today in listening to the distant sound of the firing of my men. As I can be of no further use here I respectfully ask that if there is a probability of the conflict being renewed tomorrow I may be permitted to go to the scene of battle with my staff — merely to be with my own men if nothing more — they will fight none the worse for my being with them.

If it is not deemed best to entrust me with the command even of my own Army I simply ask to be permitted to share their fate on the field of battle. Please reply to this to night.[2]

I have been engaged for the last few hours in doing what I can to make arrangements for the wounded. I have started out all the ambulances now landed.

G B McClellan
Maj Genl

Maj Genl Halleck
Comdg USA Washington

As I have sent my escort to the front I would be glad to take some of Gregg's Cavalry with me if allowed to go.

ALS (telegram sent), Records of the Office of the Secretary of War, RG 107 (M-504:65), National Archives. *OR*, Ser. 1, XI, Part 1, pp. 101–102.

1. Halleck had telegraphed at 12:20 P.M.: "I think Couch should land at Alexandria and be immediately pushed out to Pope. Send the troops where the fighting is." *OR*, Ser. 1, XII, Part 3, pp. 747–48. 2. Halleck replied the next morning: "I cannot answer without seeing the President, as General Pope is in command, by his orders, of the department." *OR*, Ser. 1, XI, Part 1, p. 102.

To Henry W. Halleck [TELEGRAM]

Head Quarters, Army of the Potomac,
Camp near Alexandria Aug 31 3.30 am 1862

My aide just in. He reports our army as badly beaten. Our losses very heavy. Troops arriving at Centreville. Have probably lost several batteries. Some of the Corps entirely broken up into stragglers. Shall Couch continue his movement to the front?[1] We have no other tried troops in Washington. Sumner between Fairfax & Centreville. Franklin now at Centreville — having fallen back from Bull's Run. Enemy has probably suffered severely. Hammerstein is a cool head & old soldier.

G B McClellan
Maj Genl

Maj Genl Halleck
Washington

ALS (telegram sent), McClellan Papers (C-15:64), Library of Congress. *OR*, Ser. 1, XII, Part 3, pp. 771–72.

1. Halleck replied: "I think Couch's division should go forward as rapidly as possible and find the battlefield." *OR*, Ser. 1, XI, Part 1, p. 102.

To Mary Ellen McClellan

[Alexandria] Sunday [August] 31st [1862] 9.30 am.

. . . There was a severe battle yesterday, almost exactly on the old Bull Run battle ground. Pope sent in accounts during the day that he was getting on splendidly, driving the enemy all day, gaining a glorious victory etc etc. About 3 this morning Hammerstein returned from the field (where I had sent him to procure information) & told me that we were badly whipped. McDowell & Sigel's Corps broken — the troops of my own army that were present (Porter & Heintzelman) badly cut up, but in perfect order. Banks was not engaged. Franklin had arrived & was in position at Centreville. Sumner must have got up by this time. Couch's Division is about starting. It is probable that the enemy are too much fatigued to renew the attack this morning, perhaps not at all today. So that time may be given to our people to make such arrangements as will enable them to hold their own. I telegraphed last evening asking permission to be with my troops, received a reply about half an hour ago from Halleck that he would have to consult the Presdt first!! If they refuse to let me go out I think I shall feel obliged to insist upon a leave or something of the kind the moment the question of the existing battle is settled. I feel like a fool here — sucking my thumbs & doing nothing but what ought to be done by junior officers. I leave it all in the hands of the Almighty — I will try to do my best in the position that may be assigned to me & be as patient as I can. . . .

10.45 [A.M.] . . . I feel in that state of excitement & anxiety that I can hardly keep still for a moment. I learn from Hammerstein that the men in front are all very anxious for me to be with them — it is *too* cruel!

12 1/2 pm. A short time since I saw the order defining commands etc[1] — mine is that part of the Army of the Potomac *not* sent to Pope — as all is sent there I am left in command of *nothing* — a command I feel fully competent to exercise, & to which I can do full justice. I am going to write a quiet moderate letter to Mr. Aspinwall presently, explaining to him the exact state of the case, without comment, so that my friends in New York may know all. . . .

Everything is too uncertain & unsafe around Washington at present for you to dream of going there. As a matter of self respect I cannot go there. . . .

I do not regard Washn as safe against the rebels. If I can quietly slip over there I will send your silver off.[2] There is an order forbidding anyone going there without permission from the War Dept, & I do not care to ask them even for so slight a favor as that. . . .

AL copy, McClellan Papers (C-7 :63), Library of Congress.

1. Adj. Gen.'s Office, Special Order 89, Aug. 30, 1862, read, in part: "General McClellan commands that portion of the Army of the Potomac that has not been sent forward to General Pope's command." *OR*, Ser. 1, XI, Part 1, p. 103. 2. Mrs. McClellan had expressed concern over their possessions in Washington. She wrote on Aug. 30, for example: "I don't like to trouble you . . . but I really do feel a little nervous about the silver & dont know what had better be done about it. It is in a trunk at Corcoran & Riggs Bank. . . ." McClellan Papers (B-11 :48)

To Henry W. Halleck [TELEGRAM]

Head-Quarters, Army of the Potomac,
Camp near Alexandria Aug 31 1862 2.30 pm

Maj Haller[1] is at Fairfax Station with my Provost & Head Quarters Guards & other troops. I have requested (4) four more companies to be sent at once & the precautions you direct to be taken.[2]

Under the War Department order of yesterday[3] I have no control over anything except my staff some one hundred men in my camp here & the few remaining near Fort Monroe. I have no control over the new regiments, do not know where they are or anything about them except some of those near here. Their commanding officers & those of the works are not under me. When I have seen evils existing under my eye I have corrected them. I think it is the business of Genl Casey to prepare the new regiments for the field & a matter between him & Genl Barnard to order others to vicinity of Chain Bridge. Neither of them is under my command & by the War Dept order I have no right to give them orders.

G B McClellan

Genl Halleck
Washington

ALS (telegram sent), Records of the Office of the Secretary of War, RG 107 (M-504 :65), National Archives. *OR*, Ser. 1, XI, Part 1, p. 102.

1. Maj. G. O. Haller, 7th U.S. Infantry. 2. At 12:45 P.M. Halleck had telegraphed: "The Subsistence Department are making Fairfax Station their principal depot. It should be well guarded . . . As many as possible of the new regiments should be prepared to take the field. Perhaps some more should be sent to the vicinity of Chain Bridge." *OR*, Ser. 1, XI, Part 1, p. 102. 3. See GBM to his wife, Aug. 31, note 1, *supra*.

To Henry W. Halleck [TELEGRAM]

Camp near Alexandria Aug 31 [1862] 7.30 pm

Having been informed that there were some (20,000) twenty thousand stragglers from Popes army between this & Centreville all of Gregg's cavalry have been sent to endeavor to drive them back to their regiments.

Two hundred of 8th Illinois Cavalry will be ready in the morning, and two hundred & fifty (250) more as soon as disembarked. The armament of Forts Buffalo & Ramsay is very incomplete.

G B McClellan
Maj Genl

Maj Genl Halleck
Washington D.C.

ALS (telegram sent), Records of the Office of the Secretary of War, RG 107 (M-504:65), National Archives. *OR*, Ser. 1, XII, Part 3, p. 773.

To Henry W. Halleck [TELEGRAM]

Head Quarters, Army of the Potomac,
Camp near Alexandria Aug 31 10.25 pm 1862

I am ready to afford you every assistance in my power, but you will readily perceive how difficult an undefined position such as I now hold must be.[1]

At what hour in the morning can I see you alone, either at your own house or the office?

G B McClellan
Maj Genl

Maj Genl Halleck
Washington D.C.

ALS (telegram sent), McClellan Papers (C-15:64), Library of Congress. *OR*, Ser. 1, XII, Part 3, p. 773.

1. Halleck had telegraphed at 10:07 P.M.: "You will retain the command of everything in this vicinity not temporarily belonging to Pope's army in the field. I beg of you to assist me in this crisis with your ability and experience. I am utterly tired out." *OR*, Ser. 1, XI, Part 1, pp. 102–103.

To Henry W. Halleck [TELEGRAM]

Camp near Alexandria Aug 31 [1862] 11 1/2 pm

The squadron of 2nd regular Cavalry that I sent with General Sumner was captured today about 2 pm some 3 miles from Fairfax CH beyond it on the Little River Pike by Fitzhugh Lee[1] with (3,000) Cavalry & three (3) light batteries. I have conversed with the 1st Sergeant who says that when he last saw them they were within a mile of Fairfax. Pope has no troops on that road, this squadron getting there by mistake. There is nothing of ours on the right of Centreville but Sumner's Corps. There was much Artillery firing during the day. A rebel Major told the sergeant that the rebels had driven in our center & left today. He says the road is filled with wagons & stragglers coming towards Alexandria. It is clear from the Sergeant's account that we were badly beaten yesterday & that Pope's right is entirely exposed.

I recommend that no more of Couch's Division be sent to the front, that Burnside be brought here as soon as practicable, & that everything available this side of Fairfax be drawn in at once including the mass of the troops on the Railroad. I apprehend that the enemy will, or have by this time, occupied Fairfax CH & cut off Pope entirely unless he falls back tonight via Sangster's & Fairfax Station.

I think these orders should be sent at once — I have no confidence in the dispositions made as I gather them — to speak frankly, & the occasion requires it, there appears to be a total absence of brains & I fear the total destruction of the Army. I have some Cavalry here that can carry out any orders you may have to send.

The occasion is grave & demands grave measures. The question is the salvation of the country.

I learn that our loss yesterday amounted to (15,000) fifteen thousand — we cannot afford such losses without an object. It is my deliberate opinion that the interests of the nation demand that Pope should fall back tonight if possible and not one moment is to be lost.

I will use all the Cavalry I have to watch our right. Please answer at once.[2] I feel confident that you can rely upon the information I give you — I shall be up all night & ready to obey any orders you give me.

G B McClellan
Maj Genl

Genl Halleck
Washington

ALS (telegram sent), Records of the Office of the Secretary of War, RG 107 (M-504:65), National Archives. *OR*, Ser. 1, XI, Part 1, p. 103.

1. Brig. Gen. Fitzhugh Lee, commanding a brigade of Stuart's cavalry division. 2. Halleck replied at 1:30 A.M. on Sept. 1: "I must wait for more definitive information before I can order a retreat, as the falling back on the line of works must necessarily be directed in case of a serious disaster.... I am fully aware of the gravity of the crisis and have been for weeks." *OR*, Ser. 1, XII, Part 3, p. 786.

To Mary Ellen McClellan

Sept 1 [1862] Washington 2 pm.

I have only time to tell you that I have been placed in command of Washn & all the garrison etc in the vicinity — to do the best I can with it. The decisive battle will be fought today near Fairfax C.H. My Hd Qtrs are to be in town. If the squall passes over & Washn is a safe place you shall come on to see me if I can't get off to see you. . . .

AL copy, McClellan Papers (C-7:63), Library of Congress.

To Fitz John Porter [TELEGRAM]

Head-Quarters of the Army,
[September 1] 1862 [5:30 P.M.]

I ask of you for my sake that of the country & of the old Army of the Potomac that you and all my friends will lend the fullest & most cordial cooperation to Genl Pope in all the operations now going on. The destinies of our country the honor of our arms are at stake, & all depends now upon the cheerful cooperation of all in the field. This week is the crisis of our fate. Say the same thing to my friends in the Army of the Potomac & that the last request I have to make of them is that for their country's sake they will extend to Genl Pope the same support they ever have to me.[1]

I am in charge of the defenses of Washington & am doing all I can to render your retreat safe should that become necessary.[2] [*crossed out:* I am now sure that the President & the Genl in Chief neither wish nor intend that the Army shall remain in its present position one moment after its safety becomes jeopardized. It is desirable that it should retain its present position if it is reasonably safe to do so but it will never be sacrificed.][3]

G B McClellan

ALS (telegram sent), McClellan Papers (A-76:30), Library of Congress. *OR*, Ser. 1, XII, Part 3, pp. 787–88.

1. This appeal was made at Lincoln's urging after Gen. Pope telegraphed Halleck on this date to report "the unsoldierly and dangerous conduct of many brigade and some division commanders of the forces sent here from the Peninsula. Every word and act and intention is discouraging, and calculated to break down the spirits of the men and produce disaster." *OR*, Ser. 1, XII, Part 2, pp. 82–83. 2. Gen. Porter replied on Sept. 2: "You may rest assured that all your friends, as well as every lover of his country, will ever give, as they have given, to General Pope their cordial co-operation and constant support. . . ." *OR*, Ser. 1, XII, Part 3, p. 798. 3. Apparently GBM intended this as a response to Porter's dispatch of Aug. 31 that read, in part, "I do not wish to see the army back . . . ; but I fear it may be kept here at the will of the enemy, to cripple it so that when it does get back it will be so crippled that it cannot defend the forts . . . ," but then thought better of it. *OR*, Ser. 1, XII, Part 3, pp. 768–69 (misdated).

To Mary Ellen McClellan

[Washington] Sept 2 [1862] 1 am.

. . . Last night [August 31] I had just finished a very severe application for a leave of absence when I received a dispatch from Halleck begging me to help him out of the scrape & take command here[1] — of course I could not refuse, so I came over this morning [September 1], mad as a March hare, & had a pretty plain talk with him & Abe — a still plainer one this evening. The result is that I have reluctantly consented to take command here & try to save the Capital — I don't know whether I can do it or not, for things are far gone — I hope I shall succeed. . . .

I will not work so hard again as I used to — for the next few days I must be at it day & night — once the pressure is over I will make the staff do the work. If when the whole army returns here (if it ever does) I am not placed in command of all I will either insist upon a long leave of absence or resign. . . .

AL copy, McClellan Papers (C-7:63), Library of Congress.

1. See GBM to Halleck, Aug. 31, 10:25 P.M., note 1, *supra*.

To Mary Ellen McClellan

[Washington] Sept 2 [1862] 12.30 pm.

I was surprised this morning when at bkft by a visit from the Presdt & Halleck — in which the former expressed the opinion that the troubles now impending could be overcome better by me than anyone else. Pope is ordered to fall back upon Washn & as he reenters everything is to come under my command again! A terrible & thankless task — yet I will do my best with God's blessing to perform it. God knows that I need his help. I am too busy to write any more now — Pray that God will help me in the great task now imposed upon me — I assume it reluctantly — with a full knowledge of all its difficulties & of the immensity of the responsibility. I only consent to take it for my country's sake & with the humble hope that God has called me to it — how I pray that he may support me! . . .

Don't be worried — my conscience is clear & I can trust in God.

AL copy, McClellan Papers (C-7:63), Library of Congress.

To Abraham Lincoln

Unofficial

Your Excellency Washington Sept 2 [1862] 12.30 pm

I have by telegraph & through my Aides placed all the garrisons on the alert, ready to cover the reentrance of the Army — have placed guards upon all the roads to collect stragglers & arranged to have them fed at once. Cavalry are out hastening in Genl Pope's trains so as to clear the roads as rapidly as possible & get everything out of the way of the troops. The wagons are being placed in secure spots where they will not interfere with the free movement of troops in the event of an action. A brigade of Couch's Division (Abercrombie's) is ordered to Chain Bridge. Col Kelton[1] informed me that he saw no stragglers this side of Fairfax. I shall be on the ground before any stragglers of moment or any troops arrive — in the mean time I have been & am busily engaged in transmitting the necessary orders & obtaining the requisite information. If Pope retires promptly & in good order all will yet go well. I have telegraphed to Burnside to learn the state of affairs with him.

You may rest certain that nothing I can think of shall be left undone.

Most respectfully your obdt svt
Geo B. McClellan
Maj Genl Comdg

His Excellency the President

ALS, Lincoln Papers, Library of Congress.

1. Col. John C. Kelton, Halleck's assistant adjutant general.

To John Pope

Maj. Gen. John Pope
Commanding Army of Virginia: Headquarters,
General: Washington, September 2, 1862.

General Halleck instructed me to repeat to you the order he sent this morning to withdraw your army to Washington without unnecessary delay.[1] He feared that his message might miss you, and desired to take this double precaution.

In order to bring troops upon ground with which they are already familiar, it would be best to move Porter's corps upon Upton's Hill, that it may occupy Hall's Hill, &c.; McDowell's to Upton's Hill; Franklin's to the works in front of Alexandria; Heintzelman's to the same vicinity; Couch to Fort Corcoran, or, if practicable, to the Chain Bridge; Sumner either to Fort Albany or to Alexandria, as may be most convenient.

In haste, general, very truly, yours
Geo. B. McClellan
Major-General, U.S. Army.

OR, Ser. 1, XIX, Part 1, p. 38.

1. Halleck's dispatch to Pope read, in part: "You will bring your forces as best you can within or near the line of fortification. General McClellan has charge of all the defenses,

and you will consider any direction, as to disposition of the troops as they arrive, given by him as coming from me.'' *OR*, Ser. 1, XII, Part 3, p. 797.

To Henry W. Halleck

Major-General Halleck:
My dear Halleck: [Washington] September 2 [1862] 1.20 p.m.

My ordnance officer (Lieutenant Porter)[1] informs me that General Ripley says that he has just received an order from the Secretary of War to ship everything from this arsenal to New York.

I had sent to General Ripley to learn what small arms were here, so that I might be prepared to arm stragglers, &c. I do not think this order ought to be carried out so promptly. I do not despair of saving the capital. Better destroy all there is there at the eleventh hour than to send them off now. Will you not say something as to this?[2]

In haste, truly, yours,
Geo. B. McClellan

I am pushing things through and shall soon have everything we have in readiness.

McC

OR, Ser. 1, XII, Part 3, p. 802.

1. Lt. Horace Porter, the Army of the Potomac's chief ordnance officer. 2. Halleck replied on this date: ''At least 50,000 or 60,000 arms will be left and a large number of pieces of artillery.'' *OR*, Ser. 1, XII, Part 3, p. 805.

To Abraham Lincoln

Unofficial
Your Excellency [Washington] Sept 2 [1862] 3 pm

Several excellent batteries of field Artillery have arrived, also some more Cavalry & are all rapidly disembarking.

I now have members of my staff examining everything except the works south (*east*) of the East Branch, with distinct instructions as to what is to be done in every work in case of attack, & of the disposition to be made of the troops outside of the works. I have nothing yet from Burnside. I hope to be able to inform you by 8 tonight that everything I have in hand is prepared for action.

It is right that Pope should now fall back with the utmost rapidity consistent with good order. In my view we must now prepare at once to cover the Chain Bridge, & be ready to attack the enemy in flank should they venture to cross the upper Potomac. As it is *possible* I do not say *probable* that our Railway communication with Baltimore may be cut off, I would respectfully suggest that the *mass* of Comm. Wilkes' James River Flotilla be ordered to the Potomac to ensure our water communication.[1] If orders can be given to the Commodore to bring to the Potomac whatever he thinks necessary I am sure that there will be no trouble on that score — for he has ever evinced the strongest disposition to assist the Army, instead of waiting to be called upon for aid, he *volunteers* it — he can arrange the matter with me in a few minutes. I am about riding to the front & as I am anxious about the Chain Bridge will return that way — & will endeavor to pass by the Soldiers Home to report to you the state of affairs unless called elsewhere. I am still confident, altho' I fully appreciate the magnitude of the task committed to me.

With the highest respect I am your Excellency's obd svt

Geo B McClellan

His Excellency the President
Executive Mansion

ALS, Lincoln Papers, Library of Congress.

1. This action had already been taken, beginning with Wilkes's appointment to command the Potomac flotilla on Aug. 29, *NOR*, Ser. 1, VII, pp. 687–88.

To Mary Ellen McClellan

[Alexandria] Sept 3 [1862] 11.30 am.

. . . I am now about to jump into the saddle & will be off all day. I did not return from my ride last night until after midnight — I rode out to meet the troops & place them in position. Colburn & I rode out several miles to the front. All is quiet today, & I think the Capital is safe. Just as I was starting off yesterday to gather up the army, supposing that I would find it savagely followed up by the rebels & that I might have dangerous work before me I commenced the enclosed scrawl on a scrap of paper as a good bye — could not even finish it. It may amuse you now that the danger is over.

[*enclosure*]

Sept 2 4 pm. I am just about starting out to pick up the Army of the Potomac. Don't know whether I will get back — but can't resist saying one last word to you before I start. . . .

AL copy, McClellan Papers (C-7:63), Library of Congress.

To Henry W. Halleck

Head Quarters, Washington
Sept 4 [1862] 12 1/2 pm

General

Banks' Corps is on the march for Rockville, Poolesville etc to watch & check the enemy should he attempt to cross the Potomac below the

Point of Rocks. Sumner is in position near Tennallytown — Couch's division is probably by this time concentrated at Chain Bridge.

Have ordered more cavalry & a battery to Edwards Ferry. The troops are being rested & refitted as well as circumstances will permit — no time has been lost in doing this. I am not quite well enough to ride out today, except in case of necessity, but have sent my aides in all directions. The shelling of the canal boats is an old amusement of the rebels — it is probably a pretty strong proof that they do not intend to cross at Edwards' Ferry.[1]

Very respectfully yours
Geo B McClellan
Maj Genl

Maj Genl H W Halleck
Comdr in Chief

ALS, Records of the Adjutant General's Office, RG 94 (159: Halleck Papers), National Archives. *OR*, Ser. 1, XIX, Part 2, pp. 174–75.

1. Halleck forwarded a report on this date that the enemy was firing on boats in the Chesapeake and Ohio Canal. *OR*, Ser. 1, XIX, Part 2, p. 175.

EIGHT

THE MARYLAND CAMPAIGN AND ANTIETAM

SEPTEMBER 5–19, 1862

THE MARYLAND CAMPAIGN was the climax of George McClellan's military career and Antietam his greatest and most important battle. His description of Antietam for his wife as "the most terrible battle of the age" was a fair enough statement for 1862, and its cost — combined casualties in the two armies of nearly 23,000 men — has never been surpassed on any single day of warfare in the nation's history. Lee's first invasion of the North was turned back and (so McClellan told General Halleck) "Maryland & Penna. are now safe."

Lacking the weaponry and manpower to besiege Washington after Second Bull Run, General Lee had elected to cross the Potomac into Maryland to shift the theater of war to what he called the Confederacy's northern frontier. He did so to retain the strategic initiative and to provision his men and forage his animals on Northern soil, but primarily he went north to force a battle he believed would be decisive for the South's independence. He intended to draw McClellan far from his Washington base and fight him on a battleground of his own choosing somewhere in the Cumberland Valley of Maryland and Pennsylvania. McClellan followed slowly into Maryland, guarding Washington and Baltimore against attack and reorganizing his army and his command system.

In the first days of the campaign McClellan's letters to his wife reveal him to be confident of his prospects, but this tone is soon replaced by the more familiar litany of the daunting odds that faced him. Although his intelligence came now from Alfred Pleasonton's cavalry and from civilian informants, its counts of the enemy were as grossly inflated as anything Allan Pinkerton had produced on the Peninsula — and General McClellan was as predisposed as ever to accept them. The figure of 120,000 he settled on for Lee's army and reported to Washington on September

10 came to him from a church elder who had heard it from talkative Rebels. It was three times Lee's actual strength.

The campaign, and Lee's plan for it, was abruptly and fundamentally altered by the Lost Order. The copy of his operational plan lost by a Confederate courier and found on September 13 by a Union soldier revealed to McClellan that Lee had divided his army to surround and capture the Federal garrison at Harper's Ferry, and gave the location of each of the widely scattered commands. As McClellan himself phrased it, the Lost Order presented him with the unique opportunity "to cut the enemy in two & beat him in detail." His dispatches on September 13 reveal his reaction to the find, and also the hedging in his report to General Halleck as to when he learned of it and what it contained. Indeed, many of his dispatches on this and the next few days are notable for their distortions and their exaggeration of the speed of his movements and the magnitude of what he accomplished.

The five days beginning on September 13 witnessed the discovery of the Lost Order, the fighting at South Mountain, the surrender of Harper's Ferry, the movement to Sharpsburg, and the great battle there on the seventeenth; yet during this momentous period McClellan wrote comparatively few dispatches and they are less revealing than those written (for example) during the Seven Days. His sole description of a tactical plan is his letter of September 13 to General Franklin, outlining his intentions for breaking through South Mountain the following day. His failure in those days to write down anything of how he planned to fight the Battle of Antietam leaves the largest single gap in his contemporaneous military record. The telegram he sent to General Halleck during the fighting on the seventeenth gives only a very brief description of actions already taken.

The scarcity of battlefield communications in the Maryland fighting is due in part to the nature of the operations there. While movements on the Peninsula had been deliberate enough to allow time to link the various commands by field telegraph, there was no similar opportunity at South Mountain and Antietam. Flag signals and couriers took the place of the telegraph. Rather than writing out orders and messages himself, in these actions McClellan seems to have communicated almost entirely through oral commands and directions to his aides. In that event, his actions at Antietam spoke louder than his words.

To Mary Ellen McClellan

[Washington] Sept 5 [1862] 11 am.

... Again I have been called upon to save the country — the case is desperate, but with God's help I will try unselfishly to do my best & if he wills it accomplish the salvation of the nation.[1] My men are true & will stand by me to the last. I still hope for success & will leave nothing undone to gain it....

How weary I am of this struggle against adversity. But one thing sustains me — & that is my trust in God — I know that the interests at stake are so great as to justify his interference — not for me, but for the innocent thousands, millions rather, who have been plunged in misery by no fault of theirs. It is probable that our communications will be cut off in a day or two — but don't be worried. You may rest assured that I am doing all I can for my country & that no shame shall rest upon you willfully brought upon you by me....

My hands are full, so is my heart....

4 pm. ... It makes my heart bleed to see the poor shattered remnants of my noble Army of the Potomac, poor fellows! and to see how they love me even now. I hear them calling out to me as I ride among them — "George — don't leave us again!" "They *shan't* take you away from us again" etc etc. I can hardly restrain myself when I see how fearfully they are reduced in numbers & realize how many of them lie unburied on the field of battle where their lives were uselessly sacrificed. It is the most terrible trial I ever experienced — Truly God is trying me in the fire....

AL copy, McClellan Papers (C-7:63), Library of Congress.

1. Earlier that morning President Lincoln directed GBM to take command in the field against the Confederate invaders in Maryland.

To Abraham Lincoln

Your Excellency Washington Sept 5 [1862]

I have ordered a portion of the Provost Guard of the Army of the Potomac to take post at the Soldiers' Home for the purpose of guarding your Excellency's residence.[1]

The officer in command is instructed to deliver this note & receive your orders.

Very respectfully yr obdt svt
Geo B McClellan
Maj Genl

His Excellency the President

ALS, Lincoln Papers, Library of Congress.

1. During the summer months the president often stayed in a cottage on the grounds of the Soldiers' Home, on the northern outskirts of Washington.

To Henry W. Halleck

Head-Quarters, Army of the Potomac,
General [Washington] Sept 6 1862

Genl Sumner reports the enemy moving towards Rockville. It will save a great deal of trouble & invaluable time if you will suspend the operation of the order in regard to Franklin & Porter until I can see my way out of this difficulty. I wish to move Franklin's Corps to the front at once. To prevent a change in Burnside's command while on the march I would urgently recommend that Hooker be assigned to McDowell's Corps.[1]

The Secty[2] told me he would cheerfully agree to anything of this kind that met your approval, & I really feel it necessary for me to ask for these things at once.

Very truly yours
Geo B McClellan
Maj Genl

Maj Genl Halleck

ALS, Records of the Adjutant General's Office, RG 94 (159: Halleck Papers), National Archives. *OR*, Ser. 1, XIX, Part 2, pp. 189–90.

1. In Army Hd. Qtrs., Special Orders 223 (Sept. 5) and 224 (Sept. 6), Porter and Franklin and Brig. Gen. Charles Griffin were relieved from duty while charges against them stemming from the Second Bull Run battle were investigated, Hooker was assigned command of Porter's corps, and Jesse L. Reno relieved McDowell as a corps commander. *OR*, Ser. 1, XIX, Part 2, pp. 188, 197. The orders were suspended, and Hooker was put in command of McDowell's corps. 2. Secretary of War Stanton.

To Abraham Lincoln

Confidential Head-Quarters, Army of the Potomac,
Your Excellency [Washington] Sept 6 1862

I venture to say a few words in regard to a note I have just written to Genl Halleck[1] asking that Genl Hooker may be assigned to the command of McDowell's Corps instead of Genl Reno — I ask this altho' an intimate friend & an admirer of Genl Reno. Hooker has more experience with troops & is *perfectly* disposable — to take Reno now is to break up Burnside's Corps the temporary command of which will fall to Reno the moment I have placed Burnside *in command of a wing*. I also asked that the order removing Porter, Franklin & Griffin from their commands may be suspended until I have got through with the present crisis. I would not ask these things did I not feel that they were necessary in the present crisis. The Secretary of War (with whom I had a very pleasant interview) promised me that he would cheerfully agree to anything of this kind that I regarded as necessary.

Asking, with all due respect, a prompt decision on these important points[2]

I am respectfully your obt svt
Geo B McClellan
Maj Genl

ALS, McClellan Papers (A-77:31), Library of Congress.

1. GBM to Halleck, Sept. 6, *supra*. 2. The president returned this letter to GBM with the endorsement: "With entire respect, I must repeat that Gen. Halleck must control these questions."

To Edwin M. Stanton

Headquarters Army of the Potomac,
Sir: [Washington], September 7, 1862.

I have been applied to by General Stone for permission to serve with the Army during the impending movements, even if only as a spectator.

I have no doubt as to the loyalty and devotion of General Stone, but am unwilling to use his services unless I know that it meets the approval of the Government.

I not only have no objection to his employment in this army, but, more than that, would be glad to avail myself of his services as soon as circumstances permit.[1]

Very truly, yours,
Geo. B. McClellan,
Major-General

Hon. E. M. Stanton, Secretary of War.

OR, Ser. 1, V, p. 342.

1. Gen. Stone, who had been released from imprisonment on Aug. 16, did not serve in the Army of the Potomac during the Maryland campaign. For the circumstances of his arrest, see GBM to Andrew Porter, Feb. 8, 1862, note 2, *supra*, and GBM to Stone, Dec. 5, 1862, *infra*.

To Mary Ellen McClellan

[Washington] Sept. 7th [1862] 2.30 pm. Sunday

...I leave in a couple of hours to take command of the army in the field. I shall go to Rockville tonight & start out after the rebels tomorrow. I shall have nearly 100,000 men, old & new, & hope with God's blessing to gain a decisive victory. I think we shall win for the men are now in good spirits — confident in their General & all united in sentiment. Pope & McDowell have morally killed themselves — & are relieved from command — a signal instance of retributive justice. I have done nothing towards this — it has done itself. I have now the entire confidence of the Govt & the love of the army — my enemies are crushed, silent & disarmed — if I defeat the rebels I shall be master of the situation. . . .

AL copy, McClellan Papers (C-7 :63), Library of Congress.

To Mary Ellen McClellan [TELEGRAM]

Washington Sept 7/62 2.50 pm.

We are all well & the entire army is now united, cheerful & confident. You need not fear the result for I believe that God will give us the victory. I leave here this afternoon to take command of the troops in the field. The feeling of the Govt towards me, I am sure, is kind & trusting. I hope with God's blessing, to justify the great confidence they now repose in me, & will bury the past in oblivion. A victory now & we will soon be together. I send short letter today. God bless & reward your trust in him & all will be well.

G. B. McC

AL copy, McClellan Papers (C-7 :63), Library of Congress.

To Henry W. Halleck [TELEGRAM]

Head Quarters, Army of the Potomac,
Camp near Rockville Sept 8 8 pm 1862

Nothing new to report except that I have heard from the cavalry at Mechanicsville who report railroad destroyed by rebels from Monrovia to the Monocacy & that a force of about (7000) seven thousand reached Frederick yesterday, they being a part of Jackson's force. The cavalry skirmishes today near the Monocacy were quite successful so far as heard from. I have ordered reconnaissances in all directions tomorrow including one well to the north & north west. I think that we are now in position to prevent any attacks in force on Baltimore, while we cover Washington on this side. I am rather weak in cavalry on the right but am hourly expecting more of Averell's Brigade. We are prepared to attack anything that crosses the Potomac this side of the Monocacy. I am by no means satisfied yet that the enemy have crossed the river in very large force — our information is still entirely too indefinite to justify definite action. I am ready to push in any direction & hope very soon to have the supplies & transportation so regulated that we can safely move farther from Washn & clear Maryland of the rebels.[1] The time occupied in ascertaining their position, strength & intentions will enable me to place the Army in fair condition. I do not feel sure that there is no force in front of Washington. I think I can now answer for it that they shall not cross the river this side of Monocacy & that they shall not take Baltimore without defeating this Army — I am also in position to hasten to the assistance of Washington if necessary. As soon as I find out where to strike I will be after them without an hour's delay.

G B McClellan
Maj Genl

Maj Genl Halleck
Washington D.C.

ALS (telegram sent), McClellan Papers (C-15:64), Library of Congress. *OR*, Ser. 1, XIX, Part 2, p. 211.

1. At 1:05 P.M. Halleck had telegraphed that the Confederates were reported at Leesburg. "If so, it seems to me that a sufficient number of your forces to meet the enemy should move rapidly forward, leaving a reserve in reach of you and Washington at the same time." *OR*, Ser. 1, XIX, Part 2, p. 210.

To Andrew G. Curtin [TELEGRAM]

To His Excy Gov Curtin
Harrisburg

Hd Qrs Army Potomac
Rockville Md Sept 8 1862 9 pm

My information about the enemy comes from unreliable sources & is vague & conflicting. This army is in position to move against the Rebels whatever their plan may be. If they intend an advance towards your state I shall act with all possible vigor. I can scarcely believe that such is their purpose. I shall use every effort to ascertain the actual state of the fact & trust that you will do whatever you can in the same direction & that you will keep me advised of whatever you may learn. It would be well for you to push your investigations towards Frederick as far as possible.[1]

Geo B. McClellan
M.G. Comdg.

Retained copy, Records of the Office of the Secretary of War, RG 107 (M-504:66), National Archives. *OR*, Ser. 1, XIX, Part 2, p. 216.

1. At 3:15 A.M. on Sept. 9 Gov. Curtin replied, in part: "No doubt appears to exist as to the intention of the enemy to invade our state & are now probably now on or over our border. I will telegraph you all reliable information received by me. . . ." McClellan Papers (A-78:31), Library of Congress.

To Mary Ellen McClellan

Sept 8 [September 9, 1862] Camp near Rockville[1]

In coming to Rockville, we reached there somewhere about midnight [September 7] & had no baggage. Sacket[2] & I found a room together in the house of a Miss Beall, an old maid of strong Union sentiment, who refused to receive any pay &c. Yesterday we came out to this camp which is about half a mile from the town, & in a pleasant situation in a clover field, on a hill where we have all the air that is stirring.

You don't know what a task has been imposed upon me! I have been obliged to do the best I could with the broken & discouraged fragments of two armies defeated by no fault of mine — nothing but a desire to do my duty could have induced me to accept the command under such circumstances — not feeling at all sure that I could do anything I felt that under the circumstances no one else *could* save the country, & I have not shrunk from the terrible task. Pope has subsided into oblivion with the contempt of all — he has proved to be a perfect failure & all acknowledge it. McDowell had to flee for his life — his own men would have killed him had he made his appearance among them — even his staff did not dare to go among his men. Did you ever hear of a more striking instance of retributive justice — the man who wickedly turned against me when I had done all I could to aid him has now no friends left — utterly despised, entirely lost, *he* has also been consigned to oblivion — I can afford to forgive & forget him. I saw Pope & McD for a few moments at Upton's Hill when I rode out to meet the troops & assume command — I have not seen them since — I hope never to lay eyes on them again — between them they are responsible for the lives of many of my best & bravest men — they have done all they could (unintentionally I hope) to ruin & destroy the country — I can never forgive them for that. Pope has been foolish enough to try to throw the blame of his defeat on the Army of the Potomac — the resulting inquiry will beyond a doubt be most disastrous to him & nail him as an incompetent General. He would have been wiser to have accepted his defeat without complaint. I will probably move some 4 or 5 miles further to the front tomorrow [September 9] — as I have ordered the whole army forward. I expect to fight a great battle & to do my best at it — I do not think secesh will catch me very badly — the men & officers have complete confidence in me & I pray to God that he will justify their trust.

AL copy; copy, McClellan Papers (C-7:63/D-10:72), Library of Congress.

1. It appears that this letter was written in the early hours of the morning, shortly after midnight. 2. Col. Delos B. Sacket, GBM's inspector general.

To Henry W. Halleck [TELEGRAM]

Maj Gen H. W. Halleck Camp near Rockville Md
Gen in Chief Sept. 9th [1862] 7.30 am

Rebel scouts last night at Lisbon. In the Cavalry skirmish at Poolesville yesterday the Rebels lost one Captain & fifteen men killed & wounded besides six prisoners. 3rd Ind Cavalry one squadron did the work very handsomely on our side. Last reports that the Rebels were not in sight near Poolesville & Hyattstown. Our Cavalry are pushing forward in all directions while the Army will at least occupy the line of the Seneca today. Pleasonton's report of last night that there were 100,000 Rebels on this side of the river was derived from the notorious Capt White; it is not fully reliable.[1] We shall know better today. I will keep you fully informed.

G. B. McClellan
Maj Genl

Received copy, Records of the Office of the Secretary of War, RG 107 (M-473:50), National Archives. *OR*, Ser. 1, XIX, Part 2, pp. 218–19.

1. Pleasonton's dispatch read, in part: "Most reliable information has been obtained that the enemy has crossed the River in force over 100,000 strong. They are to march to *Frederick* thence to *Gettysburg* thence to *York* & thence to *Baltimore.*" Capt. Elijah V. White acted as a guide for the Confederates. McClellan Papers (A-78:31), Library of Congress.

To Mary Ellen McClellan

[Rockville] Tuesday morning [September 9, 1862] 8 1/2 am.

... I hope to learn this morning something definite as to the movements of secesh to be enabled to regulate my own. I hardly expect to equal the genius of Mr. Pope but I hope to waste fewer lives & to accomplish something more than lame defeat. I have ordered a general advance of a few miles today — which will bring us on the line of the Seneca & near enough to secesh to find out what he is doing & take measures accordingly. I shall follow him wherever he goes & do my best to beat him — if I accomplish that it is all over with him & the campaign will be ended.

9.30 [A.M.] ... The fact is that commanding such an army as this — picked up after a defeat, is no very easy thing — it does take a great deal of time & infinite labor. In coming to Rockville we arrived about midnight. Yesterday we came out to this camp, which is about 1/2 a mile from the town. I am still uncertain whether I shall move Hd Qtrs today, or on which road, as that depends on the information I receive as to the enemy. I probably won't go more than four or five miles in a central direction....

It is something of a triumph that my enemies have been put down so completely, & if to that I can add the defeat of secesh I think I ought to be entitled to fall back into private life....

AL copy, McClellan Papers (C-7:63), Library of Congress.

To Henry W. Halleck [TELEGRAM]

Head Quarters, Army of the Potomac,
Camp near Rockville Sept 9 3.30 pm 1862

At noon today all the troops ordered forward were in motion for their new positions. The latest information from the front indicates the enemy in large force near Frederick. Our cavalry have taken several prisoners

& the standard of a rebel regiment of cavalry today. From the parties now out I hope to know soon something definite as to the strength, position & intentions of the enemy. They talk of going to Gettysburg & York. I do not think they have yet left Frederick in any force. I am anxious for the prompt arrival of the rest of my cavalry from Fort Monroe. When the prisoners get in I shall learn something of them. Thus far my cavalry have gained the advantage.

G B McClellan
Maj Genl

Maj Genl Halleck
Washington D.C.

ALS (telegram sent), McClellan Papers (C-15 :64), Library of Congress. *OR*, Ser. 1, XIX, Part 2, p. 219.

To Mary Ellen McClellan

Sept 9 [1862] Camp near Rockville 5 pm.

... Am going out in a few minutes to ride over to the camp of the Regulars, whom I have not been to see for a long time, & who welcomed me so cordially the other night — brave fellows that they are.

It is hard to get accurate news from the front — the last reports from Pleasonton are that the enemy have 110,000 on this side of the river.[1] I have not so many, so I must watch them closely & try to catch them in some mistake, which I hope to do. My people are mostly in front of here — some 6 to 10 miles — moved forward today. They are I think well placed to be concentrated wherever it may be necessary & I want now a little breathing time to get them rested & in good order for fighting. Most of them will do well now — a few days will compose them still further, increase my cavalry force & put me in better condition generally. I think my present positions will check their advance into Penna & give me time to get some reinforcements that I need very much....

I have this moment learned that in addition to the force on this side of the river the enemy have *also* a large force near Leesburg — so McC has a difficult game to play, but will do his best & try to do his duty.

AL copy, McClellan Papers (C-7 :63), Library of Congress.

1. Pleasonton's dispatch to this effect was sent at 3:15 P.M. GBM forwarded the estimate to Gen. Halleck at 6:00 P.M. McClellan Papers (A-78 :31); *OR*, Ser. 1, XIX, Part 2, p. 219.

To Fitz John Porter [TELEGRAM]

Maj Genl F. J. Porter
Arlington Rockville 8.40 pm Sept 9 1862

Dispatch rec'd.[1] Our Cavalry have had some handsome affairs today fully maintaining the morale they gained in the Peninsula. We have regained Barnsville & Sugar Loaf Mt. The Army is tonight well posted to act in any direction the moment the enemy develops his movements. I am now in condition to watch him closely & he will find it hard to escape me if he commits a blunder. We shall do our best & I think that will suffice.

G B McClellan
MG

Retained copy, Records of the Office of the Secretary of War, RG 107 (M-504 :66), National Archives. *OR*, Ser. 1, XIX, Part 2, p. 221.

1. Porter's telegram of this date reported on the condition of his forces in the Washington lines. *OR*, Ser. 1, XIX, Part 2, p. 220.

To Abraham Lincoln [TELEGRAM]

Head Quarters,
Army of the Potomac,
Camp near Rockville
His Excellency the President Sept. 10th 12m 1862

In reply to your dispatch of this morning[1] I have the honor to state that Genl Pleasonton at Barnesville reports that a movement of the enemy last night is said to have been made across the Potomac from this side to the other side. We shall know the truth of this rumor soon. Pleasonton is watching all the fords as high as Conrad's Ferry & has pickets out to the mouth of the Monocacy. He has sent out this morning to occupy Sugar Loaf Mt. from which a large extent of country can be seen in all directions. Genl Burnside had his scouts out last night at Ridgeville & within (3) three miles of Newmarket. No enemy seen with the exception of a few pickets. They were told that Stuart's cavalry (5000) five thousand in number occupied Newmarket, & that the main Rebel forces under Jackson were still at Frederick. Burnside has sent a strong reconnaissance today to the mountain pass at Ridgeville. I propose if the information I have rec'd proves reliable regarding the natural strength of this position, to occupy it with a sufficient force to resist an advance of the enemy in that direction. I have scouts and spies pushed forward in every direction and shall soon be in possession of reliable & definite information. The statements I get regarding the enemy's forces that have crossed to this side range from eighty (80) to one hundred & fifty (150) thousand. I am perfectly certain that none of the enemy's troops have crossed the Potomac within the last twenty four hours below the mouth of the Monocacy. I was informed last night by Genl Pleasonton that his information rendered it probable that Jackson's force had advanced to Newmarket with Stuart's cavalry at Urbanna.[2] In view of this I ordered the Army forward this morning to the line along the high ridge from Ridgeville, thro' Damascus, Clarksburg &c. But the information subsequently obtained from Genl Burnside's scouts that the mass of the enemy was still at Frederick induced to suspend the movement of the right wing until I could verify the truth of the reports by means of Burnside's reconnaissances in force today.[3] My extreme left advances to Poolesville this morning. The work of re-organization & refitting is progressing very satisfactorily under the new heads of Staff Departments. Despatch this instant rec'd from Genl Pleasonton dated Barnesville 10.30 a.m. says "my scouts occupy the ferry at the mouth of the Monocacy. They found no enemy except a few pickets on the other side of the Monocacy. At Licksville about (3) three miles from that stream it was reported there was a force of six thousand (6000) men."

Geo B McClellan
Maj Genl Comdg

LS (telegram sent), McClellan Papers (C-16:65), Library of Congress. *OR*, Ser. 1, XIX, Part 2, p. 233.

1. The president telegraphed: "How does it look now?" *OR*, Ser. 1, XIX, Part 2, p. 232. 2. Pleasonton's dispatch to this effect was sent at 7:30 P.M. on Sept. 9. McClellan Papers (A-78:31). 3. Burnside's dispatch of this date read, in part: "A large force is reported at Frederick under Lee & Jackson but all the reports are indefinite, am trying to get more definite information through citizens." McClellan Papers (A-78:31).

To Henry W. Halleck

Maj. Genl. H. W. Halleck,
General-in-Chief.
General:

Hd. Qtrs. Camp near Rockville,
Septr. 11th [September 10] 1862.[1]

At the time this army moved from Washington, it was not known what the intentions of the Rebels were in placing their forces on this side of the Potomac. It might have been a feint to draw away our troops from Washington, for the purpose of throwing their main army into the city as soon as we were out of the way, or it might have been supposed to be precisely what they are now doing. In view of this uncertain condition of things, I left what I conceived to be a sufficient force to defend the city against any army they could bring against it from the Virginia side of the Potomac.

This uncertainty, in my judgment, exists no longer. All the evidence that has accumulated from various sources since we left Washington goes to prove most conclusively that almost the entire Rebel army in Virginia, amounting to not less than 120,000 men, is in the vicinity of Frederick City.

These troops, for the most part, consist of their oldest regiments, and are commanded by their best Generals. Several brigades joined them yesterday direct from Richmond, two deserters from which say that they saw no other troops between Richmond and Leesburg. Every thing seems to indicate that they intend to hazard all upon the issue of the coming battle. They are probably aware that their forces are numerically superior to ours by at least twenty-five per cent. This, with the prestige of their recent successes, will, without doubt, inspire them with a confidence which will cause them to fight well. The momentous consequences involved in the struggle of the next few days impel me, at the risk of being considered slow and overcautious, to most earnestly recommend that every available man be at once added to this army.

I believe this army fully appreciates the importance of a victory at this time, and will fight well. But the result of a general battle, with such odds as the enemy now appears to have against us, might, to say the least, be doubtful; and if we should be defeated, the consequences to the country would be disastrous in the extreme. Under these circumstances, I would recommend that one or two of the three army corps now on the Potomac, opposite Washington, be at once withdrawn and sent to reinforce this army. I would also advise that the force of Colonel Miles,[2] at Harper's Ferry, where it can be of but little use and is continually exposed to be cut off by the enemy, be immediately ordered here. This would add about twenty-five thousand old troops to our present force, and would greatly strengthen us.

If there are any Rebel forces remaining on the other side of the Potomac, they must be so few that the troops left in the forts, after the two corps shall have been withdrawn, will be sufficient to check them; and with the large cavalry force now on that side kept well out in front to give warning of the distant approach of any very large army, a part of this army might be sent back within the entrenchments to assist in repelling an attack. But even if Washington should be taken while these armies are confronting each other, this would not, in my judgment, bear comparison with the ruin and disasters which would follow a signal defeat of this Army. If we should be successful in conquering the gigantic rebel army before us, we would have no difficulty in recovering it. On the other hand, should their force prove sufficiently powerful to defeat us, would all the forces now around Washington be sufficient to prevent such a victorious army from carrying the works on this side the Potomac, after they are uncovered by our Army? I think not.

From the moment the rebels commenced the policy of concentrating their forces, with their large masses of troops operating against our scattered forces, they have been successful. They are undoubtedly pursuing the same policy now, and are prepared to take advantage of any division of our troops in future.

I therefore most respectfully, but strenuously urge upon you the absolute necessity, at this critical juncture, of uniting all our disposable forces. Every other consideration should yield to this; and if we defeat the army now arrayed before us, the rebellion is crushed; for I do not believe they can organize another army. But if we should be so unfortunate as to meet with defeat, our country is at their mercy.[3]

Very respectfully, Your obt. svt.
Geo B McClellan
Maj. Genl.

Copy, Stanton Papers, Library of Congress. *OR*, Ser. 1, XIX, Part 2, pp. 254–55.

1. Although this War Dept. copy is dated Sept. 11 (and so appears in the *Official Records*), a copy by Gen. Marcy is dated Sept. 10, and in his reply Halleck refers to "your letter of the 10th." McClellan Papers (A-80:32), Library of Congress; *OR*, Ser. 1, XIX, Part 2, p. 280. Furthermore, it is logical that GBM's telegraphed calls for the troops at Harper's Ferry and for specific reinforcements from Washington (*infra*) would follow the writing of this letter rather than precede it. 2. Col. Dixon S. Miles. 3. In his reply on Sept. 13, Halleck wrote: "You attach too little importance to the capital. I assure you that you are wrong. The capture of this place will throw us back six months, if it should not destroy us." *OR*, Ser. 1, XIX, Part 2, pp. 280–81.

To Andrew G. Curtin [TELEGRAM]

Headquarters Army of the Potomac,
[Brookeville, Md.]
September 10, 1862 — 10.30 p.m.

Andrew G. Curtin
Governor of Pennsylvania:

Everything that we can learn induces me to believe that the information you have received is substantially correct.[1] I think the enemy are checked in the directions of Baltimore and Gettysburg. You should concentrate all the troops you can in the vicinity of Chambersburg, not entirely neglecting Gettysburg. I will follow them up as rapidly as possible, and do all I can to check their movements into Pennsylvania. Call out the militia, especially mounted men, and do everything in your power to impede the enemy by the action of light troops; attack them in flank, destroying their trains and any property which must inevitably come into their possession. You may be sure that I will follow them as closely as I can, and fight them whenever I can find them. It is as much my interest as yours to preserve the soil of Pennsylvania from invasion, or, failing in that, to destroy any army that may have the temerity to attempt it.

Geo. B. McClellan
Major-General

OR, Ser. 1, XIX, Part 2, pp. 248–49.

1. Curtin's telegram of 10:00 A.M. on this date reported intelligence that the Confederate force "around Frederick is not less than 120,000 men.... From all we can learn, the enemy has selected his ground and massed his force near Frederick, to give you battle, the result of which will probably decide the future of our country." *OR*, Ser. 1, XIX, Part 2, p. 248.

To Henry W. Halleck [TELEGRAM]

Maj Gen Halleck Brookeville Sept 10th [1862] 11.55 pm

I have ordered a general advance tomorrow. Send me up all the troops you can spare.

Geo B McClellan
Maj Genl

Received copy, Records of the Office of the Secretary of War, RG 107 (M-473:50), National Archives. *OR*, Ser. 1, XIX, Part 2, p. 234.

To Henry W. Halleck [TELEGRAM]

Major General Halleck
Washington

Head Quarters, Army of the Potomac,
Camp near Rockville Sept. 11, 1862 9.45 am

Colonel Miles is at or near Harper's Ferry, I understand with nine thousand troops. He can do nothing where he is, but could be of great service if ordered to join me. I suggest that he be ordered at once to join me by the most practicable route.

Geo. B. McClellan
Maj. Gen. Comdg.

Retained copy, McClellan Papers (C-18:65), Library of Congress. *OR*, Ser. 1, XIX, Part 1, p. 758.

1. Halleck replied at 2:00 P.M.: "There is no way for Colonel Miles to join you at present. His only chance is to defend his works till you can open communication with him. When you do so he will be subject to your orders." *OR*, Ser. 1, XIX, Part 1, p. 758.

To Henry W. Halleck [TELEGRAM]

Major Gen Halleck
General in Chief,
Washington

Head Quarters, Army of the Potomac,
Camp near Rockville Sept 11 1862 3.45 pm

Please send forward all the troops you can spare from Washington, particularly Porter, Heintzelman, Sigel and all other old troops.[1] Please send them to Brookville via Leesboro, as soon as possible. General Banks reports seventy two thousand five hundred troops in and about Washington.[2] If the enemy has left for Pennsylvania, I will follow him rapidly. I move my head quarters to Middlebrook immediately.

Geo. B. McClellan
Maj Genl Comdg

Retained copy, McClellan Papers (C-18:65), Library of Congress. *OR*, Ser. 1, XIX, Part 2, p. 253.

1. The three field corps left at Washington were commanded by Porter, Heintzelman, and Maj. Gen. Franz Sigel, formerly of the Army of Virginia. 2. The president telegraphed at 6:00 P.M. that Porter "is ordered to-night to join you as quick as possible. I am for sending you all that can be spared, & I hope others can follow Porter very soon." *Collected Works of Lincoln*, V, p. 415.

To Henry W. Halleck [TELEGRAM]

Head Quarters, Army of the Potomac,
Major General Halleck — Middleburg [Middlebrook]
Genl in Chief, Washington — Sept. 11, 1862 11.30 pm

My signals have today been established on Sugar Loaf Mountain. At last advices Burnside's troops were within two miles of New Market. I have ordered him tomorrow to advance if possible to Frederick and occupy it. Sumner and Franklin to advance early in the morning to Urbana. Couch following the movement after leaving a force to guard the fords below the Monocacy. I am much obliged to you for sending me Porter's Corps and should like the remainder of Keyes' Corps as soon as possible. I shall follow up the rebels as rapidly as possible.

Geo. B. McClellan
Maj Genl Comdg

Retained copy, McClellan papers (C-16:65), Library of Congress. *OR*, Ser. 1, XIX, Part 2, p. 255.

To Henry W. Halleck [TELEGRAM]

Gen H W Halleck — Hd Qrs A.P. Clarksburg Sept 12, 1862 10 am

My columns are pushing on rapidly to Frederick. I feel perfectly confident that the enemy has abandoned Frederick moving in two directions. Viz. on the Hagerstown & Harpers Ferry roads.

Fitz Lee with 4 Regts of Cavalry & 6 pieces Artillery left New Market yesterday for Liberty. They are being followed by Burnside's Cavalry.

G B McClellan
MGC

Received copy, Records of the Office of the Secretary of War, RG 107 (M-473:50), National Archives. *OR*, Ser. 1, XIX, Part 2, pp. 270–71.

To Mary Ellen McClellan

Sept 12 [1862] 3 pm. Camp near Urbana

As our wagons are not yet up & won't be for a couple of hours or more I avail myself of the "advantages of the situation" to scrawl a few lines to you. I am sitting on a saddle blanket, under a tree — tore this paper from the back of a dispatch sent to me this morning, & am using my "Album" (the Photograph Gallery you gave me) as a writing desk. I stopped half an hour this morning at a little place called Clarksburg. Some Union people invited me into the house, when presently one of the young ladies, brought me with great pride a large photograph album & showed me that the first picture in the book was one of those we had taken together. They were all so anxious to know whether it resembled you, that I showed them some of those in *my* collection, which *happened* to be in my pocket at the time — don't you think it was a lucky *accident* that brought it there. The place selected for our camp tonight is where I am writing, in a beautiful grove on the summit of a hill; one of the prettiest camps we have yet had. We are travelling now thro' one of the most lovely regions I have ever seen — quite broken with lovely valleys in all directions, & some fine mountains in the distance.

From all I can gather secesh is skedadelling & I don't think I can catch him unless he is really moving into Penna — in that case I shall catch him before he has made much headway towards the interior. I begin to think that he is making off to get out of the scrape by recrossing the river at Williamsport — in which case my only chance of bagging him will be to cross lower down & cut into his communications near Winchester. He evidently don't want to fight me — for some reason or other. . . .

The doctrines enunciated by Mr. Mahan[1] are very excellent, but I don't see the application to myself in respect of McDowell. I have never injured McD — therefore I am not called upon to make any advances to him as the Prof. seems to think I ought. I bear no hatred to the man — I simply regard him as a scoundrel a liar & a fool who in seeking to injure me has killed himself — I have the most thorough contempt for him — nothing more. All I ask is that I may never set eyes on him again — as for ever having any friendly relations with him it is simply absurd. . . .

7 1/2 pm. My tent has been pitched some time. I have given all the orders necessary for tomorrow & they have all gone to the various corps. . . .

I believe that I have done all in my power & that the arrangement of the troops is good. I learned an hour or two ago thro' the signal that our troops were entering Frederic. We certainly ought to be there in respectable force by this time — my only apprehension now is that secesh will manage to get back across the Potomac at Wmsport before I can catch him. If he goes to Penna I think I must overhaul him before long & give him a good lesson. If he does go to Penna I feel quite confident that I can so arrange things that the chances will be that he will never return — but I presume he is smart enough to know that & to act accordingly....

Interrupted here by the news that we really have Frederic — Burnside & Pleasonton both there. The next trouble is to save the garrison of Harper's Ferry, which is I fear in danger of being captured by the rebels. They were not placed under my orders until this afternoon, altho' before I left Washn I strongly urged that they should be withdrawn at once as I feared they would be captured. But other counsels prevailed & I am rather anxious as to the result. If they are not taken by this time I think I can save them — at all events nothing in my power shall be left undone to accomplish this result. I feel sure of one thing now, & that is that my men will fight well. The only doubtful ones are McD's old troops, who are in bad condition as to discipline & everything else. Hooker will however soon bring them out of the kinks, & will make them fight if anyone can. The moment I hear that Harper's Ferry is safe I shall feel quite sure of the result....

I learn that the people cheered the troops tremendously when they entered Frederic. I have thus far found the Union sentiment much stronger in this region than I had expected — people are disposed to be very kind & polite to me — invite me into their houses, offer me dinner & various other acts of kindness that were quite unknown in the Peninsula.

AL copy; copy, McClellan Papers (C-7:63/D-10:72), Library of Congress.

1. Dennis Hart Mahan, of the West Point faculty. Apparently he had written to Mrs. McClellan.

To Henry W. Halleck [TELEGRAM]

Head Qrs Army Potomac,
Maj Gen Halleck Near Urbana Sept. 12 [1862] 5.30 pm

I have just learned by signal from Sugar Loaf that our troops are entering Frederick. The remainder of Burnside's troops are between Frederick & New Market. Sumner is near Urbana with an advanced guard thrown out to the Monocacy, Williams on his right, Franklin on his left, Couch at Barnesville. Cavalry has been sent towards Point of Rocks to ascertain whether there is any force of the enemy in that direction. Burnside has cavalry in pursuit of Fitz Hugh Lee towards Westminster. Should the enemy go towards Penna I shall follow him. Should he attempt to recross the Potomac I shall endeavor to cut off his retreat. My movements tomorrow will be dependent upon information to be received during the night. The troops have marched today as far as was possible and proper for them to move.

Geo. B. McClellan
Maj Gen Comdg

P.S. I have ordered Banks to send eight new Regts to relieve parts of Couch's command I left at Offutts' cross roads, Seneca and Conrads & Edwards Ferries. How soon may I expect these troops. Their presence at the points indicated are very necessary.[1]

G B McClellan

Received copy, Records of the Office of the Secretary of War, RG 107 (M-473 :50), National Archives. *OR*, Ser. 1, XIX, Part 2, p. 271.

1. Halleck replied on Sept. 13 that Gen. Banks, in command of Washington's defenses, "cannot safely spare eight new regiments from here.... Until you know more certainly the enemy's force south of the Potomac, you are wrong in thus uncovering the capital. I am of opinion that the enemy will send a small column toward Pennsylvania, so as to draw your forces in that direction; then suddenly move on Washington...." *OR*, Ser. 1, XIX, Part 2, pp. 280–81.

To Henry W. Halleck [TELEGRAM]

Hd Qrs Army Potomac
Maj Gen Halleck Near Urbana Sept 12 [1862] 6 pm

I learn nothing reliable as to the enemy south of Potomac.[1] I this morning ordered Cavalry to endeavor to open communication with Harper's Ferry and in my orders of movement for tomorrow have arranged so that I go or send to his[2] relief if necessary. I have heard no firing in that direction & if he resists at all I think cannot only relieve him but place the rebels who attack him in great danger of being cut off. Everything moves at daylight tomorrow. Your message to him this moment received. Will forward by first opportunity.[3]

G B McClellan
Maj Genl Comdg

Received copy, Records of the Office of the Secretary of War, RG 107 (M-473 :50), National Archives. *OR*, Ser. 1, XIX, Part 2, pp. 271–72.

1. Halleck had telegraphed at 1:45 P.M.: "Have you any reliable information of enemy's force south of the Potomac? Is it not possible to open communication with Harper's Ferry, so that Colonel Miles' forces can co-operate with you?" *OR*, Ser. 1, XIX, Part 2, p. 271. 2. Col. Miles. 3. Halleck's dispatch of this date to Miles read: "You will obey such orders as General McClellan may give you. You will endeavor to open communication with him and unite your forces to his at the earliest possible moment." *OR*, Ser. 1, XIX, Part 1, p. 758.

To Abraham Lincoln [TELEGRAM]

Head Quarters, Army of the Potomac,
Camp near Urbana Sept 12 1862 9 pm

You will have learned by my telegrams to Genl Halleck that we hold Frederick & the line of the Monocacy.[1]

I have taken all possible means to communicate with Harper's Ferry so that I may send to its relief if necessary. Cavalry are in pursuit of the Westminster party with orders to catch them at all hazards. The main body of my cavalry & horse artillery are ordered after the enemy's main column with orders to check its march as much as possible that I may overtake it. If Harper's Ferry is still in our possession I think I can save the garrison if they fight at all. If the rebels are really moving into Penna I shall soon be up with them. My apprehension is that they may make for Williamsport & get across the river before I can catch them.

G B McClellan
Maj Genl

His Excellency the President

ALS (telegram sent), McClellan Papers (C-15:64), Library of Congress. *OR*, Ser. 1, XIX, Part 2, p. 272.

1. The president had telegraphed at 5:45 P.M. that information received "corroborates the idea that the enemy is recrossing the Potomac. Please do not let him get off without being hurt." *Collected Works of Lincoln*, V, p. 418.

To Lorenzo Thomas

Brigadier General L. Thomas
Adjutant General, U.S. Army
General:

Head Quarters Army of the Potomac,
[Frederick] September 13th 1862.

There is no more important arm of the military service than the regular artillery, and none which during the existing war has achieved more and upon which, hope for the future success during the contest, is to rely. It is of the greatest consequence to maintain it in a condition of efficiency. For this end it must be recruited. Out of the twenty six regular batteries in this army, ten are now but four gun batteries, when it is of great importance that they should be of six guns, and this for want of cannoneers and drivers. The volunteers serving with the batteries in many cases have demanded to be returned to their regiments and I have been compelled since they have a sort of right to it to return them. During the present month and the fall months, the terms of service of many men will expire. Thus the condition of the regular artillery is precarious, unless some stimulus is given to the recruiting service. I view it of the highest importance to the country and the service, that the six gun batteries should be increased to eight gun batteries. We would thus need fewer volunteer batteries; would have a more manageable artillery force at less expense than we have now, and would have one vastly more reliable.

To carry the ten, four gun batteries up to eight gun batteries would require one hundred men each, say one thousand men. To carry the sixteen six gun batteries up to eight gun batteries, would require sixty men each, say nine hundred sixty men.

To fill up the twenty six batteries, to full batteries of six guns each, with the proper complement of men, would require from one thousand to twelve hundred men.

I earnestly invite the serious attention of the Adjutant General and the War Department to the subject of filling up the Artillery; and I ask that every means be exhausted to procure two thousand men for the Artillery.

I also enclose a memorandum of the number of recruits needed for the regular Infantry.[1] The regular Infantry regiments, are the most reliable foot troops that we have. Their existence is threatened by the paucity and continual diminution of their numbers. I earnestly request, that if the resources of the War Department can control the matter, that they be used to their utmost to reinforce the thinned ranks of these regiments.[2]

I am Very Respectfully Your obedient Servant,
[George B. McClellan]
Major General Commanding

Retained copy, Records of U.S. Army Continental Commands, RG 393 (3946: Army of the Potomac), National Archives. *OR*, Ser. 1, XIX, Part 2, pp. 282–83.

1. Not found. 2. For efforts to recruit for the regular army from the ranks of the volunteers, see Adj. Gen.'s Office, General Order 154, Oct. 9, 1862, *OR*, Ser. 3, II, p. 654.

To Abraham Lincoln [TELEGRAM]

2.35 AM[1]

To the President Hd Qrs Frederick Sept 13th [1862] 12 M

I have the whole Rebel force in front of me but am confident and no time shall be lost. I have a difficult task to perform but with Gods blessing will accomplish it. I think Lee has made a gross mistake and that he will be severely punished for it. The Army is in motion as rapidly as possible. I hope for a great success if the plans of the Rebels remain unchanged. We have possession of Cotocktane.[2] I have all the plans of the Rebels[3] and will catch them in their own trap if my men are equal to the emergency. I now feel that I can count on them as of old. All forces of Pennsylvania should be placed to cooperate at Chambersburg. My respects to Mrs Lincoln.

Received most enthusiastically by the ladies.[4] Will send you trophies. All well and with Gods Blessing will accomplish it.

Geo B. McClellan

Received copy, Records of the Office of the Secretary of War, RG 107 (M-473:50), National Archives. *OR*, Ser. 1, XIX, Part 2, p. 281.

1. Telegraphic communication was not yet re-established between Frederick and Washington, and this dispatch, written at noon (12 M, or meridian) on Sept. 13, was relayed by courier or flag signal to an intermediate telegraph station and received in Washington at 2:35 A.M. on Sept. 14. 2. The Catoctin range, west of Frederick. 3. The so-called Lost Order, a copy of Gen. Lee's Special Orders No. 191 found that morning near Frederick by a Federal soldier. 4. A reference to GBM's welcome in Frederick.

To William B. Franklin

Head Quarters, Army of the Potomac,
Camp near Frederick
Sept. 13 1862 6.20 pm

Maj. Genl. W. B. Franklin
Comdg. 6th Corps

Genl: I have now full information as to the movements & intentions of the enemy.

Jackson has crossed the Upper Potomac to capture the garrison at Martinsburg & cut off Miles' retreat towards the west. A division on the south side of the Potomac was to carry Loudoun Heights & cut off his retreat in that direction. McLaws with his own command & the division of R. H. Anderson[1] was to move by Boonsboro & Rohrersville to carry the Maryland Heights. The signal officers inform me that he is now in Pleasant Valley. The firing shows that Miles still holds out.

Longstreet was to move to Boonsboro & there halt with the reserve trains, D. H. Hill to form the rear guard, Stuart's cavalry to bring up stragglers etc. We have cleared out all the cavalry this side of the mountains & north of us. The last I heard from Pleasonton he occupied Middletown after several sharp skirmishes. A division of Burnside's command started several hours ago to support him. The whole of Burnside's command, including Hooker's Corps march this evening & early tomorrow morning followed by the Corps of Sumner & Banks & Sykes' Divn upon Boonsboro to carry that position. Couch has been ordered to concentrate his divn & join you as rapidly as possible. Without waiting for the whole of that divn to join you, you will move at daybreak in the morning by Jefferson & Burkittsville upon the road to Rohrersville. I have reliable information that the mountain pass by this road[2] is practicable for artillery & wagons. If this pass is not occupied by the enemy in force seize it as soon as practicable & debouch upon Rohrersville in order to cut off the retreat or destroy McLaws' command. If you find the pass held by the enemy in large force make all your dispositions for the attack & commence it about half an hour after you hear severe firing at the pass on the Hagerstown pike,[3] where the main column will attack. Having gained the pass your duty will be first to cut off, destroy or capture McLaws' command & relieve Col Miles. If you effect this you will order him to join you at once with all his disposable troops, first destroying the bridges over the Potomac if not already done & leaving a sufficient garrison to prevent the enemy from passing the ford. You will then return by Rohrersville on the direct road to Boonsboro, if the main column has not succeeded in its attack. If it has succeeded take the road from Rohrersville to Sharpsburg & Williamsport in order either to cut off the retreat of Hill & Longstreet towards the Potomac, or to prevent the repassage of Jackson. My general idea is to cut the enemy in two & beat him in detail. I believe I have sufficiently explained my intentions. I ask of you at this important moment all your intellect & the utmost activity that a general can exercise. Knowing my views & intentions you are fully authorized to change any of the details of this order as circumstances may change, provided the purpose is carried out — that purpose being to attack the enemy in detail & beat him.

Genl Smith's dispatch of 4 p.m. with your comments is received.[4] If with a full knowledge of all the circumstances you consider it preferable to crush the enemy at Petersville before undertaking the movement I have directed, you are at liberty to do so, but you will readily perceive that no slight advantage should for a moment interfere with the decisive results I propose to gain. I cannot too strongly impress upon you the absolute necessity of informing me every hour during the day of your movements & frequently during the night. Force your Colonels to prevent straggling & bring every available man into action.

I think the force you have is, with good management, sufficient for the end in view. If you differ widely from me & being on the spot you know better than I do the circumstances of the case, inform me at once & I will do my best to reinforce you. Inform me at the same time how many more troops you think you should have.

Until 5 a.m. tomorrow Genl Hd Qtrs will be at this place. At that hour they will move upon the main road to Hagerstown.[5]

I am, Genl, very respt yr obt svt
Geo B McClellan
Maj Genl Comdg

LS retained copy, McClellan Papers (C-16:65), Library of Congress. *OR*, Ser. 1, XIX, Part 1, pp. 45–46, LI, Part 1, pp. 826–27.

1. Maj. Gens. Lafayette McLaws and Richard H. Anderson. 2. Crampton's Gap, in South Mountain. 3. Turner's Gap. 4. Maj. Gen. William F. Smith's message to Franklin reported strong enemy forces at Petersville, and proposed an attack on the rear of those besieging Harper's Ferry from Pleasant Valley. McClellan Papers (A-79:31). 5. Franklin replied at 10:00 P.M.: "I have rec'd your orders..., understand them, and will do my best to carry them out. My command will commence its movement at 5 1/2 A.M." McClellan Papers (A-79:31).

To Henry W. Halleck [TELEGRAM]

Maj. Gen. H. W. Halleck
Genl in Chief, Washington

Head Quarters, Army of the Potomac,
Frederick, Sept. 13, 1862 8.45 pm

We occupy Middletown and Jefferson. The whole force of the enemy in front. They are not retreating into Virginia. Look well to Chambersburg. Shall lose no time. Will soon have decisive battle.[1]

G. B. McClellan
Maj. Gen. Comdg.

Retained copy, McClellan Papers (C-18:65), Library of Congress. *OR*, Ser. 1, XIX, Part 2, p. 288 (misdated).

1. Halleck replied on Sept. 14: "Scouts report a large force still on Virginia side of the Potomac, near Leesburg. If so, I fear you are exposing your left flank, and that the enemy can cross in your rear. . . . I do not understand what you mean by asking me to look out for Chambersburg. I have no troops to send there." *OR*, Ser. 1, XIX, Part 2, p. 289.

To Henry W. Halleck [TELEGRAM]

Head-Quarters, Army of the Potomac,
Frederick City Sept. 13, 11 p.m. 1862

An order of Genl. R. E. Lee addressed to Genl. D. H. Hill which has accidentally come into my hands this evening the authenticity of which is unquestionable discloses some of the plans of the enemy and shows most conclusively that the main rebel army is now before us including Longstreet's, Jackson's, the two Hill's, McLaws', Walker's, R. H. Anderson's & Hood's commands.[1] That army was ordered to march on the 10th and to attack and capture our forces at Harper's Ferry and Martinsburg yesterday, by surrounding them with such a heavy force that they conceived it impossible they could escape. They were also ordered to take possession of the B. & O. Railroad & afterward to concentrate again at Boonsboro or Hagerstown. That this was the plan of campaign on the 9th is confirmed by the fact that heavy firing has been heard in the direction of Harper's Ferry this afternoon and that the columns took the roads specified in the order.

It may therefore in my judgment be regarded as certain that this rebel army which I have good reason for believing amounts to 120,000 men or more and known to be commanded by Lee in person intended to attempt penetrating Pennsylvania. The Officers told their friends here that they were going to Harrisburg and Philadelphia. My advance has pushed forward to day and overtaken the enemy on the Middletown and Harper's Ferry roads and several slight engagements have taken place in which our troops have driven the enemy from their positions. A train of wagons about 3/4 of a mile long was destroyed today by the rebels in their flight. We took over fifty prisoners.

This Army marches forward early tomorrow morning and will make forced marches to endeavor to relieve Col. Miles, but I fear unless he makes a stout resistance we may be too late. A report came in just this moment that Miles was attacked today and repulsed the enemy but I do not know what credit to attach to the statement.[2] I shall do everything in my power to save Miles if he still holds out.

Portions of Burnside's and Franklin's Corps moved forward this evening. I have received your dispatch of 10 am today.[3] You will perceive from what I have stated that there is but little probability of the enemy being in much force south of the Potomac. I do not by any means wish to be understood as undervaluing the importance of holding Washington. It is of great consequence, but upon the success of this Army the fate of the nation depends.

It was for this reason that I said everything else should be made subordinate to placing this Army in a proper condition to meet the large rebel force in our front.

Unless Genl Lee has changed his plans I expect a severe general engagement tomorrow. I feel confident that there is now no rebel force immediately threatening Washington or Baltimore but that I have the mass of their troops to contend with & they outnumber me when united.

Geo B McClellan
Maj Genl

Genl H. W. Halleck
Genl in Chief Washington

Retained copy, McClellan Papers (A-79:31), Library of Congress. *OR*, Ser. 1, XIX, Part 2, pp. 281–82.

1. Longstreet and Jackson were in fact corps commanders. The Confederate infantry divisions were led by D. H. Hill, A. P. Hill, Lafayette McLaws, John G. Walker, John B. Hood, David R. Jones, John R. Jones, and Alexander R. Lawton. 2. In a dispatch sent at 6:15 P.M. Pleasonton wrote: "Report from Harper's Ferry says Longstreet attacked them today & was repulsed, & started up the river with his wagons. A man from Harper's Ferry brought this news." McClellan Papers (A-79:31). 3. See GBM to Halleck, Sept. 11 [Sept. 10], note 3, *supra*.

To Henry W. Halleck [TELEGRAM]

Genl H. W. Halleck
Genl in Chief, Washington

Head Quarters, Army of the Potomac,
Near Frederick Sept. 14th 1862 [9 A.M.]

Courier from Col Miles who left in the night has just arrived and says Col Miles is surrounded by a large force of the enemy but thinks he can hold out two days. Genl White[1] has joined him with his command from Martinsburg.

Miles is in possession of Harper's Ferry & Loudoun Heights. If he holds out today I can probably save him. The whole Army is moving as rapidly as possible. The enemy is in possession of Maryland Heights.

Geo. B. McClellan
Maj Genl

Retained copy, McClellan Papers (C-16:65), Library of Congress. *OR*, Ser. 1, XIX, Part 1, p. 758.

1. Brig. Gen. Julius White.

To Mary Ellen McClellan

Sept 14th [1862] Frederick am.

I have only time to say good morning this bright sunny Sunday & then start to the front to try to relieve Harper's Ferry, which is sorely pressed by secesh. It is probable that we shall have a serious engagement today & perhaps a general battle — if we have one at all during this operation it ought to be today or tomorrow. I feel as reasonably confident of success as any one well can who trusts in a higher power & does not know what its decision will be. I can't describe to you for want of time the enthusiastic reception we met with yesterday at Frederic — I was nearly overwhelmed & pulled to pieces. I enclose with this a little flag that some enthusiastic lady thrust into or upon Dan's bridle. As to flowers!! — they came in crowds! In truth I was seldom more affected than by the scenes I saw yesterday & the reception I met with — it would have gratified you very much....

AL copy, McClellan Papers (C-7:63), Library of Congress.

To William B. Franklin

Maj Gen Franklin — Head Quarters, Army of the Potomac.
General. — Middletown, Sept. 14, 11.45 am 1862

The enemy occupies the main pass in front of Middletown with infantry and artillery. Pleasonton has silenced one battery, and our infantry are now endeavoring to turn the pass by our left. I have just been informed that the enemy have about 1500 cavalry and some artillery at Burkheadsville[1] and that they are in considerable force in vicinity of Boonsboro. I learned this morning by a messenger direct from Colonel Miles that he had abandoned the Maryland Heights yesterday afternoon and occupied the Loudon and Bolivar Heights and that the garrison of Martinsburg had joined him. Reno's Corps is partially engaged in front of here, and Hooker is arriving rapidly. Please lose no time in driving the rebel cavalry out of Burkheadsville, and occupying the pass. Have Saunders[2] keep the communication open between us and keep me informed of everything transpiring at the pass before you. Let me know first whether the enemy occupies the pass and if so the strength of their force there.

Continue to bear in mind the necessity of relieving Colonel Miles if possible.

I am, General very respectfully your ob't servt
Geo B. McClellan
Maj Genl Comdg

LS retained copy, McClellan Papers (C-18:65), Library of Congress. *OR*, Ser. 1, LI, Part 1, p. 833.

1. Burkittsville. The report was from Pleasonton. *OR*, XIX, Part 2, p. 290. 2. Capt. William P. Sanders, 6th U.S. Cavalry.

To Dixon S. Miles

Triplicates sent by Maj. Allen's men.[1]

Col D S Miles — Head Quarters, Army of the Potomac,
Col — Middletown 1 pm Sept 14 1862

The Army is being rapidly concentrated here. We are now attacking the pass in the Hagerstown Road over the Blue Ridge.[2] A column is about attacking the Burkittsville and Boonsboro pass.[3] You may count on our making every effort to relieve you. You may count upon my accomplishing that object. Hold out to the last extremity. If it is possible reoccupy the Maryland Heights with your whole force. If you can do that, I will certainly be able to relieve you. As the Catoctin Valley is in our possession, you can safely cross at Berlin or its vicinity so far as opposition on this side of the river is concerned. Hold out to the last.

Geo B. McClellan
Maj Gen Comdg

LS retained copy, McClellan Papers (C-18:65), Library of Congress. *OR*, Ser. 1, XIX, Part 1, p. 45.

1. Civilians employed by Allan Pinkerton. None of them reached Col. Miles. 2. Turner's Gap in South Mountain. 3. Crampton's Gap.

To William B. Franklin

Head Quarters, Army of the Potomac
Maj. Gen. Franklin — Frederic [Middletown] Sept 14 2 pm 1862

Your dispatch of 12.30 just received.[1] Send back to hurry up Couch. Mass your troops and carry Burkittsville at any cost. We shall have strong opposition at both passes. As fast as the troops come up, I will hold a reserve in readiness to support you. If you find the enemy in very great force at the pass let me know at once, and amuse them as best you can so as to retain them there. In that event I will probably throw the mass of the Army on the pass in front of here. If I carry that it will clear the way for you, and you must then follow the enemy as rapidly as possible.[2]

Geo B McClellan
Maj Genl Comdg

LS retained copy, McClellan Papers (C-18:65), Library of Congress. *OR*, Ser. 1, XIX, Part 1, p. 46.

1. Franklin reported that the enemy on his front was reinforced by artillery. "I think from appearances that we may have a heavy fight to get the pass." McClellan Papers (A-79:31). 2. In his reply of 5:20 P.M., Franklin wrote: "I report that I have been severely engaged with the enemy for the last hour. . . . The force of the enemy is too great for us to take the pass to night I am afraid. I shall await further orders here & shall attack again in the morning without further orders." McClellan Papers (A-81:32).

To Henry W. Halleck [TELEGRAM]

Headquarters Army of the Potomac
Sept 14 4 pm 1862 In front of Middletown

We are forcing the passage of the Blue Ridge. Have possession of the heights on left of Hagerstown pike & are now attacking on the right. Franklin is attacking the Rohrersville pass through same range. Thus far all goes well. Have taken about a hundred (100) prisoners already. I have the troops well in hand & they are very confident. Hope to have full possession of the passes by dark. Firing near Harper's Ferry within last hour.

G B. McClellan
Maj Genl

Maj Genl Halleck
Washington DC

ALS (telegram sent), Chicago Historical Society. *OR*, Ser. 1, XIX, Part 2, p. 289.

To Joseph Hooker

Head Qrs Army of Potomac
Maj. Gen. Hooker [Bolivar, Md.] Sept 14, 1862 9 p.m.

General Reno has succeeded in carrying the heights on the left of the main pike.

Please hold your present position at all hazards. General Richardson has been placed under your orders.[1] Let me know at daybreak tomorrow morning the state of affairs in your vicinity, and whether you will need further reinforcements. I presume, however, that Richardson's division is all that will be required by you.

Franklin has had a severe contest with the enemy at pass in front of Jefferson, the result of which is not yet known to me.

G B McClellan
Maj Genl Comdg

LS, Hooker Papers, Huntington Library. *OR*, Ser. 1, LI, Part 1, p. 831.

1. Brig. Gen. Richardson commanded a division in Sumner's Second Corps.

To Henry W. Halleck [TELEGRAM]

Maj Genl Halleck — Head Quarters Army of the Potomac
Genl in Chief — Beyond Middletown Sept 14th [1862] 9.40 pm

After a very severe engagement the Corps of Hooker and Reno have carried the heights commanding the Hagerstown road.

The troops behaved magnificently. They never fought better. Franklin has been hotly engaged on the extreme left. I do not yet know the result except that firing indicated progress on his part. The action continued until after dark and terminated leaving us in possession of the entire crest.

It has been a glorious victory; I cannot yet tell whether the enemy will retreat during the night or appear in increased force in the morning. I am hurrying up everything from the rear to be prepared for any eventuality.

I regret to add that the gallant and able Genl Reno is killed.

G B McClellan

Received copy, Records of the Office of the Secretary of War, RG 107 (M-473 :50), National Archives. *OR*, Ser. 1, XIX, Part 2, p. 289.

To Mary Ellen McClellan [TELEGRAM]

Mrs. McClellan — Hd Qrs Army of the Potomac
New London Conn. — Bolivar [September] 14 1862 9.40 pm

We have carried the Heights near here after a hard engagement & gained a glorious victory. All your particular friends well.

G B McClellan
Maj Genl USA

Received copy (War Dept.), Records of the Office of the Secretary of War, RG 107 (M-504 :66), National Archives.

To Henry W. Halleck [TELEGRAM]

Maj Genl H. W. Halleck — Head Quarters, Army of the Potomac,
Genl in Chief, Washn — Hd Qtrs Bolivar Sept 15th 8 am 1862

I am happy to inform you that Franklin's success on the left was as complete as that in the center & right & resulted in his getting possession of the Burkittsville Gap after a severe engagement. On all parts of the line the troops, old & new, behaved with the utmost steadiness & gallantry, carrying with but little assistance from our own artillery, very strong positions defended by artillery & infantry. I do not think our loss very severe. The Corps of D. H. Hill & Longstreet were engaged with our right. We have taken a considerable number of prisoners. The enemy disappeared during the night. Our troops are now advancing in pursuit of them. I do not yet know where he will next be found. The morale of our own men is now restored.

Geo B McClellan
Maj Genl Comdg

LS (telegram sent), McClellan Papers (C-16:65), Library of Congress. *OR*, Ser. 1, XIX, Part 2, p. 294.

To Henry W. Halleck [TELEGRAM]

Maj Genl H. W. Halleck
Comdr in Chief

Head Quarters, Army of the Potomac,
Bolivar, Sept. 15 8.30 am 1862

I have just learned from Genl Hooker in the advance, who states that the information is perfectly reliable, that the enemy is making for Shepherdstown in a perfect panic, & that Genl Lee last night stated publicly that he must admit they had been shockingly whipped.[1]

I am hurrying everything forward to endeavor to press their retreat to the utmost.

Geo B McClellan
Maj Genl Comdg

LS (telegram sent), McClellan Papers (C-16:65), Library of Congress. *OR*, Ser. 1, XIX, Part 2, p. 294.

1. GBM is quoting from Hooker's dispatch, sent about 8:00 A.M., the source of which was "some citizens from Boonsboro." McClellan Papers (A-79:31).

To Nathaniel P. Banks [TELEGRAM]

Maj. Gen. Banks
Washington

Head Quarters, Army of the Potomac,
Bolivar — three miles beyond Middletown
Sept. 15, 1862 9 am

I think that under present circumstances it will be well for you to move the greater part of your command to the south side of the Potomac. I do not consider that any danger to Washington is now to be feared from the north side of the river.[1]

Geo. B. McClellan
Maj. Genl. Commandg

Retained copy, McClellan Papers (C-18:65), Library of Congress. *OR*, Ser. 1, XIX, Part 2, p. 294.

1. Banks replied at 2:00 P.M. that forces would be sent from Washington to cover the Potomac crossings downstream from Harper's Ferry, and that he would "carry out your instructions as far as practicable." *OR*, Ser. 1, XIX, Part 2, pp. 298–99.

To Mary Ellen McClellan

Sept 15 [1862] Monday 9.30 am. Bolivar

. . . Just sent you a telegram[1] informing you that we yesterday gained a glorious & complete victory: every moment adds to its importance. R E Lee wounded, Hill D H reported killed — Lee is *reported* to state his loss at 15,000 yesterday.[2] I am pushing everything after them with the greatest rapidity & expect to gain great results. I thank God most humbly for his great mercy. How glad I am for my country that it is delivered from immediate peril. I am about starting with the pursuit & must close this. . . .

If I can believe one tenth of what is reported, God has seldom given an army a greater victory than this. . . .

AL copy, McClellan Papers (C-7:63), Library of Congress.

1. His telegram, sent at 9:00 A.M., read: "Have just learned that the enemy are retreating in a panic & that our victory is complete. We are pushing everything after them." Records of the Office of the Secretary of War, RG 107 (M-504:66), National Archives. 2. This is taken from a dispatch sent from the front by Capt. George A. Custer of GBM's staff. Gen. Lee had injured his hands in a fall several days before. Gen. Hill was unhurt in the previous day's fighting. McClellan Papers (A-79:31).

To Henry W. Halleck [TELEGRAM]

Maj. Gen. H. W. Halleck
Comdr in Chief, Washington

Head Quarters, Army of the Potomac,
Bolivar Sept. 15th 10 am 1862

There are already about seven hundred rebel prisoners at Frederick, under very insufficient guard, and shall probably send in a larger number today. It would be well to have them either paroled or other wise disposed of as Frederick is an inconvenient place for them. Information this moment rec'd completely confirms the rout & demoralization of the rebel Army. Genl. Lee is reported wounded & Garland killed.[1] Hooker alone has over a thousand more prisoners. It is stated that Lee gives his loss as fifteen thousand. We are following as rapidly as the men can move.[2]

Geo B McClellan
Maj Genl Comdg

LS (telegram sent), McClellan Papers (C-16:65), Library of Congress. *OR*, Ser. 1, XIX, Part 2, pp. 294–95.

1. Brig. Gen. Samuel Garland was killed at Fox's Gap. 2. That afternoon President Lincoln telegraphed: "Your dispatches of to-day received. God bless you, and all with you. Destroy the rebel army, if possible." *Collected Works of Lincoln*, V, p. 426.

To Winfield Scott [TELEGRAM]

Lieut Gen Winfield Scott
West Point Camp near Boonsboro Md Sept 15th 1862

We attacked a large force of the enemy yesterday occupying a strong mountain pass four miles west of Middletown. Our troops old and new regiments behaved most valiantly & gained a signal victory. R E Lee in command. The Rebels routed and retreating in disorder this morning. We are pursuing closely and taking many prisoners.[1]

Geo. B. McClellan
Major General

Copy, Records of the Office of the Secretary of War, RG 107 (M-473 :50), National Archives. *OR*, Ser. 1, XIX, Part 2, p. 295.

1. Gen. Scott replied on Sept. 16: "Bravo my Dear General — twice more & its done." McClellan Papers (A-80 :32), Library of Congress.

To William B. Franklin

Headquarters Army of the Potomac
[Boonsboro, September 15, 1862, 1 :20 P.M.]

Burnside's Corps & Sykes' Division are moving on Porterstown & Sharpsburg by the road almost 1 mile south of Hagerstown Pike with orders to turn & attack a force of the enemy supposed to be at Centreville.[1] I will instruct them to communicate with you at Rohrersville & if necessary reinforce you. It is important to drive in the enemy in your front but be cautious in doing it until you have some idea of his force.[2]

The Corps of Sumner, Hooker & Banks[3] are moving to Boonsboro on the main pike. At least one Division has already passed down towards Centreville. I will direct a portion to turn to the left at the first road beyond the mountain (west) so as to be in position to reinforce you or to move on Portersville. Sykes will be at the Boonsboro & Rohrersville road in about 1 1/2 hours Burnside following close. Thus far our success is complete but let us follow up closely but warily. Attack whenever you see a fair chance of success. Lose no time in communicating with Sykes & Burnside.[4]

McC

To Franklin

ALS retained copy, McClellan Papers (A-79 :31), Library of Congress. *OR*, Ser. 1, LI, Part 1, p. 836.

1. At the time more commonly known as Keedysville. 2. Franklin had reported at 8 :50 A.M. that the Confederates on his front were drawn up in line of battle across Pleasant Valley. "If Harper's Ferry has fallen — and the cessation of firing makes me fear that it has — it is my opinion that I should be strongly re-enforced." *OR*, Ser. 1, XIX, Part 1, p.

47. 3. The Twelfth Corps was formerly Banks's Second Corps of the Army of Virginia. Maj. Gen. Joseph K. F. Mansfield took command that day. 4. Franklin replied at 3:00 P.M. that the enemy was withdrawing swiftly down Pleasant Valley toward Harper's Ferry. "Under your last orders, I do not feel justified in putting my whole command in motion toward the front, but shall act according to the dictates of my judgment, as circumstances may occur." *OR*, Ser. 1, XIX, Part 2, p. 296.

To Ambrose E. Burnside

Major Genl Burnside — Head Quarters, Army of the Potomac,
General — [Boonsboro] Sept. 15, 1862 3.45 pm

The last news received is that the enemy is drawn up in line of battle about two miles beyond Centreville, which will bring them on the west and behind Antietam Creek. They are represented to be in considerable force under Longstreet.[1] Our troops are rapidly moving up. If not too late I think you had better move on Rohresville communicating meantime with Franklin. If with your assistance, he can defeat the enemy in front of him, join him at once. If however he can hold his own, march direct on Sharpsburg & cooperate with us unless that place should be evacuated by the enemy. In that case, move at once to cooperate with Franklin. Porter of course will continue on his march to Sharpsburg.

Very Resp'y Yr ob't Servt
G B McC

Retained copy, McClellan Papers (C-18:65), Library of Congress. *OR*, Ser. 1, LI, Part 1, pp. 837–38.

1. Capt. Custer had reported: "The enemy is drawn up in line of battle on a ridge about two miles beyond [Keedysville]. They are in full view. Their line is a perfect one about a mile and a half long.... Longstreet is in command and has forty cannon that we know of." McClellan Papers (A-80:32).

To Henry W. Halleck [TELEGRAM]

Head Quarters, Army of the Potomac,
Maj Gen H. W. Halleck — Bivouac near Sharpsburg
Comdr in Chief, Washington — Sept. 16th 7 am 1862

The enemy yesterday held a position just in front of Sharpsburg. When our troops arrived in sufficient force it was too late in the day to attack. This morning a heavy fog has thus far prevented our doing more than to ascertain that some of the enemy are still there. Do not yet know in what force. Will attack as soon as situation of the enemy is developed. I hear that Miles surrendered at 8 a.m. yesterday unconditionally. I fear his resistance was not as stubborn as it ought to have been. Had he held the Maryland Heights he would inevitably have been saved.

The time lost on account of the fog is being occupied in getting up supplies for the want of which many of our men are suffering.[1]

Geo B McClellan
Maj Genl Comdg

LS (telegram sent), McClellan Papers (C-16:65), Library of Congress. *OR*, Ser. 1, XIX, Part 2, pp. 307–308.

1. Halleck replied on this date, in part: "I think ... you will find that the whole force of the enemy in your front has crossed the river. I fear now more than ever that they will recross at Harper's Ferry or below, and turn your left, thus cutting you off from Washington. This has appeared to me to be a part of their plan, and hence my anxiety on the subject." *OR*, Ser. 1, XIX, Part 1, p. 41.

To Mary Ellen McClellan [TELEGRAM]

Mrs. McClellan
Care J W Alsop
Middletown Conn

Hd Qrs AP [September] 16th [1862] 7 am
Near Sharpsburg

Have reached thus far & have no doubt delivered Penna & Maryland. All well & in excellent spirits.

G B McClellan

Received copy (War Dept.), Records of the Office of the Secretary of War, RG 107 (M-504:66), National Archives.

To William B. Franklin

Major Genl Franklin
General

Head Quarters, Army of the Potomac,
Centreville Sept 16, 1862 7.45 am

The man O'Sullivan[1] who passed through your lines yesterday as a bearer of dispatches to Colonel Miles has returned, and informs me that Miles surrendered unconditionally at 8 o'clock yesterday morning — and that the rebels on this side of the river were rapidly recrossing to the Virginia side by our pontoon bridge at Harper's Ferry. He did not see this with his own eyes, but was so informed by persons in whom he has implicit confidence. I think the enemy has abandoned the position in front of us, but the fog is so dense that I have not yet been enabled to determine. If the enemy is in force here, I shall attack him this morning. The instant I know whether he is still here or not I shall inform you. I would again caution you to watch Knoxville and Berlin with a small cavalry force, so that no enemy can get in your rear.

Very Resp'y Yr. obt Servt.
Geo B McClellan
Maj Genl Comdg

LS retained copy, McClellan Papers (C-18:65), Library of Congress. *OR*, Ser. 1, LI, Part 1, p. 839.

1. Probably T. O'Sullivan, one of Pinkerton's men.

To Alfred Pleasonton

Genl Pleasonton [Before Sharpsburg] Sept 17 [1862] 11:45 am

Do not expose your batteries without necessity unless they are inflicting on the enemy a loss commensurate with what we suffer. How goes it with you.

G B McClellan

P.S. Can you do any good by a cavalry charge?[1]

ALS, Private Collection.

1. Gen. Pleasonton's cavalry and horse artillery were posted at the center of the Federal line.

To Henry W. Halleck [TELEGRAM]

Headquarters Army of the Potomac
[Before Sharpsburg] Sept 17 [1862] 1.25 pm

Please take military possession of the Chambersburg & Hagerstown rail road that our ammunition & supplies may be hurried up without delay.[1]

We are in the midst of the most terrible battle of the war, perhaps of history — thus far it looks well but I have great odds against me. Hurry up all the troops possible. Our loss has been terrific, but we have gained much ground. I have thrown the mass of the Army on their left flank. Burnside is now attacking their right & I hold my small reserve consisting of Porters (5th Corps) ready to attack the center as soon as the flank movements are developed. [*Crossed out:* It will be either a great defeat or a most glorious victory. I think & hope that God will give us the latter.] I hope that God will give us a glorious victory.

G B McClellan
Maj Genl

Maj Genl Halleck
Genl in Chief Washn

ALS (telegram sent), McClellan Papers (A-80:32), Library of Congress. *OR*, Ser. 1, XIX, Part 2, p. 312.

1. Halleck telegraphed that evening to Gen. Wool, in command at Baltimore, to send all possible reinforcements to GBM. "Also, see that all ammunition and other supplies are

forwarded as expeditiously as possible. If necessary, take military possession of the railroads for that purpose." *OR*, Ser. 1, XIX, Part 2, p. 319.

To Mary Ellen McClellan [TELEGRAM]

Mrs. McClellan Hd Qrs A.P. near Sharpsburg
Care J. W. Alsop Middletown Ct 1.45 p.m. [September] 17 [1862]

We are in the midst of the most terrible battle of the age.

So far God has given us success but with many variations during the day. The battle is not yet over & I write this in the midst of it.

I trust that God will smile upon our cause. I am well. None of your immediate friends killed that I hear of. Your father with me quite safe.

G B. McClellan
M.G.C.

Received copy (War Dept.), Records of the Office of the Secretary of War, RG 107 (M-504:66), National Archives.

To James W. Ripley [TELEGRAM]

Brig Gen Ripley Hd Qrs A.P. [near Sharpsburg]
Chf Ordn Via Hagerstown Sept 17th 1862

If you can possibly do it force some 20 pdr Parrott ammunition through tonight via Hagerstown & Chambersburg to us near Sharpsburg Md.

G B McClellan
Maj Genl Comdg

Received copy, Records of the Office of the Secretary of War, RG 107 (M-473:50), National Archives. *OR*, Ser. 1, XIX, Part 2, p. 312.

1. This telegram was endorsed in the Ordnance Office: "Attended to at once, September 17 — 11 p.m."

To Henry W. Halleck [TELEGRAM]

Major General Halleck Head Quarters, Army of the Potomac,
General-in-Chief, Washington Keedysville Sept. 18, 1862 8 am

The battle of yesterday continued for fourteen hours, and until after dark. We held all we gained except a portion of the extreme left that was obliged to abandon a part of what it had gained. Our losses very heavy, especially in General officers. The battle will probably be renewed today. Send all the troops you can by the most expeditious route.

G. B. McClellan
Maj. Genl. Comdg.

Retained copy, McClellan Papers (C-18:65), Library of Congress. *OR*, Ser. 1, XIX, Part 2, p. 322.

To Mary Ellen McClellan [TELEGRAM]

Headquarters Army of the Potomac
[Keedysville] Sept 18 [1862] 8 am

The battle of yesterday a desperate one. We hold all we gained. The contest will probably be renewed today. Your father & I well.

G. B. McClellan
Maj Genl

Mrs McClellan
Care J W Alsop Esq Middletown Conn

ALS (telegram sent), McClellan Papers (A-80:32), Library of Congress.

To Mary Ellen McClellan

Sept 18 [1862] 8 am. Camp near Sharpsburg

. . . We fought yesterday a terrible battle against the entire rebel army. The battle continued *14* hours & was terrific — the fighting on both sides was superb. The general result was in our favor, that is to say we gained a great deal of ground & held it. It was a success, but whether a decided victory depends upon what occurs today. I hope that God has given us a great success. It is all in his hands, where I am content to leave it. The spectacle yesterday was the grandest I could conceive of — nothing could be more sublime. Those in whose judgment I rely tell me that I fought the battle splendidly & that it was a masterpiece of art. I am well nigh tired out by anxiety & want of sleep. . . .

God has been good in sparing the lives of all my staff. Genls Hooker, Sedgwick, Dana, Richardson & Hartsuff & several other general officers wounded. Mansfield is dead I fear, but am not certain — I just learn that he is not mortally wounded[1] . . .

AL copy, McClellan Papers (C-7:63), Library of Congress.

1. For a later count of officer casualties, see GBM to his wife, Sept. 20, 1862, note 1, *infra.*

To Mary Ellen McClellan [TELEGRAM]

Mrs McClellan
Care J. W. Alsop Middletown Ct

Hd Qrs near Sharpsburg
8 am [September] 19 [1862]

Our victory complete. Enemy has left his dead & wounded on the field. Our people now in pursuit. Your father and I are well.

G. B. McClellan

Retained copy, Records of the Office of the Secretary of War, RG 107 (M-504:66), National Archives.

To Henry W. Halleck [TELEGRAM]

Headquarters Army of the Potomac
Near Sharpsburg Sept. 19 [1862] 8.30 am

But little occurred yesterday except skirmishing, we being fully occupied in replenishing ammunition, taking care of wounded, etc. Last night the enemy abandoned his position leaving his dead & wounded on the field. We are again in pursuit. I do not yet know whether he is falling back to an interior position or crossing the river. We may safely claim a complete victory.

G B. McClellan
Maj Gen

Maj Genl Halleck
Comdr in Chief

ALS (telegram sent), McClellan Papers (A-80 :32), Library of Congress. *OR*, Ser. 1, XIX, Part 2, p. 330.

To Henry W. Halleck [TELEGRAM]

Headquarters Army of the Potomac
[Near Sharpsburg] Sept 19 10.30 am 1862

Pleasonton is driving the enemy across the river. Our victory was complete. The enemy is driven back into Virginia. Maryland & Penna. are now safe.

G B McClellan
Maj Genl

Genl H W Halleck
Comdr in chief

ALS (telegram sent), McClellan Papers (A-80 :32), Library of Congress. *OR*, Ser. 1, XIX, Part 2, p. 330.

To Henry W. Halleck [TELEGRAM]

Maj. Gen. H. W. Halleck
Comdg in Chief

Head Quarters, Army of the Potomac,
Sharpsburg, Sept. 19 1.30 pm 1862

I have the honor to report that Maryland is entirely freed from the presence of the enemy, who has been driven across the Potomac. No fears need now be entertained for the safety of Pennsylvania. I shall at once reoccupy Harper's Ferry.

G. B. McClellan
Maj. Genl. Comdg.

Retained copy, McClellan Papers (C-18 :65), Library of Congress. *OR*, Ser. 1, XIX, Part 1, p. 68.

NINE

AN END TO ACTIVE SERVICE

SEPTEMBER 20–NOVEMBER 10, 1862

THERE IS NOTHING in General McClellan's correspondence following the Battle of Antietam to indicate he recognized the unique opportunity he had missed for a decisive victory on that field. Instead he was gratified simply to have saved his army from defeat and the North from invasion. What he witnessed on the Maryland battlefields caused no change in his mental picture of the Confederate army. "In the last battles the enemy was undoubtedly greatly superior to us in number, and it was only by very hard fighting that we gained the advantage we did . . . ," he assured General Halleck on September 27. Nor is there any suggestion here that in his final weeks of command of the Army of the Potomac he understood anything closer to the truth about his foe than in his first weeks.

Indeed, as he wrote Mrs. McClellan on September 20, he measured the results of Antietam as entitling him to insist on the removal of his immediate superiors, General-in-Chief Halleck and Secretary of War Stanton. He expected to accomplish this through the intervention of Northern state governors and of "certain friends of mine . . . ," and to regain for himself the post of general-in-chief. In reality, the far greater pressure exerted on President Lincoln was for the removal of General McClellan.

The president's preliminary Emancipation Proclamation and his suspension of the privilege of habeas corpus soon afterward were deeply shocking to McClellan. In the interval between his angry initial reaction, as reflected in letters to his wife and to William H. Aspinwall (September 25 and 26), and the general order he issued on October 7 advising his army of its duty to support these actions by the chief executive, he was repeatedly advised by friends and political supporters not to publicly oppose the government on these issues. Afterward, however, his letters suggest a growing reluctance to serve the Lincoln administration any further. (For part of this period his views on matters are stated less explicitly than usual due to the absence for some two weeks of letters to his wife, who during this time was with him at his camp in Pleasant Valley, near Harper's Ferry.)

Throughout the correspondence in this section McClellan was unwavering in his opposition to taking the Army of the Potomac on campaign once more. He insisted that his troops were unprepared in numbers, organization, morale, supplies, and equipment to renew the contest against Lee anytime soon, and he stubbornly resisted the president's urgings and then his direct order to begin an advance. "These people don't know what an army requires & therefore act stupidly," he told his wife on October 2. On October 30, finally crossing the Potomac into Virginia to begin what proved to be his last march as army commander, he telegraphed Lincoln a listing of reasons he opposed the advance, and added, "I write this only to place the responsibility where it belongs . . . ."

The course he advocated instead was first to secure the line of the Potomac and the Shenandoah Valley against further Confederate incursions, a process requiring extensive bridge-building and railroad construction and fortification, and then (as he told Halleck on October 7) "to adopt a new & decisive line of operations which shall strike at the heart of the rebellion." Behind this generalized objective was his unstated desire to return his army to the Peninsula, in the spring of 1863, to repeat his advance on Richmond.

The president's basic reason for relieving McClellan of command — and for seeking his replacement at least twice before — was the general's reluctance to fight. Lincoln had urged him to cross the Potomac and march rapidly (as rapidly as the Confederates customarily marched, he told him) so as to threaten Lee's communications with Richmond and bring him to battle at the earliest opportunity. Privately he made that the test: if McClellan allowed the Rebels to get ahead of him and block his path he would be dismissed. In the event, McClellan moved with his usual deliberation, requiring nine days just to cross the Potomac, and on November 4 it was reported to Washington that the enemy was at Culpeper Court House, on the Federals' line of advance. That day also saw the last of the midterm elections in the Northern states, another important factor in the timing of the president's decision. General McClellan had let himself be made the most visible symbol of political opposition to the administration, and that fact, when added to his military shortcomings, made his dismissal inevitable — and would be a decisive factor, over the next two years, in preventing his reinstatement.

To Mary Ellen McClellan

Sept 20 [1862] 8 am. Camp near Sharpsburg

. . . Yesterday the enemy completed his evacuation of Maryland — completely beaten — we got many prisoners, muskets, colors, cannon etc — his loss in killed & wounded was very great — so was ours, unfortunately.

Genl Mansfield was killed (or rather died of his wounds) — Genls Sedgwick, Richardson, Dana, Brooks, Hooker, Weber, Rodman — & two others whose names I cannot recall were wounded on Wednesday. Poor Henry Kingsbury died of his wounds the day after the battle.[1]

The battle lasted 14 hours & was without doubt the most severe ever fought on this continent, & few more desperate were ever fought anywhere.

9 am. . . . Am glad to say that I am much better today — for to tell you the truth I have been under the weather since the battle — the want of rest & anxiety brought on my old disease. The battle of Wednesday *was* a terrible one. I presume the loss will prove not less than 10,000 on each side.[2] Our victory was complete & the disorganized rebel army has rapidly returned to Virginia — its dreams of "invading Penna" dissipated for ever. I feel some little pride in having with a beaten and demoralized army defeated Lee so utterly, & saved the North so completely. Well — one of these days history will I trust do me justice in deciding that it was not my fault that the campaign of the Peninsula was not successful. An opportunity has presented itself through the Governors of some of the states to enable me to take my stand — I have insisted that Stanton shall be removed & that Halleck shall give way to me as Comdr in Chief.[3] I will *not* serve under him — for he is an incompetent fool — in no way fit for the important place he holds. Since I left Washn Stanton has again asserted that *I* not *Pope* lost the battle of Manassas No 2! The only safety for the country & for me is to get rid of both of them — no success is possible with them. I am tired of fighting against such disadvantages & feel that it is now time for the country to come to my help, & remove these difficulties from my path. If my countrymen will not open their eyes & assert themselves they must pardon me if I decline longer to pursue the thankless avocation of serving them. . . .

Thank Heaven for one thing — my military reputation is cleared — I have shown that I can fight battles & *win* them! I think my enemies are pretty effectively killed by this time! May they remain so!!

AL copy, McClellan Papers (C-7:63), Library of Congress.

1. Maj. Gens. Joseph K. F. Mansfield, John Sedgwick, Israel B. Richardson, Joseph Hooker; Brig. Gens. N. J. T. Dana, W. T. H. Brooks, Max Weber, Isaac P. Rodman; Col. Henry W. Kingsbury, 11th Connecticut. Brig. Gens. George L. Hartsuff and Samuel W. Crawford were the two others wounded. The wounds of Richardson and Rodman were mortal. 2.

Losses at Antietam would be later calculated as 12,401 Federal, 10,318 Confederate. 3. GBM refers here to a conference of Northern governors scheduled for Sept. 24 at Altoona, Pa. The tenor of the meeting proved strongly anti-McClellan, however, with only Andrew G. Curtin of Pennsylvania, David Tod of Ohio, and Augustus W. Bradford of Maryland opposing demands for his removal. *New York Herald,* Sept. 26, 1862.

To Joseph Hooker

Maj. Gen. Joseph Hooker
Commanding Corps
My dear Hooker:

Headquarters Army of the Potomac
Sharpsburg, September 20, 1862.

I have been very sick the last few days, and just able to go where my presence was absolutely necessary, so I could not come to see you and thank you for what you did the other day, and express my intense regret and sympathy for your unfortunate wound. Had you not been wounded and when you were, I believe the result of the battle would have been the entire destruction of the rebel army, for I *know* that, with you at its head, your corps would have kept on until it gained the main road. As a slight expression of what I think you merit, I have requested that the brigadier-general's commission rendered vacant by Mansfield's death may be given to you. I will this evening write a private note to the President on the subject, and I am glad to assure you that, so far as I can learn, it is the universal feeling of the army that you are the most deserving in it.

With the sincere hope that your health may soon be restored, so that you may again be with us in the field,

I am, my dear general, your sincere friend,
Geo. B. McClellan
Major-General

OR, Ser. 1, XIX, Part 1, p. 219.

To Abraham Lincoln

Head-Quarters, Army of the Potomac,
[Sharpsburg, September 20] 1862

Your Excellency

I would most respectfully ask that the commission of Brig Genl in the regular army rendered vacant by the death of Brig Genl Mansfield may be conferred upon Maj Genl J Hooker US Vols.

The able & gallant services of this most excellent officer upon many a hard-fought field render him eminently deserving of it; no one has rendered greater service to his country & I am confident that I but express the general feeling of the army when I ask this appointment for him —

it cannot be better disposed of, nor to a more deserving, able & gallant officer.[1]

I am very respectfully your obdt svt

AL retained copy, Records of the U.S. Army Continental Commands, RG 393 (3964: Army of the Potomac), National Archives.

1. GBM had telegraphed Gen. Halleck to the same effect on Sept. 19. *OR,* Ser. 1, XIX, Part 1, p. 182. The appointment was made, effective on this date.

To Henry W. Halleck [TELEGRAM]

Major General Halleck
General-in-Chief, Washington

Head Quarters, Army of the Potomac,
Near Sharpsburg, Sept 20, 1862 8 pm

Your telegram of to day is received.[1] I telegraphed you yesterday all I knew, and had nothing more to inform you of until this evening. Williams' Corps (Banks') occupied Maryland Heights at 1 p.m. to day. The rest of the Army is near here, except Couch's division which is at this moment engaged with the enemy in front of Williamsport. The enemy is retiring via Charlestown and Martinsburg on Winchester. He last night reoccupied Williamsport by a small force, but will be out of it by morning. I think he has a force of infantry near Shepherdstown.

I regret that you find it necessary to couch every dispatch I have the honor to receive from you, in a spirit of fault finding, and that you have not yet found leisure to say one word in commendation of the recent achievements of this Army, or even to allude to them. I have abstained from giving the number of guns, colors, small arms, prisoners, etc. captured, until I could do so with some accuracy. I hope by tomorrow evening to be able to give at least an approximate statement.[2].

G. B. McClellan
Maj. Gen. Comdg.

Retained copy, McClellan Papers (C-18:65), Library of Congress. *OR,* Ser. 1, XIX, Part 1, pp. 68–69.

1. Halleck's telegram of this date read: "We are still left entirely in the dark in regard to your own movements and those of the enemy. This should not be so. You should keep me advised of both, so far as you know them." *OR,* Ser. 1, XIX, Part 1, p. 68. 2. Halleck replied on Sept. 21, in part: "The Government has been most anxious for the last two days to obtain the information given in yours of yesterday . . . , and you have entirely misconstrued the urgency of my request for it. Except your short dispatch, in regard to Pleasonton's pursuit [Sept. 19, 1862, 10:30 A.M., *supra*], I had no official information of what had taken place since the battle of the 17th." *OR,* Ser. 1, XIX, Part 2, p. 339.

To Mary Ellen McClellan

Sept 20 [1862] 9 pm. Camp near Sharpsburg

. . . I hope that my future will be determined this week. Thro' certain friends of mine I have taken the stand that Stanton must leave & that Halleck must restore my old place to me. Unless these two conditions are fulfilled I will leave the service. I feel that I have done all that can be asked in twice saving the country. If I continue in its service I have at least the right to demand a guarantee that I shall not be interfered with — I know I cannot have that assurance so long as Stanton continues in the position of Secy of War & Halleck as Genl in Chief. You will understand that it is a matter of indifference to me whether they come to terms or not.

I now feel that my military reputation is safe & that I can retire from the service for sufficient reasons without leaving any stain upon my reputation. I feel now that this last short campaign is a sufficient legacy for our child, so far as honor is concerned. . . .

You should see my soldiers *now*! You never saw anything like their enthusiasm — it surpasses anything you ever imagined, & I don't believe that Napoleon even ever possessed the love & confidence of his men more fully than I do of mine. . . .

My tent is filled quite to overflowing with trophies in the way of captured rebel battle flags. We have more than have been taken in all battles put together — & all sorts of inscriptions on them. . . .

AL copy, McClellan Papers (C–7:63), Library of Congress.

To Henry B. Whipple

Head Quarters, Army of the Potomac
Camp near Sharpsburg Sept. 21, 1862

My dear Bishop,

Will you do me the favor to perform Divine service in my Camp this evening. If you can give me a couple of hours notice I would be glad of it that I may be able to inform the Corps in the vicinity. After the great success that God has vouchsafed us, I feel that we cannot do less than avail ourselves of the first opportunity, to render to Him the thanks due to Him alone. I for one feel that the great result is the result of His great mercy, and would be glad that you should be the medium to offer the thanks which I feel due from the Army and from the Country. Earnestly hoping that you will accede to my request[1]

I am very Respectfully your humble servant,
[George B. McClellan]
Maj Genl Comdg

Retained copy, McClellan Papers (B-12:48), Library of Congress. Whipple was Episcopal bishop of Minnesota.

1. Bishop Whipple was then visiting the army's wounded. He wrote GBM on Sept. 23: "I... cannot close without telling you how sweet is the remembrance of the pleasant service held in your Camp, nor to assure you, that it is a pleasure every day to ask God to bless you." Society Collection, Historical Society of Pennsylvania.

To Mary Ellen McClellan

[Sharpsburg] Sept 21st [1862] Sunday am.

...Do you know that I have not had one word from Halleck, the Presdt nor the Secy of War about the last great battle! All, except fault finding, that I have had since leaving Washn was one from *Abe* about the Sunday battle [South Mountain] in which he says "God bless you & all with you" — that is all I have — but plenty from Halleck couched in almost insulting language & prophesying disaster! I telegraphed him last night that I regretted the uniformly fault finding tone of his dispatches & that he had not as yet found leisure to notice the recent achievements of my army....

AL copy, McClellan Papers (C-7:63), Library of Congress.

To Mary Ellen McClellan

[Sharpsburg] Sept 22 [1862] 9 am.

...I rode out on the battle field yesterday — the burial of the dead is by this time completed & a terrible work it has been — for the slain counted by thousands on each side....

I look upon the campaign as substantially ended & my present intention is to seize Harper's Ferry & hold it with a strong force. Then go to work to reorganize the army ready for another campaign....

I shall not go to Washn if I can help it, but will try to reorganize the army somewhere near Harper's Ferry or Frederic....

It may be that now that the Govt is pretty well over their scare they will begin again with their persecutions & throw me overboard again. I don't care if they do. I have the satisfaction of knowing that God has in his mercy a second time made me the instrument for saving the nation & am content with the honor that has fallen to my lot. I feel that the short campaign just terminated will vindicate my professional honor & I have seen enough of public life. No motive of ambition can now retain me in the service — the only thing that *can* keep me there will be the conviction that my country needs my services & that circumstances make it necessary for me to render them. I am confident that the poison still rankles in the veins of my enemies at Washn & that so long as they live it will remain there....

I have received no papers containing the news of the last battle & do not know the effect it has produced on the Northern mind. I trust it has been a good one & that I am reestablished in the confidence of the best people of the nation....

Everything quiet today — not a shot fired as yet — I am moving troops down to Harper's Ferry & hope to occupy it tomorrow — then I will have the Potomac clear....

AL copy, McClellan Papers (C-7:63), Library of Congress.

To Henry W. Halleck [TELEGRAM]

Head Quarters,
Army of the Potomac,
Camp near the Potomac
Sept. 22d 1862 [noon]

Maj. Gen. H. W. Halleck
Commander in Chief, Washington

When I was assigned to the command of the Army in Washington it was suffering under the disheartening influences of defeat, it had been greatly reduced by casualties in Genl Pope's campaign, and its efficiency had been much impaired.

The sanguinary battles fought by these troops at South Mountain and Antietam Creek have resulted in a loss to us of ten General officers & many regimental and Company officers, besides a large number of enlisted men. Two Army Corps have been sadly cut up and scattered by the overwhelming numbers brought against them in the battle of the 17th inst, and the entire Army has been greatly exhausted by unavoidable overwork, hunger, & want of sleep & rest. When the enemy recrossed the Potomac the means of transportation at my disposal was inadequate to furnish a single day's supply of subsistence in advance. Under these circumstances I did not feel authorized to cross the river in pursuit of the retreating enemy, & thereby place that stream, which is liable at any time to rise above a fording stage, between this Army & its base of supply.

As soon as the exigencies of the service will admit of it, this Army should be re-organized. It is absolutely necessary to secure its efficiency that the old skeleton regiments should be filled up at once, & officers appointed to supply the numerous existing vacancies. There are instances where Captains are commanding Regiments & Companies are without a single commissioned officer.

Franklin's Corps marched to Wmsport yesterday morning to reinforce Couch. They now occupy that place, the enemy having retreated on their approach.

Williams' (Banks') Corps occupies Maryland Heights. Sumner's Corps is en route for the same point, & Meade's (Hooker's) Corps will probably follow it soon. I propose as soon as the pontoon bridge can be relaid (it is expected to arrive there today) to cross these troops and occupy Harper's Ferry & Charlestown, with a view of pushing them out into the Shenandoah Valley as soon as practicable. Burnside's & Porter's Corps are here. The enemy still continues to show his pickets along the river & with a large force drove back the last reconnaissance that was attempted on the other side. A large body of the enemy was reported last night as moving from Charlestown towards Bunker Hill, and I am of opinion that the mass of their Army is retreating in that direction. I am sending out scouts in every direction, and will keep you advised of all I learn of the movements of the enemy.

Geo B McClellan
Maj Gen Comdg

LS (telegram sent), McClellan Papers (C-16:65), Library of Congress. *OR*, Ser. 1, XIX, Part 2, pp. 342–43.

To Henry W. Halleck [TELEGRAM]

Head Quarters, Army of the Potomac,
Near Shepherdstown,
Sept 23, 1862 9.30 am

Major General Halleck
General in Chief Washington

From several different sources I learn that Gen. R E Lee is still opposite to my position at Leestown, between Shepherdstown and Martinsburg, and that General Jackson is on the Opequon Creek about three miles above its mouth, both with large forces. There are also indications of heavy reinforcements moving towards them from Winchester and Charlestown. I have therefore ordered Gen Franklin to take position with his Corps at the crossroads about one mile northwest of Bakersville on the Bakersville and Williamsport road, and Gen Couch to establish his division near Downsville, leaving sufficient force at Williamsport to watch and guard the ford at that place. The fact of the enemy's remaining so long in our front, and the indications of an advance of reinforcements seem to indicate that he will give us another battle, with all his available force. As I mentioned to you before our Army has been very much reduced by casualties in the recent battles, and in my judgment all the reinforcements of old troops that can possibly be dispensed with around Washington and other places should be instantly pushed forward by rail to this Army via Harper's Ferry and Hagerstown. A defeat at this juncture would be ruinous to our cause. I cannot think it possible that the enemy will bring any forces to bear upon Washington till after the question is decided here; — but if he should troops can soon be sent back from this Army by rail to reinforce the garrison there.[1]

The evidence I have that reinforcements are coming to the rebel army consists in the fact that long columns of dust extending from Winchester to Charlestown and from Charlestown in this direction and also troops moving this way were seen last evening. This is corroborated by the statements of citizens.

G. B. McClellan
Maj. Genl. Comdg.

P.S. Gen. Sumner with his Corps & Williams (Banks) occupies Harper's Ferry and the surrounding heights. I think he will be able to hold his position till reinforcements arrive.

G. B. McC.

Retained copy, McClellan Papers (C-18:65), Library of Congress. *OR,* Ser. 1, XIX, Part 1, p. 70.

1. Halleck telegraphed on Sept. 24, in part: ''Sigel's corps is the only old one here.... On what point would you prefer it to move?'' *OR,* Ser. 1, XIX, Part 2, p. 353.

To Henry W. Halleck [TELEGRAM]

Head Quarters, Army of the Potomac,
Major General Halleck — Near Shepherdstown
General in Chief Washington — Sept. 24, 1862 11 am

The enemy's pickets occupy the Virginia side of the river near Shepherdstown, and he is still said to be in position with large forces between Shepherdstown and Martinsburg. It has been raining for several hours. If the storm continues the river will probably be raised above a fording stage. Should this occur, I propose to concentrate the greater portion of the Army in the vicinity of Harper's Ferry, ready to act against the enemy in the direction of Winchester. The pontoon bridge arrived at Harper's Ferry last evening and is probably laid by this time.

A reconnaissance made from Harper's Ferry yesterday found the enemy's artillery, infantry and cavalry in force drawn up in line near Charlestown.

G. B. McClellan
Maj. Genl. Comdg.

Retained copy, McClellan Papers (C-18:65), Library of Congress. *OR,* Ser. 1, XIX, Part 2, p. 353.

To Henry W. Halleck [TELEGRAM]

Maj Gen Halleck — Head Quarters, Army of the Potomac,
Gen-in-Chief Washington — [Sharpsburg] Sept 24, 1862 10 pm

It is necessary to build a permanent double track wagon bridge over the Potomac at Harper's Ferry — also a wagon bridge over the Shenandoah at the same place on the piers now standing. The Potomac bridge must probably be built on crib piers filled with stone and will be about nine hundred feet in length, the Shenandoah bridge about four hundred feet long. I have to request that Colonel D. C. McCallum may be placed in charge of this work, and instructed to report to me at Harper's Ferry without delay. He should take steps before leaving Washington to organize the gangs of workmen and to procure all the material possible. I cannot too strongly urge the importance of expedition in this matter. Until this or the rail road bridge is finished it is scarcely possible to advance from Harper's Ferry in force, and as that is clearly our true line of operations, I need not urge upon you the necessity of completing our communications there.[1]

G. B. McClellan
Maj. Genl. Comdg.

Retained copy, McClellan Papers (C-18:65), Library of Congress. *OR,* Ser. 1, XIX, Part 2, pp. 354–55.

1. In his reply on Sept. 26, Halleck wrote that there must be agreement on a general plan of operations before bridge-building was undertaken. "I had hoped that, instead of crossing at Harper's Ferry . . . , you would be able to cross lower down the Potomac, so as to cover Washington. . . . It seems to me that Washington is the real base of operations, and that it should not under any circumstances be exposed." *OR,* Ser. 1, XIX, Part 2, p. 360.

To Mary Ellen McClellan

[Sharpsburg] Sept 25 [1862] 7.30 am.

. . . We are so near the mountains that it is quite cold at night. . . .

I think the health of our men is improving much — they look a great deal better than they did on the Peninsula — eyes look brighter — & faces better. . . .

My plans are easily given — for I really do not know whether I am to do as I choose or not. I shall keep on doing what seems best until brought up with a round turn — *then* I'll kick up *my* heels. My own judgment is to watch the line of the Potomac until the water rises, then to concentrate everything near Harper's Ferry — reorganize the army as promptly as possible & then if secesh remains near Winchester to attack him — if he retires to follow him up & attack him near Richmond. . . .

It is very doubtful whether I shall remain in the service after the rebels have left this vicinity. The Presdt's late Proclamation,[1] the continuation of Stanton & Halleck in office render it almost impossible for me to retain my commission & self respect at the same time. I cannot make up my mind to fight for such an accursed doctrine as that of a servile insurrection — it is too infamous. Stanton is as great a villain as ever & Halleck as great a fool — he has no brains whatever! . . .

It *is* a mercy of God that none of my staff have been hit considering how much they have been exposed to danger — they have had plenty of horses killed, sabres hit, clothes cut etc — but have thus far escaped unhurt. Am going on a visit to Harper's Ferry this morning....

AL copy, McClellan Papers (C-7 :63), Library of Congress.

1. The preliminary Emancipation Proclamation, issued Sept. 22. *Collected Works of Lincoln,* V, pp. 433–36.

To William H. Aspinwall

Head-Quarters Army of the Potomac,
Sharpsburg Sept 26, 1862

My dear Sir

I am very anxious to know how you and men like you regard the recent Proclamations of the Presdt inaugurating servile war, emancipating the slaves, & at one stroke of the pen changing our free institutions into a despotism — for such I regard as the natural effect of the last Proclamation suspending the Habeas Corpus throughout the land.[1]

I shall probably be in this vicinity for some days &, if you regard the matter as gravely as I do, would be glad to communicate with you.[2]

In haste I am sincerely yours
Geo B McClellan

Wm H Aspinwall esq
New York City

ALS, Civil War Collection, Huntington Library.

1. GBM refers to the preliminary Emancipation Proclamation and to the president's proclamation of Sept. 24 suspending the writ of habeas corpus as it applied to persons accused of "discouraging volunteer enlistments, resisting militia drafts, or guilty of any disloyal practice, affording aid and comfort to Rebels...." *Collected Works of Lincoln,* V, pp. 436–37. 2. Aspinwall visited GBM at his camp a short time later. See GBM to his wife, Oct. 5, 1862, *infra.*

To Henry W. Halleck [TELEGRAM]

Maj. Gen. Halleck
Genl in Chief Washington

Head Quarters, Army of the Potomac,
[Sharpsburg] Sept. 27, 1862 10 am

All the information in my possession goes to prove that the main body of the enemy is concentrated not far from Martinsburg with some troops at Charlestown — not many in Winchester.[1] Their movements of late have been an extension towards our right and beyond it. They are receiving reinforcements in Winchester, mainly I think of conscripts, perhaps entirely so. This Army is not now in condition to undertake another campaign nor to bring on another battle, unless great advantages are offered by some mistake of the enemy or pressing military exigencies render it necessary. We are greatly deficient in officers. Many of the old regiments are reduced to mere skeletons, the new regiments need instruction. Not a day should be lost in filling the old regiments, our main dependence, and in supplying vacancies among the officers by promotion. My present purpose is to hold the Army about as it now is, rendering Harper's Ferry secure and watching the river closely, intending to attack the enemy should he attempt to cross to this side.

Our possession of Harper's Ferry gives us the great advantage of a secure debouche; but we cannot avail ourselves of it until the railroad bridge is finished, because we cannot otherwise supply a greater number of troops than we now have on the Virginia side at that point. When the river rises so that the enemy cannot cross in force, I propose concentrating the Army somewhere near Harper's Ferry and then acting according to circumstances viz, moving on Winchester if from the position and attitude of the enemy we are likely to gain a great advantage by doing so; or else devoting a reasonable time to the organization of the Army and instruction of the new troops preparatory to an advance on whatever line may be determined. In any event I regard it as absolutely necessary to send new regiments at once to the old Corps for purposes of instruction, and that the old regiments be filled at once.

I have no fear as to an attack on Washington by the line of Manassas; holding Harper's Ferry as I do, they will not run the risk of an attack on their flank and rear while they have the garrison of Washington in their front. I rather apprehend a renewal of the attempt in Maryland, should the river remain low for a great length of time and should they receive considerable addition to their force. I would be glad to have Peck's division as soon as possible.[2] I am surprised that Sigel's men have been sent to Western Virginia without my knowledge. The last I heard from you on the subject was that they were at my disposition.

In the last battles the enemy was undoubtedly greatly superior to us in number, and it was only by very hard fighting that we gained the advantage we did; as it was, the result was at one period very doubtful and we had all we could do to win the day. If the enemy receives considerable reinforcements and we none, it is possible that I may have too much on my hands in the next battle.

My own view of the proper policy to be pursued is to retain in Washington merely the force necessary to garrison it and to send everything else available to reinforce this Army. The railways give us the means of promptly reinforcing Washington should it become necessary. If I am reinforced as I ask, and am allowed to take my own course, I will hold myself responsible for the safety of Washington.

Several persons recently from Richmond say that there are no troops there except conscripts and they few in number.

I hope to be able to give you details as to the late battles by this evening.[3] I am about starting again for Harper's Ferry.

G. B. McClellan
Maj. Genl. Comdg.

Retained copy, McClellan Papers (C-18:65), Library of Congress. *OR*, Ser. 1, XIX, Part 1, pp. 70–71.

1. Halleck had telegraphed on Sept. 26, in part: "Before more troops are moved from here into the field, we ought to have a full understanding in respect to your future operations. As I now understand, you propose to cross the Potomac at or above Harper's Ferry, and move up the valley. Will not this line again expose Washington, and compel us to keep a large force here? The enemy is repairing bridges on the Rapidan and Rappahannock, preparatory to throwing a force on Washington.... Cannot your army move, so as to cover Washington, by keeping between it and the enemy? I particularly wish your views on this subject." *OR*, Ser. 1, XIX, Part 2, pp. 359–60. 2. Maj. Gen. John J. Peck's division was at Yorktown. 3. See GBM to Halleck, Sept. 29, 1862, *OR*, Ser. 1, XIX, Part 1, p. 181.

To Lorenzo Thomas

To Brig Genl L Thomas,
Adjt. Genl. U.S. Army

Head Quarters Army of the Potomac
[Sharpsburg] September 28th 1862.

General:

The reduced condition of the old regiments, and the futility of dependence upon the recruiting service for the replenishing of their ranks, points to the necessity of earnest endeavor to collect all the absent officers and men belonging to these organizations. I am aware that this subject has already occupied the attention of the War Department, but I am now more especially alluding to the class of absentees employed on extra duty in the hospital and other staff departments of the Army, who are the most valuable of the absentees (for many absent men are runaways) and who can be sent to their regiments now without difficulty, inasmuch as their places can be readily supplied from new troops.

I am now getting together stragglers and convalescents from hospitals, and if I could get extra duty men also, a very considerable addition would be made to the diminished ranks of the old regiments.

In order to carry this into effect, I respectfully suggest than an order be issued fixing a time, say the 15th of October, when all hospital attendants and other extra duty men shall be relieved and sent to the Convalescent Camp at Alexandria in depot, from which they can be drawn and sent to their regiments as soon as a sufficient number have accumulated to justify the sending for them. The order should prohibit any officer retaining a soldier of the old regiments without the consent of the War Department or of the Commander of the Army or Department to which the soldier belongs. I suggest that every hospital and staff office be inspected within the month of October, by, if necessary, scores of officers detailed for the purpose, to ferret out the old soldiers hidden away therein. Such an inspection would produce more fruit in one week, than the recruiting service can in three months.

And finally I suggest to the War Department the employment of the deputy provost marshals throughout the north more particularly in the arrest of deserters. Convalescent soldiers leave hospitals and have done so for the past year and return home, habitually. It is the experience of every Army Commander, that not more than a tenth of the soldiers who are left behind sick, ever rejoin. A regiment here, which has been employed pretty much during the whole year as depot guard &c., has had in the course of the year some five hundred sick sent to hospitals in the rear. Of these, it has received back some fifteen or twenty. The stragglers too, are numerous in every division of the Army; many of these desert. The States of the North are flooded with deserters, absentees, &c. One Corps of this Army has 13,000 and odd men present and 15,000 and odd absent. Of this 15,000, 8,000 probably are at work at home, deserters. They can be secured and returned — and I beg that the fullest exercise of the power of the government may be devoted if necessary to the accomplishment of this end. It will have the happiest result in swelling the ranks of the old regiments and in preventing their future reduction.[1]

I am General Very Respectfully, Your obedient servant,
[George B. McClellan]
Major General Commanding

P.S. Since writing the above G.O. No. 140 of Sept. 24 1862 has come to my notice. The Department has therefore anticipated my suggestions with regard to the employment of Deputy Provost Marshals.[2]

Retained copy, Records of the U.S. Army Continental Commands, RG 393 (3964: Army of the Potomac), National Archives. *OR,* Ser. 1, XIX, Part 2, p. 365.

1. On Oct. 7 Halleck replied that every effort was being made to collect the absentees. He urged GBM to take stronger measures against straggling and to increase the army's mobility. "The country is becoming very impatient at the want of activity of your army, and we must push it on.... If we compare the average distances marched per month by our troops for the last year with that of the rebels, or with European armies in the field, we will see why our troops march no better. They are not sufficiently exercised to make them good and efficient soldiers." *OR,* Ser. 1, XIX, Part 2, pp. 394–95. 2. Issued by the Adjutant General's Office: *OR,* Ser. 3, II, p. 586.

To Mary Ellen McClellan

Sept 29 [1862] Sharpsburg am.

. . . I think secesh has gone to Winchester — the last I heard last night was to that effect. If he has gone there I will be able to arrange my troops more with a view to comfort & if it will only rain a little so as to raise the river will feel quite justified in asking for a short leave. . . .

We are having fine weather. . . .

I don't know what will be done about Stanton etc. I only feel that I cannot in justice to myself remain in the service if he continues in office. Not yet even have I a word from anyone in Washn about the battle of the Antietam & nothing in regard to South Mountain except from the Presdt in the following *beautiful* language. "Your dispatch received. God bless you & all with you. Can't you beat them some more before they get off?"!!![1] I don't look for any thanks at their hands & believe that they scarcely pretend to conceal their malevolence. I still hope that the indignant people will punish them as they deserve. I fully agree with you that forbearance is no longer a virtue. I shall make it only a matter of interest. If by pushing a little the people will take the matter in hand that will be the best solution.

11 pm. . . . I have been hard at work all day upon a mere preliminary report of the recent battles & find that in order to arrive at anything like the truth, I must tomorrow take all my aides to the ground and talk with them there. I would really prefer *fighting three* battles to *writing* the report of one. You can hardly imagine the difficulties of such a task. You are necessarily combating the amour propre, the vanity of every officer concerned when you say one word in commendation of anybody else. Each one is firmly convinced of the fact that no one *but* he had anything to do with the result, every commander of a brigade even becomes firmly convinced that he fought the whole battle & that he arranged the general plan, of which he knew simply nothing.

I *ought* to rap Burnside *very* severely & probably will — yet I hate to do it. He is very slow & is not fit to command more than a regiment. If I rap him as he deserves he will be my mortal enemy hereafter — if I do not praise him as he thinks he deserves & as I know he does *not*, he will be at least a very lukewarm friend. I mention this merely as an instance that you will comprehend. . . .

AL copy; copy, McClellan Papers (C-7:63/D-10:72), Library of Congress.

1. See GBM to Halleck, Sept. 15, 1862, 10:00 A.M., note 2, *supra*.

To Henry W. Halleck [TELEGRAM]

General H. W. Halleck
General in Chief

Head Quarters, Army of the Potomac,
[Sharpsburg] Sept. 30 10 am 1862

From all the information I can obtain I am satisfied that the mass of the Rebel Army has left Martinsburg and marched for Winchester where it is said they will make a stand and await our approach.

They have been forcing every man they could find capable of bearing arms into their ranks. They have compelled the farmers to bring their grain to their Army and they have thereby caused great dissatisfaction among the people of Northern Virginia.

Geo. B. McClellan
Maj Genl

Retained copy, McClellan Papers (C-16:65), Library of Congress. *OR,* Ser. 1, XIX, Part 2, p. 371.

To Mary Ellen McClellan

[Sharpsburg] Oct 1 [1862] 7.30 am.

. . . A cloudy day. If it does not rain I think I will go to Wmsport & Hagerstown today — to see that part of the country, for there is no telling but that I might have to fight a battle there one of these days & it is very convenient to know the ground. In this last battle the rebels possessed an immense advantage in knowing every part of the ground, while I knew only what I could see from a distance. . . .

I rode all over the battle field again yesterday — so as to be sure that I understand it all before writing my report. I was but the more impressed with the great difficulties of the undertaking & the magnitude of the success. Did I tell you that our losses at South Mt & Antietam amounted to within one or two hundred of 15,000, that we took some 6000 prisoners, 39 colors, 14 guns, 14,500 small arms etc etc. Pretty fair trophies after a battle so stubbornly contested. . . .

Yesterday I received at last a telegram from Halleck about the battle of Antietam[1]. . . .

I don't know where we are drifting but do not like the looks of things — time will show. . . .

I do not yet know what are the military plans of the gigantic intellects at the head of the Govt! . . .

AL copy, McClellan Papers (C-7:63), Library of Congress.

1. Halleck telegraphed on Sept. 30: "Your report of yesterday giving the results of the battles of South Mountain and Antietam has been received and submitted to the president. These were hard fought battles but well earned and decided victories. The valor and endurance of your army in the several conflicts . . . are creditable alike to the troops & to the officers who commanded them. A grateful country while mourning the lamented dead will not be unmindful of the honors due the living." McClellan Papers (A-81:32).

To Henry W. Halleck [TELEGRAM]

Maj. Gen. Halleck
General in Chief, Washington

Head Quarters, Army of the Potomac,
[Sharpsburg] October 1 1862 11 a.m.

I take it for granted that we will hereafter hold Harper's Ferry as a permanent arrangement, whatever line of operations may be adopted for the main Army. In this event a permanent and reliable bridge is needed there across the Shenandoah. Mr. Roebling[1] can build a double track suspension bridge on the existing piers in three or four weeks. The wire is now in possession of government and the cost will be some five thousand dollars ($5000) besides the wire. No pontoon nor trestle bridge can be made to resist the freshets. I ask authority to have this work undertaken at once. I would also renew the recommendation that a permanent wagon bridge be made across the Potomac at Harper's Ferry.[2] This without reference to the future operations of the main Army, but simply as a necessity for the proper defence of Harper's Ferry itself.[3]

G B McClellan
Major Genl Comdg

Retained copy, McClellan Papers (C-18:65), Library of Congress. *OR,* Ser. 1, XIX, Part 1, p. 10.

1. Bridge builder John A. Roebling. 2. See GBM to Halleck, Sept. 24, 10:00 P.M., *supra.* 3. Halleck replied on this date that "the Government does not contemplate the delay in your movements for the length of time required to build permanent bridges." He repeated his view that the army should cross downstream from Harper's Ferry "and compel the enemy to fall back or to give you battle," an operation that should be started at once. *OR,* Ser. 1, XIX, Part 1, p. 10.

To Mary Ellen McClellan

[Sharpsburg] Oct 2 [1862] am.

. . . I do think that man Halleck is the most stupid idiot I ever heard of — either that or he drinks hard — for he cannot even comprehend the English language.[1] . . .

I found the Presdt at Genl Sumner's qtrs at Harper's Ferry — none of the Cabinet were with him, merely some Western officers such as McClernand & others.[2] His ostensible purpose is to see the troops & the battle fields. I incline to think that the real purpose of his visit is to push me into a premature advance into Virginia. I may be mistaken, but think not. The real truth is that my army is not fit to advance — the old rgts are reduced to mere skeletons & are completely tired out — they need rest and filling up. The new rgts are not fit for the field. The remains of Pope's army are pretty well broken up & ought not to be made to fight for some little time yet. Cavalry & artillery horses are broken down — so it goes.

These people don't know what an army requires & therefore act stupidly. . . .

AL copy, McClellan Papers (C-7:63), Library of Congress.

1. Presumably this refers to the exchange of telegrams with Halleck the previous day. 2. On Oct. 1–4 President Lincoln visited the Army of the Potomac. Brig. Gen. John A. McClernand was among those in his party.

To Israel Washburn

Headquarters Army of the Potomac,
Camp near Sharpsburg, Md.,
October 4, 1862.

To His Excellency the Governor
of the State of Maine:
Sir,

In view of the reduced and shattered condition of the Seventh Regiment of Maine Volunteers, the result of arduous service and exposure during the campaigns on the Peninsula and in Maryland, I made on the 2d inst. a special application to the War Department that the regiment should be sent to report to you in Maine, that it might be recruited and reorganized under your personal supervision.[1] I yesterday received the necessary authority, as you will observe by the copy of Special Order No. 271 from these headquarters, inclosed herein. I send the regiment to you for the purpose indicated. I beg that when this purpose shall have been accomplished, that the regiment may be ordered to report to me with all practical dispatch.

In returning this gallant remnant of a noble body of men, whose bravery has been exhibited on every field almost in the campaigns cited, to the State whose pride it is to have sent them forth, I feel happy that it has been in my power to signify, even in this insufficient manner, my appreciation of their services and of their value to this army, and I will venture on the latter account to ask your Excellency's best endeavors to fill at once their diminished ranks, that I may again see their standard in the Army of the Potomac.[2] I am, with much respect,

Your obedient sevant,
Geo. B. McClellan
Major-General, U.S.A.

Thomas W. Hyde, *Following the Greek Cross or, Memories of the Sixth Army Corps* (Boston, 1895), pp. 110–11.

1. In his telegram to Adj. Gen. Thomas on Oct. 2, GBM noted that the 7th Maine was reduced to sixty-five men. McClellan Papers (A-82:33), Library of Congress. 2. The regiment returned to the Army of the Potomac in February 1863.

To Mary Ellen McClellan

[Sharpsburg] Oct 5th [1862] Sunday 7.30 am

. . . The Presdt left us about 11 yesterday morning. I went with him as far as over the battle field of South Mtn & on my way thither was quite surprised to meet Mr. Aspinwall en route to my camp. . . .

The Presdt was very kind personally — told me he was convinced I was the best general in the country etc etc. He was very affable & I really think he does feel very kindly towards me personally. I showed him the battle fields & am sure he departed with a more vivid idea of the great difficulty of the task we had accomplished. Mr. Aspinwall is decidedly of the opinion that it is my duty to submit to the Presdt's proclamation & quietly continue doing my duty as a soldier. I presume he is right & am at least sure that he is honest in his opinion. I shall surely give his views full consideration. He is of the opinion that the nation cannot stand the burdens of the war much longer & that a speedy solution is necessary — in this he is no doubt correct — & I hope sincerely that another successful battle may conclude my part of the work. I will try to find time to think over the whole affair today & tonight, & do my best to hit upon some plan of campaign that will enable me to drive the rebels entirely away from this part of the country forever.

AL copy, McClellan Papers (C-7:63), Library of Congress.

To William H. Aspinwall

Head-Quarters Army of the Potomac,
Camp near Sharpsburg Oct 5 1862

My dear Sir

Will you allow me to present to you the accompanying piece of the color staff of the flag of a Texas Regt of Hood's Brigade. The color & staff were captured by the U.S. Army of the Potomac at the battle of the Antietam Sept 17 1862. The staff was broken by a ball — the colors are deposited at Washington.

Please accept this staff as a slight token of my personal friendship for you & as a memento of our trip over the field of Antietam today.

Very truly & sincerely your friend
Geo B. McClellan
Maj Genl Comdg

W H Aspinwall Esq
New York

ALS, Miscellaneous Collections, Huntington Library.

To Robert E. Lee

Headquarters Army of the Potomac,
[Sharpsburg] October 5, 1862.

General R. E. Lee,
Commanding Army
of Northern Virginia:
General:

I have the honor to acknowledge the receipt of your letter of the 4th instant, inclosing a letter to Mrs. Philip Kearny, and, at the same time, committing to my care the sword, horse, and saddle of Major-General

Kearny, to the end that, in accordance with the expressed wish of Mrs. Kearny, they may be placed in her keeping.[1] The articles have been received, and, with the letter, will be forwarded to Mrs. Kearny by the earliest opportunity. I beg you to accept my thanks for your courteous and humane attention to the request of the widow of this lamented officer. I shall be happy to reciprocate the courtesy when circumstances shall place it in my power to do so.

Very respectfully, your obedient servant,
Geo. B. McClellan
Major-General, Commanding.

OR, Ser. 1, XIX, Part 2, p. 384.

1. Lee to McClellan, Oct. 4, *OR,* Ser. 1, XIX, Part 2, p. 381. Gen. Kearny was killed on Sept. 1 at the Battle of Chantilly. His body had been returned earlier.

To Henry W. Halleck [TELEGRAM]

Genl H. W. Halleck
Genl. in Chief

Head-Quarters, Army of the Potomac,
[Sharpsburg] Oct. 6, 4.30 pm 1862

Your telegram ordering Cox's division to Clarksburg was received before the one directing the movement across the Potomac.[1] Is it still intended that Cox shall march at once.

It is important in making my decision regarding the route to be taken by the Army that I should know 1st what description of troops I am to be reinforced with upon the Shenandoah route, and also upon the other route between the enemy & Washington, whether they are to be old or new troops or what proportion of each. If possible I should be glad to have Pecks division sent to me if it can be got here within a reasonable time.

2d Will you inform me what the present condition of the Alexandria and Leesburg Rail Road is, also the Manassas Gap Rail Road, and what time it would require to put them in working order.

It is believed that the Harpers Ferry & Winchester Rail Road is not materially injured.[2]

Geo. B. McClellan
Maj Genl

Retained copy, McClellan Papers (A-82:33), Library of Congress. *OR,* Ser. 1, XIX, Part 2, p. 387.

1. Halleck's telegram of this date ordered the Kanawha Division to western Virginia. *OR,* Ser. 1, XIX, Part 2, p. 387. Also on Oct. 6 Halleck telegraphed, in part: "The President directs that you cross the Potomac and give battle to the enemy or drive him south. Your army must move now while the roads are good. If you cross the river between the enemy and Washington, and cover the latter by your operations, you can be re-enforced with 30,000 men. If you move up the Valley of the Shenandoah, not more than 12,000 or 15,000

can be sent to you. The President advises the interior line, between Washington and the enemy, but does not order it.... I am directed to add that the Secretary of War and the General-in-Chief fully concur with the President...." *OR*, Ser. 1, XIX, Part 1, p. 72. 2. Halleck replied on Oct. 7: "Cox's division must go west at once. [Peck's] division is at Yorktown and Suffolk. The Manassas Gap road can be repaired in a few days. The Leesburg road is much more injured. Your army can reach the former in less time than would be required to repair the latter. The troops to be sent you will be partly new and partly old — mostly new." *OR*, Ser. 1, XIX, Part 2, p. 393.

To Mary Ellen McClellan

[Sharpsburg] Oct 7 [1862] 8 am.

... I yesterday afternoon received orders to advance & attack the enemy or drive him south (this is confidential). I can't go far for the reason that I cannot carry many supplies. So far as I can see the little campaign can't last many days for when it is once fought some other line of operations will have to be taken as the one up here leads to no final result.

AL copy, McClellan Papers (C-7:63), Library of Congress.

To Henry W. Halleck [TELEGRAM]

[Sharpsburg, October 7, 1862, 1 P.M.]

After a full consultation with the Corps Commanders in my vicinity I have determined to adopt the line of the Shenandoah for immediate operations against the enemy now near Winchester. On no other line north of Washn can the Army be supplied nor can it on any other cover Maryland and Penna. Were we to cross the river below the mouth of the Shenandoah we would leave it in the power of the enemy to recross into Maryland & thus check the movement. In the same case we would voluntarily give him the advantage of the strong line of the Shenandoah no point of which could be reached by us in advance of him. I see no objective point of strategical value to be gained or sought for by a movement between the Shenandoah & Washn. I wish to state distinctly that I do not regard the line of the Shenandoah valley as important for ulterior objects — it is important only so long as the enemy remains near Winchester & we cannot follow that line far beyond that point simply because the country is destitute of supplies & we have not sufficient means of transportation to enable us to advance more than 20 or 25 miles beyond a railway or canal terminus. If the enemy abandons Winchester & falls back upon Staunton it will be impossible for us to pursue him by that route, & we must then take a new line of operations based upon water or railway communication. The only possible object to be gained by an advance from this vicinity is to fight the enemy near Winchester — if they retreat we have nothing to gain by pursuing them, & in fact cannot do so to any great distance. The objects I propose to myself are to fight the enemy if they remain near Winchester, or failing in that to force them to abandon the valley of the Shenandoah — then to adopt a new & decisive line of operations which shall strike at the heart of the rebellion.

I have taken all possible measures to insure the most prompt equipment of the troops, but from all that I can learn it will be at least three days before the 1st, 5th & 6th Corps are in condition to move from their present camps — they need shoes & other indispensible articles of clothing, as well as shelter tents &c. I beg to assure you that not an hour shall be lost in carrying your instructions into effect.

Please send the reinforcements to Harper's Ferry — I would prefer that the new regts be sent as regts — not brigaded — unless already done so with old troops. I would again ask for Peck's Div & if possible Heintzelman's Corps. If the enemy give battle near Winchester it will be a desperate affair, requiring all our resources.

I hope that no time will be lost in sending forward the reinforcements, that I may get them in hand as soon as possible.

G B McC

Maj Genl H W Halleck
Washn

ALS (telegram sent), McClellan Papers (A-83 :33), Library of Congress. *OR,* Ser. 1, XIX, Part 1, pp. 11–12.

To Abraham Lincoln [TELEGRAM]

Hd Quarters Army Potomac
The President, U.S. [Sharpsburg, October] 7th [1862, 11:35 P.M.]

I have issued the following order on your proclamation.

"Hd Quarters Army Potomac Camp near Sharpsburg Md Oct 7th 1862 Genl Order No. 163. The attention of the officers & soldiers of the Army of the Potomac is called to Genl Order No. 139 War Dept Sept 24th 1862, publishing to the Army the Presidents proclamation of Sept 22d.[1]

A proclamation of such grave moment to the Nation officially communicated to the Army affords to the Genl Commanding an opportunity of defining specifically to the officers & soldiers under his Command the relation borne by all persons in the Military service of the U.S. towards the Civil Authorities of the Government. The Constitution confides to the Civil Authorities legislative judicial and executive, the power and duty of making expounding & executing the federal laws. Armed forces are raised & supported simply to sustain the Civil Authorities and are to be held in strict subordination thereto in all respects. This fundamental rule of our political system is essential to the security of our Republican Institutions & should be thoroughly understood & observed by every soldier. The principle upon which & the objects for which Armies shall be employed in suppressing Rebellion must be determined & declared by the Civil Authorities and the Chief Executive, who is charged with the administration of the National affairs, is the proper & only source through which the views & orders of the Government can be made known to the Armies of the Nation. Discussions by officers & soldiers concerning public measures determined upon and declared by the Government when carried at all beyond temperate and respectful expressions of opinion tend greatly to impair & destroy the discipline & efficiency of troops by substituting the spirit of political faction for that firm steady & earnest support of the Authority of the Government which is the highest duty of the American soldier. The remedy for political error if any are committed is to be found only in the action of the people at the polls. In thus calling the attention of this Army to the true relation between the soldiers and the Government the Genl Commanding merely adverts to an evil against which it has been thought advisable during our whole history to guard the Armies of the Republic & in so doing he will [not] be considered by any right minded person as casting any reflection upon that loyalty & good conduct which has been so fully illustrated upon so many battle fields. In carrying out all measures of public policy this Army will of course be guided by the same rules of mercy and Christianity that have ever controlled its conduct toward the defenceless.

By Command of Maj Genl McClellan. James Hardie Lt Col Aide de Camp Acting Ajt. A Genl."

Geo B McClellan
M.G. Comdg

Received copy, Lincoln Papers, Library of Congress. *OR*, Ser. 1, XIX, Part 2, p. 395.

1. The preliminary Emancipation Proclamation.

To Henry W. Halleck [TELEGRAM]

Major Genl Halleck
General in Chief Washington

Head Quarters, Army of the Potomac,
[Knoxville, Md.] Oct 10, 1862, 10 pm

Every disposition has been made to cut off the retreat of the enemy's cavalry that today made the raid into Maryland and Pennsylvania.

G. B. McClellan
Maj Genl Comdg

Retained copy, McClellan Papers (C-18:65), Library of Congress. *OR*, Ser. 1, XIX, Part 2, p. 59.

To Henry W. Halleck [TELEGRAM]

Genl H. W. Halleck
Genl-in-Chief

Head Quarters, Army of the Potomac,
[Knoxville] October 11 9 am 1862

An engine has been sent from Hagerstown towards Chambersburg this morning and I shall probably hear from there in a short time. I have made such disposition of troops along the river that I think we will intercept the rebels on their return. All of my available Cavalry was ordered in pursuit last night but as yet nothing has been heard from it.

Cox's division is loaded in cars at Hancock with Cavalry well out towards the Penna. line, and if the rebels attempt to return above Hancock that division will be certain to intercept them. If they attempt to cross below Hancock I have infantry at or near all the different fords.

I have six Regiments of Cavalry now up the river between Hancock and Cumberland. All of these troops have been ordered to keep a sharp lookout for the return of the rebels.

The force which crossed the river I learn from several different sources consists of four Regiments of Cavalry with four guns (about 2500 men). I have given every order necessary to insure the capture or destruction of these forces, and I hope we may be able to teach them a lesson they will not soon forget. The great difficulty we labor under is the want of Cavalry, as many of our horses are overworked and unserviceable.

We have been making every effort to get supplies of clothing for this Army, and Colonel Ingalls[1] has received advices that it has been forwarded by rail road. But owing to bad management on the Roads or from some other cause it comes in very slowly and it will take a much longer time than was anticipated to get articles that are absolutely indispensable to the Army unless the Rail Road managers forward supplies more rapidly.

Geo. B. McClellan
Maj Genl

Retained copy, McClellan Papers (C-16:65), Library of Congress. *OR*, Ser. 1, XIX, Part 2, p. 66.

1. Lt. Col. Rufus Ingalls, chief quartermaster of the Army of the Potomac.

To Henry W. Halleck [TELEGRAM]

Maj Gen H. W. Halleck
Com in Chief, Washington

Head Quarters, Army of the Potomac,
[Knoxville] Oct. 11th 1862 [3:30 P.M.]

I am compelled again to call your attention to the great deficiency of shoes & other indispensable articles of clothing that still exists in some of the Corps of this Army. Upon the assurances of the Chf Qtr Master who based his calculations upon information rec'd from Washington that clothing would be forwarded at certain times, Corps commanders sent their wagons to Hagerstown & Harper's Ferry for it. It did not arrive as promised & has not yet arrived. Unless some measures are taken to insure the prompt forwarding of these supplies there will necessarily be a corresponding delay in getting the Army ready to move, as the men cannot march without shoes. Everything has been done that can be done at these Head Qtrs to accomplish the desired result.

G. B. McClellan
Maj Genl Comdg

LS (telegram sent), McClellan Papers (C-16:65), Library of Congress. *OR*, Ser. 1, XIX, Part 1, p. 12.

To Henry W. Halleck [TELEGRAM]

Major General Halleck
General in Chief

Head Quarters, Army of the Potomac,
[Knoxville] October 12, 1862 12.45 pm

It is absolutely necessary that some energetic means be taken to supply the cavalry of this Army with remount horses. The present rate of supply is (1050) ten hundred and fifty per week,[1] for the entire Army here and in front of Washington. From this number the Artillery draw for their batteries.[2]

Geo. B. McClellan
Maj. Genl. Comdg.

Retained copy, McClellan Papers (C-16:65), Library of Congress. *OR*, Ser. 1, XIX, Part 1, p. 13.

1. As the telegram was received at the War Dept., due to a telegrapher's error this figure was written as 150. Records of the Office of the Secretary of War, RG 107 (M-473:50), National Archives. 2. Halleck replied on Oct. 14: "I have caused the matters complained of in your telegrams of the 11th and 12th to be investigated. I am now informed by the Quartermaster-General that every requisition from you for shoes and clothing had been filled and the articles forwarded as directed. . . ." He enclosed a report from Quartermaster General Meigs that an average of 1,459 horses had been supplied in each of the previous six weeks, and that the total number of animals with GBM's army was 31,000. "It is believed that your present proportion of cavalry and of animals is much larger than that of any other of our armies," Halleck wrote. *OR*, Ser. 1, XIX, Part 1, p. 15.

To Henry W. Halleck [TELEGRAM]

General H. W. Halleck
Genl in Chief

Head Quarters, Army of the Potomac,
[Knoxville] October 12 5 pm 1862

The Rebel Cavalry under Stuart which left Chambersburg yesterday morning in the direction of Gettysburg reached the Potomac near the mouth of the Monocacy at about 9 a.m. today having marched about one hundred miles in twenty four hours. General Stoneman who was at Poolsville near where they passed was ordered by telegraph at 1 o'clock p.m. yesterday to keep his cavalry well out on all the different approaches from the direction of Frederick so as to give him time to mass his forces to resist their re-crossing into Virginia.[1]

As you will see from the dispatch of Genl Pleasonton just received and herewith transmitted it does not appear that he complied with this order.[2] He will be called upon for an explanation of this matter.[3] It would seem that Pleasonton's forces although within a short distance of Poolsville received but little assistance from Stoneman.

Geo. B. McClellan
Maj. Genl.

Retained copy, McClellan Papers (C-16:65), Library of Congress. *OR*, Ser. 1, XIX, Part 2, p. 30.

1. Marcy to Stoneman, Oct. 11, *OR*, Ser. 1, XIX, Part 2, pp. 76–77. Brig. Gen. George Stoneman commanded a division of the Third Corps. 2. Pleasonton reported at 1:30 P.M. on this date that he had skirmished with the enemy cavalry but could not prevent them recrossing the Potomac. "There was no artillery at this point, and, with the exception of a few infantry companies, I had no assistance." *OR*, Ser. 1, XIX, Part 2, p. 30. 3. Marcy to Stoneman, Oct. 12, *OR*, Ser. 1, LI, Part 1, pp. 881–82. Stoneman replied on Oct. 13 that with thirty miles of the Potomac to cover he considered his dispositions judicious, but they were "rendered nugatory by the rapidity and uncertainty of the enemy's movements." *OR*, Ser. 1, XIX, Part 2, pp. 42–44.

To Henry W. Halleck [TELEGRAM]

Gen H W Halleck
Gen in Chief

Hd Qrs Army of Potomac
[Knoxville] Oct. 13 [1862] 7.30 p.m.

The recent raid of Stuart who in spite of all the precautions I could take with the means at my disposal went entirely around this Army has shown most conclusively how greatly the service suffers from our deficiency in the Cavalry Arm. The great extent of the River line from Washn to Cumberland the major portion of which in the present stage of water is fordable at almost every point renders it necessary to scatter our Cavalry for a very great distance in order to watch the numerous crossings. At the time Stuart crossed it so happened that the greater part of our Cavalry was absent near Cumberland in pursuit of another Rebel Cavalry force which had made its appearance at the Little Cacapon and other points on the upper Potomac destroying RR bridges etc. I had pickets at McCoy's Ferry where Stuart crossed but they were captured by his men and in consequence of this I did not learn of the crossing for some hours afterwards. All the Cavalry that could be collected to pursue Stuart only amounted to less than one thousand men. With these Pleasonton marched seventy eight miles in twenty four hours with a horse battery but only came up with Stuart at the Potomac after he had marched over ninety miles during the same time with change of horses.

The track of the Rebels was entirely outside of our Infantry until he came near Gen Stoneman at Poolesville who has not as yet explained why he did not mass his troops and engage him as he was ordered. The rapid movement of the rebel Cavalry precluded the possibility of marching our Infantry from any point of our lines with a probability of intercepting them. Cavalry is the only description of force that can prevent these raids. Our Cavalry has been constantly occupied in scouting and reconnaissances and this severe labor has worked down the horses and rendered many of them unserviceable so that at this time no more than one half of our Cavalry are fit for active service in the field. The enemy is well provided with Cavalry while our Cavalry force even with every man well mounted would be inadequate to the requirement of the service and to the large Infantry force with the Army. I therefore again most strenuously urge upon the Dept the imperative necessity of at once supplying this Army including the command of Gen Banks with a sufficient number of horses to remount every dismounted Cavalry soldier within the shortest possible time. If this is not done we shall be constantly exposed to Rebel Cavalry raids.[1]

Geo B McClellan
Maj Genl

Received copy, Records of the Office of the Secretary of War, RG 107 (M-473 :50), National Archives. *OR,* Ser. 1, XIX, Part 2, p. 417.

1. Halleck replied on Oct. 14 that "the Government has been, and is, making every possible effort to increase the cavalry force.... The President has read your telegram, and directs me to suggest that, if the enemy had more occupation south of the river, his cavalry would not be so likely to make raids north of it." *OR,* Ser. 1, XIX, Part 2, p. 421.

To Henry W. Halleck [TELEGRAM]

Genl. H. W. Halleck
Genl-in-Chief

Head Quarters, Army of the Potomac,
[Knoxville] October 14 7 pm 1862

Your dispatch of today received.[1] The only force that could operate to the least advantage against such a force as has been reported near Leesburg is Cavalry. At the present time I have but one regiment available in addition to the one with Genl. Stoneman, and that one is needed in front of Harper's Ferry where I have but two weak squadrons. Moreover if I had a regiment or two more they would only be exposed to capture if they were sent across the river in the face of such a force as was reported to be there. Stoneman has been instructed to watch all the fords as high as the mouth of the Monocacy. I would suggest that a sufficient guard of Infantry & Artillery be sent from Washington to hold the fords from Great Falls to the Seneca Creek. This would enable Stoneman to concentrate his forces more upon his line.

With my small Cavalry force it is impossible for me to watch the line of the Potomac properly or even make the reconnaissances that are necessary for our movements. This makes it necessary for me to weaken my line very much by extending the infantry to guard the innumerable fords. This will continue until the river rises and it will be next to impossible to prevent the rebel Cavalry raids. My Cavalry force as I urged this morning should be largely & immediately increased under any hypothesis — whether to guard the river or advance on the enemy or both.

Geo. B. McClellan
Maj Genl

Retained copy, McClellan Papers (C-16 :65), Library of Congress. *OR,* Ser. 1, XIX, Part 2, pp. 421–22.

1. See GBM to Halleck, Oct. 13, note 1, *supra.*

To Abraham Lincoln

His Excellency the President
Sir

Head-Quarters Army Potomac,
Camp in Pleasant Valley Oct 17 1862

Your letter of the 13th inst reached me yesterday morning by the hands of Col Perkins.[1]

I had sent out strong reconnaissances early in the morning in the direction of Charlestown Leetown etc, & as sharp artillery firing was heard I felt it incumbent to go to the front. I did not leave Charlestown until dark so that I have been unable to give to your Excellency's letter that full & respectful consideration which it merits at my hands.

I do not wish to detain Col Perkins beyond this morning's train, I therefore think it best to send him back with this simple acknowledgment of the receipt of your Excellency's letter. I am not wedded to any particular plan of operations — I hope to have today reliable information as to the position of the enemy, whom I still believe to be between Bunker Hill and Winchester. I promise you that I will give to your views the fullest & most unprejudiced consideration, & that it is my intention to advance the moment my men are shod & my cavalry are sufficiently remounted to be serviceable.

Your Excellency may be assured that I will not adopt a course which differs at all from your views without first fully explaining my reasons & giving you time to issue such instructions as may seem best to you.

I am Sir very respectfully your obdt Servant
Geo B McClellan
Maj Gen USA

ALS, Lincoln Papers, Library of Congress. *OR,* Ser. 1, XIX, Part 1, p. 16.

1. In a long and carefully reasoned letter dated Oct. 13, delivered to GBM by Col. Delavan D. Perkins, Lincoln outlined his views on the Army of the Potomac's future operations. "You remember my speaking to you of what I called your over-cautiousness," he wrote. "Are you not over-cautious when you assume that you can not do what the enemy is constantly doing? Should you not claim to be at least his equal in prowess, and act upon the claim?" If the Confederate army in the Shenandoah Valley could subsist far from a railhead, he asked, why could not GBM advance beyond his own rail supply line? To wait for railroad construction "ignores the question of *time,* which can not, and must not be ignored." He proposed that the Army of the Potomac advance swiftly on a line east of the Blue Ridge, by which it should reach Richmond before the enemy. "His route is the arc of a circle, while yours is the chord." Should Lee instead cross the Potomac and march on Pennsylvania, GBM would be squarely on his supply line, "and you have nothing to do but to follow, and ruin him...." If Lee moved toward Richmond to protect his communications, the president wrote, "I would press closely to him, fight him if a favorable opportunity should present, and, at least, try to beat him to Richmond on the inside track. I say 'try'; if we never try, we shall never succeed." After reviewing in detail the advantages of the route he suggested, he concluded by saying, "It is all easy if our troops march as well as the enemy; and it is unmanly to say they can not do it. This letter is in no sense an order." *Collected Works of Lincoln,* V, pp. 460–61.

To Henry W. Halleck [TELEGRAM]

Head Quarters,
Army of the Potomac,
[Pleasant Valley] Oct 17th 1862

Maj. Gen. H. W. Halleck
Commander in Chief, Washington

As the draft is now in progress in some of the States I beg to recall to your attention the necessity of filling up the old regiments at the earliest possible moment, and to urge that the first results of the draft be at once applied towards accomplishing this object, which will so greatly and so rapidly increase the efficiency of this Army.[1]

Geo B McClellan
Maj Gen Comdg

LS (telegram sent), McClellan Papers (C-16:65), Library of Congress. *OR,* Ser. 1, XIX, Part 2, p. 439.

1. These were drafts of militia to meet any shortfall in a state's quota of volunteers.

To Samuel L. M. Barlow

Head-Quarters Army of the Potomac,
[Pleasant Valley] Oct 17 1862

My dear Barlow

Your letter of the 14th has just reached me — I cry peccavi & bow down submissively under the weight of your righteous indignation — hit me again & I won't murmur — except a confession that I have been very wrong in so long neglecting to write to so good a friend as you are. The cause of the omission has by no means been that I have forgotten you — but the truth is that I have very little time or inclination to write. When I manage to write to my wife I feel that a great feat has been accomplished, & I am in these days even too lazy to telegraph except by proxy.

I am much obliged to you for Van Buren's speech — which one of these days I hope to have leisure to read.[1] I am *rather* glad to hear this morning that the democrats have carried Penna[2] — the only trouble about their carrying N.Y. also may be in the rather ultra tone of Seymour's first speech. If N.Y. goes democratic some of our dear friends in Washn will feel a little crest fallen. I must confess a double motive for desiring the defeat of Wadsworth — I have so thorough a contempt for the man & regard him as such a vile traitorous miscreant that I do not wish to see the great state of N.Y. disgraced by having such a thing at its head.[3]

I should have been glad to have seen *that* meeting incognito — no doubt it was very exciting.

My wife is with me here — in a quiet old fashioned little farm house near my camp — Mrs Marcy is also here & we are having a very quiet & pleasant time all by ourselves.

Lee is still near Winchester & will probably remain there until I am prepared to move upon him — I am badly in need of two things now, besides men — viz: horses & shoes for the men — I hope for still further success when I next advance.

Now don't wait for answers from me — write when you feel in the humor, & I will try to be a better correspondent in the future — in any event never doubt my sincere friendship for you, & don't get any absurd notions in your head because I seldom write. Why, man alive, I have not written to my own Mother for nearly a year! — I haven't written to my wife for more than a week. With my kindest regards to the Madame in which my wife & Mrs M join

I am sincerely your friend
Geo B McClellan

S L M B. Q. A. D. X. K. Barlow Esq[4]
New York City

ALS, Barlow Papers, Huntington Library.

1. No doubt the speech of New York Democratic state chairman John Van Buren, delivered to a meeting on Oct. 13 that ratified the party's nominees for the state elections. 2. The Pennsylvania election for congressional seats and state offices was held on Oct. 14. 3. In New York's gubernatorial election Democrat Horatio Seymour was opposed by Republican James S. Wadsworth. Wadsworth had served in the Army of the Potomac and as military governor in Washington. The election, on Nov. 4, went to Seymour. 4. GBM often teased Barlow on his use of initials.

To Henry W. Halleck

Head Qrs Army of the Potomac
October 18th 1862

General,

Your letter of the 14th inst, enclosing a copy of one to you of the same date from the Quarter Master General, has been received.[1]

In this letter you say you are informed by the Quarter Master General that every requisition from me for Shoes and Clothing has been filled, and the articles forwarded as directed. General Meigs may have ordered these articles to be forwarded, but they have not yet reached our Depots; and unless greater effort to insure prompt transmission is made by the Department of which General Meigs is the head, they might as well remain in New York or Philadelphia so far as this Army is concerned.

I am officially informed by one Corps Commander that there is a deficiency of five thousand pairs of Shoes in the amount he called for; and other commanders are continually making similar complaints. The soldiers of this Army have for some time past been suffering for Clothing, and I am constrained to believe it in a great degree owing to the want of proper action on the part of the Quarter Master's Department.

Genl Meigs states further that the Army of the Potomac has, since the battles in front of Washington, received 9254 horses to replace losses; and in this connection inquires most seriously if there is an instance of record of such drain and destruction of horses.

When I marched this Army from Washington on the 8th day of September, it was greatly deficient in Cavalry horses, — the hard service to which they had been subjected in front of Washington having rendered about one half of them unserviceable. Nearly all the horses that this Army has received since then have been to replace those that were broken down at that time; but there have not been anything like the number named by the Quarter Master General. The following statement furnished at my order by Lt Col Myers, Asst Chf Qr Master, gives the actual number of horses received by this Army since September 8th 1862 —

By Capt. J. C. Crane, A.Q.M. Frederick	
Horses from Frederick	732
By Capt. Weeks, A.Q.M. Hagerstown	
Horses from Hagerstown	134
By Capt. Pitkin, A.Q.M. Harpers Ferry	
Horses from Washington	201
By Capt. Bliss, A.Q.M. Harpers Ferry	
Horses from Washington	498
By Capt. J. B. Howard, A.Q.M. Hd Qr	
Horses from Washington	399
Total Rec'd Horses	1964
So stated by Quarter Mas. Genl	9254
Difference	7290

From this statement it will be seen that the total number of horses received by this Army since the commencement of the present campaign is only 1964 — 7290 less than the number given by the Quarter Master General. Of those delivered, very many were totally unfitted for the service, and should never have been received. General Pleasonton Comdg a Cavalry Division, says in a report made yesterday. — "The horses now purchased for Cavalry service are much inferior to those first obtained, and are not suitable for the hard service of Cavalry Horses."[2]

I am very respectfully your obt servt
Geo B McClellan
Maj Genl U.S.A.

Major Genl Halleck

LS, Records of the Adjutant General's Office, RG 94 (159: Halleck Papers), National Archives. *OR,* Ser. 1, XIX, Part 1, pp. 16–17.

1. See GBM to Halleck, Oct. 12, 12:45 P.M., note 2, *supra.* 2. Gen. Meigs reported at length to Halleck on Oct. 21, and by telegram to GBM on Oct. 22, that inefficient transportation and the failure to unload supplies at the army's depots were the primary causes of the delays. As to the supplying of horses, he said that by order they had only been issued under GBM's authorization, and the "missing" horses must have gone to the forces at Washington. "Had you so ordered, not less than 10,000 so distributed to troops under your command would have been sent to Harper's Ferry or Frederick." *OR,* Ser. 1, XIX, Part 1, pp. 17–20, Part 2, pp. 464–65.

To Augustus W. Bradford

Head Quarters
Army of the Potomac
Pleasant Valley Md.
October 18th 1862

To His Excellency A. W. Bradford,
Governor of Maryland
Governor:

I have the honor to acknowledge the receipt of your Excellency's Order of September 29th,[1] in which you advert in such flattering terms to the conduct of this Army in the recent battles fought upon the soil of your State.

It was with the utmost pride and gratification that I received this most prompt acknowledgement of the skill of the Officers and the gallantry of the men of the Army of the Potomac; we felt it all the more deeply because it emanated from the Executive of the State whose inhabitants had witnessed our efforts, and whose fields were rescued from the invader.

Your praise will stimulate this Army to renewed efforts in the sacred cause of the Union.

Permit me, Governor, in the name of the Army of the Potomac, to thank you for your appreciation of its victories.

With the sincere hope and belief that no Rebel Army shall again pollute the loyal State of Maryland, and committing to you as a sacred trust, the remains of our gallant comrades who now rest beneath its soil

I am, Governor, with high respect Your obedient Servant
Geo. B. McClellan
Maj. Genl. U.S.A.

Copy, Bradford Papers, Maryland Historical Society Library.

1. McClellan Papers (A-81:32), Library of Congress.

To Henry W. Halleck [TELEGRAM]

Maj. Gen. H. W. Halleck
Comdr in Chief, Washington

Head Quarters, Army of the Potomac,
[Pleasant Valley] Oct. 21st 1862

Since the receipt of the President's order to move on the enemy I have been making every exertion to get this Army supplied with clothing absolutely necessary for marching. This I am happy to say is now nearly accomplished. I have also during the same time repeatedly urged upon you the importance of supplying Cavalry and Artillery horses to replace those broken down by hard service, and steps have been taken to insure a prompt delivery. Our Cavalry even when well supplied with horses is much inferior in numbers to that of the enemy, but in efficiency has proved itself superior. So forcibly has this been impressed upon our old Cavalry Regts by repeated successes that the men are fully persuaded that they are equal to twice their number of rebel Cavalry.

Exclusive of the Cavalry force now engaged in picketing the river, I have not at present over about one thousand (1000) horses for service. Officers have been sent in various directions to purchase horses, & I expect them soon. Without more Cavalry horses our communications from the moment we march would be at the mercy of the large Cavalry forces of the enemy, and it would not be possible for us to cover our flanks properly or to obtain the necessary information of the position & movements of the enemy in such a way as to insure success. My experience has shown the necessity of a large & efficient Cavalry force. Under the foregoing circumstances I beg leave to ask whether the President desires me to march on the enemy at once, or to await the reception of the new horses, every possible step having been taken to insure their prompt arrival.[1]

Geo B McClellan
Maj Genl Comdg

LS (telegram sent), McClellan Papers (C-16:65), Library of Congress. *OR,* Ser. 1, XIX, Part 1, p. 81.

1. Halleck replied at 3:00 P.M. that the president "directs me to say that he has no change to make in his order of the 6th instant. If you have not been and are not now in condition to obey it, you will be able to show such want of ability. The President does not expect impossibilities, but he is very anxious that all this good weather should not be wasted in inactivity." *OR,* Ser. 1, XIX, Part 1, p. 81.

To Montgomery C. Meigs [TELEGRAM]

Brig. Genl. M. C. Meigs
Qtr Mastr Genl U.S.A.
Washington DC

Head Qtrs Army Potomac
[Pleasant Valley] Oct 22d 1862

Your dispatch of this date received.[1] I have never intended in any letter or dispatch to make any accusation against yourself or your department for not furnishing or forwarding clothing as rapidly as it was possible for you to do. I believe that everything has been done that could be done in this respect both by yourself and the Dept. The idea that I have tried to convey was that certain portions of the command were without clothing and the Army could not move until it was supplied.

G B McClellan
Maj Genl Comdg

Retained copy, McClellan Papers (A-85:34), Library of Congress. *OR*, Ser. 1, XIX, Part 1, pp. 9–10.

1. See GBM to Halleck, Oct. 18, note 2, *supra*.

To Henry W. Halleck [TELEGRAM]

Head Quarters, Army of the Potomac,
Pleasant Valley Oct 22 1862 [2:30 P.M.]

Your dispatch of the 22nd (twenty second) [October 21] is received.[1] After full consultation I have decided to move upon the line indicated by the Presdt in his letter of the 13th inst[2] and have accordingly taken steps to execute the movement. I will inform you from time to time of the occupation of Leesburg, Hillsboro', Snickersville etc. I shall need all the cavalry & other reinforcements you can send me from Washington.

G B McClellan
Maj Genl

Maj Genl Halleck
Genl in Chief Washington D.C.

ALS (telegram sent), McClellan Papers (C-15:64), Library of Congress. *OR*, Ser. 1, XIX, Part 2, p. 464.

1. See GBM to Halleck, Oct. 21, note 1, *supra*. 2. See GBM to Lincoln, Oct. 17, note 1, *supra*.

To Henry W. Halleck [TELEGRAM]

Head Quarters, Army of the Potomac,
Pleasant Valley Oct 24th 1862 [3:30 P.M.]

Referring to your telegram of 3.30 pm yesterday I understand the (20,000) twenty thousand reinforcements to be made up of Heintzelman

& Sigel's Corps.[1] Am I right in this or do you intend giving me (20,000) twenty thousand men in addition to these two Corps?[2]

If some of Bayard's Cavalry could join me by way of Leesburg it would expedite my movement considerably.[3] The trouble will be with the cavalry. I expect large numbers of horses early in the week. Of course I shall not wait for a complete remount.

G B McClellan
Maj Genl

Maj Genl Halleck
Genl in Chief Washington DC

ALS (telegram sent), McClellan Papers (C-15:64), Library of Congress. *OR*, Ser. 1, XIX, Part 2, p. 476.

1. Halleck had proposed in an Oct. 23 telegram to reinforce GBM with the corps of Heintzelman and Sigel from Washington, to join him by way of the Manassas Gap Railroad at Thoroughfare Gap in the Bull Run Mountains. *OR*, Ser. 1, XIX, Part 2, p. 470. 2. Halleck replied the next day that the figure of 20,000 men represented the two corps. *OR*, Ser. 1, XIX, Part 2, p. 483. 3. Brig. Gen. George D. Bayard commanded a cavalry brigade in the Third Corps.

To Henry W. Halleck

Brig Genl H W Halleck
Genl in Chief USA
General

Head-Quarters Army of the Potomac,
Pleasant Valley Oct 24 1862

Your letter of the 20th reached me only this morning.[1] As I stated in my dispatch of last evening[2] I had not contemplated the erection of other than field works in the vicinity of Harper's Ferry. On the heights there is little or no earth & the only recourse is to build blockhouses of dry or loose stone & timber. I have advocated the defence of Harper's Ferry on account of its importance in covering the line of the Potomac & not as a base of operations.

I hope that the boats will all be in position today for the construction of a bridge at Berlin. As soon as the bridge is finished I will place Stoneman at Leesburg, & occupy Waterford & Hillsboro. I will thus be in position, as soon as my cavalry is in reasonably good condition, to bring down the three Corps now near Sharpsburg & to effect rapidly the junction with Genls Heintzelman & Sigel as you propose. I think the occupation of Thorofare Gap a wise measure.

This will be handed to you by my aide de camp Lt Col Colburn who can explain to you the general state of affairs here, & who will receive your views as to the troops to be left in garrison at Harper's Ferry.

AL retained copy, McClellan Papers (A-85:34), Library of Congress.

1. In his letter of Oct. 20 Halleck rejected the idea of anything more elaborate than field works for the defense of Harper's Ferry. "Harper's Ferry is not, in my opinion, a proper

base of military operations, and it would be an error to expend time and money there for such an object." *OR,* Ser. 1, XIX, Part 2, p. 451. 2. GBM to Halleck, Oct. 23, *OR,* Ser. 1, XIX, Part 2, p. 469.

To Mary Ellen McClellan

[Pleasant Valley] Oct 25 [1862] am.

I hope my bridge at Berlin is finished & if so I can cross some troops today & shall be all ready to march the moment the cavalry is ready, which will be shortly. I don't think Lee will fight me nearer than Richmond — I expect no fight in this vicinity....

My report is at last finished & will I presume be copied today....

I see that there is much impatience throughout the country for a move — I am just as anxious as anyone, but am crippled by want of horses....

I sent Bishop McIlvaine[1] over to Harper's Ferry in my ambulance. He is accompanied by the Rev. Mr. Clements.

AL copy, McClellan Papers (C-7:63), Library of Congress.

1. Charles P. McIlvaine, Episcopal bishop of Ohio.

To Alexander S. Webb

Head-Quarters Army of the Potomac
[Pleasant Valley] Oct 25 1862

My dear Webb

I return herewith your Father's[1] letter which you were kind enough to send me. When you write to him tell him that I am most highly gratified by the kind feelings he entertains towards me, & that in the midst of the abuse with which I have been so roundly & frequently pursued it is indeed a comfort to find that I possess the good opinion of such a person as he is — it more than counterbalances the abuse.

I am sincerely your friend
Geo B McClellan

Col A S Webb

ALS, Alexander Stewart Webb Papers, Yale University Library. Lt. Col. Webb was chief of staff of the Fifth Corps.

1. James Watson Webb, minister to Brazil and former owner of the *New York Courier and Enquirer.*

To Albert V. Colburn [TELEGRAM]

[Pleasant Valley, October 25, 1862]

Remain as you propose. Explain to Genl Halleck exactly the condition of our cavalry & what measures have been taken to obtain horses promptly. Also that it is yet impossible for me to fix the exact time when I will be at the points agreed upon. I hope by Monday [October 27] to be able to fix the day.[1]

G B McClellan
Maj Genl

Lt Col A V Colburn
Washington DC

ALS (telegram sent), McClellan Papers (A-86 :34), Library of Congress. Lt. Col. Colburn was GBM's assistant adjutant general.

1. Colburn replied on this date that he had just seen Halleck. "There was no use of trying to explain matters to him because he would not listen to anything. When I spoke to him about the cavalry horses he said that that was the Quarter Masters business & he had nothing to do with it. I will try again but think it no use." McClellan Papers (A-86 :34).

To Abraham Lincoln [TELEGRAM]

Head Qrs Army of Potomac
His Excellency the President [Pleasant Valley] Oct. 25 6 pm 1862

In reply to your telegram of this date,[1] I have the honor to state that from the time this Army left Washington on the 7th of Sept my Cavalry has been constantly employed in making reconnaissances, scouting and picketing. Since the battle of Antietam six Regiments have made one trip of two hundred miles, marching fifty five miles in one day while endeavoring to reach Stewart's[2] Cavalry. General Pleasonton in his official report, states that he with the remainder of our available Cavalry while on Stewart's track marched seventy eight miles in twenty four hours. Besides these two remarkable expeditions our Cavalry has been engaged in picketing and scouting one hundred and fifty miles of river front, ever since the battle of Antietam, and has made repeated reconnaissances since that time, engaging the enemy on every occasion. Indeed it has performed harder service since the battle than before. I beg you will also consider that this same Cavalry was brought from the Peninsula where it encountered most laborious service, and was at the commencement of this campaign in low condition and from that time to the present it has had no time to recruit.

If any instance can be found where overworked Cavalry has performed more labor than mine since the battle of Antietam I am not conscious of it.[3]

Geo. B. McClellan
Maj. Genl.

Retained copy, McClellan Papers (A-86 :34), Library of Congress. *OR*, Ser. 1, XIX, Part 2, p. 485.

1. The president had seen a cavalry officer's report, forwarded by GBM, which stated that his horses were "absolutely broken down with fatigue and want of flesh," and he tele-

graphed, "Will you pardon me for asking what the horses of your army have done since the battle of Antietam that fatigue anything?" *OR,* Ser. 1, XIX, Part 2, pp. 484–85; *Collected Works of Lincoln,* V, p. 474. 2. Maj. Gen. J. E. B. Stuart. 3. On Oct. 26 GBM sent Lincoln a lengthy chronicle of the cavalry's record, and concluded, "I feel confident you will concur with me that our Cavalry is equally as efficient as that of the rebels." *OR,* Ser. 1, XIX, Part 2, pp. 490–91.

To Henry W. Halleck [TELEGRAM]

Head Quarters, Army of the Potomac,
Maj General Halleck [Pleasant Valley] October 25, 1862
General in Chief Washington 10.45 pm

As the moment is at hand for the advance of this Army a question arises for the decision of the General in Chief, which although perhaps implicitly decided by the President in his letter of the 13th should be clearly presented by me as I do not regard it as in my province to determine it. This question is the extent to which the line of the Potomac should be guarded after this Army leaves, in order to cover Maryland and Pennsylvania from invasion by large or small parties of the enemy. It will always be somewhat difficult to guard the immediate line of the river, owing to its great extent and the numerous passages which exist. It has long appeared to me that the best way of covering this line would be occupying Front Royal, Strasburg, Wardensville and Moorefield at the debouches of the several vallies in which they are situated. These points, or suitable places in their vicinity, should be strongly intrenched and permanently held. One great advantage of this arrangement would be the covering of the Baltimore and Ohio Railroad, and an essential part of the system would be the construction of the link of railway from Winchester to Strasburg, and the rebuilding of the Manassas Gap Railway bridge over the Shenandoah. The intrenchment of Manassas Junction would complete the system for the defence of the approaches to Washington and the Upper Potomac. Many months ago I recommended this arrangement, in fact gave orders for it to be carried into effect.[1] I still regard it as essential under all circumstances.

The views of the Chief Engineer of this Army in regard to the defences and garrisons of Harper's Ferry and its dependencies are in your possession.[2] The only troops under my command outside of the organization of the Army of the Potomac are the Maryland Brigade under Gen. Kenly, the 54 Pennsylvania, Col. Voss' 12th Illinois Cavalry, Col Davis' 8th New York Cavalry — total 2894 Infantry, one battery and about 900 cavalrymen. There are also two of my regiments of Cavalry (about 750 men) guarding the Balto. and Ohio R. Road between Hancock and Cumberland.

As I have no Department and command simply an active Army in the field, my responsibility for the safety of the line of the Potomac and the states north of it must terminate the moment I advance so far beyond that line as to adopt another for my base of operations. The question for the General in Chief to decide and which I regard as beyond my province is this:

1st Shall the safety of Harper's Ferry and the line of the Potomac be regarded as assured by the advance of the Army south of the Blue Ridge and the line left to take care of itself?

2nd If it is deemed necessary to hold the line, or that herein before indicated in advance of it, how many troops shall be placed there, at what points, (and in what numbers and of what composition at each), and where shall they be supplied; i.e. from this Army or from other sources?

Omitting the detached troops mentioned above and the small garrisons of Boonsboro and Frederick, the last returns show the strength of this Army for duty to be about 116,000 officers and men. This includes the divisions of Stoneman and Whipple, but does not include Heintzelman, Sigel and Bayard.

If Harper's Ferry and the river above are rendered fully secure it is possible that the active army, if it supplies the garrisons may be reduced so much as to be inadequate to the purposes contemplated; if it is preserved intact Maryland, Pennsylvania and the Balto. & Ohio R. Road may be unduly exposed. I leave the decision of these grave questions to the General in Chief. I know nothing of the number of troops at Baltimore, etcetera.

An important element in the solution of this problem is the fact that a great portion of Bragg's Army is probably now at liberty to unite itself with Lee's command.

I commence crossing the river at Berlin in the morning, and must ask a prompt decision of the questions proposed herein.[3]

G. B. McClellan
Maj Genl Comdg

Retained copy, McClellan Papers (C-19:66), Library of Congress. *OR,* Ser. 1, XIX, Part 1, p. 84.

1. See GBM to Nathaniel P. Banks, Mar. 16, 1862, *supra.* 2. GBM to Halleck, with enclosures, Oct. 18, *OR,* Ser. 1, XIX, Part 2, pp. 441–42. 3. Halleck replied on Oct. 26, in part: "The Government has intrusted you with defeating and driving back the rebel army in your front.... You are informed of my views, but the President has left you at liberty to adopt them or not, as you may deem best. You will also exercise your own discretion in regard to what points on the Potomac and the Baltimore and Ohio Railroad are to be occupied or fortified.... I think it will be time enough to decide upon fortifying Front Royal, Strasburg, Wardensville, and Moorefield when the enemy is driven south of them and they come into our possession. I do not think that we need have any immediate fear of Bragg's army. You are within 20 miles of Lee's, while Bragg is distant about 400 miles." *OR,* Ser. 1, XIX, Part 1, pp. 84–85.

To Mary Ellen McClellan

[Pleasant Valley] Oct 26th [1862] am

... I move a respectable number of troops across the Potomac today — the beginning of the general movement, which will however require several days to accomplish — for the cavalry is still terribly off. I was mad as a "march hare" yesterday at a telegram received from the Presdt asking what my "cavalry had done since the battle of Antietam to fatigue anything" — it was one of those dirty little flings that I can't get used to when they are not merited.

AL copy, McClellan Papers (C-7 :63), Library of Congress.

To Herman Haupt [TELEGRAM]

Brigadier General Herman Haupt
Superintendant Mil. Railways
Washington

Head Quarters, Army of
Potomac [Pleasant Valley]
October 26th 1862 10.45 am

I have the honor to request you to ascertain how far the Leesburg R. Road is practicable.

I have also to request you to be ready to supply this Army via Orange and Alexandria and Manassas Gap Railroads; to take steps at once to reestablish the wharves etc. at Acquia, and to be prepared to rebuild the Railroad bridge over the Rappahannock at Fredericksburg, and to supply that road with rolling stock.[1]

Geo. B. McClellan
Maj. Gen. Comdg.

Retained copy, McClellan Papers (C-19 :66), Library of Congress. *OR,* Ser. 1, XIX, Part 2, p. 494.

1. Haupt replied that afternoon that rebuilding the railroad from Washington to Leesburg was impracticable for any present campaign, but that he was prepared to repair the Orange and Alexandria and Manassas Gap railroads. Federal troops had destroyed the line between Aquia Creek and Fredericksburg and four months would be needed to rebuild the wharves and facilities at Aquia Landing. Considering the great effort involved, he requested instructions "as to the relative military importance of these roads & the order of priority in which they should be prepared for service." McClellan Papers (A-86 :34).

To Abraham Lincoln [TELEGRAM]

Head Quarters Army of Potomac
[Pleasant Valley] October 27 1862 3 pm

His Excellency the President

Your Excellency is aware of the very great reduction of numbers that has taken place in most of the old regiments of this command, and how necessary it is to fill up these skeletons before taking them again into action.

I have the honor therefore to request that the order to fill up the old regiments with drafted men may at once be issued.[1]

Geo. B. McClellan
Maj Genl Comdg

Retained copy, McClellan Papers (C-19:66), Library of Congress. *OR*, Ser. 1, XIX, Part 2, p. 496.

1. Lincoln replied on this date that the request "would be complied with as far as practicable. And now I ask a distinct answer to the question, Is it your purpose not to go into action again until the men now being drafted in the States are incorporated into the old regiments?" *OR*, Ser. 1, XIX, Part 2, p. 497.

To Abraham Lincoln [TELEGRAM]

His Excellency the President
Washington

Head Qrs Army of Potomac
[Pleasant Valley] Oct 27 1862 7.15 pm

I have the honor to acknowledge the receipt of your dispatch of 5.10 pm today. Feeling deeply impressed with the importance of filling up the old regiments at the earliest practicable moment, I have upon several different occasions urged this measure upon the War Dept as well as upon Your Excellency, as the most speedy and effectual method of giving us effective troops for future operations. Some time ago an agent of the Governor of Pennsylvania informed me that an order from the War Dept was necessary to authorize the transfer of drafted men to the old regiments. On the 17 inst I requested Gen Halleck to have the necessary order given.[1] I received no reply to this, and learned this afternoon that no such order had been issued. In the press of business I then called an aide and telling him that I had conversed with you upon this subject, I directed him to write for me a dispatch asking Your Excellency to have the necessary order given. I regret to say that this officer after writing the dispatch, finding me still engaged, sent it to the telegraph office without first submitting it to me, under the impression that he had communicated my views. He however unfortunately added "before taking them into action again." This phrase was not authorized or intended by me. It has conveyed altogether an erroneous impression as to my plans and intentions.

To Your Excellency's question I answer distinctly that I have not and have not had any idea of postponing the advance until the old regiments are filled by drafted men.

I commenced crossing the Army into Virginia yesterday and shall push forward as rapidly as possible to endeavor to meet the enemy. Burnside's Corps and part of Slocum's have been crossing yesterday and today, and Reynolds' Corps is ready to follow. Pleasonton with the cavalry is at Purcellville this evening. The crossing will be continued as rapidly as the means at hand will permit. Nothing but the physical difficulties of the operation shall delay it.

Geo. B. McClellan
Maj. Genl Comdg.

Retained copy, McClellan Papers (C-19:66), Library of Congress. *OR*, Ser. 1, XIX, Part 2, pp. 497–98.

1. GBM to Halleck, Oct. 17, *supra*.

To Herman Haupt [TELEGRAM]

Brigadier Gen Haupt
Supt Military Railways — Head Quarters Army of Potomac
Washington — [Pleasant Valley] Oct 27 1862 10 pm

Please take immediate steps to enable you to forward supplies via Orange & Alexandria & Manassas Gap Railroads for this Army, at the rate of seven hundred (700) tons per day. Also be prepared to repair the Orange and Alexandria Railroad beyond Manassas Junction, wherever it may be damaged. Please communicate to the General in Chief the information you gave me yesterday[1] in regard to the Fredericksburg Railroad and consult with him as to the possibility of repairing that road in season to use it for the purposes of this campaign.

Geo. B. McClellan
Maj Genl Comdg

Retained copy, McClellan Papers (C-19:66), Library of Congress. *OR*, Ser. 1, XIX, Part 2, p. 498.

1. See GBM to Haupt, Oct. 26, note 1, *supra*.

To Henry W. Halleck [TELEGRAM]

Major Gen Halleck — Head Quarters Army of Potomac
Gen-in-Chief Washington — [Berlin, Md.] October 29, 1862 1.15 pm

On the 25th Inst I sent you a dispatch requesting you to decide what steps should be taken to guard the line of the Potomac when this Army leaves here. To this I received your reply that I had been intrusted by the President with defeating and driving away the rebel Army; that you had given me no orders heretofore, did not give me any then, etc.[1]

Under these circumstances I have only to make such arrangements for guarding this extended line as the means at my disposal will permit,— at the same time keeping in view the supreme necessity of maintaining the moving Army in adequate force to meet the rebel Army before us.

The dispositions I have ordered are as follows, viz:

Ten thousand men to be left at Harper's Ferry — One brigade of infantry in front of Sharpsburg — Kenly's brigade of infantry at Williamsport — Kelley's brigade including Col. Campbell's 54 Penna Infantry at Cumberland and between that point and Hancock — I have also left four small cavalry regiments to patrol and watch the river and the Baltimore & Ohio Railroad from Cumberland down to Harper's Ferry.

I do not regard this force as sufficient to cover securely this great extent of line, but I do not feel justified in detaching any more troops from the moving columns. I would therefore recommend that some new regiments of infantry and cavalry be sent to strengthen the forces left by me.

There should be a brigade of infantry and section of artillery in the vicinity of Cherry Run; another brigade at Hancock, an additional brigade at Williamsport, one regiment at Hagerstown, and one at Chambersburg with a section of artillery at each place if possible. This is on the supposition that the enemy retain a considerable cavalry force west of the Blue Ridge. If they go east of it the occupation of the points named in my dispatch of the 25th Inst. will obviate the necessity of keeping many of these troops on the river. There are now several hundred of our wounded including General Richardson in the vicinity of Sharpsburg that cannot possibly be moved at present.

I repeat that I do not look upon the forces I have been able to leave from this Army as sufficient to prevent cavalry raids into Maryland and Pennsylvania, as cavalry is the only description of troops adequate to this service and I am, as you are aware, deficient in this arm.[2]

Geo. B. McClellan
Maj Genl Comdg

Retained copy, McClellan Papers (C-19:66), Library of Congress. *OR*, Ser. 1, XIX, Part 1, p. 85.

1. GBM to Halleck, Oct. 25, and note 3, *supra*. 2. Halleck replied on Oct. 30, in part: "The troops proposed for Thoroughfare Gap will be sent to that place whenever you are in position for their co-operation, as previously stated, but no new regiments can be sent from here to the Upper Potomac. The guarding of that line is left to your own discretion with the troops now under your command." *OR*, Ser. 1, XIX, Part 1, p. 85.

To Mary Ellen McClellan

Berlin Oct [c. 29, 1862]

. . . It will not do for me to visit Washn now — the tone of the telegrams I receive from the authorities is such as to show that they will take advantage of anything possible to do me all the harm they can & if I went down I should at once be accused by the Presdt of purposely delaying the movement. Moreover the condition of things is such that I *ought not* leave just now — the army is in the midst of the preliminary movements for the main march & I must be at hand in this critical moment of the operation. . . .

If you could know the mean & dirty character of the dispatches I receive you would boil over with anger — when it is possible to misunderstand, & when it is not possible, whenever there is a chance of a wretched innuendo — there it comes. But the good of the country requires me to submit to all this from men whom I know to be greatly my inferiors socially, intellectually & morally! There never was a truer epithet applied to a certain individual than that of the "Gorilla."

AL copy, McClellan Papers (C-7:63), Library of Congress.

To Mary Ellen McClellan

Berlin Oct 30th [1862]

. . . I have just been put in an *excellent* humor (?) by seeing that instead of sending the drafted men to fill the old rgts (as had been promised me) they are forming them into new rgts. Also that in face of the great want of cavalry with this army they are sending the new cavalry rgts from Penna to Louisville instead of hither!! Blind & foolish they will continue to the end.

AL copy, McClellan Papers (C-7:63), Library of Congress.

To Andrew G. Curtin [TELEGRAM]

His Excellency A. G. Curtin
Governor of Pennsylvania
Harrisburg Pa.

Head Quarters Army of Potomac
[Berlin] October 30, 1862 9.30 pm

I am about leaving this line and leave behind me all the troops I can safely spare to hold Harper's Ferry and the line of the upper Potomac, but I do not consider the force sufficient to prevent raids and have so represented to General Halleck who informed me that he has no more troops to send. I leave Major Gen. Morell at Hagerstown in command from mouth of Antietam up to Cumberland. I urge that you expedite as much as possible the organization of the nine month drafted men that some of them may be sent with the least possible delay to Chambersburg, Hagerstown, Sharpsburg, Williamsport and Hancock to prevent the possibility of raids. If I could have filled the old Pennsylvania regiments with the drafted men I could have left men enough to have made your frontier reasonably safe. As it is I cannot do it with due regard to the success of the main Army, and beg to warn you in time. Without reference to the safety of the frontier I wish to urge again in the strongest terms the absolute necessity of filling the old regiments with drafted men.[1]

Geo. B. McClellan
Maj. Gen. Comdg.

Retained copy, McClellan Papers (C-19:66), Library of Congress. *OR,* Ser. 1, XIX, Part 2, p. 510. The same dispatch was sent to President Lincoln.

1. Curtin replied on Nov. 1 that troops raised in Pennsylvania were "under the command of the authorities of the United States, who, no doubt . . . will direct the proper dispositions to be made, unless, indeed, you have yourself the power to make them. . . . On behalf of this loyal commonwealth, . . . I have the right to, and I do, demand that her frontier shall be properly protected." *OR,* Ser. 1, XIX, Part 2, p. 528.

To Abraham Lincoln [TELEGRAM]

Head Quarters, Army of the Potomac,
Berlin Oct 30 11.30 pm 1862

Reynolds has crossed. All the Army is in motion to follow the general movement. I ask your attention to my dispatches calling the notice of the General in Chief to the insufficiency of the preparations I leave behind me for resisting a raid, also to the fact that we are to have no reinforcements for the old Penna regts from the drafted men. No greater mistake has been made than the total failure to reinforce the old regiments. Please remember that I have clearly stated what troops I leave behind & that I regard the number insufficient to prevent a raid & that while the responsibility has been thrown upon me by Genl Halleck he has given me only limited means to accomplish the object.

I write this only to place the responsibility where it belongs & wish you to show this to Genl Halleck. I also wish before entering upon this important campaign again to inform you that I am most ill provided with cavalry & artillery horses, & that any statements to the effect that I have received for the active army under my command more than (2500) twenty five hundred horses for cavalry & artillery are totally untrue & that it is not until today that I have clothing enough in hand to supply the pressing wants of my men.

Destructive diseases are breaking out among the horses.

ALS (telegram sent), McClellan Papers (C-15:64), Library of Congress. The last page of this dispatch is missing.

To Mary Ellen McClellan

[Berlin] Oct 31 [1862] pm.

If I am successful in this campaign I think it will end in driving Stanton out — as he was good enough to say that he held office only for the purpose of crushing me, it will afford me great pleasure if I can in any honorable & open way be instrumental in consigning the rascal to the infamous fate he deserves. If I can crush him I will — relentlessly & without remorse. . . .

After midnight. . . . From the dispatches just received I think I will move Hd Qtrs over the river tomorrow — the advance is getting a little too far away from me & I wish to have everything well under my own hands, as I am responsible.

AL copy, McClellan Papers (C-7:63), Library of Congress.

To Abraham Lincoln [TELEGRAM]

Head Qrs, Army of Potomac
His Excellency the President [Berlin] Nov. 1 9.45 am 1862

I have the honor to inform you that all the Corps of this Army have crossed the Potomac except Franklin's which comes up this morning.

I have ordered an advance this morning and shall go forward from day to day as rapidly as possible.

The enemy in considerable force occupied Snickers Gap yesterday. They will be driven out today or tomorrow as soon as we can reach the position with sufficient force.

Geo. B. McClellan
Maj Genl

Retained copy, McClellan Papers (C-20:66), Library of Congress. *OR,* Ser. 1, XIX, Part 2, p. 523.

To Abraham Lincoln [TELEGRAM]

Head Quarters, Army of the Potomac,
Purcellville [Va., November 2] 1862 4.40 pm.

A good deal of artillery firing on the front & right. I do not yet know whether it is at Snicker's Gap or Pleasonton at Uniontown. I go towards the sound at once. It seems that there will be serious resistance not far from here, but you can fully rely upon it that the Army of the Potomac will retain its reputation. The troops are not all yet up, but are moving as rapidly as they can. I directed Franklin to remain near the Potomac today, or a part of it, to obtain necessary articles of clothing. We are still entirely too weak in cavalry — [*crossed out:* every step in the power of the Govt should be taken to strengthen us in this arm at once] but I will do the best I can with what I have got — as I close the artillery firing is heavy.

G B McClellan
Maj Genl

A Lincoln
Presdt US

ALS (telegram sent), McClellan Papers (A-88:35), Library of Congress. *OR,* Ser. 1, XIX, Part 2, p. 532.

To Mary Ellen McClellan [TELEGRAM]

Mrs McClellan
Government House Trenton NJ

Hd Qrs near Middleburg
[November] 4 [1862] 11 pm

I am very well. Your father has gone back sick but nothing serious so do not be worried in the least. All goes well except secesh who are travelling too fast to meet my views. Expect no letters or teleghs for some days. Will write a few lines tonight. We have Ashbys Gap.

G B McClellan
MG

Received copy (War Dept.), Records of the Office of the Secretary of War, RG 107 (M-504:66), National Archives.

To Mary Ellen McClellan

Nov 4th [1862] 11.30 pm near Middleburg

...We are in the full tide of success so far as it is or can be successful to advance without a battle....

Tomorrow night I hope to strike the RR & telegraph again — no telegraph within 25 miles of this....

AL copy, McClellan Papers (C-7:63), Library of Congress.

To Mary Ellen McClellan

Nov 5 [1862] 9 pm camp near Rectortown

...After a considerable amount of marching & skirmishing we have worked our way thus far down into rebeldom. We have had delightful weather for marching & a beautiful country to travel through.

...We left Berlin on Sunday morning [November 2], the Hd Qtrs stopping at Wheatland, but I heard firing & rode to the front — going all the way to Snicker's Gap (to the top of the mountain) & spending the night in Snickersville. Next morning I rode to meet the train, but heard some more firing — & rode again towards the front, & spent the night near Bloomfield — camping some miles back. At Snickersville I got a bed in a house to sleep in — at Bloomfield I slept under a tree in the woods — so that last night I was very glad after another long ride to get to my tent again....

Pleasonton has been doing very well again — has had some skirmishing pretty much every day — today he came across Jeb Stuart & thrashed him badly. Jeb outnumbered him two to one, but was well whipped — there were some very pretty charges made.

AL copy, McClellan Papers (C-7:63), Library of Congress.

To Mary Ellen McClellan

Nov 6 [1862] 1 pm camp near Rectortown

The army still advances, but the machine is so huge & complicated that it is slow in its motions.

AL copy, McClellan Papers (C-7:63), Library of Congress.

To Abraham Lincoln [TELEGRAM]

Head Quarters, Army of the Potomac,
Rectorstown Nov 7 11.30 a.m. 1862

A heavy snow storm today. No rations yet arrived here but hope for them within an hour or two. Burnside on the Rappahannock.

G B McClellan
Maj Genl

His Ex A Lincoln
Presdt Washington DC

ALS (telegram sent), McClellan Papers (C-14:64), Library of Congress. *OR,* Ser. 1, XIX, Part 2, p. 549.

To Abraham Lincoln [TELEGRAM]

His Excellency the President
Washington

Head Quarters Army of the Potomac
[Rectortown] Nov. 7, 1862 4 pm

The Manassas Gap Railroad is in such poor running condition that I shall be obliged to establish my depot for supplies for the whole Army at Gainesville, until the Orange and Alexandria Railroad can be repaired beyond Manassas Junction. I am now concentrating my troops in the direction of Warrenton and have telegraphed Gen Haupt to repair the Orange and Alexandria railroad to the line of the Rappahannock as soon as it can be covered by our troops. The storm continues unabated.

Geo. B. McClellan
Maj Gen Comdg

Retained copy, McClellan Papers (C-19:66), Library of Congress. *OR,* Ser. 1, XIX, Part 2, p. 549.

To Mary Ellen McClellan

[Rectortown] Nov 7 [1862] 2 pm

. . . Sumner returned last night. Howard returned this morning. I go to Warrenton tomorrow. Reynolds is there now, Burnside at Waterloo — Bayard in front — Pleasonton & Averill are trying to catch Jeb Stuart again near Flint Hills. Couch is here & moves tomorrow towards Warrenton. Porter & Franklin are at White Plains. Porter moves tomorrow to New Baltimore, thence next day to Warrenton. Franklin moves day after tomorrow to New Baltimore. Sigel will remain at Thoroughfare Gap & the vicinity. The Manassas Gap road is in such bad order that we cannot depend upon it this far up for supplies. Gainesville will be the depot until the O & Alex. RR is open to Warrenton. We will have great difficulty in getting supplies by the O & Alex. RR — its capacity has been overrated. Lee is at Gordonsville — G. W. Smith was yesterday driven out of Warrenton. . . .

11 1/2 pm. Another interruption — this time more important. It was in the shape of dear good old Burnside accompanied by Genl Buckingham, the Secy's Adjt Genl — they brought with them the order relieving me from the command of the Army of the Potomac, & assigning Burnside to the command. No cause is given. I am ordered to turn over the command immediately & repair to Trenton N.J. & on my arrival there to report by telegraph for future orders ! ![1]. . . .

Poor Burn feels dreadfully, almost crazy — I am sorry for him, & he never showed himself a better man or truer friend than now. Of course I was much surprised — but as I read the order in the presence of Genl Buckingham, I am sure that not a muscle quivered nor was the slightest expression of feeling visible on my face, which he watched closely. They shall not have that triumph. They have made a great mistake — alas for my poor country — I know in my innermost heart she never had a truer servant. I have informally turned over the command to Burnside — but will go tomorrow to Warrenton with him, & perhaps remain a day or two there in order to give him all the information in my power. . . .

Do not be at all worried — I am not. I have done the best I could for my country — to the last I have done my duty as I understand it. That I must have made many mistakes I cannot deny — I do not see any great blunders — but no one can judge of himself. Our consolation must be that we have tried to do what was right — if we have failed it was not our fault. . . .

8 am [November 8] . . . I am about starting for Warrenton. . . .

AL copy, McClellan Papers (C-7 :63), Library of Congress.

1. On Nov. 5 Lincoln addressed the order for GBM's dismissal to Halleck, authorizing him to execute it. The order was delivered by Brig. Gen. Catharinus P. Buckingham of the War Dept. *OR*, Ser. 1, XIX, Part 2, p. 549.

To the Army of the Potomac

Head Quarters, Army of the Potomac
Camp near Rectorstown Va.
Nov 7th 1862

Officers & Soldiers
of the Army of the Potomac

An order of the President devolves upon Maj. Gen. Burnside the command of this Army.

In parting from you I cannot express the love and gratitude I bear for you. As an Army you have grown up under my care. In you I have never found doubt or coldness. The battles you have fought under my command will proudly live in our Nation's history. The glory you have achieved, our mutual perils & fatigues, the graves of our comrades fallen in battle & by disease, the broken forms of those whom wounds & sickness have disabled — the strongest associations which can exist among men, unite us still by an indissoluble tie. [*Crossed out:* Farewell!] We shall also ever be comrades in supporting the Constitution of our country & the nationality of our people.[1]

Geo B McClellan
Maj Genl USA

DS (in part ADS), Alexander Stewart Webb Papers, Yale University Library. *OR,* Ser. 1, XIX, Part 2, p. 551.

1. An endorsement by Lt. Col. Webb reads: "McC wrote the last part on this sheet for the first time. It is in his hand writing. Alex S Webb." The concluding sentence does not appear in the broadside issued to the troops at the time, which ends with the salute "Farewell!," but does appear in official publications. McClellan Papers (B-12:48), Library of Congress.

To Mary B. Burnside

My dear Mrs B — Warrenton Nov 8 1862 6 pm

From the bottom of my heart I console with you & congratulate my wife. In the midst of your troubles I am sure that you will fully appreciate the cordial feeling existing between Burn & myself. He is as sorry to assume command as I am to give it up. Much more so. Be sure that all will yet come out well. Old Burn is true & honest — his future will be all that you can wish. I hope to see you before many days. In the meantime

I am most truly your friend
Geo B McClellan

Mrs. A. E. B.

ALS, Charles B. Phillips Library, Aurora University.

To Mary Ellen McClellan

Warrenton Sunday am. November [9, 1862]

. . . I expect to start tomorrow morning & may get to Washn in time to take the afternoon train. . . .

I shall not stop in Washn longer than for the next train & will not go to see anybody. I shall go on just as quietly as I can & make as little fuss as possible. . . .

The officers & men feel terribly about the change — none worse than

Burnside who is almost crazy. I learn today that the men are very sullen & have lost their good spirits entirely. It made me feel very badly yesterday when I rode among them & saw how bright & cheerful they looked & how glad they were to see me. Poor fellows, they did not know the change that had occurred....

AL copy, McClellan Papers (C-7 :63), Library of Congress.

To Mary Ellen McClellan

Warrenton Nov 10th [1862] 2 pm

...I am very well & taking leave of the men. I did not know before how much they loved me nor how dear they were to me. Gray haired men came to me with tears streaming down their cheeks. I never before had to exercise so much self control. The scenes of today repay me for all that I have endured. I will leave here early tomorrow morning & hope to leave Washn at 3 pm....

AL copy, McClellan Papers (C-7 :63), Library of Congress.

TEN

THE CALL TO POLITICS

NOVEMBER 12, 1862–AUGUST 28, 1864

THE NEARLY twenty-two months covered in this section record General McClellan's version of his transition from soldier to presidential candidate. In July 1864, some five weeks before the Democratic nominating convention officially completed the transition, he spelled out his view of presidential ambition. "It is my firm conviction," he wrote, "that no man should seek that high office, and that no true man should refuse it, if it is spontaneously conferred upon him, & he is satisfied that he can do good to his country by accepting it. . . . " This idealized picture of the democratic process left unsaid the fact that over the months, with careful deliberation, he had made himself available should his party choose to confer the nomination upon him.

Throughout this period, although he was the senior general on the active list, he performed no military duties beyond writing a lengthy report of his fifteen months as commander of the Army of the Potomac and helping organize a militia call-up in New York State. Largely unstated in the correspondence presented here — nearly all of it previously unpublished — was the expectation of a return to command in some capacity. Each Union military crisis — the defeats at Fredericksburg in December 1862 and at Chancellorsville in May 1863, and the Confederate invasion of the North that was checked at Gettysburg in July 1863 — brought with it renewed pressure on the president to recall General McClellan. In 1864 the Blair family mounted an effort to see him returned to active service in exchange for his renunciation of all presidential ambitions — a scheme that McClellan describes here in a memorandum to Samuel Barlow and an unsent letter to Francis P. Blair — but this too failed of accomplishment. He retained his commission, taking as his example General Winfield Scott, who had run for the presidency in 1852 without resigning from the army.

Initially assigned to Trenton, New Jersey, by the War Department, McClellan soon changed his posting to New York City. There, as his letters indicate, his associations were largely with leading figures in the Democratic party, among them Barlow, August Belmont, and the editors of the two leading Democratic newspapers, Manton M. Marble of the *New York World* and William C. Prime of the *Journal of Commerce*. During the summer of 1863 the McClellans moved out of New York to a house on Orange Mountain in New Jersey, which would remain their residence until early 1865. Convinced that he was kept under surveillance by agents of Secretary Stanton and that his mail was opened, he entrusted the delivery of his correspondence to friends or messengers whenever possible. When forced to resort to the mails, he often referred in his letters to matters he dared not commit to paper but would tell his correspondent when they met.

Although it is not until writing his mother on December 6, 1863, that McClellan first recorded his thoughts on being a presidential candidate, he had committed himself publicly to the Democratic opposition some two months earlier, with the so-called Woodward letter. His endorsement of George W. Woodward, a Democrat of extreme conservatism and a representative of the peace wing of the party, for governor of Pennsylvania (October 12) was a decision pressed on him by that state's party leaders, who made the endorsement the price of their support of his presidential candidacy. Thereafter his correspondence becomes increasingly political in nature, covering relations with party leaders, his positions on major issues (particularly his stand on the war and on bringing it to a peaceful conclusion), and his replies to attacks on him by the Republican opposition.

In such letters as that of June 25, 1864, to Manton Marble, McClellan left no doubt that he intended to distance himself from the peace-at-any-price segment of the party. He believed (correctly) that the peace men were behind the postponement of the national convention to late August, and if their influence was that great, he told Marble, he would refuse to be the candidate. Marble and other supporters downplayed the peace wing's importance and persuaded him to accept if nominated. On the eve of the convention's opening on August 29, he seemed assured of being the Democrats' candidate, and all the signs seemed to point to his election in November.

To Henry W. Halleck [TELEGRAM]

Maj General H W Halleck
Gen in Chief Trenton NJ Nov 12 '62

I have the honor to report my arrival here with a portion of my staff at four this morning.

G B McClellan
Maj Genl USA

Received copy, Records of the Office of the Secretary of War, RG 107 (M-473 :50), National Archives. *OR,* Ser. 1, XIX, Part 2, p. 574.

To Samuel L. M. Barlow

My dear Barlow Trenton Friday am [November 14, 1862]

I have been trying in vain to reply to your kind notes to Madame & myself & can now say only a few words to thank you for your kind feeling — which is no more than I expected. I telegraphed you this morning, asking you to come to see me. I expect to go to Phila for one day on Monday [November 17] & shall probably go to New York on Thursday next — of that we will talk when I see you, which I hope will be today or tomorrow — as I shall try to shut myself up on Sunday. With my kindest regards, & those of Madame, to you & the "other Madame"

I am ever your friend
McClellan

S L M Barlow Esq

ALS, Barlow Papers, Huntington Library.

To Terrence Farley

Terrence Farley Esq
Chairman Comm on National Affairs
Dear Sir New York Nov 22 1862

I have the pleasure to acknowledge the receipt of your letter of today embodying the Resolutions of the Municipal authorities of the City of New York tendering to me the distinguished honor of the hospitalities of the Metropolis.

I appreciate fully and feel most deeply this action of the Municipality — which I regard as one of the highest compliments that can be paid to a citizen of our country. At this particular moment it is especially gratifying to me to be thus assured that I possess the kind feeling & regard of the authorities of our greatest City. I trust that they reflect the sentiments of their constituents.

At any other time I would gratefully accept the hospitalities of the city, but I do not feel that it would be right for me to do so while so many of my former comrades are enduring the privations of war & perhaps sacrificing their lives for our country.

I trust therefore that you will permit me to decline a compliment I so little deserve, and that you will convey to the Honorable Mayor & Council my warmest & most grateful thanks for the great honor they have conferred upon me.

I am my dear sir with high respect your obdt svt
Geo B McClellan

ALS retained copy, McClellan Papers (A-88:35), Library of Congress. Farley was a New York City councilman.

To Charles P. Stone

Brig Genl C P Stone
US Volunteers Washington D.C. — 5th Avenue Hotel New York City
General: — Dec 5 1862

I have the honor to acknowledge the receipt of your letter of the 1st inst.[1]

The order for your arrest in February last was given by the Secretary of War — I had the order in his hand writing several days before it was finally carried into effect.

When the order was first given by the Secy he informed me that it was at the solicitation of the Congressional Committee on the Conduct of the War and based upon testimony taken by them.

On the evening when you were arrested I submitted to the Secy the written result of the examination of a refugee from Leesburg;[2] this information to a certain extent agreed with the evidence stated to have been taken by the Congressional Committee; & upon its being imparted to the Secretary he again instructed me to cause you to be arrested — which I at once did.[3]

At that time I stated to the Secy that I could not from the information in my possession understand how charges could be framed against you, that the case was too indefinite. On several occasions after your arrest I called the attention of the Secy to the propriety of giving you a prompt trial, but the reply always was either that there was no time to attend to the case or that the Congressional Committee was still engaged in collecting additional evidence in your case & were not yet fully prepared to frame the charges.

[*Crossed out:* You will remember that I ordered you to Washington a few days before your arrest — I at that time had the Secy's written order for your arrest, and it may not be irrelevant to state that on the morning of your arrival in Washington I went to the room of the Congl Comm. & there met the Hon Z Chandler,[4] whom I informed that you were in the city, *not* in arrest, & whom I requested to say to the Comm that I would be glad if they would send for you & confront you fully with all the witnesses & testimony against you, as I was confident that you would from your innocence of all improper motives, & could explain whatever facts were alleged against you. I believe that I some time since informed you verbally that when directed to order certain witnesses from your command to present themselves before the Congl Committee I officially informed the Chairman of the Committee[5] that these particular witnesses were in arrest under disgraceful charges — this was done that the Committee might know all the circumstances which might affect the weight due to their statements.[6]]

AL retained copy, McClellan Papers (A-88:35), Library of Congress. *OR*, Ser. 1, V, p. 345.

1. In his letter of Dec. 1 Stone called for a copy of the charges on which GBM had ordered his arrest on Feb. 8, 1862. *OR*, Ser. 1, V, pp. 344–45. 2. Allan Pinkerton to GBM, Feb. 6, 1862. McClellan Papers (A-39:16). 3. See GBM to Andrew Porter, Feb. 8, 1862, *supra*. 4. Sen. Zachariah Chandler. 5. Sen. Benjamin F. Wade. 6. One such witness was Col. George W. B. Tomkins, charged with "misbehavior before the enemy" at the Battle of Bull Run. GBM to Edwin M. Stanton, Mar. 24, 1862, Lincoln Papers, Library of Congress.

To Edward Everett

My dear Mr Everett 5th Avenue Hotel Dec 7 /62

I owe you a very full apology for my long delay in replying to your most kind note of the 17th ulto.[1] I received it when very busy with preparations to go from Trenton to N.Y., & since my arrival here have had but few moments to myself.

I cannot express too warmly my very grateful appreciation of your kind feeling & good opinion of me, & I assure you that the approval of such as you far more than compensates me for whatever of abuse & detractions I may have undergone.

I am content to await the arbitrament of the future, conscious that I have at least endeavored to do my best for the cause of our country & that my mistakes were not intentional.

With the hope that you have ere this regained your health & again thanking you for your kindness

I am sincerely & respectfully your friend
Geo B McClellan

The Hon Edward Everett

ALS, Everett Papers, Massachusetts Historical Society. The statesman and orator Edward Everett had been governor of Massachusetts, congressman and senator, and minister to Great Britain.

1. Everett wrote on Nov. 17 to offer "the tribute of my admiration, not only for the consummate talent you have evinced in organizing and leading our armies... but of the discretion & dignity, with which you have conducted yourself, in the trying circumstances in which you have been placed," and to express the hope "that you will soon be recalled to the field...." McClellan Papers (A-88:35), Library of Congress.

To August Belmont

My dear Mr Belmont — 5th Avenue Hotel Dec 7 1862

I owe you an apology for my delay in returning the copies of your letters which you were so good as to lend me.[1]

In reading them my greatest regret is that the administration could not be induced to act in accordance with your views — some such policy as that you urged must yet be adopted or we are lost.

I leave for Washington this evening, & hope to return in two or three days.

Your sincere friend
Geo B McClellan

August Belmont Esq

ALS, Belmont Family Collection, Rare Book and Manuscript Library, Columbia University. Belmont was national chairman of the Democratic party.

1. Letters Belmont had written to the president and other administration officials.

To Lorenzo Thomas

To the Adjutant General
Head Qrs of the Army
Sir. Washington D.C. Dec 9, 1862.

I have the honor to request that the instructions requiring me to await orders at Trenton New Jersey may be so far modified as to authorize my taking post in the City of New York.

I propose to commence at once the labor of preparing my full official reports of the battles of the Peninsula and of the campaign in Maryland. I shall need for this purpose the assistance of a number of officers who were on my staff during those campaigns. I give their names herein below and ask that they may be assigned to temporary duty in the City of New York to report to me for the service indicated. The officers referred to are as follows:

1.	Brigadier Genl. R. B. Marcy	late Chief of Staff HQ. AP
2.	Brig. Genl. S. Williams	Asst Adjt Genl " "
3.	Brig. Genl. Jas Hardie	Actg Asst Adjt Genl " "
4.	Colonel T. M. Key	A.D.C.
5.	Lt Col. E. McK. Hudson	"
6.	Lt Col. N. B. Sweitzer	"
7.	Lt Col. A. V. Colburn	"
8.	Lt Col. P. de Radowitz	"
9.	Capt. Arthur McClellan	"
10.	Capt. W. F. Biddle	"
11.	Capt. W. P. Mason	"
12.	Capt. J. C. Duane, Engr Corps	late Chief Engr

It is probable that the services of a few other officers late of my staff or under my command may also be necessary to me. For them I will make special applications as the necessity arises.[1]

Very Respectfully Your Obdt Servant

Retained copy, McClellan Papers (A-88:35), Library of Congress.

1. A memorandum in the McClellan Papers (A-107:42) indicates that Hudson, Sweitzer, Biddle, Mason, Lt. Col. Edward H. Wright, and Maj. Herbert Hammerstein drafted portions of the report.

To Leslie Combs

My dear Sir Washington, December 11, 1862

Your very kind letter of the 4th[1] has at last reached me, the envelope opened and the letter evidently read by some of the Government officials. I only hope that they were as well satisfied with the contents as I was. I thank you most sincerely for the kind judgment you — an old soldier — express of the last battles fought by the Army of the Potomac under my command. I am ready to stake all, upon my opinion, that the true line of operations against Richmond is by the Peninsula and that the greatest military blunder of the war was made when I was withdrawn from there.

McDowell could and ought to have joined me at Hanover Court-House, and the result of his junction with me, would have been the capture of Richmond. It was perfectly practicable and possible to reinforce me up to the time I abandoned the line of the James River. I believe that you are entirely right in your surmises that Mr. Lincoln and Mr. Stanton are the "high officials" who originated the idea of withdrawing the Army from James River. I will not venture upon criticism now, for I feel that this letter will, in all probability, be read by others than yourself before it reaches you. I will only say, that I think you are entirely correct in the judgment you pass upon *"Officials."* I hope that the one you mention is simply an "ass" but I fear he is a "knave" as well.[2] Permit me to express my high appreciation of the commendation you bestow upon the final operations of the Maryland Campaign. I *do* believe that something more was deserved than the reward of being placed upon the shelf. I accept however the case as it stands. I am not now disposed to complain, but I am confident that, before long, the time will come when the whole truth will be known.

With my warmest thanks for your kind feeling and sympathy,

I am my dear Sir, Yours
Geo. B. McClellan
Maj. Genl.

To Hon Leslie Combs

Copy, McClellan Papers (A-72:29), Library of Congress. Combs was a veteran of the War of 1812 and a onetime leader of the Whig party in Kentucky.

1. Combs's letter of Dec. 4 commented on Halleck's recently published report as general-in-chief, dated Nov. 25. Terming the withdrawal from the Peninsula "military madness," Combs was critical of Halleck and McDowell. Regarding the Maryland campaign, he wrote: "Considering the materials you had to work with — *raw* and *dispirited* troops — I think your battle of Antietam, the most remarkable triumph in history, certainly our history." McClellan Papers (A-88:35). 2. The reference is to Secretary Stanton.

To Mary Ellen McClellan

[Washington] Dec 12, 1862

I did not get back from Mr. Blair's until three this morning. I met there Gov. Dennison & the chairman of the Mil. Com. of the House & was drawn into a very long explanation of the past.[1] I have sent over to the Court a written answer to the only remaining questions they seem to desire to ask, & if they do not require me to go there in person, I will be free from them. I have been summoned in Porter's case, but he will not be ready for me for some days, & I shall leave tomorrow morning & be with you in the evening....

Just summoned again to the Court!!

4.30 pm. I went through quite an inquisition & was kept some time....

I then went to see the Surgeon Genl about our cripples & afterwards to the Comm. of Pensions to try to hurry up the papers of some of those poor cripples whom we saw, but the Commissioner had left his office & I failed in the object of my visit. I am writing now in Porter's rooms — those that Seth[2] had last winter. Fitz & I are the "great tabooed" — you would laugh to see how *some* officials fight shy in public, & then come to me privately to protest their devotion! It is too funny! I am to dine with Mr. Crittenden[3] & the Kentucky delegation this evening & have arranged to leave in the eleven o'clock train tomorrow morning & will be with you by ten that night....

I have not had a moment to myself & am more than ever tired of this wretched place. I hear that a battle is in progress on the Rappahannock — nothing yet indicates much progress — I fear the result will not be favorable & that Burnside will fail in his attempt.[4] I must close now & get ready for dinner.

Copy, McClellan Papers (D-10:72), Library of Congress.

1. GBM was in Washington to testify at a court of inquiry investigating Gen. McDowell. His meeting was with Postmaster General Montgomery Blair, former Ohio governor William Dennison, and Congressman Abraham B. Olin. 2. Seth Williams, of GBM's staff. 3. Congressman John J. Crittenden, of Kentucky. 4. The Battle of Fredericksburg.

To John Van Buren

5th Avenue Hotel
My dear Sir Sunday am [December 14, 1862]

Mrs McClellan desires me to express her thanks for the beautiful flowers we found awaiting us on our return home last evening — and which are some consolation for our inability to dine with you. Mrs McC is not at all well this morning, so much so that I did not think it well for her to go out this damp day. We have therefore staid at home quietly instead of accepting your kind invitation to your pew.

I feel with you great anxiety as to the result of the battle now impending on the Rappahannock — I do not see that anything decisive was effected yesterday on our side, but as Franklin seems to have met with partial success & there are no indications of Hooker having been engaged I still hope for something better today.

Very truly yours
Geo B McClellan

John Van Buren Esq
Fourth Avenue

ALS, Miscellaneous Collections, Huntington Library. Van Buren was state chairman of the Democratic party in New York.

To August Belmont

5th Avenue Hotel
My dear Mr Belmont Sunday evg [December 14, 1862]

When I sent you the copies of the letters you were so good as to lend me I thought that the accompanying was enclosed — I was in a great hurry at the time, just starting for Washington. I hope you will excuse my unaccountable delay in the return of these letters, all of which I have read with much interest.[1]

I fear that Mr L is busily engaged in breaking the rest of the eggs in the basket!

Is this the blackest hour which precedes the dawn?

Ever yours
Geo B McC

August Belmont Esq.

ALS, Belmont Family Collection, Rare Book and Manuscript Library, Columbia University.

1. See GBM to Belmont, Dec. 7, *supra.*

To Fitz John Porter

5th Avenue Hotel
My dear old Fitz Friday [December 19, 1862]

Your notes received. I have not dared to reply to them by mail — so much do I distrust the honesty of certain surroundings.

I am much disappointed in not receiving from Washington the telegrams I sent for. Tell Colburn that the copies of your dispatches to Burnside which were sent to me at Alexandria *must* be boxed up in Washington *or* at the Hd Qtrs of the Army of the Potomac. Have Colburn hunt them up & give them to you. I have *one* in my desk at Trenton which I will get for you & send by safe hand.[1]

I have only a few minutes to write & will therefore be brief. I *do* remember the Wms Burg reprimand, & the subsequent explanation which was fully satisfactory to me.[2] I can testify & I am confident that Marcy will do the same (tho' I have had no chance to talk with him about it) that if I had *any* fault to find with you it was on account of your extreme anxiety to get established & be off to Acquia.

You unquestionably gained time by leaving Wms Burg as you did & were right in so doing. Ask Colburn whether he can testify to these facts. If Marcy can I will simply write you "Marcy remembers." Of course I do not wish to go to Washn as a witness or anything else if it is unnecessary, but you must be sure that I am ready to go any where or to do anything in my power that will aid you — so don't hesitate to call upon me in any case of necessity.

You lost no time either on the Peninsula or at Fredericksburg.

I have a copy of my dispatch to you at Centreville — my memory is not clear about receiving a copy — have Colburn look it up.

I have no earthly doubt, Fitz, as to the result of your trial — you will come out brighter than ever & the wretched conspiracy against you will utterly fail.

I did not reply to your questions about the members of the Court — 1st because I did not believe I could get a letter to you unopened — 2nd because I really know but little of the members.

Hunter I distrust. I never saw him — but he is an enemy of mine. Buford I knew in Illinois — he is a graduate & *was* a good man & a good friend of mine. Garfield I don't know at all.[3]

I will work with you in this matter Fitz to any extent — our cause is the same & we must crush these fellows.

Marcy has just come in — he recollects my not liking your leaving Wms Burg, but knows nothing about the letter (the intercepted one).

So long as I am here you had better enclose your letters (except when private hand can be availed of) to Dr E E Marcy[4] 22 East 21st Street New York City.

In great haste ever yours
McC

F.J.P.

I am surprised at the feeling in my favor all over the North — it is almost unanimous.

ALS, Porter Papers, Library of Congress.

1. The reference is to dispatches sent by Porter during the Second Bull Run campaign, sought for his pending court-martial on charges of military misconduct during that operation. 2. See GBM to Porter, Aug. 17, 1862, *supra*. 3. Maj. Gen. David Hunter, Brig. Gen. N. B. Buford, Brig. Gen. James A. Garfield. 4. Mrs. McClellan's uncle.

To Fitz John Porter

My dear Fitz [New York] Saturday [December 20, 1862]

I hoped to get the enclosed ready in time to go by Marble[1] but was disappointed. I send a copy of a letter you wrote me from Sharpsburg which I thought *might* be of interest or service to you.

The original of the letter from Centreville has a word or two missing as you will observe in the copy.[2]

Yours of the 15th reached me.

The monied men & the respectable men of this city are up in arms, their patience is exhausted & unless the Presdt comprehends the gravity of his situation I see great danger ahead.

Burnside must have conducted his withdrawal very skilfully to have succeeded so well — poor fellow how I pity him! I have defended him to the best of my ability.

The sacrifice of Saturday was an useless one — nothing gained, not even honor. Banks ought to have gone to the James River, & to the last moment I hoped that it was so.

The future looks dark & threatening — alas for our poor country! I still trust in God & bow to his will — he will bring us victory when we deserve it. A change *must* come ere long — the present state of affairs *cannot* last.

When will you probably want me as a witness? Will the Court sit during the holidays?

Ever yours
McC

I shudder, Fitz, when I think of those poor fellows of ours so uselessly killed at Fredericksburg!

ALS, Porter Papers, Library of Congress.

1. Manton M. Marble, editor of the *New York World*. 2. Probably Porter to GBM, Aug. 31, 1862. *OR,* Ser. 1, XII, Part 3, pp. 768–69 (misdated).

To Fitz John Porter

Dear Fitz [Philadelphia] Thursday [January] 8th [1863]

Your two notes of 4th & 6th received.

The Hooker rumor has reached here — I hardly believe it true. I think the story about Burn, his resignation & recommendation to the Presdt is true.[1]

Of course the Presdt told a falsehood when he said that I had recommended a withdrawal — he had no grounds for such a statement & knew it to be false when he made it.[2]

I will take care that Halleck's way of urging Burn to advance of his own free will & accord is well known — I will quietly repeat it.

I fully agree with your views as to the crossing of the Rappahannock — it would be sheer madness & folly. You are certainly not far wrong in your estimate of the force now required to operate on Richmond — the whole aspect of affairs has changed & must be looked in the face or we shall only repeat the blunders of previous years.

I take it for granted that the fortifications of Richmond are now so strong that they must be reduced by "starvation, heavy guns & trenches."

Don't leave the service yet — be content to wait a while without a command & watch the boiling of the pot a little longer. Your notion about Rosecran's affair agree with mine — the result at Vicksburg fully explains it to my mind.

Joe Johnston regarded Vicksburg as the most important point — when he has got rid of Sherman he will take Grant & Rosecranz in hand — & concentrate upon them in succession.[3]

I shall be only too glad, Fitz, if my testimony has done you any good — your faithful service through so many long months should of itself have cleared you without the necessity of my opening my mouth.

I cannot imagine the possibility of your being hurt by the Court upon the evidence which has been given.

It is impossible for me to get on with Stanton — Harris[4] is entirely mistaken in regard to that. In fact a complete change of Cabinet & policy is necessary before any honest man of his country can do good. You may be sure that I will not be recalled until the Presdt is prepared to make an entire change.

I see in this morning's papers that *I* had *a long private interview with Genl Butler yesterday, that we were "fast & sincere friends" etc.*[5] I need hardly assure you that I did not see *Genl Butler at all* during his stay here, nor had I any interview with him in any way. I don't know that all this amounts to anything — but you are authorized to tell the truth if you think it worth while to correct the statement.

I expect to leave here on Monday — to stay over one day in Trenton — then after remaining a few days in N.Y. to go to Boston for a few days. I look anxiously for your defence & the finding of the Court — for although strong as adamant in the conviction that you merit reward instead of censure, I distrust so much all connected with the Administration that I cannot but be anxious.[6] I must close now, old fellow — God bless & preserve you.

Ever your true friend
McC

F.J.P.

ALS, Porter Papers, Library of Congress.

1. On Jan. 1 Burnside wrote the president that he, Secretary of War Stanton, and General-in-Chief Halleck had all lost the confidence of the country, and he offered to resign. *OR*, Ser. 1, XXI, pp. 941–42. 2. This appears to relate to the withdrawal from the Peninsula. 3. On Dec. 31, 1862, and Jan. 2, 1863, William S. Rosecrans fought the indecisive Battle of Stone's River, in Tennessee, and on Dec. 29, 1862, in Mississippi, William T. Sherman was repulsed in an attack on the defenses of Vicksburg. 4. Sen. Ira Harris, of New York. 5. Maj. Gen. Benjamin F. Butler. 6. On Jan. 10 Porter was found guilty and sentenced to be cashiered from the service.

To Samuel L. M. Barlow

My dear Sir New York Jany 20 1863

Mrs McClellan desires me to acknowledge the receipt of your kind letter of yesterday, accompanying the title papers & insurance policies of the house No 22 West 31st Street.[1]

In doing so I cannot refrain from expressing the deep gratitude we both feel for this munificent token of personal regard on the part of gentlemen whose esteem & friendship we value so much — doubly pleasant from the fact that it makes us citizens of New York, & fixes our residence in the midst of so many kind friends.

For my own part, if I am again called to the field of battle, I shall go with a much lighter heart from the consciousness that my wife & child are no longer homeless.

With our most sincere thanks to you and your friends

I am truly yours
Geo B McClellan
Maj Genl USA

S L M Barlow Esq
New York

ALS, Barlow Papers, Huntington Library.

1. The house was a gift to Mrs. McClellan from several prominent New Yorkers, including Barlow, William H. Aspinwall, and John Jacob Astor, Jr.

To A. W. H. Clapp

Hon. A. W. H. Clapp, Portland:
Dear Sir, Boston, Feb. 4, 1863.

I have the pleasure to acknowledge the receipt of the letter of Mr. Emery[1] accompanying the resolutions, adopted at a Convention of the citizens of Portland, inviting me to visit their city. I regret that I am still obliged to repeat the reply so reluctantly given to the deputation of gentlemen who did me the honor to call upon me on Monday — that it is not in my power at present to accept the very flattering invitation conveyed by them. Please convey to Mr. Emery and the gentlemen he represents my warm and sincere appreciation of the honor they have conferred upon me, and my heartfelt gratitude for their approval of my course as a public officer. If in the future I am again called upon to exercise active command, it will be with the same devotion to the cause of the Constitution and the Union that has actuated me in the past, and I trust I may be permitted to say that I shall feel all the stronger that I have gained the approval of so many of the citizens of Portland.

Again expressing my warmest thanks,

I am very respectfully and truly yours,
Geo. B. McClellan
Major General, U.S.A.

Boston Post, Feb. 6, 1863. Clapp headed a delegation that invited GBM to visit Portland, Me.

1. George F. Emery was chairman of a Portland citizens' committee.

To Horatio Seymour

Hon Horatio Seymour
Governor of New York
Governor New York Feb 13/63

I take the liberty of presenting to you Captain Razderachin of the Russian Artillery, who desires to procure a commission in some one of our regiments or batteries that he may be enabled to see service during this war.

Difficulties have been thrown in his way — I think some rule has been made preventing any one from being with Head Quarters in the field unless they hold a commission — & I understand [from] Capt R. that it is mainly for this reason that he desires to obtain a commission.

When in Europe I received so many courtesies from the Russian Govt that I would esteem it as a special favor should circumstances enable you to gratify the desire of this young officer.

He will be able to show you his Russian Commission & other papers authenticating his position.[1]

I am, Governor, with sentiments of the highest respect
your friend & servant
Geo B McClellan

ALS, Western Reserve Historical Society. Seymour had assumed the governorship of New York on Jan. 1.

1. Valerian Razderachin was commissioned a captain and appointed to a staff position in the Army of the Potomac.

To Edward Everett

22 West 31st Street
New York Feb 20/63

My dear Mr Everett

Your very welcome note of the 18th reached me yesterday.[1] Mrs McClellan & I were both of us much disappointed in not having the pleasure of your company from Hartford — will you permit me to offer our sincere sympathy in the family affliction which detained you.

I am much obliged to you for the very interesting note from the Prince de Joinville — I admire him so much that it affords me great pleasure to read *anything* from his pen.

I have been somewhat amused by the action of the Albany Senate — had they concurred in the House Resolutions I should simply have declined the proffered compliment as gracefully as I could, & the whole affair would soon have been forgotten — as it is they have probably injured themselves more than they have me.

I had a very pleasant interview with Gov Seymour a day or two ago & was much pleased with him — he quite won my heart & head, & I am glad to feel assured that he is a conservative as well as an able man. It is most fortunate that the State of New York may be regarded as in safe hands in these tumultuous times.

I will be glad to profit by your hint in regard to the "lenteur Americaine" — I had not observed the application made of it by Mr Stille, as I have not read his pamphlet with any care — in fact I merely glanced at a paragraph here & there — I am obliged to you for the suggestion.

The Report is making good progress, although it is a tedious, difficult, & disagreeable task — It is much easier to conduct campaigns & fight battles than to write their history — at least I find it so.

I cannot express to you the pleasure with which we look back upon our Boston visit — I never met with more warmth of feeling & sincere kindness.

By no means the least pleasant of the associations of the trip is the fact that we feel that we can now claim personal friendship with yourself.

Mrs McC desires me to enclose with this the photograph which you were so kind as to ask for — with her kindest regards as well as my own

I am most respectfully & sincerely your friend
Geo B McClellan

Hon Edward Everett

ALS, Everett Papers, Massachusetts Historical Society.

1. In his letter Everett remarked on the recent division in the New York legislature over a resolution in GBM's behalf. He also enclosed a copy of a letter from the Prince de Joinville, written July 10, 1862, expressing the hope that radical influences would not cause the Civil War to "degenerate into a war of extermination without end, ruinous to the North, and odious to the remainder of the world." Everett suggested that in his report GBM counter Joinville's theory, in his *Army of the Potomac,* of an American affinity for slowness *(la lenteur Américaine),* "which Mr. [Charles Janeway] Stillé, in his pamphlet called 'How a free People conduct a long war,' endeavors to make an invidious application to yourself." McClellan Papers (A-89:35), Library of Congress.

To Benjamin F. Wade [TELEGRAM]

New York, February 23, 1863.

If you can do me the favor to inform me upon what points the committee desire my testimony, I can greatly facilitate their objects and save much time by refreshing my memory by consulting papers before starting.[1]

George B. McClellan
Major General

Hon. B. F. Wade
Chairman on Conduct of War

Report of the Joint Committee on the Conduct of the War, I (1863), p. 108. Sen. Wade was chairman of the Joint Committee.

1. On Feb. 19 Wade had notified GBM that his testimony was desired. In his response on this date, Wade said information was wanted "generally on your military administration," and it was not possible to be more specific. *Report of the Joint Committee,* I (1863), pp. 107–108.

To Mary Ellen McClellan

Washington Wednesday 5 pm.
[February 25, 1863]

My own dearest little one

When we started from N.Y. we found no sleeping car & did the best we could with the very uncomfortable arrangements of the Jersey RR — when we got to Trenton we looked out for Wright[1] — but no Wright was to be found, & the delinquency was explained by a telegram from him today saying that the servants failed to awaken him, & that he will be here this evening. We were promised sleeping car at Phila, in chase of which we took a ride of 5 miles (it seemed 50) in street RR cars & reached the depot of the Baltimore Road just in time to strike the train & to ascertain the melancholy fact that there was not the slightest suspicion of a sleeping car there either. So we had to work through. I came the Caesar on myself, threw my cape over my head & retired into the privacy of private life to think of my own dearest little Nelly — (& you may be sure, sweetest one, that I *did* think of you all night long, when you, no doubt, were sound asleep) — so we reached Washn. As soon as we arrived I sent a note to the Hon B F Wade telling him that I was here & ready to be examined, he replied that he was too ill to attend, but that if I would go down any time after 12 they would call the Committee together & examine me. Then Hudson & I breakfasted, dressed & went down to the Capitol. I found only one member of the Committee (Cavode)[2] who told me that they would not be ready for me until ten tomorrow. Then I drove up town & fished up Sackett, with whom I went to call upon his poor wife. Since then I have seen Barry, Davis, Buford, Fox, Welles etc etc — *all* very friendly.[3] Rip van Winkle sent his kindest regards to you & John.[4] I also went to the office of L Thomas[5] to report my arrival — saw L who was disposed to be *very* friendly — also saw McDowell who was inclined to be my confrere, but he was met so coldly & politely that he was rather dumbfounded — I cut him very short.

Aspinwall telegraphed me today that Gen Morgan wished me to call on the Presdt — I will probably do so after dinner & will tell you the result.[6] I have invited Sackett, Davis, Ingalls, Buford & one or two others to dine with me today.

I will try to write again tonight — to my own sweet love, my own dearest darling Nelly

Ever with truest love your own
George

ALS, McClellan Papers (B-40:60), Library of Congress.

1. Lt. Col. Edward H. Wright; GBM was traveling with Lt. Col. Edward McK. Hudson, of his staff. 2. Congressman John Covode, of Pennsylvania. 3. Col. Delos B. Sacket, Brig. Gen. William F. Barry, Maj. Nelson H. Davis, Brig. Gen. John Buford, Gustavus V. Fox, Gideon Welles. 4. Presumably Col. Wright; John H. B. McClellan, GBM's brother. 5. Adj. Gen. Lorenzo Thomas. 6. Former New York governor Edwin D. Morgan. GBM does not mention a meeting with the president in the two letters that follow, and presumably it did not take place. It may have been intended to deal with his recall to the post of general-in-chief, which Montgomery Blair discussed with him the previous day in New York. However, when Blair returned to Washington he found Lincoln opposed to the idea. *Diary of Gideon Welles,* I, p. 345.

To Mary Ellen McClellan

My own dearest Nelly, Washington
my own sweet wife Thursday Feby 26 [1863] 3 1/2 pm

I went before the Committee today — they were very polite — & gave me something to do which will occupy me for a couple of days at least. I have sent for Key[1] to help me in preparing my record. I have many — very many — bitter enemies here — they are making their last grand attack. I *must & will* defeat them, for I know that I am right & that I have tried to do my duty. It is possible, not probable, that I may be detained here over Sunday — be sure my own dearest darling that I will not stay away one hour more than I can help. I am in a *battle* & must fight it out. I pray that God will aid me & give the right success. Kiss the dear little baby for me — God bless her — & believe me to be with truest love from your own fond husband

Geo McC

ALS, McClellan Papers (B-12:48), Library of Congress.

1. Col. Thomas M. Key.

To Mary Ellen McClellan

[Washington] Willards Saturday
My own dearest darling midnight [February 28, 1863]

Although I am tired nearly to death I can't go to bed without saying good night to you my own dearest one. I have just got back from that confounded Committee & have to appear before them again on Monday morning. I have been under their hands for several hours & you may imagine that my brain is *rather* tired out. I have been tramping up & down the Committee room for I don't know how long — my brain on a constant stretch, watching like a hawk for the training of every question, for fear that I should be tripped in some way or other. I dined yesterday very pleasantly with the Wyse's & after dinner Wright & I dropped in upon the Stoeckles — it was perfectly ridiculous the effect. We found the whole Diplomatic Corps there except Gerolt & it was very clear that they all thought there was some hidden meaning to the visit. Lord Lyons would not let me get out of his sight![1] Mrs. S was charming as ever. I saw Miss Robbins too, who is staying there. Today I half dined at Montgomery Blairs — that is I dropped in there for an hour while the Committee took a recess. I met there old Mr. Blair, head of the House, Fox & some ladies — a very pleasant party. I learn here that the Blairs have been strong consistent friends of mine through all the troubles of the past few months. I have all sorts of kind & pleasant messages for you from everyone I met. I am very sorry that I did not bring you on, for I find that I have no chance in Washn without you! Mrs. Stoeckle sent all sorts of kind messages for you — as did every one else that I met, & I sincerely believe, you little scamp, that you are far more popular in Washn today than your husband is.

I have been interrupted so often since I began this that it is after one o'clock & I have lost the thread of what I wanted to say, except that I miss you more than I can express, you dear little sweet darling. I can't help thinking when here of that awful morning when I had the confidential interview with you, when you did *not* love me, by a great deal.[2] I am foolish enough sometimes to feel sadly about it — to regret that the time *once was* when I did not possess your whole heart & soul. I can't realize *now* that such a state of things ever *could* exist, but it does make me feel sadly when I pass by the corner where we had those meetings, & I think how little you then realized the intense love I bore you. *Will* you understand it now — you do know *now* how I worship the ground you stand upon, God bless you. I *must* say good night now you dearest darling. I *hope* that I will be able to leave here Monday, but I don't know now. With fervent love, your own

George

ALS, McClellan Papers (B-12:48), Library of Congress.

1. The diplomats mentioned are Baron Stoeckel, of Russia; Baron Gerold, of Prussia; and Lord Lyons, of Great Britain. 2. GBM refers here to his first proposal of marriage, in June 1854, which was rejected.

To Fitz John Porter

My dear Fitz [New York] March 11 1863

If your engagements will at all permit you to do so you can help us out very much by taking up the siege of Yorktown & putting it in shape. Hardie[1] has all the papers.

From your position at the time I think you can do the subject justice better than any one else.

When could you take it up — if at all?[2]

I have nothing new — have you?

Ever yours
Geo B McC

Maj Genl F J Porter

ALS, Rare Book Collection, Huntington Library.

1. Lt. Col. James A. Hardie. 2. Apparently Porter wrote, or at least edited, the Yorktown section of GBM's report. Porter to GBM, Mar. 18, 1863, McClellan Papers (A-89:35), Library of Congress.

To Elizabeth B. McClellan

My dear Mother [New York] Sunday March 15 [1863]

Nelly wrote to you yesterday a note, that will go with this, asking you to come on and make us a visit — we are both most sincerely anxious that you should do so, for we shall not regard ourselves as fairly settled in our new home until you have been here to see what it is like. It is a very pleasant house & I am sure that you would like it very much. It is a bright cheerful house in itself, & in one of the most pleasant portions of the City — a part that was well in the country when you knew New York long ago, but now in the heart of the City. We are having a quiet time this evening — as we do not see company on Sunday when we can avoid it — for even in New York I think that one is entitled to one quiet day in the week. The baby has improved beyond description — has grown much, is as rugged as a young bear & talks a great deal — she is active as a cat & is never quiet for a moment except when asleep.

By way of compensation for the unnatural weather we have had during the winter, we are now luxuriating in cold weather — I presume you have the same — the skaters are rejoiced & the ice dealers more encouraged than they were.

When I returned from Washington I passed through Philadelphia at about 4 in the morning — as that was a rather unreasonable hour I did not think it worth while to wake you up & passed through without stopping — more especially as I had been absent longer than I expected when I left home. I hope not to be obliged to go to Washn again for a long time, but to be allowed to remain quietly in New York at least until my report is completed, which will be in a few weeks — for it is an immense task & will be a frightfully long production. Miss Helen Reece came to see Nelly yesterday — I did not see her — she told Nell that she had not seen me since I was 5 years old — but I think she must have been mistaken as I remember the family very well.

I hope that you *will* bring Mary on to see us. We are both very earnestly desirous of seeing you here & think you will enjoy it. Don't let anything prevent you from doing so. Nell's love & mine to Mary, John, Maria & the children — also to the Coxes & Phillips etc.

Ever your affectionate son
Geo B McClellan

ALS, McClellan Papers (B-41:61), Library of Congress.

To Robert C. Winthrop

22 West 31st St
My dear Mr Winthrop New York March 25 [1863]

My conscience reproaches me for allowing your kind note of the 13th to remain so long unanswered. Permit me now to thank you for it, as well as for the Eulogy — which I have read with much interest.

I often wish that I could luxuriate among the books of the [*illegible*] Library & gratify my love for reading! We *are* really at housekeeping, & I can assure you that no two persons in the world enjoy the possession of a home more than my wife and myself. We have been such wanderers all our lives that the prospect of a permanent home is perfectly delightful to us.

The Eulogy has taken its place in my library — not a very large one, I must confess, for a vagrant soldier collects almost as few books as a rolling stone does moss — but still large enough to give me employment in the few leisure hours I have. In unpacking my books I find an old parchment bound copy of "Bernal Diaz" — the first edition, published in 1632. I purchased it from the library of a "Convento" in Puebla in /47 — is it of any interest or value to collectors? I never met with any other copy of that edition — but I do not know whether it is rare or the reverse.[1]

I remember that neither the "Padre Guardian" of the Convent, nor any of his "compadres" had ever read the book , or were even cognizant of its existence in their library until I unearthed it in my search for something readable among their shelves of bad theology!

We have not yet recovered, & I trust that we never shall, from the pleasant impressions made by our Boston visit. It is one of my dreams now to go there *quietly* and to enjoy Boston in a very leisurely manner.

Mrs McClellan desires me to send her kindest regards to your daughter & yourself — in which I beg leave to join, & to express the hope that we may soon see you in New York.

I am my dear sir most sincerely & respectfully
Your friend
Geo B McClellan

Hon Robert C Winthrop

ALS, Winthrop Papers, Massachusetts Historical Society. Winthrop, a long-time political figure in Massachusetts, had served in both houses of Congress.

1. Winthrop replied on Apr. 2 that a first edition of *The True History of the Conquest of New Spain* was not of great value at the time, but suggested GBM record the story of its acquisition on the flyleaf, and one day "I am sure it will command a price which might now seem fabulous." McClellan Papers (A-89:35), Library of Congress.

To R. J. Atkinson

R J Atkinson Esq
3rd Auditor Treasury Dept Washington D.C. New York
Sir: April 16 1863

I have the honor to acknowledge the receipt of your letter of the 18th Nov last in reference to expenditure of monies advanced by the State of Ohio for secret service.[1]

From the early part of May 1861 I placed the conduct of the secret service Dept in the hands of Mr Allen Pinkerton & turned over to him the money I received from the State of Ohio for that purpose. I enclose with this Mr Pinkerton's account in detail of the monies thus expended, this account being made out in the same form & in all respects on the same basis as his accounts for similar services with the War Dept during the last two years.

The amount expended is in excess of that drawn from the State of Ohio, & was advanced from private means to meet exigencies as they arose.

The balance found due should be paid Mr Allen Pinkerton whose address is Chicago Illinois.

With the hope that this account will prove satisfactory to you

I am, Sir, very respectfully your obdt svt
Geo B McClellan
Maj Genl USA

ALS retained copy, McClellan Papers (A-90:35), Library of Congress.

1. Atkinson's letter of Nov. 18, 1862, requested documentation for some $12,000 in secret service funds for which the state of Ohio was seeking reimbursement from the federal government. McClellan Papers (A-88:35).

To Andrew A. Humphreys

Brig. Gen. A. A. Humphreys,
Fifth Corps, Army of the Potomac,
Falmouth, Va.:
General: New York, April 21, 1863

Your letter of the 13th instant is received.[1] It will afford me pleasure to make the corrections your letter suggests in the full and final report I am now preparing. My impression has been that your command was not in condition to be thrown into action until near the close of the 18th, if then; but I never attributed any blame to you or your troops for it, regarding it as the necessary result of circumstances beyond your control.

I do not now see that any censure upon yourself could be implied from the paragraph you quote. None was intended.

I am, very respectfully, your obedient servant,
Geo. B. McClellan
Major-General, U.S. Army

Copy, Fitz John Porter Papers, Library of Congress. *OR*, Ser. 1, LI, Part 1, p. 1009. Humphreys had commanded a Fifth Corps division in the Maryland campaign.

1. Humphreys wrote that GBM was in error in his recently published preliminary report on Antietam, dated Oct. 15, 1862, in giving as one reason he did not renew the fighting on Sept. 18 that "Humphreys's division of new troops, fatigued with forced marches, were arriving throughout the day, but were not available until near its close." *OR*, Ser. 1, LI, Part 1, pp. 1005–1006.

To Richard Wallach

Richard Wallach Esq
Mayor of the City of Washington
Sir: New York May 14 1863

I have the honor to acknowledge the receipt, through Mr. Altermehle and the Committee, of the Resolutions passed by the Board of Aldermen & Common Council of the City of Washington, expression of the appreciation of its citizens of my services in its defence, & tendering me their thanks.

I receive this expression of confidence with unusual pride and satisfaction, for I must confess that the most anxious hours of my life, and my most unremitting labors have been bestowed upon the safety of our Capital; which I once found entirely open & defenceless, and on another occasion threatened by a powerful & victorious army.

That those most deeply interested in the safety of the City are satisfied with the efforts of the troops I commanded, & their results, is a sufficient reward for our exertions. I beg that you will offer my sincere thanks to the gentlemen of the Board of Aldermen & of the Common Council, for the great honor they have bestowed upon me, and, with my thanks to you personally,[1]

believe me to be very truly & respectfully your obedient servant
Geo B McClellan
Maj Genl USA

ALS retained copy, McClellan Papers (A-90:35), Library of Congress.

1. In addition to Washington and New York, a number of cities tendered similar resolutions of appreciation to GBM, including Baltimore, Albany, Buffalo, and Utica.

To James A. Hardie

Lt Col Jas A Hardie
Asst Adjt General Washington D.C.
Sir: New York May 25 1863

I have the honor to acknowledge the receipt of a copy of a letter from Maj Genl Butler to the Secty of War, dated May 1 1863, with your endorsement thereon.[1]

Genl Butler has made an entirely erroneous statement in regard to my case.

As the facts really are his argument proves that I am unquestionably the senior Major General on the active list, whether of Regulars or Volunteers.

I shall therefore make no comments upon his argument, but correct his misstatements as they occur in his letter.

I was appointed a Major General in the Regular Army *not on the 24th of July 1861,* as he states, *but on the 14th of May 1861.*

I was notified by telegram of the fact on the evening of that day, and have now in my possession the original letter of appointment *dated & issued on May 14th,* received in due course of mail, and at once accepted.

General Butler asserts that he was appointed a Major General of Volunteers, was actually in the active service of the U.S. in command of a Department two weeks before any letter of appointment issued to any other Major General of the U.S. Army or Volunteers, and more than two months before any Major Genl of the U.S. Army was appointed after the rebellion, & that his letter of appointment was dated *May 16* 1861 & that he assumed command of the Dept. of S.E. Virginia on the 22d May.

Now the truth is that my appointment as a Major General of the Regular Army was *dated* and *issued* on the 14th of May 1861 — two days before his appointment as a Maj Genl of Vols, and six days before he assumed command of the Dept of S E Virginia; it will presently appear that I was already in command of a Dept under another & earlier commission.

Genl Butler also says that he was assigned to the command of the Dept of Annapolis (as a Brig. Genl) on the *27th April 1861* and that "at this time Generals McClellan and Banks were drawing their salaries as officers in their respective railroads." The fact is that on the *23rd of April 1861* I was commissioned and mustered in as a "Major General of the Ohio Militia *mustered into the service of the U.S.* under requisition of the Presdt dated April 15 1861." I entered upon the performance of my duty as a Major General on the same day — April 23 1861 — and from that date devoted my entire time and attention to my military duties, so that at the time specified by Genl Butler, April 27 1861, I was actively engaged in the command and organization of the Ohio troops.

There will be found on file in the Adjt Genl's office official letters from me of the date of *April 27* 1861 & earlier.

On the 3rd of May 1861 I was (as Major General of the Ohio Volunteers) assigned by the War Dept to the command of the Department of the Ohio, then consisting of the states of Ohio, Indiana & Illinois — prior to that my command was confined to the State of Ohio.

Thus instead of Genl Butler's appointment *being senior to mine by two months,* mine as a *Major General of the regular Army* is *senior to his in the Vols* by *two days,* while my appointment as a Maj Genl of Vols in the U.S. service is *senior to his* by *23 days,* & *senior even to his service as a Brig Genl.* In brief, I claim to be the senior Major Genl on the active list, whether of the Regular Army or Volunteers, because my actual appointment as a Major General of the Regular Army is prior to that of any other Major Genl, & because when I received *that* appointment I was actually performing the duty of the grade (comdg a Dept etc) under a Volunteer Commission under which I had been mustered into the U.S. service 21 days earlier than the date of my commission in the Regular Army.

So far as General Butler is concerned, I had received the appointment and entered upon the active duties of a Major General before the time he claims to have entered upon duty even as a Brig Genl.

By referring to the history of the present war it will be found that, prior to the date upon which General Butler erroneously says that I was appointed, I had as a Maj Genl of the Regular Army organized an Army & conducted a successful campaign, by which Western Virginia was restored to the Genl Govt, & an Army of the enemy destroyed.

I had supposed that every General Officer knew that I held a commission during that campaign. I respectfully request that you will lay this statement before the Secty of War, & that you will acknowledge its receipt.

I have the honor to be very respectfully your obedient servant
Geo B McClellan
Maj Genl USA

ALS retained copy, McClellan Papers (A-90:36), Library of Congress. Hardie, formerly of GBM's staff, was now serving at army headquarters in Washington.

1. Gen. Butler's eleven-page letter is fairly summarized by GBM. Seniority, Butler wrote, is "a right won in the service of the country, an honor to be prized, [and] I know you will commend me if I insist, with pertinacious firmness upon its complete acknowledgment." In his endorsement, Hardie asked for arguments on the matter so that it might be submitted to a board of officers. GBM's argument was correct in all respects. McClellan Papers (A-90:35).

To Charles C. Fulton

Private
Chas C Fulton Esq
Dear Sir New York May 28 /63

Your letter of the 27 is received.[1] I regarded our conversation as entirely a private one, brought on in consequence of the note of introduction you brought to me from Judge Blair;[2] I had no idea of talking for the public, nor that our interview should lead to any letters for publication.

Your letter as a general thing expresses my views, which you have made in some cases rather stronger & wider than I intended, & in others less so. But, for reasons which I need not explain, I have made it a rule to avoid writing letters for publication, & have sought to remain as quiet as possible, & I do not feel that the time has yet arrived for me to depart from my custom, & I therefore request that my conversation may not be regarded as a subject for publication.

With many thanks for your good opinion & kind feeling

I am etc etc
G B McC —

ALS retained copy, McClellan Papers (A-90:35), Library of Congress. Fulton was editor of the *Baltimore American*.

1. Fulton had an interview with GBM on May 26, which he sought permission to publish. He had understood GBM to say, he wrote, "that all talk of 'terms of peace' and 'conciliation' and 'compromise,' with men arrayed in armed hostility to the Government, was simply ridiculous, and never had or ever could receive any consideration or favor from you." He further understood GBM's motto to be "Union first — peace last," and that whatever stood in the way of reunion, "whether it be property in men, or property of other descriptions, must be thrust aside, and that a cordial and enthusiastic support is due to the President and the Government...." McClellan Papers (A-90:35). 2. Montgomery Blair.

To Samuel S. Cox

Hon S S Cox
Columbus Ohio
Dear Sir New York June 8/63

I have the pleasure to acknowledge the receipt of your letter of the 31st intimating that it is possible that my name may be presented to the Democratic State Convention of Ohio as a candidate for nomination as Governor of that State.[1]

I feel the strongest interest in the welfare of a State whose gallant sons have done so much for the country in its time of peril, & to which I am indebted for the Major Generalship that called me again to the military service of the U.S. but I should be compelled to decline the nomination were it offered me.

Accept for yourself & offer to our friends my sincere thanks for this new evidence of their good opinion.

& believe me to be very truly yours,
G B McClellan

ALS retained copy, McClellan Papers (A-90:35), Library of Congress. Cox was a Democratic congressman from Ohio.

1. "You can be nominated with a perfect furor," Cox wrote on May 31, "and an election would be a foregone conclusion." If GBM did not accept the nomination, he added, he feared it would be captured by the peace Democrat Clement L. Vallandigham. McClellan Papers (A-90:35).

To Thurlow Weed

Private

My dear Sir

Oaklands[1] — June 13/63

Your kind note is just received.[2]

For what I cannot doubt that you would consider good reasons I have determined to decline the compliment of presiding over the proposed meeting of Monday next [June 15].

I fully concur with you in the conviction that an honorable peace is not now possible, and that the war must be prosecuted to save the Union and the Government at whatever cost of time treasure & blood.

I am clear, also, in the conviction that the policy governing the conduct of the war should be one looking not only to military success, but also to ultimate reunion, & that it should consequently be such as to preserve the rights of all Union loving citizens — wherever they may be — as far as compatible with military necessity.

My views as to the prosecution of the war remain substantially as they have been from the beginning of the contest — these views I have often made known officially.

I will endeavor to write to you more fully before Monday —

In the mean time

believe me to be in great haste truly your friend
Geo B McClellan

Hon Thurlow Weed
New York

ALS, Thurlow Weed Papers, Rush Rhees Library, University of Rochester. Weed was a veteran New York political manager associated with William H. Seward.

1. A country estate in the Hudson Valley, where the McClellans were visiting. 2. Weed wrote GBM on June 12 urging him to preside at a mass meeting in New York to rally support for the war, "availing yourself of the occasion to say that this Government and Union must be preserved; that both are worth all it may cost to save them; . . . and that

there can be no Peace until the authority of the Government is re-established.... Some such avowals from your lips, just now, would refresh the country.'' McClellan Papers (A-90:35), Library of Congress.

To Samuel L. M. Barlow

My dear Sam Oaklands June 15 [1863]

I enclose a reply to the invitation — read it & send in if you think it will do — it is written very hurriedly & therefore must be bad.[1]

I had a telegram from Gov Seymour this evg. asking me to go to Albany to assist him in organizing troops called for from Washn — I replied asking when he wanted me & expect to go there tomorrow.[2]

I will see you within a few days, but this unexpected call overturns my calculations — I shall remain with the Gov as long as I can be of any real service to him. Will probably have my staff join me there, & try my hand at hard work again.

I will write to you from there — was sorry to miss you on Friday, but I had not time to go to your office.

Ever yours
McC

S L M X Q B

ALS, Barlow Papers, Huntington Library.

1. Either GBM's letter of June 13 to Thurlow Weed, *supra,* or a similar letter of June 11 to James T. Brady, an organizer of the mass meeting. McClellan Papers (A-90:35), Library of Congress. 2. Secretary Stanton had called for militia to meet an invasion of Maryland and Pennsylvania by Gen. Lee's army.

To Edward Everett

My dear Mr Everett Orange New Jersey July 6 1863

On my arrival here a few days ago I found your kind note of the 18th ulto, with the enclosure, awaiting me.[1] Permit me again to express my thanks for the light in which you choose to view my relations with the present crisis, & for the kind manner in which you have written to the Presdt about me.

If one can believe the news this morning, the country, thanks to Genl Meade & the magnificent Army of the Potomac, is safe for the present at least — for it would seem that Lee will find full occupation in making his way homeward again.[2] What the effect may be upon the general policy of the Administration I cannot forsee — but it will clearly enable them to keep me in retirement, & I am only too glad that my services may not now be necessary.

After some unexpected & vexatious delays my report is now in the hands of the copyists, & will — I hope — be finished this week. If circumstances are such as to enable me to hold it back long enough I will take the liberty of sending it to you for revision — although it is possible that I may be obliged to send it in without further delay.

I am happy to say that quiet & country air have quite restored Mrs McClellan's health. She desires me to send her kindest regards to you

I am my dear Sir, in haste, most respectfully & truly,
Your friend
Geo B McClellan

Hon Edward Everett
Boston

ALS, Everett Papers, Massachusetts Historical Society.

1. With his letter of June 18 Everett enclosed an extract of a letter he had written President Lincoln on June 16 urging that GBM be restored to command of the Army of the Potomac. "Your order to that effect would be worth 50,000 men . . . and it is a certain fact that General McClellan has the confidence of the entire Democratic party of both wings; of the Conservative party; and of the Conservative wing of the Republican party to a great extent." Everett urged GBM to accept the command if offered, even though it was unjust "to keep placing you, in moments of peril, at the head of demoralized armies. . . ." McClellan Papers (A-90:35), Library of Congress. 2. The Battle of Gettysburg was fought on July 1–3.

To George G. Meade

My dear General: New York, July 11, 1863.

I have abstained from writing to you simply because I hear that you have no time to read letters — but I will say a word now, anyhow.

I wish to offer you my sincere and heartfelt congratulations upon the glorious victory you have achieved, and the splendid way in which you assumed control of our noble old army under such trying circumstances.

You have done all that could be done and the Army of the Potomac has supported you nobly. I don't know that, situated as I am, my opinion is worth much to any of you — but I can trust saying that I feel very proud of you and my old Army. I don't flatter myself that your work is over — I believe that you have another severe battle to fight, but I am confident that you will win.[1]

That God may bless you and your army in its future conflicts is the prayer of

Your sincere friend
Geo. B. McClellan

Maj. Gen'l G. G. Meade
Comdg. Army of Potomac

George G. Meade, *The Life and Letters of George Gordon Meade* (New York, 1913), II, p. 312.

1. Meade replied on July 14 that already he detected a counter-reaction to his victory, "Lee having crossed the [Potomac] river last night without waiting for me to attack him in one of the strongest positions he has ever occupied. I do assure you General I appreciate in the highest degree, the value of your favorable opinion, and the A. of the Potomac will be delighted to know that their old & cherished commander watches & is gratified at their success." McClellan Papers (A-90:35), Library of Congress.

To Samuel S. Cox

My dear Cox Orange New Jersey July 14 [1863]

Your kind letter of a month ago reached me some time after it was written, as I was for several weeks absent from home.[1]

I am very much obliged to you for the manner in which you managed the whole affair — I would have made no suggestions for any change.

I think you are quite right in not having my letter published — I hoped that no publication would be necessary, & felt sure that you would keep the affair as quiet as possible.

It seems that they had a terrible time in New York yesterday — & no one seems to know whether the disturbance is at an end or not — God help our poor country![2] I sometimes almost despair when I see so few who really comprehend the state of affairs! The Govt must come back to the true & original issues before it can hope to have the support of the great mass of the people — & without their cordial support I see but little hope for ultimate success.

With the hope that Morgan[3] wont reach Columbus & my sincere well wishes for you

I am ever your friend
Geo B McC

Hon S S Cox

ALS, Thomas F. Madigan Collection, Rare Books and Manuscripts Division, New York Public Library.

1. Cox wrote on June 13 that he had not read GBM's letter [June 8, *supra*] to the Ohio Democratic nominating convention, "so that no sort of embarrassment has been produced by the suggestion of your name" as a candidate for governor. "I have not had your letter published, altho' it would read well enough to the public, but it is best as it is." McClellan Papers (A-90:35), Library of Congress. Vallandigham won the Democratic nomination, but lost the election on Oct. 13. 2. GBM refers to the New York draft riot. 3. The Confederate cavalry raider John Hunt Morgan.

To Allan Pinkerton

My dear Allan: Orange, New Jersey July 17, 1863

Yours of the 10th was delayed a little in reaching me on account of my absence from the city, but it came I think in due course of mail. I am much obliged to you for it. I can well imagine the state of affairs you describe during the Battle of Gettysburg. I suppose, "How does it look now?" often passed over the wires.[1] To be trapped like a rat? What you say about Meade having been some days in command before it was announced, is very new to me — and not yet improbable — what is to be done with Hooker now?

James D. Horan, *The Pinkertons: The Detective Dynasty That Made History* (New York, 1967), pp. 136–37.

1. The president several times had sent this query to GBM during the Maryland campaign.

To Erastus Corning

Private

My dear Mr Corning New York Aug 1 1863

I trust that I need not apologize to you for taking the great liberty of asking a favor.

I wish to call your attention to the case of Genl Fitz John Porter, in the hope that it may be in your power to do something for him. To explain the case better than I can in my own words I will give you an extract from a *private* note I received from Porter a few days ago — he says "I was anxious for occupation then — but now that the invasion of Maryland has rendered entirely dependent upon me my mother and my nephew (an invalid & a cripple) I am anxious for and am trying to get employment. Others are or soon will be dependent on my exertions. I did expect to weather the storm till another administration — but my sails have been rent, & my ship waterlogged. When in service my nephew & mother were dependent upon me — & what could be spared from my family went to them. Hence I saved nothing.... If there is any place coming to your knowledge which you think I can fill & get, I will thank you most kindly to speak a favorable word. I think I can do almost anything — or can make myself capable in a short time — and a will to please will be carried to my work. Do you know of any opening on railroads, or any supervision work?"

As this was in a private letter I would be glad that you should regard it as confidential.

I believe you know Porter & what he is — I will answer for his integrity, energy & ability.

If there *is* any opening on the Central R.R. I am sure that you would find a man of Porter's character & caliber invaluable.

I need not say to you how grateful I should be could you find it in your power to do anything for Porter. If *you* can do nothing, will you do me the favor to advise me in what direction to direct my efforts in his behalf.[1]

With my kindest regards to the ladies

I am sincerely your friend
Geo B McClellan

Hon Erastus Corning

ALS, Simon Gratz Autograph Collection, Historical Society of Pennsylvania. Corning was a New York financier and the president of the New York Central Railroad.

1. Some six months later Porter found employment in a mining venture in Colorado Territory.

To Lorenzo Thomas

Brig Genl L Thomas
Adjt Genl USA
General New York Aug 4 1863

I have the honor to forward herewith my Report of the operations of the Army of the Potomac while under my command, together with accompanying documents.

They will be handed to you by my Aide de Camp Captain Arthur McClellan whom I send to Washington for this purpose.

In view of all the circumstances of the case I respectfully request permission to publish the Report.

I am sir very respectfully your obdt svt
Geo B McClellan
Maj Genl USA

ALS retained copy, McClellan Papers (A-90:35), Library of Congress.

To Edward Everett

My dear Mr Everett New York Aug 4/63

Your very kind letter of the 25th reached me after some little delay.[1]

I thank you sincerely for your kind suggestions.

I agree with you fully that the Report of the Committee on the Conduct of the War merits little if any attention.

I had not, until I received your letter, heard of the rumor to which you allude, in regard to intentions entertained by leaders of the Democratic party of marching on Washington. I am satisfied that there is not one word of truth in the report, & you may rest assured that had such a thing been contemplated it would have received no countenance from me. I am sure that the Democracy have no intention of making any other opposition to the Administration than a strictly legal one.

I supposed that the prompt & energetic action of Gov Seymour in sending troops to Penna before the battle of Gettysburg would have convinced the most prejudiced of the entire loyalty of that gentleman, & all who act & think with him.

I write more fully to Mr Lawrence in regard to the other topic of your letter, & shall request him to show my letter to you.

We leave tomorrow for a quiet place at the sea side — East Hampton, Long Island — where we expect to spend a few weeks.

Mrs. McC — whose health is much improved — desires me to send her kind regards.

I am, my dear Sir, in haste most respectfully & truly yours
Geo B McClellan

Hon Edward Everett
Boston

ALS, Everett Papers, Massachusetts Historical Society.

1. Everett wrote on July 25 that the *Report of the Joint Committee on the Conduct of the War*, published earlier in the year, "made no impression on the public mind to your disadvantage. . . ." He also reported an "absurd rumor" current in Boston "that before Lee's repulse at Gettysburg, there was a project formed by certain Democratic leaders in New York & elsewhere, to raise a force, with you at the head, to march on Washington, and expel the present administration." To dispel such rumors, he seconded a proposal by fellow Bostonian James Lawrence that GBM clarify his views on the prosecution of the war so that neither friends nor enemies could continue to benefit by his silence. McClellan Papers (A-90:35), Library of Congress.

To Elizabeth B. McClellan

My dear Mother East Hampton L.I. Aug 9 1863

I had fully intended to run on to see you before coming to this place, but was prevented by the delay in getting my Report finished — so that I was kept in N.Y. until the very day before starting hither.

This is a quiet old village — quite a jumping off place — way beyond railways & such modern inventions of the enemy. It is a village founded in 1649 which retains pretty much unchanged the habits & customs of that somewhat distant period. It is about one mile from the sea — by the road a little less in a direct line. There are no Hotels — no such modern inventions having reached here yet, & it being the sincere & continual prayer of the inhabitants that they may be preserved from "Hotels, Railways, Telegraphs, Mails, Newspapers, Bad Whiskey & all other pestilences." We have rooms in one quiet old house, & take our meals in another — the residence of a retired & one eyed Captain of a whale ship. Quite a number of people are boarding in the village in the same manner — but they seem to have a happy faculty of minding their own affairs, & don't trouble us much more than we do them — occasionally a wagon load of aborigines ride out to look at the wild beast — but soon depart quite contented with a frightened shake of the hands & a good stare.

We breakfast at 7 1/2 — loaf until 10 — then go to bathe — at least shall do so if they stop drowning people — dine at one — sleep in the afternoon — then walk or drive — tea at 6 — another talk or walk & then go to sleep! An unfortunate boy was drowned on Friday — so that bathing was suspended yesterday. But if nobody else is drowned meanwhile we will try it again tomorrow. Nelly and the baby are quite well — but suffering from the heat which happens by some strange chance to be quite intense just now — fortunately there are no mosquitoes & we have strong hopes that it will be cool again in a day or two.

Arthur tells me that the Coxe family was pretty generally drafted! I hope they will put Arthur on Sedgwick's staff & I presume they will.

Give my best love to Mary, John, Maria & the children — remember me kindly to the Coxes

& believe me ever with warmest love from Nelly & the baby
your affectionate son
Geo B McC

ALS, McClellan Papers (B-13:49), Library of Congress.

To Samuel L. M. Barlow

My dear S L M — East Hampton L I Aug 11 1863

I have received your two kind notes, & am most obliged to you for them.[1]

I am very glad to learn that the Report is actually turned in, & that Arthur was assigned to Sedgwick's staff[2] — Arthur promised to write to me, but has not yet done so. I will write to Grant & Banks at an early day — within two or three days. We have had terribly hot weather here, & were almost discouraged, but a fine sea breeze has sprung up this evening & we hope for better things. If Crocker can give us rooms it is possible that we will go to New London next week — somewhere about the 18th or 20th. There are very few here whom I ever met before, & not a particularly interesting lot — but the bathing is superb.

With my kindest regards to Mrs Barlow when you write, & to Prime & Marble.[3]

I am ever sincerely yours
Geo McC

Won't you drop in at my house some day & see whether there are any letters of importance for me, expecially from Corning about F.J.P.
McC

ALS, Barlow Papers, Huntington Library.

1. In an Aug. 8 letter Barlow cited a *New York Herald* account that GBM's report had been filed at the War Dept. 2. Arthur McClellan was posted to the staff of Maj. Gen. John Sedgwick of the Sixth Corps. 3. Editors William C. Prime, of the *Journal of Commerce,* and Manton Marble, of the *New York World.*

To Samuel L. M. Barlow

My dear S L M East Hampton L I Aug 17 1863

Your last note with the enclosed letters reached me on Saturday.

I have a note from Ketchum[1] urging me to let him take the Report to his office — & I think it will be best to do so. I have written to him that he might have it — but said to him that it was my only copy & that you were having another made by your clerks in their leisure hours. I am half sorry he wants it, but he has taken so much trouble for me & acted such a friendly part that I do not feel that I ought to disoblige him. We shall not get to New London before Friday [August 21] — & *perhaps* not then, as we have not heard from Crocker, to whom I wrote about a week ago. I hope, however to hear from him this evening.

We have nothing new here, & I am not bothered by news from other parts of the world.

In haste ever yours
McC

S L M Barlow Esq

ALS, Barlow Papers, Huntington Library.

1. Hiram Ketchum, who frequently wrote to newspapers in GBM's defense.

To Samuel L. M. Barlow

Pequot House [New London, Conn.]
My dear Sam Thursday [August 27, 1863]

I take the liberty of addressing to you the commission of Baron Ordustrom, a Swedish officer sent to me by Gov. Seymour. I have written to him to call for it at your office, & have done so because I am not certain that a note to the care of the Swedish Consul would reach him. Had a very pleasant sail, & fishing to a comfortable extent. Can get the Madgie for Monday if Prime will take the Fisher's Island trip. Do come on Sunday if you can.

Ever yours
McC

Hudson writes that they are devoting themselves to "paperasse"[1] & red tape in the Army of the Potomac, & that the soldiers have altered the close of their favorite song to read as follows

"McClellan was our leader, now he is gone.
God help us all as we are marching along!"[2]

ALS, Barlow Papers, Huntington Library.

1. "Official papers." 2. The standard chorus of William B. Bradford's "Marching Along" included the lines, "McClellan's our leader, he's gallant and strong / For God and our country we are marching along."

To Samuel L. M. Barlow

My dear Barlow [New York, c. September 25, 1863]

From what I hear I doubt whether the performance tonight will be through in time for me to see you this evening.

I have heard about all that can be said in regard to the Penna proposition & shall give it full & fair consideration[1] — but I see that I can do nothing in the way of cool thinking here — so I shall do that part of it in Orange.

Say to Gov Church[2] that I shall not be prepared to give a final answer tomorrow morning, & that I will write to you on the subject tomorrow.

The matter is at that point where more talking will do no good — I must decide it for myself & in my own way. Further pressure would only induce a negative decision — to which I confess that I am inclined.

Marcy arrives tomorrow morning.

In great haste ever yours
McClellan

S.L.M.B.

ALS, Barlow Papers, Huntington Library.

1. The matter of endorsing the Democratic candidate for governor of Pennsylvania. See GBM to Charles J. Biddle, Oct. 12, *infra*. The immediate question was whether GBM should make an appearance in Philadelphia. He did so, arriving on Sept. 29. 2. Sanford E. Church, former lieutenant governor of New York. Church and Gov. Seymour, Barlow wrote GBM on Sept. 26, "honestly believe that you can save the election in Pa. by your mere presence. The same opinion is expressed by very many of your warmest personal, political and army friends." McClellan Papers (B-23:53), Library of Congress.

To Charles J. Biddle

Hon Chas J Biddle
Phila
Dear Sir Orange New Jersey Oct 12 1863 —

My attention has been called to an article in the Phila Press asserting that I had written to the Managers of a Democratic meeting at Allentown disapproving the objects of the meeting, that if I voted or spoke it would be in favor of Gov Curtin.[1]

I am informed that similar assertions have been made throughout the state [*crossed out:* for the purpose of inducing persons supposed to be friendly to me to cast their influence against Judge Woodward in the coming election].

It has been my earnest endeavor, heretofore, to avoid participation in party politics, & I had determined to adhere to this course [*crossed out:* so long as my regard for the interests of the country would permit, for my profession is that of a soldier, not a politician].

But it is obvious that I cannot longer maintain silence under such misrepresentations. I therefore request you to deny that I have written any such letter or entertained any such views as those attributed to me in the Phila Press, and I desire to state clearly and distinctly that, having some few days ago had a full conversation with Judge Woodward, I find that our views agree and I regard his election as Governor of Penna called for by the interests of the nation.

I understand Judge Woodward to be in favor of the prosecution of the war with all the means at the command of the loyal states, until the military [*crossed out:* & political] power of the rebellion is destroyed; I understand him to be of the opinion that, while the war is waged with all possible decision and energy, the policy directing it should be in consonance with the principles of humanity & civilization, working no injury to private rights & property not demanded by military necessity & recognized by military law among civilized nations; and, finally, I understand him to agree with me in the opinion that the *sole* great objects of this war are the restoration of the unity of the nation, the preservation of the Constitution, & the supremacy of the laws of the country.

Believing that our opinions entirely agree upon these points, & that he feels, as I do, that the maintainance of our national unity is of vital necessity, I would, were it in my power, give to Judge Woodward my voice & my vote.[2]

Geo B McClellan

ALS retained copy, McClellan Papers, Illinois State Historical Library. Biddle was state chairman of the Democratic party in Pennsylvania.

1. In the Pennsylvania gubernatorial election, Republican governor Curtin was being challenged by Democrat George W. Woodward, of the state supreme court. See also GBM to Henry M. Naglee, Sept. 23, 1864, *infra.* 2. As published in the *Philadelphia Press* on Oct. 13, the day of the election, this closing sentence read: "Believing that our opinions entirely agree upon these points, I would, were it in my power, give to Judge Woodward my voice and my vote."

To William Adams

My dear Doctor — Orange New Jersey Nov 18 1863

Next to seeing you en propre personne your kind letter of the 16 was the most acceptable event.

I regret very much that you cannot yet see the way clear to making us a visit, & that I missed you the other day. When we were last in the city it was a business visit & we were fully occupied — so that we really had no leisure to see any of our friends — but I will see you when I next visit the city.

We have not yet decided when to return to the city — probably not before the beginning of December if then. We shall remain here as long as the weather will permit — it is so much more quiet here.

I can hardly express my gratitude to Mr Stokes for his friendly thoughtfulness in regard to the seats in Church — I shall write to him on the subject, but will you, if you chance to see him in the mean time, say to him how warmly Mrs McC & I thank him for his goodness, & how fully we appreciate his regard.

I will try to write something for the Round Table. How many pages manuscript would be required? I don't think I should care to have my name appear. I must confess that situated as I am at present I would not object to increasing my income somewhat by the use of my pen.[1]

With *our* warmest regards to your family & yourself

I am as ever your sincere friend
Geo B McC

Rev Wm Adams

ALS, George B. McClellan, Jr., Papers, Library of Congress. Adams was pastor of the Madison Avenue Presbyterian Church in New York.

1. Between December 1863 and March 1864 *The Round Table,* a new journal of opinion, would publish five unsigned articles of military analysis by GBM.

To Abraham Lincoln

His Ex Abraham Lincoln etc
Your Excellency New York Nov 1863[1]

When the present war commenced I was successfully engaged in private life. Actuated solely by the desire to serve my country, I sacrificed all my personal interests, and accepted the Commission of Maj Genl in the Regular Army which you bestowed upon me without any solicitation from me. I have never applied to you directly or indirectly for any particular command position or duty, but have contented myself with performing to the best of my ability whatever duties you imposed upon me. It was in this spirit that I conducted the campaign of Western Virginia, and after its successful close I assumed control at Washington of the troops just defeated at the first battle of Manassas, organized and commanded the Army of the Potomac, received without being asked and gave up without complaining the position of Commander in Chief of the U.S. Armies, conducted the Peninsular Campaign, witnessed the transfer of my army to the command of Genl Pope, resumed it when the combined forces had been defeated and the Capital was in hourly peril, carried on the Maryland Campaign, and, thanks to my noble and tried comrades, gained the battles of South Mountain and Antietam, and it was in this spirit that, when in full advance with every probability of a successful battle impending, I again, and finally, yielded the command of that Army to which I was united by those inexpressibly close bonds which a soldier alone can appreciate.

I have been now for more than a year unemployed, and it is evident that my services are no longer desired by your Excellency. Under these circumstances I feel that I can be of no present use to my country by retaining my Commission, and I am unwilling longer to receive pay while performing no service.

It is now my duty to consult my private interests and those of my family — which I have entirely ignored and sacrificed during my continuance in service.

As a fitting opportunity has offered, and my conscience tells me that I have faithfully performed all the service I at present can for the benefit of my country, I have determined to return to private life, and have sent to the Adjt Genl the resignation of my Commission, which I beg may be at once accepted. Should unexpected, and I trust improbable, vicissitudes of fortune ever again, as heretofore, render my sword necessary to the nation, I shall again be ready to use it in her cause at any sacrifice to myself.

It would have been gratifying to me to have retired from the service with the knowledge that I still retained the approbation of your Excellency — as it is, I thank you for the confidence and kind feeling you once entertained for me, and which I am unconscious of having justly forfeited. I cannot, nor ought I to restrain myself from bidding through you a last farewell to the heroic men who so long fought under my command.

Neither time nor space can divide them from my heart; whatever fate the future may have in store for me, my pulse will ever beat more quickly, and my blood warm at the thought of the soldiers who were with me during the trying scenes of the Peninsula, at South Mountain & at Antietam.

I am grateful to Providence that it was permitted me that my last service should be to free the Capital a second time from danger and the loyal states from invasion.

I am content to bear as a legacy to my descendants the connection which already exists between my name and that of the proud Army of the Potomac. It can have far abler Commanders than myself, and may win even more glorious victories than those which now grace its annals, but it can have no General who will love it so well as I did.

I invoke upon it and the other Armies of the Republic the highest blessings of the Almighty, and in severing my official connection with your Excellency I pray that God may bless you, and so direct your counsels that you may succeed in restoring to this distracted land the inestimable boon of peace founded on the preservation of our Union and the mutual respect & sympathy of the now discordant and contending sections of our once happy country.

Geo B McClellan

ALS, McClellan Papers (A-91:36), Library of Congress.

1. GBM seems to have written this letter of resignation in anticipation of taking the presidency of the New Jersey Railroad and Transportation Co., offered to him on Nov. 19. He did not take the post, however, and the letter was not sent. J. J. Astor, Jr., to GBM, Nov. 19, 1863, McClellan Papers (A-91:36).

To Elizabeth B. McClellan

My dear Mother Orange New Jersey Dec 6 1863

Your kind & welcome letter of the 3rd reached me all right. I did not suppose that you would forget my birthday, but it was very pleasant to receive a letter from you written on that day. It so happened that we spent the most of that day in Newark — Col Wright's[1] little boy was to be christened & I was his God-father — so we went over early in the day, went to Church for the christening & then back to the house for a lunch, & reached home almost dark. The ceremony went off very well — as the baby did not cry & I did not drop him!! You see I am becoming quite skilful. We have not seen Mason[2] & his wife yet — he promised to let us know when they returned to New York, so we will probably see them during the coming week. I received the letter from Arthur which Mary[3] sent me on the 25 ulto & enclose with this a reply which I will be glad to have sent to him by the underground military.

I don't think Grant's army will get far enough down in Alabama to disturb Frederica[4] at their plantation — they are likely to remain quiet even if Mobile should be taken, as no gun boat of any size could get that far up the Alabama river. We have not fully decided as to remaining out here all winter, but shall almost certainly do so until Christmas. It is probable that it may prove too unpleasant in Jany & Feby — but if no change occurs in my own situation meantime, it is quite likely that we will remain here all winter. It is splendid for the baby — who rushes about in the open air looking more like the inhabitant of a shanty than anything else. Nell has a pretty good photograph of May which she will send you this week — I think you will like it. May talks now almost like anybody else — & moves anywhere & everywhere. We go in town this week on a visit of two or three days at Mrs. Alsop's — May goes with us. There are two or three weddings to come off which we can't well avoid attending, so we will kill two birds with one stone.

Marcy has just been ordered off on another tour of inspection — the Dept of Missouri this time — he will probably start tomorrow. He & Mrs M went into the city yesterday so that Nell & I have been entirely alone — a good quiet time. We had quite a bonfire on the Mountain a few nights ago — a house (not quite finished) burned down — we knew nothing of it until the next day, as it was at some distance from us. We are altogether alone on the Mountain now — all the families whom we know having some time since moved into the city. There are six houses in all on the Mountain. Has Eck Coxe[5] come back to be drafted? If he don't look out he may go down to pay Arthur a longer visit than he expected — in that event advise Arty to take him as his orderly!!! I feel very indifferent about the White House — for very many reasons I do not wish it — I shall do nothing to get it & trust that Providence will decide the matter as is best for the country.[6] Nell & the baby send their best love to you & Mary — Marcy & Mrs. M would were they here. Give Nell's love & mine to John, Maria & the children — to the Coxes & Boxes, & Phillips also. Tell Mary to write — & I wish you would oftener, my dear Mother — I will anyhow —

Ever your affectionate son
Geo B McC

ALS, McClellan Papers (B-13:49), Library of Congress.

1. Col. Edward H. Wright. 2. Capt. William P. Mason. 3. GBM's brother and sister. 4. Frederica M. English, GBM's married sister. 5. Eckby Coxe, a family friend. 6. In her letter Mrs. McClellan had written: "The Democrats say, the *War Democrats,* that George B. McClellan, is to be the next President...." McClellan Papers (B-22:52).

To Samuel L. M. Barlow

My dear S L M [Orange] Dec 25 [1863]

The insurance on the house expires on Jany 3d as you supposed.

I find a copy signed by Sheldon & Co of an agreement to publish my report & pay me 15% copyright.[1] I fancy I signed a similar copy, but am not certain as I left the matter pretty much to Marcy.

I did not have time to see them about it before I left town — if you think of it when passing by will you speak to them & see what they want to do now?

On my return here I found Arthur. He was on a 10 days leave & has gone back to Phila — so I have had no time to think more about H's introduction.[2] I will write to you about it by tomorrow for certain unless I find that I am going to the city on Monday.

Merry Christmas!

Ever your friend
McC

ALS, Barlow Papers, Huntington Library

1. GBM's *Report on the Organization of the Army of the Potomac, and of Its Campaigns in Virginia and Maryland* would be published by the Government Printing Office in Feb. 1864. In March an edition enlarged to include GBM's account of the western Virginia campaign was issued by the New York publisher Sheldon & Co. 2. Apparently this is a reference to G. S. Hillard's *Life and Campaigns of George B. McClellan,* which would be published in Aug. 1864.

To Robert C. Winthrop

My dear Mr Winthrop Orange New Jersey Jany 1 1864

Your very kind note of the 24th reached me only yesterday, as I had not visited the city for several days, for we are still residing in the country. I trust it is not necessary for me to assure you of my extreme gratification at hearing from you again, & knowing that my wife and myself are still so kindly remembered by you & your daughter.

In these days when I sometimes hear that one old friend is angry with me because I said something, another because I said nothing, a third because I would not do something that was impossible to do, a fourth because I did something that I could not avoid doing, it is most gratifying to hear that I still have some such friends left as Dr Adams & yourself — who have charity & exercise it.

You may be sure that we will both read your book,[1] & I know that we will find it of great interest, for the longer I live & the more I see of men the deeper interest do I feel in the words of the past, which seem to me ever to show that the passions of poor human nature have not changed much from the earliest ages.

The passions which have brought us to our present unhappy condition surely are not new ones, but simply the outcropping of those which have agitated the world from the beginning of its history.

Mrs McClellan desires me to thank you most warmly for your kind remembrance of her, & to unite with me in wishing a *very* happy New Year to your daughter & yourself. God grant that the New Year may be a happier one than the past for our poor country!

With kindest regards to you & yours

I am most truly & respectfully your friend
Geo B McClellan

Hon Robt C Winthrop
Boston

ALS, Winthrop Papers, Massachusetts Historical Society.

1. The recently published *Life and Letters of John Winthrop.*

To Samuel S. Cox

Private

My dear Cox — Orange Feby 12 [1864]

Your kind note of yesterday is received.[1] I have no personal objection to the passage of Schenck's bill — I would rather be fired out of the service than resign. If I am turned out by such a bill I fancy that I shall retain a claim (in equity at least) to the Seniority of Rank which I now hold & of which it is sought to deprive me. Some future Administration may recognize this claim. I would rather, in the present state of affairs, be a private citizen again — & as I have said before I would rather be turned out than go of my own accord.

As to the Maryland Legislature affair I do not think that I initiated the matter — it came I *think* from Seward. I doubt very much whether there is any letter of mine in the War Dept on the subject. The facts of the case, for your private benefit, are these:

At the time of the arrest the Army at Washington was still weak & not in condition to take the field & fight a general battle. Intelligence reached us, I *think* through Seward, that the Secesh members of the Maryland Legislature intended to meet at Frederick (an illegal act under the Constitution of Md), secretly pass a Secession Ordinance, secretly send it to Jo Johnston, who was at once to move into Maryland & raise a general disturbance. This information seemed at the time to be thoroughly reliable. The danger was great — in a military point of view we were not prepared to resist an invasion of Maryland — the only chance was to nip the whole affair in the bud — which was promptly done, as a matter necessary for the safety of the military position of Washington & the troops there. I look upon this as an entirely different matter from the arbitrary arrests in loyal states, & have no apology to make.[2]

I will write to one or two who were then with me who will probably remember more of the details as to the way in which it was initiated than I now do & inform you.

Please don't fail to let me see you when you next come this way — I want a "talk" with you.

In haste sincerely your friend
Geo B McC

Hon S S Cox

ALS, Charlton L. Lewis Papers, Yale University Library.

1. Cox wrote on Feb. 11: "There is a bill today introduced by [Robert C.] Schenck to retire Generals. It is a blow at you." He also reported that "the Republicans have a letter of yours, or rather that it is in the War office, initiating the arrest of the Maryland legislature [in Sept. 1861] . . . ; some of your friends are anxious about it." McClellan Papers (B-14:49), Library of Congress. 2. See GBM to Banks, Sept. 12, 1861, *supra.*

To Edward Everett

My dear Mr Everett New York Feby 17 1864

I beg that you will receive for yourself, and convey to the other gentlemen to whom I am so much indebted, my grateful thanks for the unexpected and most agreeable evidence of continued regard which I have just received from you.

You could not have determined upon a gift more delightful and useful to me than the books which you have been so good as to present to me.[1]

In no other form could I be so constantly reminded, were a memento necessary, of the kind friends whom I am so fortunate and proud to possess in Boston.

It may gratify you to know that had I been consulted as to the selection I would not have changed the list, and that it contains works which I have long been most anxious to possess.

I will do my best to make good use of them, and if, after the quiet life which now seems to be my lot, I should ever again be called upon to serve my country, I trust that the use I shall meantime have made of your magnificent gift will have changed my views and made me better fitted to do good.

As I cannot thank each of our friends individually I hope you will be good enough to convey to them my most sincere thanks for the most acceptable and superb mark of their regard & friendship

And believe me ever your sincere & respectful friend
Geo B McClellan

Hon Edward Everett
Boston

ALS, Everett Papers, Massachusetts Historical Society.

1. In his letter of Jan. 29 Everett wrote that he and a number of GBM's Boston friends were making him a gift of books "interesting to the statesman, the student of history, and the general reader... as a small token of our gratitude for your public services, and of our respect for your personal character." He enclosed a list of the forty-seven titles, many of them multi-volume works. McClellan Papers (B-14:49), Library of Congress.

To Edward H. Wright

My dear Wright Orange March 2/64

Yours from Newark & that of 13th Feb reached me, but I have been so much occupied with the N.Y. edition of the Report that it has been impossible for me to reply to any letters until today, & now I can do no more than write a line to let you know why I am so dilatory & to urge you to write to me often. I hear from all quarters that the Report is doing much good, & opening many eyes. I am glad that you have directed your share to the Army — for I am especially anxious that it should be circulated there.

I shall be free to write you a long letter in a few days — when I get my desk cleared off — now I only send my kindest regards to Madame & to your Father & Mother — in which my wife joins — & baby sends her love to Minnie — about [*torn*] she constantly prattles at a great rate. My wife stopped at your house in Newark the other day, & came away richer by a banquet.

In haste ever your friend
McC

E.H.W.

ALS, Miscellaneous Collections, Huntington Library.

To William C. Prime

My dear Prime [Orange, c. March 8, 1864]

The writer of the accompanying was a Col in the Vols & wrote to ask me if I had any objection to his translating my Report into French.[1] I replied that he was very welcome to do so, and received the note on the other side. I don't understand the working of these things. Would his proposition, request rather, interfere with Sheldon? What shall I tell him?

It is immaterial to me whether it is translated or not — tho' I suppose it would be very well to have it circulate in as many languages as possible, not omitting Sanscrit & Chinese.

In haste ever yours
McC

W.C.P.

ALS, McClellan Papers (B-14:49), Library of Congress.

1. In a letter dated March 5, Lionel J. D'Epineuil, formerly a colonel in the 53rd New York, requested the exclusive right to prepare a French translation.

To Samuel L. M. Barlow

My dear S L M New York March 9/64

Sheldon sent me this morning a check for $1500 as part payment etc.[1] I have sent $1000 to pay my other debt & send with this the balance ($500) as part payment on my account with you.

Won't you ask Taylor to let me know at once how much more I owe you — for I am very anxious to feel that I am out of debt so far as owing you — tho' I never can, nor wish to, pay you back all the kindness I have received from you. I wont have time to see you to day — as I am very busy.

Ever yours
Geo McC

S L M B

ALS, Barlow Papers, Huntington Library.

1. An advance against royalties for the Sheldon & Co. edition of GBM's *Report*.

To Reverdy Johnson

Personal

My dear Senator — Orange New Jersey March 9 1864

Yours of the 3d being directed to me in New York reached me only yesterday as I happened not to visit the city for several days. An unexpected visit from my brother has rendered it out of my power to reply to it until this moment. Please accept my apology for my apparent neglect in so long delaying a reply.

It is entirely untrue that I was on a gun boat during the battle of Malvern Hill. In the morning, after having arranged the lines of battle & made every preparation I went on a gun boat with Capt Rodgers to do what I did not wish to trust to anyone else — i.e. examine the final position to which the Army was to fall back. I returned immediately and was with Genl Porter near the left of the line before the enemy made his first attack, nor did I leave the land during the continuance of the battle. You will find the whole story in my report. I can conscientiously say that during the whole Seven Days my personal movements were made in accordance solely with my sense of duty — that I went wherever I thought my presence as the Comdr was of most benefit to my Army.

I confess that I have grown callous to the multiplied attacks made upon me, for I know that my men understand me and that history will do me justice. I suppose you have seen the last absurd falsehood of the Tribune in regard to a supposed interview with Genl Lee during, or just after, the battle of Antietam.[1] It fortunately happens that during that campaign I did not have any communication with Genl Lee, or any other rebel officer, even upon the subject of prisoners, wounded etc — communications which usually follow every battle of consequence. Of course I need not say to you that the whole story is made from the whole cloth.

I feel perfectly contented to allow these people to lie to their hearts content — I don't believe any respectable people credit what they say. I had a note from Mr Ketchum this evening, enclosing yours of the 7th to him.

Allow me, my dear Mr Johnson, to thank you most warmly & sincerely for the able & friendly way in which you sprang to my vindication — I shall ever be most grateful to you for it, as I was already for the friendship you evinced towards my persecuted & most wronged friend Fitz John Porter.

Again apologizing for the length of time that has elapsed without my replying to your letter

I am ever, most respectfully, your sincere friend
Geo B McClellan

Hon Reverdy Johnson
U.S. Senate

ALS, Reverdy Johnson Papers, Library of Congress. Johnson was senator from Maryland.

1. On Mar. 7 the *Washington Chronicle* and the *New York Tribune* first reported the tale of one Francis Waldron, who claimed GBM and Lee met at Antietam and agreed that the Confederate army would withdraw unopposed. Waldron proved to be an alcoholic and the story a hoax.

To William C. Prime

My dear Prime Orange [March] 10th [1864]

Is it absolutely authentic that the exchange of prisoners has been resumed — and if so is it to such an extent as to render it advisable to discontinue all efforts in regard to replying to those prisoners' letters?

I see they have *my* bill up in the House[1] — I hope Cox & the rest of them do not intend to waste their time by spending weeks in making speeches about it.

If I were not principled against taking any steps in such a matter I should write to Cox & say that it would gratify me if nothing should be said by the Democrats on the subject — that some *one*, Cox for example, should rise & simply state the fact that the bill would dismiss me if passed & then let the vote be taken. Do you know that it sometimes occurs to me that if I am really the one aimed at it would be no more than decent for me to save the necks of other innocent men by throwing up my commission at once & stating the reason thereupon! Can you find out what the real animus is?

In great haste ever yours
McC

W.C.P.

ALS, McClellan Papers (B-41:61), Library of Congress.

1. See GBM to Cox, Feb. 12, *supra*.

To Manton M. Marble

My dear Marble Orange N.J. March 12 1864

I enclose a note & slip received from Cox. I have told him that I hardly think it worth while to notice it, but that I would leave it to your judgment.

Of course there is not a word of truth in it. I have not seen Lee since April 1855 — when on my way to Europe — and had no communication whatever with him during the Maryland campaign. Nor did I see any envoy of Lee's in any way that could possibly give color to the lie — I don't think I ever saw Mr F Waldron (if he is the liar) in my life. I gave no safe conduct for any rebel officer to come through my lines — So much for that.[1]

What will they start next? What are you doing stealing my thunder from the Round Table & copying it into the World?[2] Somebody will accuse me next of helping you and S.L.M.[3] in the work of editing that "awful" paper!

Ever yours
McC

Manton Marble Esq

ALS, Marble Papers, Library of Congress.

1. See GBM to Johnson, Mar. 9, note 1, *supra*. 2. GBM's articles of military analysis were being published anonymously in *The Round Table*. 3. Samuel L. M. Barlow was a major investor in the *World*.

To Elizabeth B. McClellan

My dearest Mother Orange New Jersey March 13 1864

Time flies so rapidly and so quietly in this out of the way place that I really have nothing new to tell — unless I would commit to paper the wise sayings and new pranks of the baby who is improving every day & is certainly an improvement on all other babies who have been heard of or described heretofore. She is very quiet — strange to say — this Sunday afternoon, but I will venture to guess that her voice will be heard, or she will rush in here on a raid before I finish this scrawl. She is quite an intelligent being in these days — talks, in her own way, quite as much to her own satisfaction as any one else of more mature years can, & rules the house generally. But she is as good a child as ever was, never gets mad unless she loses her temper, or has some other equally good reason for it, & is very tractable, especially when her general views agree with those of those around her. There! I knew it! Here she is — large as life & quite as important! She has managed to blacken her face & is quite proud of the achievement. As Nell is lying down I suppose there is a lark on foot & a general frolic — if it is Sunday! Seriously speaking, & without prejudice, I think she is the brightest & best little thing that ever was. She is in perfect health, & runs about in the most ready fashion with but little regard to weather. This year in the country has been a splendid thing both for her & for Nell — who is stronger, in better health, & looking more beautiful than for years past — probably since she left school.

I think it was a good thing for all of us that we were able to pass this winter quietly in the country, instead of in the midst of the excitement and worry of New York life — which is all very well in its way, but decidedly fatiguing. Little George[1] is here, & improving very rapidly I think — he looks better & says that he is stronger. I fear the little fellow finds it very dull, as there is no one in the vicinity of his own age — but if the weather continues good he can be out in the air most of the time & soon pick up. Nell & I are obliged to go to the city tomorrow for a few hours & will take him with us. New York is quite busy at present with preparations for the Sanitary Fair[2] — how it will turn out I have no means of knowing, but people expect a great success — it certainly ought to produce more than any of the others, tho' many of the cities have done very well. I am sorry to see that Meade's health is reported bad — I fear it is only a dodge to get rid of him, & put some more pliant man in his place.

I am inclined to think that it is time that Grant desires Smith W F to be in command of the Army of the Potomac. So Grant has his Lieut Generalcy![3] Well — they might have found many much worse men to give it to, & I am glad to see that he wears his great honors so modestly — it is a very good feature in his character. I suppose *my bill* will pass this week — dismissing me from the service, with Buell etc. I shall be glad of it, as I wish to serve this Administration no longer, & do not like to resign.[4] I shall be glad to be once more in private life, & it will be very difficult to get me out of it again. But I know that all things will prove in the end to have been arranged for the best and am quite willing to accept what I cannot avoid. Genl Marcy is still in Missouri inspecting — we don't know when to expect him home, as he may be ordered elsewhere at once. Mrs. M & Nelly send their love to all. Give mine to Mary, John & Maria, & tell the latter not to be at all worried about George, as he is getting on very well. I heard from Arthur last week — he was quite well.

Do write to your affectionate son
Geo B McClellan

ALS, McClellan Papers (B-14:49), Library of Congress.

1. George McClellan, GBM's nephew. 2. Sponsored by the U.S. Sanitary Commission, the New York Sanitary Fair, like other similar fairs, was designed to raise money for the benefit of Union troops. 3. Grant had been appointed lieutenant general and general-in-chief of the Union armies. 4. See GBM to Cox, Feb. 12, *supra*. The bill had become highly politicized and would fail of passage.

To Edward H. Wright

My dear Wright Orange New Jersey March 19 1864

On my return here yesterday after an absence of two days in New York I found yours of the 15th awaiting me.[1] We were all exceedingly grieved to learn of your father's serious illness, and most sincerely pray that he is in this restored to health. I think you are quite right in urging him to remain quietly at home in his present state of health — the excitement and inconveniences of Washington life certainly can do him no good, and may injure him much. I trust that you will succeed in persuading him to remain quiet until his health is completely restored.

The Fremont interview was a strange one, & confirms many little hints that had reached my ears — we will talk over it more fully when we meet than would be prudent in a letter in these days when the mails are so [*torn*]. I am really sorry that the bill for turning me out has been defeated, as it appears to have been — I do not wish to resign, but I would be very glad to be in civil life again without any action of my own — I am very tired of hanging by the eye lids & am really anxious to begin the world anew in private life. But whatever the result may be I shall accept it as the best.

The Report is going off grandly — it has already paid my debts & lifted a great load off my shoulders.

The Waldron lie *has* exploded — the more things of that kind the better — they always wait upon their authors.

Baldy[2] is climbing rapidly — Maj Genl of the regular army! I learn that it disquiets Rosecrans and others exceedingly.

Mrs Marcy & my wife join me in love to all — Baby sends her love to "Minnie Ight" & often talks about her. Now that the roads are rapidly becoming good we feel the want of you more than ever.

Tell your father how rejoiced we all are that he has recovered from the attack & that we hope he will take such good care of himself as to avoid another.

Ever your friend
McC

Col E H Wright

My wife desires her thanks for the photograph.

ALS, Miscellaneous Collections, Huntington Library.

1. In his letter of Mar. 15 Wright reported an interview with a spokesman for John Charles Frémont, who was angling for a presidential bid and wanted to join with GBM to oppose the so-called unemployed generals bill. Wright said he was told that if Frémont was elected president he would name GBM general-in-chief, and he expected a reciprocal arrangement if GBM was elected. McClellan Papers (B-14:49), Library of Congress. 2. Gen. William F. Smith.

To Horatio Seymour

His Ex Horatio Seymour
Governor of New York
Governor New York April 5/64

I take pleasure in addressing you in behalf of a meritorious officer who informs me that he has got into trouble on account of language used in the heat of a political discussion. I allude to Lieut E. H. Underhill 1st N.Y. Artillery. I know nothing of the merits of the particular question — I do not know what may be Lt U's politics or what the trouble is, but I know that he is a gallant and meritorious officer who has won his way on fields of battle from the position of a private soldier to that of a 1st Lt, & that he has received very strong recommendations for promotion from his immediate and superior commanders. I therefore feel at liberty to direct your attention to these facts and to ask as a matter of justice to a gallant soldier such kind consideration as it may be in your power to give whenever the case comes before you.[1]

Very truly your friend
Geo B. McClellan

ALS, McClellan Papers, New-York Historical Society.

1. Apparently no action was taken against Lt. Underhill, who remained on duty with his battery.

To Samuel S. Cox

My dear Cox Orange April 22 [1864]

Your kind note of the 12th with its enclosures was waiting for me here when I returned from a two weeks visit to New York, two or three days ago — as I was obliged to run over there again on business this is my first chance to reply to it.

I am very sorry that I missed you again, but sincerely hope for better luck next time. The letters you send me are of great interest — I return them after having taken some notes from them which may be of some use to me hereafter. Some of these days the whole mass of evidence which corroborates the ground I have taken in my report, & on which I acted at the time, will come out & I shall be justified in the eyes of all but the willfully blind.

The boy has just come for the mail — so I will let this note go unfinished & retain the letters which will send you in a day or two.

In the mean time believe me ever your friend
Geo B McC

ALS, Thomas F. Madigan Collection, Rare Books and Manuscripts Division, New York Public Library.

To Samuel L. M. Barlow

[Orange, c. May 3, 1864]

Mr B. insinuates that while in command of the Army of the Potomac I entertained political aspirations and that my course was guided by them.[1]

In this he is entirely mistaken — my thoughts & time were devoted solely to the military affairs committed to me, and whatever political opinions I expressed were expressed officially & frankly to the Govt as a part of my duty as the Comdr of the Army, or of one of the great armies of the nation. I never looked to the Presidency & no official or personal act letter or conversation of mine will bear a contrary interpretation. I deny that my course of conduct while in command was calculated to produce the impression that I was ready as a General to lend myself to any party to supplant the Chief Magistrate etc.

Mr Blair then intimates an attempt on my part to get control of the Govt by throwing myself into a party hostile to its Administration etc & cites the example of Lee & others as a proper course.[2]

I have already stated the facts as to my conduct while in command. Since then, when assailed in every way by the Administration & its partisans, I have but once raised my voice — the Woodward letter[3] — & in this I exercised the right of a citizen to repel attack & express an opinion.

Mr B. here assumes that the reelection of Mr L & the retention of power by his party are essential to our success — I differ from him & regard success as possible only by a change of Administration & policy, therefore I should be wanting to my country did I support a party & a policy which I conscientiously believe will bring ruin upon us all.

The insinuation in regard to the Harrison Bar letter[4] scarcely needs a comment — it was prepared without an "arrière pensée,"[5] & the singularity of its coincidence with the Woodward letter arises from the fact that the two are based upon the same general idea & that I had not changed my views in the interval. Let Mr B. prove that the principles contained in the Harrison Bar & Woodward letters are wrong before he asks me or my friends to condemn them.

If Mr B., as he strongly intimates, regards a comparison of the two letters as proving a desire on my part to conciliate the peace party — I can only deny that any such intention existed, & regret that I cannot see the force of the argument by which he reaches his conclusion.

I have not sought & do not intend to seek political preferment, but I do not see how I am to carry into effect Mr Blair's wishes without proving false to my country, for I could only comply with his request by coming out in favor of Mr Lincoln & his policy — that I cannot do.

I will not sacrifice my friends my country & my reputation for a command. I can make no communication to Mr Lincoln on the subject.

AD, McClellan Papers (B-23:53), Library of Congress.

1. In the spring of 1864 Barlow and Montgomery Blair exchanged a series of lengthy letters dealing with GBM's political beliefs and the possibility of his being the Democratic nominee for the presidency. This memorandum was prepared by GBM as a response to Blair's letter to Barlow of May 1, and served as the basis for Barlow's reply to Blair of May 3 (both: Barlow Papers, Huntington Library). GBM fairly summarizes the main points in Blair's letter. Blair concluded: "I believe if he would unbosom himself unreservedly & in confidence directly with the President that he would give him a military place in which he could be most useful... & in such event the political alliance in which he has to some extent been involved might be turned to the best possible account for the country." 2. Blair maintained that Lee and others were "bitterly hostile" to Jefferson Davis but remained silent for the sake of Confederate unity. 3. GBM to Biddle, Oct. 12, 1863, *supra*. 4. GBM to Lincoln, July 7, 1862, *supra*. 5. Ulterior motive.

To Elizabeth B. McClellan

My dearest Mother Orange May 8 1864 8 pm.

I do not know whether the telegraph has relieved the suspense of the thousands of anxious hearts in the great cities by this hour — here we are out of its reach and must wait as calmly as we may until tomorrow to learn the result of the advance across the Rapidan.[1] I have seen the morning Herald, but it gives nothing tangible and satisfactory — the absence of certain news does not tend to reassure my mind as to the issue. If we had gained a decided success it is more than probable that we should have heard something definite in regard to it, for the maxim that "no news is good news" hardly applies in such a case as this. I have implicit faith in the ability of my poor old Army to accomplish anything that troops can effect, but there is such a thing as expecting impossibilities, and such may have been the task now set before it.

I am inclined to think that Lee *did* attack & that the result was that he stopped or checked the advance of the army — it may well be that after the attack, finding that he could not drive them in retreat he fell back upon his defences at Mine Run, or somewhere in that vicinity, & I am not confident that we can easily force the position. How disgraceful it will be if it becomes necessary to retire again behind the line of the Rappahannock! It makes my heart sick when I think of the thousands of brave men who have been sacrificed by the blunders of our rulers — our sins as a nation must have been great indeed to merit such a punishment, & I fear that the end is not yet. Heaven knows that my heart will feel lighter if it proves that Lee has been badly defeated & driven in upon Richmond. Whatever the result may be God grant that Arty may go safely through it — I have strong faith that he will, & never forget to pray that he may — I have no guess as to that — but I shall be very glad when I know that the battle is over, & that some of my friends are safe. I am very sorry for poor Hayes — he was a good fellow & a fine soldier — he behaved very gallantly on the Peninsula & was an old friend of mine. Bartlett, too, who is reported wounded, was an excellent officer who was with me throughout the whole Peninsula campaign.[2]

People are very anxious in New York — they do not seem to have much confidence & I think they are prepared for disaster — which I still hope & trust will be arrested. I presume we shall know tomorrow something definite as to the result of the battles — I should not be at all surprised to hear that Butler had been beaten back to his boats — I doubt whether he has force enough for his part of the undertaking.[3] I will write again as soon as we have something definite. Nell and Mrs. Marcy would send their love did they know I was writing. Nell has just recovered from a severe sore throat etc contracted at the Fair. All well now.

With love to Mary John Maria etc

Ever your affectionate son
Geo B McClellan

I enclose a photograph taken a few days since — also an Eugénie for Mary, which is I think very good.

ALS, McClellan Papers (B-15:49), Library of Congress.

1. The Battle of the Wilderness was fought on May 5–7. 2. Brig. Gen. Alexander Hays was killed in the Wilderness fighting. Col. William F. Bartlett, wounded in the Wilderness, is no doubt confused here with Brig. Gen. Joseph J. Bartlett. 3. Gen. Butler's operation south of the James River failed.

To Mary McClellan

My dear Mary — Orange May 12 1864

Yours of Tuesday was awaiting me on my return from the city this evening. I am *very* much obliged to you for the copy of Arthur's note[1] — please don't fail to let me know anything you hear from him at once. I have been utterly upset by poor Sedgwick's death — a sad sad blow to the Army & the country. How many more might have been so much better spared! But it is doubtless all for the best.

They must have had a terrible time down there! But how splendidly my noble old Army has fought — nothing could have been finer than their conduct. God give them victory! I shall if possible attend Sedgwick's funeral. I am very tired so I will say good night — love to Mother and all.

Ever your affectionate brother
Geo B McClellan

ALS, McClellan Papers (B-15:49), Library of Congress.

1. Arthur McClellan wrote on May 9: "Gen. Sedgwick was killed this morning by a sharpshooter; the ball passed through the lower part of the brain & he died instantly. We are all in the lowest spirits, for the Gen. was loved by us all." McClellan Papers (B-15:49).

To Abram S. Hewitt

My dear Hewitt Orange June 10 /64

Since receiving yours I have been "ordered" not to use my eyes as they are suffering from overwork. I was in the city afterwards & expected to see you but was detained up town so long that I could not get down to Burling Slip. I went with Mr Bassinger on Tuesday & Wednesday to Phillipsburg.[1] I think he has about the best line that can be had under the circumstances, but would call your attention to the fact that there must be far more vigor in the work if you ever expect to get the endeavor through. I urged Mr B. to devote himself entirely for the present to procuring the right of way so that work may be commenced. It will be better for all concerned that nothing be done in regard to the Boonton line until that other matter is well straightened out — which ought to be done in two weeks. There are some heavy cuts & fills where the right of way should be obtained *at once*. I will try to see you tomorrow & explain myself more fully than my eyes will now permit me to do in writing. The compensation proposition will be quite satisfactory to me.

In haste your friend
Geo B McC

Mr A S Hewitt

ALS, Allan Nevins Papers, Rare Book and Manuscript Library, Columbia University. The industrialist Hewitt operated, among other ventures, the Cooper-Hewitt ironworks in Newark.

1. GBM had undertaken for Hewitt an engineering study for a proposed extension of the Morris and Essex Railroad. Hewitt to GBM, May 29, McClellan Papers (B-16:50), Library of Congress.

To Samuel L. M. Barlow

Private

My dear S L M West Point June 17 [1864]

I enclose a couple of letters for your edification. The Gov has been here & is in favor of postponing the Convention — he has much to say in that connection — I listened and said nothing.[1]

If I have any penetration whatever you may rest assured that the postponement is urged by & is in the interest not only of the Peace men, but also of the "Nelson" men, who may by some strange accident finally prove to be "Seymour" men — *probably to their own surprise!!*[2]

I am afraid that I scared a red headed politician out of several weeks growth two days since — he came to see me about "the meeting that had been arranged with F" etc — I shut him up so promptly that I don't think any one else will have the impertinence to renew the subject. He left somewhat hurriedly, & I am satisfied decidedly impressed with the idea that there had been a mistake *somewhere*, & that I was not yet entirely in the power of the politicians.[3] I wish you would impress our [*torn*] friend with the idea that I don't care to meet his friends[4] — I have got certain obstinate ideas in my head lately that I dont care to put on paper, but which I will explain when I see you — In the mean time my advice to you is to follow my example — clear out of town, let the politicians go where they belong viz: to the old gentleman with cloven feet, & take a good rest.

I think we shall move on to Saratoga tomorrow to pass Sunday & a day or two next week.

Yours of yesterday this moment reached me.[5] Am very glad you like the Address. I have no objection whatever to its being printed & would be glad to correct the proofs.

I was not aware that the regulars were at Vicksburg, & I don't think it deserves as much mention as Yorktown anyhow.

I wish they had kept Vallandigham down south when they had him there!

I will see you as I pass thru' town, & will try to stay overnight.

Ever yours in haste
McC

ALS, Barlow Papers, Huntington Library.

1. On June 15 GBM delivered an address dedicating the site of a monument to be erected at West Point to honor the Civil War dead of the regular army. New York's Gov. Horatio Seymour attended, and discussed with GBM postponement of the Democratic nominating convention scheduled for July 4. 2. Supreme Court Justice Samuel Nelson and Gov. Seymour, both potential candidates for the nomination. 3. In a draft for this letter, dated June 16, GBM gave a fuller account of this incident: "I was strongly tempted yesterday to throw a man out of the window — a red haired little scamp calling himself McClosky . . . came to see me and said that he wished to see 'about that interview with Fremont' — I asked him what he meant — He said it had all been arranged in Washington and asked whether the Gov had not explained it to me — I told him no & asked who had dared to do such a thing without my knowledge. . . ." McClellan Papers (B-15:49), Library of Congress. Apparently rumor had invented a proposed meeting between GBM and Frémont. See GBM to Wright, Mar. 19, note 1, *supra*. 4. On the evidence of GBM's draft, this appears to be a reference to a peace faction centering around Gov. Thomas H. Seymour of Connecticut. 5. Barlow's letter of June 16 congratulated GBM on his West Point address, and proposed it be printed as a campaign document. He added: "Vallandigham's advent will I fear give serious trouble. It will at all events compel a decided platform of action, before the [convention] meeting in Chicago." McClellan Papers (B-15:50). Peace Democrat Vallandigham had been banished to the Confederacy in May 1863 for supposedly treasonous utterances. Returning through Canada to Ohio, he was again deeply involved in Democratic politics.

To Samuel S. Cox

My dear Cox Saratoga June 20 [1864]

I have not found a moment to reply to yours of the 9th until now — it reached me at West Point.[1]

I fully agree with you, and although I had a long conversation with Gov S[2] I was not convinced by his arguments in favor of a postponement, but as the matter would seem to involve me personally I cannot express myself as I otherwise would.

I do not appreciate the weight of the arguments against a postponement,[3] & the coolest, most disinterested, men I have seen are in favor of the meeting as first announced.

I have been careful, especially since receiving your letter, to act upon your suggestion, & to observe great caution in expressing an opinion. I shall return to Orange some time next week & hope to see you the *next time* you visit New York.

Ever your friend
McC

Hon S S Cox

ALS, Thomas F. Madigan Collection, Rare Books and Manuscripts Division, New York Public Library.

1. In his letter of June 9 Cox spoke of the movement to postpone the Democratic convention: "It is believed that Grant will fail in his object & that his failure will give great impulse to the *Peace* men who expect to be able either to control the nomination, if it be made later, or to have force enough to divide the Convention. . . . My object in writing is to guard you against the matter lest some one may torture some expression of yours into favoring the postponement." McClellan Papers (B-15:50), Library of Congress. 2. Gov. Seymour of New York. 3. GBM surely meant to say he did not appreciate the arguments favoring postponement.

To Manton M. Marble

My dear Marble Lake George June 25 [1864]

Your two kind notes of the 13th & 16th duly reached me, but I have been so much on the move that it has been very difficult to write.[1] I need not tell you how truly I was gratified that the West Point oration met with your approval, & that I regretted exceedingly that you could not be there.

I don't know whether I shall be able to take up Halleck's book, but will if possible.

I expect to leave for home on Monday or Tuesday [June 27 or 28] when I shall try to bring to a focus the railway matter I undertook — if I can finish it at once, it is probable that we will take a cottage on the shore of this lake some 10 miles from Caldwell, at a little village named

Bolton — where I can pass the summer & fall without fear of being disturbed by politicians etc.

I shall however see you soon after my return home. So the Convention is postponed![2] Probably I don't know enough of the state of affairs to judge, but my instinct is against the movement, & I feel now perfectly free from any obligation to allow myself to be used as a candidate. It is very doubtful whether anything could now induce me to consent to have my name used. I will tell you when we meet more than I care to in a letter — in the mean time I shall keep as quiet & say as little as possible.

I suppose Barlow is at Saratoga — I shan't be able to see him on my way home.

It is almost too hot to write even here — so with my sincere congratulations upon the recent happy change in your condition & with my kind regards to Mrs Marble[3]

I am your friend
Geo B McClellan

Mr. Manton Marble

ALS, Marble Papers, Library of Congress.

1. In his letters of June 13 and 16 Marble asked GBM to review a newly published American edition of Henri Jomini's *Life of Napoleon,* edited by Henry Halleck, and congratulated him on his West Point address: "I do not hesitate to say that it is far superior to Mr Everett's Gettysburgh address in all essential respects — if the object of oratory be to touch the hearts & move the minds of men." McClellan Papers (B-15:50), Library of Congress. 2. The Democratic convention was rescheduled to open in Chicago on Aug. 29. 3. Marble was married on May 25.

To Henry B. Carrington

My dear Colonel — Orange New Jersey July 2 1864

Yours of the 18 reached me only two days since, in consequence of my unusually long absence from home — so I trust you will pardon my delay in acknowledging its receipt.[1]

I am sincerely gratified that you like the West Point address, and you will be glad to know that it has met the approval of very many of our best men.

I do not think that you will ever have reason to repent of the unswerving friendship you have entertained towards me, and you may be sure that there never can be anything in common between myself and the men you allude to.

In great haste ever your friend
Geo B McClellan

Col H B Carrington

ALS, Carrington Family Papers, Yale University Library. Brig. Gen. Carrington commanded the military district of Indiana, with headquarters in Indianapolis.

1. In his letter of June 18, Carrington warned that Vallandigham and his followers were "preparing for open rupture with the Government. I know that they have repudiated you and dare not trust your high-toned honor with their plans." McClellan Papers (B-16:50), Library of Congress.

To Elizabeth B. McClellan

My dear Mother Orange Sunday July 3 [1864]

We returned here on Wednesday [June 29] after, what was for us, quite a long trip to West Point, Saratoga, Lake George & Ticonderoga. Went to West Point on the 13th and remained there until the last of the week. The Address seemed to pass off very well and gave satisfaction to all except Messrs Lincoln Stanton & Co who have ordered off Bowman & Clitz for being concerned in the heinous crime of inviting so great a reprobate as myself to the Point — such paltry spite cannot remain long unpunished and I trust that the day is not far distant when those wretches will receive at the hands of an outraged people the punishment they so richly deserve.[1] From West Point we went to Saratoga where we remained from Saturday until Tuesday — drinking the usual quantity of water & taking the usual drive to our dinner at Saratoga Lake — a quiet pretty spot where good plain dinners are supplied at rather exorbitant prices — but it is the fashion — so we accepted an invitation & went there. But few persons had reached Saratoga when we were there — so we had a very quiet & pleasant time — the more so as it happened that among the few guests at our Hotel were some of our Boston friends whom we were very glad to see. From Saratoga we went to Lake George where we spent just a week.

Nothing could have been kinder than the reception we met with everywhere — we were quite overpowered with kindness & found numberless friends among people we had never seen or heard of before.

We took a very pleasant trip to Ticonderoga and drove & toured & steamed about in every direction — so that we now know that region of country very well.

The only drawback to the trip was that we found it impossible to keep as quiet as we desired to — but we submitted with a good grace & got through very pleasantly.

I am very glad to hear that the Phila Fair passed off so pleasantly & successfully — it must have been a very great and interesting spectacle — and I am told that it presented a fine & more striking display than the New York Fair. Towards the close an invitation was sent to me by Mr. Welsh, but I did not receive it until the Fair was over — although it is not probable that I should have accepted it in any event — as I do not care to be much in Phila until it is a little more thoroughly whitewashed. The panic in money affairs & the resignation of Mr Chase have created quite a stir in New York — I never knew of a man so universally detested & despised as is Mr Chase by the monied men of this part of the world — he is politically dead beyond the power of a resurrection — so will it soon be with his late associates — nothing can save them for any length of time.[2]

I saw in the Herald the other day that 2nd Lt G M English, 31st Alabama Vols, was taken prisoner with a number of other secesh — I presume it is our enterprising young relation — if I had any idea as to where they have sent him I would try to help him in the way of any little comforts he might need.[3]

I wrote to Arthur while we were away from here — I have not heard from the little fellow since we left home three weeks ago — if you receive any letters from him please send me copies — I am anxious to know how he is, & what he is doing.

We had a vain attempt at a rain storm yesterday which passed away without giving us by any means as much rain as seems to be needed — for the country is very dry here & in New York State. From the quiet which pervades the house I imagine all are asleep — but as I know they would send their love if they knew that I was writing I will send them anyhow. Fanny has returned from school "for good."

Love to Mary, Maria & the children

Ever your affectionate son
Geo McC

My love to the Coxes and Phillips —

ALS, McClellan Papers (B-41:61), Library of Congress.

1. On orders from Secretary Stanton, the committee that invited GBM to deliver his West Point address — Lt. Col. Henry B. Clitz, Lt. C. C. Parsons, and Lt. Col. Henry Bowman, superintendent of the Military Academy — were transferred or dismissed. 2. Secretary of the Treasury Chase's resignation was accepted by the president on June 30. 3. Lt. English was GBM's nephew.

To L. Edgerton

Personal

My Dear Sir: Oaklands, July 20 [1864]

Yours of the 15th reached me when on the point of starting from home, and too late to reply to it.[1]

I regret that my absence will deprive me of the pleasure of meeting your brother, although I confess that I would prefer seeing him after the Chicago Convention rather than before it, as it is my desire and purpose to take no step, directly or indirectly, to influence, in any manner, the action of that body.

With my thanks for your kind feeling and my respects to your brother,

I am, very truly yours,
George B. McClellan

Mr. L. Edgerton, New-York

New York World, Oct. 10, 1864.

1. Edgerton's letter introduced his brother, Alfred P. Edgerton, a delegate to the Democratic convention from Indiana, who wanted to meet GBM.

To Francis P. Blair

My dear Sir [Oaklands, N.Y., c. July 22, 1864]

I have endeavored to give to the suggestions made by you in our late interview[1] that careful consideration which they merit alike from the grave importance of the subjects involved and from the respect & high personal regard I entertain for you & your long experience in public affairs. As the conclusions of my deliberate judgment are not finally in accordance with your views and wishes I feel it due to you that I should explain the chief reasons which have influenced my mind in making its conclusions.[2]

In the course of our conversation its basis, the predominating idea, was your proposition that I should write a letter to the Presdt distinctly stating that I would not permit my name to be used as a candidate for the Presidency in opposition to the present incumbent, and that in that event — not otherwise — I would be actively employed by him in a position befitting my rank, & that thus the nation would have the benefit of what you are pleased to regard as valuable services on my part. That another officer of high rank General Grant had written such a letter was mentioned by you as an argument in favor of my pursuing a similar course.

Here let me repeat the statement, which you are aware I have more than once made, that I have not taken a single step nor said one word for the purpose of influencing the action of any political Convention, & that I am not an aspirant for nomination for the Presidency. It is my firm conviction that no man should seek that high office, and that no true man should refuse it, if it is spontaneously conferred upon him, & he is satisfied that he can do good to his country by accepting it. Whoever is nominated for the Presidency in opposition to the present incumbent, it will be upon principles differing widely from those which have controlled his course. Should the result of the election be in his favor — no harm will have inured to him from the contest. Should a majority of the loyal voters of the country decide in favor of his opponent it will be upon a struggle of principles not of men. Now, situated as your country is, its fate trembling in the balance, anyone who pledges himself not to oppose the reelection of the actual incumbent as a condition of obtaining office or employment places himself upon the horns of a dilemma.

If he does not conscientiously approve the policy of the incumbent, he simply sells his self respect honor & truth — as well as his country — for a price.

Or he says by implication at least, that he does fully approve of all the measures of the incumbent, & that he regards the question as merely a choice of men, & not of principles or measures.

No one who knows me will suppose that I could accept the first alternative. The second is inadmissable for the reason that I do not approve of the policy and measures of the present President.

To prevent the possibility of misunderstanding permit me to mention a few important points in regard to which I differ very widely from the President — I shall not attempt to go over the whole ground because it is not necessary to do so.

By retaining my commission as I have done at a great personal sacrifice, I have shown my constant readiness to perform any proper duty to which I might be assigned. If the cause of my being removed from command & being kept so long unemployed was a want of confidence in my ability as a soldier it would have been idle for me to ask for command. But I am not permitted to adopt this solution, for the reason that it was only a short time before my removal from command that the President took occasion to express to me his high confidence in my value as a soldier.

If political considerations caused my displacement I can merely assert that no thought, word or act of mine justified such a course, and the onus of undoing the work, together with all its consequences, must rest with those who are alone responsible for it.

I conceive that I should forfeit my own self respect, & be wanting in that respect due the high office of the President of the U.S. should I seek for employment — "I sit upon the bank & patiently watch the wind."

I think that the original object of the war, as declared by the Govt., viz: the preservation of the Union, its Constitution & its laws, has been lost sight of, or very widely departed from, & that other issues have been brought into the foreground which either should be entirely secondary, or are wrong or impossible of attainment.

I think the war has been permitted to take a course which unnecessarily embitters the inimical feeling between the two sections, & much increases the difficulty of attaining the true objects for which we ought to fight. Convinced that the Union of the States should never be abandoned so long as there is a hope that it can be made to secure the welfare & happiness of the people of all the States, I deprecate a policy which far from tending to that end tends in the contrary direction.

I think that in such a contest as this policy should ever accompany the use of arms, & that our antagonists should be made to know that we are ever ready to extend the olive branch, & make an honorable peace on the basis of the Union of all the states.

ADf, McClellan Papers (B-16:50), Library of Congress. Blair had been a major figure in national politics since the Jackson administration.

1. This interview, held at Blair's behest, took place in the Astor House in New York on July 21. As Blair later described it in a letter to the *National Intelligencer,* published on Oct. 8, it was undertaken without the president's knowledge. 2. It is highly probable that after drafting this letter GBM determined not to send it. It has not been found among Blair's papers. Further, Blair's account in the *Intelligencer* gives no indication that he ever received a response from GBM to the proposal that he write Lincoln to seek reinstatement in the army (although this draft clearly states GBM's negative response), and states that in fact he told the president when he returned to Washington that he might be receiving such a request from the general.

To Ann Mary Coleman

My dear Mrs Coleman The Oaklands July 27 1864

Your kind note of the 23rd has reached me.[1]

I regret extremely that our movements for the next week are to be such that it will not be in my power to go to the city nor even to visit Orange, so that I shall not have the pleasure of seeing you at present.

I sincerely hope, however, that the time may not be far distant when I shall be so fortunate as to make the acquaintance of the daughter of one whose memory I love and respect as I do that of John J Crittenden — would that it have pleased God to have spared him to aid his country with his wise and unselfish councils — I fear we have too few like him remaining to us.

I am very sorry that it has been and still is impossible for me to call upon you at Bound Brook and beg that you will when next you write give my warmest regards to the General

and believe me, my dear Madame
very truly & respectfully your friend
Geo B McClellan

Mrs A M Coleman

ALS, John Jordan Crittenden Papers, William R. Perkins Library, Duke University. Mrs. Coleman was the daughter of John J. Crittenden of Kentucky.

1. In her letter of July 23 Mrs. Coleman explained that she was visiting in New Jersey and hoped to meet GBM and pay him the respects of her brother, Maj. Gen. Thomas L. Crittenden. She wrote that her two sons had joined the Confederate service (typifying the war-divided Crittenden family), "but I am a great admirer of Gen. McClellan!!" McClellan Papers (B-16:50), Library of Congress.

To Samuel L. M. Barlow

My dear S L M New York Aug 8 [1864]

If you don't know Key[1] know him by this & talk with the utmost freedom to him. What you say to him is as if said to me.

I don't expect to see you before the 29th unless you come to Orange. I shan't come again to N.Y. & don't send to me any d — d politicians.

Ever your friend
Geo B McClellan

S L M B Esq

ALS, Barlow Papers, Huntington Library.

1. Thomas M. Key, formerly of GBM's staff.

To William C. Prime

Private

My dear Prime Orange Aug 10 /64

I enclose some papers which will explain themselves — I don't know that the article Mr. Rush encloses amounts to enough to make it worth while to take much trouble — don't let his "confidential" note go out of your hands.[1]

If you see Key today tell him that I could not come in on account of the illness of my child — I may get in tomorrow, but it will depend entirely upon the child, who is a little better today. I don't think it desirable to write anything either to Blair or to Hanna[2] — I receive so many suggestions that I have determined to follow my own judgment in these matters. Morgan is very anxious that I should write a letter suggesting an *armistice*!!!![3]

If these fools will ruin the country I won't help them. I am very sorry that Blair interview got into the papers as it did — I expect that it was through Blair himself, & cannot but feel that I am partly accountable for a thing that is not exactly as it ought to be — I regret it exceedingly.[4]

My kindest regards to Barlow — don't send any politicians out here — I'll snub them if they come — confound them!

Sincerely your friend
Geo B McClellan

W. C. P.

ALS, McClellan Papers (B-17:50), Library of Congress.

1. On Aug. 1 Benjamin Rush sent his article supporting GBM that he wanted placed in a widely circulated newspaper. McClellan Papers (B-16:50). **2.** Francis P. Blair; James M. Hanna, an Indiana delegate to the Democratic convention. **3.** George W. Morgan, an Ohio politician, wrote on Aug. 4 that a call for an armistice by GBM "would double our chances at Chicago." McClellan Papers (B-16:50). **4.** A report of Francis P. Blair's interview with

GBM (see GBM to Blair, c. July 22, *supra*) had appeared in the *New York Herald* on Aug. 4.

To Samuel L. M. Barlow

My dear Sam Orange Sunday [August 28, 1864] 6.20 pm

Your messenger has just reached me.[1] Much obliged for the trouble you have taken. Things are just as I would have them — if we win we win everything and are free as air. If we lose we lose like gentlemen. I would not for the world have given any powers to make bargains. I will not come to town unless you send word to me that I *must*. If I am nominated I hope you will come out yourself as I shall want to talk to you about many things. In the contrary case I shall want to see you within a day or two in regard to my resigning. Baby has been sick again — better now.

With a thousand thanks for your kind forethought.

Ever your friend
McC

S L M B

ALS, Barlow Papers, Huntington Library.

1. Writing at 3:00 A.M. on this date, Barlow described the preconvention political maneuvering as reported to him by telegraph from Chicago: "It is plain to me that but for [Dean] Richmond, [Samuel J.] Tilden and Marble, the peace men, Lincoln men, and Seymour men, would have had it all their own way. As it stands if we win at all, we win everything, and shall have a wise platform and a good V.P.... As to 'private powers' I am glad none were given and delighted that I remained at home.... I do not see how you can safely come to town at all, just now, if you are nominated. You will be *crowded* out of sight." McClellan Papers (B-22:52), Library of Congress.

ELEVEN

CANDIDATE FOR PRESIDENT
SEPTEMBER 4, 1864–JULY 4, 1865

As the Democrats were gathering in Chicago to nominate their candidate for 1864, President Lincoln predicted that in the campaign he would be facing either a war Democrat running on a peace platform, or a peace Democrat on a war platform. It was a perceptive observation. In the event, General McClellan won the presidential nomination without significant opposition, but the peace wing of the party forced through a platform containing a plank terming the war a failure and calling for an armistice without preconditions, and for good measure nominated a peace man, George H. Pendleton, of Ohio, as McClellan's vice-presidential running mate. Few presidential candidates have been so severely handicapped by the convention that nominated them.

Included here are the two key drafts of McClellan's letter accepting the nomination (of the six drafts he wrote) that demonstrate his uncompromising rejection of the peace plank and his efforts to clothe the rejection in palatable language and render the party's split as inconspicuous as possible. His correspondence relating to the acceptance letter reveals that his stance was based not only on principle but also on his awareness of political realities; accepting the Chicago platform would lose him the states of New York and Pennsylvania, which between them contained half the electoral votes needed for victory in November. Nothing in the campaign gave him more satisfaction than this affirmation that the precondition of peace between North and South must be reunion.

He left the direction of the campaign to August Belmont, Samuel Barlow, and newspaper editors Manton Marble and William Prime. He made just two public appearances, at rallies in Newark and in New York City; as he told a supporter on October 3, "I have made up my mind on reflection that it would be better for me not to participate in person in the canvass." He dutifully corresponded with some political figures and met others who visited him, but it is clear from these letters that presidential politics was not to George McClellan's liking, and midway through the campaign he secluded himself and his wife for a week at the country home of his friend Joseph W. Alsop, in Connecticut.

McClellan devoted most of his campaign efforts to the army vote. Thirteen states had made some provision for their soldiers to vote, and it was expected that the general's great popularity with the men in the ranks during his time in command would be reflected in the 1864 balloting. He sought out officers friendly to him to distribute Democratic campaign literature to the troops, and encouraged the formation of such military clubs as the McClellan Legion to rally ex-soldiers and men home on furlough and sick leave to his cause. Despite these efforts, however, no other segment of the electorate rejected his candidacy so strongly. In the final election count Lincoln would capture 55 percent of the vote; among the soldiers the president's count was 78 percent. In spite of his acceptance letter, Northern soldiers perceived General McClellan as representing the party advocating peace at any price, and they turned against him by an overwhelming margin.

Lincoln's comfortable advantage in the popular vote (403,000) and his substantial edge in the electoral vote (212 to 21) were due in part to the encouraging military news during the campaign, especially Sherman's capture of Atlanta and Sheridan's victories in the Shenandoah Valley, but perhaps of equal consequence was the effect of the Chicago platform on McClellan's campaign. Before the convention he had feared becoming the tool of the peace faction, but in the end he became its victim.

The presidential contest of 1864 was the last role George McClellan would play in the Civil War. On Election Day he resigned his army commission, and in January 1865, some three months before the war concluded, he sailed with his family for Europe. The final sampling here of the letters he wrote in Europe reflects his interest in the war's progress and its outcome, but also the sense that he was living in a self-imposed exile. He would not return to the United States for three and a half years.

To Samuel L. M. Barlow

My dear Sam Orange Sept 4 [1864]

Your package duly reached me thro' Duncan[1] — much obliged for it.

Duncan suggested that it would be better that I should see Belmont Tilden etc on *Tuesday* evening [September 6] — to which I assented. It will suit me better as I must go in on Tuesday to see my wife off to New London. Please let me know by Douglas Robinson[2] if the arrangement suits. I suggested that Duncan should telegraph Dean Richmond to be there on Tuesday evening also. Is that all right? I want to see Prime also.[3]

I shall be at my house on Tuesday a little after 10 am — by 10 1/2 at latest — can you drop in for a moment before going down town?

I have not changed my mind since I saw you.

Ever yours
McC

S. L. M. B.

ALS, Barlow Papers, Huntington Library.

1. Probably the New York banker William B. Duncan. 2. Family friend Douglas Robinson acted as GBM's courier between New York and Orange. 3. This meeting concerned GBM's acceptance of the nomination.

To the Democratic Nomination Committee

Gentlemen [Orange, c. September 4, 1864][1]

I have the honor to acknowledge the receipt of your letter of the __ inst informing me of my nomination by the National Democratic Committee recently assembled at Chicago, as their Candidate for the Presidency at the next election.

It is unnecessary for me to say to you that this nomination comes to me unsought, and since the record of my brief public life has been open to the world, I may fairly assume that that record was kept in view when the nomination was made. The effect of long & varied service in the Army, during war & peace, has been to strengthen & render indelible in my mind & heart the love & reverence for the Union, Constitution, Laws & Flag of our nation impressed upon me in early youth. These feelings have thus far guided the course of my life, & must continue to do so in the future.

I cannot realize that the existence of more than one Government over the region which once owned our Flag is compatible with the peace, the power & the happiness of the people. While in my judgment the restoration and maintainance of our Union is the real, the sole object for which the war should be waged, I cannot be blind to the fact that that Union was originally formed by the exercise of a spirit of conciliation & compromise, and that to restore & preserve it the same spirit must prevail in our councils.[2] We have fought enough to satisfy the military honor of both sections, & to satiate the vengeance of the most vindictive.

It is, then, my opinion that, while the restoration of the Union in all its integrity is and must continue to be the indispensable condition in any settlement of the questions at issue in this war, we should as soon as it is clear, or seems probable, that our present adversaries are willing to negotiate upon the basis of the immediate restoration of the Federal Union of the States,[3] exhaust all practicable means, consistent with the honor & safety of the country, to secure that restoration of the Union, with the Constitutional rights of all the States fully guaranteed for all future time. But if an honest frank & full effort to obtain this object results in failure then I am of the opinion that we must continue the resort to the dread arbitrament of war, a war conducted strictly in accordance with those principles which I had so often had occasion to communicate when in command of Armies.[4] For it is better to fight for the restoration of the Union than for the adjustment of the inevitable questions of a boundary line, division of territories and other kindred subjects of dispute. I, for one, could not look in the face of my gallant comrades of the Army & Navy who have survived so many bloody battles, & tell them that their labors and the sacrifices of such numbers of their slain & crippled brethren had been in vain — that we had abandoned that Union for which we had so often risked our lives. I believe that a vast majority of our people, whether in the Army & Navy or at home, would, with me hail with unbounded joy the permanent restoration of peace on the basis of the Federal Union of the States without the effusion of another drop of blood; but if all honest & honorable efforts to secure this blessing should fail, I have such confidence in the patriotism & devotion of the people that I am sure they would without a murmur make the further sacrifices necessary to maintain their honor and secure a permanent reunion of the States. Believing that the views I have expressed are those of the Convention you represent, and are in harmony with the intentions of its Resolutions, I accept the nomination.

That this nomination has aroused feelings of deep satisfaction within me I neither can nor would wish to deny, for I feel the full force of such an honor emanating from so large a portion of the people.

But that which under happier circumstances might well call forth sentiments of high exultation has in the present instance merely caused me to realize my own weakness, and the terrible grandeur of the responsibility to be assumed should a majority of the people ratify your choice. Should that event occur I can only promise to seek fervently the guidance of the Almighty, & with his powerful aid do my best to restore Union & Peace to our distracted land, & to secure all the liberties & rights of the people guaranteed by the Constitution. Through you, gentlemen, I beg to thank the Convention you represent, & the people who elected you for this unsought & most weighty honor. Whatever expectations the people may build upon me I shall not willingly disappoint.

AL, McClellan Papers (B-21:52), Library of Congress.

1. This is the second of six drafts GBM wrote of his letter of acceptance of the Democratic presidential nomination, and was composed between Sept. 1 and Sept. 6, the first known date of any of the drafts (draft four). Drafts one, two, three, and five are in the McClellan Papers; drafts four and six are in the Barlow Papers, Huntington Library. This second draft is essentially a clean copy of GBM's heavily edited "1st rough draft" — the substantive changes are noted below — and represents his initial reaction to the platform adopted by the convention. His primary problem was responding to the platform's second plank, written by Clement Vallandigham, that in effect called for an unconditional armistice: "*Resolved,* That this convention does explicitly declare ... that after four years of failure to restore the Union by the experiment of war, ... justice, humanity, liberty and the public welfare demand that immediate efforts be made for a cessation of hostilities, with a view to an ultimate convention of the States, or other peaceable means, to the end that at the earliest practicable moment peace may be restored on the basis of the Federal Union of the States." 2. At this point the first draft had contained the sentence: "Nor am I ignorant that in order that a restored Union may be useful and permanent a feeling of mutual confidence & respect must exist between the two sections now unhappily at war." 3. The foregoing phrasing, beginning with "we should as soon as it is clear ...," originally read: "we should use our best endeavors to attain a pacific solution of the controversy without further effusion of blood." 4. This concluding phrase was added in the second draft.

To Samuel L. M. Barlow

My dear Sam [New York, September 6, 1864] 3 p.m.

I enclose a note I found awaiting me from Mr Wall[1] — I think it may be well for Belmont to see it in confidence this evening — if you agree with me please let him see it. I would be glad to have it again sometime.

I look upon it as of great importance in showing that so ultra a man is willing to unite with us on the proper platform. I can't stay in town tonight — will see you on Thursday [September 8], & will appropriate Friday evg for a long talk with you.

In haste ever yours.
McC

S L M B Esq etc

ALS, Barlow Papers, Huntington Library.

1. Former New Jersey senator James W. Wall, a peace Democrat, wrote on Sept. 1 that he had spoken in support of GBM at a rally, and pledged his aid in the campaign. Of vice-presidential candidate George H. Pendleton he wrote: "My friend Pendleton ... is an elevated high toned gentleman of rare ability." McClellan Papers (B-18:51), Library of Congress.

To Mary Ellen McClellan

Orange Tuesday 11pm.
[September 6, 1864]

My own dear little darling

You don't know, my own dear Nelly, how lonely it is without you — when I came back this evening I "took to" the May as you do & felt a double responsibility.[1] The dear little thing is perfectly well, & was wonderfully bright & affectionate — but she could not understand how "her own dear Mama had gone away" — she misses you terribly, & seemed to cling to me more than ever — little darling.

If you could have seen her you would have made up your mind that she does love you *very* much. I saw Dr Adams[2] — he was much pleased with my letter. I have recopied it tonight after a careful revision of *my own,* & have added the following just after what I said about "looking my comrades in the face etc" —

"The sentiments of my living comrades, the memory of the heroic dead, the traditions handed down from our Fathers, the Glory of our great nation, the hopes of our children, the preservation of our personal liberties, my own acts and words, all my antecedents, all that I prize on earth unite in rendering it impossible for me ever to consent to the disruption of the Union, with its direful consequences of exhaustive wars, financial ruin, anarchy & misrule, even should I of all in this broad land stand alone in this conviction." The changes I have made — & they are my style — are my own & add to the strength of the letter.[3] I think I have it now in an admirable shape & am not afraid to go down to posterity on it.

I found 32 letters awaiting me tonight — all but about 4 on this subject & all agreeing in sentiment. There can be no doubt as to the feeling of the people in this part of the world — they are with me. I had a letter from Mr. Aspinwall — just like the others. I shall write a few lines to him tonight. I go in again tomorrow morning & shall do my best to join you on Thursday night [September 8] — but I am as yet entirely in the dark as to the movements of the Committee.[4]

Fan[5] goes to visit Susie Adams on Friday — I should think it would be a relief to your mother — I asked Fan this evening if she had not been chasing her bull with gunpowder! She went to bed a little while ago in a more pacific frame of mind. Had a letter from Arthur.

Ever with fondest & truest love, my own sweet Nelly

Your own
George

ALS, McClellan Papers (B-25:54), Library of Congress.

1. Mrs. McClellan had left that morning to visit family friends in New London, Conn. 2. Presbyterian minister William Adams. 3. The sentence quoted was incorporated in the

fourth draft of GBM's acceptance letter, but subsequently deleted. 4. The Democratic nomination committee, headed by Horatio Seymour. 5. Fanny Marcy, GBM's sister-in-law.

To William H. Aspinwall

Orange Tuesday 11 PM
[September 6, 1864]

My dear Mr Aspinwall

Your welcome letter of the 4th reached me this evening.[1] Many thanks for it. My letter of acceptance is ready — you need have no fears on the subject — it is true to the country & to myself & in entire consistency with my record. I will either accept on my own terms (you know what they are) or I will decline the whole affair. In my judgment my letter will be acceptable to all true patriots, & will only drive off the real adherents of Jeff Davis this side of the line. Do not allow yourself to be anxious for one moment. — Whatever the result of the election may be my name will go down unsullied & you will never have cause to be ashamed that you have been one of my best & truest friends. — I received your kind letter enclosing that of Mr ——. You are perfectly right in telling him that the platform will be "the Union at any cost." Rest assured that I have the boldness to speak out my own mind, & the nerve to risk anything for my country. No politicians can make [me] their tool, & I both am & shall continue to be unpledged to any men except the real patriots of the land who value the "Union" above all things on earth. — I have earnestly sought the guidance of the Almighty & I cannot help feel he has vouchsafed to answer my prayers. I believe that the course I have determined to pursue is in accordance with his will, & that it will save the country. I hope that whatever my future may be you will always write & talk to me in the same spirit of friendly frankness that has always characterised yr course toward me. Your trust shall not be misplaced. Should it be convenient or agreeable to you I would be glad to have you meet me at my house on Thursday next [September 8] when I meet the committee. I presume about 12 o clock tho' the time is not fixed, & in truth I have seen none of them yet.

Ever your sincere friend
Geo B McClellan

To Wm Aspinwall Esq.

Copy, James S. Schoff Collection, William L. Clements Library, University of Michigan.

1. In his letter of Sept. 4 Aspinwall wrote, in part: "Your future influence & independence will depend much on the response you give to the nomination — if you have the boldness to speak out your own mind . . . , you will put to rest the assertions of your opponents that you are to be the tool in the hands of trading politicians. . . . The Chicago platform is simply an effort to unite the opposing elements of the Democratic party, & is unworthy of the crisis in which our nation is placed." McClellan Papers (A-91:36), Library of Congress.

To the Democratic Nomination Committee

Gentlemen Orange New Jersey Sept 8 1864[1]

I have the honor to acknowledge the receipt of your letter informing me of my nomination by the Democratic National Convention, recently assembled at Chicago, as their candidate, at the next election, for President of the United States.

It is unnecessary for me to say to you that this nomination comes to me unsought. [*Crossed out:* Since the record of my public life has been open to the world, I assume that that record was kept in view] I am happy to know that when the nomination was made the record of my public life was kept in view. The effect of long and varied service in the Army, during war and peace, has been to strengthen and make indelible in my mind and heart the love and reverence for the Union, Constitution, Laws and Flag of our country impressed upon me in early youth.

These feelings have thus far guided the course of my life, and must continue to do so to its end.

The existence of more than one Government over the region which once owned our flag is incompatible with the peace, the power, and the happiness of the people.

The preservation of our Union was the sole avowed object for which the war was commenced.

It should have been conducted for that object only, and in accordance with those principles which I took occasion to declare when in [*crossed out:* command of armies, and especially in my letter to the President from Harrison's Landing.] active service. Thus conducted, the work of reconciliation would have been easy, and we might have reaped the benefits of our many victories on land and sea.

The Union was originally formed by the exercise of a spirit of conciliation and compromise.

To restore and preserve it the same spirit must prevail in our Councils, and in the hearts of the people. The reestablishment of the Union in all its integrity is, and must continue to be, the indispensable condition in any settlement [*crossed out:* of the questions at issue in this war]. So soon as it is clear, or even possible, that our present adversaries are ready for peace upon the basis of the Union, we should exhaust all the resources of statesmanship practiced by civilized nations, and taught by the traditions of the American people, consistent with the honor and interests of the country, to secure such peace, reestablish the Union, and guarantee for the future the Constitutional rights of every State. The Union is [*crossed out:* our only] the one condition of peace. We ask no more.[2]

Let me add what I doubt not was, although unexpressed, the sentiment of the Convention, as it is of the people they represent, that when any one State is willing to return to the Union, it should be received at once, with a full guarantee of all its Constitutional rights.

But if a frank, earnest and persistent effort to achieve these objects should fail, [*crossed out:* it will be necessary to insist upon the preservation of the Union at all hazards, and] the responsibility for ulterior consequences will fall upon those who remain in arms against the Union. But the Union must be preserved at all hazards. I could not look in the face of my gallant comrades of the Army and Navy, who have survived so many bloody battles, and tell them that their labors, and the sacrifice of so many of our slain and wounded brethren had been in vain — that we had abandoned that Union for which we have so often perilled our lives.

A vast majority of our people, whether in the Army and Navy or at home, would, as I would, hail with unbounded joy the permanent restoration of peace, on the basis of the Union under the Constitution, without the effusion of another drop of blood. But no peace can be permanent without Union.

As to the other subjects presented in the resolutions of the Convention, I need only say that I should seek in the Constitution of the United States, and the laws framed in accordance therewith, the rule of my duty and the limitations of executive power, — endeavor to restore economy in public expenditure, reestablish the supremacy of law, [*crossed out:* and assert for our country and people that commanding position to which our history & our principles entitle us among the nations of the world.] & by the assertion of a more vigorous nationality reserve our commanding position among the nations of the Earth.[3] The condition of our finances, the depreciation of the paper currency, and the burdens thus imposed on labor, [*crossed out:* industry] & capital show the necessity of a return to a sound financial system; while the rights of citizens and the rights of States, and the binding authority of law over President, Army and people are subjects of not less vital importance in war than in peace. Believing that the views here expressed are those of the Convention and the people you represent, I accept the nomination.

I realize the weight of the responsibility to be borne should the people ratify your choice.

Conscious of my own weakness, I can only seek fervently the guidance of the Ruler of the Universe, and, relying on His all-powerful aid, do my best to restore Union and Peace to a suffering people, and to establish and guard their liberties and rights.

I am, Gentlemen very respectfully your obedient servant

Geo B McClellan

Hon Horatio Seymour
and others, Committee etc.

ALS, Barlow Papers, Huntington Library.

1. This sixth and final draft of GBM's acceptance letter was the product of intensive revisions on Sept. 7 and 8 in company with Samuel Barlow, and perhaps other advisers, in New York. It is a copy of the much-altered fifth draft, with the additional final revisions indicated. 2. These last two sentences are in Barlow's handwriting. 3. The phrasing replacing the crossed-out section is by Barlow.

To Mary Ellen McClellan

[New York] Friday 3 pm
[September 9, 1864]

My own dearest darling

I had hoped to run on for you to day but am not well enough yet to go on & return at once so I send one of Barlow's young men (Mac) to bring you back tomorrow morning. I am almost well to day, but John[1] who is here says that I must keep quiet to day & that I ought not to go on unless I could stay there a day or two — & from your dear letter I see that you want to return tomorrow.

I caught cold that day we came in & the Mexican disease[2] returned upon me — the two in connection with unusual mental excitement & no sleep have rather used me up. I have spent the day on the sofa perfectly quiet & believe I am entirely well. Fan was here just now with Fanny Keith — they go to spend two days with Susie Adams. She says May is *perfectly* well & bright this morning — also your mother. I shall remain in town tonight & meet you at the cars at the Depot. Should I not, for any reason, you will find me at Barlow's — but I expect to meet you. My letter was not handed in until midnight last night. The effect thus far has been electric — the peace men are the only ones who squirm — but all the good men are delighted with it.

John came on last evening — returning this evening — he, of course, is pleased as punch. I am *very* glad that you got on so very comfortably. I am *very* sorry that it is not best for me to go for you — but you must not be in the slightest degree worried about me — it is only a measure of prudence insisted on by the Doctor that I should not go & return at once.

I can't tell you how anxious I am to see you again, my own darling — more than I can express. I telegraphed you last night — but have no answer.

Come in the morning train.

Ever with fondest love your own loving
George

Give my love to Maria & all the family & tell them how much I am disappointed that I cannot see them now.

ALS, McClellan Papers (B-12:48), Library of Congress.

1. Dr. John H. B. McClellan, GBM's brother. 2. Malaria, contracted during the Mexican War.

To Samuel L. M. Barlow

Dear S L M — Orange Sept 13 [1864]

I have letters from Phila to the effect that Randall Reed etc give way — L. W. Cass, Glancy Jones & others write to me in the best of humor — all I hear from every direction is favorable.[1]

I am much better — have kept very quiet — & have been pretty sick, but now regard myself as well.

Sincerely yours
Geo McC

Received yours enclosing the letter from my brother.[2]

ALS, Barlow Papers, Huntington Library.

1. Congressman Samuel J. Randall, and William B. Reed, L. W. Cass, and Glancy Jones were peace Democrats. 2. Barlow's letter of Sept. 12 expressed concern about vice-presidential nominee Pendleton: "If he is all right & don't bolt, so as to lose us Inda. & Illinois I think we are safe. If he does, it will be very doubtful.... Everything is first rate (even the Herald) but much depends on Pendleton, to whom all of our friends are telegraphing." John H. B. McClellan's letter of Sept. 12 to Barlow read, in part: "Everything here looks most favorable — the General's letter has worked wonders. Some of the peace men kicked very hard but all will have to come in." McClellan Papers (B-19:51), Library of Congress.

To Samuel S. Cox

My dear Cox Orange Sept 15 [1864]

Your kind note of the 9th reached me a few days since[1] — I have been too busy & too sick to write any letters or you may be assured I should ere this have replied to it. It reached me too late for the letter of acceptance — nothing less than that letter would have answered in this part of the world — without it, on the simple platform, there was no chance whatever for Penn & New York — more than that, I could not have run on the platform as everybody interpreted it in this part of the world without violating all my antecedents — which I would not do for a thousand Presidencies. I have heard of the hard work you did at Chicago.

I shall not have time to have any *visites* taken — I have had so many applications in regard to similar things that I found my only safety was to decide to have *none* taken.

With my kindest regards to Mrs Cox

I am, in great haste, ever your friend
Geo B McClellan

Hon S S Cox

ALS, Thomas F. Madigan Collection, Rare Books and Manuscripts Division, New York Public Library.

1. In his letter of Sept. 9, Cox suggested that a passage from GBM's *Report* — military victory "should be accompanied and followed by conciliatory measures" — was "in substantial harmony with our platform" and should be part of his acceptance letter. McClellan Papers (B-19:51), Library of Congress.

To Manton M. Marble

My dear Marble — Orange Sept 17 [1864]

On my return last night I found yours of the 12[1] — many thanks. I return the enclosures herewith.

I send in another envelope three or four letters that you may perhaps attend to with advantage. Pretty much all the letters I receive are in one direction. I got an indignant protest from some Maryland secessionists!! So much the better. I will attend to your suggestions — I have many letters from privates & *ex*-soldiers — *all* right.

I am nearly worn out with writing & will say good bye.

Ever your friend
McC

M.M.

ALS, Marble Papers, Library of Congress.

1. In his letter of Sept. 12, Marble suggested that GBM "keep up a diligent *friendly* correspondence with all your old friends in the Army. You know how the platform hurts us there, & how confidently Mr. Lincoln counts upon the ambition of the Army officers & the votes of the soldiers to assist in his re-election." McClellan Papers (B-19:51), Library of Congress.

To William C. Prime

My dear Prime — Orange Sept 20 [1864]

I enclose a letter received last night — for your perusal. Would not the writer's suggestion as to military clubs be a good thing?[1]

It seems to me that the state of affairs described ought to be shown up. Would it not be a good idea to publish extracts from the letter — omitting of course the name of the writer — simply stating its authenticity? I think that such things as he states ought to be made known far & wide.

Ever your friend
Geo B McC

W.C.P.

ALS, McClellan Papers (B-41:61), Library of Congress.

1. In his letter of Sept. 13 Charles D. Deshler, signing himself "State Military Asst. for New Jersey," recounted incidents of what he termed intimidation of soldiers supporting

the Democratic ticket. To counter this, he proposed the formation of "'Soldiers' McClellan Clubs" across the North, made up of ex-soldiers and men home on leave or recovering from wounds. McClellan Papers (B-19:51).

To Robert C. Winthrop

My dear Mr Winthrop Orange Sept 20 [1864]

Your very welcome letter of yesterday has just reached me.[1] I regret extremely that I was not so fortunate as to meet you, but it was not in my power to visit the city on Saturday [September 17], or I certainly should have done so.

I cannot express to you the gratification I felt upon being assured of your entire approval of the course I have taken — in what I did I was actuated solely by what seemed right, not by any notions of policy, & it is a source of great gratification to me to know that you, for whom I entertain so great respect & regard, agree with me. It matters not to me, personally, whether I am elected or not — but it is all important that my course should meet the affirmation of good men.

I was extremely gratified by your speech — which was so far above the tone of so many of the political speeches of the present day & so like those of better days of the Republic.[2] I hope that I may have the pleasure of seeing you ere long — in the mean time, with kindest regards to Miss Winthrop, in which, as well as to yourself Mrs McClellan desires most cordially to unite

I am, respectfully, your sincere friend
Geo B McClellan

Hon Robt C Winthrop
Boston

ALS, Winthrop Papers, Massachusetts Historical Society.

1. In his letter of Sept. 19 Winthrop commented on GBM's acceptance letter: "It relieved your friends from a world of anxiety & embarrassment, & has placed you in a position which is better than the Presidency. If the election shall go as we hope, you will have won the victory by your own pen, as surely as you won Antietam by your sword." McClellan Papers (A-80:32), Library of Congress. 2. Winthrop had addressed a Democratic campaign rally in New York's Union Square on Sept. 17.

To Samuel L. M. Barlow

My dear S L M Orange Sept 21 [1864]

Yours of yesterday did not reach me until after midnight as I was absent in Newark — so I can make but a brief reply.[1]

You had better send at once for McMahon[2] (at Dix's office) & consult him — he can give you names & you can trust him to any extent. In the Army of the Potomac there is

Henry J Hunt — Brig Genl & Chf of Artillery
Jas C Duane — Maj Engrs —
H. L. Abbot — Col 1st Conn. Artillery
Chas N Turnbull — Capt Engrs
Nicholas Bowen — " " (Lt Col etc)
O. E. Babcock — Lt. Col. *but on Grant's Staff*
Genl John Gibbon
Genl M R Patrick — Provost Marshal Genl

Arthur, Sweitzer and Averell are all with Sheridan's Army — also Capt C E Morris 2nd Cavalry. With Sherman's Army you can rely on Genl Brannan, Hammerstein, Slocum (the last a Republican, but Franklin says strong in my favor) — I've no more time now, but will try to think of names today — Clarke H F — Comsry Subs. in New York is from Penna & can give you names. He is all right — Van Vliet is not & *you must not* trust him at all.

I had some confidential & reliable information yesterday — part of which is —

My steps are dogged & every person reported who comes to see me.

Grant has gone clean over to the enemy.[3]

Stanton & Presdt are not on good terms, the former now acting only under the latter's orders & not from his own discretion.

If there is any difficulty about the draft there will be martial law.

Marcy thinks Rosecrantz all right — may require a little handling in a quiet way.

When Naglee[4] returns in a day or two some of you had better see him again — he is working very hard in Penna & I am told with good effect. He has been talking to Curtin. I think you can learn much about Penna from Naglee. He was to go to Boston today — spend one day there & return.

Will you send the enclosed to Lansing.[5] He sent to me the other day for a copy of the Woodward letter & I don't want him to use it in Penna — for I think that as Curtin stands the less said about it the better — so I've written to him again not to say anything about it in his speeches. The Newark affair last night was very large.

In haste ever yours
Geo McC

S.L.M.B.

ALS, Barlow Papers, Huntington Library.

1. In his letter of Sept. 20 Barlow sought the names of army officers to whom Democratic campaign literature could be sent for distribution. Barlow Papers. 2. Lt. Col. Martin T. McMahon. 3. Apparently this is a reference to Gen. Grant's position on soldiers' voting. Barlow replied on this date, in part: "You may be right as to Grant, but if so, my information, directly from him, within ten days, shows that he has changed his mind." McClellan Papers (B-20:52), Library of Congress. 4. Henry M. Naglee, formerly a general

in the Army of the Potomac, was a Democratic campaign organizer. 5. Henry S. Lansing, also a former officer in the Army of the Potomac, wrote on Sept. 16 that he thought the Woodward letter — GBM to Charles J. Biddle, Oct. 12, 1863, *supra* — would effectively demonstrate GBM's views in Pennsylvania. McClellan Papers (B-20:51).

To Henry M. Naglee

My dear Genl Orange Sept 23 [1864]

The conversation between us in regard to the "Woodward letter" has deeply impressed me.

That letter was not called forth by any personal feeling in regard to either of the candidates — simply by the misrepresentations made in regard to me & my course. My acquaintance with Judge Woodward was very slight — to the present day I have met him but twice — while on the other hand my intercourse with Gov Curtin has extended over a considerable period of time & I am under obligations to him for many acts of personal & official kindness.

I regret extremely that the letter caused any unpleasant personal feeling on the part of the Governor — which was far from my intention.

Please say as much to the Governor for me

and oblige your sincere friend
Geo B McClellan

Genl H M Naglee

ALS retained copy, McClellan Papers (B-20:52), Library of Congress.

To Samuel L. M. Barlow

My dear S.L.M. Orange Sept 23 [1864]

I enclose a bill of lading just received for a photograph of Lord Clyde sent to me from England by the Persia — will you do me the favor to ask Taylor to get it for me & send by express to this place.

I shall be in town on Monday morning [September 26] & will be at my house a little after 10 when I shall be delighted to see you.

In haste ever yours
Geo B McClellan

S.L.M.B.

I open this to say that I have just received yours of the 23rd.[1] I have carefully thought over the matter & cannot think of anything I ever wrote or said that could be tortured into giving Lincoln the advice in question. You may be sure that it is a lie out of the whole cloth.

Sincerely yours
McC

I can't imagine what I ought to write Thomson about — and I don't feel disposed to go far out of my way to see a man of whom I entertain the opinion I do of *R*!![2]

Lansing writes to know whether I have heard from Pendleton — if you see him tell him not a word.[3]

ALS, Barlow Papers, Huntington Library.

1. Barlow wrote: "Lincoln pretends to have a letter of yours to himself, written in 1861, I believe, in which you advised him to assume dictatorial powers, arrest members of Congress &c &c. This story is likely to hurt us very much in certain quarters. Have you a copy of any such letter and if not, can you give me the substance." McClellan Papers (B-20:52), Library of Congress. 2. Barlow suggested GBM write J. Edgar Thomson, head of the Pennsylvania Railroad, and William B. Reed in regard to the contest in Pennsylvania. 3. Lansing wrote on Sept. 22 that a letter from the vice-presidential nominee, of the peace wing of the party, supporting GBM's acceptance letter would help in the East "but might be disastrous in the West." McClellan Papers (B-20:52).

To Samuel S. Cox

My dear Cox — Orange Sept 24 [1864]

Yours of the 21st has just reached me.[1]

Although tired out I cannot refrain from acknowledging it at once. I *know* you have had a hard fight, & how nobly you have fought it — I shall be glad when the election is over that you may have a little rest and quietness — for I am sure you will need it by that time.

I am very glad that the letter of acceptance seems wise to you after a calm survey of the state of affairs — it certainly has done much good in this part of the country — we should have been whipped without it. I dare not trust mine to the mail & will await a better opportunity of writing more fully.

In the mean time, with my kindest regards to Mrs Cox, in which as well as to yourself Mrs McClellan desires to unite

I am your friend
Geo B McClellan

Hon S S Cox

ALS, Thomas F. Madigan Collection, Rare Books and Manuscripts Division, New York Public Library.

1. Cox wrote from Ohio on Sept. 21 that he had been "anxious about your [acceptance] letter. I would not now, 'for the world,' have you done otherwise.... I knew we would have a storm. We have had it. It has mostly passed away.... I am working like a beaver. A fair response from the Army for us, will elect all our old Congressmen & give us the state." McClellan Papers (B-20:52), Library of Congress.

To William T. Sherman

My dear General Orange New Jersey Sept 26 1864

Events have crowded upon me so thickly of late that I have been unable to congratulate you as I had wished & intended to do.[1] But on the principle that it is better late than never I will even at this late day express to you my sincere & heartfelt appreciation of the remarkable campaign you have just completed. I confess that at the beginning I trembled for your long line of communications, and I have watched with the most intense interest the admirable manner in which you overcame the difficulty. Your campaign will go down to history as one of the memorable ones of the world, & will be even more highly appreciated in the future than it is in the present. How beautifully you have illustrated the tenderness of communications, by your operations against the enemy's!

But I will not now pretend to do more than offer you my heartfelt congratulations upon the manner in which you have served your country and illustrated your own name — nor can I avoid congratulating you also upon the superb conduct of your troops during the whole campaign.

Poor Macpherson's loss grieved me very much — it must have been a serious personal as well as official one to you — connected as he had been with you for a long time.[2] I am starting for the city & beg you to excuse this hurried screed, & accept it simply as the hearty congratulations[3]

of your sincere friend
Geo B McClellan

Genl W T Sherman
Atlanta

ALS, Sherman Papers, Library of Congress.

1. Atlanta had fallen to Sherman on Sept. 1. 2. Maj. Gen. James B. McPherson, commander of the Army of the Tennessee, was killed at Atlanta on July 22. 3. Sherman acknowledged GBM's complimentary letter on Oct. 11: "Coming from so high a source I cannot but esteem it. . . . I think I understand the purpose of the South properly and that the best way to deal with them is to meet them fair & square on any issue — we must fight them. Cut into them — not talk [to] them, and pursue till they cry enough. If we relax one bit we could never hold up our head again. They would ride us roughshod." McClellan Papers (B-21:52), Library of Congress.

To Charles A. Whittier

My dear Major Orange Sept 27 [1864]

I received yesterday your kind letter of the 17th accompanying Genl Sedgwick's badge.[1]

I can hardly tell you how deeply I thank you for it — you could have sent it to no one who would prize it more, for I am sure that no one was more warmly attached to John Sedgwick than I was.

His death was the severest blow that has fallen to me in this war — for I knew that no one ever possessed a truer and more attached friend than he was to me. I will keep the badge with the most sacred care, & should the wish of my heart ever be realized — and that is to command the Army of the Potomac in one more great campaign — that badge shall go with me, & share whatever of good or ill fortune I may meet with.

Should it ever be my fortune again to be in power and command I hope that you & your comrades will understand that I shall consider Sedgwick's staff as left to my especial care, & that I should be only too glad to gather them around me.

I congratulate you most sincerely upon the brilliant successes just gained in the valley, & hope that they may result in our permanent possession of that troublesome region. Give my love to Arthur & say to him that I will write to him today or tomorrow. With my kind regards to Genl Wright[2] & such others of my friends as may be near you

I am your sincere friend
Geo B McClellan

Maj C A Whittier

So you have lost poor Russell too![3]

When you next write to Miss Sedgwick will you do me the favor to convey to her my sincere thanks for her kindness in permitting me to have this relic of my deceased friend.

McC

ALS, William Alvord Papers, Bancroft Library, University of California at Berkeley. Maj. Whittier was on the staff of the Sixth Corps.

1. Whittier wrote on Sept. 17 enclosing Gen. Sedgwick's corps badge, explaining that the general's sister wanted GBM to have it. McClellan Papers (A-91:36), Library of Congress. 2. Maj. Gen. Horatio G. Wright succeeded Sedgwick as commander of the Sixth Corps. 3. Brig. Gen. David A. Russell, killed at the Battle of Opequon Creek.

To Samuel L. M. Barlow

My dear Saml [Orange] Sept 27 [1864]

Yours just received. The dispatch is from Marcy & is — "McKinstry has just received Fremont's withdrawal from the canvass, to be published on telegraph notice from him. Says Fremont had an interview with Chase & Wilson; they promised him a position in the Cabinet & a dismissal of the two Blairs if he would withdraw and advocate Lincoln. He replied that it was an insult. Fremont said and" — here it breaks off & further this deponent knoweth not.[1] I had a letter from the Gov.[2] this evening — he thinks it better for him to turn all his efforts to N.Y. — I have replied telling him that he is no doubt the best judge — the letter came & the reply goes thro' Duncan who can tell you in detail what both are. I will meet Mr Curtis as you suggest — also Thos Scott.[3] Will arrange with you about the evening on Thursday [September 29] when I come in. Can I get a dinner in Madison Avenue or don't you receive poor people — Hitchcock is a good friend of mine & I can get a meal at the 5th Avenue on him if you have become proud.

In haste sincerely yours
Geo B McC

Wrote to Guthrie — Sherman — Dix & Gov S etc last night.[4]

ALS, Barlow Papers, Huntington Library.

1. This telegram, sent to GBM in cipher by Marcy on Sept. 22, was suppressed by a telegraph official in Pittsburgh. The telegrapher there sent it secretly to GBM by mail. Edward W. Kulgan to GBM, Sept. 23, McClellan Papers (B-20:52), Library of Congress. Justus McKinstry, spokesman for third-party candidate Frémont, was Marcy's authority for saying that Frémont was approached by Republican emissaries Salmon P. Chase and Henry Wilson. 2. Gov. Horatio Seymour wrote GBM on Sept. 26 that he would be unable to campaign in Pennsylvania. McClellan Papers (B-20:52). 3. Presumably George Ticknor Curtis; Thomas A. Scott, of the Pennsylvania Railroad. 4. James Guthrie of Kentucky, Gen. Sherman, Gen. Dix, Gov. Seymour.

To William C. Prime

My dear Prime — Orange Sept 28 [1864]

Please denote enclosed to "Col R B Marcy — Planters Hotel St Louis" & oblige me etc.

I saw H. Ketchum[1] last night who is exceedingly desirous to have me see about 100 of the head men of his concern — I suppose I ought to see some of them, but don't want to see so many. K. was to see me again tomorrow at 12 1/2. Can't you invent *some* way of getting me out of the scrape?

I expect to see you tomorrow also.

Ever yours
McC

W.C.P.

ALS, McClellan Papers (B-41:61), Library of Congress.

1. Hiram Ketchum was an active Democratic campaigner, particularly in writing and distributing campaign literature.

To Mary Ellen McClellan

My own little darling wife — New York Friday [September 30, 1864]

I was obliged to remain in town last night, & have been at work all the morning to complete the inventory of the books — it is now finished & I have seen the glazier who will put in the glass tomorrow, so that I can think of nothing else to be done but the plumber's work & copying the inventories, which I shall do tomorrow. I told Ellen to tell everybody who comes to the house that we no longer live there, & that the house is Mr Goodridge's — for I think it will be better that I should not see any more people there.[1] I have brought the two bundles you left for Marion to take out so that she need not go to the house. Ellen is cleaning the parlors today. I have heard nothing from Orange, so I take it for granted that May is all well — or "better." I had a long and very pleasant interview with Mr Cisco[2] yesterday — I like him much. I am waiting here (at Mr Alsop's) to see Mr A who will be in in a few minutes — so that I can arrange with him about my going to Asawann & prevent any mistakes.[3]

A very beautiful present has come here for you — I enclose the note accompanying it that you may answer it. It is a large casket — almost 18 inches or two feet square — of wood, beautifully carved & heavily gilded — the man & his wife are ordinary workmen & have been engaged upon it ever since the battle of Antietam — it is really very handsome. I have asked Michael to keep it here.

Give my love to Fan & to the Shipmans & Robinsons — & kind regards to all my friends — especially the Brownwells.

If you knew how lonely I am without you I don't think you would move away any more for a while! Prime yesterday told me that all the letters he received were very encouraging.

Ever with fondest love, my own sweet little Nelly,

Your own true husband
George

ALS, McClellan Papers (B-40:60), Library of Congress.

1. GBM had arranged to rent his New York house. 2. John J. Cisco, former assistant secretary of the treasury. 3. Mrs. McClellan was stopping in Hartford before visiting the Joseph W. Alsops at their country home in Middletown, Conn., where GBM was to join her.

To Mary Ellen McClellan

My own dearest little wife Orange Sunday evg [October 2, 1864]

Your dear letter of Friday morning reached me yesterday — many thanks for it — & was delighted that you reached H. so comfortably — it *must* have been a great comfort to be quiet all the way.

I had quite a number of visitors yesterday — Rush was here for a couple of hours in the morning — afterwards Col Peterson who remained a long time — afterwards Wright, the Doctor, Robinson, Raymond etc etc.[1]

It commenced raining a little before dark & continued pretty much all night & through today — so much so that we could not go to church. Emma, Raymond & Bobbie went to the Tableaux & remained all night at the Pillott's — returning about noon today. The only other visitors there were the Redmonds — Marie was afraid of the weather & very sensibly determined not to go. There was a telegram from your Father saying that your Mother would start — or had started — on Thursday & would reach here early in the week[2] — so I suppose she has remained over Sunday in Cincinnati, & will reach home on Tuesday — at least I hope so for it will be rather lonely for your Aunt & Marie without her. I had a note from Boston saying that Jms Lawrence is all right & has come out openly on our side — also a letter published from Mr. Gray taking ground openly.[3] I had a note from John Astor who evidently feels very badly & as his wife sails for Europe within a week I should not be at all surprised if he in the end came out all right. I think Jim Kilburn ought to feel highly flattered by the truthfulness of his representation of H. Greeley! I will bring the baby's gamp without fail.

I have several things to do tomorrow & Wright is coming to clear out my desk — on those accounts & because the weather will no doubt be bad & I want to see your mother I shall wait until Tuesday [October 4], when I will come in the boat & reach you Wednesday am before you are up. May sends her best love to her dear Mama & sends a letter which before she retired she insisted that I should send you — dear little thing, I hate to leave her, & if the weather were decent should be much tempted to take her along. Your Aunt & Marie send much love — & I send as much as a letter can carry. It don't pay to have you away — it's awfully lonely, & every time I see the baby (& I've been with her nearly all day) it makes me miss you all the more.

Ever with fondness, my own Nelly
your devoted husband George

My best love to the Alsops — in which May joins.

ALS, McClellan Papers (B-40:60), Library of Congress.

1. Among GBM's visitors were Richard R. Rush, Edward H. Wright, and Edward A. Raymond. 2. Mrs. Marcy was visiting her husband in St. Louis. 3. James Lawrence, William Gray.

To Charles Mason

My dear Sir. Orange Oct 3, 1864

I hasten to acknowledge the receipt of your letter of the 29th Sept suggesting the propriety of my visiting Pennsylvania before the coming election.[1]

I fully appreciate the importance of carrying that State, and I would do everything in my power to aid in securing that result, but I have made up my mind on reflection that it would be better for me not to participate in person in the canvass.

Trusting you will appreciate my motives in pursuing this mode of action

I am my dear Sir your obedient Servant
Geo B McClellan

Hon Charles Mason

LS, Mason Papers, State Historical Society of Iowa. Mason headed the Democratic Resident Committee, a political club in Washington.

1. Mason urged GBM to make an appearance in Pennsylvania before the state and congressional elections there on Oct. 11, where his mere presence "at some of the great political meetings which will be held next week would greatly promote their interest...." McClellan Papers (B-21:52), Library of Congress.

To Mary Ellen McClellan

Monday night — rather late
[Orange, October 3, 1864]

My own dearest little Nelly

I can't well go to bed quietly without saying a word to you & telling you how much I miss you although I have been very busy all day. After breakfast I walked to Maywood for a few minutes & then went to work copying the list of my books. While at that Wright came — upon which I brought him up to this little room where we went to work at my letters, & by dinner time had the desk cleared!! that with the exception of one or two letters that it was necessary for me to write myself. I had begun at those when Col Ramsey of Penna came & kept me a long while. In the meantime Marie's husband arrived! When they had gone I went to work pasting letters in your autograph book, until towards dusk when I took care of May for about half an hour & was rather edified by her brightness — she *is* bright as a brand new button. Then I took a short walk & found tea ready on my return — which your Aunt & I took alone — Marie being at the Doctor's. After tea I read while your Aunt & Lewis played cribbage, until the May got fairly asleep when I watched her while Maggie had her tea. Then Mrs Robinson came in & soon after Raymond, Kilburn & Marie. When they left your Aunt & I played a few games of cribbage, & when the rest of the family returned I came up & went to work at my list of books & am now pretty well tired out.

Your aunt had a letter from Mama this morning. She intended to pass Saturday & Sunday in Cincinnati, leaving for home on Monday a.m. She had a very pleasant time at St Louis, & I presume will return as good as new. Your father goes down the river this week — but not farther south than Helena. Under all the circumstances I shall not leave until Wednesday — I shall thus see your mother, bring the latest news from her

& have all my little affairs arranged so that you need not worry about returning in a hurry. I have an idea of taking a wagon & pair of horses at Middletown & driving across to New London — qu'en pensez-vous?[1] *I* think it would be splendid, & in order to be prepared for it shall bring my black carpet bag. May is sound asleep or she would send reams of love. When I come remind me to tell you of one of her remarks about you that cannot be translated to paper without losing all its effect.

Dear little thing — she has been as good as a kitten & I hate to leave her — it is like pulling eye teeth! Give my love to Fan & all the Alsops. Goodnight my own dear little darling wife — my own little Nell — I wish I was with you now.

Ever with fondest love your own
George

ALS, McClellan Papers (B-40:60), Library of Congress.

1. "What do you think of it?"

To Samuel L. M. Barlow

Dear S L M Orange Tuesday evening [October 4, 1864]

Yours of today rec'd. I heard from Naglee today[1] — he says that all looks well — wants me to go to Phila which I wont do — & have so written. I fancy N & McK know more than Phillips — who perhaps don't amount to much.[2]

I doubt whether I can be in New York on Saturday [October 8] & don't want anyone to know where I am. Should I be able to be in N.Y. on Saturday I will let you know, but it is very doubtful whether I shall be for a week.

As I have written of late to all the men you speak of except A's friend I guess it don't make much difference if I don't see them provided I don't avoid them.

Should I miss Prime in the morning will you send word to him to attend to my state room

& oblige ever yours
Geo B McC

S L M B Esq

ALS, Barlow Papers, Huntington Library.

1. Naglee wrote from Philadelphia on Oct. 2: "If you will come here you will not be annoyed by those you refer to. . . . Everything looks well — we can do without the soldiers' vote in Nov. here." McClellan Papers (B-21:52), Library of Congress. 2. GBM no doubt refers to Pennsylvania political figures.

To William C. Prime

My dear Prime [New York] Wednesday am [October 5, 1864]

I was caught here so that I could not get to your house until after one, & returned at once in hopes that I might find you. I enclose a letter received yesterday from Genl Hunt (Chief of Artillery) — I think some of his suggestions are worth attending to.[1] Please let me have the letter again when you are through with it.

John Van B.[2] was here to see me this morning and wishes to use in a speech the Blair interview and propositions. So far as it is a public matter there is no objection to it — the only doubt I feel is simply a feeling of delicacy about my being in any manner instrumental in regard to its being brought out (altho' there was no seal of secrecy about it), also that I don't care to move personally in the campaign even to that extent. I wanted particularly to talk to you about it & am very sorry that I have missed you. In a matter that concerns myself so nearly I hardly feel competent to judge. It seems to me, however, that since the elder Blair was the means of the affair getting into the Herald, & the younger brought it into his speech that all obligations of secrecy upon me (if any ever existed) are removed.[3]

With this idea I enclose a note to John Van B — which I would be glad to have you read &, if you *entirely agree* with me, send it to him this evening if you can. If you for *any reason* think it better for me not to give my consent please suppress the note & simply write a note to John telling him that, leaving in a hurry, I requested you to say that nothing had better *come from me* about it for the present. If there is *any doubt* the safe course is necessarily the better.[4]

Don't let Barlow telegraph for me unless it is *absolutely* necessary — my own judgment is that the fewer men I see the better, unless of the class of Cisco etc. I can't find any real use in seeing the politicians — rather the contrary.

In haste sincerely yours
McC

W.C.P.

ALS, McClellan Papers (B-41:61), Library of Congress.

1. In his letter of Sept. 27 Henry J. Hunt suggested stressing that the experience of the Mexican War was proof an armistice could effectively lead to peace; and that the Democratic platform was addressed to the South, "to detach the people from their leaders." McClellan Papers (B-21:52 / B-41:61). 2. John Van Buren, state party chairman in New York. 3. GBM refers here to his interview with Francis P. Blair in New York in July — see GBM to Blair, c. July 22, 1864, *supra* — a report of which had appeared in the *New York Herald* on Aug. 4, and to a campaign speech by Montgomery Blair on Sept. 27 in which he remarked that President Lincoln had "concerted with General Grant" to recall GBM "into the field as his adjunct." 4. In his speech, delivered in Philadelphia, Van

Buren said nothing more about the Blair propositions than had already appeared in the press. Van Buren to Samuel L. M. Barlow, Oct. 14, Barlow Papers, Huntington Library.

To J. Henry Liebenau

My Dear Sir: Orange Oct. 13 [1864]

In consequence of an absence of several days from home your letter of the 8th did not meet my eye until to-day.[1]

I accept with pride the honorary membership of the legion you have done me the honor to call by my name.

No greater compliment could have been paid to me than this association of my name with a society composed of my comrades in the present war. My love and gratitude for them have remained unchanged during our long separation, and I have watched with the most intense interest their noble and persistent gallantry in the many battles they have fought under the commanders who have succeeded me in the Army of the Potomac.

You, and they, may rest satisfied that I remain the same man that I was when I had the honor to command the Army of the Potomac, and that I shall never willingly disappoint their confidence.

With my sincere thanks for the compliment you have paid me, and my earnest wishes for the prosperity of my former comrades, and of our country,

I am, very respectfully and truly, your friend,
George B. McClellan

Mr. H. Liebenau, Corresponding Secretary
McClellan Legion, 534 Broadway

New York World, Oct. 16, 1864. Liebenau, former quartermaster of the 71st New York regiment, was an officer of the New York McClellan Legion.

1. Liebenau wrote on Oct. 8 that his veterans' political club ''repudiated the Chicago platform, as an insult to the soldier'' and instead embraced ''your frank and honest Letter of Acceptance....'' McClellan Papers (B-21:52), Library of Congress.

To Sidney Herbert

My dear Major Orange New Jersey October 13 1864

In consequence of my absence from home your note of the 6th has reached my eye only this morning.[1]

I trust that I need not assure you that I regard with the greatest interest your efforts in the organization of the ''old soldiers.''

My feeling of personal attachment towards the gallant veterans whom it is my pride that I have commanded & whose achievement I so strongly appreciate remains unchanged. In the present political contest I should doubly savor success and be quite reconciled to defeat if I felt that my old comrades still clung to the commander whom they never failed in battle.

AL retained copy, McClellan Papers (B-21:52), Library of Congress. Herbert, a former officer in the Army of the Potomac, organized a McClellan Legion club in Boston.

1. Herbert wrote GBM on Oct. 6: "A word of encouragement &c from you . . . will do more to give success to my efforts than the most eloquent oration of modern time." McClellan Papers (B-21:52).

To William C. Prime

My dear Prime Orange Oct 13 [1864]

I enclose among other letters, two of special interest — one from Col Ferry which I think it might be well to have published — omitting names & dates — anything which could identify Ferry. The letter from Camp Parole is of interest as giving a name to which documents may be sent.[1] I also enclose a letter from McMahon which please regard as *private* & return to me — note his suggestions.[2]

Ever yours
McC

What is your *private* opinion of Mather?[3]

ALS, McClellan Papers (B-21:52), Library of Congress.

1. Col. John H. Ferry wrote on Oct. 3 that his commission was revoked after he was seen at the Chicago Democratic convention. R. W. Vincent, awaiting prisoner exchange at Camp Parole at Annapolis, wrote on Oct. 8 for campaign literature. McClellan Papers (B-21:52). 2. In his letter of Oct. 10 Col. McMahon suggested increasing the number of campaign documents and Democratic newspapers sent to the Army of the Potomac, addressing them to officers loyal to the party to insure their distribution. McClellan Papers (B-21:52). 3. John C. Mather wrote on Oct. 13 that a visit to Pennsylvania by GBM would carry the state for the Democrats in November. McClellan Papers (B-21:52).

To Samuel L. M. Barlow

Private

My dear S L M Orange Oct 13 [1864]

Yours of today received. I return the last two letters with many thanks.

Lansing was a bad selection — he is not popular down there & I am sorry he has gone. I delayed replying to B's letter because I could not at once think of exactly the right man & wished to consult Wright.[1] I had written to B. but destroyed the letter when I received yours.

I shan't give him a letter to Grant — it would hardly do. Hancock is on the fence — waiting to see which is to be the winning side — so with many Genls including Meade. Gibbon, Hunt, Bartlett & Patrick are perfectly sound.[2] It would do harm, I think, for me to give letters to L. for the reason that it would give the impression that he was sent by me & was a particularly confidential friend which would do us no especial good down there — quite the contrary.

It's too late to mend the matter now, & he had better go on his letters from Belmont & his personal acquaintance with the Army. He will work hard & be energetic — but he is not, or was not, very popular.

In great haste ever yours
McC

S L M B

Are not matters a little mixed? What *is* the matter with Indiana?[3]

Ask Prime to show you McMahon's letter — I told him to consider it private.

ALS, Barlow Papers, Huntington Library.

1. August Belmont wrote GBM on Oct. 11 to report that "General Grant is very favorably disposed & intends to see fair play & our rights protected" in the matter of soldier voting. He suggested sending Henry Lansing to the Army of the Potomac to handle the details of the voting arrangements. McClellan Papers (B-21:52), Library of Congress. 2. The source of these appraisals was McMahon's letter to GBM of Oct. 10. McClellan Papers (B-21:52). 3. The Democrats were defeated in Indiana, as they were in Pennsylvania and Ohio, in the Oct. 11 elections.

To August Belmont

My dear Mr. Belmont — Orange Oct 13 [1864]

I wrote to you today, in reply to your last, saying that I did not think Lansing was exactly the man to go to the Army & that if you would tell me precisely what was to be done I would try to find the proper man. But Barlow writes that Lansing has gone — so I destroy the letter & we must let it go.

I hear but little out here — but my letters from the Army are encouraging.

In great haste
Sincerely your friend
Geo B McClellan

Mr A. Belmont

ALS, Belmont Family Collection, Rare Book and Manuscript Library, Columbia University.

To Allan Pinkerton

My dear Allan [Orange] Oct. 20 [1864]

I presumed the association of my name with Vallandigham was abandoned — I take it for granted my letter[1] effectually knocked on the head any ideas of bringing in the Peace Party. I intend to destroy any and all pretense for any possible association of my name to the Peace Party.

Many of my conservative friends regret that I wrote that letter.

I did not. I tried to do what was right and I trust that the future will vindicate the wisdom of my course by showing that the letter in question did very much toward breaking up the Copperheads in the North.

James D. Horan, *The Pinkertons: The Detective Dynasty That Made History* (New York, 1967), p. 145.

1. GBM's letter accepting the nomination.

To William C. Prime

My dear Prime Orange Oct 20 [1864]

I enclose a note just received from Langenschwartz. Can't something be done for him? I've no doubt he has sacrificed much — & that he would be made perfectly happy by being sent somewhere & having his expenses paid.[1]

In haste ever yours
McC

W.C.P.

I enclose a letter from a private soldier — can't you send him Docs. & tickets?

Friday [October 21] am.

Thank you for yours of yesterday.[2] I had a note from Barlow to the effect that Pendleton was to be in city today. I have engagements with some Penna people which will prevent me from coming in the morning. Is it advisable that I should take any part in the discussion? I decidedly doubt it. Answer by Robinson if possible.

McC

ALS, McClellan Papers (B-22:52), Library of Congress.

1. In his letter of Oct. 17 Max Langenschwartz complained that he had exhausted his resources in campaigning for the Democrats among German-speaking citizens. McClellan Papers (B-21:52). 2. Prime's letter of Oct. 20 included a calculation of the electoral vote in the coming election, with GBM winning. "We are gaining daily in my opinion. . . . We can't tell what will happen within a fortnight or three weeks, but the *set* of the tide is now with us." McClellan Papers (B-22:52).

To Robert C. Winthrop

My dear Mr. Winthrop Orange Oct 22 [1864]

I had intended to write to you yesterday, but was prevented by a constant stream of callers during the day.

I wished simply to thank you for your noble oration delivered at New

London.[1] The country owes you its thanks for such a calm dignified & able & exhaustive exposition of the questions at issue. Would that the whole contest could be conducted in the spirit with which you approach it!

I know of no political speech of the present or the past that will bear comparison with yours, and I rejoice at the reception it has met with from all the good and honest men whom I have heard from in regard to it.

There is hope for our country so long as such orations can be delivered and listened to.

Mrs McClellan unites with me in kindest regards to your daughter & yourself

And I am ever your friend
Geo B McClellan

Hon Robt C Winthrop
Boston

ALS, Winthrop Papers, Massachusetts Historical Society.

1. In his address, delivered on Oct. 18, Winthrop charged that the administration's policy "has been calculated to extinguish every spark of Union sentiment in the Southern States.... I, for one, have never had a particle of faith that a sudden, sweeping forcible emancipation could result in anything but mischief and misery for the black race, as well as the white.... We are not for wading through seas of blood in order to reorganize the whole social structure of the South."

To Samuel L. M. Barlow

My dear Barlow Orange Oct 27 [1864] Thursday

I enclose a note from Naglee which contains a good suggestion.

Gov Seymour writes that all is favorable in New York,[1] & I hear that the Penna people feel very jubilant.

In haste truly yours
Geo B McClellan

Mr S L M Barlow

ALS, Barlow Papers, Huntington Library.

1. On Oct. 23 Seymour wrote: "I have for many years canvassed this state and I have never seen so much spirit and enthusiasm in the Democratic party.... I may be mistaken, but I feel a great political revolution is going on." McClellan Papers (B-22:52), Library of Congress.

To Samuel L. M. Barlow

My dear Barlow Orange Thursday night [October 27, 1864]

Yours of this morning has reached me.[1] I expect definite intelligence from Curtin tomorrow which will enable me to act in the Penna matter.

Tomorrow night or Saturday morning I shall have reliable information in regard to some of the plans of the Govt — I can now only conjecture what they are, but have sent a confidential friend to receive the information which my informant dares not trust to the mail or to any but the most reliable person.[2] I would advise that any of the party in the West who have papers which could in any way commit them should be at once advised to destroy them or to conceal them. A similar course may be advisable in the East. But I shall know pretty much all they intend to do within a couple of days & will then be able to make definite suggestions even if I can't give reasons. But if you have the means it can do no harm to give the cautions I have suggested. I pity you in the midst of your hard work — I am a good deal overrun, but not so much as you are. Don't work yourself entirely to death.

In haste sincerely yours
Geo B McClellan

S L M B

All the news I hear is *very* favorable. There is every reason to be most hopeful.

ALS, Barlow Papers, Huntington Library.

1. On Oct. 27 Barlow wrote: "You can have no idea of the work we are doing. I have hardly ate or slept for ten days, while my house has become a miniature Tammany Hall. . . . I think the case may be fairly stated to be this — we have an even chance of success . . . ; but today we hear, that under pretense of fraud, the Govt. is stopping the boxes containing our ballots." Barlow Papers. 2. GBM suspected a conspiracy by the administration going beyond interference with the soldier vote. The informant mentioned here was Allan Pinkerton, who had sent GBM a message on Oct. 26 that he possessed information of the gravest consequence to the McClellan campaign. The "confidential friend" sent to meet Pinkerton was Edward H. Wright. By Wright's later account, Pinkerton told him the government had report of a plot by "friends of McClellan," among them August Belmont, Thomas M. Key, George Ticknor Curtis, and Wright, to assassinate President Lincoln. They were watched "and on the slightest movement on their part all would be arrested and hung," Pinkerton said. Wright reported on the meeting on Oct. 29, and, he wrote, "Gen. McClellan treated the conspiracy nonsense as I had, and said he would not insult any of his friends by repeating such a charge to them." There is not the slightest evidence of such a plot, and the source of Pinkerton's information is unknown. Wright to Curtis, Dec. 28, 1886, McClellan Papers (B-39:60), Library of Congress.

To William C. Prime

My dear Prime [New York] Monday am. [November 7, 1864]

We leave this morning. What do you & Barlow think now about my resigning my commission tomorrow?

Let me hear how things look by Mrs Robinson this afternoon.

In haste ever yours
McC

W.C.P.

ALS, McClellan Papers (B-22:52), Library of Congress.

To E. D. Townsend

Col E D Townsend, Asst Adj Genl
Washington D C
Sir: Orange New Jersey Nov 8 1864

I have the honor to resign my commission as a Major General in the Army of the U.S.A., with the request that it may be accepted to take effect today.[1]

I am, sir, very respectfully,
Geo B McClellan
Maj Genl USA

ALS, Records of the Adjutant General's Office, RG 94 (M-619:278), National Archives.

1. On Nov. 13 Townsend replied: "Your resignation dated November 8th reached this Department at two o'clock on the 10th instant and was accepted by order of the President." McClellan Papers (A-91:36), Library of Congress.

To Samuel L. M. Barlow

My dear Sam Orange Nov 10/64

Yours of yesterday reached me in the evening.[1] It is a noble letter and just such as would have been most grateful had I been depressed and in need of consolation — I value it none the less from the fact that I was fully prepared for the result and not in the slightest degree overcome by it.

For my country's sake I deplore the result — but the people have decided with their eyes wide open and I feel that a great weight is removed from my mind. I have sent in my resignation and have abandoned public life forever — I can imagine no combination of circumstances that can ever induce me to enter it again — I say this in no spirit of pique or mortification — it is simply the result of cool judgment. I shall hereafter devote myself to my family and friends, & leave to others the grateful task of serving an intelligent, enlightened and appreciative people! I am still quite at sea as to my future — it is of course useless to think much about it for a few days, that is until my resignation is accepted, & the excitement has somewhat subsided. I should be delighted if a miracle should occur which would give me something to do that would take me to Europe for a few months — but that would be too good to think of. I shall determine on nothing until I see you — which will be in a few days. I don't know exactly what I shall do, but have no doubt that a flock of ravens will turn up somewhere, & alight in my neighborhood.

I fully appreciate the work that my friends have done, & their motives — no man, I think, ever had more or truer or nobler friends than I — would that I could thank them all, as I do you, for the devotion with which they have fought this bitter & desperate fight — if we have been unsuccessful we have at least, thank God, no cause to be ashamed. I am sure that when the future has made things more clear & has applied the sad test of experience to the principles of the two parties, that our position in defeat will be more enviable than that of our antagonists in success. God grant that our poor country may not be ruined in the course of proving that we were right. Give my kind regards to Mr. Belmont when you see him, & my warmest to Marble, Prime etc etc. Mrs McC unites with me in love to the Madame, children & yourself — & says that she appreciated your letter more than she can express.

Ever your friend
Geo B McClellan

S.L.M.B.

ALS, Barlow Papers, Huntington Library.

1. Barlow's letter of Nov. 9 read, in part: "For your want of success I am sorry. I believed that in your election lay the only hope of peace with Union. Under Mr. Lincoln, I see little prospect of anything, but fruitless war, disgraceful peace, & ruinous bankruptcy. But I cannot resist the feeling . . . that if you had been triumphantly chosen, you would be today more to be pitied, than envied. The fearful responsibility to be assumed by a president next March, with an empty treasury, a wasted army, and a defiant and apparently united people in rebellion, is enough to appal anyone. . . ." McClellan Papers (B-22:52), Library of Congress.

To Elizabeth B. McClellan

My dear Mother Orange Nov 11 /64

The smoke has cleared away and we are beaten!

All we can do is to accept it as the will of God & to pray that he will so turn the hearts of our rulers that they may open a way of salvation for the country to emerge from its troubles. Personally I am glad that the dreadful responsibility of the government of the nation is not to devolve upon my shoulders — my only regret is for my country & my friends — so many of whom have suffered on account of their devotion to me. It could have been a most pleasant thing to me to have had it in my power to redress their wrongs, but that is impossible now, & I can repay them only by sincere gratitude. I do not yet believe that God can have given over our country — & although I do not yet see the daylight, I cannot doubt that it will break forth when least expected, & I have full confidence that if we deserve to be saved He will save us.

I sent in my resignation a couple of days ago, & have not yet heard whether it is accepted or not. I shall now remain in private life — and I can imagine no combination of circumstances that will draw me into public life again. I feel that I have sacrificed as much for my country as any one can reasonably expect unless I could effect some good object which no one else could — & I do not flatter myself that that can ever be the case. I have not yet determined upon my plans, but as soon as the excitement has subsided & my resignation is accepted I shall very promptly determine what to do. I am still young enough, strong enough, & hopeful enough to begin life anew & have no regret for the past — because I feel that I have simply tried to do my duty to the country & to God. I never felt less regret for anything in my life than for the personal consequences of the late defeat. A great weight is removed from my shoulders & I feel that I am once more a free citizen — as good as any body else! As soon as things are quiet & the excitement has subsided I shall quietly come on to Phila for a few days. We are all very well — including the baby. All send much love to all of you. Like wise to Mary & John & Maria & Mr Chisolm. Have you heard from Arthur since his return to the Army? I hope & trust that you will not let the state of the country worry you at all — it is in the hands of God & in him we must trust to carry us through.

Ever, my dearest Mother
Your affectionate son
Geo McC

Mrs. E. S. B. McC
Love to the Coxes, Phillips etc etc

ALS, McClellan Papers (B-22:52), Library of Congress.

To Samuel L. M. Barlow

My dear S L M Orange Tuesday evg [November 15, 1864]

Upon my return this evening I found awaiting me the acceptance of my resignation dated the 13th — it is accepted "by order of the Presdt." — so that I am at last a free man once more! No comments are made — it is simply a formal acceptance by the Adjt Genl.

Will you do me the favor to ascertain for me & let me know by Mr Robinson tomorrow (Wednesday) evg whether any Morris & Essex shares are in the market & if so what price. Advise —

Ever yours
Geo B McClellan

S.L.M.B.
Please inform Prime of the acceptance.

ALS, Barlow Papers, Huntington Library.

To Charles Lanman

My dear Mr Lanman Orange Nov 16/64

Your kind note of the 10th duly reached me.[1]

If I entertained any sentiment of personal chagrin at the result of the late election it would have been at once dispelled by the many evidences of regard and friendship I have since received from those whom I most respect. Fortunately, perhaps, I regarded the contest from the beginning as one inviting the great interests of the nation, & as of too great magnitude to leave any room for personal feelings or ambition, so that when the end came there was no personal mortification to be soothed. But I am none the less grateful to my friends for the warm interest they display in me, & shall never cease to entertain the most sincere gratitude towards them.

I do not yet despair of the Republic, but believe that after many trials & sufferings we shall at last recover our old institutions & our former glory, & come out of the fiery furnace purified & strengthened.

At all events our course is clear, & that is to stand firmly by the great principles we have advocated & never forget that we have still a country to save whenever God permits us to act in its behalf. I beg that you will express to Mr Seaton & Mr Welling[2] my high appreciation of the noble course they have pursued

& believe me ever your friend
Geo B McClellan

Mr Chas Lanman
Georgetown

ALS, McClellan Papers, New-York Historical Society. Lanman was librarian of the House of Representatives and of the War Department.

1. In his letter of Nov. 10 Lanman wrote: "May our poor unhappy country become worthy of such a son, ... in the fiery trials of both a civil and a political war." McClellan Papers (B-91:36), Library of Congress. 2. William W. Seaton and James C. Welling were editors at the *National Intelligencer*.

To Robert C. Winthrop

My dear Mr Winthrop Orange New Jersey Nov 16 1864

Your very welcome letter of the 14th reached me today.[1] I am truly rejoiced to find so entire unanimity of sentiment among those whose opinion I respect, as to the light in which we should view the actual state of affairs. Up to the close of the Chicago Convention there is much to regret, yet it is possible, perhaps probable, that no course could have resulted otherwise than that actually pursued — so great was the power wielded by the Administration. Since the Convention I think the fight has been a noble one & that we have no cause to be ashamed, tho' we have much to deplore for the country's sake.

Had it been ordained that we should succeed I can readily understand the great difficulties in our path, yet I was confident that, with God's blessing and the aid of the good men I had hoped to gather around me, I could see a way clear by which it was at least possible to restore the Union of our Fathers without injury to the self respect of either nation. I am glad that I can truly say that no feeling of personal disappointment has crossed my mind — personally I cheerfully acquiese in the result. I wrote my resignation on the day of the election before I could know the result, & yesterday was notified that it had been accepted — I am therefore even now a private citizen, & shall direct myself to the active pursuits of civil life. I shall never cease to thank you, my dear Mr Winthrop, for the exertions you have made in behalf of our common country, & for the many endeavors of personal regard you have given me. I trust & ask that, although neither of us may ever again be called upon to cooperate in public life, that the acquaintance — and I hope I may say friendship — which has sprung up between us may in the future be closer than in the past. Mrs McClellan unites with me in kindest regards to your daughter & yourself

And I am, my dear sir, ever your sincere friend
Geo B McClellan

Hon Robt C Winthrop
Boston

ALS, Winthrop Papers, Massachusetts Historical Society.

1. Winthrop wrote: "The prospects for the future are so dark & the difficulties of the present so formidable that any one who escapes the responsibility of holding the helm at such a moment, may well be felicitated." Although he had doubted the prospects for victory, he added, "Our defeat is rather more sweeping than I had anticipated...." McClellan Papers (A-91:36), Library of Congress.

To Arthur McClellan

My dear Arthur — Orange Nov 20th [1864]

Your welcome letter of the 12th reached me only yesterday morning — many thanks for it.[1]

Until we meet it is hardly worth while to discuss the late election further than to say that it was very close so far as the popular vote was concerned; & that as we were defeated we have nothing to do but to acquiesce in the result & pray that the country may pass safely through the ordeal of the next four years. Personally I am glad that I have escaped the troubles & trials of the charge of the nation at such a time — had the result been otherwise I should have accepted the trust with a full sense of its difficulties, & simply from a sense of duty. Of course you now know that my resignation was accepted & that Sheridan has the vacancy[2] — it seems probable that he was the best man for it — & I hope sincerely that he may not succeed to the cares which it brought to me. I am again a free man & a great weight is lifted from me. What the future may bring to me I do not yet know — I find that the miserable feeling of political failure is carried to the extent of operating against me even in obtaining employment in civil life — but I am sure that I shall in some way make my way & there are other lands than this should I have to shake the dust from my shoes here.

I suppose my arrangements will be made before it is necessary for you to carry out the intention you expressed[3] & I hope that there will be much that I can aid you as to your own future in civil life. As soon as I know definitely what I am to do I will inform you. Nelly & the baby send their love. Give my kind regards to Whittier & my other friends — not forgetting Wright & Getty.

Your affectionate brother
Geo McC

ALS, McClellan Papers (B-41:61), Library of Congress.

1. GBM's brother wrote on Nov. 12: "If the people have been blind enough to wish for four years more of the present dynasty they deserve to suffer.... At any rate you have lost no dignity by defeat and your way of managing the campaign will contrast favorably with Mr. Lincoln's." McClellan Papers (B-21:52). 2. Philip Sheridan was appointed major general in the regular army in GBM's place. 3. Arthur McClellan had considered resigning his commission, but did not.

To Charles G. Halpine

My dear Sir — Orange New Jersey Nov 25 1864

Your very kind and welcome letter of the 19th has reached me,[1] but I have been unable to reply to it until now in consequence of my continued absence from home.

I had entirely forgotten the "Hunter" articles until you reminded me of them — in truth they made no lasting impression on my mind. I have not the slightest recollection that I ever associated your name with them, & suspect that Genl Halleck was mistaken in the matter. If I ever thought that you had anything to do with them the idea passed from my mind even more completely than the letters themselves — so much so that when I met you the association was not in any manner recalled to my mind.

I sincerely thank you for your friendship & kind feeling — and assure you that I value them most highly.

If I had felt any personal mortification or disappointment upon the result of the late election — which I did not — I should have felt amply compensated by the assurances I not infrequently receive of the regard of those whose good opinion I most value.

With the hope that we may in the future see more of each other

I am very sincerely yours
Geo B McClellan

Mr Chas G Halpine
New York

ALS, Halpine Papers, Huntington Library. Halpine was a reporter for the *New York Herald*.

1. Halpine wrote GBM on Nov. 19 to explain that he was not the author "of certain articles hostile to you which appeared in the spring of 1862 in the Chicago Tribune. That you *thought* me the author, Gen. Halleck informed me; that they were evidently inspired from Gen. [David] Hunter's headquarters, was obvious to any reader; but they were not by me...." McClellan Papers (A-91:36), Library of Congress.

To Manton M. Marble

My dear Marble Orange New Jersey Nov 28 1864

Your very welcome letter of the 13th duly reached me.[1]

I failed to reply to it for the reason that I have been but little at home of late, & my mind has been occupied in — thus far — unsuccessful attempts to settle down in private life.

I do not know what the future has in store for me — I do not know where my lot will be cast — whether I can remain here or seek my future in some new country — but I can now at least look calmly back upon the eventful episodes through which we have passed — none of us insignificant actors in the scene.

We have aided in "making history" — and that too a history which some yet unborn Homer or Milton will some day clothe in verse. As I look back upon it it seems to me a subject replete with dignity — a struggle of honor patriotism & truth against deceit selfishness & fanaticism, and I think that we have well played our parts. The mistakes made were not of our making — & before the curtain falls upon the final act of the drama I trust that we will see that these apparent mistakes were a part of the grand plan of the Almighty, who designed that the cup should be drained even to the bitter dregs, that the people might be made worthy of being saved. At all events I accept the result, & calmly abide the issue — be it good or evil. But now — while I stand on the middle height — not embittered by disappointment, not yet regretting the brilliant prize which has escaped us, nor daring to look hopefully into the future — I cannot fail to appreciate the noble course of such true friends as Barlow & yourself, & to thank you for it. You have done nothing that I regret — much that I admire & am grateful for. It is not probable that I shall again emerge from a private station — but I hope that in that sphere the ties of friendship formed in the exciting period through which we have passed, will only be drawn more closely, and that if it has not been permitted us to save our country, we can at least enjoy the satisfaction of thwarting the efforts of others to destroy it & of enjoying ourselves in our own quiet way during the remainder of our lives.

I thank you not only for your letter, but for your continued & unselfish friendship, and with my kindest regards to Mrs M,

I am ever your sincere friend
Geo B McClellan

Mr Manton Marble

ALS, Marble Papers, Library of Congress.

1. Marble wrote on Nov. 13, in part: "I never have despaired of a constitutional restoration of things at the South. The election shows that we had more reason to despair of constitutional restoration of things at the North. . . . But because that bitter lesson has not yet been learned, because the North in its secret soul is still stubborn and stiff-necked in its refusal of constitutional rights to those who saw its temper and sought a lawless & wicked remedy . . . the time was not ripe for our success, the fullness of time had not yet come, & success, if we had achieved it at the polls, would have been transient, temporary and lacking in all that made success there . . . worthy to be won." McClellan Papers (A-91:36), Library of Congress.

To Samuel L. M. Barlow

My dear Sam Orange Nov 28 [1864]

The M & E has gone up — political reasons entirely![1] I suppose I must make up my mind now to shake the dust off my shoes & go elsewhere — so be it. I feel that I owe nothing to a country which denies me the privilege of earning an honest living merely because a great and honest party chose to make me their leader. I shall leave it without regret — I shall regret only the kind, true & dear friends that remain.

Were it not for the house in 31st St I should now be almost penniless — that alone enables me to live — & for that I know that I am indebted to you — & to you alone — so that if it is ever a consolation to you & your children to know that you have kept above water the head of a miserable fellow like myself you have that satisfaction. I don't care to *talk* more with *Marie* — he *talks* too much — may I trouble you to send word to him thro' Flandin that I would like to have a *definite* proposition as to compensation & the *means of reaching Guatemala*. I want the details — not generalities.[2] Tomorrow I go to finish my engineering work on the M & E. I may come to town on Wednesday — but if you can (& have time to waste on a forlornity) write me tomorrow (Tuesday) by Robinson.

Confound the whole concern — I am strongly tempted to convert what

I have into gold & offer my sword & brains (if I have any) to Maximilian or Alexander.[3] How about the gold investment. I think Sherman will come to grief.[4]

Ever yours
McC

S.L.M.B.

ALS, Barlow Papers, Huntington Library.

1. Abram S. Hewitt had recommended GBM for the post of president of the Morris and Essex Railroad at a salary of $8,000. On Nov. 26 Hewitt wrote GBM that the Morris and Essex's board of directors, out of concern for the railroad's dealings with the New Jersey legislature and the federal government, "did not think it expedient to make you President...." McClellan Papers (B-23:53 / B-22:52), Library of Congress. 2. Apparently this is a reference to an engineering position on a proposed interocean canal. See Edward W. Serrell to GBM, Nov. 19, McClellan Papers (B-22:52). 3. Ferdinand Maximilian Joseph, the puppet emperor of the French in Mexico; Alexander II of Russia. 4. Gen. Sherman had set off on his March to the Sea on Nov. 15.

To Samuel L. M. Barlow

My dear Sam Orange Dec 30/64

Yours of the 27th reached me — much obliged for your kindness in attending to the gold matter for me. Many thanks for your attending to the tax matter for me too.[1] Alas that the fates prevented me from turning over Montauk Light House as a faint mark of appreciation! Never mind — when Quicksilver goes to 200 you can afford to build a private Light House on your own account![2]

You say that Fitz[3] writes that he has written to me several times. I have never received a line from him, except two or three lines of a note of introduction for a Mr. Biddle. I presume friend Stanton has read the letters, whatever they might be — much good may they do him. Wright tells me that Reverdy Johnson says that Fitz is making a great deal of money, & that he will soon be able to return to civilization a rich man.

I shall write to Fitz today — when you write to him say that I have not received his letters, & that I have sent frequent messages to him by Mr. Lathrop etc etc. I have thought very seriously over the European matter, & unless something unsuspected occurs shall go as early in February as possible.[4]

We shall be in town most of next week.

In great haste ever yours
McC

S.L.M.B.

P.S. I enclose a letter for *Fitz John Porter*, will you have it directed & mailed — I think it will go more safely than if I send it from here.

ALS, Barlow Papers, Huntington Library.

1. Barlow had arranged for a transaction in gold for GBM, and also for the payment of taxes on his New York house. McClellan Papers (B-23 :53), Library of Congress. 2. Barlow and GBM were investors in the New Alexander Quicksilver Mining Co. 3. Fitz John Porter, then engaged in mining ventures in Colorado Territory. 4. The McClellans would sail for Europe on Jan. 25, 1865.

To August Belmont

My dear Mr Belmont Rome March 19 1865

Your very kind note of the 2nd, with the enclosed letter, duly reached me — many thanks to you for both. You can readily imagine how difficult it is to find time to write during one's first visit to Rome, so that I am sure you will accept my apology for the delay in acknowledging the receipt of your letter.

We reached here just in time for the two last days of the Carnival, which we enjoyed exceedingly — altho' I confess that I should not care to put myself to any inconvenience for the sake of seeing it again — once is quite enough. We are with our friends the Story's in the Barberini Palace,[1] & are enjoying our visit extremely — our only regret is that we cannot remain here months instead of weeks — for I can clearly see that we shall carry away only a very superficial idea of this great city.

We shall remain until after Easter week, & then go to Naples for two or three weeks. The weather has not been pleasant here until within a day or two — but at Naples and in Sicily all accounts say that it has been literally infamous. I don't know whether the natives here talk of the weather as we are very apt to do about the mosquitos at home, but they all say that the spring has been thus far unusually late & disagreeable — the leaves have not yet commenced to bud, & we have had only three really pleasant days since our arrival.

Saw the Pope last week — he was quite amicable. It seems hardly necessary to say that in spite of the weather we have enjoyed ourselves exceedingly here, & are in no regard disappointed. We have taken a first glance at most of the galleries & will be able to devote a good deal of the pleasant weather (if we ever have any) to the environs. I shall not fail to call upon Baron Rothschild immediately upon our return to Paris, & I regretted exceedingly that I could not do so before our departure. We are in rather an excited state of mind here — consequent upon the arrival of the fragment of a telegraphic dispatch stating that a battle was in progress between Sherman & Joe Johnston with "undecided" results. I hope that we may hear something definite in a day or two. With Johnston in front of him Sherman's progress will at least be much slackened & less of a triumphal march than heretofore. There is one item that seems very favorable if it is true — that is a line or two to the effect that the Richmond papers are abusing Johnston for something — what for is not stated.

I trust that your return voyage will be much smoother than our last passage[2] & that your health will be entirely restored by the time you reach New York. Mrs McClellan desires to unite with me in kind regards to Mrs Belmont & yourself

and I am sincerely yours
Geo B McClellan

Mr August Belmont
New York

ALS, Belmont Family Collection, Rare Book and Manuscript Library, Columbia University.

1. The sculptor William Wetmore Story and his wife, the sister of GBM's sister-in-law Maria Eldredge McClellan. 2. The Belmonts and the McClellans had sailed for Europe together aboard the *China*.

To Samuel L. M. Barlow

My dear Sam — Rome April 15/65

I know that there are one or two unanswered letters of yours lying around loose, but I cannot place my hands upon them — perhaps I can before this is committed to the mercies of the Pontifical Post Office.

The fact is that Rome is not favorable to letter writing — especially when one is staying at a private house — sight seeing all day & expected to play the agreeable all the evening when not dining out etc — so that I have not written a line for weeks, & it is purely accidental that I can do so now. As you know, we have been here some seven weeks, & I begin to feel that I am in a condition to appreciate this wonderful city.

We will probably leave for Naples next week, without having by any means accomplished all the most pleasant excursions that can be made in the vicinity. Apart from riding & driving over the Campagna, we have only been to Frascati, Tusculum & Veii — but hope to accomplish Tivoli next week. We will probably remain two or three weeks at Naples — making Head Quarters at Sorrento — then take up the line of march to Florence & Venice. Where to spend the summer we have not yet quite decided — probably either in Switzerland or Germany — depending upon what we find when we arrive in that part of the world — the desideratum is a cheap & quiet place, off the crowded routes of travel — that such places exist, I know — the only trouble is, to find them. The more I think of the state of affairs at home the better satisfied I am that I did well in coming abroad, & the less do I feel inclined to return until the latest possible moment. It is very clear that I can be of no use at present, & I am much inclined to think that my day of public usefulness is probably passed. The manner in which we have been received abroad has been very gratifying — here all is on the bright side — I hear no slanders — all treat me as a gentleman, & seem disposed to exaggerate very much the importance of my part in the war, & to give me a much higher position than I merit. Here we are the equals of the best — at home there is always the wretched feeling of partisan to be encountered. I should be glad to be able to remain abroad until the expiration of Uncle Abraham's term of service — if gold keeps down, & quicksilver up, I may be able to do it. My only regret is the absence of a few of my best & truest friends, & I could be very happy to be here many years if some of you would come over.

Let me know what the amount of my income tax was. I hope it was not overwhelming — there is at all events one great consolation — it will not be very large next year! Does the quicksilver still look like paying another 5% dividend in July, & keeping up the same good habit in the future? I sincerely hope that it will. Mr Aspinwall left here some two weeks ago — he was as kind as ever. He wrote from here to M'Henry about the Atlantic & Great Western road, but received a reply that L'Hammedieu had the place — so that is knocked on the head.[1]

I suppose that if I were at home now, there would probably be nothing for me to do but to go into exile in Nevada or Utah for some years — not altogether a pleasant prospect in contrast with Europe. What are the prospects of your coming over this year — this side of the water is far more pleasant I assure you. We are in daily expectation of hearing something decisive from Sherman — the last meagre accounts we have look very much as if Secesh were pretty nearly on his last legs — tho' war is a very uncertain game. Do write often — I will write you a long long letter from Sorrento, if it is the pleasant place it is said to be. Nell joins me in love to you & yours. May sends hers to Elsie & Pierre. Mrs Marcy & Fanny seem to have had a very pleasant winter in New York.

Ever your sincere friend
Geo B McC

S.L.M.B. etc

Give my kindest regards to Willy Duncan & tell him I shall write to him from Sorrento. What has become of Lansing? Remember me to him when you see him. Also to John Van Buren — Curtis — Barton. Give my love to Marble & tell him to send me a Weekly World once in a while. Direct through Morgan & Co — London.

April 17 — have just heard the glorious news that Richmond is taken!

ALS, Barlow Papers, Huntington Library.

1. Aspinwall wrote GBM on Dec. 16, 1864, that he had recommended him for the presidency of the Atlantic and Great Western Railroad. McClellan Papers (B-23:53), Library of Congress.

To William Adams

Dear Doctor Sorrento May 4 1865

While in Rome I once or twice commenced letters to you, but for some reason or other they were never finished. The truth is that we were very busy while there, for in addition to the obligatory sight seeing we were so situated that we could not avoid mixing a good deal in Society & very rarely had any leisure time to ourselves — but now we are in charming Sorrento where everything is a delight & where a quiet life is most enjoyable. You will no doubt have learned from Mrs Marcy our general movements from time to time, & how first-rate our trip has thus far been.

We were in Rome just two months — long enough to see quite thoroughly most that is worth seeing — from the Colosseum & the Baths of Caracalla to the galleries — from Carnival to Easter Week. Of course our stay there could not be otherwise than most instructive & most pleasant — for it will afford food for thought for many a long year hereafter. The spectacle presented by the Eternal City with its singular contrasts between the past & the present — the glorious grandeur of the Old Rome, the petty feuding of the Papacy — is almost enough to make one doubt the boasted progress of the human race, fortunately however we are not confined to Rome in making the contrast. The sturdy obstinacy of the Papal Govt in refusing to learn anything is truly sublime, & one cannot help admire their entire consistency. Yet the Pope individually is quite prepossessing, and when we saw him I could with difficulty realize that the genial pleasant old gentleman before me was the author of the encyclical, the "non possumus"[1] of the age — I fear that common report is true, & that this mild old man raises "the adversary" when excited. I can safely say that I passed through the ordeal of Rome without the slightest danger of being converted, and that all I saw of processions of penitent "sacare" nobles, of streams of trusting pilgrims working their weary way up the Scala Spagna, of numerous priests, of the moving harmony of the Messiah, of the gorgeous spectacle of Easter Sunday & the Bacchanalia have only served to attach me still more strongly to our own simple worship of the Deity, & to cause me to thank him from the bottom of my heart that I was born & bred in a Protestant country. I am fully sensible of the grandeur of St Peters, and I trust that I never entered a Catholic Church — however simple — with other than a feeling of reverence, but I always felt stronger and better satisfied with our own faith when I realized how independent it is of all the externals which form so large a part of the Catholic worship.

We remained only three days in Naples — fearing to keep May too long there — and in that time merely had a passing glance at the Museum, and made the trip to Baia, Lake Avernus etc. I can hardly tell whether I shall read the Aeneid again with as much interest as of old since I have seen the base slopes that bound Avernus! We had a delightful trip hither, & are so pleasantly situated that we are enjoying ourselves exceedingly. We are at the Hotel Rispoli — if you remember its location — have the best rooms in the house, with a piazza facing over the water & commanding a view of the entire bay. The weather, the air — everything has been most charming since our arrival, & we are perfectly enchanted with the place. I could be well contented to live here did circumstances permit. Yesterday we went to Capri, & entered the Blue Grotto. We were all disappointed, although it was very beautiful — still I should not care to repeat the trip simply for the sake of the Grotto. Afterwards we went to the Villa Jovis — that is I did — and enjoyed the sublime view from that wonderful point. That was well worth the trouble of the trip many times over. If you were there you must remember that striking view down into the sea from the "Salto." Tiberius was clearly a man of taste if he was a great scamp. We have not yet been to Pompeii nor to Paestum & Amalfi — will probably go there early next week. But as we came here to rest & shall probably remain at least two or three weeks longer we are in no haste. Day before yesterday I took the charming walk to the Conti de' Fontinelli, where one has that beautiful view over the two bays of Naples & Salerno. But while we have been enjoying ourselves amongst these magnificent scenes, you at home have passed through the most wonderful transition of which history bears record. How strange it is that the military death of the rebellion should have been followed with such tragic quickness by the atrocious murder of Mr Lincoln! Now I cannot but forget all that had been unpleasant between us, & remember only the brighter parts of our intercourse. Most sincerely do I join in the sentiment of unmingled horror & regret with which his sad end seems to have inspired everyone. Would for our country's sake that a better man had succeeded him. I fear that the destinies of the nation are not safe in the hands of the person whom fate & party folly have elevated to the head of the Government.

We can only leave the result in the hands of God & pray that he may not deem it well to punish us still further. I have still unshaken faith in the great destinies of my country & in the belief that God intends it to play a great part in the history of the world. Nell joins me in best love to Mrs Adams, Miss Maria and yourself as well as to the "boys." Do write when you have a leisure moment & send under care to J.S. Morgan & Co., London.

Ever affectionately and sincerely yours
Geo B McClellan

Rev Wm Adams D.D.

ALS, George B. McClellan, Jr., Papers, Library of Congress.

1. "We cannot," presumably in reference to Pius IX's 1864 encyclical *Quanta cura.*

To Charles E. Whitehead

To Chas. E. Whitehead Esq
Secty etc. Hotel Byron, Villeneuve
My dear Sir: Lake Geneva July 4 1865

I have received your very polite invitation, in behalf of the Citizens of the U.S. of America who are in Geneva, to Mrs. McClellan and myself to join them at dinner today.

I regret that it will not be in our power to do ourselves the pleasure of uniting with you in the celebration of this most interesting anniversary of the most sacred day in the American calendar.

Although I cannot meet you in person, I hope that you will permit me to express the intense joy and pride with which, in common with all true Americans, I look upon the recent glorious successes of our gallant Armies under Grant & Sherman.

As these victories have finally crushed the armed opposition to the General Government, and have brought back the whole of the National Domain under the folds of our Flag, I trust that this anniversary of the Nation's Birthday will be the opening of a new era in our history: — when brotherly love shall again prevail between the people of the once contending sections, — when all the causes of the late war shall have disappeared, — when the idea of Secession shall be regarded as a thing entirely of the past, never again to be revived, — and during which we shall become a stronger, more united and more prosperous nation than ever before.

I most sincerely unite with you in the feelings of sorrow and indignation which have been so universally expressed for the cowardly murder which deprived the country of its Chief Magistrate, — and in the desire to afford the most loyal support to his successor.

I trust, too, that you will unite with me in the hope that, since we have completely vindicated our national strength and military honor by the entire defeat & ruin of our late enemies, our people will pursue a magnanimous and merciful course towards a fallen foe — one that will tend to soften the bitter feelings inevitably caused by a long & earnest war, & to restore the confidence and kind feeling that should exist between those who owe allegiance to the same Government & belong to the same People.

Begging that you will convey to the Committee, & the Gentlemen they represent, my sincere thanks for their very courteous invitation[1]

I am, my dear Sir, very truly & respectfully yours
Geo B McClellan

ALS, Chicago Historical Society. Whitehead represented a group of American expatriates living in Geneva.

1. Whitehead wrote GBM on July 6: "Your letter of the 4th was rec'd while we were at table, and I read it with feelings of the greatest pleasure & satisfaction to the 44 Americans who dined together. Such expressions from influential Americans will do much good in allaying the bitterness of feeling that still exists." McClellan Papers (B-23:53), Library of Congress. GBM replied on July 8: "You are most fully welcome to make any use you may deem fit of my note of the 4th . . . , and I shall be but too glad if it should aid in modifying the opinion of even a single American." Chicago Historical Society.

ACKNOWLEDGMENTS

MORE than one hundred institutions were surveyed for McClellan correspondence, and thanks are due the staffs of all of them for their generous and informed assistance. Special gratitude is owed the following: Michael P. Musick at the Navy and Old Army Branch, National Archives; James H. Hutson and his staff at the Manuscript Division, Library of Congress; Harriet McLoone at the Huntington Library, San Marino, California; Galen R. Wilson at the William L. Clements Library, University of Michigan; Emily C. Walhout at the Houghton Library, Harvard University; Bernard R. Crystal at the Rare Book and Manuscript Library, Columbia University; Nancy Boothe Parker at the Woodson Research Center, Rice University; Thomas Dunnings at the New-York Historical Society, New York City; Carl A. Lane at the New Jersey Historical Society, Newark; John D. Cushing at the Massachusetts Historical Society, Boston; Gary J. Arnold at the Ohio Historical Society, Columbus; Herbert Cahoon at the Pierpont Morgan Library, New York City; and Enid H. Douglass at the Chase Papers project, Claremont Graduate School, Claremont, California.

INDEX OF ADDRESSEES

GENERAL INDEX

For a complete listing of addressees, consult the Index of Addressees